"*****…this is a concise, practical, and comprehensive directory on how to reduce anxiety. A highly regarded and widely known resource."

—*Authoritative Guide to Self-Help Resources in Mental Health, Revised Edition*

"A great resource for a holistic approach."

—Reid Wilson, author of *Don't Panic*

"Extremely well done."

—Christopher McCullough, author of *Managing Your Anxiety*

"Any who've struggled with panic attacks and fears will find this packed with self-help exercises and guidelines to overcoming anxiety and stress, from understanding how to assert oneself to creating a positive recovery strategy."

—*Midwest Book Review*

"This workbook offers a practical and comprehensive guide to anyone struggling to cope with the many-faceted manifestations of panic and anxiety."

—*Child and Behavior Therapy*

The Anxiety & Phobia WORKBOOK

FIFTH EDITION

EDMUND J. BOURNE, PhD

New Harbinger Publications, Inc.

Distributed in Canada by Raincoast Books

Copyright © 2010 by Edmund J. Bourne
New Harbinger Publications, Inc.
5674 Shattuck Avenue
Oakland, CA 94609
www.newharbinger.com

Cover design by Amy Shoup
Text design by Tracy Marie Carlson
Acquired by Catharine Sutker
Edited by Jean Blomquist

Library of Congress Cataloging-in-Publication Data

Bourne, Edmund J.
    The anxiety and phobia workbook / Edmund J. Bourne. -- 5th ed.
        p. cm.
    title: Anxiety & phobia workbook
    Includes bibliographical references.
    ISBN 978-1-57224-891-5 (pbk.) -- ISBN 978-1-57224-892-2 (pdf ebook) 1. Anxiety disorders--Popular works. 2. Phobias--Popular works. I. Title. II. Title: Anxiety & phobia workbook.
    RC531.B67 2010
    616.85'22--dc22

                                        2010040275

15   14   13

15   14   13   12   11   10   9   8

This book is dedicated to anyone who has struggled with anxiety or an incomprehensible fear.

But do not distress yourself with imaginings. Many fears are born of fatigue and loneliness. Beyond a wholesome discipline, be gentle with yourself.

 —Max Ehrmann
  "Desiderata"

Contents

Grateful Acknowledgment

To all the staff at New Harbinger who contributed to this edition: Jean Blomquist, Heather Garnos, Catharine Sutker, Amy Shoup, Tracy Carlson, and others. Thank you for the care and attention you gave to the fifth edition of this book and for your flexibility and patience in working with me over the year it took to bring the project to completion.

Preface to the Fifth Edition

Twenty-one years have passed since this book was first published as a broad summary of the diverse approaches for treating anxiety disorders. To my surprise and appreciation, the book has been well received, reaching many places around the world. During the two decades that have passed, the field of anxiety disorders itself has grown and evolved in many ways. The 1990s saw the growth of cognitive behavioral therapy as the dominant treatment approach for all anxiety disorders. During the first half of the recent decade, there was increasing specialization in the field, with numerous books, programs, and special organizations devoted to each of the anxiety disorders (for example, the Obsessive Compulsive Foundation). The early 2000s also saw a proliferation of websites presenting information on anxiety. Popular new approaches similar to, yet outside of, the mainstream cognitive behavioral treatment model showed up and were propagated on the Internet (for example, Charles Linden's method that has many cognitive elements but also emphasizes distraction). In the past few years, another new approach has been gaining prominence and research support in the field: acceptance and commitment therapy (abbreviated ACT). This new approach differs from cognitive behavioral therapy (CBT) in emphasizing mindfulness toward anxious feelings and thoughts, rather than challenging and changing fear-producing thoughts, as in CBT. ACT is really the opposite of distraction, as it encourages you simply to "be with" anxiety, mindfully observing it. It teaches ways to gain distance from fearful thoughts, instead of becoming entangled with them. A more detailed discussion of acceptance and commitment therapy can be found in chapter 19.

Readers familiar with the fourth edition of this book will find some noticeable changes in this edition. Two new chapters have been added. Chapter 11 examines the nature, causes, and treatment of ten common phobias. It was written in response to my readers and clients requesting more specific information on some particularly common phobias. Chapter 19, as mentioned, explores acceptance and commitment therapy as a treatment approach to anxiety, including a number of exercises for implementing this approach. Other changes in the fifth edition include

- Updated material on each of the major anxiety disorders (chapter 1)

- Updated information on the neurobiology of certain anxiety disorders (chapter 2)

- Updated material on the use of CDs and MP3 downloads (rather than audiotapes) for relaxing visualizations (chapter 4)

- Updated information on nutrition (chapter 15)

- Augmented information on medications to include descriptions of a few newer medications used to treat anxiety disorders such as Cymbalta, Pristiq, and Lyrica (chapter 17)

As the second decade of the twenty-first century begins, the causes of anxiety in contemporary society are legion. In my opinion, the collective level of anxiety in society is even more pressing and stressful than ten years ago. From broad issues—such as economic recession, environmental breakdown, political polarization, and multiple wars—to more immediate problems with the health care system, schools, urban congestion, the food industry, and technological complexity, we all live in increasingly stressful times. It is my hope that the variety of interventions offered in this book will provide you with a wide range of resources to better cope with anxiety in all the forms in which it can show up in these times of change.

Introduction

Research conducted by the National Institute of Mental Health has shown that anxiety disorders are the number one mental health problem among American women and are second only to alcohol and drug abuse among men. Approximately 17 percent of the population of the United States, or nearly fifty million people, have suffered from panic attacks, phobias, or other anxiety disorders in the past year. Nearly a quarter of the adult population will suffer from an anxiety disorder at some time during their life. Yet only a small proportion of these people receive treatment. During the past twenty years, panic and anxiety reached epidemic proportions, with much coverage of these disorders in the media. Now, at the end of the first decade of the twenty-first century, a trend toward increasing collective anxiety has appeared in the wake of new uncertainties about economic instability, rapid deterioration of the environment, and global terrorism.

Why are problems with panic, phobias, and anxiety so prevalent? It has been my impression that anxiety disorders are an outcome of cumulative stress acting over time. Certainly there are numerous factors which cause a person to develop panic attacks, phobias, or obsessions—but stress over time plays a key role. Of course each of us creates much of our own stress, yet the society in which we live affects us deeply. People living in Western society are currently experiencing more stress than they have at any previous time in history, and it is this stress that explains the increased incidence of anxiety disorders. While it can be argued that human beings have always had to deal with stressful societal conditions (wars, famines, plagues, economic depression, and so forth), there are two reasons for suggesting that the overall stress level is higher now than before.

First, our environment and social order have changed more in the last thirty years than they have in the previous three hundred years. Digital information technology has changed our lives drastically in less than twenty years. The increased pace of modern society—and the increased rate of technological change—have deprived people of adequate time to adjust to these changes.

To compound this situation, there are rapidly increasing uncertainties about the future of all of our lives. The worst economic downturn since the Great Depression has affected people throughout the world since late 2008, and many uncertainties remain as this book goes to press in late 2010. Future prospects for the world's environment are seriously in question, as a large number of scientists believe we have already reached a tipping point for climate change, extreme weather events, loss of biodiversity, and destruction of natural habitats all over the world. Once these tipping points are crossed, it's very difficult returning to the world to which we are accustomed. In addition, nuclear proliferation has led to the grim possibility of terrorists developing and using nuclear weapons against developed countries. The list of uncertainties could go on, but conditions such as these provide a social context for anxiety. When a society becomes more anxious and uncertain, this shows up as an increased incidence of anxiety disorders in the population.

Finally, cultural values are unclear. We lack a consistent, externally sanctioned set of values (traditionally prescribed by society and religion). This leaves a vacuum in which people are left to fend for themselves. Faced with a barrage of inconsistent worldviews and standards presented by the media, people must learn to cope with the responsibility of creating their own meaning and moral order.

All of these factors make it difficult for many individuals in modern society to experience a sense of stability or consistency in their lives. Anxiety disorders are simply one outcome of a diminished ability to cope with the resulting stress, as are addictive disorders, depression, and the increased incidence of degenerative diseases.

Many good books on anxiety disorders have appeared during the past twenty years. Most of these popular books tend to be primarily descriptive. Although several of them have spoken of methods of treatment and offered practical recovery strategies, the emphasis has been on providing readers with a basic understanding of the anxiety disorders.

In writing this workbook, my intention has been to 1) describe specific skills that you need to overcome problems with panic, anxiety, and phobias, and 2) provide step-by-step procedures and exercises for mastering these skills. Although there is quite a bit of descriptive material, what makes this a *workbook* is its emphasis on coping strategies and skills along with exercises to foster your recovery.

There is probably little in this book that is altogether new. The chapters on relaxation, exercise, coping skills for panic attacks, exposure, identifying and expressing feelings, asserting yourself, self-esteem, nutrition, medications, and meditation summarize concepts that have been dealt with in greater detail in the books listed at the end of each chapter. It has been my hope to define in a single volume the full range of strategies necessary to overcome problems with anxiety. The more of these strategies you can incorporate into your own recovery program, the more efficient and rapid your progress will be.

The approach of this workbook is strongly holistic. It presents interventions that will affect your life on many levels: body, behavior, feelings, mind, interpersonal relations, self-esteem, and spirituality. A majority of the previous popular approaches to panic and phobias have emphasized primarily behavioral and cognitive (or mental) strategies. These are very important and still constitute the core of any successful program for treating all anxiety disorders. Such approaches are covered in four chapters of this workbook. Chapter 6 offers concepts and coping strategies that are crucial for learning to handle panic attacks. Chapter 7 details the process of exposure, which is necessary to any program for recovering from agoraphobia, social phobia, or other specific phobias. Chapters 8 and 9 present methods for learning to counter unhelpful "self-talk" and mistaken beliefs that tend to perpetuate anxiety on a day-to-day basis.

Relaxation and personal wellness are also of prime importance. As previously mentioned, anxiety disorders develop as the result of cumulative, long-term stress. This stress is apparent in the well-known fact that most people with anxiety disorders tend to be in a chronic state of physiological hyperarousal. Recovery depends on adopting lifestyle changes that promote a more relaxed, balanced, and healthy approach to life: in short, changes that upgrade your level of *physical well-being.* The strategies and skills presented in the chapters on relaxation, exercise, and nutrition constitute a necessary *foundation* on which the other skills presented throughout this workbook rest. It is much easier, for example, to implement exposure if you have first learned how to effectively enter a deep state of relaxation. You will also find it easier to identify and change counterproductive self-talk when you are feeling physically healthy and relaxed. Just as learning habits of positive self-talk will help you feel better, so improving your physical health through proper relaxation, exercise, and nutrition will reduce your *predisposition* to counterproductive attitudes and self-talk. In short, when you feel well, you will think well.

At the other end of the spectrum, a lack of direction or personal meaning in your life can lead to an increased vulnerability to anxiety disorders. Panic attacks and agoraphobia—especially when they involve a fear of being closed in or unable to escape—may symbolize a sense of having "nowhere to go" or being "stuck" within your life. Given the complexity of contemporary society and the lack of any externally prescribed set of values, it is common to feel confused and uncertain about the meaning and direction of your life. By getting more in touch with a larger sense of purpose, and, where appropriate, cultivating your own spirituality, you can gain a sense of meaning that will help to diminish your problems with anxiety. This is an important area to consider in dealing with anxiety disorders and probably most other behavior disorders as well (see chapter 20).

In sum, a holistic model incorporating all of the approaches presented in this workbook is necessary for a full and lasting solution to anxiety disorders. Recovery from anxiety depends upon intervening at all levels of the whole person.

A final important point bears mentioning. It will take a strong commitment and consistent motivation on your part to successfully utilize the skills presented in this workbook. If you are self-motivated and disciplined, it is possible to achieve a lasting recovery on your own. At the same time, it is not always preferable or even most effective to go it alone. Many readers will decide to use this workbook in conjunction with seeing a therapist who has expertise in treating anxiety disorders. A therapist can provide structure and support, and can help you fine-tune the concepts and strategies found in this workbook to your own individual situation. Some of you may also find support groups or treatment groups (especially for agoraphobia and social phobia) to be very valuable. A group format can motivate you and maintain your enthusiasm for learning the skills necessary for recovery. A number of people seem to benefit from the inspiration, structure, and support that a group can provide.

Ultimately you will need to choose the best way for yourself. If you decide to seek outside help for your problem, you will want to contact a specialist in the treatment of anxiety disorders to help you decide what treatment format is best for you. A list of such specialists in the United States and Canada is offered by the Anxiety Disorders Association of America (ADAA). Go to their website, adaa.org, and enter your city or zip code (see appendix 1 for further information). ADAA also offers a list of support groups for anxiety disorders by state.

It is quite possible to overcome your problem with panic, phobias, or anxiety on your own through the use of the strategies and exercises presented in this workbook. Yet it is equally valuable and appropriate, if you feel so inclined, to use this book as an adjunct to working with a therapist or group treatment program. Whatever approach you choose, know that there is much help available. Problems with anxiety can improve or can be entirely resolved when you make a commitment and follow through consistently with the type of approach described in this book.

1

Anxiety Disorders

Susan awakens suddenly almost every night, a couple of hours after going to sleep, with a tightness in her throat, a racing heart, dizziness, and a fear that she's going to die. Although she's shaking all over, she hasn't a clue why. After many nights of getting up and pacing her living room floor in an attempt to get a grip on herself, she decides to go see her doctor to find out whether something is wrong with her heart.

Cindy, a medical secretary, has been having attacks like Susan's whenever she's in a confined public situation. Not only does she fear losing control over herself, but she dreads what others might think of her if this were to happen. Recently she has been avoiding going into any kind of store other than the local 7-Eleven unless her boyfriend is with her. She has also needed to leave restaurants and movie theaters during dates. Now she is beginning to wonder whether she can cope with her job. She has been forcing herself to go into work, yet after a few minutes among her office mates, she starts to fear that she's losing control of herself. Suddenly she feels as though she *has* to leave.

Steve has a responsible position as a software engineer but feels he is unable to advance because of his inability to contribute in group meetings. It's almost more than he can bear just to sit in on meetings, let alone offer his opinions. Yesterday his boss asked him whether he would be available to make a presentation on his segment of a large project. At that point, Steve became extremely nervous and tongue-tied. He walked out of the room, stammering that he would let his boss know by the next day about the presentation. Privately, he thought about resigning.

Mike is so embarrassed about a peculiar fear he's had over the past few months that he can't tell anyone, not even his wife. While driving he is frequently gripped by the fear that he has run over someone or perhaps an animal. Even though there is no "thud" suggesting that anything like this has happened, he feels compelled to make a U-turn and retrace the route he's just driven to make absolutely sure. In fact, recently, his paranoia about having hit someone has grown so strong that he has to retrace his route three or four times to assure himself that nothing has happened. Mike is a bright, successful professional and feels utterly humiliated about his compulsion to check. He's beginning to wonder if he's going crazy.

Susan, Cindy, Steve, and Mike are all confronted by anxiety. Yet it is not ordinary anxiety. Their experiences differ in two fundamental respects from the "normal" anxiety people experience in response to everyday life. First, their anxiety has gone out of control. In each case, the individual feels powerless to direct what's happening. This sense of powerlessness in turn creates even more anxiety. Second, the anxiety is interfering with the normal functioning of their lives. Susan's sleep is disrupted. Cindy and Steve may lose their jobs. And Mike has lost the ability to drive in an efficient and timely manner.

The examples of Susan, Cindy, Steve, and Mike illustrate four types of anxiety disorder: panic disorder, agoraphobia, social phobia, and obsessive-compulsive disorder. Later in this chapter, you can find detailed descriptions of the characteristics of each specific anxiety disorder. But I would first like you to consider the common theme that runs through them all. What is the nature of anxiety itself?

What Is Anxiety?

You can better understand the nature of anxiety by looking at both what it is and what it is not. For example, anxiety can be distinguished from fear in several ways. When you are afraid, your fear is usually directed toward some concrete external object or situation. The event that you fear usually is within the bounds of possibility. You might fear not meeting a deadline, failing an exam, being unable to pay your bills, or being rejected by someone you want to please. When you experience anxiety, on the other hand, you often can't specify what it is you're anxious about. The focus of anxiety is more internal than external. It seems to be a response to a vague, distant, or even unrecognized danger. You might be anxious about "losing control" of yourself or some situation. Or you might feel a vague anxiety about "something bad happening."

Anxiety affects your whole being. It is a physiological, behavioral, and psychological reaction all at once. On a physiological level, anxiety may include bodily reactions such as rapid heartbeat, muscle tension, queasiness, dry mouth, or sweating. On a behavioral level, it can sabotage your ability to act, express yourself, or deal with certain everyday situations.

Psychologically, anxiety is a subjective state of apprehension and uneasiness. In its most extreme form, it can cause you to feel detached from yourself and even fearful of dying or going crazy.

The fact that anxiety can affect you on a physiological, behavioral, and psychological level has important implications for your attempts to recover. A complete program of recovery from an anxiety disorder must intervene at all three levels to

1.   Reduce physiological reactivity

2.   Eliminate avoidance behavior

3.   Change subjective interpretations (or "self-talk") which perpetuate a state of apprehension and worry

Anxiety can appear in different forms and at different levels of intensity. It can range in severity from a mere twinge of uneasiness to a full-blown panic attack marked by heart palpitations, disorientation, and terror. Anxiety that is not connected with any particular situation, that comes "out of the blue," is called free-floating anxiety or, in more severe instances, a *spontaneous panic attack*. The difference between an episode of free-floating anxiety and a spontaneous panic attack can be defined by whether you experience four or more of the following symptoms at the same time (the occurrence of four or more symptoms defines a panic attack):

- Shortness of breath

- Heart palpitations (rapid or irregular heartbeat)

- Trembling or shaking

- Sweating

- Choking

- Nausea or abdominal distress

- Numbness

- Dizziness or unsteadiness

- Feeling of detachment or being out of touch with yourself

- Hot flashes or chills

- Fear of dying

- Fear of going crazy or out of control

If your anxiety arises *only* in response to a specific situation, it is called *situational anxiety* or *phobic anxiety*. Situational anxiety is different from everyday fear in that it tends to be out of proportion or unrealistic. If you have a disproportionate apprehension about driving on freeways, going to the doctor, or confronting your spouse, this may qualify as situational anxiety. Situational anxiety becomes *phobic* when you actually start to *avoid* the situation: if you give up driving on freeways, going to doctors, or confronting your spouse altogether. In other words, phobic anxiety is situational anxiety that includes persistent avoidance of the situation.

Often anxiety can be brought on merely by thinking about a particular situation. When you feel distressed about what might happen when or if you have to face one of your phobic situations, you are experiencing what is called *anticipatory anxiety*. In its milder forms, anticipatory anxiety is indistinguishable from ordinary "worrying." But sometimes anticipatory anxiety becomes intense enough to be called *anticipatory panic*.

There is an important difference between spontaneous anxiety (or panic) and anticipatory anxiety (or panic). Spontaneous anxiety tends to come out of the blue, peaks to a high level very rapidly, and then subsides gradually. The peak is usually reached within five minutes, followed by a gradual tapering-off period of an hour or more. Anticipatory anxiety, on the other hand, tends to build up more gradually in response to encountering—or simply thinking about—a threatening situation and then usually falls off quickly. You may "worry yourself into a frenzy" about something for an hour or more and then let go of the worry as you find something else to occupy your mind.

Anxiety vs. Anxiety Disorders

Anxiety is an inevitable part of life in contemporary society. It's important to realize that there are many situations that come up in everyday life in which it is *appropriate* and *reasonable* to react with some anxiety. If you didn't feel *any* anxiety in response to everyday challenges involving potential loss or failure, something would be wrong. This workbook can be of use to anyone experiencing normal, ordinary anxiety reactions (everyone, in other words). It is also intended for those of you who are dealing with specific anxiety disorders. Incorporating exercise, breathing skills, relaxation, and good nutritional habits into your daily life—as well as paying attention to self-talk, mistaken beliefs, feelings, assertiveness, and self-esteem—can all contribute to making your life more balanced and less anxious, regardless of the nature and extent of the anxiety you happen to be dealing with.

Anxiety disorders are distinguished from everyday, normal anxiety in that they involve anxiety that 1) *is more intense* (for example, panic attacks), 2) *lasts longer* (anxiety that may persist for months instead of going away after a stressful situation has passed), or 3) *leads to phobias* that interfere with your life.

Criteria for diagnosing specific anxiety disorders have been established by the American Psychiatric Association and are listed in a well-known diagnostic manual used by mental health professionals. This manual is called the *DSM–IV* (*Diagnostic and Statistical Manual of Mental Disorders*—fourth edition). The following descriptions of various anxiety disorders are based on the criteria in the *DSM–IV*, as is the self-diagnosis questionnaire at the end of this chapter. This workbook can help you even if your specific anxiety disorder or reaction doesn't fit any of the *DSM–IV*'s diagnostic categories. On the other hand, don't be unduly concerned if your reaction is perfectly described by one of the diagnostic categories. Approximately 15 percent of the people in the United States would find themselves in your company.

Panic Disorder

Panic disorder is characterized by sudden episodes of acute apprehension or intense fear that occur "out of the blue," without any apparent cause. Intense panic usually lasts no more than a few minutes, but, in rare instances, can return in "waves" for a period of up to two hours. During the panic itself, any of the following symptoms can occur:

- Shortness of breath or a feeling of being smothered
- Heart palpitations—pounding heart or accelerated heart rate
- Dizziness, unsteadiness, or faintness
- Trembling or shaking
- A feeling of choking
- Sweating
- Nausea or abdominal distress

- A feeling of unreality—as if you're "not all there" (*depersonalization*)

- Numbness or tingling in hands and feet

- Hot and cold flashes

- Chest pain or discomfort

- Fears of going crazy or losing control

- Fears of dying

At least four of these symptoms are present in a full-blown panic attack, while having two or three of them is referred to as a *limited-symptom attack*.

Your symptoms would be diagnosed as panic disorder if 1) you have had two or more panic attacks and 2) at least one of these attacks has been followed by one month (or more) of persistent concern about having another panic attack, or worry about the possible implications of having another panic attack. It's important to recognize that panic disorder, by itself, does not involve any phobias. The panic doesn't occur because you are thinking about, approaching, or actually entering a phobic situation. Instead, it occurs spontaneously, unexpectedly, and for no apparent reason. Also, the panic attacks are not due to the physiological effects of a drug (prescription or recreational) or a medical condition.

You may have two or three panic attacks without ever having another one again or without having another one for years. Or you may have several panic attacks followed by a panic-free period, only to have the panic return a month or two later. Sometimes an initial panic attack may be followed by recurring attacks three or more times per week unremittingly until you seek treatment. In all of these cases, there is a tendency to develop *anticipatory anxiety* or apprehension between panic attacks focusing on fear of having another one. This apprehension about having another panic attack is one of the hallmarks of panic disorder.

If you are suffering from panic disorder, you may be very frightened by your symptoms and consult with doctors to find a medical cause. Heart palpitations and an irregular heartbeat may lead to EKG and other cardiac tests, which, in most cases, turn out normal. (Sometimes mitral valve prolapse, a benign arrhythmia of the heart, may coexist with panic disorder.) Fortunately, an increasing number of physicians have some knowledge of panic disorder and are able to distinguish it from purely physical complaints.

A diagnosis of panic disorder is made only after possible medical causes—including hypoglycemia, hyperthyroidism, reaction to excess caffeine, or withdrawal from alcohol, tranquilizers, or sedatives—have been ruled out. The causes of panic disorder involve a combination of heredity, chemical imbalances in the brain, and personal stress. Sudden losses or major life changes may trigger the onset of panic attacks.

People tend to develop panic disorder during late adolescence or in their twenties. About half of the people who have panic disorder develop it before the age of twenty-four. In about a third of cases, panic is complicated by the development of agoraphobia (as described in the following section). Between 1 and 2 percent of the population have "pure" panic disorder, while about 5 percent, or one in every twenty people, suffer from panic attacks complicated by agoraphobia. Women are about twice as likely as men to develop panic disorder.

Cigarette smoking increases the risk of panic disorder (Isensee et al. 2003). About 30 percent of people with panic disorder use alcohol to self-medicate (Mental Health America 2007), which often worsens their symptoms when the effects of alcohol wear off. Cannabis often precipitates panic in some people.

Panic disorder is in part influenced by excessive activity in parts of the brain known as the amygdala and the hypothalamus. See chapter 2 for more detailed information on the neurobiology of panic disorder.

Current Treatment

All of the following strategies are considered state-of-the-art treatments for panic disorder.

Relaxation Training. Practicing abdominal breathing and some form of deep muscle relaxation (such as progressive muscle relaxation) on a daily basis. This helps to reduce the *physical* symptoms of panic as well as anticipatory anxiety you might experience about having a panic attack. A physical exercise program may also be recommended to reduce anxiety. (See chapters 4 and 5.)

Panic-Control Therapy. Identifying and eliminating catastrophic thoughts (such as "I'm trapped!" "I'm going to go crazy!" or "I'm going to have a heart attack!") that tend to trigger panic attacks. (See chapter 6.)

Interoceptive Desensitization. Practicing voluntary habituation to the *bodily symptoms* of panic, such as rapid heartbeat, sweaty hands, shortness of breath, or dizziness. Such symptoms are created deliberately, usually in the therapist's office. For example, dizziness might be induced by spinning in a chair or rapid heartbeat by running up and down stairs. Repeated exposure to unpleasant bodily symptoms promotes *desensitization*, which basically means getting used to them to the point that they no longer frighten you. (See chapter 7.)

Medication. SSRI antidepressant medications such as Zoloft, Lexapro, Celexa, or Cymbalta—or benzodiazepine medications such as Xanax, Ativan, or Klonopin—may be used to reduce severity of panic symptoms. Such medications are best used in conjunction with the first three strategies above. (See chapter 17.)

Lifestyle and Personality Changes. Some of the lifestyle changes that can reduce your tendency to have panic attacks include stress management, regular exercise, eliminating stimulants and sugar from your diet, slowing down and creating "downtime," and altering your attitudes about perfectionism, the excessive need to please, and the excessive need to control. (Chapters 4, 5, 10, and 15 address these issues.)

Agoraphobia

The word *agoraphobia* means fear of open spaces; however, the essence of agoraphobia is a fear of panic attacks. If you suffer from agoraphobia, you are afraid of being in situations from which escape might be difficult—or in which help might be unavailable—if you suddenly had a panic attack. You may avoid grocery stores or freeways, for example, not so much because of their inherent characteristics but because these are situations from which escape might be difficult or embarrassing in the event of panic. Fear of embarrassment plays a key role. Most agoraphobics fear not only having panic attacks but *what other people will think* should they be seen having a panic attack.

It is common for the agoraphobic to avoid a variety of situations. Some of the more common ones include

- Crowded public places such as grocery stores, department stores, or restaurants

- Enclosed or confined places such as tunnels, bridges, or the hairdresser's chair

- Public transportation such as trains, buses, subways, or planes

- Being at home alone

Perhaps the most common feature of agoraphobia is anxiety about being far away from home or far from a "safe person" (usually your spouse, partner, a parent, or anyone to whom you have a primary attachment). You may completely avoid driving alone or may be afraid of driving alone beyond a certain short distance from home. In more severe cases, you might be able to walk alone only a few yards from home or you might be housebound altogether. I know of one agoraphobic who was unable to leave her bedroom without being accompanied.

If you have agoraphobia, you are not only phobic about a variety of situations but tend to be anxious much of the time. This anxiety arises from *anticipating* that you *might* be stuck in a situation in which you would panic. What would happen, for example, if you were asked to go somewhere you ordinarily avoid and have to explain your way out of it? Or what would happen if you suddenly were left alone? Because of the severe restrictions in your activities and life, you may also be depressed. Depression arises from feeling in the grip of a condition over which you have no control or that you are powerless to change.

Agoraphobia, in most cases, appears to be engendered by panic disorder. At first you simply have panic attacks that occur for no apparent reason (panic disorder). After a while, though, you become aware that your attacks occur more frequently in confined situations away from home or when you are by yourself. You begin to be afraid of these situations. At the point where you actually start to avoid these situations for fear of panicking, you've started to develop agoraphobia. From that point you might go on to develop a mild, moderate, or severe problem. In a mild case, you might feel uncomfortable in confined situations but not actually avoid them. You continue to work or shop on your own but do not want to go far from home otherwise. In a moderate case, you might start to avoid some situations, such as public transportation, elevators, driving far from home, or being in restaurants. However, your restriction is only partial, and there are certain situations away from home or your safe person that you can handle on your own, even with some discomfort. Severe agoraphobia is marked by an all-inclusive restriction of activities to the point where you are unable to leave your house without being accompanied.

Just why some people with panic attacks develop agoraphobia and others do not is unknown at this time. (There are a few people who develop only agoraphobia without any panic attacks.) Nor is it understood why some people develop much more severe cases than others. What is known is that agoraphobia is caused by a combination of heredity and environment. Agoraphobics may have a parent, sibling, or other relative who also has the problem. When one identical twin is agoraphobic, the other has a high likelihood of being agoraphobic, too. On the environmental side, there are certain types of childhood circumstances that predispose a child to agoraphobia. These include growing up with parents who are 1) perfectionist and overcritical, 2) overprotective, and/or 3) overly anxious to the point of communicating to their child that the world is a "dangerous place." The hereditary and environmental origins of agoraphobia and other anxiety disorders will be explored in greater depth in the following chapter.

Agoraphobia affects people in all walks of life and at all levels of the socioeconomic scale. Approximately 80 percent of agoraphobics are women, although this percentage has been dropping recently. It is possible to speculate that as women are increasingly expected to hold down full-time jobs (making a housebound lifestyle less socially acceptable), the percentage of women and men with agoraphobia may tend to equalize.

Current Treatment

Relaxation Training, Panic Control Therapy, and Interoceptive Desensitization. Since agoraphobia is usually based on a fear of panic attacks, the same treatments as were described for panic disorder are utilized. (See chapters 4 and 6.)

Exposure. Exposure therapy means you face, or expose, yourself to a feared situation. Situations that you have avoided are gradually confronted through a process of small incremental steps. Such exposures are conducted first in imagination and then in real life (see chapter 7). For example, if you were fearful of driving far from home, you would gradually increase the distance you drive in small increments. A support person might accompany you in the same car at first, then drive in a second car behind you, and then, finally, you would practice driving alone. Or, if you were fearful of being home alone, the person who usually stays with you would leave for only a few minutes at first and then gradually increase the time away. Over time you learn to confront and enter into all of the situations you have been avoiding.

Cognitive Therapy. The aim of cognitive therapy is to help you replace exaggerated, fearful thinking about panic and phobias with more realistic and supportive mental habits. You learn to identify, challenge, and replace counterproductive thoughts with constructive ones. (See chapters 8 and 9.)

Medication. Current treatment for agoraphobia often utilizes medication. SSRIs such as Zoloft, Lexapro, Celexa, or Cymbalta are especially likely to be used for more severe cases where a person is housebound or highly restricted in what they are able to do. Low doses of tranquilizers such as Xanax or Klonopin may also be used to help people negotiate the early stages of exposure. (See chapter 17.)

Assertiveness Training. Since agoraphobics often have difficulty standing up for themselves and their rights, assertiveness training is frequently part of the treatment. (See chapter 13.)

Group Therapy. Treatment for agoraphobia can be done very effectively in a group setting. There is much support available in a group, both for realizing that you are not alone and for completing week-to-week homework assignments.

Social Anxiety Disorder

Social anxiety disorder (also known as social phobia) is one of the more common anxiety disorders. It involves fear of embarrassment or humiliation in situations where you are exposed to the scrutiny of others or you must perform. This fear is much stronger than the normal anxiety most nonphobic people experience in social or performance situations. Usually it's so strong that it causes you to avoid the situation altogether, although some people with social phobia endure social situations, albeit with considerable anxiety. Typically, your concern is that you will say or do something that will cause others to judge you as being anxious, weak, "crazy," or stupid. Your concern is generally out of proportion with the situation, and you recognize that it's excessive (children with social phobia, however, do not recognize the excessiveness of their fear).

The most common social phobia is fear of public speaking. In fact, this is the most common of all phobias and affects performers, speakers, people whose jobs require them to make presentations, and students who have to speak before their class. Public-speaking phobia affects a large percentage of the population and is equally prevalent among men and women.

Other common social phobias include

- Fear of blushing in public

- Fear of choking on or spilling food while eating in public

- Fear of being watched at work

- Fear of using public toilets

- Fear of writing or signing documents in the presence of others

- Fear of crowds

- Fear of taking examinations

Sometimes social phobia is less specific and involves a generalized fear of *any* social or group situation where you feel that you might be watched or evaluated. When your fear is of a wide range of social situations (for example, initiating conversations, participating in small groups, speaking to authority figures, dating, attending parties, and so on), the condition is referred to as *generalized social phobia.*

Common symptoms of social anxiety disorder include blushing, sweating, trembling, heart palpitations, and nausea. Many people who are unaware that they are socially phobic use alcohol to reduce these symptoms, which, in some cases, can lead to alcoholism.

While social anxieties are common, you would be given a formal diagnosis of social phobia only if your avoidance interferes with work, social activities, or important relationships, and/or if it causes you considerable distress. As with agoraphobia, panic attacks can accompany social phobia, although your panic is related more to being embarrassed or humiliated than to being confined or trapped. Also, the panic arises only in connection with a specific type of social situation.

Social phobias tend to develop earlier than agoraphobia and can begin in late childhood or adolescence, often between ages eleven and nineteen. They often develop in shy children around the time they are faced with increased peer pressure at school. Typically these phobias persist (without treatment) through adolescence and young adulthood but have a tendency to decrease in severity later in life. Recent studies suggest that social phobia affects between 3 to 7 percent of the U.S. population and may be more prevalent among men than women. Up to 14 percent of adults experience social phobia at some time in their lives. Social anxiety disorder occurs almost twice as often in women, but men are more likely to seek treatment for it (U.S. Department of Health and Human Services 1999).

A significant percentage of people with social anxiety disorder are clinically depressed, have another anxiety disorder such as panic disorder or generalized anxiety disorder, or are dealing with substance abuse.

As with other anxiety disorders, there are both genetic and environmental components in the causes of social anxiety disorder. If one identical twin has the problem, the other twin is 30 to 50 percent more likely to have the problem. At the same time, social anxiety in adoptive parents is significantly correlated with social anxiety in their children (Kendler, Karkowski, and Prescott 1999).

Current Treatment

All of the following interventions are part of the current treatment for social phobia:

Relaxation Training. Abdominal breathing and deep relaxation techniques are practiced on a regular basis to assuage physical symptoms of anxiety. (See chapter 4.)

Cognitive Therapy. Fearful thoughts that tend to perpetuate social phobias are identified, challenged, and replaced with more realistic thoughts. For example, the thought "I'll make a fool of myself if I speak up" would be replaced with the idea "It's okay if I'm a bit awkward at first when I speak up—most people won't be bothered."

Cognitive therapists tend to focus on three specific types of cognitive distortions: an excessive focus on anxiety symptoms and how they might appear to others, distortions in self-concept about your social attractiveness, and the tendency to overestimate the likelihood of a negative evaluation.

Exposure. Exposure involves gradually and incrementally facing the social situation or situations you're phobic about. You might do this first in imagery and then in real life. For example, if you're phobic of public speaking, you might start out giving a one-minute talk to a friend and then *gradually* increase, through many steps, both the duration of your talk and the number of people you speak to. Or, if you have difficulty speaking up in groups, you'd gradually increase both the length and degree of self-disclosure of remarks made in a group setting. (See chapter 7.) After each exposure, you'd review and challenge any unrealistic thinking that caused anxiety. While the treatment for social phobia can be done on an individual basis, group therapy is the ideal treatment format. This allows *direct* exposure to the situation and stimuli that evoke anxiety in the first place.

Staying on Task. People with social phobia tend to focus a lot on how they are doing or try to gauge other people's reactions while speaking in a social situation. Treatment includes training yourself to focus only on the task at hand, whether conversing with a boss, speaking up in class, or presenting information to a group.

Medication. SSRI medications such as Zoloft, Luvox, Cymbalta, or Lexapro, or low doses of benzodiazepine tranquilizers such as Xanax or Klonopin, may be used as an adjunct to the cognitive and exposure-based treatments described above. Sometimes MAO-inhibitor medications such as Nardil or Parnate are used to treat social phobia with success. (See chapter 17.)

Social Skills Training. In some cases, learning basic social skills such as smiling and making eye contact, maintaining a conversation, self-disclosure, and active listening are part of the treatment for social phobia.

Assertiveness Training. Training in assertiveness, the ability to ask directly for what you want or to say no to what you don't want, is often included in the treatment. (See chapter 13.)

Specific Phobia

A specific phobia typically involves a strong fear and avoidance of *one particular* type of object or situation. There are no spontaneous panic attacks, and there is no fear of panic attacks, as in agoraphobia. There is also no fear of humiliation or embarrassment in social situations, as in social phobia. Direct exposure to the feared object or situation may elicit a panic reaction, however. The fear and avoidance are strong enough to interfere with your normal routines, work, or relationships and to cause you significant distress. Even though you recognize its irrationalities, a specific phobia can cause you considerable anxiety.

Among the most common specific phobias are the following:

Animal Phobias. These can include fear and avoidance of snakes, bats, rats, spiders, bees, dogs, and other creatures. Often these phobias begin in childhood, when they are considered normal fears. Only when they persist into adulthood and disrupt your life or cause significant distress do they come to be classified as specific phobias.

Acrophobia (fear of heights). With acrophobia, you tend to be afraid of high floors of buildings or of finding yourself atop mountains, hills, or high-level bridges. In such situations you may experience 1) vertigo (dizziness) or 2) an urge to jump, usually experienced as some external force drawing you to the edge.

Elevator Phobia. This phobia may involve a fear that the cables will break and the elevator will crash *or* a fear that the elevator will get stuck and you will be trapped inside. You may have panic reactions, but you have no history of panic disorder or agoraphobia.

Airplane Phobia. This most often involves a fear that the plane will crash. Alternatively, it can involve a fear that the cabin will depressurize, causing you to asphyxiate. More recently, phobias about planes being hijacked or bombed have become common. When flying, you may have a panic attack. Otherwise you have no history of panic disorder or agoraphobia. Fear of flying is a very common phobia. Approximately 10 percent of the population will not fly at all, while an additional 20 percent experience considerable anxiety while flying.

Doctor or Dentist Phobias. This can begin as a fear of painful procedures (injections, having teeth filled) conducted in a doctor's or dentist's office. Later it can generalize to anything having to do with doctors or dentists. The danger is that you may avoid needed medical treatment.

Phobias of Thunder and/or Lightning. Almost invariably, phobias of thunder and lightning begin in childhood. When they persist beyond adolescence, they are classified as specific phobias.

Blood-Injury Phobia. This is a unique phobia in that you have a tendency to faint (rather than panic) if exposed to blood or your own pain through injections or inadvertent injury. People with blood-injury phobia tend to be both physically and psychologically healthy in other regards.

Disease Phobia (Hypochondria). Usually this phobia involves a fear of contracting and/or ultimately succumbing to a specific illness, such as a heart attack or cancer. With disease phobias, you tend to seek constant reassurance from doctors and will avoid any situation that reminds you of the dreaded disease.

Specific phobias are common and affect approximately 10 percent of the population. However, since they do not always result in severe impairment, only a minority of people with specific phobias actually seek treatment. These types of phobias occur in men and women about equally. Animal phobias tend to be more common in women, while disease phobias are more common in men. In general, women are twice as likely to report specific phobias as men, but this may reflect a difference in who seeks treatment (Cameron 2004).

As previously mentioned, specific phobias are often childhood fears that were never outgrown. In other instances, they may develop after a traumatic event, such as an accident, a natural disaster, an illness, or a visit to the dentist—in other words, as a result of conditioning. A final cause is childhood *modeling*. Repeated observation of a parent with a specific phobia can lead a child to develop it as well.

Current Treatment

Since specific phobias generally do not involve spontaneous panic attacks, some of the treatments for panic, such as panic-control therapy, interoceptive desensitization, and medication, are usually not included.

Relaxation Training. Abdominal breathing and deep muscle relaxation are practiced on a regular basis to reduce symptoms of anxiety that occur both when facing the specific phobia and when experiencing worry (anticipatory anxiety) about having to deal with the phobic situation. (See chapter 4.)

Cognitive Therapy. Fearful thoughts that tend to perpetuate the specific phobia are challenged and replaced. For example, "What if I panic because I feel trapped aboard an airplane?" would be replaced with more realistic and supportive thoughts, such as "While I may not be able to leave the airplane for two hours, I *can* move around, such as leaving my seat to go to the bathroom several times if needed. If I start to feel panicky, I have many strategies for coping that I can use, including abdominal breathing, talking to my companion, listening to a relaxing tape, or taking medication, if necessary." Coping statements, such as "I've handled this before and I can handle it again" or "This is just a thought; it has no validity," are also useful. These supportive coping statements are rehearsed until they are internalized. (See chapter 8.)

Exposure. This involves gradually facing the phobic situation through a series of incremental steps. For example, fear of flying would be faced first in imagination only (imagery desensitization), then by watching planes land and take off, then by boarding a grounded plane, then by taking a short flight, and, finally, by taking a longer flight. A support person would accompany you first through all the steps, then you'd try them on your own.

For some phobias, it's difficult to do real-life exposure. For example, if you're afraid of earthquakes, treatment would emphasize cognitive therapy and then exposure to imagined scenes of earthquakes (or watching movies about earthquakes). Imagery and real-life exposure are described in chapter 7.

To sum up, specific phobia is usually a benign disorder, particularly if it begins as a common childhood fear. Though it may last for years, it rarely gets worse and it often diminishes over time. Typically it is not associated with other psychiatric disturbances. People with specific phobias are usually functioning at a high level in all other respects.

Generalized Anxiety Disorder

Generalized anxiety disorder is characterized by chronic anxiety that persists for at least six months *but is unaccompanied by panic attacks, phobias, or obsessions.* You simply experience persistent anxiety and worry without the complicating features of other anxiety disorders. To be given a diagnosis of generalized anxiety disorder, your anxiety and worry must focus on two or more stressful life circumstances (such as finances, relationships, health, work problems, or school performance) a majority of days during a six-month period. It's common, if you're dealing with generalized anxiety disorder, to have a large number of worries and to spend a lot of your time worrying. Yet you find it difficult to exercise much control over your worrying. Moreover, the intensity and frequency of the worry are always out of proportion to the actual likelihood of the feared events happening.

In addition to frequent, hard-to-control worry, generalized anxiety disorder involves having at least three of the following six symptoms (with some symptoms present more days than not over the past six months):

- Tense—feeling keyed up

- Being easily fatigued

- Difficulty concentrating

- Irritability

- Muscle tightness

- Difficulties with sleep

Generalized anxiety disorder is frequently associated with physical symptoms such as tension headaches, irritable bowel syndrome, high blood pressure, insomnia, and even osteoporosis. However, the presence of any or all of these physical problems does not necessarily imply a diagnosis of generalized anxiety disorder, which is based primarily on the presence of ongoing worry.

You are likely to receive a diagnosis of generalized anxiety disorder if your worry and associated symptoms cause you significant distress and/or interfere with your ability to function occupationally, socially, or in other important areas.

If a doctor tells you that you suffer from generalized anxiety disorder, he or she has probably ruled out possible medical causes of chronic anxiety, such as hyperventilation, thyroid problems, or drug-induced anxiety (alcohol or benzodiazepine withdrawal). Generalized anxiety disorder often occurs together with depression, a condition sometimes referred to as "mixed anxiety-depressive disorder." In such instances, a careful history will usually reveal which disorder—the generalized anxiety or the depression—came first.

Generalized anxiety disorder can develop at any age. In children and adolescents, the focus of worry often tends to be on performance in school or sports events. In adults, the focus can vary. This disorder affects approximately 5 percent of the American population and may be slightly more common in females than males (55 to 60 percent of those diagnosed with the disorder are female).

Although there are no specific phobias associated with generalized anxiety disorder, one view propounded by Aaron Beck and Gary Emery suggests that the disorder is sustained by "basic fears" of a broader nature than specific phobias, such as

- Fear of losing control

- Fear of not being able to cope

- Fear of failure

- Fear of rejection or abandonment

- Fear of death and disease

Generalized anxiety disorder can be aggravated by any stressful situation that elicits these fears, such as increased demands for performance, intensified marital conflict, physical illness, or *any situation that heightens your perception of danger or threat.*

The underlying causes of generalized anxiety disorder are unknown. It is likely to involve a combination of heredity, neurobiology, and predisposing childhood experiences, such as excessive parental expectations or parental abandonment and rejection, or parents modeling worry behavior.

Current Treatment

Relaxation Training. Abdominal breathing and deep relaxation techniques are practiced on a regular basis to directly reduce anxiety. A physical exercise program may also be included in the treatment. (See chapters 4 and 5.)

Cognitive Therapy. Fearful self-talk underlying specific worry themes is identified, challenged, and replaced with more realistic thinking. When you worry, you overestimate the odds of something negative happening and underestimate your ability to cope if something bad did, in fact, happen. Cognitive therapy aims to correct both types of distorted thinking. You would also work on changing negative beliefs, or "metabeliefs," about worry itself. These include both beliefs that worry will help you avoid something negative, such as "If I worry about it, it won't happen," as well as fearful beliefs about worry itself, such as "My worries are uncontrollable" or "I'll go crazy from worrying." Realistic self-statements are consistently practiced and internalized over time. Guided imagery may also be used to help redirect your mind from preoccupation with worry to more optimistic themes.

Worry Exposure. In worry exposure, you do repeated and prolonged exposure to fearful images (your worst-case scenarios) of what you're worried about. In these images you include strategies you would use to reduce anxiety and cope with the situation.

Reducing Worry Behaviors. You identify overly cautious "safety behaviors" that tend to reinforce worrying. For example, if you tend to call your spouse or child several times a day to check on them, you would reduce the frequency of this behavior.

Problem Solving. This means taking systematic action to solve the problem you're worried about. In short, you focus on solutions to the problem that worries you instead of the worry itself. If there is no practical solution, you work on changing your attitude toward the situation—that is, learning to accept what you can't change.

Distraction. A variety of distraction techniques can be helpful for worries that do not lend themselves easily to cognitive therapy or problem solving. Common diversionary activities include talking to a friend, journaling, listening to music, gardening, exercise, puzzle solving, arts and crafts, cooking, and using the Internet.

Medication. For moderate to severe cases of generalized anxiety disorder, SSRI medications such as Zoloft, Luvox, Lexapro, or Celexa may be used. The SNRI medication Effexor has also been found to be effective in treating generalized anxiety disorder. Another medication, BuSpar, has been used for fifteen years to treat worry and generalized anxiety. It is no longer considered a first-line medication, however, as the SSRIs appear to be slightly more effective. BuSpar may sometimes be combined with an SSRI to enhance the SSRI's effectiveness. Benzodiazepines such as Xanax, Ativan, and Klonopin are often used in primary care but are not considered a first-line treatment by psychiatrists because of their potential for tolerance, dependence, and abuse.

Mindfulness Practice. Mindfulness is an attitude of simply witnessing the ongoing stream of your thoughts and feelings in the present moment without judgment. It originated in Buddhist meditation practice but is now being used as a common treatment for stress, depression, and generalized anxiety. For further information about mindfulness practice, see chapter 18.

Lifestyle and Personality Changes. Such changes are basically similar to the methods described for panic disorder: stress management, increased downtime, regular exercise, eliminating stimulants/sweets from your diet, resolving interpersonal conflicts, and changing attitudes toward perfectionism, an excessive need to please others, or the excessive need to control.

Obsessive-Compulsive Disorder

Some people naturally tend to be more neat, tidy, and orderly than others. These traits can be useful in many situations, both at work and at home. In obsessive-compulsive disorder, however, they are carried to an extreme and disruptive degree. Obsessive-compulsive people can spend many hours cleaning, tidying, checking, or ordering, to the point that these activities interfere with the rest of the business of their lives.

Obsessions are recurring ideas, thoughts, images, or impulses that seem senseless but nonetheless continue to intrude into your mind. Examples include images of violence, thoughts of doing violence to someone else, or fears of leaving on lights or the stove or leaving your door unlocked. You recognize that these thoughts or fears are irrational and you try to suppress them, but they continue to intrude into your mind for hours, days, weeks, or longer. These thoughts or images are not merely excessive worries about real-life problems and are usually unrelated to a real-life problem.

Compulsions are behaviors or rituals that you perform to dispel the anxiety brought up by obsessions. For example, you may wash your hands numerous times to dispel a fear of being contaminated, check the stove again and again to see if it is turned off, or look continually in your rearview mirror while driving to assuage anxiety about having hit somebody. You realize that these rituals are unreasonable, yet you feel compelled to perform them to ward off the anxiety associated with your particular obsession. The conflict between your wish to be free of the compulsive ritual and the irresistible desire to perform it is a source of anxiety, shame, and even despair. Eventually you may cease struggling with your compulsions and give over to them entirely.

Obsessions may occur by themselves, without necessarily being accompanied by compulsions. In fact, about 20 percent of the people who suffer from obsessive-compulsive disorder only have obsessions, and these often center around fears of causing harm to a loved one or having disquieting sexual thoughts.

The most common compulsions include washing, checking, and counting. If you are a washer, you are constantly concerned about avoiding contamination. You avoid touching doorknobs, shaking hands, or coming into contact with any object you associate with germs, filth, or a toxic substance. You can spend literally hours washing hands or showering to reduce anxiety about being contaminated. Women more often have this compulsion than men. Men outnumber women as checkers, however. Doors have to be repeatedly checked to dispel obsessions about being robbed; stoves are repeatedly checked to dispel obsessions about starting a fire; or roads repeatedly checked to dispel obsessions about having hit someone. In the counting compulsion, you must count up to a certain number or repeat a word a certain number of times to dispel anxiety about harm befalling you or someone else.

Obsessive-compulsive disorder is often accompanied by depression. Preoccupation with obsessions, in fact, tends to wax and wane with depression. This disorder is also typically accompanied by phobic avoidance—such as when a person with an obsession about dirt avoids public restrooms or touching doorknobs. Sometimes avoidance interferes with the person's social or occupational functioning.

It is very important to realize that as bizarre as obsessive-compulsive behavior may sound, it has nothing to do with "being crazy." You always recognize the irrationality and senselessness of your thoughts and behavior, and you are very frustrated (as well as depressed) about your inability to control them.

Obsessive-compulsive disorder is different from compulsive behavior disorders such as gambling and overeating. People with compulsive behavior disorders derive some pleasure from their compulsive activities, whereas people with OCD neither want to perform their compulsions (except to reduce fear) nor derive any pleasure from doing so.

Obsessive-compulsive disorder used to be considered a rare behavior disturbance. However, recent studies have shown that about *2 to 3 percent of the general population* may suffer, to varying degrees, from obsessive-compulsive disorder. The reason prevalence rates have been underestimated up to now is that most sufferers have been very reluctant to tell anyone about their problem. This disorder appears to affect men and women in equal numbers. Although many cases of obsessive-compulsive disorder begin in adolescence and young adulthood, about half begin in childhood. The age of onset tends to be earlier in males than females.

The causes of obsessive-compulsive disorder are unclear. There is some evidence that a deficiency of a neurotransmitter substance in the brain known as serotonin, or a disturbance in serotonin metabolism, is associated with the disorder. This is borne out by the fact that many sufferers improve when they take medications that increase brain serotonin levels, such as clomipramine (Anafranil) or specific serotonin-enhancing antidepressants such as fluoxetine (Prozac), fluvoxamine (Luvox), sertraline (Zoloft), or escitalopram (Lexapro). It also appears that persons with OCD have excessive activity in certain parts of the brain, such as the prefrontal cortex and the caudate nucleus. See chapter 2 for a more detailed description of the latest research on the neurobiology of obsessive-compulsive disorder.

Current Treatment

Relaxation Training. As with all of the anxiety disorders, abdominal breathing and deep relaxation skills are practiced on a daily basis to help reduce anxiety symptoms. (See chapter 4.)

Cognitive Therapy. Fearful, superstitious, or guilty thoughts associated with obsessions are identified, challenged, and replaced. For example, the idea "If I have a thought of doing harm to my child, I might act on it" is replaced with "The thought of doing harm is just 'random noise' caused by the OCD. It has no significance. Just having the thought doesn't mean I'll do it." (See chapter 8.)

Exposure and Response Prevention (ERP). This technique consists of exposure to situations that aggravate obsessions, followed by enforced prevention from performing rituals or compulsions. For example, if you've been washing your hands every time you touch a doorknob, you'd be instructed to touch doorknobs and either reduce the number of times you wash your hands or refrain from washing at all. Similarly, if you check the door five times whenever you leave your house, you would be required to gradually reduce the number of checks to one.

You and your therapist devise a variety of situations, preferably in your home setting. Then you continually practice exposing yourself to these situations and desist from performing the compulsions (response prevention). Usually your therapist or a support person accompanies you to monitor your compliance in not performing compulsions.

When your problem involves obsessions only, without compulsions, any neutralizing thoughts or covert rituals you use to reduce anxiety caused by your obsessions need to be stopped. You would also work on accepting your obsessions without trying to make them go away. (For further information on exposure and response prevention in treating OCD, see the book *Stop Obsessing: How to Overcome Your Obsessions and Compulsions* by Edna Foa and Reid Wilson, or *The OCD Workbook* by Bruce Hyman and Cherry Pedrick.)

Medication. Medications such as Anafranil and the SSRI medications, including Prozac, Luvox, Lexapro, Cymbalta, and Zoloft, help about 60 to 70 percent of those with OCD. Long-term use of medication is fairly common with OCD, although in some cases the cognitive and exposure/response prevention strategies described above may suffice. Effective doses of SSRI medications are usually higher for OCD than for other anxiety disorders, and benefits from these medications tend to appear only after two to three months at higher doses. Low doses of antipsychotic medications such as Zyprexa and Resperdal have been found to be useful adjuncts in the treatment of OCD for some people, which indicates that part of the brain mechanisms underlying OCD involve the role of dopamine receptors.

Lifestyle and Personality Changes. Essentially, the same lifestyle and personality changes described for panic disorder and generalized anxiety disorder apply to OCD.

The strategies presented in this workbook will be helpful if you are affected by obsessive-compulsive disorder. Yet the primary mode of treatment I would suggest is to consult a professional who is well versed in the use of behavioral methods, such as exposure and response prevention, as well as in the use of appropriate medications. This workbook can complement behavioral and pharmacological treatment approaches.

Post-Traumatic Stress Disorder

The essential feature of post-traumatic stress disorder (PTSD) is the development of disabling psychological symptoms following a traumatic event. It was first identified during World War I, when soldiers were observed to suffer chronic anxiety, nightmares, and flashbacks for weeks, months, or even years following combat. This condition came to be known as shell shock.

Post-traumatic stress disorder can occur in anyone in the wake of a severe trauma outside the normal range of human experience. These are traumas that would produce intense fear, terror, and feelings of helplessness in anyone and include natural disasters, such as earthquakes or tornadoes; car or plane crashes; and rape, assault, or other violent crimes against you or your immediate family. It appears that the symptoms are more intense and longer lasting when the trauma is personal, as in rape or other violent crimes. Observation of someone else suffering a severe trauma can be sufficient to induce post-traumatic stress disorder.

Among the variety of symptoms that can occur with post-traumatic stress disorder, the following nine are particularly common:

- Repetitive, distressing thoughts about the event

- Nightmares related to the event

- Flashbacks so intense that you feel or act as though the trauma were occurring all over again

- An attempt to avoid thoughts or feelings associated with the trauma

- An attempt to avoid activities or external situations associated with the trauma—such as developing a phobia about driving after you have been in an auto accident

- Emotional numbness—being out of touch with your feelings

- Feelings of detachment or estrangement from others

- Losing interest in activities that used to give you pleasure

- Persistent symptoms of increased anxiety, such as difficulty falling or staying asleep, difficulty concentrating, startling easily, or irritability and outbursts of anger

For you to receive a diagnosis of post-traumatic stress disorder, these symptoms need to have persisted for at least one month (with less than one month's duration, the appropriate diagnosis is acute stress disorder—see below). In addition, the disturbance must be causing you significant distress, interfering with social, vocational, or other important areas of your life.

If you suffer from post-traumatic stress disorder, you tend to be anxious and depressed. Sometimes you will find yourself acting impulsively, suddenly changing residence or going on a trip with hardly any plans. If you have been through a trauma where others around you died, you may suffer from guilt about having survived.

Post-traumatic stress disorder can occur at any age and affects about 8 percent of the population. Children with the disorder tend not to relive the trauma consciously but continually reenact it in their play or in distressing dreams.

There is some evidence that susceptibility to post-traumatic stress disorder is hereditary. For identical twins exposed to combat in Vietnam, if one identical twin developed the disorder, the odds were higher that the other identical twin would, as compared with fraternal twins (True, Rice, and Eisen 1993).

Current Treatment

Treatment for post-traumatic stress disorder is complex and multifaceted. Many of the strategies described above for other anxiety disorders are helpful, but additional techniques may be used as well.

Relaxation Training. Abdominal breathing and progressive muscle relaxation techniques are practiced to better control anxiety symptoms. (See chapter 4.)

Cognitive Therapy. Fearful or depressed thinking is identified, challenged, and replaced with more productive thinking. For example, guilt about having been responsible for the trauma—or having survived when someone you loved did not—would be challenged. You would reinforce yourself with supportive, constructive thoughts, such as "What happened was horrible, and I accept that there is nothing I could have done to prevent it. I'm learning now that I can go on." (See chapters 8 and 9.)

Exposure Therapy. A therapist or support person helps you confront fearful situations that you want to avoid because they trigger strong anxiety. In imaginal exposure, you would repeatedly go back over fearful memories of events, objects, and persons associated with the original trauma. In real-life exposure, you would return to the actual situation where the trauma occurred. For example, if you were assaulted in an elevator, you would return to the elevator several times. Repeated exposure helps you to understand that the fearful situation is no longer dangerous. (See chapter 7.)

Medication. SSRI medications such as Zoloft, Luvox, Prozac, or Celexa are often helpful in alleviating PTSD symptoms. Especially when these symptoms are severe and long-lasting, a course of medication lasting one or two years might be utilized. Tranquilizers such as Xanax or Klonopin might be used on a short-term basis. (See chapter 17.)

Support Groups. Support groups are particularly helpful in enabling PTSD victims to realize that they are not alone. Support groups for rape or crime survivors are often available in larger metropolitan areas. Considerable research indicates that social support offers protective effects in both avoiding and recovering from the disorder.

EMDR or Hypnotherapy. Eye-movement desensitization and reprocessing (EMDR) or hypnotherapy are often helpful in enabling PTSD victims to retrieve and work through memories of the original traumatic incident. These techniques may be used to accelerate the course of therapy and/or overcome resistance to exposure. Studies have found these techniques to be equally effective as cognitive behavioral therapy and exposure (Seidler and Wagner 2006).

It's important to add that the treatment for any anxiety disorder may include marital or family therapy. Interpersonal problems with spouses and/or family may serve to perpetuate anxiety and undermine the success of treatment until these issues are addressed. Family therapy is also useful in educating family members about how to understand, support, and, in some cases, set limits with the family member suffering with the anxiety disorder.

Additional Anxiety Disorders in the *DSM–IV*

The anxiety disorders described above have been recognized by professionals in the field for over twenty years. When the fourth edition of *The Diagnostic and Statistical Manual of Mental Disorders* was published in 1994, the following four disorders were added.

Acute Stress Disorder

Like post-traumatic stress disorder, acute stress disorder involves developing anxiety and other disabling symptoms after exposure to a traumatic event. The principal distinction is that the symptoms subside in less than one month; if the symptoms last beyond one month, the diagnosis is changed from acute stress disorder to post-traumatic stress disorder. As with post-traumatic stress disorder, the initial trauma involves exposure to an event that carries the threat of death or serious injury (for example, military combat, violent personal assault, sexual assault, a natural or man-made disaster, a car accident, or being diagnosed with a life-threatening illness). Either during or after the traumatic incident, you have symptoms such as numbness, detachment, or feelings of unreality or depersonalization. Later you tend to avoid anything that reminds you of the incident and have persistent symptoms of anxiety (difficulty sleeping, irritability, poor concentration, exaggerated startle response, restlessness). This disturbance typically interferes with your work and your significant relationships but, as indicated, lasts no longer than four weeks following the traumatic event.

Agoraphobia Without a History of Panic Disorder

This particular anxiety disorder has all of the same features as agoraphobia—such as avoidance of a variety of situations—but there is no history of having had full-blown panic attacks. Instead, the focus of your fear is on only *one or two* symptoms among all those listed for panic disorder. For example, you might be afraid *only* of having heart palpitations if you venture too far from home or go to a crowded public place. Sometimes the fear is of an incapacitating symptom not on the list of panic attack symptoms. For example, you might be afraid to drive long distances and/or to be far from a town because of a fear of losing bladder control or having a bout of diarrhea.

Only a small percentage of people with agoraphobia do not have a history of panic disorder (estimates range from 5 to 15 percent). Treatment emphasizes relaxation, cognitive therapy, and *in vivo* exposure.

Anxiety Disorder Due to a General Medical Condition

This diagnostic category is reserved for situations in which significant anxiety (in the form of either panic attacks or generalized anxiety) is a direct physiological effect of a specific medical condition. Numerous types of medical conditions can cause anxiety, including endocrine conditions (hyper- and hypothyroidism, pheochromocytoma, hypoglycemia), cardiovascular conditions (congestive heart failure, pulmonary embolism), metabolic conditions (vitamin B_{12} deficiency, porphyria), and neurological conditions (vestibular problems, encephalitis). For a more complete listing, see the section in chapter 2 entitled "Medical Conditions That Can Cause Panic Attacks or Anxiety."

Substance-Induced Anxiety Disorder

This category is used when generalized anxiety or panic attacks are determined to be the direct physiological effect of a substance, whether a drug of abuse, a medication, or toxin exposure. The anxiety may be a result either of exposure to the substance or of withdrawal from it. For example, if you had no previous history of an anxiety disorder, then suddenly developed panic attacks as a result of withdrawing too quickly from a medication, you would receive this diagnosis.

Self-Diagnosis Questionnaire

The following questionnaire is designed to help you identify which particular anxiety disorder you may be dealing with. It is based on the official classification of anxiety disorders used by mental health professionals and known as the *DSM–IV (Diagnostic and Statistical Manual of Mental Disorders*—fourth edition).

1. Do you have spontaneous anxiety attacks that come out of the blue? (Only answer "yes" if you do *not* have any phobias.)   Yes ____   No ____

2. Have you had at least one such attack in the last month?   Yes ____   No ____

3. If you had an anxiety attack in the last month, did you worry about having another one? Or did you worry about the implications of your attack for your physical or mental health?   Yes ____   No ____

4. In your worst experience with anxiety, did you have more than three of the following symptoms?

    ☐   Shortness of breath or a smothering sensation

- [ ] Dizziness or an unsteady feeling

- [ ] Heart palpitations or rapid heartbeat

- [ ] Trembling or shaking

- [ ] Sweating

- [ ] Choking

- [ ] Nausea or abdominal distress

- [ ] Feelings of being detached or out of touch with your body

- [ ] Numbness or tingling sensations

- [ ] Flushes or chills

- [ ] Chest pain or discomfort

- [ ] Fear of dying

- [ ] Fear of going crazy or doing something out of control

If your answers to 1, 2, 3, and 4 were yes, stop. You've met the conditions for **panic disorder**.

If your answer to 1 was yes, but your anxiety reaction involved three or fewer of the symptoms listed under 4, you're experiencing what are called *limited-symptom attacks*, but do not have full-blown panic disorder.

If you have panic attacks *and* phobias, go on.

5. Does fear of having panic attacks cause you to avoid going into certain situations? Yes _____ No _____

If your answer to 5 was yes, stop. It is likely that you are dealing with **agoraphobia**. See question 6 to determine the extent of your agoraphobia.

6. Which of the following situations do you avoid because you are afraid of panicking?

- [ ] Going far away from home

- [ ] Shopping in a grocery store

- [ ] Standing in a grocery store line

- [ ] Going to department stores

- [ ] Going to shopping malls

- [ ] Driving on freeways

- [ ] Driving on surface streets far from home

- [ ] Driving anywhere by yourself

- [ ] Using public transportation (buses, trains, etc.)

- ☐ Going over bridges (whether you're the driver or the passenger)
- ☐ Going through tunnels (as driver or passenger)
- ☐ Flying in planes
- ☐ Riding in elevators
- ☐ Being in high places
- ☐ Going to a dentist's or doctor's office
- ☐ Sitting in a barber's or beautician's chair
- ☐ Eating in restaurants
- ☐ Going to work
- ☐ Being too far from a safe person or safe place
- ☐ Being alone
- ☐ Going outside your house
- ☐ Other _____

The number of situations you checked above indicates the extent of your agoraphobia and the degree to which it limits your activity.

If your answer to 5 was no, but you do have phobias, go on.

7.   Do you avoid certain situations *not* primarily because you are afraid of panicking but because you're afraid of being embarrassed or negatively evaluated by other people (which could subsequently lead you to panic)?   Yes _____   No _____

If your answer to 7 was yes, stop. It's likely that you are dealing with **social phobia**. See question 8 to determine the extent of your social phobia.

8.   Which of the following situations do you avoid because of a fear of embarrassing or humiliating yourself?

- ☐ Sitting in any kind of group (for example, at work, in school classrooms, in social organizations, or in self-help groups)
- ☐ Giving a talk or presentation before a small group of people
- ☐ Giving a talk or presentation before a large group of people
- ☐ Parties and social functions
- ☐ Using public restrooms
- ☐ Eating in front of others
- ☐ Writing or signing your name in the presence of others
- ☐ Dating
- ☐ Any situation in which you might say something foolish

☐   Other _____

The number of situations you checked indicates the extent to which social phobia limits your activities.

If your answers to questions 5 and 7 were no, but you have other phobias, continue.

9.   Do you fear and avoid any one (or more than one) of the following?

☐   Insects or animals, such as spiders, bees, snakes, rats, bats, or dogs

☐   Heights (high floors in buildings, tops of hills or mountains, high-level bridges)

☐   Driving

☐   Tunnels

☐   Bridges

☐   Elevators

☐   Airplanes (flying)

☐   Doctors or dentists

☐   Thunder or lightning

☐   Water

☐   Blood

☐   Injections or medical procedures

☐   Illness such as heart attacks or cancer

☐   Darkness

☐   Other _____

10.   Do you have high degrees of anxiety usually *only* when you have to face one of these situations?   Yes _____   No _____

If you checked one or more items in 9 and answered yes to 10, stop. It's likely that you're dealing with a **specific phobia**. If not, proceed.

11.   Do you feel quite anxious much of the time but do *not* have distinct panic attacks, do *not* have phobias, and do *not* have specific obsessions or compulsions?   Yes _____   No .

12.   Have you been prone to excessive worry for at least the last six months? Yes _____   No _____

13.   Has your anxiety and worry been associated with at least three of the following six symptoms?

☐   Tense—feeling keyed up

☐   Being easily fatigued

    ☐   Difficulty concentrating or mind going blank

    ☐   Irritability

    ☐   Muscle tension

    ☐   Sleep disturbance (difficulty falling or staying asleep, or restless and unsatisfying sleep)

If your answers to 11, 12, and 13 were yes, stop. It's likely that you're dealing with **generalized anxiety disorder**. If you answered yes to 11 but no to 12 or 13, you're dealing with an anxiety condition that is not severe enough to qualify as generalized anxiety disorder.

14.   Do you have recurring intrusive thoughts such as about hurting or harming a close relative, about being contaminated with dirt or a toxic substance, fearing you forgot to lock your door or turn off an appliance, or an unpleasant fantasy of catastrophe? (You recognize that these thoughts are irrational but you can't keep them from coming into your mind.)   Yes ____   No ____

15.   Do you perform ritualistic actions such as washing your hands, checking, or counting to relieve anxiety over irrational fears that enter your mind?   Yes ____   No ____

If you answered yes to 14 but no to 15, you are probably dealing with **obsessive-compulsive disorder**, but have obsessions only.

If you answered yes to 14 and 15, you're probably dealing with **obsessive-compulsive disorder**, with both obsessions and compulsions.

If you answered no to 14 and 15 and most or all of the preceding questions, but you still have anxiety or anxiety-related symptoms, you may be dealing with **post-traumatic stress disorder** or a nonspecific anxiety condition. Use the section in this chapter on post-traumatic stress disorder to determine whether your symptoms fit this category.

Co-Occurrence of Anxiety Disorders

In the years that have passed since the first edition of *The Anxiety & Phobia Workbook* was published, it has become increasingly apparent that many people are dealing with more than one anxiety disorder. For example, one survey of people with panic disorder found that 15 to 30 percent also have social phobia, 10 to 20 percent have a specific phobia, 25 percent have generalized anxiety disorder, and 8 to 10 percent have obsessive-compulsive disorder. People with agoraphobia quite often have social phobias and/or obsessive-compulsive difficulties. If you find that your particular condition fits the description for more than one anxiety disorder, you are not alone.

Further Reading

Panic Disorder

Barlow, David, and Michelle Craske. *Mastery of Your Anxiety and Panic: Workbook.* Fourth edition. New York: Oxford University Press, 2007.

Beckfield, Denise F. *Master Your Panic and Take Back Your Life.* Second edition. San Luis Obispo, CA: Impact Publishers, 1998.

Wilson, Reid. *Don't Panic: Taking Control of Anxiety Attacks.* Revised edition. New York: HarperCollins, 1996.

Zuercher-White, Elke. *An End to Panic.* Second edition. Oakland, CA: New Harbinger Publications, 1998.

Agoraphobia

Beckfield, Denise F. *Master Your Panic and Take Back Your Life.* Second edition. San Luis Obispo, CA: Impact Publishers, 1998.

Feninger, Mani. *Journey from Anxiety to Freedom.* Rocklin, CA: Prima Publishers, 1998.

Zuercher-White, Elke. *The Agoraphobia Workbook.* Oakland, CA: New Harbinger Publications, 2003.

Social Phobia

Antony, Martin, and Richard Swinson. *The Shyness & Social Anxiety Workbook.* Second edition. Oakland, CA: New Harbinger Publications, 2008.

Butler, Gillian. *Overcoming Social Anxiety and Shyness: A Self-Help Guide Using Cognitive-Behavioral Techniques.* New York: Basic Books, 2008.

Rapee, Ronald. *Overcoming Shyness and Social Phobia.* Northvale, NJ: Jason Aronson, 1998.

Schneier, Franklin, and Lawrence Welkowitz. *The Hidden Face of Shyness: Understanding and Overcoming Social Anxiety.* New York: Avon Books, 1996.

Specific Phobia

Bourne, Edmund J. *Overcoming Specific Phobia: Therapist Protocol & Client Manual.* Oakland, CA: New Harbinger Publications, 1998.

Brown, Duane. *Flying Without Fear.* Oakland, CA: New Harbinger Publications, 1996.

Generalized Anxiety Disorder

Copeland, Mary Ellen. *The Worry Control Workbook.* Oakland, CA: New Harbinger Publications, 1998.

White, John. *Overcoming Generalized Anxiety Disorder: Therapist Protocol and Client Manual.* Oakland, CA: New Harbinger Publications, 1998.

Obsessive-Compulsive Disorder

Foa, Edna, and Reid Wilson. *Stop Obsessing: How to Overcome Your Obsessions and Compulsions.* Revised edition. New York: Bantam, 2001.

Hyman, Bruce, and Troy Dufrene. *Coping With OCD: Practical Strategies for Living Well with Obsessive-Compulsive Disorder.* Oakland, CA: New Harbinger Publications, 2008.

Hyman, Bruce M., and Cherry Pedrick. *The OCD Workbook.* Second edition. Oakland, CA: New Harbinger Publications, 2005.

Schwartz, Jeffrey M. *Brain Lock: Free Yourself from Obsessive-Compulsive Behavior.* New York: Regan Books, 1996.

Steketee, Gail. *Stuff: Compulsive Hoarding and the Meaning of Things.* New York: Houghton Mifflin Harcourt, 2010.

Post-Traumatic Stress Disorder

Allen, Jon G. *Coping with Trauma: A Guide to Self-Understanding.* Washington, DC: American Psychiatric Press, 1999.

England, Diane. *The Post-Traumatic Stress Disorder Relationship.* Avon, MA: Adams Media, 2009.

Matsakis, Aphrodite. *Trust After Trauma: A Guide to Relationships for Survivors and Those Who Love Them.* Oakland, CA: New Harbinger Publications, 1998.

Schiraldi, Glenn. *The Post-Traumatic Stress Disorder Sourcebook: A Guide to Healing, Recovery, and Growth.* Second edition. New York: McGraw-Hill, 2009.

2

Major Causes of Anxiety Disorders

If you are dealing with one of the anxiety disorders, you are likely to be concerned with the causes of your problem. You probably ask yourself, "Why do I have panic attacks? Is it something hereditary, or is it the way I was brought up? What causes phobias to develop? Why am I afraid of something I know isn't dangerous? What causes obsessions and compulsions?"

The symptoms of anxiety disorders often seem irrational and inexplicable: it is only natural to raise the question "Why?" But before considering in detail the various causes of anxiety disorders, there are two general points you should bear in mind. First, although learning about the causes of anxiety disorders can give you insight into how these problems develop, such knowledge is not necessary to overcome your particular difficulty. The various strategies for overcoming anxiety disorders presented in this workbook—such as relaxation, exercise, desensitization, changing self-talk and mistaken beliefs, or dealing with feelings— do not depend on a knowledge of underlying causes to be effective. However interesting the information in this chapter may be, it is not necessarily what "cures." Second, be wary of the notion that there is one primary cause, or type of cause, for any of the anxiety disorders. Whether you are dealing with panic attacks, social phobia, generalized anxiety, or obsessive-compulsive disorder, recognize that there is no one cause which, if removed, would eliminate the problem. Anxiety problems are brought about by a variety of causes operating on numerous different levels: heredity, biology, family background and upbringing, conditioning, recent stressors, your self-talk and personal belief system, your ability to express feelings, and so on. The range of chapters in this book indicates the many different levels on which you can understand the causes of and the means of recovering from anxiety disorders.

Some experts in the field of anxiety disorders propose "single-cause" theories. Such theories tend to greatly oversimplify anxiety disorders and are susceptible to one of two mistaken lines of reasoning: the *biological fallacy* and the *psychological fallacy*. The biological fallacy assumes that a particular type of anxiety disorder is caused *solely* by some biological or physiological imbalance in the brain or body. For example, there has recently been a tendency to reduce the causation of panic disorder, as well as obsessive-compulsive disorder, to a strictly biological level. Panic disorder is viewed as arising from a dysfunction in parts of the brain, such as the *amygdala* and the *locus coeruleus*. Obsessive-compulsive disorder is thought to be caused by a deficiency in a particular neurotransmitter substance in the brain called *serotonin*—or a dysregulation in the serotonin system of neurons in the brain. (A *neurotransmitter* is a chemical substance that allows nerve impulses to be transmitted from one nerve cell to another.)

It is helpful to know that there may be physiological dysfunctions involved in panic disorder and obsessive-compulsive disorder. This certainly has implications for treatment of these problems. But this does not mean that panic attacks and obsessive-compulsive disorder are physiological disturbances only. The question remains: *What caused the physiological disturbance itself?* Perhaps chronic stress due to psychological conflict causes the amygdala and locus coeruleus to malfunction in panic disorder. Or perhaps chronically suppressed anger sets up a disturbance in brain serotonin levels that is a contributing cause of obsessive-compulsive disorder. Psychological conflicts and repressed anger may, in turn, have been caused by a person's upbringing. Because any particular physiological disturbance may have originally been set up by stress or other psychological factors, it is a fallacy to assume that anxiety disorders are solely (or even primarily) caused by physiological imbalances.

The psychological fallacy makes the same kind of mistake in the opposite direction. It assumes that, say, social phobia or generalized anxiety disorder is caused by having grown up with parents who neglected, abandoned, or abused you, resulting in a deep-seated sense of insecurity or shame that causes your current phobic avoidance and anxiety as an adult. While it may be true that your family background *contributed* in an important way to your current problems, is it reasonable to assume that this is the *only* cause? Again, not really. To do so overlooks the possible contributions of hereditary and biological factors. After all, not all children who grow up in dysfunctional families develop anxiety disorders. It is more plausible to assume that your problem is a result of *both* 1) a hereditary predisposition toward anxiety (and possibly phobia) *and* 2) early childhood conditions that fostered a sense of shame and/or insecurity.

In sum, the idea that your particular difficulties are *just* a physiological disturbance or *just* a psychological disturbance neglects the fact that nature and nurture are interactive. Biological disturbances may be "set up" by stress or psychological factors; psychological problems, in turn, may be influenced by inborn biological disturbances. There is simply no way to say which came first or which is the so-called ultimate cause. By the same token, a comprehensive approach to recovery from panic, phobias, or anxiety cannot restrict itself to treating physiological or psychological causes in isolation. A variety of strategies dealing with several different levels, including biological, behavioral, emotional, mental, interpersonal, and even spiritual factors, is necessary for a full and lasting recovery. This multidimensional approach to recovery is discussed in the next chapter and assumed throughout this book.

The causes of anxiety disorders vary not only according to the level at which they occur but also according to the time period over which they operate. Some are *predisposing causes*, which set you up from birth or childhood to develop panic or anxiety later on. Some are *recent* or *short-term* causes—circumstances that *trigger* the onset of, say, panic attacks or agoraphobia. Others are *maintaining* causes—factors in your current lifestyle, attitudes, and behavior that serve to keep anxiety disorders going once they have developed. The remainder of this chapter examines each of these types of causes in more detail. A section on biological causes is included to acquaint you with some of the better-known hypotheses about the role of the brain in causing panic attacks and anxiety.

An outline of the causes of anxiety disorders follows.

Causes of Anxiety Disorders

Long-Term, Predisposing Causes

1.   Heredity

2.   Childhood Circumstances

   • Your Parents Communicate an Overly Cautious View of the World

   • Your Parents Are Overly Critical and Set Excessively High Standards

   • Emotional Insecurity and Dependence

   • Your Parents Suppress Your Expression of Feelings and Self-Assertiveness

3.   Cumulative Stress over Time

Biological Causes

1.   The physiology of Panic

2.   Panic Attacks

3.   Generalized Anxiety

4.   Obsessive-Compulsive Disorder

5.   Medical Conditions That Can Cause Panic Attacks or Anxiety

Short-Term, Triggering Causes

1.   Stressors That Precipitate Panic Attacks

   • Significant Personal Loss

   • Significant Life Change

   • Stimulants and Recreational Drugs

2.   Conditioning and the Origin of Phobias

3.   Trauma, Simple Phobias, and Post-Traumatic Stress Disorder

Maintaining Causes

1.   Avoidance of Phobic Situations

2.   Anxious Self-Talk

3.   Mistaken Beliefs

4.   Withheld Feelings

5.   Lack of Assertiveness

6.   Lack of Self-Nurturing Skills

7.   Muscle Tension

8.   Stimulants and Other Dietary Factors

9.   High-Stress Lifestyle

10.   Lack of Meaning or Sense of Purpose

Long-Term, Predisposing Causes

Heredity

Are anxiety disorders inherited? The limited evidence that exists to date would argue that they are—at least in part. For example, it is estimated that 15 to 25 percent of children growing up with at least one agoraphobic parent become agoraphobic themselves, while the rate of agoraphobia in the general population is only 5 percent. This fact in itself doesn't prove that agoraphobia is inherited, however, because it could be argued that children *learn* from their parents to be agoraphobic.

More compelling evidence comes from studies of identical twins, who, of course, have exactly the same genetic makeup. If one identical twin has an anxiety disorder, the probability of the other identical twin having an anxiety disorder ranges from 31 to 88 percent, depending on the study you're looking at. By comparison, when fraternal twins (whose genes are no more similar than those of siblings born at different times) are studied, the probability is much lower. If one fraternal twin has an anxiety disorder, the odds of the other having an anxiety disorder range from about 0 to 38 percent—again, depending on the study. Having the same genetic makeup as someone else with phobias or anxiety makes it *more than twice as likely* that you will have a similar problem. Interestingly, the percentages for fraternal twins are generally higher than the incidence of anxiety disorders in the population (about 8 to 10 percent). This would argue that growing up in the same family—having the same parenting—contributes at least something to the development of anxiety disorders. Both nature and nurture seem to have an impact.

What is it that is inherited? Based on what is known at this time, it seems that you don't inherit agoraphobia, social phobia, or even panic attacks specifically from your parents. What is inherited seems to be a *general personality type* that predisposes you to be overly anxious.

This is a volatile, excitable, reactive personality that is more easily set off by any slightly threatening stimulus than is the personality of individuals without anxiety disorders. Once you are born with this highly reactive personality, you might develop one or another anxiety disorder, depending on your particular environment and upbringing. For example, whether you develop agoraphobia or social phobia might depend on how much you learned to feel ashamed in situations where you were expected to perform. Whether you develop panic attacks or not might depend on the nature and degree of stress you're exposed to during adolescence and early adulthood. In short, while heredity might cause you to be born with a more reactive, excitable nervous system, childhood experiences, conditioning, and stress all serve to shape the particular type of anxiety disorder you subsequently develop.

Recent research in the field of behavior genetics has begun to hone in on specific genes associated with anxiety disorders. For example, the seventeenth chromosome (we all have 23) contains a gene known as SERT (serotonin transfer gene), which functions in the manufacture of the brain neurotransmitter serotonin. People with the "short" form of the gene tend to be more predisposed to develop anxiety disorders (as well as mood disorders such as depression), while people with the "long" form of the gene have a degree of protection, in spite of childhood and adult stress, from developing problems with anxiety.

Childhood Circumstances

What childhood experiences or family environments might predispose you to develop a particular anxiety disorder? Unfortunately, very little research on this topic has been done. Researchers have found that panic attacks and agoraphobia in adulthood are often preceded by separation anxiety disorder in childhood. This is a condition in which children experience anxiety, panic, or somatic symptoms when separated from their parents, as when going to school or even before going to sleep. Later on as adults, these same people experience anxiety when separated from a "safe" person or place. The conditions that might lead to separation anxiety disorder in the first place are matters for speculation.

What follows is a list of childhood circumstances that might predispose you to develop anxiety disorders. The list is based on my own experience with clients over several years. These factors are especially relevant if you are dealing with agoraphobia or social phobia, but may be applicable to other anxiety disorders as well.

- ***Your Parents Communicate an Overly Cautious View of the World***

Parents of people with phobias either tend to have phobias themselves or are more fearful and anxious than average. Often they are overly concerned about potential dangers to their child. They are likely to say things like "Don't go out in the rain—you'll catch a cold," "Don't watch TV so much. You'll ruin your eyes," or "Be very careful," again and again. The more they communicate a fearful, overcautious attitude toward their child, the more that child comes to view the world as a "dangerous" place. When you learn that the outside world is threatening, you automatically restrict your exploration and risk taking. You grow up with a tendency to worry excessively and be overly concerned with safety.

- ### *Your Parents Are Overly Critical and Set Excessively High Standards*

Children growing up with critical, perfectionist parents are never quite sure of their own acceptability. There is always some doubt about whether you are "good enough," or sufficiently worthy. As a result, you are constantly striving to please your parents and maintain their approval. As an adult, you may be overly eager to please, "look good," and "be nice" at the expense of your true feelings and capacity for assertiveness. Having grown up always feeling insecure, you may become very dependent on a safe person or safe place, and may restrict yourself from entering public or social situations where there is a risk of "losing face." You often come to internalize your parents' values, becoming exceptionally perfectionist and self-critical (as well as critical of others).

- ### *Emotional Insecurity and Dependence*

Up to the age of four or five, children are utterly dependent on their parents, especially their mother. Any conditions that create insecurity during this time can lead to excessive dependency and clinging later on. Excessive criticism and perfectionist standards on the part of parents seem to be a common source of insecurity for people who later develop anxiety disorders. *However, experiences of neglect, rejection, abandonment through divorce or death, and physical or sexual abuse can also produce the kind of basic insecurity (as well as emotional dependency) that forms a background for anxiety disorders.*

Growing up in a family in which one or both parents are alcoholic is also a common contributing factor in 20 to 25 percent of the clients I've seen. As described in a number of popular books on the subject, adult children of alcoholics grow up with characteristics such as 1) obsession with control, 2) avoidance of feelings, 3) difficulty trusting others, 4) overresponsibility, 5) all-or-nothing thinking, and 6) excessive eagerness to please, at the expense of their own needs. Although not all adult children of alcoholics develop anxiety disorders, the above characteristics are commonly seen in many people who have problems with panic and/or phobias.

A common denominator in the background of adult children of alcoholics, adult survivors of other forms of abuse, and most people who develop anxiety disorders is a deep-seated sense of insecurity. Perhaps the degree of insecurity and the way children respond to it will determine whether they later develop a specific type of anxiety disorder—as opposed to, say, an addictive personality or some other behavior disturbance. When children respond to insecurity with *excessive dependency*, the stage is set for overreliance on a safe person or safe place later in life. This is a common background for agoraphobia.

- ### *Your Parents Suppress Your Expression of Feelings and Self-Assertiveness*

Parents not only may foster dependency but may suppress your innate capacity to express your feelings and assert yourself. For example, as a child you may have been continually reprimanded or punished for speaking out, acting impulsively, or getting angry. Subsequently you grew up exerting a restrictive, even punitive, attitude toward your own expression of impulses and feelings. If these impulses and feelings are suppressed over a long period of time, their sudden recurrence under stress may produce anxiety or even panic. Frequently, people who learned to bottle up their feelings and self-expression as children are tense, more prone to be anxious, and unable to express themselves as adults. Of course, this form of suppression in childhood can also lead to depression and passivity later on. In both cases, learning to express your feelings and becoming more assertive can have a very beneficial effect.

Reading about the four factors just discussed may have stimulated you to think about what happened in your own childhood. Use the *Family Background Questionnaire* on the next page to further explore what circumstances in your family may have contributed to your own problems with anxiety.

Family Background Questionnaire

Use the following questionnaire to reflect on your childhood. Can you identify what conditions might have contributed to your current problem with anxiety?

1. Did either of your parents suffer from panic attacks or phobias?

2. Did you have a brother, sister, grandparent, or other relative who had panic attacks or phobias?

3. Did either of your parents seem excessively prone to worry?

4. Did either of your parents seem overly concerned about potential dangers that could befall you or other family members?

5. Did your parents encourage exploration of the outside world, or did they cultivate an attitude of caution, suspicion, or distrust?

6. Do you feel that your parents were overly critical or demanding of you? If so, how did you feel in response to this criticism?
    - ☐ Put down or diminished
    - ☐ Ashamed or guilty
    - ☐ Hurt or rejected
    - ☐ Angry or rebellious

7. As a child, did you feel free to express your feelings and impulses? How were feelings dealt with in your family?
    - ☐ Openly expressed
    - ☐ Punished
    - ☐ Denied

8. Was it okay for you to cry? How did your parents respond when you cried?

9. Was it okay to express anger? How did your parents respond when you got angry?

10. What was your role in the family? How were you perceived relative to other children in the family?

11. Do you feel that you grew up feeling insecure? Which of the following might have contributed to your insecurity:
    - ☐ Excessive criticism by your parents

    ☐   Excessive punishment

    ☐   Your parents made you feel ashamed

    ☐   Your parents made you feel guilty

    ☐   Your parents neglected you

    ☐   One or both parents abandoned you through death or divorce

    ☐   Physical abuse

    ☐   Sexual abuse

    ☐   Parental alcoholism

12.   If you grew up insecure, how did you respond to your feelings of insecurity?

    ☐   By becoming very dependent on your family (Did you have difficulty leaving home?)

    ☐   By becoming very independent of your family (Did you leave home early?)

    ☐   By becoming angry or rebellious

Cumulative Stress over Time

A third contributing factor in the development of anxiety disorders is the influence of *cumulative* stress over time. When stress persists without letup over a period of time, such as several months or years, it tends to accumulate. This sort of stress is more enduring than the normal, temporary stresses of moving, the Christmas season, or a short-term financial setback. Cumulative stress can arise from unresolved psychological conflicts lasting over many years. Or it can be due to difficulties in one area of your life—such as problems with your marriage or physical health—that persist over a long period of time. Finally, it may be due to the accretion of a large number of *life events*. Life events include changes in the course of your life that require an adjustment and reordering of your priorities, such as going off to college, changing jobs, getting married or leaving an intimate relationship, moving to a new location, having a baby, or having your children leave home. While one or two life events every year is a common and manageable experience, a series of many of them stretching over one or two years' time can lead to a state of chronic stress and exhaustion.

The concept of life events arose from the work of Dr. Richard Holmes and Dr. Thomas Rahe, who developed an instrument called the *Life Events Survey* (also known as *The Social Readjustment Scale*) to assess the number and severity of life events that occur in a two-year period. They used the survey specifically to predict a person's risk of developing physical disease. However, the survey can also be used as a general measure of cumulative stress. You can get an estimate of your own level of cumulative stress by completing the *Life Events Survey* in this chapter.

Life Events Survey

Life Event	Average Stress Score
Death of spouse	100
Divorce	73
Marital separation	65
Jail term	63
Death of close family member	63
Personal injury or illness	53
Marriage	50
Being fired from work	47
Marital problems	45
Retirement	45
Change in health of family member	44
Pregnancy	40
Sexual difficulties	39
Gain of new family member	39
Business readjustment	39
Change in finances	38
Death of close friend	37
Change to different line of work	36
Change in number of arguments with spouse	35
Mortgage or loan for major purchase (such as a home)	31
Foreclosure of mortgage or loan	30
Change in responsibilities at work	29
Son or daughter leaving home	29
Trouble with in-laws	29
Outstanding personal achievement	28
Spouse begins or stops work	26
Beginning or finishing school	26
Change in living conditions	25
Revision of personal habits	24
Trouble with boss	23
Change in work hours or conditions	20
Change in residence	20
Change in school	20
Change in recreation	19
Change in church activities	19
Change in social activities	18
Mortgage or loan for lesser purchase (such as a car or TV)	17
Change in sleeping habits	16
Change in number of family get-together	15
Change in eating habits	15
Vacation	13
Christmas	12
Minor violations of the law	11

Determine which life events have occurred in your life over the past two years and add up your total stress score. For example, if you got married, changed to a different line of work, changed residence, and took two vacations, your total stress score would be 50 + 36 + 20 + 13 + 13 = 132. If your total stress score is under 150, you are less likely to be suffering the effects of cumulative stress. If it is between 150 and 300, you may be suffering from chronic stress, depending on how you perceived and coped with the particular life events that occurred. If your score is over 300, it is likely you are experiencing some detrimental effects of cumulative stress. Please note that the stress scores on the above survey are averaged over many people. The degree to which any particular event is stressful to you will depend on how you perceive it.

For many years, it has been known that stress can increase your risk of developing psychosomatic disorders, such as high blood pressure, headaches, or ulcers. Only recently has it been recognized that *psychological disorders* may also be an outcome of cumulative stress. Over time, stress can affect the neuroendocrine regulatory systems of the brain, which play an important role in mood disorders, such as depression and anxiety disorders. Stress is nonspecific in its action; it simply has the greatest impact on the weakest point in your system. If this happens to be your cardiovascular system, you may develop high blood pressure or migraine headaches. If it is the neuroendocrine and neurotransmitter systems of your brain, you will be more subject to developing a behavior disorder such as mood swings, generalized anxiety, or panic disorder. In short, cumulative stress might produce headaches, fatigue, or panic attacks, depending on your particular point of greatest vulnerability. That point of vulnerability may, in turn, be influenced by heredity. It is likely then that genes, cumulative stress, and childhood circumstances all contribute to the genesis of a particular anxiety disorder, as suggested in this diagram:

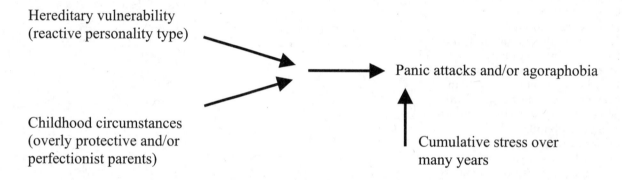

When you examine long-term causes, it turns out that no *one* of them may be sufficient, by itself, to produce a particular anxiety disorder. You may live twenty years with a hereditary vulnerability to panic attacks and yet never have one. Then life events in your twenties might produce enough cumulative stress to activate what had been only a potential—and you have your first panic attack. If you grew up feeling insecure and were taught that the outside world is dangerous, you may go on to develop agoraphobia. If you grew up feeling ashamed when you performed, perhaps your particular type of phobic avoidance will be less territorial and more social (in other words, a social phobia).

Biological Causes

Biological causes refer to physiological imbalances in the body or brain that are associated with anxiety disorders. It is important to recognize that such imbalances are not necessarily the *ultimate causes* of anxiety disorders and may *themselves* be caused by

- A specific hereditary vulnerability
- Cumulative stress over time

- A hereditary vulnerability that is *brought out* by cumulative stress

Once again, it is likely that genes, life history, and stress all work together to bring about the disturbances underlying anxiety disorders.

Recent research has pointed to different types of biological explanations for different types of anxiety disorders. The type of malfunction associated with spontaneous panic attacks is probably different from the type associated with generalized anxiety disorder. And both of these, in turn, are different from physiological imbalances associated with obsessive-compulsive disorder. Each of these is discussed separately below.

I can't overemphasize that our state of knowledge about biological causes underlying anxiety disorders is still very tentative and incomplete. The brain mechanisms considered below, which are discussed after an initial section on the physiology of panic, should be viewed as hypothetical—not proven facts.

Finally, it is important to realize that even though there may be a physiological imbalance in the brain underlying your particular anxiety disorder, there is no reason to assume you can't correct it. *If you are willing to make lifestyle changes to reduce stress and upgrade your level of physical wellness, any physiological imbalances associated with panic, phobias, anxiety, or obsessions will tend to diminish and perhaps disappear altogether.* These lifestyle changes include making time for daily relaxation, an exercise program, good nutrition, social support, and self-nurturing activities (see the relevant chapters in this workbook). An alternative way to correct a biological imbalance is to rely on prescription medications that specifically alter the functioning of your brain. Medications work well in overcoming the physiological causes of anxiety disorders—though, in my opinion, they should be viewed as a last line of defense. It is often possible to correct physical imbalances *simply* by upgrading your level of health and wellness.

Later in this section you will read about mechanisms in the brain that are thought, based on recent research, to underlie panic attacks, generalized anxiety, and obsessive-compulsive disorder. First, however, is a description of the basic physiology of a panic attack—something that is much better understood.

The Physiology of Panic

What happens to your body during a panic attack? Panic is an extreme version of an alarm reaction your body *naturally* goes through in response to any type of threat. Years ago, Walter Cannon described this as the *fight-or-flight response*. It is a built-in mechanism that enables all higher animals to mobilize a great deal of energy quickly in order to cope with predators or other immediate threats to their survival. This alarm reaction serves us well in situations that are realistically dangerous. Unfortunately, most of us also experience the fight-or-flight reaction in response to any situation that is viewed as *psychologically* dangerous, threatening, or overwhelming. An argument with your spouse or having to get up and go to work after a bad night's sleep can cause a pronounced stress response because *you perceive* it as threatening or overwhelming, even though it poses no direct risk to your survival.

In the case of a panic attack, there may be no perceived threat at all—the reaction may come on "out of the blue," without any noticeable provocation. Somehow the natural fight-

or-flight response has gotten out of control. That it occurs out of context and without apparent reason suggests that the brain mechanisms that control the response aren't functioning properly. The current hypothesis about the nature of this dysfunction is described in the next section. The physiology of panic itself, however, is better known.

Your nervous system has two separate actions: *voluntary* and *involuntary*. There is a voluntary nervous system that moves your muscles and obeys your direct command. Your involuntary nervous system, on the other hand, regulates automatic functions ordinarily outside voluntary control, such as your heartbeat, respiration, and digestion. This involuntary system is itself divided into two branches: the *sympathetic* and *parasympathetic* nervous systems. The sympathetic nervous system is responsible for mobilizing a number of reactions throughout your body whenever you're emotional or excited. The parasympathetic nervous system has an opposite function. It maintains normal, smooth functioning of your various internal organs during times when you are calm and at rest.

In a panic attack, your sympathetic nervous system sets off several different bodily reactions rapidly and intensely. First, it causes your adrenal glands to release large amounts of adrenaline. What you feel is a sudden "jolt," often accompanied by a feeling of dread or terror. Within seconds, the excess adrenaline can cause 1) your heart to race, 2) your respiration to become rapid and shallow, 3) profuse sweating, 4) trembling and shaking, and 5) cold hands and feet. Your sympathetic nervous system also produces muscle contractions (the most extreme case of this is when animals "freeze" in fear), possibly leading you to experience strong contractions in your chest or throat along with a fear of not being able to breathe. Other reactions caused by the sympathetic nervous system include excess release of stomach acid, inhibition of digestion, release of red blood cells by the spleen, release of stored-up sugar by the liver, an increase in metabolic rate, and dilation of the pupils.

All of these reactions occur to a lesser degree when you are emotional or excited. The problem in panic is that they peak to such an extreme level that you feel overwhelmed, feel terrified, and have a strong urge to run. It is important to realize that the adrenaline released during panic tends to be reabsorbed by the liver and kidneys within a few minutes. If you can "ride out" the bodily symptoms of panic without fighting them or telling yourself how horrible they are, they will tend to subside within a short time. Chapter 6 will describe strategies for learning to observe rather than react to the bodily symptoms of panic. By breathing properly and making supportive, calming statements to yourself, you can learn to manage panic instead of scaring yourself into a much more intense reaction.

While the physiology of panic is well understood, the mechanisms in the brain that initiate these physiological reactions are less well understood. The following section presents a recent hypothesis about a particular imbalance in the brain thought to be responsible for panic attacks.

Panic Attacks

Your brain is by far the most complex system in your body, consisting of over one hundred billion brain cells or neurons. At any given moment in time, millions of nerve impulses are being transmitted along multiple pathways which interconnect various regions of your brain.

Every time a single nerve impulse moves from one nerve cell to the next, it must cross a space. Individual nerve cells are not connected but are separated by tiny spaces called *synapses*. It has been known for some time that the process by which a nerve impulse moves across a synapse is chemical in nature. Microscopic amounts of chemicals secreted into the synapse allow transmission of a nerve impulse from one neuron to the next. These chemicals are called *neurotransmitters*; there are over twenty different types of them in the brain.

It appears that there are different systems in the brain that are especially sensitive to particular neurotransmitters. Each system consists of a vast network of nerve cells (*neurons*) that are sensitive to a particular neurotransmitter. One system, called the *noradrenergic system*, seems to be especially sensitive to a neurotransmitter substance called *norepinephrine*. Another system, the *serotonergic* system, contains neurons especially sensitive to a neurotransmitter substance called *serotonin*. Both systems have a large number of receptor sites (sites on nerve cells that respond to neurotransmitters) in some of the major structures of the brain that are activated during a panic attack. Specifically, the *amygdala*—a structure in your brain—is thought to play a key role in instigating panic. Research has found that the amygdala does not act alone but works in concert with a variety of other structures that all contribute to stimulating panic. These structures include "higher" brain centers such as the prefrontal cortex and insula, which serve to modulate sensory information, interpreting it as "dangerous" or "safe." Such information is stored in memory in a part of the brain called the *hippocampus*. The higher brain centers and the hippocampus interface directly with the amygdala. The amygdala, in turn, instigates panic by stimulating a variety of other brain structures, including 1) the *locus coeruleus*, which contributes to general behavioral and physiological arousal, 2) the *hypothalamus*, which regulates the release of adrenaline (via the pituitary gland, stimulating your adrenal glands) and also stimulates your sympathetic nervous system (see the previous section), 3) the *periaqueductal gray region*, which stimulates defensive and avoidance behavior, and, finally, 4) the *parabrachial nucleus*, which stimulates increased respiration.

Within your brain, panic attacks are more likely to occur when this entire system is *overly sensitized*, perhaps from having been previously activated too frequently, too intensely, or both. Thus the neurological basis for panic is not exactly a "chemical imbalance," as your doctor may have told you, but an overly sensitized "fear system," including all of the above brain structures. Researchers believe that deficiencies of the neurotransmitters serotonin and norepinephrine may contribute to *insufficient inhibition* of the amygdala, locus coeruleus, and associated structures that make up this fear system. That is why SSRI (selective serotonin reuptake inhibitors) or tricyclic antidepressant medications, which increase the amounts of serotonin and norepinepherine available throughout your brain, can diminish panic attacks. Over a period of two to four weeks, these medications seem to be able to *stabilize* and *desensitize* an overly sensitized amygdala, locus coeruleus, and associated fear system.

What *causes* the original oversensitization of the fear system remains unclear at this time. One hypothesis is that changes in this system can take place as a result of acute stress or as the long-term result of multiple stressors over time. Although this hypothesis remains unproven, it seems likely that *cumulative stress contributes in an important way to the onset of panic attacks* (as discussed earlier in this chapter). If this hypothesis about stress altering the amygdala and the fear system turns out to be true, an important implication follows: *the most effective long-term treatment for brain dysfunctions associated with panic disorder is a consistent and comprehensive program for reducing stress in your life.* Medications can certainly help restabilize structures in your brain that contribute to panic and anxiety in the short run. Yet without changes in your lifestyle (such as regular relaxation and exercise, good time management, proper nutrition, personal support, and constructive attitudes)—changes that allow you to live more simply and peacefully—panic and anxiety will tend to return after the medications are withdrawn.

Generalized Anxiety

Benzodiazepine tranquilizers, such as Xanax, Ativan, or Klonopin, can very effectively reduce generalized anxiety (as well as anticipatory anxiety in panic and phobic disorders). It has been discovered that a specific system in the brain, the GABA system, is uniquely sensitive to benzodiazepine drugs. This system consists of neurons that are sensitive to the neurotransmitter gamma-aminobutyric acid (GABA for short). GABA functions naturally in the brain as an inhibitory neurotransmitter—it tends to inhibit, or "tone down," brain activity, particularly in the limbic system, which is the brain's center for emotions. Thus GABA is associated with the brain's own natural calming response. When you give people GABA directly, or give them drugs that increase the activity of the GABA system, their anxiety decreases.

It appears that benzodiazepine tranquilizers like Xanax stimulate the GABA system to be more active, just as the neurotransmitter GABA itself does. That is why these tranquilizers tone down anxiety, as well as any other form of emotional arousal.

What is going on with the GABA system in persons who are chronically anxious? Several hypotheses have been proposed. There may be a deficiency of GABA itself, resulting in less inhibitory activity of the GABA system. Or there may be a deficiency of some naturally occurring benzodiazepine substance in the brain (yet to be identified) which leads to reduced activity of the GABA system. Perhaps there are too many GABA receptors relative to the amount of GABA available. The situation is quite complicated because brain activation (hence anxiety) is controlled not only by the GABA system but by the serotonin and norepinephrine systems (and even other neurotransmitter systems) as well. Moreover, brain research has found that these systems all interact and modulate each other. Suffice it to say that the GABA system plays a major role in the neurobiological basis of generalized anxiety. Deficient activation of the GABA system results in insufficient inhibition of limbic system structures, such as the amygdala and locus coeruleus, which contributes to all forms of anxiety.

Obsessive-Compulsive Disorder

The same reasoning that applied to generalized anxiety disorder also applies to obsessive-compulsive disorder (OCD). The effectiveness of specific drugs, such as clomipramine (Anafranil) and SSRI antidepressants (selective serotonin reuptake inhibitors)—fluoxetine (Prozac), sertraline (Zoloft), paroxetine (Paxil), and fluvoxamine (Luvox)—in reducing obsessive-compulsive symptoms tells us something about the possible biological mechanisms for obsessive-compulsive disorder. These drugs are known to increase the amount of a specific neurotransmitter substance, serotonin, in the brain. They do so more effectively than most other antidepressant medications. So we know that serotonin (and the serotonin system of the brain) plays an important role in the neurobiological basis of OCD.

Recent brain research has identified an OCD "neurocircuit" in the brain involving three brain structures: the *orbitofrontal cortex, thalamus,* and *caudate nucleus.* These structures define a circuit, or "loop," that brain imaging studies have found to be overly active in persons with OCD. When you worry, the orbitofrontal cortex sends a worry signal to the thalamus, which in turn sends the signal back (via the caudate) to the orbitofrontal cortex for interpretation. In normal people, this cycle happens only once or a few times. In people with OCD, however, because of a problem in the caudate nucleus, the signal goes back and forth and "loops" many, many times. It appears that SSRIs work by toning down excess activity of this OCD circuit. Many serotonin neurons in the brain are inhibitory in function, and there appears to be an abundance of these inhibitory neurons in the structures that make up the OCD loop. Thus increasing serotonin in the brain increases the activity of the inhibitory serotonin neurons, which in turn "brakes" excess activity in the OCD circuit.

Another brain structure involved in OCD is the *anterior cingulate gyrus.* One function of the cingulate is to enable you to flexibly shift attention from one topic to another. When the cingulate isn't functioning properly, you can more easily get "stuck" or get locked into a particular theme, as is the case when you are obsessing on something. It appears that SSRI medications help the cingulate to function better. Brain imaging research has also found that cognitive behavioral therapy, specifically exposure and response prevention, can normalize brain function in the structures associated with OCD. It's quite exciting to see that a strictly psychological intervention can result in lasting changes in brain function similar to what drugs can accomplish.

Medical Conditions That Can Cause Panic Attacks or Anxiety

The physiology of panic described at the beginning of this section is well established. But the various proposed explanations of the biological mechanisms involving different neurotransmitter systems of the brain are, at present, still hypothetical. It is important to keep in mind that these biological hypotheses apply to a majority *but not all cases* of panic attacks and generalized anxiety. Sometimes panic reactions or anxiety can arise from medical conditions that are quite separate from recognized anxiety disorders. Hyperthyroidism and hypoglycemia, for example, can cause panic attacks that are by all appearances identical to those seen in panic disorder. A calcium or magnesium deficiency or an allergy to certain food additives can also produce panic or anxiety. When these conditions are corrected, the anxiety disappears.

Any of the following conditions might be a cause of panic attacks or generalized anxiety. The first six are the ones most frequently seen.

- ### Hyperventilation Syndrome

Rapid, shallow breathing at the level of your chest can sometimes lead to excessive lowering of carbon dioxide in your bloodstream. This results in symptoms very similar to those of a panic attack, including light-headedness, dizziness, feelings of unreality, shortness of breath, trembling, and/or tingling in your hands, feet, or lips. These symptoms, in turn, may be perceived as dangerous and may stimulate a bona fide panic attack. (See the section on abdominal breathing in chapter 4 for further discussion of hyperventilation.)

- *Hypoglycemia*

For a large number of people, blood sugar levels can fall too low as a result of improper diet or simply stress. When this happens, such people experience a variety of symptoms similar to a panic reaction, including anxiety, shakiness, dizziness, weakness, and disorientation. Hypoglycemia can cause panic attacks, or, more often, can aggravate panic reactions that are caused by other factors. (See chapter 15 for a detailed discussion.)

- *Hyperthyroidism*

Excessive secretion of thyroid hormone can lead to heart palpitations (rapid heartbeat), sweating, and generalized anxiety. Other symptoms of hyperthyroidism include weight loss, elevated body temperature, insomnia, and bulging eyes. If you have several of the above symptoms, you might want to have your doctor do a thyroid panel to see if this condition is contributing to your anxiety or panic symptoms. (See chapter 16 for more information about how thyroid conditions can affect anxiety.)

- *Mitral Valve Prolapse*

Mitral valve prolapse is a harmless condition that causes heart palpitations. It is caused by a slight defect in the valve separating the upper and lower chambers on the left side of your heart. Blood moves through the mitral valve as it passes from the upper to the lower chamber. With mitral valve prolapse, the valve doesn't close completely and some of the blood can flow back from the lower to upper chamber, causing the heart to beat out of rhythm. The resulting rhythm disturbance can be disconcerting enough to cause some people to panic—but it is *not* dangerous. Mitral valve prolapse is *not* a cause of heart attacks.

For reasons that are unclear, mitral valve prolapse occurs more frequently in people with panic disorder than in the population at large. In severe cases, it can be treated through the use of beta-blocking drugs such as Inderal.

- *Premenstrual Syndrome (PMS)*

If you are a woman, it is important to observe whether your panic reactions (or generalized anxiety) worsen around the time just before your period. If so, treating your PMS may be enough to alleviate your problem with panic or anxiety. Treatment usually involves improvements in diet and exercise, taking supplements such as vitamin B_6, and in some cases taking natural progesterone. (See chapter 16 for a more detailed discussion.)

- *Inner Ear Disturbances*

For a small proportion of the population, panic attacks seem to be associated with a disturbance in balance caused by swelling of the inner ear (due to infection, allergy, Ménière's syndrome, or other problems). If dizziness, light-headedness, and/or unsteadiness are a *promi-

nent part of your problem with anxiety or panic, you may want to consult an otolaryngologist to check the labyrinth system of your inner ear.

Other medical conditions that can cause panic or anxiety include the following:

- Acute reaction to cocaine, amphetamines, caffeine, aspartame, appetite suppressants, asthma medications, steroids, or other stimulants

- Withdrawal from alcohol, sedatives, or tranquilizers

- Thyrotoxicosis

- Cushing's syndrome

- Adrenal tumor

- Parathyroid disease

- Partial complex seizures (temporal lobe epilepsy)

- Post-concussion syndrome

- Deficiencies of calcium, magnesium, potassium, niacin, vitamin B_{12}

- Emphysema

- Pulmonary embolism

- Cardiac arrhythmias

- Congestive heart failure

- Essential hypertension

- Environmental toxins such as mercury, carbon dioxide, hydrocarbons, food additives, pesticides

To adequately rule out any medical conditions that could be causing or aggravating your particular problem, have your doctor give you a thorough physical examination, including a blood panel, before adopting behavioral and psychological strategies for recovery. Keep in mind, though, that the above medical conditions (with the exception of hyperventilation and hypoglycemia) contribute to panic or anxiety in only a minority of cases.

Short-Term, Triggering Causes

Long-term causes such as heredity, childhood environment, and cumulative stress create a *predisposition* to anxiety disorders. Yet it takes more specific conditions, operating over a short period of time, to actually trigger panic attacks or cause a phobia to develop. In this section we will briefly consider

- Specific stressors that often precede a first panic attack

- Conditioning processes that produce phobias

- The role of trauma in certain simple phobias and post-traumatic stress disorder

Stressors That Precipitate Panic Attacks

A first panic attack is often preceded by a stressful event or situation. In my experience with people already vulnerable to panic disorder as a result of the predisposing factors previously described, I have found that the following three types of stressors often preceded their first panic attack:

- ### Significant Personal Loss

Loss of a significant person through death, divorce, or separation seems very frequently to be a trigger of a first panic attack. Other major losses, such as loss of employment, loss of health through illness, or a major financial reversal, can also precipitate a first panic attack.

- ### Significant Life Change

A major life event causing a period of adjustment lasting several months can sometimes precipitate a first panic attack. Examples of such an event might include getting married, having a baby, going off to college, changing jobs, going into the military, making a geographical move, or developing a protracted physical illness.

It may be that *any major stressor,* whether it is a significant loss or a major life change, can trigger a first panic attack in an individual who is already vulnerable for other reasons.

- ### Stimulants and Recreational Drugs

It is not uncommon for a first panic attack to occur after excessive intake of caffeine. Often people are unaware that their use of caffeine is excessive until a full-blown panic attack brings it to their attention.

Even more common is the incidence of panic attacks in people using cocaine. Cocaine is such a strong stimulant that it may cause panic attacks even in people who are *not* predisposed to panic disorder by the long-term factors previously described. Amphetamines ("speed"), PCP, LSD, high doses of marijuana, and withdrawal from narcotics, barbiturates, or tranquilizers can also jolt a person into a first panic attack.

Conditioning and the Origin of Phobias

A phobia is a persistent and unreasonable fear of a specific object, activity, or situation that results in a compelling desire to avoid that dreaded object, activity, or situation. There are three characteristics that distinguish a phobia from ordinary, everyday fears. First, you are *persistently* afraid of the object or situation over a long period of time. Second, you know that your fear is *unreasonable,* even though this recognition does not help to dispel it. Finally, what is most characteristic of a phobia is your *avoidance* of the feared situation. Being unreasonably afraid of something is not yet a phobia; the phobia begins when you actually start avoiding what you fear.

What is avoided tends to vary among the different types of phobias. If you are agoraphobic, you tend to avoid situations where you're afraid you can't easily escape if you have a panic attack—examples include checkout lines in grocery stores, freeways, elevators, and bridges. If you have a social phobia, you tend to avoid situations where you fear you might humiliate or embarrass yourself in front of others—examples include public speaking, parties, public restrooms, and job interviews. Simple phobias cause you to fear potential death or injury from causes such as natural disasters or certain animals. Or you may have an enormous fear of being trapped.

How do these phobias develop? There are two types of processes that are most commonly responsible: *conditioning* and *trauma*. Trauma isn't always involved in the creation of a phobia, but conditioning processes are always present. There are two types of conditioning that contribute to the formation of a phobia: 1) *conditioning by association* and 2) *conditioning by avoidance*.

In *conditioning by association*, a situation that was originally neutral begins to elicit strong anxiety because on one particular day you panicked or had a strong anxiety reaction in that same situation. For example, you're driving on the freeway and spontaneously have a panic attack. The panic is made worse by fearful thoughts, such as "How do I get out of here?" or "What if I get into an accident?" Your mind forms a strong association between being on the freeway and experiencing anxiety, so that later, being on, being near, or even thinking about freeways elicits anxiety. In short, you have *learned* an association between freeways and anxiety. By the same token, experiencing strong anxiety the first time you try public speaking may lead to an association between the two. Subsequently, every time you attempt to speak before others, or even think about doing so, strong anxiety is automatically triggered.

Conditioning by association may cause you to develop a fear toward a particular situation or object, but it does not by itself create a phobia. Only when you start to *avoid* that situation or object do you "learn" to be phobic. A time-honored principle in behavioral psychology is that any behavior that is rewarded tends to be repeated. Avoiding a situation you're anxious about is obviously rewarded—the reward being the reduction of anxiety. Each time you avoid the situation, the reward of being relieved of anxiety follows, and so your avoidance behavior gets strengthened and tends to be repeated. Your avoidance works very well in saving you from anxiety.

Learning to stay away from a fearful situation because it is rewarding to do so is what constitutes *conditioning by avoidance*. Avoidance conditioning is the most critical process in the formation of any phobia. It is directly reversed and overcome by the processes of imagery and real-life exposure described in chapter 7.

Trauma, Simple Phobias, and Post-Traumatic Stress Disorder

Agoraphobia and social phobia tend to develop primarily as a result of the conditioning processes just described. Certain simple phobias, on the other hand, can develop in the wake of specific traumatic experiences. As a child, I had a phobia about bees as a result of having picked up a bee and getting stung when I was two years old. This is really an example of conditioning by association. The fear I felt at the time I got stung caused me to develop an association between bees and fear. Avoidance conditioning came into play when I later started running away from bees whenever I saw them near me. By the same token, being in an auto accident can cause a person to subsequently fear driving or even being in a car. Or nearly drowning may lead to a subsequent phobia about water. Many simple phobias can be traced back to some kind of traumatic incident in childhood. Others—especially those we have from a very early age, like the fear of darkness or fears of insects—may be part of our evolutionary heritage. Such fears may have been biologically programmed into the nervous systems of all mammals to promote survival of the species. These inborn fears people often grow up with cannot be considered phobias unless 1) they lead to persistent avoidance and 2) they persist into adulthood.

A different outcome of trauma is the occurrence of post-traumatic stress disorder, which was described in chapter 1. No specific phobias develop; instead you tend to develop an array of symptoms that "re-create" the original trauma. Distressing recollections and dreams about what happened are the mind's attempt to gain control of the original event and to neutralize the emotional charge it carries.

Maintaining Causes

The maintaining causes of anxiety disorders are what tend to keep them going. They involve ways of thinking, feeling, and coping that serve to perpetuate anxiety, panic, or phobias. Much of this workbook is devoted to helping you deal with these maintaining causes. Of the four types of causes we are considering, only the maintaining ones operate in the here and now and are thus the easiest to deal with. The following list of maintaining causes isn't exhaustive and includes only those that are most obvious. Maintaining causes will be considered in greater detail throughout the rest of this workbook.

Avoidance of Phobic Situations

Phobias develop because it is very rewarding to avoid facing situations that cause you anxiety. As long as you continue to avoid dealing with a phobic situation, activity, or object, the phobia will remain securely in place. Trying to think or reason your way out of a phobia simply won't work if you continue to avoid confronting it directly. As long as you avoid a situation, you will be prone to worry about whether you can ever handle it.

Overcoming a phobia means that you unlearn certain responses while relearning others. When you finally begin to face the situation, you *unlearn* both 1) the "fear-in-advance," the anticipatory anxiety about possibly panicking in the situation, and 2) the avoidance of the situation itself. At the same time, you give yourself the opportunity to *learn* that you can enter—and remain in—a phobic situation without undue anxiety. You can learn to tolerate and eventually be comfortable in any phobic situation if you approach it in sufficiently small steps. The imagery and real-life desensitization processes discussed in chapter 7 are intended to foster this type of learning.

Anxious Self-Talk

Self-talk is what you say to yourself in your own mind. It is the internal monologue that you engage in much of the time, although it may be so automatic and subtle that you don't notice it unless you step back and pay attention. Much of your anxiety is created by statements you make to yourself beginning with the words "what if"—for example, "What if I have another panic attack?" "What if I lose control of myself while driving?" "What will people think if I get anxious while standing in line?" This type of self-talk *anticipates* the worst before it even happens. The more common term for it is simply *worry*.

Self-talk can also contribute to creating a full-blown panic attack. Such an attack may start off with bodily symptoms such as tightness in the chest and heart palpitations. If you can accept and "flow with" these symptoms without letting them scare you, they will soon peak and then subside. However, all too often you tell yourself such things as "Oh no—I'm going to panic!" "What if I have a heart attack?" "I've got to get out of here, but I can't!" "People will think I'm weird if I have to rest or lean on something for a minute because my legs feel weak." This scare-talk only aggravates the physical symptoms, which in turn produce even more extreme scare-talk, leading to a vicious circle that produces a full-blown panic attack.

The good news is that you can learn to recognize anxiety-provoking self-talk, stop it, and replace it with more supportive and calming statements to yourself. The subject of self-talk is dealt with in detail in chapter 8.

Mistaken Beliefs

Your negative self-talk comes from underlying mistaken beliefs about yourself, others, and "the way the world is." For example, if you believe that you can't be safely alone, you will talk yourself and everyone else into assuming that there must always be someone with you. If you truly believe that life is always a struggle, then you will tell yourself that something is wrong when you start to feel better or when others offer you help. A belief that the outside world is dangerous does not promote an attitude of trust or a willingness to take risks necessary to overcome a condition like agoraphobia.

Revamping your basic beliefs about yourself and your life takes more time and work than simply reversing anxious self-talk. Yet to do so will have far-reaching effects on your self-esteem, your willingness to accept imperfections in yourself and others, and your long-term peace of mind. The subject of mistaken beliefs is considered in detail in chapter 9.

Withheld Feelings

Denying feelings of anger, frustration, sadness, or even excitement can contribute to a state of *free-floating anxiety*. Free-floating anxiety is when you feel vaguely anxious without knowing why. You may have noticed that after you let out your angry feelings or have a good cry you feel calmer and more at ease. Expressing feelings can have a distinct physiological effect that results in a reduced level of anxiety.

As mentioned earlier, anxiety-prone people are often born with a predisposition to be more emotionally reactive or volatile. Yet they often grow up in families where obtaining parental approval takes precedence over expressing their needs and feelings. As adults, they still feel it is more important to attain perfection or always be pleasing than to express strong feelings. This tendency to deny deep emotions can lead to a chronic state of tension and anxiety. It is believed by some that the *external* danger avoided by the phobic is actually a stand-in for a deeper-lying *internal* danger: the fear of long-repressed feelings resurfacing. Panic may occur when such feelings "threaten" to break through. For example, if you have a phobia about water, this might be viewed as a stand-in for a deeper-lying fear of denied feelings. Or a fear of ferocious animals might symbolize a deeper-lying fear of experiencing your own anger and the unmet needs from which it flows. In my view, this emotion-based theory of phobias may be at least partially right.

Fortunately, it is possible to *learn* to recognize and express your feelings more easily and frequently. Excessive ventilation of feelings, especially anger, may not always be productive, yet it is important to at least know *what* you are feeling and then allow your feelings some form of expression. Doing so will substantially lower your level of anxiety and reduce your tendency to panic. This topic is dealt with in chapter 12.

Lack of Assertiveness

In order to express feelings to other people, it is important that you develop an assertive style of communicating that allows you to express yourself in a direct, forthright manner. Assertive communication strikes the right balance between submissiveness, where you are afraid to ask for what you want at all, and aggressiveness, where you demand what you want through coercion or threat. If you are prone to anxiety and phobias, you will tend to act submissively. You avoid asking directly for what you want and are afraid to express strong feelings, especially anger. Often you are afraid of imposing on others; you don't want to compromise your self-image as someone who is pleasing and nice. Or you are afraid that assertive communication will alienate the one person you feel dependent on for your basic sense of security. The problem with a lack of assertiveness is that it breeds feelings within yourself of resentment and confinement. And resentment and a sense of confinement are notorious for aggravating anxiety and phobias.

It's possible to *learn* to be assertive and directly express your wants and feelings. An introduction to this type of communication is presented in chapter 13.

Lack of Self-Nurturing Skills

Common to the background of many people with anxiety disorders is a pervasive sense of insecurity. This is especially apparent in agoraphobia, where the need to stay close to a safe place or safe person can be so strong. Such insecurity arises from a variety of conditions in childhood, including parental neglect, abandonment, abuse, overprotection, or overcriticism, as well as alcoholism or chemical dependency in the family. Since they never received consistent or reliable nurturing as children, adult survivors of these various forms of deprivation often lack the capacity to properly take care of their own needs. Unaware of how to love and nurture themselves, they suffer low self-esteem and may feel anxious or overwhelmed in the face of adult demands and responsibilities. This lack of self-nurturing skills only serves to perpetuate anxiety.

The most lasting solution to parental abuse and deprivation is to become a good parent to yourself. Methods for gaining awareness of your needs, healing the "child within," and becoming more nurturing toward yourself are presented in chapter 14.

Muscle Tension

When your muscles are tense, you feel "uptight." Muscle tension tends to restrict your breathing. And when your breathing is shallow and restricted, you are more likely to experience anxiety. Tense muscles also help to keep your feelings suppressed, which, as discussed above, can increase anxiety. You may have noticed that when your body is tense, your mind has a greater tendency to race. As you relax the muscles throughout your body, your mind will begin to slow down and become calmer. A founder of systematic methods of relaxation, Edmund Jacobson, once said, "An anxious mind cannot exist in a relaxed body." Body and mind are inextricably related in anxiety.

You can reduce your level of muscle tension on a consistent basis by maintaining daily programs of deep relaxation as well as vigorous exercise. Either one of these alone can reduce muscle tension, but the combination has an even more profound effect. Detailed guidelines for incorporating relaxation and exercise into your lifestyle are presented in chapters 4 and 5.

Stimulants and Other Dietary Factors

Stimulants such as caffeine and nicotine can aggravate anxiety and leave you more vulnerable to panic attacks. You may not even be aware of their impact until you reduce or eliminate them from your life. In two cases, I have seen panic attacks go away completely when clients eliminated caffeine from their diet (this was caffeine from not only coffee but also tea, cola beverages, and over-the-counter medications). For some people, other dietary factors, such as sugar and food additives, can aggravate or occasionally even cause panic reactions.

The nutrition–anxiety connection has hardly been explored in either popular or technical books on anxiety disorders. Chapter 15 of this book takes a detailed look at this connection.

High-Stress Lifestyle

The role of stress both as a predisposing agent and as a short-term cause of anxiety disorders has been described earlier. It is not surprising that a stressful lifestyle perpetuates problems with anxiety. The frequency of panic attacks and severity of phobias tends to wax and wane depending on how well you cope with the daily stresses of living. Getting a handle on all of the maintaining causes of anxiety discussed in this section—self-talk, mistaken beliefs, withheld feelings, lack of assertiveness, lack of support, muscle tension, and diet—will go a long way toward reducing stress in your life. Other factors associated with stress that are not dealt with in this workbook include time management, Type A personality, and communication. These have been discussed in many excellent popular books on stress management. I can recommend the following: *Guide to Stress Reduction* by John Mason and *The Relaxation & Stress Reduction Workbook* by Martha Davis, Elizabeth Eshelman, and Matthew McKay. (See the reading list at the end of this chapter.)

Lack of Meaning or Sense of Purpose

It has been my repeated experience that clients experience relief from anxiety as well as phobias when they come to feel that their life has meaning, purpose, and a sense of direction. Until you discover something larger than self-gratification—something that gives your life a sense of purpose—you may be prone to feelings of boredom and a vague sense of confinement because you are not realizing all your potential. This sense of confinement can be a potent breeding ground for anxiety, phobias, and even panic attacks.

Issues of meaninglessness and purposelessness, and their relationship to psychological well-being, have been dealt with in depth by existential psychologists such as Victor Frankl and Rollo May. Several ways of confronting and working on these issues in your own life are presented in chapter 20.

Exercise

1. Which of the following factors do you feel might be helping to maintain your particular difficulty?

    ☐   Avoidance of phobic situations

    ☐   Anxious self-talk

    ☐   Mistaken beliefs

    ☐   Withheld feelings

    ☐   Lack of assertiveness

    ☐   Lack of self-nurturing skills

    ☐   Muscle tension

    ☐   Stimulants and other dietary factors

    ☐   High-stress lifestyle

    ☐   Lack of meaning or sense of purpose

2. Can you rank these maintaining causes according to how much you feel they influence your condition? Which ones do you feel are most important for you to work on?

3. Specify three maintaining causes that you would seriously be willing to work on in the next month.

_____

_____

_____

Further Reading

Davis, Martha, Elizabeth Robbins Eshelman, and Matthew McKay. *The Relaxation & Stress Reduction Workbook*. Sixth edition. Oakland, CA: New Harbinger Publications, 2008.

Holmes, Thomas, and Richard Rahe. Social readjustment rating scale. *Journal of Psychosomatic Research* 11:213–218, 1967.

Mason, John. *Guide to Stress Reduction*. Berkeley, CA: Celestial Arts, 1985.

Preston, John, John O'Neal, and Mary C. Talaga. *Handbook of Clinical Psychopharmacology for Therapists*. Sixth edition. Oakland, CA: New Harbinger Publications, 2010.

3

Recovery: A Comprehensive Approach

Chapter 2 demonstrated how many different types of factors are contributing causes of anxiety disorders. Heredity, physiological imbalances in the brain, childhood deprivation and faulty parenting, and the cumulative effect of stress over time can all work to bring about the onset of panic attacks, agoraphobia, or any of the other anxiety disorders. The maintaining causes of these disorders—what keeps them going—are many and varied as well. Such factors can operate at the level of your body (for example, shallow breathing, muscle tension, or poor nutrition), emotions (such as withheld feelings), behavior (avoidance of phobic situations), mind (anxious self-talk and mistaken beliefs), and "whole self" (such as low self-esteem or a lack of self-nurturing skills).

If the causes of anxiety disorders are so varied, then an adequate approach to recovery needs to be, too. It is the basic philosophy of this workbook that the most effective approach for treating panic, phobias, or any other problem with anxiety is one that addresses the *full range* of factors contributing to these conditions. This type of approach can be called "comprehensive." It assumes that you can't just give someone the "right" medication and expect panic or generalized anxiety to go away. Nor can you just deal with childhood deprivation, having someone work through the emotional consequences of bad parenting, and expect the problems to disappear. By the same token, you can't just teach people new behaviors and new ways of talking to themselves and expect these things alone to resolve their problems. Some therapists still treat anxiety disorders solely as psychiatric conditions which can be "cured" by medication, or solely as childhood developmental problems, or solely as behavior problems; but the trend in recent years has been away from such single-gauged approaches. Many practitioners have discovered that problems with anxiety go away only temporarily when merely one or two contributing causes are dealt with. Lasting recovery is achieved when you are willing to make basic and comprehensive changes in habit, attitude, and lifestyle.

This chapter outlines and illustrates a comprehensive approach to recovery that has evolved over the years during which I have treated anxiety problems. What makes this approach truly comprehensive is that it offers interventions addressing seven different levels of contributing causes. These levels are as follows:

- Physical

- Emotional

- Behavioral

- Mental

- Interpersonal

- Whole Self

- Existential and spiritual

Some brief descriptions of these levels, and a preview of the rest of the chapters in this workbook, follow.

Physical Level

Physical-level causes include possible physiological imbalances in the brain and body (see the section on biological causes in chapter 2). Such causes also include 1) shallow breathing, 2) muscle tension, 3) bodily effects of cumulative stress, and 4) nutritional and dietary factors (such as excess caffeine or sugar in your diet). Strategies for dealing with physical-level causes can be found in five different chapters in this workbook. Chapter 4 offers breathing techniques to help modify your breathing pattern from the shallow, chest-level breathing that contributes to anxiety. That chapter also provides two deep relaxation techniques designed to reduce muscle tension and the effects of stress—progressive muscle relaxation and meditation. When practiced on a regular basis, either of these techniques can help you feel calmer in general, often making it unnecessary to rely on tranquilizers.

Chapter 5 on exercise makes a strong case for getting involved in a program of regular aerobic exercise. Many of my clients have found regular exercise to be the *single most effective* strategy for reducing muscle tension, stress, and hence anxiety (both chronic and acute). Chapter 15 discusses a variety of dietary changes that can help reduce anxiety. These include eliminating stimulants and substances that stress the body and relying more on foods and supplements that promote a calmer disposition. Chapter 16 examines a variety of health issues that can aggravate anxiety—conditions such as adrenal exhaustion, PMS, seasonal affective disorder, and insomnia. All need to be dealt with in a comprehensive program for overcoming anxiety. Finally, chapter 17 discusses situations where it is *appropriate* for you to take medication, along with the risks and benefits of each of the major types of medications used to treat anxiety disorders.

Emotional Level

Suppressed feelings—especially withheld anger—can be a very important contributing cause to both chronic anxiety and panic attacks. Often feelings of panic are merely a front for buried feelings of anger, frustration, grief, or desperation. Many people with anxiety disorders grew up in families that discouraged the expression of feelings. As an adult you may have difficulty just identifying what you *are* feeling, let alone expressing those feelings. Chapter 12 provides specific guidelines and strategies for

- Recognizing symptoms of suppressed feelings

- Identifying what you are feeling

- Learning to express your feelings
- Communicating your feelings to someone else

Behavioral Level

Phobias persist because of a single behavior: avoidance. As long as you avoid driving free-ways, crossing bridges, speaking in public, or being in your home alone, your fear about these situations will persist. Your phobia is maintained because your avoidance behavior is so well rewarded: you don't have to reckon with the anxiety you'd experience if you confronted what you fear. Chapter 7 describes strategies that have been found to be very effective in dealing with phobias. Desensitization through imagery allows you to first confront your fear men-tally, imagining over and over that you can handle it well. Real-life desensitization involves confronting your phobia in actuality—but with the help of a support person and in small increments. Perhaps the most important feature of both types of desensitization is that they break down into small steps the process of confronting what you fear.

Certain behaviors tend to encourage panic attacks. Trying to fight or resist panic will usually only aggravate it. Most of the time it is impossible to will your way out of panic. Chapter 6 suggests strategies you can use to minimize panic when it first develops. Learning to observe and "go with it" instead of reacting to the bodily symptoms of panic is perhaps the most important behavioral shift you can make. Specific techniques such as talking to another person, distracting your mind, becoming physically active, expressing needs and feelings, doing abdominal breathing, and repeating affirmations can all foster an increased capacity to *actively cope* with, rather than passively react to, the bodily symptoms of panic.

Mental Level

What you say to yourself internally—what is called *self-talk*—has a major effect on your state of anxiety. People with all types of anxiety disorders tend to engage in excessive "what-if" thinking, imagining the worst possible outcome in advance of facing what they fear. Scaring yourself through what-if scenarios is what has traditionally been called "worry." Self-critical thinking and perfectionist self-talk (statements to yourself that start with "I should," "I have to," or "I must") also promote anxiety.

Chapter 8 presents specific strategies for recognizing and *countering* destructive thinking patterns. By reconstructing negative self-talk into more supportive, confidence-building state-ments, you can begin to undo the long-standing habits of worry, self-criticism, and perfection-ism that perpetuate anxiety.

Beneath anxiety-provoking self-talk are *mistaken beliefs* about yourself, others, and the world that produce anxiety in very basic ways. For example, if you see yourself as inadequate compared to others—or view the outside world as a dangerous place—you'll tend to remain anxious until you revise these basic attitudes. Chapter 9 offers strategies for both identifying and countering mistaken beliefs that contribute to anxiety.

Interpersonal Level

Much of the anxiety people experience arises from difficulties in interpersonal relationships. When you have difficulty communicating your real feelings and needs to others, you may find yourself swallowing frustration to the point where you're chronically tense and anxious. The same is true when you're unable to set limits or say no to unwanted demands or requests from others. Chapter 13 offers a variety of strategies for learning to stand up for your rights and express your true wants and feelings. Assertive communication provides ways to express what you want or don't want in a manner that preserves respect for other people. Learning to be assertive is a very important part of the recovery process, especially if you're dealing with agoraphobia or social phobia.

Being able to talk about your condition with others is also an important step in the recovery process. Ways to do this are discussed at the end of chapter 6.

"Whole Self" Level (Self-Esteem)

Of all the contributing causes to anxiety disorders, low self-esteem is among the deepest. You may have grown up in a dysfunctional family, which, through various forms of deprivation, abuse, or neglect, fostered your low sense of self-worth. As a result, you may carry into adulthood deep-seated feelings of insecurity, shame, and inadequacy, which tend to show up, on a more noticeable level, as panic attacks, fear of confronting the outside world (agoraphobia), fear of humiliation (social phobia), or generalized anxiety. Frequently, low self-esteem is tied in with all of the various contributing causes described above—in particular, lack of assertiveness, self-critical or perfectionist self-talk, and difficulty expressing feelings.

There are many ways to build self-esteem. Developing a positive body image, working toward and achieving concrete goals, and countering negative self-talk with validating affirmations can all help. Many of my clients have found it particularly worthwhile to cultivate a relationship with their own *inner child*. The inner child is the part of you that is spontaneous and playful but also carries the insecurity, shame, or pain that may be left over from your childhood. It is quite possible to make up for the inadequate parenting you may have received by becoming a strong, nurturing parent to your own child within. Chapter 14 provides specific strategies and exercises for strengthening your feelings of self-worth.

Existential and Spiritual Level

Sometimes people can improve on all of the levels previously described and yet remain anxious and unsettled. They seem to have a vague sense of dissatisfaction, emptiness, or boredom about life, which can lead to panic or to chronic, generalized anxiety. Certain of my clients have found that the ultimate "solution" to their problem with anxiety was to find a broad purpose or direction that gave their life greater meaning. Frequently, this involved taking up a vocation that fulfilled their true talents and interests. In one case it involved developing an artistic talent that provided a creative outlet. Anxiety symptoms (as well as depression) can be the psyche's way of pushing you to explore and actualize an unrealized potential in your life, whether this involves intellectual development, emotional development, or even getting more in touch with your body. Instead of regarding your panic or phobias *merely* as a reaction to negative physical, emotional, or mental factors, you may be surprised to discover that they represent a call to realize your full potential.

For many individuals, a deep spiritual commitment and involvement provides a significant pathway to recovery from anxiety problems. Twelve-step programs have demonstrated the potency of spiritual awakening in the area of addictions—and the same is true for recovery from anxiety disorders. Developing a connection with a Higher Power (call it God, Spirit, or whatever you like) can provide a profound means for achieving inner security, strength, peace of mind, and an attitude that the outer world is a benevolent place. An existential-spiritual level of recovery is considered in chapter 20.

Four Examples of a Comprehensive Recovery Program

The preceding section may have helped to broaden your understanding of the various levels that come into play in a comprehensive approach to recovery from anxiety disorders. To make this more concrete, I want you to consider what such an approach would look like in four specific cases. These four examples are the same ones that were presented at the beginning of chapter 1 and reflect the four most common types of anxiety disorder seen by therapists: panic attacks, agoraphobia, social phobia, and obsessive-compulsive disorder. As you read through each of the examples, you may begin to formulate what strategies you want to include in your own recovery program. The *Problem Effectiveness Chart* and *Weekly Practice Record* that follow these examples will enable you to work out your own unique program in greater detail.

Susan: Panic Disorder

You may remember from chapter 1 that Susan was awakened every night by panic attacks marked by heart palpitations, dizziness, and a fear that she was going to die. She would get up and try to make these symptoms go away, becoming more and more anxious when they didn't, to the point where she might spend an hour or more walking about her house. Terrified and confused, she worried about whether she was going to have a heart attack. After a week of recurring panic episodes, she made an appointment with a cardiologist.

Let's suppose that her cardiologist was enlightened about anxiety disorders. After ruling out any heart problems, the cardiologist diagnosed her panic disorder and sent her to a therapist who specialized in the treatment of phobias and panic. This therapist utilized a comprehensive treatment approach with a number of components designed to diminish Susan's problem on a physical, emotional, and mental level.

First, the therapist sent her back to a medical doctor, an internist, to rule out any other possible physical bases for her problem, such as hyperthyroidism, hypoglycemia, mitral valve prolapse, or a calcium-magnesium deficiency. Once these possible medical conditions ruled out, Susan began her recovery program by learning abdominal breathing technique (see chapter 4) that helped her to slow down the physiological arousal response that accompanies a panic attack. She was also asked to practice progressive muscle relaxation on a daily basis (chapter 4) to train her body to enter into a relaxed state easily. Regular practice of progressive muscle relaxation had a cumulative effect (the same would be true for regular practice of any other deep relaxation technique, such as visualization or meditation). After several weeks, Susan noticed that she was feeling more relaxed *all the time*. In addition to breathing and deep relaxation techniques, she was asked to maintain a program of regular, vigorous exercise (see chapter 5). She had discretion in choosing the type of exercise to do, but preferably it was to be aerobic exercise lasting for a half hour four to five times per week. Regular exercise worked together with the breathing techniques and deep relaxation to help relieve excess muscle tension, metabolize excess adrenaline, reduce vulnerability to sudden surges of anxiety, and increase Susan's overall sense of well-being. This combination of relaxation and exercise alone went a long way to significantly reduce the intensity and frequency of her panic attacks.

Susan's therapist also discovered that she was drinking three to four cups of coffee per day. Although for some people this might be a manageable amount, most individuals dealing with panic disorder find that their condition is aggravated by even small amounts of caffeine. Susan was asked to gradually taper off her caffeine consumption and replace regular with decaffeinated coffee. Her therapist also recommended a balanced diet, consisting largely of whole, unprocessed foods with minimal sugar and salt. She was also advised to take high-potency vitamin B-complex, vitamin C, and calcium-magnesium supplements (see chapter 15).

Susan was then taught specific techniques for interrupting the onset of panic when she first began to notice the approach of symptoms (see chapter 6). These techniques included calling a friend, physically exerting herself by doing housework, or writing out her feelings in a journal if she was feeling angry or frustrated. Special emphasis was given to her self-talk—what she said to herself at the very onset of feeling panic symptoms (see chapter 8). Her therapist found that Susan had a tendency to scare herself into a high state of panic by internally saying such things as "What if I have a heart attack?" "I can't stand this!" or "I've got to get out of here!" She was taught to replace this "scare-talk" with more positive, self-supportive statements, such as "I can handle these sensations," "I can flow with this and wait for my anxiety to diminish," or "I can let my body do its thing and this will pass." After practicing these "coping affirmations" many times, Susan found that she could simply *observe* her bodily symptoms rather than react to them. After a while she was able to avoid severe panic reactions altogether. Her therapist also helped Susan to identify some of the fundamental mistaken beliefs underlying much of her behavior (see chapter 9). She began to let go of such basic assumptions about herself, such as "I have to be completely successful at everything I do," "Life is a struggle," and "Everything must be totally predictable and in control." She was able to take life a little more easily and view its inevitable challenges with more perspective. The net result was a significant reduction in her overall level of anxiety.

A final issue associated with Susan's panic reactions was her tendency to completely suppress her anger and frustration. Early on, her therapist noticed that Susan was most vulnerable to panic on days when she had encountered numerous frustrating situations at work. She had grown up in a family where everyone was supposed to always do their best without ever complaining. Direct expression of feelings and needs was discouraged—she had learned to keep up a pleasant front both to strangers and friends, no matter how she was feeling inside. Although Susan couldn't believe it at first, she eventually concluded that her panic reactions were sometimes nothing more than intense feelings of frustration and anger in disguise. Her exercise program helped her to discharge some of these feelings. She also found it helpful to write her feelings down in a journal whenever she noticed herself beginning to feel on edge.

Susan's recovery program consisted of a variety of interventions on a physical, behavioral, emotional, and mental level, as summarized below.

Physical	Breathing exercises
	Regular practice of deep relaxation
	Regular aerobic exercise
	Elimination of caffeine
	Nutritional improvements, including vitamin supplements
Behavioral	Coping techniques to abort panic reactions at their onset— such as abdominal breathing and distraction techniques
Emotional	Identifying some panic reactions as anger in disguise
	Learning to express frustrations verbally and in writing
Mental	Changing scare-talk at the onset of panic to supportive, calming self-talk
	Practicing coping affirmations
	Reevaluating underlying mistaken beliefs and adopting a more relaxed, easygoing perspective on life

It was through a combination of all these interventions that Susan was able to find lasting relief from her panic attacks. Six months from the time she began her program, she was still occasionally anxious but only rarely experienced symptoms of panic. On those occasions when she did, she had a variety of tools that allowed her to dissipate the reaction before it gained momentum.

For Susan it was possible to achieve a lasting recovery from panic without the use of prescription medications. This is not always the case. When panic is so frequent or severe that it interferes with your work, relationships, or general ability to function (or when it does not yield to approaches like those discussed above), it may be appropriate to take medication. An antidepressant medication such as Zoloft (sertraline), taken over a period of six months to one year, can often be quite helpful in these instances (see chapter 17).

Cindy: Agoraphobia

You may recall Cindy's case from the example in the first chapter. She not only had panic attacks but was beginning to avoid situations such as grocery stores, restaurants, and movie theaters, where she was afraid she might have an attack. She was also very concerned that she might have to stop going to work. This avoidance of situations out of fear of panic is the hallmark of agoraphobia. What would a comprehensive recovery program for Cindy look like?

Just about all the interventions described in the example of Susan were also used in Cindy's case, because she, too, was experiencing panic attacks. Breathing techniques, regular practice of progressive muscle relaxation, regular (if possible, aerobic) exercise, and nutritional improvements were all necessary to help her reduce the physiological component of panic (see the corresponding chapters in this workbook). She also learned the same coping techniques for panic so that she was able to *act* rather than *react* when she felt the first bodily symptoms of panic coming on (see chapter 6). Cindy also worked on changing counterproductive self-talk (see chapter 8). In her case, this was especially important—not only for coping with panic itself but for curbing her excessive tendency to worry about panicking when she went to work. Finally, Cindy, just like Susan, needed to reexamine some of her basic mistaken beliefs about herself, such as "I can't make mistakes," "I must always be pleasing to everybody," and "Success is everything." She developed affirmations to counter these beliefs and made an audio recording that she listened to every night as she went to sleep (see chapter 9).

It was important for Cindy to work not only on her panic reactions but on her avoidance behavior as well. At the outset, she was avoiding crowded public situations, such as grocery stores, restaurants, and movie theaters, and had nearly reached the point where she was afraid to go to work. In only a few weeks, she had severely limited where she would go. It was through the processes of imagery and real-life desensitization that she learned to reenter all these situations and be comfortable with them (see chapter 7). There were three phases in this process. First, she broke down the goal of reentering each specific situation into a series of steps. For example, in the case of the grocery store, she had eight steps:

1. Spending one minute near the entrance of the store
2. Spending one minute inside the door of the store
3. Going halfway to the back of the store, spending one minute, and then leaving
4. Going to the back of the store, spending one minute, and then leaving
5. Spending three minutes in the store without buying anything
6. Buying one item and going through the express checkout line
7. Buying three items and going through the express checkout line
8. Buying three items and going through a regular checkout line

The second phase involved practicing imagery desensitization—going through each of these steps in her *imagination* until she could visualize the final step in detail without feeling any anxiety.

Third, Cindy practiced real-life desensitization, going through each of the eight steps in real life. She practiced each step several times at first with the help of a support person—usually her boyfriend—and then tried it out alone. For example, after she had mastered step 3 by herself, she started practicing step 4 with her support person. She found that the process worked best if she temporarily stopped or retreated any time she felt anxiety coming on so strongly that she felt it might get out of control. It was easier to advance from one step to the next if she didn't "overexpose" or resensitize herself by pushing herself to the point of feeling intense anxiety.

Cindy undertook this three-phase process—1) breaking the goal down into steps, 2) imagery desensitization, and 3) real-life desensitization—with each of her specific phobias. By practicing desensitization on a regular basis, she was able after three months to reenter all the situations she had previously avoided and to feel comfortable with them.

Cindy had a high degree of self-motivation. The consistent encouragement and reinforcement she got from her boyfriend, who always accompanied her on her first run of entering a phobic situation, sped up her progress considerably.

The most direct and efficient way to overcome any fear is simply to face it. If you are agoraphobic, however, the prospect of confronting long-standing fears can seem overwhelming at first. Cindy learned that this confrontation process can be made manageable if it is broken down into sufficiently small steps that are first negotiated in imagination.

Apart from overcoming her phobias, another important part of Cindy's recovery was learning to be assertive (see chapter 13). A major part of the stress that contributed to her first panic attack came from her inability to say no to unreasonable demands placed on her by her boss. Cindy's friends also noted that she couldn't stand up for her rights or say no to her boyfriend for fear of his leaving her. She had grown up in a family where her father had left when she was eight. In addition, her mother was very demanding and critical. Consequently, Cindy was never quite sure that she was loved, and she had a deep-seated insecurity about being abandoned. As a child she feared that standing up for herself would jeopardize the tenuous and conditional love she received from her mother. Cindy carried this pattern of dependency and fear of abandonment into adulthood and replayed it in her relationship with her boyfriend. In subtle ways, it actually served to reinforce her agoraphobia. On an unconscious level, she felt that if she were dependent on her boyfriend to take care of her, he would never leave her.

During her recovery, Cindy realized that she wanted to rework her "life script." She was feeling increasingly frustrated about always accommodating everyone else, and she began to recognize the need to develop a stronger sense of herself and her own rights. Through learning to be assertive, she discovered that she could ask for what she wanted, say no to what she didn't want, and still obtain the love and support she needed from her boyfriend and others. In fact, she was surprised to find that everyone, including her boyfriend, respected her more for being able to stand up for herself. The independence Cindy gained from learning to confront situations she had previously avoided went hand in hand with the independence she gained from developing a more assertive interpersonal style. There was no longer any need for her agoraphobia because there was no longer any need for the dependency that maintained it.

Because of the insecurity and fear of abandonment left over from her childhood, it was also critical for Cindy to work on self-esteem (see chapter 14). She discovered that the only remedy for the inadequate parenting she had received was to become a good parent to herself. She did this in part by improving her body image and countering her *inner critic* (self-critical inner dialogue) with affirmations of self-acceptance and self-worth. What she found most helpful, though, was cultivating a relationship with her *inner child*. (The inner child is that part of you which is playful and creative but also carries old wounds—the pain, insecurity, or sense of inadequacy you may have felt since childhood.) Cindy learned to relabel moods in which she felt insecure or frightened as requests for nurturing from her inner child. She gained considerable inner strength and self-confidence as she learned a variety of ways to support, nurture, and care for her own child within.

In sum, Cindy's recovery program for agoraphobia contained all of the elements of Susan's program for panic attacks *plus* imagery and real-life desensitization to overcome her specific avoidances. It was also necessary for Cindy to address assertiveness and self-esteem issues. She needed to overcome feelings of insecurity and a fear of abandonment that she had carried over from childhood—an insecurity and fear that tended to reinforce her agoraphobia. Her total program involved interventions on six different levels:

Physical	Breathing exercises
	Regular practice of deep relaxation
	Regular aerobic exercise
	Nutritional improvements, including vitamin supplements
Behavioral	Coping techniques to abort panic reactions at their onset
	Imagery and real-life desensitization to overcome specific phobias
Emotional	Learning to identify and express feelings
Mental	Countering negative self-talk that contributed to panic attacks as well as worry about panicking
	Countering underlying mistaken beliefs with self-supporting affirmations
Interpersonal	Developing a more assertive interpersonal style
Whole Self	Developing self-esteem through

- working on her body image
- overcoming her inner critic
- cultivating a relationship with her inner child

It took Cindy about a year to fully implement these interventions. At the end of one year, she was close to being free of her agoraphobia as well as panic attacks. She decided to go back to school part-time to train to become a registered nurse while continuing her job as a medical secretary.

Steve: Social Phobia

You may recall from chapter 1 that Steve had difficulty attending meetings at work. He would clam up in group sessions and feared that his coworkers would look upon him critically for not contributing. His very worst fear was of being asked to give a presentation before a group. When this finally happened, he was so terrified that he felt he might have to quit his job.

Steve's problem fits the picture of a social phobia very well—he feared embarrassment and humiliation as a result of being unable to perform in a group situation. His recovery program depended heavily on the processes of imagery and real-life desensitization.

Like Susan and Cindy, Steve required a comprehensive treatment approach. Because he tended generally to be anxious much of the time, the same strategies were needed that were used to reduce the physical component of anxiety for Susan and Cindy. Steve first learned abdominal breathing techniques to reduce anxiety on a short-term basis. He found these to be very helpful in reducing the apprehension that came up when he was asked to attend meetings at work. He also practiced a deep relaxation technique twice a day. In Steve's case, meditation seemed to work better than progressive muscle relaxation for soothing his active mind (see chapter 18). He also found that jogging four times a week made a substantial improvement in his level of tension and anxiety (see chapter 5). Finally, he learned that when he reduced his consumption of refined sugar, his mood swings diminished and he was less prone to bouts of depression (see chapter 15). By upgrading his overall health and wellness, Steve became more confident about tackling his social phobia.

The phobia of being in meetings at work was dealt with first through imagery desensitization. As in Cindy's case, Steve broke down the goal of being able to handle meetings into steps:

1. Sitting in a small group (fewer than five people) for fifteen minutes

2. Sitting in a small group for forty-five minutes to one hour

3. Sitting in a larger group for fifteen minutes

4. Sitting in a larger group for forty-five minutes to one hour

5. Repeating steps 1 to 4, but making at least one comment during the course of the meeting

6. Repeating steps 1 to 4, but making at least two comments during the meeting

7. Giving a one-minute presentation before a small group

8. Giving a three-minute presentation before a small group

9. Giving a five- to ten-minute presentation before a small group

10. Repeating steps 7 to 9 with a larger group

The next phase was to go through each of the steps in detail in his imagination. Steve would keep working with a particular step until he no longer felt any anxiety and then would go on to the next one. If at any point his anxiety started to come on very strong—to the point where he felt it might get out of control—he would "switch off" the scene he was visualizing and retreat in his mind to a very peaceful, relaxing scene. Steve found it useful to make an audio recording which guided him through visualizing all ten of the steps in his program.

After he had successfully desensitized himself in his imagination, Steve undertook the mission to conquer his fear of groups in real life (see chapter 7). First, he sat down with his boss and discussed his problem. He explained that he wanted to be able to participate in meetings and was working through a specific step-by-step program to overcome his phobia. He made an arrangement with his boss to attend only small, short meetings; he had permission to temporarily leave if his anxiety level became too high. After mastering small, brief meetings, he would be able to progress to larger and longer ones. Knowing he would always be free to retreat if he needed to, he felt more willing to undertake real-life desensitization. After working up to a point where he could verbally participate in large meetings, he began to work on his fear of making a presentation. Instead of starting out trying to do this at work, Steve decided to take a course in public speaking at a local junior college. The demands for performance in a classroom setting, where everyone was learning, seemed less intense than the expectations at work. After completing the public speaking class, he arranged to make a brief presentation at work before a small group of coworkers he knew well. From there he progressed to larger groups, to longer presentations, and finally to speaking before groups of strangers.

Steve continued to feel anxious when he got up before a group, but he was now able to *handle* his anxiety through a combination of abdominal breathing techniques and coping affirmations: "I can ride through this anxiety and be fine"; "As soon as I get started, I'll be fine"; "What I have to say is worthwhile—everyone will be interested." With time and practice, he got to the point where he no longer feared making presentations and, in fact, looked forward to them as an opportunity to contribute his own insights and ideas.

Besides practicing imagery and real-life desensitization, Steve, like Cindy, worked on assertiveness and self-esteem (see chapters 13 and 14). He had grown up in a family where he was the youngest of three brothers. Always being bossed around by his older brothers, he had learned to suppress his own feelings and ideas. Throughout his life, he had been afraid to stand up for himself. This fear played no small role in his difficulty with speaking up or making presentations before a group. Through practicing assertiveness skills, he learned how to express his feelings and wants to others directly. He was pleasantly surprised to find that others usually appreciated and were interested in what he had to say.

As the youngest child in his family, Steve had also been "babied" during childhood. He grew up with an underlying fear of standing up as his own person and assuming full responsibility as an adult. He had to work on self-esteem to realize that he was just as valuable, important, and able to contribute as anyone else. Overcoming his social phobia certainly helped, but, like Cindy, Steve also worked on developing a relationship with his inner child. By consistently validating and supporting the little boy within, he gradually overcame the feelings of inadequacy and shame that had fed his phobia.

Steve's program for recovery from social phobia contained many of the same components as Cindy's program for recovery from agoraphobia. The only significant difference was that Steve didn't have to deal with panic; his phobia centered around fears of embarrassment and humiliation rather than fears of losing control during a panic attack. All of the following strategies contributed to his recovery, with real-life desensitization perhaps being the most crucial:

Physical	Breathing exercises
	Regular practice of deep relaxation
	Regular aerobic exercise
	Nutritional improvements (specifically, reducing sugar intake and thus hypoglycemic mood swings)
Behavioral	Imagery desensitization
	Real-life desensitization, including taking a public speaking class prior to making presentations at work
Emotional	Learning to identify and express feelings
Mental	Countering negative self-talk
	Countering mistaken beliefs
Interpersonal	Developing an assertive interpersonal style
Whole Self	Developing self-esteem by cultivating a relationship with his inner child

Mike: Obsessive-Compulsive Disorder

Mike, you may recall, was a successful businessman who had a recurring, irrational fear while driving that he had run over a person or animal. So strong and insistent was this fear that he continually had to retrace the route he'd just driven to assure himself that no one was lying in the street. By the time he sought treatment, his compulsion to check was so strong that he needed to retrace his route three or four times before he could go on. Because he felt both ashamed and powerless to control his behavior, he was also significantly depressed—a common complaint of people with obsessive-compulsive disorder. Mike's problem was an example of the "checking" type of obsessive-compulsive disorder. But the comprehensive recovery program he undertook could apply equally well to other forms of obsessive-compulsive disorder, including washing, counting, or other compulsions.

In many respects Mike's road to recovery was similar to that of Susan, Cindy, and Steve in the preceding examples. His therapist asked him to practice breathing exercises, progressive muscle relaxation, and aerobic exercise on a daily basis to reduce the physiological component of his anxiety. Mike also reduced the amount of caffeine and sugar in his diet and started taking high-potency B-complex and vitamin C supplements with breakfast and dinner. Mike felt so much better from these practices alone that there were certain days that he didn't need to retrace his driving route at all. However, his problem didn't disappear altogether.

Mike worked on changing his inner dialogue, or self-talk, while driving. Instead of always asking himself, "What if I hit someone?" he learned to counter with the statement, "If I hit anything, I certainly would hear it or feel it. But this hasn't happened, so I'm okay."

Repeating this reassuring statement over and over helped him to reduce the number of times he needed to retrace his route from three or four to one or two, but it didn't dispel his obsession completely.

Another helpful intervention was learning to identify and express his angry feelings. Mike found that by getting angry with his compulsion to check and shouting "No!" very loudly in his car, he could sometimes dissipate his anxiety enough so that he didn't have to check. Getting in touch with and acknowledging his frustrations also helped him to reduce stress in other areas of his life apart from his specific problem with checking. Yet expressing needs and feelings was not enough, any more than the physical and mental strategies he had tried, to completely resolve his obsessive-compulsive problem.

From his reading on the subject, Mike learned that obsessive-compulsive disorder responds best to the combination of two specific interventions:

- A behavioral intervention called *exposure and response prevention*

- Medication—specifically, antidepressant medications such as clomipramine (Anafranil) and fluoxetine (Prozac)

Under the supervision of his therapist, Mike practiced exposure and response prevention in two steps. First, he was instructed to reduce to one the number of times he retraced his route. He had already brought the frequency down from four or five repetitions to two or three, and over the course of a month he was able to reduce the number further, to one. At this point his therapist rode with him in the car and instructed Mike, whenever he felt the urge to retrace, to pull the car over to the side of the road and stop. Mike then waited several minutes for the anxiety he felt about not retracing his route to subside. Then he resumed his driving. After two weeks of practicing response prevention with his therapist, Mike was finally able to do it on his own. It was very liberating to Mike not to have to spend so much time and energy on retracing his driving route.

A problem that remained, though, was that he couldn't get the obsession about having run over someone out of his mind completely—even though positive self-talk had helped somewhat. He continued to be vigilant while driving and was depressed that he had so little control over his thoughts.

Mike's therapist referred him to a psychiatrist who instructed him about the medication clomipramine, a drug that has been effective in eliminating or reducing the symptoms of obsessive-compulsive disorder in about 60 percent of the cases in which it has been used. Within three weeks of starting the medication, Mike found that his obsessions had disappeared altogether and that his depression had lifted significantly. He began to relax and enjoy driving again, free of any concern about having hit someone. His doctor told him that he would need to stay on the medication for one year, at which point Mike would gradually taper off the dose and see if he could continue to live free of obsessions without taking medication.

Although Mike's obsessive-compulsive disorder responded quite well to the combination of interventions described above, he continued to feel depressed from time to time. It became apparent to his therapist that Mike was feeling somewhat bored with his line of work and with his life in general. The final phase of his recovery program involved making two major adjustments that added meaning and direction to his life. First, he decided to make a career change. Over the course of a year, he moved from a corporate position in marketing to starting a small retail business of his own. All his life, Mike had had a strong interest in music but had never done anything to fulfill it. So, as a second step, he began taking piano lessons. After a year, he took this pursuit a step further, bought a synthesizer, and began to compose his own original piano pieces. This creative outlet added a new dimension to Mike's life and enabled him to express a previously unrealized potential. It was after this that his depression fully lifted.

The most critical component of Mike's recovery from obsessive-compulsive disorder was the combination of response prevention and medication. The crux of his recovery from depression was the combination of overcoming his obsessive-compulsive disorder *and* developing a creative outlet that gave his life a new dimension of meaning. His total program for recovery can be summarized as follows:

Physical	Breathing exercises
	Regular practice of deep relaxation
	Regular aerobic exercise
	Nutritional improvements plus vitamin supplements
Behavioral	Exposure and response prevention to eliminate checking
Emotional	Learning to identify and express anger and frustration
Mental	Self-talk to counter fears about having run over someone
Medication	Taking clomipramine for one year
Existential-Spiritual	Pursuing a creative interest in playing the piano and musical composition

Developing Your Own Recovery Program

By this point I hope that you've gained an idea about three things: 1) the wide range of strategies used in a comprehensive recovery program, 2) the specific types of strategies employed, and 3) how such strategies are actually implemented in specific cases.

You can now begin to develop your own recovery program. The following two charts are designed to assist you with this. The first is the *Problem Effectiveness Chart*. It correlates different types of anxiety disorders with specific chapters in this workbook. Chapters that are particularly relevant for *everyone* with the disorder are marked with an "X." Those chapters that are often relevant are marked with a lowercase "x." Your choice of strategies will, of course, depend on the nature and causes of your particular difficulty. After reading the first three chapters of this workbook, you should have some idea of what strategies to emphasize.

Problem Effectiveness Chart

"Ordinary" Anxiety	Post-Traumatic Stress Disorder	Obsessive-Compulsive Disorder	Generalized Anxiety Disorder	Specific Phobia	Social Phobia	Agoraphobia	Panic Attacks	
X	X	X	X	X	X	X	X	Relaxation
X	X	X	X	X	X	X	X	Exercise
					x	X	X	Coping Techniques for Panic
				X	X	X	X	Exposure
X	X	X	X	X	X	X	X	Self-Talk
X	X	X	X	X	X	X	X	Mistaken Beliefs
X	X	X	X		X	X	X	Expressing Feelings
x	x	x	x		X	X		Assertiveness
X	X	X	X	X	X	X	X	Self-Esteem
X	X	X	X	X	X	X	X	Nutrition
	X	X	x		x	x	X	Medication
x	x	x	x		x	x	x	Meaning/Spirituality

The second chart, called the *Weekly Practice Record*, enables you to outline in detail your own personal program for recovery. The chart lists all the specific strategies and skills offered in this workbook. Following each skill, in parentheses, is the recommended frequency for practice in a one-week time period. This chart enables you to check off, for each day of the week, which exercises you have practiced.

Since this is a weekly chart, I recommend that you *make fifty-two copies* of it to take you through a one-year time period. (Of course, your actual recovery may turn out to take significantly less than one year.)

At the top of the chart be sure to specify the dates of the particular week as well as your goals for that week. At the bottom of the chart, you can estimate, on a scale of 0 to 100 percent, how much you believe you have recovered up to the time of that particular week. (Note: Be prepared for your level of recovery to be marked by progressions and regressions from week to week.) It is obvious that you will not implement *all* of the strategies recommended in this workbook *every* week. As you go through each chapter, you'll likely emphasize the skills taught in that chapter. There are four skills, though, that I recommend trying to practice *five to seven times a week* for fifty-two weeks a year, regardless of the type of anxiety disorder you happen to be dealing with. These are

1. A deep relaxation technique (such as muscle relaxation, visualization, or meditation)

2. One half hour of vigorous exercise

3. Good nutritional habits

4. Countering negative self-talk or using affirmations to counter mistaken beliefs

If you happen to have phobias, there are two additional strategies I recommend practicing three to five times a week until you are phobia-free, namely

5. Imagery desensitization

6. Real-life desensitization

Beyond these guidelines, you will be working out for yourself how much time you need to spend with the various other strategies that constitute your particular recovery program.

A *consistent commitment over time* to practicing strategies that are helpful to you is what will make the difference between a partial and a complete recovery. The *Weekly Practice Record* is designed to help keep you on track with your personal program for recovery over the long haul.

Weekly Practice Record

Goals for Week   Date:

1.

2.

3.

	Mon	Tues	Wed	Thurs	Fri	Sat	Sun
Used deep breathing technique (6–7)							
Used deep relaxation technique* (5–7)							
Did one-half hour vigorous exercise (5–7)							
Used coping techniques to manage panic**							
Practiced countering negative self-talk (5–7)							
Used affirmations to counter mistaken beliefs (5–7)							
Practiced imagery desensitization (3–5)							
Practiced real-life desensitization (3–5)							
Identified/expressed feelings**							
Practiced assertive communication with significant other**							
Practiced assertive communication to avoid manipulation**							
Self-esteem: worked on improving body image**							
Self-esteem: took steps toward achieving goals**							
Self-esteem: worked on countering inner critic**							
Self-esteem: worked on nurturing inner child**							
Nutrition: eliminated caffeine/sugar/stimulants (7)							
Nutrition: ate only whole, unprocessed foods (5–7)							
Nutrition: used anti-stress supplements (5–7)							
Medication: used appropriate medications as prescribed by doctor (7)							
Meaning: worked on discovering/realizing life purpose**							
Spirituality: utilized spiritual beliefs and practices to reduce anxiety**							

Estimated percent recovery (0 percent to 100 percent): _____

* e.g., progressive muscle relaxation, visualization, or meditation

** Recommended frequency varies depending on focus

Necessary Ingredients for Undertaking Your Own Recovery Program

By now you may have some idea of the strategies you want to utilize for your own recovery. The *Weekly Practice Record* will enable you to specify, on a weekly basis, the particular strategies and skills you incorporate in your personal program. You may have already guessed, though, that recovery entails much more than just a series of strategies. Your ability to *implement* the strategies recommended in this workbook depends entirely on your attitude, commitment, and motivation to really *do* something about your problem. Your recovery depends on the extent to which you can adopt and incorporate the five necessary ingredients described below.

1. Taking Responsibility—In a Context of Support

Do you feel responsible for your problem? Or do you attribute it to some quirk of heredity, abusive parents, or the stressful people in your life? Even if you feel you aren't solely responsible for having created your disorder, you are the one who is ultimately responsible either for holding on to it or for doing something about it. It may be difficult initially to accept the idea that the decision is yours whether to maintain or whether to overcome your problem. Yet accepting full responsibility is the most empowering step you can take. If you are the one who keeps your condition going, you are also the one with the power to change and outgrow it.

Taking responsibility means you don't blame anyone else for your difficulties. It also means that you don't blame *yourself*. Is there truly any justification for blaming yourself that you have panic attacks, phobias, or obsessions and compulsions? Is it truly your fault that you developed these problems? Is it not more accurate to say that you've done the best you could in your life up to now with the knowledge and resources at your disposal? While it's up to you to change your condition, there is simply no basis for judging or blaming yourself for having it.

Taking responsibility for overcoming your condition does *not* mean that you have to do it all alone. In fact, the opposite is true: you are more likely to be willing to change and to take risks when you feel adequately supported. A most important prerequisite for undertaking your own program for recovery is to have an adequate support system. This can include your spouse or partner, one or two close friends, and/or a support group or class specifically set up to assist people with anxiety disorders.

2. Motivation—Overcoming Secondary Gains

Once you've decided to acknowledge your share of the responsibility for your problem, your ability to actually do something about it will depend on your motivation. Do you feel truly motivated to change? Enough so that you'll be willing to learn and incorporate several new habits of thought and behavior into your daily routine? Enough so that you'll be willing to make some basic changes in your lifestyle?

Psychologist David Bakan once made the observation that "suffering is the great motivator of growth." If you are experiencing considerable distress from your particular problem, you're likely to be strongly motivated to do something about it. A basic belief in your self-worth can also be a strong motivation for change. If you love yourself enough to feel that you sincerely deserve to have a fulfilling and productive life, you simply won't settle for being impeded by panic, phobias, or other anxiety symptoms. You will demand more of life than that.

This brings up the issue of what interferes with motivation. Any person, situation, or factor that consciously or unconsciously *rewards you for holding on to your condition* will tend to undermine your motivation. For example, you may want to overcome your problem with being housebound. However, if consciously or unconsciously you don't want to deal with facing the outside world, getting a job, and earning an income, you will tend to keep yourself confined. Consciously, you want to overcome agoraphobia, yet your motivation is not strong enough to overcome the unconscious "payoffs" for not recovering.

Many years ago, Sigmund Freud referred to the idea of unconscious payoffs as "secondary gains." Wherever there is strong resistance to recovering from any chronic, disabling condition—whether it is an anxiety disorder, depression, addiction, or obesity—secondary gains are often operative. If you find that you have difficulty developing or *sustaining* motivation to do something about your condition, it's important to ask yourself, "What payoffs am I getting for staying this way?" The list below enumerates some of the more common secondary gains that can keep you stuck:

- A deep-seated belief that you "don't deserve" to recover and lead a normal life—that you're unworthy of being reasonably happy. When self-punishment is a secondary gain, it is often the case that you're punishing yourself to get back at someone else. Self-punishment also can occur because you feel guilty about your condition. The way out of guilt and the tendency to hold yourself back is to work on your self-esteem (see chapter 14).

- A deep-seated belief that "it's too much work" to truly change. After all, you may already be feeling stressed out and overwhelmed. Now you are being asked to take on considerably more responsibility and work in order to recover. Unconsciously, it may just seem like too much work, leaving you discouraged about ever breaking out of your condition. The solution to this dilemma is to replace your assumption of "too much work" with more positive beliefs, such as "I don't have to be completely well tomorrow—I can take small steps toward recovering at my own pace" or "Any goal can be achieved if broken down into sufficiently small steps." (The 12-step recovery programs have abbreviated these constructive attitudes with the slogan "One day at a time.")

- If you're agoraphobic and relatively housebound, you may be attached to the payoffs you get from your spouse or partner. These include attention, being taken care of, and being financially supported, or, in general, not having to deal with adult responsibilities.

- The reverse of the last situation may also be true. Your spouse or partner may be getting payoffs from your being dependent on him or her. These can include the opportunity to take care of, control, and even take responsibility for your life (this is a case of *codependency*—see chapter 14). The payoff can also be assurance that you will never leave. That is, your partner may fear that if you fully recover and become more independent, you'll leave. You need to realize that you won't be held back by your partner's secondary gains unless you are unconsciously colluding with him or her to maintain them.

The above is only a partial list of secondary gains. They may or may not apply in your case. If you feel that you're having difficulties with motivation at any point in your recovery, it's important to raise the question "What is the payoff for avoiding change?"

3. *Making a Commitment to Yourself to Follow Through*

The initial motivation and enthusiasm you have when you first decide to do something about your problem is usually sufficient to get you started. The real test is in following through. Are you willing to make a commitment to *consistently* practice skills and strategies that work for you over the many months and sometimes years that it takes to achieve a full and lasting recovery? In my experience, it is difficult to sustain a high level of motivation over such periods of time unless you have a deep and sincere *commitment* to persist with your recovery program until you're fully satisfied with the results. On a practical level, this means going out and exercising, practicing desensitization, or working on your self-esteem even on those days when you don't feel like it. It means that you get up and keep going even after you've had a setback that makes you wonder whether you'll *ever* feel better. While your motivation may wax and wane, a personal commitment to follow through with your program is what is going to make the difference between a partial and a complete recovery.

4. *Willingness to Take Risks*

It is simply not possible to change or grow in any area of your life unless you are willing to take some risks. To recover means being willing to experiment with new ways of thinking, feeling, and acting that may be unfamiliar to you at first. It also means giving up some of the payoffs for not changing, as were described in the section on motivation. If you are dealing with phobias, the way to overcome them is simply to face those situations you've been avoiding—gradually and in your imagination at first. If you are dealing with panic attacks, it may be necessary to risk relinquishing some control and learning to flow with unpleasant bodily sensations instead of resisting and fighting them. If you're dealing with obsessions and compulsions, it may be necessary to risk experiencing anxiety when you resist engaging in compulsive behavior. Or it may be necessary to risk taking a prescription medication.

An effective program for recovery is predicated upon your willingness to risk trying out new behaviors that may cause you *more* anxiety at first yet which in the long run can be quite helpful. As in the case of taking responsibility, having support from others who believe in you and back you up will make taking risks considerably easier.

5. Defining and Visualizing Your Goals for Recovery

It's difficult to tackle and then overcome a problem unless you have a clear, concrete idea of the goal you're aiming for. Before embarking on your own program for recovery, it is important that you answer the following questions:

- "What are the most important positive changes I want to make in my life?"

- "What would a complete recovery from my present condition look like?"

- "Specifically, how will I think, feel, and act in my work, my relationships with others, and my relationship with myself once I've fully recovered?"

- "What new opportunities will I take advantage of once I've fully recovered?"

Once you've defined what your own recovery might be like, it can be very helpful to practice *visualizing* it. During the time you allocate for practicing deep relaxation, take a few minutes to imagine what your life would look like if you were entirely free of your problems. Visualize in detail any changes in your work, recreational activities, and relationships, and the body image and appearance you would like to achieve. To assist you in developing this positive scenario, use the space below or preferably a separate sheet of paper to write out a "script" of how your life would *ideally* look when you have fully recovered. Be sure to cover as many different areas of your life as possible.

Ideal Scenario for My Life After I've Recovered

In my ideal scenario for my recovered life I would have overcome my fear and anxieties and I would have another high paying job again. My family would be happy to see how far I've come. I'd be sharing my life with someone and I'd be working to create a future with her.

Practicing visualizing your goals for recovery on a daily basis (preferably in a relaxed state) will increase your confidence about succeeding. This practice will actually make a full recovery more likely. There is abundant philosophical evidence—both ancient and modern—that what you believe in with your whole heart and see with your whole mind has a strong tendency to come true.

Summary of Things to Do

1. Review the case histories in this chapter and examine the *Problem Effectiveness Chart* to determine which chapters of this workbook are relevant to your particular problem.

2. Decide in what order you're going to work with the various chapters that are relevant to you. I recommend using the chapters in the order they are presented.

3. Make fifty-two copies of the *Weekly Practice Record* to monitor your personal recovery program for one year. (Your recovery, of course, may take less than one year.)

4. Reread the final section, "Necessary Ingredients for Undertaking Your Own Recovery Program," to reinforce in your mind the five keys to a successful and complete recovery: *taking responsibility, motivation* (including overcoming secondary gains), *commitment, a willingness to take risks,* and *defining goals.*

4

Relaxation

The capacity to relax is at the very foundation of any program undertaken to overcome anxiety, phobias, or panic attacks. Many of the other skills described in this book, such as desensitization, visualization, and changing negative self-talk, build on the capacity to achieve deep relaxation.

Relaxation is more than unwinding in front of the TV set or in the bathtub at the end of the day—though, without doubt, these practices can be relaxing. The type of relaxation that really makes a difference in dealing with anxiety is the *regular, daily* practice of some form of *deep relaxation*. Deep relaxation refers to a distinct physiological state that is the exact opposite of the way your body reacts under stress or during a panic attack. This state was originally described by Herbert Benson in 1975 as the *relaxation response*. It involves a series of physiological changes including

- Decrease in heart rate
- Decrease in respiration rate
- Decrease in blood pressure
- Decrease in skeletal muscle tension
- Decrease in metabolic rate and oxygen consumption
- Decrease in analytical thinking
- Increase in skin resistance
- Increase in alpha wave activity in the brain

Regular practice of deep relaxation for twenty to thirty minutes on a daily basis can produce, over time, a generalization of relaxation to the rest of your life. That is, after several weeks of practicing deep relaxation once per day, you will tend to feel more relaxed all the time.

Numerous other benefits of deep relaxation have been documented over the past twenty years. These include

- Reduction of generalized anxiety. Many people have found that regular practice also reduces the frequency and severity of panic attacks.

- Preventing stress from becoming cumulative. Unabated stress tends to build up over time. Entering into a state of physiological quiescence once a day gives your body the opportunity to recover from the effects of stress. Even sleep can fail to break the cumulative stress cycle unless you've given yourself permission to deeply relax while awake.

- Increased energy level and productivity. (When under stress, you may work against yourself and become less efficient.)

- Improved concentration and memory. Regular practice of deep relaxation tends to increase your ability to focus and keeps your mind from "racing."

- Reduction of insomnia and fatigue. Learning to relax leads to sleep that is deeper and sounder.

- Prevention and/or reduction of psychosomatic disorders, such as hypertension, migraines, headaches, asthma, and ulcers.

- Increased self-confidence and reduced self-blame. For many people, stress and excessive self-criticism or feelings of inadequacy go hand in hand. You can perform better, as well as feel better, when you are relaxed.

- Increased availability of feelings. Muscle tension is one of the chief impediments to an awareness of your feelings.

How can you achieve a state of deep relaxation? Some of the more common methods include

1.   Abdominal breathing

2.   Progressive muscle relaxation

3.   Passive muscle relaxation

4.   Visualizing a peaceful scene

5.   Guided imagery

6.   Meditation

7.   Biofeedback

8.   Sensory deprivation

9.   Yoga

10. Calming music

For our purposes here, we will focus on the first five and the last two of these methods.

Abdominal Breathing

Your breathing directly reflects the level of tension you carry in your body. Under tension, your breathing usually becomes shallow and rapid, and your breathing occurs high in the chest. When relaxed, you breathe more fully, more deeply, and from your abdomen. It's difficult to be tense and to breathe from your abdomen at the same time.

Some of the benefits of abdominal breathing include

- Increased oxygen supply to the brain and musculature.

- Stimulation of the parasympathetic nervous system. This branch of your autonomic nervous system promotes a state of calmness and quiescence. It works in a fashion exactly opposite to the sympathetic branch of your nervous system, which stimulates a state of emotional arousal and the very physiological reactions underlying a panic attack.

- Greater feelings of connectedness between mind and body. Anxiety and worry tend to keep you "up in your head." A few minutes of deep abdominal breathing will help bring you down into your whole body.

- More efficient excretion of bodily toxins. Many toxic substances in the body are excreted through the lungs.

- Improved concentration. If your mind is racing, it's difficult to focus your attention. Abdominal breathing will help to quiet your mind.

- Abdominal breathing by itself can trigger a relaxation response.

If you suffer from phobias, panic, or other anxiety disorders, you will tend to have one or both of two types of problems with breathing. Either

1. You breathe too high up in your chest and your breathing is shallow, or

2. You tend to hyperventilate, breathing out too much carbon dioxide relative to the amount of oxygen carried in your bloodstream. Shallow, chest-level breathing, when rapid, can lead to hyperventilation. Hyperventilation, in turn, can cause physical symptoms very similar to those associated with panic attacks.

These two types of breathing are discussed in greater detail below.

Shallow, Chest-Level Breathing

Studies have found differences in the breathing patterns of anxious and shy people as opposed to those who are more relaxed and outgoing. People who are fearful and shy tend to breathe in a shallow fashion from their chest, while those who are more extroverted and relaxed breathe more slowly, deeply, and from their abdomens.

Before reading on, take a minute to notice how you are breathing right now. Is your breath slow or rapid? Deep or shallow? Does it center around a point high in your chest or down in your abdomen? You might also notice changes in your breathing pattern under stress versus when you are more relaxed.

If you find that your breathing is shallow and high in your chest, don't despair. It's quite possible to retrain yourself to breathe more deeply and from your abdomen. Practicing abdominal breathing (described below) on a regular basis will gradually help you to shift the center of your breath downward from your chest. Regular practice of full abdominal breathing will also increase your lung capacity, helping you to breathe more deeply. A program of vigorous, aerobic exercise can also be helpful.

Hyperventilation Syndrome

If you breathe from your chest, you may tend to overbreathe, exhaling excess carbon dioxide in relation to the amount of oxygen in your bloodstream. You may also tend to breathe through your mouth. The result is a cluster of symptoms, including rapid heartbeat, dizziness, and tingly sensations that are so similar to the symptoms of panic that they can be indistinguishable. Some of the physiological changes brought on by hyperventilation include

- Increased alkalinity of nerve cells, which causes them to be more excitable. The result is that you feel *nervous* and *jittery*.

- Decreased carbon dioxide in the blood, which can cause your *heart to pump harder and faster* as well as making *lights seem brighter* and *sounds louder*.

- Increased constriction of blood vessels in your brain, which can cause feelings of *dizziness, disorientation,* and even a *sense of unreality* or *separateness from your body*.

All these symptoms may be interpreted as a developing panic attack. As soon as you start responding to these bodily changes with panic-evoking mental statements to yourself, such as "I'm losing control!" or "What's happening to me?" *you actually do panic.* Symptoms that initially only mimicked panic set off a reaction that leads to genuine panic. Hyperventilation can either 1) cause physical sensations that lead you to panic *or* 2) contribute to an ongoing panic attack by aggravating unpleasant physical symptoms.

If you suspect that you are subject to hyperventilation, you might notice whether you habitually breathe shallowly from your chest and through your mouth. Notice also, when you're frightened, whether you tend to hold your breath or breathe very shallowly and quickly. The experience of tingling or numb sensations, particularly in your arms or legs, is also a sign of hyperventilation. If any of these characteristics seem to apply to you, hyperventilation may play a role in either instigating or aggravating your panic reactions or anxiety.

The traditional cure for acute hyperventilation symptoms is to breathe into a paper bag. This technique causes you to breathe in carbon dioxide, restoring the normal balance of oxygen to carbon dioxide in your bloodstream. It is a method that works. Equally effective in reducing symptoms of hyperventilation are the abdominal breathing and calming breath exercises described below. Both of them help you to slow your breathing down, which effectively reduces your intake of oxygen and brings the ratio of oxygen to carbon dioxide back into balance.

If you can recognize the symptoms of hyperventilation for what they are, then learn to curtail them by deliberately slowing your breathing, you needn't react to them with panic.

The two exercises described below can help you change your breathing pattern. By practicing them, you can achieve a state of deep relaxation in a short period of time. Just three minutes of practicing abdominal breathing or the calming breath exercise will usually induce a deep state of relaxation. Many people have successfully used one or the other technique to abort a panic attack when they felt the first signs of anxiety coming on. The techniques are also very helpful in diminishing anticipatory anxiety you may experience in advance of facing a phobic situation. While the techniques of progressive muscle relaxation and meditation described later in this chapter take up to twenty minutes to achieve their effects, the following two methods can produce a moderate to deep level of relaxation in just three to five minutes.

Abdominal Breathing Exercise

1.   Note the level of tension you're feeling. Then place one hand on your abdomen right beneath your rib cage.

2.   Inhale slowly and deeply through your nose into the "bottom" of your lungs—in other words, send the air as low down as you can. If you're breathing from your abdomen, your hand should actually *rise*. Your chest should move only slightly while your abdomen expands. (In abdominal breathing, the *diaphragm*—the muscle that separates the chest cavity from the abdominal cavity—moves downward. In so doing, it causes the muscles surrounding the abdominal cavity to push outward.)

3.   When you've taken in a full breath, pause for a moment and then exhale slowly through your nose or mouth, depending on your preference. Be sure to exhale fully. *As you exhale, allow your whole body to just let go* (you might visualize your arms and legs going loose and limp like a rag doll).

4.   Do ten slow, full abdominal breaths. Try to keep your breathing *smooth* and *regular*, without gulping in a big breath or letting your breath out all at once. It will help to slow down your breathing if you slowly count to four on the inhale (one-two-three-four) and then slowly count to four on the exhale. Remember to pause briefly at the end of each inhalation. Count from ten down to one counting backward one number with each *exhalation*. The process should go like this:

     Slow inhale … Pause … Slow exhale ("Ten.")

     Slow inhale … Pause … Slow exhale ("Nine.")

     Slow inhale … Pause … Slow exhale ("Eight.")

     and so on down to one. If you start to feel light-headed while practicing abdominal breathing, stop for fifteen to twenty seconds, then start again.

5.   Extend the exercise if you wish by doing two or three "sets" of abdominal breaths, remembering to count backward from ten to one for each set (each exhalation counts as one number). *Five full minutes* of abdominal breathing will have a pronounced effect in reducing anxiety or early symptoms of panic. Some people prefer to count from one to ten instead. Feel free to do this if it suits you.

Calming Breath Exercise

The *Calming Breath Exercise* was adapted from the ancient discipline of yoga. It is a very efficient technique for achieving a deep state of relaxation quickly.

1.   Breathing from your abdomen, inhale through your nose slowly to a count of five (count slowly "one … two … three … four … five" as you inhale).

2.   Pause and hold your breath to a count of five.

3.   Exhale slowly, through your nose or mouth, to a count of five (or more if it takes you longer). Be sure to exhale fully.

4.   When you've exhaled completely, take two breaths in your normal rhythm, then repeat steps 1 through 3 in the cycle above.

5.   Keep up the exercise for at least three to five minutes. This should involve going through *at least* ten cycles of in-five, hold-five, out-five. As you continue the exercise, you may notice that you can count higher when you exhale than when you inhale. Allow these variations in your counting to occur if they do, naturally, and just continue with the exercise for up to five minutes. Remember to take two normal breaths between each cycle. If you start to feel light-headed while practicing this exercise, stop for thirty seconds and then start again.

6.   Throughout the exercise, keep your breathing *smooth* and *regular*, without gulping in breaths or breathing out suddenly.

7.   *Optional:* Each time you exhale, you may wish to say, "Relax," "Calm," "Let go," or any other relaxing word or phrase silently to yourself. Allow your whole body to let go as you do this. If you keep this up each time you practice, eventually just saying your relaxing word by itself will bring on a mild state of relaxation.

The *Calming Breath Exercise* can be a potent technique for halting the momentum of a panic reaction when the first signs of anxiety come on. It is also useful in reducing symptoms of hyperventilation.

Practice Exercise

Practice the *Abdominal Breathing Exercise* or *Calming Breath Exercise* for *five minutes every day for at least two weeks*. If possible, find a regular time each day to do this so that your breathing exercise becomes a habit. With practice, you can learn in a short period of time to damp down the physiological reactions underlying anxiety and panic.

Once you feel you've gained some mastery in the use of either technique, apply it when you feel stressed or anxious, or when you experience the onset of panic symptoms. By extending your practice of either exercise to a month or longer, you will begin to retrain yourself to breathe from your abdomen. The more you can shift the center of your breathing from your chest to your abdomen, the more consistently you will feel relaxed on an ongoing basis.

Progressive Muscle Relaxation

Progressive muscle relaxation (PMR) is a systematic technique for achieving a deep state of relaxation. It was developed by Dr. Edmund Jacobson more than fifty years ago. Dr. Jacobson discovered that a muscle could be relaxed by first tensing it for a few seconds and then releasing it. Tensing and releasing various muscle groups throughout the body produces a deep state of relaxation, which Dr. Jacobson found capable of relieving a variety of conditions, from high blood pressure to ulcerative colitis.

In his original book, *Progressive Relaxation*, Dr. Jacobson developed a series of two hundred different muscle relaxation exercises and a training program that took months to complete. More recently, the system has been abbreviated to fifteen to twenty basic exercises, which have been found to be just as effective, if practiced regularly, as the original more elaborate system.

Progressive muscle relaxation is especially helpful for people whose anxiety is strongly associated with muscle tension. This is what often leads you to say that you are "uptight" or "tense." You may experience chronic tightness in your shoulders and neck, which can be effectively relieved by practicing progressive muscle relaxation. Other symptoms that respond well to progressive muscle relaxation include tension headaches, backaches, tightness in the jaw, tightness around the eyes, muscle spasms, high blood pressure, and insomnia. If you are troubled by racing thoughts, you may find that systematically relaxing your muscles tends to help slow down your mind. Dr. Jacobson himself once said, "An anxious mind cannot exist in a relaxed body."

The immediate effects of progressive muscle relaxation include all the benefits of the relaxation response described at the beginning of this chapter. Long-term effects of *regular* practice of progressive muscle relaxation include

- A decrease in generalized anxiety

- A decrease in anticipatory anxiety related to phobias

- Reduction in the frequency and duration of panic attacks

- Improved ability to face phobic situations through graded exposure

- Improved concentration

- An increased sense of control over moods

- Increased self-esteem

- Increased spontaneity and creativity

These long-term benefits are sometimes called *generalization effects*: the relaxation experienced during daily sessions tends, after a month or two, to *generalize* to the rest of the day. The *regular* practice of progressive muscle relaxation can go a long way toward helping you to better manage your anxiety, face your fears, overcome panic, and feel better all around.

There are no contraindications for progressive muscle relaxation unless the muscle groups to be tensed and relaxed have been injured. If you take tranquilizers, you may find that regular practice of progressive muscle relaxation will enable you to lower your dosage.

Guidelines for Practicing Progressive Muscle Relaxation (or Any Form of Deep Relaxation)

The following guidelines will help you make the most use of progressive muscle relaxation. They are also applicable to *any* form of deep relaxation you undertake to practice regularly, including self-hypnosis, guided visualization, and meditation.

1.   Practice at least *twenty minutes per day*. Two twenty-minute periods are preferable. Once a day is mandatory for obtaining generalization effects. (You may want to begin your practice with thirty-minute periods. As you gain skill in relaxation technique, you will find that the amount of time you need to experience the relaxation response will decrease.)

2.   Find a *quiet location* to practice where you won't be distracted. Don't permit the phone to ring while you're practicing. Use a fan or air conditioner to blot out background noise, if necessary.

3.   Practice at *regular times*. On awakening, before retiring, or before a meal is generally the best time. A consistent daily relaxation routine will increase the likelihood of generalization effects.

4.   Practice on an *empty stomach*. Food digestion after meals will tend to disrupt deep relaxation.

5.   Assume a *comfortable position*. Your entire body, including your head, should be supported. Lying down on a sofa or bed and sitting in a reclining chair are two ways of supporting your body most completely. (When lying down, you may want to place a pillow beneath your knees for further support.) Sitting up is preferable to lying down if you are feeling tired and sleepy. It's advantageous to experience the full depth of the relaxation response consciously, without going to sleep.

6.   *Loosen any tight garments* and take off shoes, watch, glasses, contact lenses, jewelry, and so on.

7.   *Make a decision not to worry about anything*. Give yourself permission to put aside the concerns of the day. Allow taking care of yourself and having peace of mind to take precedence over any of your worries. (Success with relaxation depends on giving peace of mind high priority in your overall scheme of values.)

8.   Assume a *passive, detached attitude*. This is probably the most important element. You want to adopt a "let it happen" attitude and be free of any worry about how well you are performing the technique. Do not *try* to relax. Do not *try* to control your body. Do not judge your performance. The point is to let go.

Progressive Muscle Relaxation Technique

Progressive muscle relaxation involves tensing and relaxing, in succession, sixteen different muscle groups of the body. The idea is to tense each muscle group hard (not so hard that you strain, however) for about ten seconds and then to let go of it suddenly. You then give yourself fifteen to twenty seconds to relax, noticing how the muscle group feels when relaxed in contrast to how it felt when tensed, before going on to the next group of muscles. You might also say to yourself, "I am relaxing," "Letting go," "Let the tension flow away," or any other relaxing phrase during each relaxation period between successive muscle groups. Throughout the exercise, maintain your focus on your muscles. When your attention wanders, bring it back to the particular muscle group you're working on. The guidelines below describe progressive muscle relaxation in detail:

- Make sure you are in a setting that is quiet and comfortable. Observe the guidelines for practicing relaxation that were previously described.

- When you tense a particular muscle group, do so vigorously, without straining, for seven to ten seconds. You may want to count "one-thousand-one," "one-thousand-two," and so on, as a way of marking off seconds.

- Concentrate on what is happening. Feel the buildup of tension in each particular muscle group. It is often helpful to visualize the particular muscle group being tensed.

- When you release the muscles, do so abruptly, and then relax, enjoying the sudden feeling of limpness. Allow the relaxation to develop for at least fifteen to twenty seconds before going on to the next group of muscles.

- Allow all the *other* muscles in your body to remain relaxed, as far as possible, while working on a particular muscle group.

- Tense and relax each muscle group once. But if a particular area feels especially tight, you can tense and relax it two or three times, waiting about twenty seconds between each cycle.

Once you are comfortably supported in a quiet place, follow the detailed instructions below:

1. To begin, take three deep abdominal breaths, exhaling slowly each time. As you exhale, imagine that tension throughout your body begins to flow away.

2. Clench your fists. Hold for seven to ten seconds and then release for fifteen to twenty seconds. *Use these same time intervals for all other muscle groups.*

3. Tighten your biceps by drawing your forearms up toward your shoulders and "making a muscle" with both arms. Hold … and then relax.

4. Tighten your *triceps*—the muscles on the undersides of your upper arms—by extending your arms out straight and locking your elbows. Hold … and then relax.

5. Tense the muscles in your forehead by raising your eyebrows as far as you can. Hold … and then relax. Imagine your forehead muscles becoming smooth and limp as they relax.

6. Tense the muscles around your eyes by clenching your eyelids tightly shut. Hold … and then relax. Imagine sensations of deep relaxation spreading all around the area of your eyes.

7. Tighten your jaw by opening your mouth so widely that you stretch the muscles around the hinges of your jaw. Hold … and then relax. Let your lips part and allow your jaw to hang loose.

8. Tighten the muscles in the back of your neck by pulling your head way back, as if you were going to touch your head to your back (be gentle with this muscle group

to avoid injury). Focus only on tensing the muscles in your neck. Hold … and then relax. (Since this area is often especially tight, it's good to do the tense-relax cycle twice.)

9.   Take a few deep breaths and tune in to the weight of your head sinking into whatever surface it is resting on.

10. Tighten your shoulders by raising them up as if you were going to touch your ears. Hold … and then relax.

11. Tighten the muscles around your shoulder blades by pushing your shoulder blades back as if you were going to touch them together. Hold the tension in your shoulder blades … and then relax. Since this area is often especially tense, you might repeat the tense-relax sequence twice.

12. Tighten the muscles of your chest by taking in a deep breath. Hold for up to ten seconds … and then release slowly. Imagine any excess tension in your chest flowing away with the exhalation.

13. Tighten your stomach muscles by sucking your stomach in. Hold… and then release. Imagine a wave of relaxation spreading through your abdomen.

14. Tighten your lower back by arching it up. (You can omit this exercise if you have lower back pain.) Hold … and then relax.

15. Tighten your buttocks by pulling them together. Hold … and then relax. Imagine the muscles in your hips going loose and limp.

16. Squeeze the muscles in your thighs all the way down to your knees. You will probably have to tighten your hips along with your thighs, since the thigh muscles attach at the pelvis. Hold … and then relax. Feel your thigh muscles smoothing out and relaxing completely.

17. Tighten your calf muscles by pulling your toes toward you (flex carefully to avoid cramps). Hold … and then relax.

18. Tighten your feet by curling your toes downward. Hold … and then relax.

19. Mentally scan your body for any residual tension. If a particular area remains tense, repeat one or two tense-relax cycles for that group of muscles.

20. Now imagine a wave of relaxation slowly spreading throughout your body, starting at your head and gradually penetrating every muscle group all the way down to your toes.

The entire progressive muscle relaxation sequence should take you twenty to thirty minutes the first time. With practice, you may decrease the time needed to fifteen to twenty minutes. You might want to make an audio recording of the above exercises to expedite your early practice sessions. Or you may wish to obtain a professionally made recording of the progressive muscle relaxation exercise. (See appendix 3.) Some people always prefer to use an audio recording, while others have the exercises so well learned after a few weeks of practice that they prefer doing them from memory.

Remember—regular practice of progressive muscle relaxation once a day will produce a significant reduction in your overall level of anxiety. It will also reduce the frequency and intensity of panic attacks. Finally, regular practice will reduce anticipatory anxiety that may arise in the course of systematically exposing yourself to phobic situations (see chapter 7).

Passive Muscle Relaxation

Progressive relaxation is an excellent technique for relaxing tight muscles. Passive muscle relaxation, an alternative technique, can induce a general state of relaxation throughout mind and body. Many people prefer it to progressive relaxation because it is effortless. There is no active tensing and relaxing of muscle groups, only focusing on each muscle group in sequence—from feet to head—and imagining each such group relaxing. Generally, it's best to lie down with your eyes closed when you practice.

The following script leads you through a passive muscle relaxation exercise. You can download passive muscle relaxation instructions to an MP3 player, use a CD, or create your own audio recording using the script below. See the Resources for Relaxation section (appendix 3) at the end of the book for websites that offer passive muscle relaxation recordings. If you make a recording, it's important to read it slowly, with pauses between the sentences.

Begin by taking two or three deep, abdominal breaths and let yourself settle back into the chair, bed, or wherever you happen to be right now. Make yourself fully comfortable. Let this be a time just for yourself, putting aside all worries and concerns of the day and making this a time just for you. (Pause.)

Let each part of your body begin to relax, starting with your feet. Just imagine your feet letting go and relaxing right now. Let go of any excess tension in your feet. Just imagine the tension draining away. (Pause.)

As your feet are relaxing, imagine relaxation moving up into your calves. Let the muscles in your calves unwind and loosen up and let go. Allow any tension you're feeling in your calves to just drain away easily and quickly. (Pause.)

Now as your calves are relaxing, allow relaxation to move up into your thighs. Let the muscles in your thighs unwind and smooth out and relax completely. You might begin to feel your legs from your waist down to your feet becoming more and more relaxed. You might notice your legs becoming heavy as they relax more and more. (Pause.)

Continue now and let relaxation move into your hips. Feel any excess tension in your hips dissolve and flow away. (Pause.)

Soon you might allow relaxation to move into your stomach area. Just let go of any stress in your stomach area—let it all go right now, imagining deep sensations of relaxation spreading all around your abdomen. (Pause.)

As your stomach is relaxing, continue to allow relaxation to move up into your chest. All the muscles in your chest can unwind and loosen up and let go. Each time you exhale, imagine breathing away any remaining tension in your chest until your chest feels completely relaxed. Let the relaxation deepen and develop throughout your chest, stomach area, and your legs. (Pause.)

Soon you might allow relaxation to move into your shoulders—just letting deep sensations of calmness and relaxation spread all through the muscles of your shoulders. Let your shoulders drop, allowing them to feel completely relaxed. Now allow the relaxation in your shoulders to move down into your arms, spreading into your upper arms, down into your elbows and forearms, and finally all the way down to your wrists and hands. Let your arms relax, enjoying the good feeling of relaxation in your arms. (Pause.)

Put aside any worries, any uncomfortable, unpleasant thoughts right now. Let yourself be totally in the present moment as you let yourself relax more and more. (Pause.)

You can feel relaxation moving into your neck now. All the muscles in your neck just unwind, smooth out, and relax completely. Just imagine the muscles in your neck loosening up just like a knotted cord unraveling. (Pause.)

Then soon, the relaxation can move into your chin and jaws. Allow your jaws to relax, letting your jaws loosen up. As they are relaxing, imagine relaxation moving into the area around your eyes. Any tension around your eyes can just dissipate and flow away as you allow your eyes to relax completely. Any eyestrain just dissolves now and your eyes can fully relax. Now let your forehead relax too—let the muscles in your forehead smooth out and relax completely, noticing the weight of your head against whatever it's resting on as you allow your entire head to relax completely. (Pause.)

Just enjoy the good feeling of relaxation all over now—letting yourself drift deeper and deeper into quietness and peace—getting more and more in touch with that place deep inside of perfect peace and serenity.

The Peaceful Scene

After completing progressive or passive muscle relaxation, it's helpful to visualize yourself in the midst of a peaceful scene. Imagining yourself in a very peaceful setting can give you a global sense of relaxation that frees you from anxious thoughts. The peaceful setting can be a quiet beach, a stream in the mountains, or a calm lake. Or it can be your bedroom or a cozy fireside on a cold winter night. Don't restrict yourself to reality; you can imagine, if you want to, floating on a cloud or flying on a magic carpet. The important thing is to visualize the scene in sufficient detail so that it completely absorbs your attention. Allowing yourself to be absorbed in a peaceful scene will deepen your state of relaxation, giving you actual physiological results. Your muscular tension lessens, your heart rate slows down, your breathing deepens, your capillaries open up and warm your hands and feet, and so on. A relaxing visualization constitutes a light form of self-hypnosis.

Here are three examples of peaceful scenes.

The Beach

You're walking along a beautiful, deserted beach. You are barefoot and can feel the firm white sand beneath your feet as you walk along the margin of the sea. You can hear the sound of the surf as the waves ebb and flow. The sound is hypnotic, relaxing you more and more. The water is a beautiful turquoise blue flecked with whitecaps far out where the waves are cresting. Near the horizon you can see a small sailboat gliding smoothly along. The sound of the waves breaking on the shore lulls you deeper and deeper into relaxation. You draw in the fresh, salty smell of the air with each breath. Your skin glows with the warmth of the sun. You can feel a gentle breeze against your cheek and ruffling your hair. Taking in the whole scene, you feel very calm and at ease.

The Forest

You're snuggled in your sleeping bag. Daylight is breaking in the forest. You can feel the rays of the sun beginning to warm your face. The dawn sky stretches above you in pastel shades of pink and orange. You can smell the fresh, piney fragrance of the surrounding woods. Nearby you can hear the rushing waters of a mountain stream. The crisp, cool morning air is refreshing and invigorating. You're feeling very cozy, comfortable, and secure.

At Home

Imagine yourself comfortably relaxing on a sofa or your bed at home. As you lie back, take some deep, abdominal breaths and set aside all of the worries and concerns of the day. The room is quiet and free of distractions. The phone is turned off and you are free of any obligations to do anything. Though people may be elsewhere in the house, they know to leave you alone. It's feeling good to be able to kick back, rest, and let your body and mind begin to slow down. You can feel your whole body starting to relax. As you continue to rest and relax, you find yourself becoming more deeply comfortable and at ease. In this quiet place, you are feeling very safe, secure, and at peace.

Note that these scenes are described in language that appeals to the senses of sight, hearing, touch, and smell. Using multisensory words increases the power of the scene to compel you, enabling you to experience it as if you were actually there. The whole point of imagining a peaceful scene is to transport you from your normal state of restless thinking into an altered state of deep relaxation.

Exercise

Use a separate sheet of paper to design your own peaceful scene. Be sure to describe it in vivid detail, appealing to as many of your senses as possible. It may help to answer the following questions:

- What does the scene look like?
- What colors are prominent?
- What sounds are present?
- What time of day is it?
- What is the temperature?
- What are you touching or in physical contact with in the scene?
- What does the air smell like?
- Are you alone or with somebody else?

Just as with progressive muscle relaxation, you may wish to record your peaceful scene so that you can conjure it up without effort. You may find it helpful to record the instructions for progressive muscle relaxation before describing your peaceful scene. You can use the script below to introduce your peaceful scene when you make your own recording:

> *Just think of relaxing every muscle in your body, from the top of your head to the tips of your toes. (Pause.)*
>
> *As you exhale, imagine releasing any remaining tension from your body, mind, or thoughts … just let that stress go. (Pause.)*
>
> *And with every breath you inhale, feel your body drifting down deeper … down deeper into total relaxation. (Pause.)*
>
> *And now imagine going to your peaceful scene … Imagine your special place as vividly as possible, as if you were really there. (Insert your peaceful scene.)*
>
> *You are very comfortable in your beautiful place, and there is no one to disturb you. … This is the most peaceful place in the world for you. … Just imagine yourself there, feeling a sense of peace flow through you and a sense of well-being. Enjoy these positive feelings. … Allow them to grow stronger and stronger. (Pause.)*
>
> *And remember, anytime you wish, you can return to this special place by just taking time to relax. (Pause.)*
>
> *These peaceful and positive feelings of relaxation can grow stronger and stronger each time you choose to relax.*

Once you have imagined your own ideal peaceful scene, practice returning to it every time you do progressive muscle relaxation, deep breathing, or any other relaxation technique. This will help to reinforce the scene in your mind. After a while, it will be so solidly established that you will be able to return to it on the spur of the moment—whenever you wish to calm yourself and turn off anxious thinking. This technique is one of the quickest and most effective tools you can use to counter ongoing anxiety or stress during the day. Fantasizing a peaceful scene is also an important part of imagery desensitization, a process for overcoming phobias described in chapter 7.

Guided Visualizations

Many people enjoy listening to guided visualizations in order to relax. Like passive muscle relaxation, no effort is required. You simply lie down, close your eyes, and listen to a CD or MP3 file on your portable audio device for twenty to thirty minutes, preferably at the same time every day. Follow the guidelines for practicing any form of deep relaxation given earlier in this chapter. See "Guidelines for Practicing Progressive Muscle Relaxation (or Any Form of Deep Relaxation)."

There are many places on the Web where you can obtain relaxing visualizations. Some popular ones you can try are drmiller.com and soundstrue.com, or you can do a search for "relaxation CDs" at amazon.com. It's a good idea to purchase at least two or three different relaxation programs to see what works best for you. Also see appendix 3 for further resources.

Meditation

From the time we awaken, until we go to bed, most of us are engaged almost continually in external activities. We tend to be only minimally in touch with our inner feelings and awareness. Even when we withdraw our senses and are falling asleep at night, we usually experience a mélange of memories, fantasies, thoughts, and feelings related to the preceding or coming day. Rarely do we get beyond all of this and experience ourselves "just being" in the present moment. For many people in Western society, in fact, the idea of doing nothing, or "just being," is difficult to comprehend.

Meditation can bring you to this place of just being. It is the one process that allows you to completely stop, let go of thoughts about the immediate past or future, and simply focus on being in the here and now. It can be a helpful discipline to practice when you find that your mind is racing or excessively busy. For a detailed discussion of meditation, both as a relaxation technique and as a general strategy for coping with anxiety, please see chapter 18.

Yoga

The word *yoga* means to "yoke" or "unify." By definition, yoga is involved with promoting unity of mind, body, and spirit. Although in the West yoga is usually thought of as a series of stretch exercises, it actually embraces a broad philosophy of life and an elaborate system for personal transformation. This system includes ethical precepts, a vegetarian diet, the familiar stretches or postures, specific practices for directing and controlling the breath, concentration practices, and deep meditation. It was originally laid out by the philosopher Pantanjali in the second century BC and is still practiced throughout the world today.

Yoga postures, by themselves, provide a very effective means to increase fitness, flexibility, and relaxation. They can be practiced alone or with a group. Many people, myself included, find that yoga simultaneously increases energy and vitality while calming the mind. Yoga may be compared to progressive muscle relaxation (PMR), in that it involves holding the body in certain flexed positions for a few moments and then relaxing. Both yoga and PMR lead to relaxation. However, I personally find yoga to be more effective than progressive muscle relaxation in freeing up blocked energy. It seems to get energy moving up and down the spine and throughout the body in a way that doesn't happen as readily with PMR. Like vigorous exercise, yoga directly promotes mind-body integration. However, in many ways, it is more specific. Each yoga posture reflects a mental attitude, whether that attitude is one of surrender, as in certain forward-bending poses, or of strengthening the will, as in a backward-bending pose. By emphasizing certain yoga postures and movements, you may be able to cultivate certain positive qualities or move through other negative, restrictive personality patterns. There is an entire school of yoga therapy that uses yoga as a methodology for addressing and working through personality issues.

If you are interested in learning yoga, the best place to start is with a class at a local health club or community college. If such classes are unavailable in your area, try working with a yoga video at home. The popular magazine *Yoga Journal* offers many excellent yoga videos.

Calming Music

Music has often been called the language of the soul. It seems to touch something deep within us. It can move you into inner spaces beyond your anxiety and worries. Relaxing music can help you to settle down into a place of serenity deep within that is impervious to the stresses and problems of daily life. It may also uplift you from a depressed mood. Whether you use music while driving, as a background while at work, or in the foreground when you want to take time out to relax, it is one of the most powerful and time-honored methods for letting go of anxiety or worry. If you use music to assuage anxiety, be sure to select pieces that are genuinely relaxing rather than stimulating or emotionally evocative.

Your portable audio device with earphones can be particularly handy at night if you don't want to disturb others around you. You may find music to be a helpful background to relaxation techniques, such as progressive muscle relaxation or guided visualizations. See appendix 3 for a list of relaxing music selections.

Some Common Obstacles to a Daily Program of Deep Relaxation

There are many difficulties you may encounter in trying to practice any form of deep relaxation on a regular basis. You may start out enthusiastically, setting aside time to practice every day. Yet after a week or so, you may find yourself "forgetting" to practice. In a fast-paced society that rewards us for speed, efficiency, and productivity, it's difficult to stop everything and simply relax for twenty to thirty minutes. We are so used to "doing" that it may seem like a chore just to "be."

If you find that you've broken your personal commitment to practice deep relaxation on a daily basis, take time to examine very carefully what you are *saying to yourself*—what excuses you make—on those days when you don't relax. If you just "don't feel like it," there is usually some more specific reason for feeling that way that can be found by examining what you're telling yourself.

Some common excuses for not practicing include

- "I don't have time to relax."

What this usually means is that you haven't given relaxation sufficient priority among all the other activities you've crowded into your schedule.

- "I don't have any place to relax."

Try creating one. You might let the kids watch their favorite TV show or play with their favorite toys while you go into another room, with instructions not to interrupt you. If you and the kids have only one room, or if they are too young to respect your privacy, then you need to practice at a time when they are out of the house or asleep. The same goes for a demanding spouse.

- "Relaxation exercises seem too slow or boring."

If you're telling yourself this, it's a good indication that you are too speeded up, too frantically pushing yourself through life. Slow down—it's good for you.

- "I feel more anxious when I relax."

In some individuals, deep relaxation may bring up suppressed feelings, which are often accompanied by sensations of anxiety. If this happens to you, be sure to start off with relatively short periods of relaxation, working up gradually to longer periods. The moment you start feeling any anxiety, simply open your eyes and stop whatever procedure you're practicing until you feel better. With time and patience, this particular problem should diminish. If it doesn't, it would be helpful to consult a professional therapist skilled in treating anxiety disorders to assist you in desensitizing yourself to relaxation.

- "I just don't have the discipline."

Often this means that you haven't persisted with practicing relaxation long enough to internalize it as a habit. You may have made similar statements to yourself in the past when you were attempting to acquire a new behavior. Brushing your teeth didn't come naturally when you first started. It took some time and diligence to reach the point where it became an honored habit. If you expend the effort to practice deep relaxation five to seven days per week for at least one month, it will likely become so ingrained that you won't need to think about doing it anymore—you'll just do it automatically.

Practicing deep relaxation is more than learning a technique: it involves making a basic shift in your attitude and lifestyle. It requires a willingness to give priority to your health and internal peace of mind over the other pressing claims of productivity, accomplishment, money, or status.

Downtime and Time Management

This chapter on relaxation would not be complete without a discussion of the concepts of downtime and time management. In fact, fully appreciating and implementing these ideas in your life is *the most important thing you can do if you would like to achieve a more relaxed lifestyle.*

You can practice deep muscle relaxation or meditation every day and feel a pleasant respite for twenty to thirty minutes. These practices can definitely enhance your overall feeling of relaxation if you practice them regularly. Yet if you're on a treadmill the rest of the time, with too much to get done and no breaks in your schedule, you're likely to remain under stress, prone to chronic anxiety or panic attacks, and ultimately headed toward burnout.

Downtime

Downtime is exactly what it sounds like—*time out* from work or other responsibilities to give yourself an opportunity to rest and replenish your energy. Without periods of downtime, any stress you experience while dealing with work or other responsibilities tends to become *cumulative*. It keeps building without any remission. You may tend to keep pushing yourself until finally you drop from exhaustion or experience an aggravation of your anxiety or phobias. Sleep at night doesn't really count as downtime. If you go to bed feeling stressed, you may sleep for eight hours and still wake up feeling tense, tired, and stressed. Downtime needs to be scheduled during the day, apart from sleep. Its primary purpose is simply to allow a break in the stress cycle—to prevent stress you're experiencing from becoming cumulative. I recommend that you give yourself the following periods of downtime:

One hour per day
One day per week
One week out of every twelve to sixteen weeks

If you don't have four weeks of paid vacation per year, then be willing to take time off without pay. During these periods of downtime, you disengage from any task you consider work, put aside all responsibilities, and don't answer the phone unless it's someone you would enjoy hearing from.

There are three kinds of downtime, each of which has an important place in developing a more relaxed lifestyle: 1) rest time, 2) recreation time, and 3) relationship time. It's important that you provide yourself enough downtime so that you have time for all three. Often recreation and relationship time can be combined. However, it's important to use rest time for just that—and nothing else.

Rest time is time when you set aside all activities and just allow yourself to *be*. You stop action and let yourself fully rest. Rest time might involve lying on the couch and doing nothing, quietly meditating, sitting in your recliner and listening to peaceful music, soaking in a Jacuzzi, or taking a catnap in the middle of the workday. The key to rest time is that it is fundamentally passive—you allow yourself to stop doing and accomplishing and just *be*. Contemporary society encourages each of us to be productive and always accomplish more and more every moment of the waking day. Rest time is a needed counterpoint. When you're under stress, one hour of rest time per day, separate from the time you sleep, is optimal.

Recreation time involves engaging in activities that help to "re-create" you—that is, serve to replenish your energy. Recreation time brightens and uplifts your spirits. In essence, it is doing anything that you experience as fun or play. Examples of such activities might include puttering in the garden, reading a novel, seeing a special movie, going on a hike, playing soccer, taking a short trip, baking a loaf of bread, or fishing. Recreation time can be done during the workweek and is most important to have on your days off from work. Such time can be spent either alone or with someone else, in which case it overlaps with the third type of downtime.

Relationship time is time when you put aside your private goals and responsibilities in order to enjoy being with another person—or, in some cases, with several people. The focus of relationship time is to honor your relationship with your partner, children, extended family members, friends, pets, and so on, and forget about your individual pursuits for a while. If you have a family, relationship time needs to be allocated equitably between time alone with your spouse, time alone with your children, and time when the entire family gets together. If you're single with a partner, time needs to be judiciously allocated between time with your partner and time with friends.

When you slow down and make time to be with others, you're less likely to neglect your basic needs for intimacy, touching, affection, validation, support, and so on (see the section called "Your Basic Needs" in chapter 14). Meeting these basic needs is absolutely vital to your well-being. Without sufficient time devoted to important relationships, you will surely suffer—and the people you most care about are bound to, as well.

How can you allow for more downtime (all three kinds) in your life? An important prerequisite is to get past workaholism. Workaholism is an addictive disorder in which work is the *only* thing that gives you a sense of inner fulfillment and self-worth. You devote all your time and energy to work, neglecting both your physical and your emotional needs. Workaholism describes an unbalanced way of life that often leads first to chronic stress, then to burnout, and ultimately to serious illness.

If you're a workaholic, it's possible to *learn* to enjoy nonwork aspects of your life, as discussed above, and achieve a more balanced approach in general. Deliberately making time for rest, recreation, and relationships may be difficult at first, but it tends to get easier and to become self-rewarding as time goes on.

Another important step is simply *to be willing to do less*. That is, you literally reduce the number of tasks and responsibilities you handle in any given day. In some cases, this may involve changing jobs; in others, it may merely involve restructuring how you allocate time for work versus rest and relaxation. For some individuals, this translates to a fundamental decision to make earning money less important and a simpler, more balanced lifestyle more important. Before you think about leaving your present job, however, consider how you can shift your values in the direction of placing more emphasis on the *process* of life ("how" you live) as opposed to accomplishments and productivity ("what" you actually do) within your current life situation.

Exercise

Take some time to reflect on how you might allocate more time for each of the three types of downtime discussed. Write your answers in the space provided below.

Rest time:

Recreation time:

Relationship time:

Time Management

A very important skill to have if you want more time away from work and responsibilities is good time management. Time management describes the way in which you organize or structure your daily activities over time. Ineffective time management can lead to stress, anxiety, burnout, and, eventually, illness. Effective time management, on the other hand, will allow you more time for the three types of downtime described above: rest, recreation, and relationships.

Developing good time management skills may necessitate giving up some cherished habits. Are any of the following tendencies true for you? Check off any of the statements below that apply:

☐   "I tend to underestimate the amount of time it takes to complete an activity or task. By the time I finish, I've taken up time I needed for something else."

☐   "I tend to squeeze too many things into too little time. As a result, I end up rushing."

☐   "I find it difficult to let go of something I'm involved in, so I end up not leaving myself enough time to get to (or complete) the next activity I need to do."

☐   "I have difficulty prioritizing activities—getting the most essential ones done before I attend to the less important ones."

☐   "I have difficulty delegating nonessential tasks to others, even when it is possible to do so."

If you checked off any of the above statements as true, you might benefit from learning and cultivating effective time management skills.

The skills described below—prioritization, delegation, allowing extra time, letting go of perfectionism, overcoming procrastination, and saying no—can help you work with, rather than against, time.

Prioritization

Prioritization means learning to discriminate between tasks or activities that are essential and those that are nonessential. You attend to what's most important and put everything else on hold (or delegate tasks to other people—see below).

You may find it useful to divide your daily tasks and responsibilities into three categories: *essential, important,* and *less important* or trivial. *Essential* tasks or activities include those that require immediate attention: they are absolutely necessary—such as getting the kids off to school. Alternatively, they can be activities that are very important to you—such as physical exercise, if you're working on reducing your anxiety. *Important* tasks and activities are those that have significant value but can be delayed for a limited time, such as spending quality one-on-one time with your spouse or partner. Important tasks cannot be delayed for a long time, however. Less important or trivial tasks can be postponed a long time without serious risk or can be delegated to others (tasks such as taking the stack of newspapers in the garage to the recycling center or deleting photos you don't want to keep on your computer).

You may find it helpful, perhaps when you first get up in the morning, to categorize the tasks facing you as *essential, important,* or *less important.* Actually divide a piece of paper into three columns and write everything down. Then start with tasks in the *essential* and *important* columns. Only move on to the tasks in the *less important* category when you're done with all the tasks in the first two columns. In general, I would advise postponing all the tasks in the *less important* column in favor of giving yourself more downtime.

If you're serious about achieving a more relaxed lifestyle, then you'll need to place downtime—time for rest, recreation, and relationships—into the *essential* category. When downtime becomes a regular and high-priority item in your schedule—something you refuse to postpone—you will begin to take life more slowly and easily. As a result, you'll feel less stressed, better able to sleep, and more capable of enjoying yourself in general. Making downtime essential requires giving up addictions to work, outer achievement, and success, as well as letting go of perfectionism.

You may also want to include under the essential column those activities that contribute to the achievement of your long-term ideals and life goals. Long-term ideals and life goals tend to remain just that for most people—postponed until the distant future—*unless* you take time to do something toward achieving them on a step-by-step basis in the present.

Delegation

Skill in delegation means being willing to let someone else take care of a task or activity that has lower priority for you or is an important task that *you* don't have to do personally. By delegating, you free up more time for those tasks that are essential and require your personal attention. Often delegation means paying someone else to do what you might do yourself if you had unlimited time: housecleaning, car washing, cooking, child care, basic repairs, and so on. At other times, delegation simply means distributing tasks equitably among family members: your spouse and the kids do their fair share of household chores. A key to delegation is a willingness to trust and rely on others' capabilities. Give up the idea that only you can do an adequate job, and be willing to entrust responsibility for a task to someone else.

Allowing Extra Time

A common problem in time management is underestimating the amount of time required to complete a task. The result is that you end up rushing to try to get something done, or else run into overtime and encroach on time that was needed for the next activity in your schedule. As a general rule, it helps to allow a little more time than you would expect for each activity during the day. It's better to err in favor of overestimating the time required for a task, leaving yourself plenty of time to proceed in a leisurely manner to the next activity.

An important prerequisite for allowing extra time is to be *willing to do fewer things*—not to cram as many tasks or activities into a given time frame. This may be very difficult for people addicted to their own adrenaline, who seem to get a certain exhilaration and fulfillment from rushing around or feeling busy. However, allowing extra time has tremendous rewards in terms of letting you proceed through your day at a more relaxed and easy pace. To do so will save you a lot of stress.

Letting Go of Perfectionism

Perfectionism essentially means setting your standards and expectations too high: there is no allowance for the inevitable mistakes, frustration, delays, and limitations that come up in the process of working toward any goal. Perfectionism can keep you on a treadmill of overwork or overdedication, to the point that you don't allow time out for your own needs. Letting go of perfectionism requires a fundamental attitude shift. It becomes all right simply to do your best, to make some mistakes along the way, and to accept the results you get, even if your best efforts fall short. It also involves learning to laugh on occasion rather than despair at the limitations inherent to human existence. (For a more in-depth discussion about letting go of perfectionism, see chapter 10.)

Overcoming Procrastination

Procrastination is always self-defeating when you leave yourself too little time. Whether preparing for an exam or preparing to go to work, putting off the inevitable leaves you harried and stressed in the end.

One reason for procrastinating can be that you really don't want to do whatever it is that needs doing in the first place. If this is your reason for stalling, the solution lies either in delegating or in prioritizing. If you can delegate an undesirable task to someone else, then by all means do so. If you can't, then get the undesirable task done *first*—in other words, prioritize it over the other things you need to do. Promising yourself to do something fun or interesting afterward as a reward for getting the undesirable task done often works well. In overcoming procrastination, the carrot usually works much better than the stick.

Another reason for procrastinating is perfectionism. If you feel that something has to be done perfectly, you may keep postponing getting started because you fear that you can't do it "just right." The solution here is to jump in and get started, whether or not you feel you're ready to do it right. An important principle to remember is that *motivation often follows behavior*. Just getting started on a task will often generate the motivation to follow through and complete it. Then you may have enough time left over to go back and rework or refine what you did during the first round. If you keep stalling, however, you can use up all the time needed to do the kind of job you'd like to do. The worst outcome is when you don't attempt the task at all because of your impossibly high standards.

Saying No

There are many reasons why people have difficulty saying no. You may always want to be pleasing and responsive to family and friends, no matter what they ask of you, so you have difficulty setting limits, even when their demands or needs become more than you can handle. Or you may be so bound up with your work that it's your primary source of identity and meaning. No matter how demanding and time-consuming work responsibilities become, you keep taking them on, because not to do so would leave you feeling empty.

In short, difficulty saying no is usually tied up with your self-image. If your image of yourself requires you to be nice all the time and always available to everyone, then there is probably no limit to what others will ask of you. If your work is who you are, then it will be hard for you to say no to work demands in order to make time for your personal needs.

Learning to say no requires a willingness to relinquish cherished beliefs about yourself—which can be one of the hardest things for anyone to do. This may involve expanding your identity beyond taking care of others, or taking care of business, and learning to take the time to nurture and attend to your own needs. It means accepting the reality that taking care of yourself—even at the expense of what you do for others—isn't selfish. Can you really offer your best to others or your work if you are tired, stressed, or burned out?

In my own case, it was necessary to go to the edge of serious illness before the importance of saying no fully sank in. In many cases, illness—whether in the form of panic attacks, depression, or some other persistent problem—may force you to reevaluate the way you live your life. Illness can be the catalyst that makes you slow down, pay attention, and learn how to live in a simpler, more balanced fashion.

Summary of Things to Do

1.   Reread the section on abdominal breathing and decide which breathing exercise you want to work with. Practice the exercise you prefer for five minutes per day for at least two weeks. Practice for one month or longer if you wish to change your breathing pattern from your chest downward toward your abdomen.

     Use the abdominal breathing or the calming breath exercise whenever you spontaneously feel symptoms of anxiety beginning to come on.

2.   Practice progressive muscle relaxation for twenty to thirty minutes per day (two practice periods per day is even better) for at least two weeks. For the first few times, have someone read you the instructions or record them—so that you can follow them effortlessly. Eventually, you'll memorize the instructions and can dispense with the recording.

3.   Visualize going to a peaceful scene following progressive muscle relaxation. It may help to record a detailed description of such a scene following your recorded instructions for progressive muscle relaxation. Try going to your peaceful scene (along with doing abdominal breathing) at those times during the day when anxiety comes up.

4.   After practicing progressive muscle relaxation for at least two weeks, you may enjoy its benefits so much that you decide to adopt it as your preferred deep relaxation technique. Alternatively, you may want to learn to meditate (see chapter 18). *The type of relaxation technique you use is less important than your willingness and commitment to practice some method of deep relaxation on a daily basis.*

5.   If you encounter difficulties in maintaining your commitment to practicing deep relaxation over the long term, reread the section called "Some Common Obstacles to a Daily Program of Deep Relaxation."

6.   Spend some time considering the section "Downtime and Time Management." Do you need to allocate more time in your life for rest, relaxation, and personal relationships? What changes would you need to make in your daily schedule to achieve this? Think about at least one change you could make, starting this week. Are you willing to commit to it?

Further Reading

Benson, Herbert. *Beyond the Relaxation Response.* New York: Berkley Books, 1985.

———. *The Relaxation Response.* Updated and expanded. New York: Quill, 2001.

Davis, Martha, Elizabeth Robbins Eshelman, and Matthew McKay. *The Relaxation & Stress Reduction Workbook.* Sixth edition. Oakland, CA: New Harbinger Publications, 2008.

Harp, David, and Nina Smiley. *The Three-Minute Meditator.* Fifth edition. Oakland, CA: New Harbinger Publications, 2007.

Kabat-Zinn, Jon. *Wherever You Go, There You Are.* Tenth anniversary edition. New York: Hyperion, 2005.

Lakein, Alan. *How to Get Control of Your Time and Your Life.* New York: Signet, 1989.

Mason, John. *Guide to Stress Reduction.* Berkeley, CA: Celestial Arts, 1985. (This book is particularly recommended as a good resource for relaxation scripts you can record for yourself.)

5

Physical Exercise

One of the most powerful and effective methods for reducing generalized anxiety and overcoming a predisposition to panic attacks is a program of regular, vigorous exercise. You have panic attacks when your body's natural fight-or-flight reaction—the sudden surge of adrenaline you experience in response to a realistic threat—becomes excessive or occurs out of context. Exercise is a natural outlet for your body when it is in the fight-or-flight mode of arousal. A majority of my clients who have undertaken a regular exercise program are less vulnerable to panic attacks and, if they do have them, find them to be less severe. Regular exercise also diminishes the tendency to experience anticipatory anxiety toward phobic situations, expediting recovery from all kinds of phobias, ranging from fear of public speaking to fear of being alone.

Regular exercise has a direct impact on several physiological factors that underlie anxiety. It brings about

- *Reduced skeletal muscle tension*, which is largely responsible for your feelings of being tense or "uptight"

- *More rapid metabolism of excess adrenaline and thyroxin* in the bloodstream, the presence of which tends to keep you in a state of arousal and vigilance

- *A discharge of pent-up frustration*, which can aggravate phobic or panic reactions

Some of the general physiological benefits of exercise include

- Enhanced oxygenation of the blood and brain, which increases alertness and concentration

- Stimulation of the production of *endorphins*, natural substances which resemble morphine both chemically and in their effects: endorphins increase your sense of well-being

- Lowered pH (increased acidity) of the blood, which increases your energy level

- Improved circulation

- Improved digestion and utilization of food

- Improved elimination (from skin, lungs, and bowels)

- Decreased cholesterol levels

- Decreased blood pressure
- Weight loss, as well as appetite suppression, in many cases
- Improved blood sugar regulation (in the case of hypoglycemia)

Several *psychological* benefits accompany these physical improvements, including

- Increased subjective feelings of well-being
- Reduced dependence on alcohol and drugs
- Reduced insomnia
- Improved concentration and memory
- Reduced depression
- Increased self-esteem
- Greater sense of control over anxiety

Symptoms of Being out of Shape

How do you know that you are out of shape and in need of exercise? Here are some common symptoms:

- Being out of breath after walking up a flight of stairs
- Long recovery time after walking up a flight of stairs
- Feeling exhausted after short periods of exertion
- Chronic muscle tension
- Poor muscle tone
- Obesity
- Muscles cramped and aching for days after participating in a sport
- General tiredness, lethargy, boredom

Your Fitness Level

The worksheet below can help you assess the extent of your fitness. Think about the most strenuous physical activity you practice in an *average week*. When you have completed the questions below, determine your fitness score and evaluate your fitness level.

INTENSITY	FREQUENCY	DURATION
How strenuous is your exercise?	How many times do you exercise per week?	How long do you exercise each time?
Heavy = 5 points (fast cycling, running, aerobic dancing)	3 or more times = 5 points	21 minutes to 1 hour = 5 points
Moderate = 3 points (jogging, cycling, very fast walking)	1 to 2 times = 2 points	11 to 20 minutes = 3 points
Light = 1 point (golf, strolling, most housework)	not at all = 0 points	10 minutes or less = 1 point
Add your score:	_____ + _____	+ _____ = Total _____

TOTAL SCORE	FITNESS LEVEL	RECOMMENDED ACTION
13 to 15	Very good	Congratulations! Maintain your present level of activity.
8 to 12	Average	You are moderately sedentary and should increase your level of activity.
7 or less	Poor	Begin planning an exercise program now!

An alternative way to assess your level of fitness is to measure your *resting pulse rate*, the average number of heartbeats per minute when you're at rest. As a rule of thumb, a resting pulse of eighty or above suggests that you could definitely improve your fitness. A resting pulse of seventy to eighty suggests that you *may* need to obtain more exercise. If you are in a fitness program and have an average resting pulse below seventy, you are likely to be in good shape. To measure your pulse, allow yourself to get relaxed, then take the number of pulse beats in twenty seconds and multiply by three.

Preparing for a Fitness Program?

If you've decided you would like to get more exercise, you need to ask yourself whether you are fully ready to do so. There are certain physical conditions that limit the amount and intensity of exercise you should undertake. If your answer to any of the questions below is yes, be sure to consult with your physician before beginning any exercise program. He or she may recommend a program of restricted or supervised exercise appropriate to your needs.

YES   NO

_____ _____   Has your physician ever said you have heart trouble?

_____ _____   Do you frequently have pains in your heart or chest?

_____ _____   Do you often feel faint or have spells of dizziness?

_____ _____   Has your physician ever told you that you have a bone or joint problem (such as arthritis) that has been or might be aggravated by exercise?

_____ _____   Has a physician ever said that your blood pressure was too high?

_____ _____   Do you have diabetes?

_____ _____   Are you over forty years old and unaccustomed to vigorous exercise?

_____ _____   Is there a physical reason, not mentioned here, why you should not undertake an exercise program?

If you answered no to all of the above questions, you can be reasonably assured that you are ready to start an exercise program. Begin slowly and increase your activity gradually over a period of weeks. If you are over forty and unaccustomed to exercise, plan to see your doctor for a physical before undertaking an exercise program.

Some individuals are reluctant to take up exercise because the state of physiological arousal accompanying vigorous exercise reminds them too much of the symptoms of panic. If this applies to you, you might want to start out doing forty-five minutes of walking on a daily basis.

Or you can *very gradually* build up to a more vigorous level of exercise. You might try just two to three minutes of jogging or cycling and then gradually increase the duration of your daily exercise a minute at a time, remembering to stop every time you feel even the slightest association with panic (see the descriptions of step-by-step desensitization in chapters 3 and 7). It might also be helpful to have a support person exercise with you initially. If you feel phobic about exercise, a program of gradual exposure will help you to desensitize to it in the same way you would to any other phobia.

Choosing an Exercise Program

There are many types of exercise to choose from. Deciding what form of exercise to do depends upon your objectives. For reducing generalized anxiety and/or a proneness to panic, *aerobic exercise* such as running, brisk walking, cycling outdoors or on a stationary bike, swimming, or aerobic dancing is the most effective for many individuals. Aerobic exercise requires sustained activity of your larger muscles. It reduces skeletal muscle tension and increases *cardiovascular conditioning*—the capacity of your circulatory system to deliver oxygen to your tissues and cells with greater efficiency. Regular aerobic exercise will reduce stress and increase your stamina.

Beyond aerobic fitness, you may have other objectives in taking up exercise. If increased muscle *strength* is important, you may want to include weight lifting or isometric exercise in your program (if you have a heart condition or angina, you should probably *not* engage in weight lifting or bodybuilding). If *socializing* is important, then racquetball, golf, or team sports, such as baseball, basketball, or volleyball, might be what you're looking for. Exercise that involves stretching, such as yoga, is ideal for developing muscular *flexibility*. If you want to *lose weight*, jogging or cycling is probably most effective. If *discharging aggression and frustration* is important, you might try competitive sports. Finally, if you just want to get outdoors, then hiking or gardening would be appropriate. Rigorous hiking (as done by the Sierra Club, for example) can increase both strength and endurance. For further information on the various benefits of different types of exercise, see Covert Bailey's book on the subject, *The New Fit or Fat*.

Many people find it helpful to *vary* the type of exercise they do. Popular combinations involve doing an aerobic type of exercise such as jogging or cycling three to four times a week and a socializing exercise (such as tennis) or a bodybuilding exercise twice a week. Maintaining a program with two distinct types of exercise prevents either one from becoming too boring. What follows are brief descriptions of some of the more common types of aerobic exercise. Each type has its advantages and possible drawbacks.

Running

For many years, running (or jogging) has been the most popular form of aerobic exercise, perhaps because of its convenience. The only equipment you need is running shoes, and in many cases you need only step out your door to begin. Running is one of the best forms of exercise for losing weight, because it burns calories quickly. Numerous studies have shown its benefits for depression, as it raises both endorphin and serotonin levels in the brain. As mentioned above, running decreases anxiety by metabolizing excess adrenaline and releasing skeletal muscle tension. A three-mile jog (approximately thirty minutes) four or five times per week can go a long way toward diminishing your vulnerability to anxiety. Work up to a pace of one mile every ten minutes.

The downside to running is that, over a period of time, it can increase your risk for injury. In particular, if you run on hard surfaces, the constant shock to your joints can lead to foot, knee, or back problems. You can minimize your risk of injury if you

- Get proper shoes—those which minimize shock to your joints.

- Run on soft surfaces—preferably grass, dirt, a track, or a hardened beach. Avoid concrete if possible; asphalt is okay if you have good shoes and don't run every day.

- Warm up to running before you begin. Try doing a minute or two of very slow jogging.

- Avoid jogging every day—alternate it with other forms of exercise.

If running outdoors is a problem because of weather, lack of a soft surface, smog, or traffic, you may want to invest in a treadmill. To make its use less boring, put it in front of your television or media player.

Swimming

Swimming is my personal favorite form of exercise. It's an especially good exercise because it uses so many different muscles throughout the body. Doctors usually recommend swimming to people with musculoskeletal problems, injuries, or arthritis because it minimizes shock to their joints. It does not promote weight loss to the same degree as running, but it will help firm up your body.

For aerobic-level conditioning, it's best to swim freestyle for twenty to thirty minutes, preferably four or five times per week. For moderate, relaxing exercise, breaststroke is an enjoyable alternative. As a rule, it's best to work out in a heated pool where the water temperature is 75 to 80 degrees Fahrenheit.

The major downside with swimming is that many pools are heavily chlorinated. This may be quite irritating to your eyes, skin, or hair—as well as the membranes in your upper respiratory passages. You can counter some of this by wearing goggles and/or nose plugs. If you're fortunate, you may be able to find a pool that uses hydrogen peroxide or bubbled-in ozone as a disinfectant. Either of these is preferable to chlorine.

Cycling

In recent years, cycling has become a very popular form of aerobic exercise. While having many of the same benefits as jogging, it's less shocking to your joints. To achieve aerobic conditioning, cycling needs to be done vigorously—at a rate of approximately fifteen miles per hour or more on a flat surface. When the weather is good, cycling can be quite enjoyable—especially if you have beautiful surroundings with little traffic or a designated bike trail. If weather precludes cycling, you need to use a stationary bike indoors.

If you want to take up outdoor cycling, you'll need to make an initial investment in a good bike. You may want to borrow someone else's bike until you feel ready to spend several hundred dollars. In purchasing a bike, I'd suggest avoiding racing bikes unless you decide you want to race. You'll probably find sitting upright when you cycle to be more enjoyable and less stressful than sitting hunched over. Make sure the bike you purchase is designed and sized correctly for your body—or it may cause you problems. A well-cushioned seat is a good investment.

When you undertake cycling, give yourself a few months to work up to a fifteen-miles-per-hour cruising speed—a mile every four minutes. One hour of cycling three to four times per week is sufficient. Be sure to wear a helmet and try to avoid riding at night.

Aerobics Classes

Most aerobics classes consist of warm-up stretches and aerobic exercises led by an instructor. These are usually done to music. Classes are generally offered by health clubs, with various levels for beginning, intermediate, and advanced participants. Since some of the exercises can be traumatic to your joints, try to find a "low-impact" aerobics class. The structured format of an aerobics class may be an excellent way to motivate you to exercise. If you are self-motivated and prefer to stay at home, there are many good aerobics videos available.

If you decide to do aerobic exercises, be sure to obtain good shoes that stabilize your feet, absorb shock, and minimize twisting. It's best to do these exercises on a wooden surface and to avoid carpets, if possible. About forty-five minutes to an hour of exercise (including warm-up) three to five times per week is sufficient.

Walking

Walking has advantages over all other forms of exercise. First, it does not require training—you already know how to do it. Second, it requires no equipment other than a pair of shoes and can be done virtually anywhere—even in a shopping mall, if necessary. The chance of injury is less than with any other type of exercise. Finally, it's the most natural exercise activity. All of us are inclined to walk. Up until society became sedentary, walking was a regular part of life.

Walking for relaxation and distraction is one thing; doing it for aerobic conditioning is another. To make walking aerobic, aim for doing it about one hour at a brisk enough pace to cover three miles. A twenty- or thirty-minute walk is generally not enough to obtain aerobic-level conditioning. If you make walking your regular form of exercise, do it four to five times per week, preferably outdoors. If you feel an hour of brisk walking is not enough of a workout, try adding hand weights or finding an area with hills.

To get the most benefit out of walking, good posture is important. If it feels natural to allow your arms to swing opposite to the stride of your legs, you'll be getting "cross-lateral conditioning," which helps to integrate the left and right hemispheres of your brain. Good walking shoes are also important. Look for padded insoles, a good arch, and firm support of the heel.

Once you can comfortably walk three or four miles without stopping, consider taking hiking trips—day or overnight—in county, state, or national parks. Hiking outdoors can revitalize your soul as much as it does your body.

Getting Started

If you haven't been exercising, it is important not to start off too fast or hard. Doing so often results in prematurely burning out on the idea of maintaining a regular exercise program. The following guidelines for getting started are recommended:

- Approach exercise gradually. Set limited goals at the outset, such as exerting only ten minutes (or to the point of being winded) every other day for the first week. Add five minutes to your workout time each successive week until you reach thirty minutes.

- Give yourself a one-month trial period. Make a commitment to stay with your program for one month, despite aches and pains, inertia, or other resistance to exercise. By the end of the first month, you may be starting to experience sufficient benefits to make the exercise self-motivating. Be aware that achieving a high level of fitness after being out of shape takes three to four months.

- Keep a record of your daily exercise practice. Use the *Daily Record of Exercise* that follows to keep track of the date, time, duration, and type of exercise you engage in on a daily basis. (You may want to make copies of the *Daily Record* so you can track your exercise program beyond the first month.) If you're doing aerobic exercise, record your pulse immediately after completing your workout and enter it under the column labeled "Pulse Rate." Also be sure to rate your level of satisfaction, using a 1 to 10 scale, where 1 equals no satisfaction at all and 10 equals total satisfaction with your exercise experience. As you begin to get into shape, your satisfaction should increase. Finally, if you fail to exercise when you intended to, indicate your reason for not doing so. Later on it may be useful to reevaluate these reasons to see if they are truly valid or "mere excuses." (See the final section of this chapter for dealing with resistance to exercise.)

- *Expect* some initial discomfort. Aches and pains when starting out are normal if you've been out of shape. You can expect the discomfort to pass as you grow in strength and endurance.

- Try to focus on the *process* of exercise rather than the product. See if you can get into the inherently enjoyable aspects of the exercise itself. If jogging or cycling is what you like, it helps to have a scenic environment. Focusing on competition with others or yourself will tend to increase rather than reduce anxiety and stress.

- Reward yourself for maintaining a commitment to your exercise program. Give yourself dinner out, a weekend trip, or new athletic clothes or equipment in exchange for sticking to your program during the first weeks and months.

- *Warm up.* Just as your car needs to warm up before you begin driving, your body needs a gradual warm-up before engaging in vigorous exercise. This is especially important if you are over forty. Five minutes of calisthenics or stretching exercises will usually be sufficient.

- After vigorous exercise, it is important to give yourself a few minutes to cool down. Walking around for two or three minutes will help bring blood back from peripheral muscles to the rest of your body.

- Avoid exercising within ninety minutes of a meal, and don't eat until one hour after exercising.

- Avoid exercising when you feel ill or overstressed (try a deep relaxation technique instead).

- Stop exercising if you experience any sudden, unexplainable bodily symptoms.

- If you find yourself feeling bored with exercising solo, find a partner to go with you or a form of exercise that requires a partner.

Daily Record of Exercise* for _____

                                                    (month)

Date	Time	Type of Exercise	Duration	Pulse Rate	Satisfaction Level	Reason for Not Exercising

* Based on a maximum frequency of six days of exercise

Optimizing the Anxiety-Reducing Effects of Exercise

Exercise needs to be of sufficient regularity, intensity, and duration to have a significant impact on anxiety. The following standards can be viewed as goals to aim for:

- Ideally exercise should be *aerobic*.

- Optimal frequency is *four to five times* per week.

- Optimal duration is *twenty to thirty minutes* or more per session.

- Optimal intensity for aerobic exercise is a heart rate of *(220 − your age) x 0.75* for at least ten minutes.

The table below indicates aerobic pulse ranges for various ages:

Age	Pulse (Heart) Rate
20–29	145–164
30–39	138–156
40–49	130–148
50–59	122–140
60–69	116–132

- *Avoid exercising only once per week.* Engaging in infrequent spurts of exercise is stressful to your body and generally does more harm than good (walking is an exception).

Obstacles to Implementing an Exercise Program

If you have difficulty starting or maintaining an exercise program, ask yourself what excuses or rationalizations you are giving yourself. What are you saying to yourself that tends to make you procrastinate? Try making a record of your opportunities and excuses. Use the one below as a model.

A Couch Potato's Logbook

Janine is fifty pounds overweight. She wants to lose weight, but she also uses her weight as an excuse not to exercise. Here is a logbook of Janine's battle with her sedentary lifestyle.

Opportunity to Exercise Not Taken	*Reason I Didn't Exercise*	*How I'll Talk Myself Into It Next Time*
Friend invited me to go to her aerobics class.	I kept thinking how grotesque I'll look in a leotard. What if my competitiveness makes me work too hard and I have a heart attack?	I'll find some loose, comfortable clothes that won't show every bulge quite so much. I'll focus on pacing myself—if I start to feel too stressed, I won't feel 'self-conscious about slowing down or just standing and stretching for a while.
Walk to the grocery store.	I'd have too much to carry home—and, anyway, it looked like rain.	I'll spread out my shopping over more trips so that I have only one bag to carry each time. I can wear a daypack to free up my hands while I'm walking home. Now that I think of it, my fold-up umbrella fits inside my pack—and, anyway, it's easy enough to carry.
Local chapter of the Sierra Club was advertising a bird walk.	I don't know the names of any of the birds. I don't have binoculars. I might get panicky if we have to climb up anywhere high.	I guess people go on these things because they *don't* know the names of the birds: I'll be in good company. Even if I don't have binoculars, it will be good for me to get out in the air—and maybe we'll see some birds close up. I'll look into borrowing some binoculars. I'll ask my friend George along—he knows about my panic attacks and he'll be able to help me if I start feeling stressed out.

Common Excuses for Not Exercising

Below is a list of common excuses people make for avoiding exercise.

- "I don't have enough time."

What you are really saying is that you're not willing to make time. You aren't assigning enough importance to the increased fitness, well-being, and improved control over anxiety you could gain from exercise. The problem is not a matter of time but one of priorities.

- "I feel too tired to exercise."

One solution is to exercise before going to work—or on your lunch break—rather than at the end of the day. If this is simply impossible, don't give up. What many nonexercisers fail to realize is that moderate exercise can actually *overcome* fatigue. Many people exercise *in spite* of feeling tired and find that they feel rejuvenated and reenergized afterward. Things will grow easier once you get past the initial inertia of starting to exercise.

- "Exercise is boring—it's no fun."

Is it really true that *all* the activities listed earlier are boring to you? Have you tried out all of them? It may be that you need to find someone to exercise with in order to have more fun. Or perhaps you need to go back and forth between two different types of exercise to stimulate your interest. Exercise can begin to feel wonderful after a few months when it becomes inherently rewarding, even if it initially bored you. If you've considered jogging but think of it as too boring, I suggest that you read *Beyond Jogging—The Inner Space of Running,* by Mike Spino.

- "It's too inconvenient to go out somewhere to exercise."

This is really no problem, as there are several ways to obtain vigorous exercise in the comfort of your home. Twenty minutes per day on a stationary bicycle will give you a good workout. If this seems boring, try listening to a portable audio device with headphones or place your stationary bike in front of the TV set. Aerobic exercise at home is convenient and fun if you have a DVD player. There are many low-impact aerobics programs available on DVD. Other indoor activities include jumping on a rebounder, calisthenics, using a rowing machine, and/or using a universal gym with adjustable weights. There are also early morning exercise programs on TV. If you can't afford exercise equipment, just put on some wild music and dance for twenty minutes. In short, it is quite possible to maintain an adequate exercise program without leaving your home.

- "I'm afraid I'll have a panic attack."

Brisk walking every day for forty-five minutes is an excellent form of exercise that is very unlikely to produce symptoms you might associate with panic. If you would prefer doing something more vigorous, start off with a very short period of two or three minutes of exercise and gradually add a minute at a time. Anytime you start to feel uneasy, simply stop, wait until you fully recover, and then try completing your designated period of exercise for that day. The principles of graded exposure described in chapter 7 can be applied effectively to a phobia about exercise.

- "Exercise causes a buildup of lactic acid—doesn't that cause panic attacks?"

It is true that exercise increases the production of lactic acid, and that lactic acid can promote panic attacks in some people who are already prone to them. However, regular exercise also increases *oxygen turnover* in your body—that is, the capacity of your body to oxidize substances it doesn't need, including lactic acid. Any increase in lactic acid produced by exercise will be offset by your body's increased capacity to remove it. The net effect of regular exercise is an overall *reduction* in your body's tendency to accumulate lactic acid.

- "I'm over forty—and that's too old to start exercising."

When clients over forty tell me "it's too late" to take up exercise, I remind them that many of the people chosen to be astronauts are in their forties. I also tell them about marathon runners who *began* running in their fifties and sixties after having not exercised at all. Unless your doctor gives you a clear medical reason for not exercising, age is never a valid excuse. With patience and persistence, it is possible to get into excellent physical shape at almost any age.

- "I'm too overweight and out of shape" or "I'm afraid I'll have a heart attack if I stress my body by exercising vigorously."

If you have physical reasons to worry about stressing your heart, be sure to design your exercise program with the help of your physician. Vigorous walking is a safe exercise for virtually everyone and is considered by some physicians to be the ideal exercise, as it rarely causes muscle or bone injuries. Swimming is also a safe bet if you're out of shape or overweight. Be sensible and realistic in the exercise program you choose. The important thing is to be consistent and committed, whether your program involves walking for one hour every day or training for a marathon.

- "I tried exercise once and it didn't work."

The question to ask here is this: *why* didn't it work? Did you start off too hard and fast? Did you get bored? Did you balk at the initial aches and pains? Did you feel lonely exercising by yourself? Perhaps it is time for you to give yourself another chance to discover all the physical and psychological benefits of a regular exercise program.

Regular exercise is an essential component of the total program for overcoming anxiety, panic, and phobias presented in this workbook. If you combine exercise with a program of regular deep relaxation, you are undoubtedly going to experience a substantial reduction in generalized anxiety and will very likely increase your resistance to panic attacks as well. Exercise and deep relaxation are the two methods *most* effective for altering a hereditary-biochemical predisposition to anxiety. The techniques described in the remaining chapters of this workbook depend for their effectiveness on your commitment to and mastery of deep relaxation and a program of regular exercise.

Summary of Things to Do

1. Evaluate your level of fitness, using the worksheet in the section "Your Fitness Level."

2. Determine whether you are ready to begin a fitness program by answering the questions in the section "Are You Ready for a Fitness Program?"

3. Choose one or more types of exercise you would prefer to do. If you're out of shape, begin with walking for periods of at least thirty minutes or with a more vigorous

form of exercise for ten to fifteen minutes. Increase the duration and intensity of your exercise gradually. Exercise at least four times per week.

4. Monitor your exercise program, using the *Daily Record of Exercise*, for at least one month.

5. Observe all the guidelines for maintaining a regular exercise program listed in the section "Getting Started." It's particularly important to give yourself time to warm up and cool down before and after engaging in vigorous exercise.

6. If you encounter resistance to exercise—or lose your motivation to keep exercising after the first week or so—reread the section "Obstacles to Implementing an Exercise Program." Try to identify what you're telling yourself about exercise that creates your resistance or lack of motivation. Work on countering your negative self-talk by giving yourself positive reasons to exercise the next time you have an opportunity.

Further Reading

Bailey, Covert. *The Ultimate Fit or Fat*. New York: Houghton Mifflin Harcourt, 2000.

Cooper, Robert K. *Health and Fitness Excellence: The Scientific Action Plan*. Boston: Houghton Mifflin, 1989.

Mannocchia, Pat. *Anatomy of Exercise: A Trainer's Inside Guide to Your Workout*. Richmond, ON, Canada: Firefly Books, 2009.

Sharkey, Brian, and Steven Gaskill. *Fitness & Health*. Champaign, IL: Human Kinetics, 2006.

Simon, Harvey. *The No Sweat Exercise Plan*. New York: McGraw-Hill, 2006.

6

Coping with Panic Attacks

A panic attack is a sudden surge of mounting physiological arousal that can occur "out of the blue" or in response to encountering (or merely thinking about) a phobic situation. *Bodily symptoms* that occur with the onset of panic can include heart palpitations, tightening in the chest or shortness of breath, choking sensations, dizziness, faintness, sweating, trembling, shaking, and/or tingling in the hands and feet. *Psychological reactions* that often accompany these bodily changes include feelings of unreality, an intense desire to run away, and fears of going crazy, dying, or doing something uncontrollable.

Anyone who has had a full-fledged panic attack knows that it is one of the most intensely uncomfortable states human beings are capable of experiencing. Your very first panic attack can have a traumatic impact, leaving you feeling terrified and helpless, with strong anticipatory anxiety about the possible recurrence of your panic symptoms. Unfortunately, in some cases, panic does come back and occurs repeatedly. Why some people have a panic attack only once—or perhaps once every few years—while others develop a chronic condition with several attacks a week is still not understood by researchers in the field.

The *good* news is that you can learn to cope with panic attacks so well that they will no longer have the power to frighten you. Over time you can actually diminish the intensity and frequency of panic attacks *if* you are willing to make some changes in your lifestyle. Lifestyle changes that are most conducive to reducing the severity of panic reactions are described in other chapters of this workbook. They include

- Regular practice of deep relaxation (see chapter 4)

- A regular program of exercise (see chapter 5)

- Elimination of stimulants (especially caffeine, sugar, and nicotine) from your diet (see chapter 15)

- Learning to acknowledge and express your feelings, especially anger and sadness (see chapter 12)

- Adopting self-talk and "core beliefs" which promote a calmer and more accepting attitude toward life (see chapters 8 and 9)

These five lifestyle changes vary in importance for different people. To the extent that you can cultivate all five of them, however, you will find that, over time, your problem with panic reactions will diminish.

The approach in this workbook is not strongly oriented toward medication. Yet there *are* some people who suffer from panic attacks for whom it's appropriate to take medication. If you're having panic attacks with sufficient intensity and frequency to interfere with your ability to work, your close personal relationships, or your sleep, or if such attacks persistently give you the feeling that you are losing your grip, then medication may be an appropriate intervention.

The two types of medications most frequently prescribed for panic attacks are antidepressants (such as Zoloft, Cymbalta, and Lexapro) and minor tranquilizers (for instance, Xanax or Ativan). For more information on the use of prescription medications in treating panic attacks, see chapter 17.

The remainder of this chapter will present some specific guidelines for dealing with panic attacks on a *short-term*, immediate basis. These are practical strategies for coping with panic attacks *at the very moment they occur*.

Deflate the Danger

A panic attack can be a very frightening and uncomfortable experience, but it is absolutely not dangerous. You may be surprised to learn that panic is an *entirely natural bodily reaction that simply occurs out of context*. It is related to the fight-or-flight reaction—an instinctual response in all mammals (not just humans) to physiologically prepare to fight or flee when their survival is threatened. This instantaneous reaction is necessary to ensure the survival of the species in life-threatening situations. It serves to protect the lives of animals in the wild when they are faced by their predators. And it serves to protect your life by informing and mobilizing your impulse to flee from danger.

Suppose, for example, that your car stalled on the railroad tracks while a train approached you from about two hundred yards away. You would experience a sudden surge of adrenaline, accompanied by feelings of panic, and a very strong and sensible urge to flee your predicament. In fact, your body would undergo a whole range of reactions, including

- An increase in your heart rate
- An increase in your respiratory rate
- A tensing of your muscles
- Constriction of your arteries and reduced blood flow to your hands and feet
- Increased blood flow to your muscles
- Release of stored sugar from your liver into your bloodstream
- Increased production of sweat

The very intensity of this reaction and the strong urge to flee are precisely what would ensure your survival. The surge of adrenaline and flow of blood to your muscles increases your alertness and physical strength. Your energy is mobilized and directed toward escape. If these reactions were less intense or less rapid, you might never get out of the way in time.

Perhaps you can recall times in your life when the flight response worked properly and served you well.

In a spontaneous panic attack, your body goes through *exactly the same* physiological flight reaction that it does in a truly life-threatening situation. The panic attack that wakes you up at night or occurs out of the blue is *physiologically indistinguishable* from your response to such experiences as your car stalling on the railroad tracks or waking to hear a robber going through your house.

What makes a panic attack unique and difficult to cope with is that these intense bodily reactions occur *in the absence of any immediate or apparent danger.* Or, in the case of agoraphobia, they occur in response to situations that have no apparent life-threatening potential (such as standing in line at the grocery store or being at home alone). In either case, you don't know why the reaction is happening. And not knowing why—not being able to make any sense out of the fact that your body is going through such an intense response—only serves to make the entire experience even more frightening. Your tendency is to react to sensations that are intense and *inexplicable* with even more fear and a heightened sense of danger.

No one fully knows at this time why spontaneous panic attacks occur—why the body's natural flight mechanism can come into play for no obvious reason or out of context. Some people believe that there is always *some* stimulus for a panic attack, even if this is not apparent. Others believe that sudden attacks arise from a temporary physiological imbalance. It *is* known that there is a greater tendency for panic attacks to occur when a person has been undergoing prolonged stress or has recently suffered a significant loss. However, only some people who have undergone stress or loss develop panic attacks, while others might develop headaches, ulcers, or reactive depression. It is also known that a disturbance in the part of the brain called the *locus coeruleus* is implicated in panic attacks, but it seems that this disturbance is only one event in a long chain of causes without being the primary cause. A full understanding of what causes panic attacks awaits future research. (For a more detailed account of what is known, see chapter 2.)

Because there is no immediate or apparent external danger in a panic attack, you may tend to *invent* or *attribute danger* to the intense bodily sensations you're going through. In the absence of any real life-threatening situation, your mind may misinterpret what's going on *inside* as being life-threatening. Your mind can very quickly go through the following process: "If I feel this bad, I must be in some danger. If there is no apparent external danger, the danger must be inside of me." And so it's very common when undergoing panic to invent any (or all) of the following "dangers":

In response to heart palpitations: "I'm going to have a heart attack" or "I'm going to die."

In response to choking sensations: "I'm going to stop breathing and suffocate."

In response to dizzy sensations: "I'm going to pass out."

In response to sensations of disorientation or feeling "not all there": "I'm going crazy."

In response to "rubbery legs": "I won't be able to walk" or "I'm going to fall."

In response to the overall intensity of your body's reactions: "I'm going to lose complete control over myself."

As soon as you tell yourself that you're feeling any of the above dangers, you multiply the intensity of your fear. This intense fear makes your bodily reactions even worse, which in turn creates still more fear, and you get caught in an upward spiral of mounting panic.

This upward spiral can be avoided if you understand that what your body is going through is *not dangerous*. All of the above dangers are illusory, a product of your imagination when you're undergoing the intense reactions that constitute panic. *There is simply no basis for any of them in reality.* Let's examine them one by one.

A panic attack cannot cause heart failure or cardiac arrest.

Rapid heartbeat and palpitations during a panic attack can be frightening sensations, but they are not dangerous. Your heart is made up of very strong and dense muscle fibers and can withstand a lot more than you might think. According to Claire Weekes (1991), a healthy heart can beat two hundred beats per minute for days—even weeks—without sustaining any damage. So, if your heart begins to race, just allow it to do so, trusting that no harm can come of it and that your heart will eventually calm down.

There's a substantial difference between what goes on with your heart during a panic attack and what happens in a heart attack. During a panic attack, your heart may race, pound, and at times miss or have extra beats. Some people even report chest pains, which pass fairly quickly, in the left-upper portion of their chest. None of these symptoms is aggravated by movement or increased physical activity. During a true heart attack, the most common symptom is continuous pain and a pressured, even crushing sensation in the center of your chest. Racing or pounding of the heart may occur but this is secondary to the pain. Moreover, the pain and pressure get worse upon exertion and may tend to diminish with rest. This is quite different from a panic attack, where racing and pounding may get worse if you stand still and lessen if you move around.

In the case of heart disease, distinct abnormalities in heart rhythm show up on an electrocardiogram (EKG) reading. It has been demonstrated that during a panic attack there are no EKG abnormalities—only rapid heartbeat. (If you want to gain additional reassurance, you may want to have your doctor perform an EKG.)

In sum, there is simply no basis for the connection between heart attacks and panic. Panic attacks are not hazardous to your heart.

A panic attack will not cause you to stop breathing or suffocate.

It is common during panic to feel your chest close down and your breathing become restricted. This might lead you to suddenly fear that you're going to suffocate. Under stress, your neck and chest muscles are tightening and reducing your respiratory capacity. Be assured that there is nothing wrong with your breathing passage or lungs, and that the tightening sensations will pass. Your brain has a built-in reflex mechanism that will eventually *force* you to breathe if you're not getting enough oxygen. If you don't believe this, try holding your breath for up to a minute and observe what happens. At a certain point you'll feel a strong reflex to take in more air. The same thing will happen in a panic attack if you're not getting enough oxygen. You'll automatically gasp and take a deep breath long before reaching the point where you could pass out from a lack of oxygen. (And even if you did pass out, you would immediately start breathing!) In sum, choking and sensations of constriction during panic, however unpleasant, are not dangerous.

A panic attack cannot cause you to faint.

The sensation of light-headedness you may feel with the onset of panic can evoke a fear of fainting. What is happening is that the blood circulation to your brain is slightly reduced, most likely because you are breathing more rapidly (see the section on hyperventilation in chapter 4). This is *not* dangerous and can be relieved by breathing slowly and regularly from your abdomen, preferably through your nose. It can also be helped by taking the first opportunity you have to walk around a bit. Let the feelings of light-headedness rise and subside without fighting them. Because your heart is pumping harder and actually increasing your circulation, you are very unlikely to faint (except in rare instances if you have a blood phobia and happen to be exposed to the sight of blood).

A panic attack cannot cause you to lose your balance.

Sometimes you may feel quite dizzy when panic comes on. It may be that tension is affecting the semicircular canal system in your inner ear, which regulates your balance. For a few moments you may feel dizzy, or it may even seem that things around you are spinning. Invariably this sensation will pass. It is not dangerous and very unlikely to be so strong that you will actually lose your balance. If sensations of pronounced dizziness persist for more than a few seconds, you may want to consult a doctor (preferably an otolaryngologist) to check if infection, allergies, or other disturbances might be affecting your inner ear.

You won't fall over or cease to walk when you feel "weak in the knees" during a panic attack.

The adrenaline released during a panic attack can dilate the blood vessels in your legs, causing blood to accumulate in your leg muscles and not fully circulate. This can produce a sensation of weakness or "jelly legs," to which you may respond with the fear that you won't be able to walk. Be assured that this sensation is just that—a sensation—and that your legs are as strong and able to carry you as ever. They won't give way! Just allow these trembling, weak sensations to pass and give your legs the chance to carry you where you need to go.

You can't "go crazy" during a panic attack.

Reduced blood flow to your brain during a panic attack is due to arterial constriction, a *normal* consequence of rapid breathing. This can result in sensations of disorientation and a feeling of unreality that can be frightening. If this sensation comes on, remind yourself that it's simply due to a slight and temporary reduction of arterial circulation in your brain and does not have anything to do with "going crazy," no matter how eerie or strange it may feel. No one has ever gone crazy from a panic attack, even though the fear of doing so is common. As bad as they feel, sensations of unreality will eventually pass and are completely harmless.

It may be helpful to know that people do not "go crazy" in a sudden or spontaneous way. Mental disorders involving behaviors that are labeled "crazy" (such as schizophrenia or manic-depressive psychosis) develop very gradually over a period of years and do not arise from panic attacks. No one has ever started to hallucinate or hear voices during a panic attack (except in rare instances where panic was induced by an overdose of a so-called recreational drug such as LSD or cocaine). In short, a panic attack cannot result in your "going crazy," no matter how disturbing or unpleasant your symptoms feel.

A panic attack cannot cause you to lose control of yourself.

Because of the intense reactions your body goes through during panic, it is easy to imagine that you could "completely lose it." But what does completely losing it mean? Becoming completely paralyzed? Acting out uncontrollably or running amok? I am aware of no reported instances of this happening. If anything, during panic, your senses and awareness are heightened with respect to a single goal: escape. Running away or trying to run away are the only ways in which you would be likely to "act out" while panicking. Complete loss of control during panic attacks is simply a myth.

The first step in learning to cope with panic reactions is to recognize that they are not dangerous. Because the bodily reactions accompanying panic feel so intense, it's easy to imagine them being dangerous. Yet in reality no danger exists. The physiological reactions underlying panic are *natural* and *protective*. In fact, *your body is designed to panic* so that you can quickly mobilize to flee situations that genuinely threaten your survival. The problem occurs when this natural, life-preserving response occurs outside the context of any immediate or apparent danger. When this happens, you can make headway in mastering panic by learning not to imagine danger where it doesn't exist.

Breaking the Connection Between Bodily Symptoms and Catastrophic Thoughts

There is an important difference between people who have panic attacks and those who do not. *Individuals who are prone to panic have a chronic tendency to interpret slightly unusual or uncomfortable bodily sensations in a catastrophic way.* For example, heart palpitations are seen as signals of an impending heart attack, chest constriction and shortness of breath are seen as signs of imminent suffocation, or dizziness is seen as a precursor to fainting or collapse. People who do not have panic attacks may notice (and not particularly like) having such bodily symptoms, *but they do not interpret them as catastrophic or dangerous.*

If you have a tendency to interpret unpleasant bodily sensations as portending something dangerous or catastrophic, you will also tend to constantly monitor your body to see if you're having those sensations. You're probably very tuned in to your internal bodily states and overreact easily if something begins to feel slightly "off" or unusual. This increased *internalization* compounds the problem, because you're more likely to notice and magnify any sudden change in your body's internal state that is slightly unusual or unpleasant.

The variety of circumstances that might cause a sudden aberration in your body's internal physiological state is legion. Sometimes the cause lies outside of your body. For example, an argument with your spouse, seeing something unpleasant on TV, hearing your alarm clock go off, or being in a hurry to get somewhere could trigger an increase in heart rate, chest constriction, stomach queasiness, or any of a wide range of bodily symptoms associated with anxiety. At other times, the cause resides in some subtle physiological shift within your body—for example, oxygen deprivation due to underbreathing, a spontaneous shift in the neuroendocrine systems of your brain, an increase in muscle tension in your neck and shoulders, or a fall in your blood sugar level. Whether the initial cause lies primarily outside or within your body, you are usually unaware of these physiological shifts until you actually feel the resultant symptoms. The above examples illustrate only a few among many possibilities, any of which might constitute the triggering event for an increase in anxiety. Whether or not you actually develop a full-blown panic attack depends on *how you perceive and respond* to the particular increase in bodily symptoms that occurs.

To sum up, people who panic are likely to experience 1) increased internalization or preoccupation with subtle shifts in bodily symptoms or mood and 2) an increased tendency to interpret slight aberrations or incremental changes in bodily symptoms as dangerous or catastrophic. The diagram that follows illustrates this tendency:

Development of Panic Attack

Phase 1   Initiating Circumstances
               (internal or external)

                      ↓

Phase 2   Slight increase in unusual or unpleasant bodily symptoms
               (i.e., heart palpitations, shortness of breath, faintness or dizziness,
               sweating, etc.)

                      ↓

Phase 3   Internalization
               (increased focus on symptoms makes them more noticeable and easily
               magnified)

                      ↓

Phase 4   Catastrophic Interpretation
               (telling yourself the symptom is dangerous—i.e., "I'll have a heart
               attack," "I'll suffocate," "I'll go completely out of control," "I must leave
               at once")

                      ↓

Phase 5   Panic

The good news is that it's possible to intervene at any point in this sequence. At phase 1, it may be *generalized stress* that leads to the initial unpleasant bodily sensations—heart palpitations, chest constriction, dizziness, and so on. Incorporating regular relaxation, exercise, low-stress nutritional habits, and other stress management techniques into your lifestyle (see chapters 4, 5, and 15) on a daily basis can go a long way toward reducing the propensity for sudden increases in your body's state of sympathetic nervous system arousal. Beyond generalized stress, you may be able to identify the particular initiating circumstances that cause your panic attacks by noting carefully what was going on just before—or in the several hours before—a panic attack occurred. You can use the *Panic Attack Record* later in this chapter to help you determine what initial circumstances may have led to a particular panic attack. You can then try to avoid or eliminate these circumstances so that they don't cause you trouble in the future. Interventions that reduce the propensity for having unpleasant bodily sensations in the first place (phases 1 and 2 in the above diagram) all require making changes in your lifestyle and attitudes.

Phase 3 of the panic cycle consists of internalization—being too focused on your internal bodily state. When you actually feel panic coming on, you can reduce internalization by using any of the active coping techniques described later in this chapter in the section "Coping Strategies to Counteract Panic at an Early Stage." These techniques serve to distract your attention away from internal bodily symptoms, and they also have a directly relaxing effect.

Perhaps the most important change you can make to defuse panic attacks, however, is to intervene at phase 4. That is, you can learn to stop interpreting unpleasant bodily sensations as being dangerous or potentially catastrophic. In fact, recent research in both the United States and England has determined that eliminating catastrophic interpretations of bodily symptoms can, *in and of itself alone,* be sufficient to relieve panic attacks. If you can learn to tolerate sensations of dizziness, tightness in your chest, rapid heartbeat, and so on as innocuous bodily symptoms—rather than read them as signs of imminent danger—you will very likely have fewer, if any, panic attacks. That is not to say that stress management techniques and coping strategies for panic are unimportant; it does imply, though, that eliminating catastrophic interpretations by itself can go a long way toward relieving panic.

To assist you in breaking the connection between bodily symptoms and catastrophic interpretations, please refer to the three worksheets that follow in a couple of pages. The first worksheet is a list of bodily symptoms that can trigger panic attacks. Rate each bodily symptom on a 0 to 5 scale, according to how much it affects you when you panic. The second worksheet is a list of common catastrophic self-statements that people who panic make in response to unpleasant bodily symptoms. Rate each of these catastrophic statements on a 1 to 4 scale, according to how much you feel it contributes to your panic attacks.

Finally, use the third worksheet to go back and connect the two lists. For each troublesome bodily symptom you rated a 4 or 5, list the specific catastrophic statements likely to be triggered by that symptom. For example, you might connect heart palpitations with "I'm having a heart attack" and "I'm going to die" or dizziness with "I'm going to pass out" or "I'm going to lose control."

When you're finished, you should have a better idea of what particular bodily symptoms and associated catastrophic interpretations trigger your panic attacks. This knowledge will likely help you break the false connection you've made between your bodily symptoms and mistaken interpretations. Keep in mind throughout this exercise that *none of the bodily symptoms you've listed is actually dangerous. However unpleasant such symptoms might feel, they are completely harmless.* Equally important, keep in mind that *none of the catastrophic thoughts you have checked off is true or valid, even though you might have convinced yourself that it is. Every one of these catastrophic thoughts is simply false—a mistaken belief that you can learn to let go of.*

How do you break the automatic connection between unpleasant bodily symptoms and false, catastrophic thoughts? The following three processes can help:

- Recognition
- Writing down alternative explanations of symptoms
- Symptom inductions

Recognition

Just recognizing your tendency to believe that harmless bodily symptoms are signs of imminent danger is the first step. Awareness of specific connections between particular symptoms and particular catastrophic thoughts, which you may have gained from the previous exercise, will help you begin defusing the danger when those symptoms come up in day-to-day life.

Writing Down Alternative Explanations for Bodily Symptoms

The catastrophic self-statements you make in an attempt to make sense of unpleasant bodily symptoms during a panic attack are simply false. It's just not true, for example, that rapid heartbeat or palpitations occur because you are having a heart attack. Nor is constriction in your chest or shortness of breath happening because you're about to suffocate. Nor are dizziness and light-headedness occurring because you're about to faint or "go crazy." In each of these cases, there is an alternative explanation that is noncatastrophic and based in fact. Alternative logical explanations might go something like this:

- An increase in heartbeat and/or heart palpitations is very likely caused by increased output of adrenaline and sympathetic nervous system activity that accompany the early stage of an anxiety reaction. Such reactions are part of the body's normal means of handling any *perceived* threat—they are part of the fight-or-flight response. They are in no way dangerous, even if they continue for some time. For example, a healthy heart can beat rapidly for hours without putting you at any risk.

- An increase in chest constriction and shortness of breath can be explained in terms of contraction of the muscles surrounding the chest cavity, also due to increased sympathetic nervous system activity. Such symptoms have nothing to do with the process of suffocating. Your chest muscles cannot contract to the point where you would be at risk of suffocating, no matter how unpleasant the tightness in your chest happens to feel.

- Becoming dizzy and becoming light-headed, common symptoms that can occur when you become anxious, are not caused by the fact that you are about to faint. They are caused by minor constrictions in the arteries of your brain, which lead to a slight reduction in blood circulation. It's extremely unlikely that you would faint, even if you feel quite light-headed. Fainting typically occurs during a drop in blood pressure; when you start to feel anxious, you usually experience an *increase* in blood pressure due to increased adrenaline and sympathetic nervous system tone.

Even less plausible is the idea that dizziness and light-headedness are caused by the fact that you're about to go crazy. The development of serious mental disorders has nothing to do with panic attacks and takes place over a much longer period of time than the duration of any panic attack.

These examples can serve as guidelines for developing your own alternative, non-catastrophic explanations for troublesome bodily symptoms. You'll likely find it helpful to refer to the first section of this chapter, "Deflate the Danger," in coming up with your own alternative explanations. The process of writing down such explanations will help strengthen your conviction that uncomfortable bodily symptoms are truly harmless rather than signs of imminent danger.

You might want to put your alternative explanations of bodily symptoms on 3 by 5 index cards—one explanation of a particular symptom per card. Keep the cards with you in your purse or wallet and take them out and read them if you feel symptoms coming on.

Symptom Inductions (Interoceptive Desensitization)

A very effective treatment for panic attacks involves voluntarily inducing bodily symptoms that can trigger panic. Many therapists refer to this technique as *interoceptive desensitization, a process of desensitizing or habituating yourself to internal bodily symptoms associated with panic,* such as those listed in the *Panic Attack Worksheet 1.* Interoceptive desensitization is typically done in a therapy session. For example, if dizziness and shortness of breath are troublesome symptoms, the therapist might have the client hyperventilate for two minutes and then stand up suddenly, to actually bring on these symptoms. This might sound like an unusual and extreme therapeutic procedure, but, in fact, it is harmless and often quite helpful. Unless the client has a respiratory disorder, hyperventilating for two minutes is harmless. Deliberately hyperventilating gives you an opportunity to *actually experience uncomfortable bodily symptoms without anything negative or dangerous happening.* The key here is that you learn on a "gut" or experiential level that nothing terrible follows bodily sensations that you used to interpret as dangerous. Repeated inductions of dizziness in this way help a panic-prone person to develop a strong conviction that dizziness is not dangerous.

Panic Attack Worksheet 1
Bodily Symptoms

Any of the following bodily symptoms can occur during a panic attack. Please evaluate each of them according to their effect when you are having an attack and indicate your answers on the 0 to 5 scale in the right-hand column.

0 = No Effect	3 = Strong Effect
1 = Mild Effect	4 = Severe Effect
2 = Medium Effect	5 = Very Severe Effect

1. Sinking feeling in stomach	0	1	2	3	4	5
2. Sweaty palms	0	1	2	3	4	5
3. Warm all over	0	1	2	3	4	5
4. Rapid or heavy heartbeat	0	1	2	3	4	5
5. Tremor of the hands	0	1	2	3	4	5
6. Weak or rubbery knees or legs	0	1	2	3	4	5
7. Shaky inside and/or outside	0	1	2	3	4	5
8. Dry mouth	0	1	2	3	4	5
9. Lump in throat	0	1	2	3	4	5
10. Tightness in chest	0	1	2	3	4	5
11. Hyperventilation	0	1	2	3	4	5
12. Nausea or diarrhea	0	1	2	3	4	5
13. Dizzy or light-headed	0	1	2	3	4	5
14. A feeling of unreality—as "in a dream"	0	1	2	3	4	5
15. Unable to think clearly	0	1	2	3	4	5
16. Blurred vision	0	1	2	3	4	5
17. A feeling of being partially paralyzed	0	1	2	3	4	5
18. A feeling of detachment or floating away	0	1	2	3	4	5
19. Palpitations or irregular heartbeat	0	1	2	3	4	5
20. Chest pain	0	1	2	3	4	5
21. Tingling in hands, feet, or face	0	1	2	3	4	5
22. Feeling faint	0	1	2	3	4	5
23. Fluttery stomach	0	1	2	3	4	5
24. Cold, clammy hands	0	1	2	3	4	5

Panic Attack Worksheet 2
Catastrophic Thoughts*

Catastrophic thoughts play a major role in aggravating panic attacks. Using the scale below, rate each of the following thoughts according to the degree to which you believe that each thought contributes to your panic attacks.

1 = Not at all   3 = Quite a lot
2 = Somewhat   4 = Very much

1. I'm going to die.	1	2	3	4
2. I'm going insane.	1	2	3	4
3. I'm losing control.	1	2	3	4
4. This will never end.	1	2	3	4
5. I'm really scared.	1	2	3	4
6. I'm having a heart attack.	1	2	3	4
7. I'm going to pass out.	1	2	3	4
8. I don't know what people will think.	1	2	3	4
9. I won't be able to get out of here.	1	2	3	4
10. I don't understand what's happening to me.	1	2	3	4
11. People will think I'm crazy.	1	2	3	4
12. I'll always be this way.	1	2	3	4
13. I'm going to throw up.	1	2	3	4
14. I must have a brain tumor.	1	2	3	4
15. I'll choke to death.	1	2	3	4
16. I'm going to act foolish.	1	2	3	4
17. I'm going blind.	1	2	3	4
18. I'll hurt someone.	1	2	3	4
19. I'm going to have a stroke.	1	2	3	4
20. I'm going to scream.	1	2	3	4
21. I'm going to babble or talk funny.	1	2	3	4
22. I'll be paralyzed by fear.	1	2	3	4
23. Something is really physically wrong with me.	1	2	3	4
24. I won't be able to breathe.	1	2	3	4
25. Something terrible will happen.	1	2	3	4
26. I'm going to make a scene.	1	2	3	4

* Adapted from "Panic Attack Cognitions Questionnaire" in *Coping with Panic: A Drug-free Approach to Dealing with Anxiety Attacks* by G. A. Clum. Copyright © 1990 by Brooks/Cole Publishing Company, a division of International Thomson Publishing Inc., Pacific Grove, CA 93950. Reprinted by permission of the publisher.

Connecting Bodily Symptoms and Catastrophic Thoughts

In the left-hand column below, list bodily symptoms you rated 5 or 4 on the first Panic Attack Worksheet. Describe your most troublesome bodily symptoms, one at a time. Then list catastrophic self-statements from the second worksheet that you rated 4 or 3. List those catastrophic statements you would be most likely to make in response to each particular bodily symptom. For example, "rapid heartbeat" is a bodily symptom that might elicit such catastrophic self-statements as "I'm having a heart attack" and "I'm going to die."

Bodily symptom: Catastrophic thoughts:

Bodily symptom: Catastrophic thoughts:

Bodily symptom: Catastrophic thoughts:

Bodily symptom: Catastrophic thoughts:

You may want to try symptom induction techniques with a professional therapist who has had experience using them. On the other hand, some people have tried these techniques on their own and found them to be quite helpful. If you decide that you want to include these techniques in your self-help program, please observe the following guidelines:

- *Check with your doctor if you are over forty or suspect that you might have any physical condition that would preclude using symptom induction procedures.* For example, you wouldn't try three minutes of hyperventilation if you have a chronic respiratory problem like asthma or emphysema. You also wouldn't run up and down stairs if you have any kind of heart condition that restricts physical exercise. Nor would you do induction procedures if you were pregnant or had epilepsy.

- Although the techniques are harmless, it's a good idea to have a friend or family member present when you first do them to provide support and encouragement. If you can get your support person to do the procedure with you, so much the better.

- You need to persist in doing each induction procedure long enough so that the sensations produced are unpleasant and/or cause an increase in anxiety. Usually this is anywhere from thirty seconds to two minutes. You *want* to simulate, if possible, the actual sensations you experience during a panic attack. The point is to expose yourself to unpleasant bodily sensations until you habituate to them. As a general rule, keep doing the procedure for about thirty seconds *after* you first notice it producing unpleasant sensations and/or anxiety. If you stop the moment you start to feel unpleasant symptoms, you'll tend to reinforce your fear of them.

- Review the *Panic Attack Worksheet 1* and identify those bodily symptoms that are most troublesome for you. Then practice any of the induction techniques below that can produce those symptoms. Practice each induction technique three or four times in a row; then repeat the practice each day for several days until it loses its ability to make you anxious. With practice, the symptoms you experience from induction procedures will lose their capacity to cause anxiety. This is precisely what you want.

Induction Techniques

After obtaining clearance from your physician, try practicing the following six symptom induction techniques:

1. Hyperventilate continuously for two minutes. This involves breathing deeply and rapidly with your mouth open. At the end of two minutes, stand up. (Symptoms: dizziness, disorientation, light-headedness)

2. Breathe through a cocktail straw while holding your nose for one minute—don't allow any air through your nose. (Symptoms: shortness of breath, suffocation)

3. Walk up and down some stairs rapidly for about ninety seconds or until your heart rate increases noticeably. Stop if you experience dizziness or your heart rate exceeds 140 beats per minute. Alternatively, you can use a stationary bike or stair-climber to increase your heart rate. (Symptoms: rapid heartbeat, heart pounding)

4. Spin—preferably in a desk chair or else standing up—for thirty seconds to one minute. It's not necessary to go a full minute if you find yourself getting significantly dizzy. Be near a chair or couch where you can sit back down easily. (Symptoms: dizziness, disorientation)

5. Tense every part of your body and hold yourself tight for one minute before releasing. (Symptom: muscle tension)

6. Put on warm clothes and turn up the heat or sit in a sauna. (Symptom: sweating)

Remember to persist with each of these procedures long enough to produce unpleasant sensations. It's ideal if you allow yourself to feel these unpleasant sensations for up to thirty seconds, although you may want to start out with a shorter period when you first try the induction. You'll get the most from this exercise if the procedure actually makes you somewhat uncomfortable or anxious. Again, the idea is to teach yourself that you can have unpleasant bodily symptoms without anything terrible or dangerous happening. To the extent that this learning carries over to real-life panic symptoms, you will likely stop having full-blown panic attacks—that is, you'll be able to withstand the unpleasant bodily sensations during the early stage of panic without reacting to them as dangerous. Keep in mind that you may need to practice the symptom induction procedures many times before you get to the point at which the symptoms don't cause you any anxiety.

After you've produced unpleasant symptoms and anxiety for thirty seconds, you can practice some coping skills that you'll learn later in this chapter. These skills include abdominal breathing, repeating coping statements, moving around, or talking to someone. You want to fully experience the unpleasant symptoms and anxiety so that you can get used to them, but you also can practice these coping skills to bring your anxiety down. Symptom inductions provide an excellent opportunity to gain confidence in your mastery of coping skills.

What if the inductions don't produce any anxiety, even from the beginning? This might happen for at least two reasons. It could happen because you feel safe doing the procedure in the comfort of your own home or with your support person. Possibly, the process of inducing body symptoms *voluntarily* may give you a sense of control over what's happening that isn't present when a real-life panic situation occurs. In order to give the symptom induction procedures a little more "charge," you can modify the conditions in which you do them as follows:

- Do the procedures alone.

- Do the procedures away from your home or safe place.

- Do them while *visualizing* yourself in your phobic situation.

- Do them (for example, hyperventilating or spinning) while actually confronting a phobic situation in real life.

For clients who want to completely master their phobias, I often recommend that they deliberately induce uncomfortable symptoms in the phobic situation (unless it could be potentially dangerous to do so, such as when driving on a busy highway).

For a more in-depth discussion of how to use and benefit from symptom inductions, please see the books by David Barlow and Michelle Craske and by Denise Beckfield listed at the end of this chapter.

Don't Fight Panic

Resisting or fighting initial panic symptoms is likely to make them worse. It's important to avoid tensing up in reaction to panic symptoms or trying to make them go away by suppressing them or gritting your teeth. Although it's important to act rather than be passive (as discussed below), you still shouldn't fight your panic. Claire Weekes, in her popular books *Hope and Help for Your Nerves* and *Peace from Nervous Suffering*, describes a four-step approach for coping with panic:

1. Face the symptoms—don't run from them.
Attempting to suppress or run away from the early symptoms of panic is a way of telling yourself that you can't handle a particular situation. In most cases, this will only create more panic. A more constructive attitude to cultivate is one that says, "Okay, here it is again. I can allow my body to go through its reactions and handle this. I've done it before."

2. Accept what your body is doing—don't fight against it.
When you try to fight panic, you simply tense up against it, which only makes you more anxious. Adopting just the opposite attitude, one of *letting go* and *allowing* your body to have its reactions (such as heart palpitations, chest constriction, sweaty palms, dizziness, and so on) will enable you to move through panic much more quickly and easily. The key is to be able to *watch* or *observe* your body's state of physiological arousal—no matter how unusual or uncomfortable it feels—without reacting to it with further fear or anxiety.

3. Float with the wave of a panic attack rather than try to force your way through it.
Claire Weekes makes a distinction between *first fear* and *second fear*. First fear consists of the physiological reactions underlying panic; second fear is when you make yourself afraid of these reactions by saying scary things to yourself like "I can't handle this!" "I've got to get out of here right now!" or "What if other people see this happening to me?" While you can't do much about first fear, you can eliminate second fear by learning to flow with the rising and falling of your body's state of arousal rather than fighting or reacting fearfully to it. Instead of scaring yourself about your body's reactions, you can move with them and make reassuring statements to yourself, such as "This too will pass," "I'll let my body do its thing and move through this," or "I've handled this before and I can handle it now." A list of such positive coping statements follows in the next section.

4. Allow time to pass.
Panic is caused by a sudden surge of adrenaline. If you can allow and float with the bodily reactions caused by this surge, much of this adrenaline will metabolize and be reabsorbed in three to five minutes. As soon as this happens, you'll start to feel better. *Panic attacks are time limited.* In most cases, panic will peak and begin to subside within only a few minutes. It is

most likely to pass quickly if you don't aggravate it by fighting against it or reacting to it wi
even more fear (causing "second fear") by saying scary things to yourself.

Coping Statements

Use any or all of the following positive statements to help yourself cultivate attitudes of accepting, "floating," and allowing time to pass during a panic attack. You may find it helpful to
repeat a single statement over and over the first minute or two when you feel panic symptoms
coming on. You may also want to do deep abdominal breathing in conjunction with repeating a coping statement. If one statement gets tiresome or seems to stop working, try another.

- This feeling isn't comfortable or pleasant, but I can accept it.

- I can be anxious and still deal with this situation.

- I can handle these symptoms or sensations.

- This isn't an emergency. It's okay to think slowly about what I need to do.

- This isn't the worst thing that could happen.

- I'm going to go with this and wait for my anxiety to decrease.

- This is an opportunity for me to learn to cope with my fears.

- I'll just let my body do its thing. This will pass.

- I'll ride this through—I don't need to let this get to me.

- I deserve to feel okay right now.

- I can take all the time I need in order to let go and relax.

- There's no need to push myself. I can take as small a step forward as I choose.

- I've survived this before and I'll survive this time, too.

- I can do my coping strategies and allow this to pass.

- This anxiety won't hurt me—even if it doesn't feel good.

- This is just anxiety—I'm not going to let it get to me.

- Nothing serious is going to happen to me.

- Fighting and resisting this isn't going to help—so I'll just let it pass.

- These are just thoughts—not reality.

- I don't need these thoughts—I can choose to think differently.

- This isn't dangerous.

- So what.

- Don't worry—be happy. (Use this to inject an element of lightness or humor.)

If you have frequent panic attacks, I suggest writing your favorite coping statements on a 3 by 5 index card and carrying it in your purse or wallet. Bring the card out and read it when you feel panic symptoms coming on.

Explore the Antecedents of Your Panic Attacks

You can increase your mastery over panic attacks by investigating the types of circumstances that tend to precede them. If you are agoraphobic, you are very familiar with these circumstances. You know that you are more likely to panic, for example, if you are far from home, driving over a bridge, or sitting in a restaurant, and so you systematically avoid these particular situations. If you have spontaneous panic attacks that come "out of the blue," you might find it helpful to monitor their occurrence for two weeks and take careful note of what was going on immediately—as well as for several hours—before each one occurs. You might observe whether any of the following conditions makes a difference in the likelihood of your having a panic reaction:

- Were you under stress?

- Were you by yourself or with someone?

- If with someone, was it a family member, a friend, or a stranger?

- What kind of mood were you in for several hours before panic came on? Anxious? Depressed? Excited? Sad? Angry? Other?

- Were you engaging in negative or fearful thoughts just before you panicked?

- Did you feel tired or rested?

- Were you experiencing some kind of loss?

- Were you feeling hot or cold?

- Were you feeling restless or calm?

- Had you consumed caffeine or sugar just before panic came on?

- Are there any other circumstances that correlate with your panic reactions?

You can use the *Panic Attack Record* that follows to monitor every panic attack you experience over a two-week period. Make copies of the form and fill one out for each separate panic attack. Answer all the questions for the entire day from the time you awoke until the time you panicked. If the attack happens at night, answer for the day preceding that night.

By making the effort to record your panic attacks and carefully observing any circumstances that consistently precede them, you are taking an important step. You are learning that you need not be a passive victim of an event that seems totally outside your control. Instead, you can begin to alter the circumstances of your daily life in a direction that significantly reduces the odds of having panic attacks.

Panic Attack Record

Fill out one form for each separate panic attack during a two-week period.

Date: _____

Time: _____

Duration (minutes): _____

Intensity of panic (rate 5 to 10 using the *Anxiety Scale* that follows): _____

Antecedents

1. Stress level during preceding day (rate on a 1 to 10 scale where 1 is the lowest stress level and 10 is the highest): _____

2. Alone or with someone? _____

3. If with someone, was it a family member, friend(s), stranger? _____

4. Your mood for three hours preceding panic attack. Anxious _____

    Depressed _____ Excited _____ Angry _____ Sad _____

    Other (specify) _____

5. Were you facing a challenge _____ or taking it easy _____ ?

6. Were you engaging in negative or fearful thoughts before you panicked? Yes ____ No ____ If so, what thoughts? _____

7. Were you tired _____ or rested _____ ?

8. Were you experiencing some kind of emotional upset or loss? Yes ____ No ____

9. Were you feeling hot _____ cold _____ neither _____ ?

10. Were you feeling restless and impatient? Yes ____ No ____

11. Were you asleep before you panicked? Yes ____ No ____

12. Did you consume caffeine or sugar within eight hours before you panicked? Yes ____ No ____ If yes, how much? _____

13. Have you noticed any other circumstances that correlate with your panic reactions? (specify)

    _____

    _____

Learn to Discriminate Early Symptoms of Panic

With practice, you can learn to identify the preliminary signs that a panic attack may be imminent. For some individuals, this might be a sudden quickening of the heartbeat. For others it might be a tightening in the chest, sweaty hands, or queasiness. Still others might experience a slight dizziness or disorientation. Most people experience some preliminary warning symptoms before reaching the "point of no return," when a full-blown panic attack is inevitable.

It's possible to distinguish among different levels or degrees of anxiety leading up to panic by using the 10-point *Anxiety Scale* (see below).

Anxiety Scale

7–10	*Major Panic Attack*	All of the symptoms in level 6 exaggerated; terror; fear of going crazy or dying; compulsion to escape
6	*Moderate Panic Attack*	Palpitations; difficulty breathing; feeling disoriented or detached (feeling of unreality); panic in response to perceived loss of control
5	*Early Panic*	Heart pounding or beating irregularly; constricted breathing; spaciness or dizziness; definite fear of losing control; compulsion to escape
4	*Marked Anxiety*	Feeling uncomfortable or "spacey"; heart beating fast; muscles tight; beginning to wonder about maintaining control
3	*Moderate Anxiety*	Feeling uncomfortable but still in control; heart starting to beat faster; more rapid breathing; sweaty palms
2	*Mild Anxiety*	Butterflies in stomach; muscle tension; definitely nervous
1	*Slight Anxiety*	Passing twinge of anxiety; feeling slightly nervous
0	*Relaxation*	Calm; a feeling of being undistracted and at peace

The symptoms at various levels of this scale are typical, although they may not correspond exactly to your specific symptoms. The important thing is to identify what constitutes a level 4 for *you*. This is the point at which—whatever symptoms you're experiencing—*you feel your control over your reaction beginning to diminish*. Up to and through level 3, you may be feeling very anxious and uncomfortable, but you still feel that you're coping. Starting at level 4, you begin to wonder whether you can manage what's happening, which can lead to further panic. With practice, you can learn to "catch yourself"—abort a panic reaction *before* it reaches this point of no return. The more adept you become at recognizing the early warning signs of panic, up through level 4 on the scale, the more control you will gain over your panic reactions. Mark this page with a paper clip or in some other fashion, as the *Anxiety Scale* will be referred to frequently here and in subsequent chapters.

Coping Strategies to Counteract Panic at an Early Stage

First you must learn to identify your own preliminary warning signs of a potential panic attack. What are your own level 4 symptoms? Once you learn the signs, it is time to *do something* about them. Fighting panic is not a good idea, but doing nothing and just remaining passive can be even less helpful. The best solution is to utilize a number of tried-and-true coping strategies.

If you've been able to detect the early symptoms of panic before they get out of control (before they reach or exceed level 5), any of the following coping strategies can be used to prevent a full-fledged panic reaction.

Practice Abdominal Breathing

Breathing slowly from your abdomen can help reduce the bodily symptoms of panic in either of two ways:

- By slowing down your respiration and breathing from your abdomen, you can reverse two of the reactions associated with the fight-or-flight response—increased respiratory rate and increased constriction of your chest wall muscles. After three or four minutes of slow, regular, abdominal breathing, you are likely to feel that you have slowed down a "runaway reaction" that was threatening to get out of control.

- Slow, abdominal breathing, especially when done through your nose, can reduce symptoms of hyperventilation that may cause or aggravate a panic attack. The dizziness, disorientation, and tingly sensations associated with hyperventilation are produced by rapid, shallow, chest-level breathing. Three or four minutes of slow, abdominal breathing reverses this process and will eliminate hyperventilation symptoms.

- Review the section on abdominal breathing in chapter 4 along with the *Abdominal Breathing* and *Calming Breath* exercises. Pick the exercise you prefer and practice it for five minutes every day until you feel that you've mastered it. (Practicing abdominal breathing every day will also help you to retrain yourself to breathe from a deeper level in your lungs.) Once you feel comfortable and confident with a particular technique, try using it anytime you feel the initial symptoms of panic coming on. Remember to keep up slow abdominal breathing for three to five minutes until you can feel your panic symptoms beginning to subside. If the breathing exercise itself causes you to feel light-headed, stop for thirty seconds and then start again.

An alternative practice that helps some people to offset panic is simply to take a deep breath and hold it as long as you can at the moment you feel panic symptoms coming on. If you still feel anxious after this, repeat the procedure two or three times.

Repeat Positive Coping Statements

One of the central points of this chapter has been to emphasize the role of negative self-talk in aggravating a panic attack. While the physical bodily reactions associated with nic (first fear) may come out of the blue, your emotional reaction to these bodily symptoms (second fear) does not. It is based on *what you tell yourself* about these symptoms. If you tell yourself that your physiological symptoms are horrible and very threatening, that you can't stand them, that you're going to lose control, or that you might die, you will scare yourself into a very high state of anxiety. On the other hand, if you accept what's happening and make calming, reassuring statements to yourself, such as "It's only anxiety—I'm not going to let it get to me," "I've been through this before and it's not dangerous," or "I can handle this until it passes," you can minimize or eliminate the escalation of your symptoms.

Use any of the positive coping statements listed earlier in this chapter when you feel the first symptoms of panic coming on. This will help divert your mind away *both* from the bodily symptoms of panic *and* from fear-inducing self-talk that can only make things worse. Again, you may find it helpful to write several coping statements down on a 3 by 5 index card that you can carry with you at all times. Should symptoms start to come on, you simply pull the card out and repeat a particular statement over and over. Keep this up for several minutes if necessary, until you feel the physiological intensity of your panic beginning to subside.

Learning to use coping statements effectively to overcome panic will take practice and perseverance. If you make the effort, you will be surprised how well coping statements can work to prevent your anxiety symptoms from going above level 4 on the *Anxiety Scale*. Positive self-talk also can help to limit a panic attack that has already gone above level 4.

In sum, the way you respond to early physical symptoms of panic will be determined largely by *what you say to yourself*, as illustrated below.

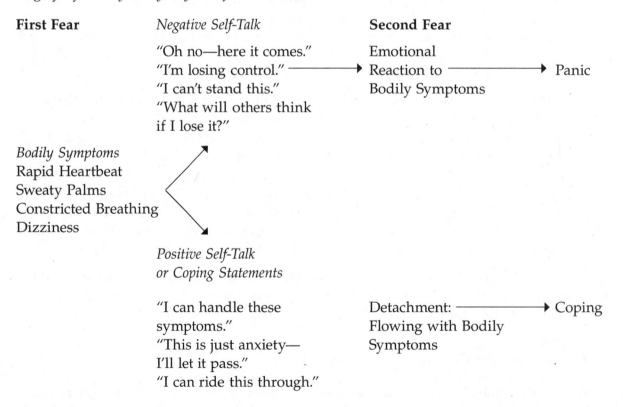

First Fear	*Negative Self-Talk*	**Second Fear**	
	"Oh no—here it comes."	Emotional	
	"I'm losing control."	Reaction to	Panic
	"I can't stand this."	Bodily Symptoms	
	"What will others think if I lose it?"		

Bodily Symptoms
Rapid Heartbeat
Sweaty Palms
Constricted Breathing
Dizziness

*Positive Self-Talk
or Coping Statements*

"I can handle these symptoms."	Detachment:	Coping	
"This is just anxiety— I'll let it pass."	Flowing with Bodily Symptoms		
"I can ride this through."			

The choice is up to you.

Use Abdominal Breathing in Combination with Coping Statements

You might find that a *combination* of abdominal breathing and repeating a positive coping statement will work best in limiting your panic. Generally, it's best to address the physical sensations of panic first with an abdominal breathing exercise and to follow up shortly thereafter with methodical repetition of a coping statement. You may prefer to completely overlap the two types of techniques or, alternatively, you may want to work exclusively on reducing your physiological arousal for a minute or two and then start working with a positive statement. Experiment to see what works better for you. I suggest that you gain some skill and familiarity with each type of strategy by itself, initially, before attempting to put them together.

Talk to a Supportive Person Nearby or on the Phone

Talking to someone can help get your mind off your anxious bodily symptoms and thoughts. Whether you are driving in a car (with a passenger or using a cell phone), standing in line at the grocery store, standing in an elevator, or flying on a plane, this can work very well. In a public speaking situation, confiding in your audience can often help to dispel initial anxiety.

Move Around or Engage in Some Physical Activity

Moving and doing something physical lets you dissipate the extra energy or adrenaline created by the fight-or-flight reaction that occurs during acute anxiety. Instead of resisting the normal physiological arousal that accompanies anxiety, you move with it. At work, you can walk to the bathroom and back or walk outdoors for ten minutes. At home, you can do household chores requiring physical activity or work out on your stationary bike or rebounder. Gardening is an excellent way to channel the physical energy of an anxiety reaction.

Stay in the Present

Focus on concrete objects around you in your immediate environment. In a grocery store, for example, you might look at the people standing around or the various magazines next to the cash register. While driving, you might focus on the cars in front of you or on the other details of the surrounding environment (so long as you don't look away from the road, of course). Staying in the present and focusing on external objects will help minimize the attention you give to troublesome physical symptoms or catastrophic "what-if" thoughts. If possible, you might try actually touching objects nearby to reinforce staying in the immediate present. Another good way to ground yourself is to focus on your legs and feet. As you're standing or walking, pay attention to your legs and feet and imagine that you are connected to the ground.

Use Simple Distraction Techniques

There are many simple repetitive acts that can help distract your attention away from your anxiety. Here are some suggestions:

- Unwrap and chew a piece of gum.

- Count backward from one hundred in threes: 100, 97, 94, and so on.

- Count the number of people in line (or all of the lines) at the grocery store.

- Count the money in your wallet.

- While driving, count the bumps on the steering wheel.

- Snap a rubber band on your wrist. This may jar your mind out of anxious thoughts.

- Take a cold shower.

- Sing.

Note: Distraction techniques are fine for helping you cope with the sudden onset of anxiety or worry. However, don't let distraction become a way of avoiding or running away from your anxiety. Ultimately, you need to directly experience anxiety and let it pass in order to habituate to it. Every time you experience a surge of anxiety and allow it to pass without trying to get away from it, you learn that you can survive whatever your nervous system dishes out. In so doing, you build confidence in your ability to manage your anxiety in any and all situations.

Get Angry with Anxiety

Anger and anxiety are incompatible responses. It's impossible to experience both at the same time. In some cases, it turns out that symptoms of anxiety are a stand-in for deeper feelings of anger, frustration, or rage. If you can get angry at your anxiety the moment it arises, you may stop it from building any further. You can do this either verbally or physically. You might say things to your symptoms such as "Get out of my way. I have things to do!" "To hell with this—I don't care what other people think!" or "This reaction is ridiculous—I'm going into this situation anyway!" This approach can be effective for some people.

Time-honored techniques for physically expressing anger include

- Pounding on a pillow on your bed with both fists

- Screaming into a pillow—or in your car alone with the windows rolled up

- Hitting a bed or a couch with a plastic baseball bat

- Throwing eggs into the bathtub (the remains wash away)

- Chopping wood

Please keep in mind that it's very important in expressing anger to direct it either into empty space or toward an object, *not at another person.* If you find yourself quite angry with someone, vent the physical charge of your anger first in one of the above ways before you attempt to communicate with that person. Rise above physical and verbal expressions of anger toward other human beings.

Experience Something Immediately Pleasurable

The feeling of pleasure is also incompatible with an anxiety state. Any of the following may help to offset anxiety, worry, or even panic:

- Have your significant other or spouse hold you (or give you a back rub).

- Take a hot shower or relax in a hot bath.

- Have a pleasurable snack or meal.

- Engage in sexual activity.

- Read humorous books or watch a comical DVD.

Learn to Observe Rather Than React to Bodily Sensations of Anxiety

You can take a major step forward by learning to detach emotionally from the first physical symptoms of panic: simply *observe* them. To the extent that you are able to *watch* the intense reactions your body goes through when aroused, and not interpret them as a threat, you will be able to save yourself considerable distress. Several of the strategies described in the previous section can help you to adopt this detached stance. By doing deep abdominal breathing, you can slow down the physiological mechanisms responsible for panic, giving yourself *time* to gain some detachment. By using positive self-talk, you replace the scare talk, which can aggravate your anxiety, with coping statements specifically designed to foster an attitude of detachment and "flowing" with the experience.

You'll find that it takes some practice to learn how to use breathing techniques and positive self-talk. Consistently working with them *will* in time enable you to reach a point where, rather than just react, you can observe and go with the bodily reactions associated with panic. This kind of detachment is the key to being able to master your panic.

What to Do When Panic Goes Above Level 4

If you are unable to arrest a panic reaction before it goes beyond your personal point of no return, observe the following guidelines:

- Get out of the panic-provoking situation if possible.

- Don't try to control or fight your symptoms—accept them and ride them out; remind yourself that panic is not dangerous and will pass.

- Call someone—express your feelings to them.

- Move around or engage in physical activity.

- Focus on simple objects around you.

- Touch the floor, touch the physical objects around you, or "ground" yourself in some other way.

- If you are in a place where you can do so, discharge tension by pounding your fists, crying, or screaming.

- Breathe slowly and regularly through your nose to reduce possible symptoms of hyperventilation.

- Use positive self-talk (coping statements) in conjunction with slow breathing.

- As a last resort, take an extra dose of a minor tranquilizer (with the general approval of your doctor).

During an intense panic attack, you may feel very confused and disoriented. Try asking yourself the following questions to increase your objectivity (you may want to write these out on a 3 by 5 index card to carry with you at all times):

- *Are these symptoms I'm feeling truly dangerous?* (Answer: "No.")

- *What is the absolute worst thing that could happen?* (Usual answer: "I might have to leave this situation quickly, or I might have to ask for assistance.")

- *Am I telling myself anything that is making this worse?*

- *What is the most supportive thing I could do for myself right now?*

Putting It All Together

In general, when anxiety symptoms start to come on, use the following three-step technique to manage them:

1. *Accept your symptoms.* Don't fight or resist them. Resisting or fleeing symptoms of anxiety tends to make them worse. The more you can adopt an attitude of acceptance, no matter how unpleasant the symptoms may be, the better will be your ability to cope. Acceptance prepares you to do something proactive about your anxiety rather than get caught up in reactions to it.

2. *Practice abdominal breathing.* When anxiety first comes up, always go to abdominal breathing first. If you've been practicing abdominal breathing regularly, merely initiating it provides a cue to your body to relax and disengage from a potential fight-or-flight response.

3. *Use a coping strategy.* After you begin to feel centered in abdominal breathing, use a coping statement or a diversion technique (for example, talking to another person or repeating coping statements) to continue to manage your feelings. Any coping strategy will reinforce the basic stance of not giving attention or energy to negative thoughts and/or uncomfortable bodily sensations. By regularly practicing coping techniques, you reinforce an attitude of mastery—instead of passive submission and victimization—in the face of your anxiety. Be aware that abdominal breathing is itself a coping strategy, and sometimes it alone will be enough.

Sharing About Your Condition

A good way to minimize the likelihood of panic in a large number of situations is simply to inform someone in charge that you have a problem with panic attacks and/or agoraphobia.

This is especially critical if you are afraid of panic attacks interfering with your capacity to perform your job. If you try to work without letting anyone know about your problem, you may come to feel increasingly trapped in the situation—trapped by your fear of what other people might think of you if you "lost it." This is likely to increase, rather than decrease, the probability of actually panicking.

If you say a little bit about your problem to your boss or a coworker, you will make your workplace into more of a "safe place." You'll worry less about what others might think if you panic, because someone important already knows. More importantly, you will have given yourself permission to temporarily leave work in the event that you do lose it. With this permission, you are much less likely to feel trapped, and any fears you might have developed about going to work are likely to dissipate.

The same applies to any other situations in which you're afraid of panicking and yet where there is someone in charge you might talk to. This includes classrooms, doctors' and dentists' offices, parties (talk to the host or hostess), or group meetings (talk to the facilitator).

To assist you in sharing about your condition, use the following *Dear Person Letter*, which is used by permission from the *TERRAP Program Manual,* by Dr. Art Hardy. (TERRAP offers group treatment programs for agoraphobia throughout the United States.) You can use the letter as the basis for developing your own script of what you want to share about your condition. The letter reprinted here deals with agoraphobia, but it can be adapted for social phobia and panic disorder as well. Either hand your letter to someone you wish to tell about your problem or read it to them.

Remember that *everyone* has experienced anxiety, and *everyone* feels uncomfortable in some situations. If you take the risk of sharing something about your condition, you'll be surprised at the support and acceptance you'll receive.

Dear Person Letter

Dear _____ :

I want to tell you something about myself. I have a problem with a type of anxiety called agoraphobia. This is *not* a mental illness, but a kind of anxiety which causes panic attacks.

Although five in one hundred people suffer from agoraphobia, some people have not heard of the condition. It is difficult for me to talk about it, but sharing this information with you is important to me.

Agoraphobia is similar to claustrophobia, except that panic attacks can be triggered by many things, such as crowds, distance from home, freeways, bridges, and/or many other situations. I can neither anticipate nor control these anxiety attacks. Because these attacks are extremely uncomfortable, sometimes terrifying, and always embarrassing, I have been avoiding situations which might arouse them.

I have found help for this problem and am making progress. At this point, I am doing some things and want to do even more, but I still need a way out of situations that are frightening to me. I have found that when other people understand that I may need to leave an uncomfortable situation, I can do better and it helps in my recovery.

It is extremely important to me to feel free to leave any given situation at any time, no matter how innocuous the situation may appear. I don't ask that you understand my condition, but I would appreciate your help.

In telling you this, I am not soliciting your sympathy, but I would like your moral support as I work toward recovery. I realize that the way I confront the problem may seem confusing and even inappropriate to you. Be assured that I have been treated by other methods but have found that the system I am using now is helping me to recover. By your acceptance, you will be working with me in licking this problem.

Summary of Things to Do

1. Reread the section "Deflate the Danger" in this chapter several times to reinforce the idea that the various symptoms of a panic attack are not dangerous.

2. Complete the first two panic attack worksheets in this chapter. Then use the third worksheet to make connections between physical sensations or symptoms that accompany your panic reactions and any catastrophic interpretations you tend to make of those sensations. Remember that it's your catastrophic self-statements that are mainly responsible for triggering panic attacks.

3. Reread the section "Don't Fight Panic" on Claire Weekes' four-step approach for coping with panic attacks to help you cultivate attitudes of acceptance and nonresistance toward panic symptoms. Learn to flow with panic rather than fight it.

4. Monitor your panic attacks for two weeks, using the *Panic Attack Record* to look for conditions and stimuli that precede your panic reactions.

5. Work on learning to recognize your own early symptoms of panic. Identify what symptoms constitute a level 4 for you on the *Anxiety Scale* (the point at which you feel like you're beginning to lose control).

6. Experiment with different coping strategies when you feel panic symptoms progressing up through level 4. Which strategies work best for you?

7. Give special attention to the following coping strategies:

   • Practice abdominal breathing (using either the *Abdominal Breathing* or the *Calming Breath* exercise from chapter 4) for five minutes per day until you've mastered the technique. Then use it to reduce arousal when you feel the initial physical symptoms of panic coming on.

   • Choose one or more coping statements and practice using them at the moment when you notice that you're starting to scare yourself with negative self-talk. Repeat your coping statements until you are able to overcome any negative self-talk going on in your head.

   • After you've gained mastery in the use of abdominal breathing and coping statements, try combining them. Start with abdominal breathing and follow this up with the repetition of a coping statement. The right combination of these techniques can be even more effective than any one of them alone.

8. Experiment with coping strategies for panic reactions *above* level 4 on the *Anxiety Scale* to find out which ones work best for you.

9. If you feel so inclined, try the symptom induction procedures. These procedures will desensitize you to physical sensations that you associate with panic. If you're working with a therapist, you may wish to ask him or her to assist you in carrying out symptom inductions.

10. Talk about your condition with a relative, a friend, or your supervisor at work, using the *Dear Person Letter* as a framework for what you say.

Further Reading

Barlow, David, and Michelle Craske. *Mastery of Your Anxiety and Panic: Workbook.* Fourth edition. New York: Oxford University Press, 2007. (Detailed presentation of the cognitive behavioral approach to treating panic.)

Beckfield, Denise F. *Master Your Panic and Take Back Your Life.* Second edition. San Luis Obispo, CA: Impact Publishers, 1998. (Thorough and useful self-help guide.)

Weekes, Claire. *Hope and Help for Your Nerves.* New York: Signet, 1991.

———. *Peace from Nervous Suffering.* New York: Bantam Books, 1978. (An excellent resource for learning to deal with panic and other forms of anxiety.)

Wilson, Reid. *Don't Panic: Taking Control of Anxiety Attacks.* Revised edition. New York: HarperCollins, 1996.

Zuercher-White, Elke. *An End to Panic.* Second edition. Oakland, CA: New Harbinger Publications, 1998.

7

Help for Phobias: Exposure

The most effective way to overcome a phobia is simply to face it. Continuing to avoid a situation that frightens you is, more than anything else, what keeps the phobia alive.

Having to face a particular situation you have been avoiding for years may at the outset seem an impossible task. Yet this task can be made manageable by breaking it down into sufficiently small steps. Instead of entering a situation all at once, you can do it very gradually in small or even minute increments.

Phobias develop as a result of *sensitization*. This is a process of becoming sensitized to a particular stimulus. In essence, you learn to associate anxiety with a particular situation. Perhaps you once panicked while sitting in a restaurant or by yourself at home. If your anxiety level was high, it's likely that you acquired a strong association between being in that particular situation and being anxious. Thereafter, being in, being near, or perhaps just thinking about that situation automatically triggered your anxiety: a connection between the situation and a strong anxiety response was established. Because this connection was automatic and seemingly beyond your control, you probably did all you could to avoid putting yourself in the situation again. Your avoidance was rewarded because it saved you from reexperiencing your anxiety. At the point where you began to *always* avoid the situation, you developed a full-fledged phobia.

Desensitization—or *exposure*—is the process of *unlearning* the connection between anxiety and a particular situation. For desensitization to occur, you need to enter a phobic situation while in a relatively relaxed state. With *real-life* desensitization, you confront a phobic situation directly, letting your anxiety rise and then subside while in the situation. (If your anxiety rises to the point where you're concerned it might get out of control, you temporarily retreat from the situation and then return to it as soon as possible.) The point is to 1) *unlearn* a connection between a phobic situation (such as driving on the freeway) and an anxiety response and 2) *reassociate* feelings of relaxation and safety with that particular situation. Repeatedly entering the situation while relaxed will eventually allow you to overcome your tendency to respond with anxiety. If you can train yourself to relax and feel safe in response to something, you will no longer feel anxious about it. Relaxation and anxiety are incompatible responses, so the goal of desensitization is to learn to remain in the phobic situation and be calm at the same time.

Real-life desensitization, or exposure, is the single most effective available treatment for phobias. In many controlled studies, direct exposure to phobic situations has consistently been found to be more effective than other, nonbehavioral treatments, such as insight therapy, cognitive therapy by itself, or medication. Nothing works better toward overcoming a fear than facing it—especially when this is done systematically and in small increments. Furthermore, improvement resulting from real-life exposure does not disappear weeks or months later. Once you've fully desensitized yourself to a phobic situation in real life, you can remain free of fear.

Real-life desensitization is the treatment of choice for agoraphobia, social phobias, and many specific phobias. It's useful in overcoming the *territorial* phobias that are common in agoraphobia—for example, fear of entering grocery stores or shopping malls, driving on bridges or freeways, riding on buses, trains, or planes, scaling heights, and being alone. *Social* phobias that respond to direct exposure include fears of public speaking, making presentations, being in groups, attending social functions, dating, using public restrooms, and taking examinations. And *specific* phobias, ranging from a fear of spiders to a fear of water or dentists, can all be overcome by direct exposure.

If real-life exposure is such an effective treatment, why are there still so many phobic people around? Why hasn't everybody availed themselves of a treatment that is so powerful? The answer is simple. For all its effectiveness, exposure isn't a particularly easy or comfortable process to go through. Not everyone is willing to tolerate the unpleasantness of facing phobic situations or to persist with practicing real-life desensitization on a regular basis. *Exposure therapy demands a strong commitment on your part.* If you're genuinely committed to your recovery, then you'll be willing to

- *Take the risk* to start facing situations you may have been avoiding for many years.

- *Tolerate the initial discomfort* that entering phobic situations—even in small increments—often involves.

- *Persist in practicing* exposure on a consistent basis, despite probable setbacks, over a long enough period of time to allow your complete recovery (generally this takes from six months to two years).

If you're ready to make a genuine commitment to real-life desensitization over a period of up to a year or two, you *will* recover from your phobias.

How to Practice Real-Life Desensitization

You can use the guidelines below to design your exposure therapy.

Set Goals

Start out by clearly defining your goals. What situations would you most like to stop avoiding? Do you want to be able to drive on the freeway alone? Buy the week's groceries by yourself? Give a presentation at work? Fly on a jet?

Be sure to make your goals specific. Instead of aiming for something as broad as being comfortable with all types of shopping, define a specific goal such as "buying the week's groceries at the local grocery store by myself" or "making a one-hour flight." Eventually you will want to remove all restrictions—in other words, be comfortable in any store or on any flight.

Once you've defined goals, set up timelines. By what date would you like to be able to give a speech, drive the freeway, or make a flight? Two months from now? One year from now? Give yourself a time frame within which to work and then make a commitment to stick with it. It's often useful to differentiate between short- and long-term goals. Use the worksheet below to define where you would like to be with your recovery process at various points in the future. Make a copy of this statement of your goals and post it in a conspicuous place to remind yourself of your plan for overcoming your fears.

GOALS

In three months:

In six months:

In one year:

Create a Hierarchy for Each Goal

For each goal you've defined, you need to create a hierarchy of exposures. A hierarchy is an incremental series of approaches to your phobic situation. You start off with a very limited exposure to the situation and then gradually, in small increments, increase your degree of exposure. For example, if you're afraid of riding in elevators, you might start out simply approaching an elevator without getting on. The next step might be to get on and off the elevator without riding it up. Then the next step would be to ride up one floor and return. After that, you would proceed to go up two floors, and so on. You can use the following guidelines, as well as sample hierarchies that appear later in the chapter, to develop your own:

1. Choose a particular phobic situation you want to work on, whether this involves going to the grocery store, driving on the freeway, or giving a talk before a group.

2. Imagine having to deal with this situation in a very limited way—one that hardly bothers you at all. In the case of going to the grocery store, this might be driving to the parking lot in front of the store and then returning home. In the case of giving a talk, this might be giving a one-minute talk to a friend in the comfort of your home. On a scale of 1 to 10, such exposures would be a 1 in intensity.

3. Now imagine what would be the strongest or most challenging exposure relating to your phobia, and place it at the opposite extreme as the highest step in your hier-

archy. For example, if you're phobic about grocery stores, your highest step might be waiting in a long line at the checkout counter by yourself. For flying, such a step might involve taking off on a transcontinental flight or encountering severe air turbulence. For public speaking, you might imagine presenting to a large crowd, giving a long presentation, or speaking on a very demanding topic. On a scale of 1 to 10, such exposures would be a 10.

4.   Now take some time to imagine six or more exposures of graduated intensity related to your phobia and rank them, on a scale of 1 to 10, according to their anxiety-provoking potential. Place these situations in ascending order between the two extremes you've already defined. Use the sample hierarchies that follow in a few pages to assist you. Then write down your list of scenes on the *Hierarchy Worksheet* later in this chapter.

Determine Scenes of Varying Intensity

Try to identify what specific parameters of your phobia make you more or less anxious and use them to develop situations of varying intensity. In the case of driving, such variables might include distance from home, whether you're driving alone or have someone with you, traffic congestion, number of stoplights, or ease of getting off the highway. In the case of public speaking, the variables might include length of the talk, the number of people you're presenting to, or how well you know the people you're presenting to.

For every phobia, there are usually one or more parameters you can use to vary the intensity of your exposure. Common variables include

- Having a support person with you (or not)
- Distance from the feared situation
- Duration of the exposure
- Proximity of an exit or way out of the situation
- General complexity of the situation (such as number of cars or people)
- Time of day

Becoming aware of the specific elements of any phobic situation that make you anxious will increase your sense of control over that situation and accelerate desensitization.

Note: If you are having difficulty moving from one step to the next in your hierarchy, you can always add an additional step. For example, suppose you're exposing yourself to grocery shopping. You've reached the point where you can stay in the store for several minutes, but you can't bring yourself to buy an item and go through the express checkout line. One intermediate step you could add would be taking an item in your basket up to the checkout line, waiting in line as long as your anxiety level remained mild, and then returning the item to where you found it. You would repeat this step without buying anything until the action became monotonous. Another example of an intermediate step would be to go through the checkout line with a support person carrying and paying for the item you picked out. After several repetitions of this, you might be ready to go through the line and buy an item on your own.

If you have a problem getting beyond a particular step, try going back to the preceding step in your hierarchy for your next practice session and working your way back up. For example, if you've mastered driving over a small bridge but have difficulty advancing to the next step, go back and repeat driving over the smaller bridge several times. The object is to get yourself so bored with the smaller bridge that you feel a strong incentive to attempt the next step up in your hierarchy. When you do, have a support person go with you.

If you have difficulty getting started with exposure therapy, try beginning with an even less challenging step than your original first step. For example, you might have a phobia about flying and you don't feel ready even to drive to the airport. As a preliminary step, watch a video that shows jets taking off and in flight, or get used to looking at photos of planes in a magazine. If you still can't make it to the airport, drive *by* it repeatedly until you feel able to drive to the airport parking lot, turn around, and return home.

Rely on a Support Person—Especially at the Beginning

It's often very helpful to rely on a person you trust (such as your spouse, your partner, a friend, or a helping professional) to accompany you on your forays into your phobia hierarchy when you first begin the process of real-life desensitization. This support person can provide reassurance and safety, distraction (by talking with you), encouragement to persist, and praise for your incremental successes.

However, your support person shouldn't push you. He or she should encourage you to enter a phobic situation without running away. But it's up to you to decide on the intensity of your exposure and to determine the point where you need to retreat. Your support person should not criticize your attempts or tell you to try harder. Yet it is good if she or he can identify any resistance on your part and help you to recognize whether such resistance is present. His or her main job is to provide encouragement and support without judging your performance. Guidelines for support people can be found at the end of this chapter.

Having a support person is often helpful and sometimes essential for getting started with exposure. However, if you want to fully conquer your phobia, you will need to eventually relinquish your support person and face your phobic situation on your own.

Optional: Try Imagery Desensitization First

Some people like to practice a technique called *imagery desensitization* before navigating a phobic situation in real life. This involves visualizing the experiences outlined in your hierarchy rather than confronting them in real life. If you wish to use this as a precursor to real-life exposure, see the section on "Imagery Desensitization" later in this chapter.

Examples of Hierarchies

Three examples follow of hierarchies developed for real-life exposure. (More examples may be found in appendix 2.) Please note that these are only sample hierarchies; your own hierarchy of phobic scenes involving elevators, grocery stores, or flying may differ depending on what aspects of the situations elicit your greatest anxiety.

Elevators

1. Look at elevators, watching them come and go.

2. Stand in a stationary elevator with your support person.

3. Stand in a stationary elevator alone.

4. Travel up or down one floor with your support person.

5. Travel up or down one floor alone, with your support person waiting outside the elevator on the floor where you will arrive.

6. Travel two to three floors with your support person.

7. Travel two to three floors alone, with your support person waiting outside the elevator on the floor where you will arrive.

8. Extend the number of floors you travel, first with your support person and then alone with your partner waiting outside the elevator.

9. Travel on an elevator alone without your support person.

Grocery Stores

1. Drive to the grocery store with your support person and spend one minute in the parking lot.

2. Drive to the grocery store with your support person and spend five minutes in the parking lot.

3. Walk up to the entrance of the grocery store and walk around outside for two minutes with your support person.

4. Repeat steps 1, 2, and 3 alone.

5. Enter the grocery store for fifteen seconds with your support person and then walk out.

6. Enter the grocery store for one minute with your support person and then walk out.

7. Walk to the back of the store with your support person and spend two minutes in the store.

8. Enter the store with your support person and go along while he or she buys one item.

9.   Enter the store with your support person and go along as he or she buys two items from different aisles.

10.   Repeat steps 5, 6, and 7 with your support person waiting outside.

11.   Enter the store with your support person and buy one item.

12.   Enter the store with your support person and buy two items from different aisles.

13.   Buy one item alone with your support person waiting outside.

14.   Buy two items alone with your support person waiting outside.

15.   Go shopping by yourself, buying only one item the first time and gradually increasing the number of items bought and your time spent inside the grocery store.

Flying

1.   Approach the airport with your support person and drive around it.

2.   Park at the airport with your support person for five minutes.

3.   Enter the terminal with your support person and walk around for five minutes.

4.   Go to the security checkpoint with your support person and stand in line for five minutes.

5.   Repeat steps 1 to 4 alone.

6.   Arrange to visit a grounded plane and spend one minute on board with your support person.

7.   Repeat step 6 but stay on board for five minutes. You might try buckling into a seat.

8.   Repeat steps 6 and 7 alone.

9.   Schedule a short flight (fifteen to thirty minutes) and go with your support person.

10.   Schedule a longer flight and go with your support person.

11.   Repeat steps 9 and 10 alone.

You can design your own hierarchy of steps for a particular phobia using the *Hierarchy Worksheet* that follows. Make several copies of this page and write down hierarchies for the specific phobias you wish to work on. You may not need all twenty steps, but try to create a minimum of eight different steps, proceeding from the least to the most challenging steps.

Hierarchy Worksheet

Hierarchy for _____

(specify phobia)

Instructions: Start with a relatively easy or mild instance of facing your phobia. Develop at least eight steps which involve progressively more challenging exposures. The final step should be your goal or even a step beyond what you've designated as your goal. Write down the date on which you complete each step as you work your way up in the hierarchy.

Step   *Date Completed*

1. _____

2. _____

3. _____

4. _____

5. _____

6. _____

7. _____

8. _____

9. _____

10. _____

11. _____

12. _____

13. _____

14. _____

15. _____

16. _____

17. _____

18. _____

19. _____

20. _____

Note: Make a copy of this sheet for each of your phobias.

Basic Procedure for Exposure

The following four steps outline what you will experience as you practice direct exposure:

1. **Enter the situation.** Proceed into your phobic situation, beginning with the first step on your hierarchy or with the one at which you last left off. Continue to proceed into the situation (or up the steps of your hierarchy) until your anxiety begins to feel somewhat uncomfortable. You can use the *Anxiety Scale* from chapter 6 to monitor your level of anxiety. In general, for exposure to proceed smoothly, you want to keep your anxiety level anywhere in the range between 1 and 4 on the scale. If it goes above level 4 for a few moments, that's fine in most cases. However, if it continues to stay above 4 or go higher, it's best to briefly retreat from the situation. If it feels manageable, great. *Just stay in your fearful situation until your anxiety begins to subside.* Even if you are uncomfortable in the situation, stay with it as long as your anxiety level does not go to the point where it begins to feel unmanageable. *Allow time to pass and let your anxiety diminish.* When undertaking exposure, it's very helpful to practice the abdominal breathing technique described in chapter 4. Breathing from your abdomen can help to diffuse some of the anxiety that comes up.

2. **Retreat if (and only if) your anxiety starts to feel "out of control."** If your anxiety feels like it's starting to get unmanageable (above 5 on the *Anxiety Scale*), then you should temporarily retreat from the situation. Retreating means briefly leaving the situation until you feel better and then returning as soon as possible. It's always best to try to stay in the situation, accept the discomfort you feel, and wait for the anxiety to subside. But if you feel you're starting to head for unmanageable anxiety or panic, it's best to retreat and then return to the situation as soon as possible.

   In many situations, this is easy to do. If you're driving on the freeway, you can pull over onto the shoulder or get off at the nearest exit. If you're sitting in a restaurant, you can retreat to the restroom and then return. If you're flying, you can't leave the plane, but you can retreat to a safe place in your mind (or use a recorded visualization—see chapter 4). Remember that retreat is not the same thing as escape—the idea is to temporarily leave the situation and then return.

Note: There are many anxiety experts who advocate continuing to expose to a phobic situation, no matter how high anxiety rises. The problem with this is that, if you actually panic during exposure, you can risk resensitizing yourself to the situation and reinforcing the strength of the phobia. While it's best to always try to endure discomfort you feel during exposure, it's also helpful to be able to temporarily retreat if your anxiety seems headed toward unmanageability or panic.

3. **Recover.** Whether you stay in the situation or temporarily retreat, eventually stay in the situation until you allow any anxiety that comes up to subside. Be sure to give yourself sufficient time for this to happen. You may find that abdominal breathing or walking around at this point helps you to recover your equanimity.

4. **Continue.** After recovering, continue to progress deeper into the situation (or further up your hierarchy). Accept anxiety symptoms if they come up and allow them to subside. Do not chastise yourself if your performance after retreating turns out to be less spectacular than it was initially. This is a common experience. In a day or two, you'll find that you'll be able to continue in your progression up your hierarchy.

    Continue going through the above cycle—expose-retreat (if necessary)-recover-continue—until you begin to feel tired or bored, then stop for the day. Progress through as many steps in your hierarchy as you feel able to. This constitutes one practice session, and it will typically take you from thirty minutes to two hours. In general, longer exposure sessions achieve more rapid results than short sessions do, but go at your own pace. For most people, one practice session per day is enough. Be aware that your progress through the steps in your hierarchy is likely to be uneven. On some days, you'll enjoy excellent progress, perhaps going through several steps. On other days, you will have to repeat the same step several times. Other days you may hardly progress at all, and on still others you will not go as far as you did on preceding days. On a given Monday, you might spend five minutes alone in the grocery store for the first time in years. On Tuesday, you may endure five minutes again but no more. Then on Wednesday, you may be unable to go into the store at all. On Thursday or Friday, however, you may then discover that you can last ten minutes in the store. This up-and-down, two-steps-forward, one-step-back phenomenon is typical of exposure therapy. Don't let it discourage you!

Making the Most of Exposure

These instructions are intended to help you get the most out of real-life desensitization:

1. *Be willing to take risks.*

    Entering a phobic situation that you've been avoiding for a long time is going to involve taking a mild to moderate risk. There's simply no risk-free way to face your fears and recover. Risk-taking is easier, however, when you start with small, limited goals and proceed incrementally. Establishing a hierarchy of phobic situations allows you to take this incremental approach toward mastering your phobias.

2. *Deal with resistance.*

    Undertaking exposure to a situation that you've been avoiding may bring up resistance. Notice if you delay getting started with your exposure sessions or find reasons to procrastinate. The mere thought of actually entering a phobic situation may elicit strong anxiety, a fear of being trapped, or self-defeating statements to yourself, such as "I'll never be able to do it" or "This is hopeless." Instead of getting stuck in resistance, try to regard the process of desensitization as a major therapeutic opportunity. By plunging in, you will learn about yourself and work through long-standing avoidance patterns that have held up your life. Give yourself pep talks about how much your life and relationships will improve when you are no longer plagued by your phobias.

You might also want to review the section on motivation under "Necessary Ingredients for Undertaking Your Own Recovery Program" in chapter 3. Consider whether there are any secondary gains that might be contributing to your resistance.

Once you get through any initial resistance to real-life exposure, the going gets easier. If you feel you're having problems with resistance at any point, you may want to consult a therapist who is familiar with exposure therapy.

3. *Be willing to tolerate some discomfort.*
    Facing situations that you've been avoiding for a long time is not particularly comfortable or pleasant. It's inevitable that you will experience some anxiety in the course of becoming desensitized. In fact, it is common to feel *worse initially,* at the outset of exposure therapy, before you feel better. Recognize that feeling worse is *not* an indication of regression but rather that exposure is really *working.* Feeling worse means that you're laying the foundation to feel better. As you gain more skill in handling symptoms of anxiety when they come up during exposure, your practice sessions will become easier and you'll gain more confidence about following through to completion.

4. *Avoid flooding—be willing to retreat.*
    Your exposure sessions are entirely different from the phobic situations you are forced into by circumstance. In the process of desensitization, you are in control of the intensity and length of your exposure to the situations that frighten you: circumstance does not offer this luxury. Always be willing to retreat from a practice situation if your anxiety exceeds level 4 on the *Anxiety Scale.* Then wait until you recover before confronting the phobic situation again. *Retreat is not cowardly*—it is the most efficient and expedient way to master a phobia. Overexposure, or *flooding,* may resensitize you to a situation and ultimately prolong the time it takes to overcome your phobia.

5. *Plan for contingencies.*
    Suppose you're practicing on an elevator and the worst happens—it stops between floors. Or suppose you are just beginning to drive on the freeway and you start to panic when you're far away from an exit. It's good to plan ahead for those worst-case scenarios whenever possible. In the first example, give yourself some insurance by practicing on an elevator that has a functioning emergency phone. Or in the case of the freeway, tell yourself in advance that it will be all right to retreat to the shoulder or at least to drive slowly with your emergency flashers on until you reach an exit. If you'll be entering a situation that doesn't have a "trapdoor," such as flying, keep your list of coping statements (see chapter 6) near at hand or bring along a relaxation audio recording and portable media player with headphones (see chapter 4 or appendix 3).

6. *Plan your exposures in advance.*
    When you first begin to practice exposure, you may be inclined to do it spontaneously, only when you most feel like it. Practicing only when you want to—on your so-called good days—may certainly help you to get started in facing situations

you've been avoiding for a long time. However, once you've made a start, it's best to plan your exposure practices ahead of time. Make the effort to do them on both your "good" and "bad" days alike. If you wait only for good days to practice, you'll tend to put it off until you feel better, which will slow your progress. While you may have more anticipatory anxiety when facing planned exposures, this anxiety will recede as you begin to have successes with your practice.

7. *Trust your own pace.*
   It's important not to regard real-life exposure as some kind of race. The goal is not to see how fast you can overcome the problem: pressuring yourself to make great strides quickly is generally not a good idea. In fact, to do so carries a risk of resensitizing yourself to your phobia if you attempt advanced steps in your hierarchy before becoming fully comfortable with earlier steps. Decide on the pace you wish to adopt in exposing yourself to a difficult situation, realizing that very small gains count for a lot in this type of work.

8. *Let go of the need for complete control.*
   Work on accepting the fact that some things are under your control while others are not. You can control the car when you're the driver, but you need to relinquish control when you're a passenger on a bus or airplane. You can control how far you choose to drive from home, but you can't control traffic, lines in the store, or how an elevator works. Use abdominal breathing and coping statements, such as "Let go and trust," "I'll do the best I can," or even "God is with me," to help you accept those situations that you can't completely control.

9. *Reward yourself for small successes.*
   It's common for people going through real-life desensitization to castigate themselves for not making sufficiently rapid progress. Bear in mind that it's important to consistently reward yourself for small successes. For example, being able to go into a phobic situation slightly further than the day before is worthy of giving yourself a reward, such as a trip to the ice cream parlor, a new plant for your garden, or a dinner out. So is being able to stay in the situation a few moments longer—or being able to tolerate anxious feelings a few moments longer. Rewarding yourself for small successes will help sustain your motivation to keep practicing.

10. *Learn to cope with the early stages of panic.*
   Use your array of coping techniques (see chapter 6) if you are unable to easily retreat from a situation when your anxiety reaches level 4. It may help to

   * Do deep abdominal breathing

   * Use affirmative self-talk

   * Converse with your support person

   * Distract yourself (such as by counting the number of blue cars on the freeway)

   * Get angry with the anxiety

Remember to maintain an overall attitude of floating, or going with your bodily sensations rather than balking or resisting them. Using abdominal breathing and positive self-talk in combination often helps. As soon as retreat becomes possible, use this option!

11. ***Use positive coping statements when entering a phobic situation.***
Repeating positive statements over and over before or during exposure sessions can be quite helpful. Repetition of coping statements serves to direct your attention away from physical symptoms of anxiety and prevents you from talking yourself into a higher level of panic. Such statements encourage a confident and composed attitude that can help you through the most difficult moments in your exposure practice. Use the list of positive coping statements provided later in this chapter. You may want to write some of them on a 3 by 5 index card that you carry with you during your practice sessions.

12. ***Practice regularly.***
Practicing methodically and regularly—rather than hurrying or pressuring yourself—will do the most to expedite your recovery. Ideally, it is good to practice real-life desensitization *three to five times per week*. Longer practice sessions, with several trials of exposure to your phobic situation, tend to produce more rapid results than shorter sessions. As long as you retreat when appropriate, it's impossible to undergo too much exposure in a given practice session (the worst that can happen is that you might end up somewhat tired or drained).

The *regularity* of your practice will determine the rate of your recovery. If you're not practicing regularly, notice what excuses you're making to yourself and sit down with someone else to evaluate them. Then find arguments for refuting those excuses the next time they come up. Regular practice of exposure is *the key* to a full and lasting recovery.

13. ***Expect and know how to handle setbacks.***
Not being able to tolerate as much exposure to a situation as you did previously is a normal part of recovery. Recovery simply doesn't proceed in a linear fashion—there will be plateaus and regressions as well as times of moving forward. Setbacks are an integral part of the recovery process.

For example, suppose you are working on overcoming a phobia about driving on freeways. Your practice sessions over a four-week period might go like this:

Week 1: During three out of five practice sessions you can drive the distance of one exit on the freeway.

Week 2: For five out of five practice sessions you can't get on the freeway at all. (This degree of regression is not at all uncommon.)

Week 3: For two out of five practice sessions you are able to drive the distance of one exit. During two other sessions you're able to drive the distance of two exits. One day you can't get on the freeway at all.

Week 4: Due to illness, you only get in two practice sessions. On one of those days, you're able to manage three exits.

It's very important not to let a setback discourage you from further practice. Simply chalk it up to a bad day or bad week and learn from it. Nothing can take away the progress you've made up to now. You can use each setback as a learning experience to tell you more about how to best proceed in mastering a particular phobic situation.

14. ***Be prepared to experience stronger emotions.***
Facing phobic situations you've been avoiding for a long time often stirs up suppressed feelings—not only of anxiety but of anger and sorrow as well. Recognize that this is a normal and expected part of the recovery process. *Allow* these feelings to surface and let yourself express them. Let yourself know that it's okay to have these feelings even though you may be uncomfortable with them. An important part of recovery from a phobic condition is learning to accept, express, and communicate your feelings (see chapter 12).

15. ***Follow through to completion.***
Finishing exposure therapy means that you reach a point where you are no longer afraid of panic attacks in *any* situation that was formerly a problem (obviously this does not include extreme situations that anyone would be afraid of). The recovery process generally takes from six months to two years to complete. Getting comfortable with most situations but still having one or two that you are afraid of is generally insufficient. To attain lasting freedom from your phobias, it's important to keep working until you get to the point where 1) you can go into any situation that non-phobic people would regard as safe and 2) you regard panic reactions themselves as manageable and not at all dangerous.

Put aside props and crutches—eventually.
In the early to middle stages of exposure, relying on props and crutches, such as a support person, a tranquilizer, a cell phone, or a lucky pendant, may be necessary and useful in helping you to reduce anxiety. If your goal is merely to be able to cope with facing difficult situations, such as driving on expressways, flying, or giving a talk, you may choose to continue to rely on such resources indefinitely. There's nothing wrong with this if your goal is simply to be able to *cope* with the situation. However, if your goal is to *fully* overcome your phobia, then you eventually will need to relinquish all such props and crutches. These devices can subtly reinforce a tendency to be afraid of a phobic situation. You unconsciously tell yourself, "I can handle the situation only with my safety crutch—without it, I can't." When you can enter into your phobic situation comfortably without a support person, medication, cell phone, or other security objects, you've achieved the highest level of mastery.

Some therapists encourage their phobic clients to dispose of any and all techniques or objects that might reduce anxiety, including such basic skills as abdominal breathing and coping statements. This seems to me a bit extreme. I would encourage you to continue to use all of the coping skills described in this chapter, but to let go of safety crutches, such as support people, cell phones, and tranquilizers, when you get toward the high end of your hierarchy. Also you should practice on days when you aren't feeling well along with the days you feel better. The point is to be able to deal with your phobic situation under any and all circumstances. Then you truly have nothing to be afraid of. You won't be telling yourself, "I can do it only if …"

Maintaining the Right Attitude

Approaching fearful situations with the *right attitude* is as important as (if not more important than) learning specific strategies for exposure. If you begin with the right attitude, then utilizing appropriate techniques becomes much easier. The following five attitudes are particularly important in increasing your ability to effectively face and overcome your fears.

Accept Bodily Symptoms of Anxiety

Recall Claire Weekes' four points, stated in chapter 6: 1) *face* your symptoms, 2) *accept* your body's reaction, 3) *float* with the wave of anxiety, and 4) *allow time to pass*. Struggling with bodily symptoms of anxiety that arise while facing something difficult will make them worse. Trying to deny or run away from them will also make them worse. *Acceptance* of the bodily symptoms of anxiety is the first thing you need to do when anxiety comes up, whether spontaneously or in a phobic situation. It's an attitude you can learn and cultivate.

Stay Grounded in the Present Moment

Anxiety begins as a physical reaction and is aggravated further by "what-if" or catastrophic thoughts. The more you can stay grounded in your body in the present moment, the less you'll be carried away by such thoughts.

Abdominal breathing is an excellent way to stay grounded in your body. Breathing is a process that is centered in your body rather than your mind. Another helpful strategy is to focus on your arms and legs while you breathe. The more attention you can bring down to your arms and legs, the less involved you're likely to be in your thoughts.

Know That Fear Always Passes

No state of anxiety is permanent—it always passes. The body metabolizes excess adrenaline in five to ten minutes, so the worst degree of panic you might ever experience is not likely to last beyond this. Lesser degrees of anxiety may persist longer than a few minutes, but they, too, will eventually pass. *Sooner or later, whatever you have constructed in your mind as threatening disappears because your mind stops focusing on it and moves on to something else.*

If You're Anxious About Something, You're Already Desensitizing to It

When you face something you fear, you almost inevitably experience some anxiety. Rather than magnifying the anxiety with further anxious thoughts, reframe it with the attitude "This anxiety is good: it means I'm already beginning to desensitize." Or you can say, "I need this anxiety—I can't desensitize without feeling it." It's true—you cannot desensitize to anxiety without at first feeling it to some extent. The path out of anxiety starts with directly experiencing it. If you know this, facing what you fear becomes easier. Every time your anxiety recurs, you can confidently remind yourself you are a step closer to being done with it.

Desensitization Always Works—with Practice

There is no fear that cannot be overcome by repeated exposure or desensitization. Habituation always defeats fear, if you're willing to persevere with facing what you fear again and again. Anxiety is based on the projection of frightening outcomes in the face of something not fully known. Once that "something" becomes fully known and familiar, it invariably loses its ability to evoke fear. Desensitization always works—with practice. Truly knowing that fact will help give you courage to persist in facing your fear, no matter how challenging it may appear at the outset.

Factors That Can Promote or Impede Your Success

Numerous studies have examined the conditions affecting the success of exposure therapy. This section summarizes the findings of this research. For a more detailed discussion, see David Barlow's *Anxiety and Its Disorders: The Nature and Treatment of Anxiety and Panic* (see especially chapter 11).

What Promotes Success

1. *Cooperation of Your Partner or Spouse*
    When your partner or spouse supports your recovery and is willing to assist you in the exposure process itself, results are often excellent. Conversely, if your partner is indifferent, is uncooperative, or consciously or unconsciously opposes your recovery, success with exposure may be difficult to attain. If you feel that your partner is interfering with your progress in overcoming your phobias, you both may want to consult a competent couples' therapist who is knowledgeable about the treatment of phobias.

2. *Willingness to Tolerate Some Discomfort*
    As discussed in the previous section, it is inevitable that you will feel more anxiety when you begin to confront phobic situations in real life. Practicing exposure

therapy is hard work and requires a willingness to tolerate some discomfort. It may be tempting not to begin or not to follow through with exposure because you dread the unpleasantness involved. That is why it is so important to reward yourself for your efforts. In some cases, *low* doses of a minor tranquilizer may be a useful adjunct in the early stages of exposure therapy. Low doses of a minor tranquilizer can reduce your anxiety just enough to make the process feasible while still allowing desensitization to occur. (See chapter 17 for a more detailed discussion of the pros and cons of using tranquilizers.)

3. *Ability to Handle the Initial Symptoms of Panic*
   Fear of having a panic attack is perhaps the greatest deterrent to undertaking a course of real-life desensitization. If you've developed a broad repertory of skills for handling the early symptoms of panic (as detailed in chapter 6), you can approach exposure with considerable confidence. These days, many phobia treatment programs train clients to cope with physical reactions associated with panic *before* beginning a program of gradual exposure.

4. *Ability to Handle Setbacks*
   Some people stop their program of exposure after experiencing one or two setbacks, failing to recognize that setbacks are a normal and predictable part of the process. Your ability to tolerate setbacks and still persist in your daily practice sessions will be a crucial determinant of your success.

5. *Willingness to Practice Regularly*
   Regular, consistent practice—in other words, three to five times per week—is unquestionably the *strongest* predictor of success with exposure. There is simply no substitute for regular practice. It has been my experience over the years that the clients who practice regularly are the ones who recover. There is no phobia that cannot be overcome by a steady and persistent commitment to practicing exposure. This is definitely an area of human experience where "persistence wins the race."

What Interferes with Success

The opposite of any of the above-mentioned conditions will tend to impede your success with exposure: lack of cooperation from your partner, your own inability to tolerate some discomfort, a lack of skills for coping with panic, an unwillingness to retreat when retreat is appropriate, an inability to handle setbacks, and/or an unwillingness to practice consistently. In addition, clinical research has shown that the following two factors can impede success with exposure therapy:

Depression
People who suffer from clinical depression associated with agoraphobia or social phobia are generally less motivated to practice exposure. They also have a tendency to discount successes and progress when they do practice. Common symptoms of clinical depression include

- Fatigue and lack of energy

- Self-reproach and feelings of worthlessness

- Loss of interest or pleasure in usual activities

- Difficulty concentrating

- Reduced appetite

- Difficulty sleeping

- Suicidal thoughts

If you feel you're experiencing three or more of the above symptoms, it would be advisable to have a clinical consultation before undertaking a self-paced program of exposure. Cognitive behavioral therapy is an extremely effective treatment for depression. In more serious cases, antidepressant medication, taken under a doctor's supervision, can help lift your mood enough to allow you to practice real-life desensitization.

Alcohol and Tranquilizers

Alcohol or high doses of minor tranquilizers tend to interfere with exposure. It's necessary to experience *some* anxiety during exposure to a phobic situation if you are to learn new and more adaptive responses to it. People who undergo exposure therapy while on high doses of minor tranquilizers often relapse when they go off the medication. This is less likely when you've been taking a low dosage (for example, 0.5 milligrams or less of Xanax per day). In fact, *low* doses of tranquilizers may in some cases be helpful toward undertaking and maintaining a program of exposure.

Using Coping Statements During Exposure

It's often helpful when doing real-life exposure to work with coping statements. These are positive statements you can say to yourself just before you begin to face your phobic situation—or during the exposure process itself. If you have a problem with public speaking, for example, you would use them before you do your presentation. With most other phobias, you can use coping statements before or during exposure.

The purpose of using coping statements is to help distract your mind from any negative, anxiety-provoking self-talk you might be prone to engage in when you face what you fear. These positive statements also help put your mind in a positive frame. They can help you relax and maintain your confidence just before or during the time you confront your phobia. Any anxiety you experience during exposure tends to make you more suggestible. By repeating positive coping statements at the time of exposure, you will induce a positive state of mind which can help keep your anxiety at a lower level.

There are two ways in which you might want to work with coping statements. First, you might want to make an audio recording of your favorite statements and listen to them right before you directly confront your phobic situation. If you have a portable media player, you might even want to listen to them during the exposure process itself.

An alternative, more active way to work with coping statements is to write them down on 3 by 5 cards—one or two statements per card. Keep the cards in your purse or wallet and then take them out and rehearse the coping statements before or during your real-life exposure sessions. Some people find repeating a single coping statement over and over to be more effective, while others like to read down a list of several coping statements at once.

Keep in mind that to get the most benefit from coping statements, you will need to practice working with them many times. They may not be as effective in offsetting anxiety the first few times you use them as they will be after repeated practice. It took many repetitions to reinforce the negative, anxiety-provoking self-statements that trigger your anxiety. By the same token, it will take repeated use of positive coping statements—before or during real-life exposure—to reach a point where you fully internalize them.

The following coping statements are divided into three categories: statements to use when you are *preparing* to face your phobic situation; statements you can use when you *first confront* the situation and *during* the exposure process; and, finally, statements you can use to help you *handle any symptoms or feelings* that come up during exposure.

Preparing to Face Your Phobia

- Today I'm willing to go just a little outside my comfort zone.

- This is an opportunity for me to learn to become comfortable with this situation.

- Facing my fear is the best way to overcome my anxiety about it.

- Each time I choose to face my fear, I take another step toward becoming free of it.

- By taking this step now, I'll eventually be able to do what I want.

- There's no right way to do this. Whatever happens is fine.

- I know I'll feel better once I'm actually in the situation.

- Whatever I do, I'll do the best I can.

- I praise myself for being willing to confront my fear.

- There's always a way to retreat from this situation if I need to.

First Confronting (and During Exposure to) Your Phobia

- I've handled this before and I can handle it now.

- Relax and go slowly. There's no need to push right now.

- I can take some abdominal breaths and take my time.

- Nothing serious is going to happen to me.

- It's okay to take my time with this and do only as much as I'm ready to do today.

- I'm going to be all right. I've succeeded with this before.

- I don't have to do this perfectly. I can let myself be human.

- I can think about being in my peaceful place as I undertake this.

- I can monitor my anxiety level and retreat from this situation if I need to.

- This is not as bad as I thought.

- As I continue to practice exposure, it will get easier.

For Feeling Trapped

- I can accept this as it is for now.

- Being "trapped" is a perception, and I can change that perception. My thinking makes me feel trapped—I can change my thinking and feel free.

Coping with Bodily Sensations and Feelings That Come Up During Exposure

- I can handle these symptoms or sensations.

- These sensations are just a reminder to use my coping skills.

- I can take some abdominal breaths and allow these feelings to pass.

- These feelings will pass and I'll be okay.

- This is just adrenaline—it will pass in a few minutes.

- This will pass soon.

- These are just thoughts—not reality.

- This is just anxiety—I'm not going to let it get to me.

- Nothing about these sensations or feelings is dangerous.

- I don't need to let these feelings and sensations stop me. I can continue to function.

- It's always okay to retreat for a while if I need to.

Guidelines for Your Support Person

Support people come in many guises, including spouses, lovers, relatives, friends, other people with phobias, recovered phobics, and therapists. The most important characteristics of an effective support person include a caring and supportive attitude, the ability to be non-judgmental, patience, and a willingness to encourage you to face your fears with persistence.

The following guidelines are intended for support people who may work with you during your exposure therapy:

1. Be familiar with the material presented in this workbook, especially the concepts of desensitization, retreat, and the *Anxiety Scale*.

2. Assist the phobic in defining specific goals for each practice session. For example, if your partner is practicing driving on the local expressway, discuss exactly how many exits he or she would like to try driving past before getting off. At what time of day and under what traffic conditions does your partner want to do exposure? Or, if your partner is practicing exposure to grocery shopping, discuss exactly how long he or she would like to try staying in the store and how far back into the store he or she wants to try to go.

3. Before beginning an exposure practice session, communicate clearly with your phobic partner about what is expected of you during practice. Does your partner want you to talk to her or him a good deal? Stay right with her or him? Follow behind? Wait outside the door to the store or at the cash register? Hold her or his hand?

4. If your partner is easily overwhelmed, help break each problem down into small, incremental steps. See the hierarchies in appendix 2 for examples.

5. It's up to the phobic—not the partner—to define the goals of a given practice session. Partners should be cooperative rather than assuming the initiative. Let the phobic decide just how far he or she is willing to go with exposure. Don't pressure your partner to do anything he or she is unready or unwilling to do.

6. Partners should be familiar with their phobic partner's early warning signs of anxiety. Encourage your partner to verbalize when he or she begins to feel initial symptoms of panic (reaching level 4 on the *Anxiety Scale*). Don't be afraid to ask from time to time how your partner is doing.

7. Create with your phobic partner a list of coping statements and relaxation procedures that you can remind him or her to use during exposure sessions.

8. Don't allow your partner's distress to rattle you, but don't fail to take it seriously. Remember that anxiety isn't necessarily rational. In case of a panic attack, quietly lead your partner away from the threatening situation, end the practice session for the day, and take your partner home. Above all, stay close by until the panic completely subsides.

9. A hug can go much further than a lot of words. If you see that your partner is frightened in a particular situation, your hug or the offer of your hand will help relieve anxiety better than any lecture about how there is no reason to be afraid.

10. Be reliable. Be where you say you're going to be during a practice session. Don't move to another location because you want to test your partner. It can be very frightening for the phobic to return to a prearranged meeting place and find you gone.

11. Don't push a person with phobias! Phobics know what's going on in their body and may panic if pushed further than they're ready to go at a particular point in their recovery. Let the phobic tell you when to end the practice session.

12. On the other hand, encourage your partner to make the most out of practice. It's better to attempt to enter a frightening situation and have to retreat than not to try at all. Your phobic partner's resistance may be making practice impossible or may be impeding progress. If your partner seems stalled or unmotivated to practice, ask what is getting in the way of proceeding. Assist, if you can, in exploring and identifying psychological resistance.

13. In spite of all your desire to help, phobics must retain responsibility for their own recovery. Be supportive and encouraging, but avoid trying to step in and do it all for them. This will only undermine their confidence. To recover, phobics need to develop their own sense of identity and self-sufficiency.

14. Try to see things from the phobic's point of view. Things that seem insignificant to others—such as walking two blocks down a street or eating in a restaurant—may involve a great deal of work and courage for the phobic to achieve, even for a short period of time. These accomplishments and the efforts leading to them should be recognized.

15. Phobics generally are very sensitive and need a great deal of praise for every step they take. Be sure to give your partner recognition for small achievements. Praise him or her for whatever is accomplished and be understanding and accepting of regressions.

16. Express confidence in the phobic. When doubts arise, let the phobic know you believe she or he can succeed in recovery with persistence.

17. Encourage practice with rewards. For example, you might say, "When you can handle restaurants, let's have lunch together somewhere special."

18. Accept the phobic's "bad" days and reinforce the idea that he or she can't have a perfect day every time. Temporary setbacks are part of the normal course of exposure therapy.

19. It may be necessary to readjust your own schedule to facilitate your partner's practice. Be sure you're willing to make a commitment to work with your partner regularly over a sustained period of time before offering to be a support person. If you're unable to see her or him through the full period of recovery (which can typically take six months to two years), let your partner know specifically how long a commitment you can make.

20. Know your own limits. Be forgiving of yourself when you're a less-than-perfect partner. If your capacity to be supportive has been stretched to the limit, take a break.

A Positive Attitude

What are some of the positive attitudes you need to be truly helpful to your phobic partner? The following ten are based on the experience of Karen Williams, a recovered agoraphobic, who now works as a paraprofessional support person. See her excellent book, *How to Help Your Loved One Recover from Agoraphobia,* for an in-depth treatment of the subject of how to be an effective support person.

1. *Acceptance.* Accept your partner just at where she or he is. Don't deny that this is a legitimate disorder or judge your partner negatively because of her or his limitations. Accepting the problem as real is a prerequisite for offering any genuine help.

2. *Understanding.* Agoraphobia appears irrational to anyone who does not understand it. Take the time to educate yourself about the problem by reading up on it and/or discussing it with your partner's therapist.

3. *Sincerity.* Sincerity means you truly care about and can get behind the agoraphobic's efforts to recover. When you offer encouraging words or praise for accomplishments, your partner can see that you really mean it.

4. *Compassion.* Even if you've never experienced agoraphobia yourself, strive to have empathy for the phobic's suffering. In short, feel for the other person. Expressing your empathy in your words and tone of voice will make a big difference.

5. *Encouragement.* It's important to encourage the phobic to keep persisting with exposure, especially during setbacks. On days when the phobic feels overwhelmed or imagines he or she just can't cope, keep instilling the attitude "You can do it."

6. *Patience.* Recognize that at times the phobic's progress may be quite slow. You will need to cultivate patience if you've made a commitment to stay with her or him over the long run.

7. *Recognition.* Remember to recognize the phobic's accomplishments, even if they are small. A steady diet of praise for small achievements will help sustain the phobic's motivation to keep practicing.

8. *Trustworthiness.* To foster a good working relationship with the phobic, you need to keep your agreements. Show up for practice sessions at the appointed time. Ask whether the phobic wants you to accompany him or her or wait at a particular location while he or she practices, and then be where you say you'll be. Be careful not to make any promises that you're unprepared to keep.

9. *Participation.* Beyond accompanying the phobic during exposure practice, it helps to participate actively in her or his treatment. If possible, arrange to attend at least one individual or group treatment session and meet the phobic's therapist. If you're a friend rather than a family member, meet the phobic's family.

10.   *Give the phobic responsibility.* A phobic person is ultimately responsible for his or her own recovery. In practicing exposure, let the phobic take the lead and decide how much he or she is willing to do. And let the phobic determine when the session is over. Your job is to support and encourage your partner's efforts. Recovery from agoraphobia (and, indeed, any anxiety disorder) is a journey toward self-sufficiency and autonomy. Be sure you encourage the phobic's *independence*—not prolonged dependence on you.

What to Avoid

What is it best to avoid doing as a support person? Use the following list of problem behaviors for quick reference.

- Avoid criticizing the phobic unless it's truly constructive.

- Avoid ridiculing, labeling, or otherwise putting the phobic down. It's true that living with a person restricted by phobias can be frustrating. However, lashing out will only cause alienation.

- Don't compare the phobic with other people, especially those who don't suffer from agoraphobia.

- Don't pressure the phobic to do anything before she or he is ready.

- Don't change the plan for a given practice session. If you and the phobic decide the goal for the session is to walk three blocks, don't suddenly suggest the idea of going an additional block or two toward the end of the session. (If the *phobic* decides to expand the goal during exposure, that's fine.)

- Don't placate the phobic. If the phobic makes excuses about not practicing, it's better to gently confront him or her about this than to simply agree. You might say, "You seem not to be doing your practice. What do you think is getting in the way of making a commitment to it?"

- Don't psychoanalyze. It's your job as a support person to offer encouragement and support, not to tell the phobic what you think is wrong with him or her or how he or she got that way.

- Don't lecture or preach. Assume a cooperative—not an authoritarian—stance. Refrain from telling the phobic what to do or not to do.

- Avoid setting time limits. Respect the phobic's own pace of recovery, even if it's slow. Pressuring someone to succeed within a time limit may sabotage progress. *If you feel the phobic is genuinely stuck, seek professional help.*

- Avoid overextending yourself. Know and express your limits in working with the phobic. You can maintain your commitment to help without doing more than you have energy and resources to handle. This may involve not always meeting the phobic's requests (or demands). Take time out from your relationship with the phobic to pursue your own creative hobbies, interests, and goals.

- Don't ever give up on the phobic. Recovery from phobias takes persistent effort over a long period of time. Your willingness to persevere and stay with the phobic, even during setbacks, will help teach him or her a similar attitude. In general, if the phobic receives appropriate treatment—and engages in that treatment—he or she should make substantial gains in one to two years.

When Are Medications Useful?

The emphasis of this chapter up to this point has been to offer practical strategies you can use to help you face and overcome your phobias in real life. If practiced regularly and conscientiously, these strategies are very effective. Direct exposure has repeatedly proven itself to be the most helpful method for overcoming phobias.

Sometimes, however, it is difficult for some people to get started with exposure. When your anxiety level is very high, or you've been avoiding particular situations for a long time, your initial resistance to beginning the first few sessions of exposure may be strong. You may, quite literally, have difficulty "getting out the door." It is in this situation that medication can sometimes be useful. While not providing a long-term solution, medication can sometimes help you get over initial blocks and barriers to getting started. Once you've gained more confidence about being able to handle previously avoided situations, your medication can gradually be phased out.

Two types of medication may be useful in facilitating early exposure. Both types can reduce the frequency and intensity of panic attacks sufficiently to help you get past your initial resistance. In so doing, they will also tend to reduce anticipatory anxiety.

- The SSRI antidepressant medications, such as Lexapro and Zoloft (see chapter 17), often help by reducing both anxiety and depression. This can certainly help increase motivation to undertake exposure. It's usually necessary to take these medications for three to four weeks before therapeutic benefits will occur. Also, if you're sensitive to these medications, it's best to start out with a *low dose, for example, one-half or even one-fourth of a tablet per day*, and gradually work up to 1 tablet per day, usually taken in the morning.

- A low dose of a benzodiazepine tranquilizer, such as .5 mg Klonopin or .25 mg Xanax, can be taken about one half hour prior to your practice session. With benzodiazepines, two conditions need to be observed. First, it's important that the dose be low, since if you take a dose high enough to mask your anxiety, you will not experience desensitization. It's always necessary to experience some anxiety for desensitization to be effective. Second, if possible, use the medication *only* before you go out to practice. Taking the medication several times per day, although this is sometimes necessary and often the way prescribed, is more likely to lead to dependence and eventual addiction. If you are not taking any medication, I suggest you try the antidepressant approach before trying a low dose of a benzodiazepine tranquilizer, since the former carries no risk of addiction. In either case, it will eventually be necessary to undertake exposure without the assistance of the medication if you wish to gain a sense of complete mastery over your fear.

See chapter 17 for further guidelines on how to use either antidepressant medications or tranquilizers.

Imagery Desensitization

What if facing your fear in real life is impractical? For example, if you fear taking a transcontinental flight, repeated real-life exposure is not a practical option. Using a technique called imagery desensitization, you can help to unravel this kind of phobia. Like real-life exposure it relies on a hierarchy of progressively anxiety-inducing steps. The difference is that you *visualize* yourself undertaking them rather than acting them out in real life. Sometimes imagery desensitization is helpful to do in advance of facing a phobic situation through real-life exposure.

Guidelines for Imagery Desensitization

To design your imagery desensitization, choose a particular phobic situation you want to work on—for example, flying. Then create your hierarchy. Imagine having to deal with this situation in a very limited way—one that hardly bothers you at all. You can create this scenario by imagining yourself somewhat removed in space or time from full exposure to the situation, such as parking in front of the airport without going in or imagining your feelings one month before you have to make a flight. Or you can diminish the difficulty of the situation by visualizing yourself with a supportive person at your side. Try in these ways to create a very mild instance of your phobia and designate it as the first step in your hierarchy. It's helpful to write out a detailed scene for this first step.

Imagine what would be the strongest or most challenging scene relating to your phobia and place it at the opposite extreme, as the highest step in your hierarchy. For flying, such a step might involve taking off on a transcontinental flight, or encountering severe air turbulence mid-flight. Again, develop your most challenging scene by writing it out in full detail.

Now take some time to imagine eight or more scenes of graduated intensity related to your phobia and rank them according to their anxiety-provoking potential. Intermediate scenes for flying might include any of the following, with the latter scenes typically being "higher" in the hierarchy:

- Arriving at the airport the day of your flight

- Checking in your bags

- Passing through security

- Waiting at the gate for your flight

- Boarding the plane

- Finding your seat on the plane

- Strapping yourself into your seat

- Hearing the flight attendant lock the door to the plane (this may be the most challenging exposure for many people)

- Taxiing to the runway

- Accelerating on the runway for takeoff

- Feeling the plane lift off the ground

If you are planning to eventually face the fear in real life, it is desirable to have these scenes correspond to things you will actually do at that time. Place your scenes in ascending order between the two extremes you've already defined. Again, develop each scene by writing it out in as much detail as possible.

Basic Procedure for Imagery Desensitization

1. Spend a few minutes getting relaxed. Use progressive muscle relaxation or any other relaxation technique that works well for you.

2. Visualize yourself in a peaceful scene (see chapter 4 for more information on imagining a peaceful scene). This is a relaxing place you can vividly picture in your mind. It can be a scene outdoors (such as a beach, a meadow, or the mountains) or indoors (curling up by a fireplace), or it can come completely from your imagination. Above all, it is a place where you feel safe. Spend about one minute there.

3. Visualize yourself in the first scene of your phobia hierarchy. Stay there for thirty seconds to one minute, trying to picture everything with as much vividness and detail as possible, as if you were right there. Imagine yourself acting and feeling calm and confident. If you feel little or no anxiety, proceed to the next scene up in your hierarchy.

4. On the other hand, if you experience mild to moderate anxiety, try to stay a full thirty seconds to one minute in the scene, allowing yourself to relax into it. You can do this by breathing away any anxious sensations in your body or by repeating a calming affirmation such as "I am calm and at ease." Picture yourself handling the situation in a calm and confident manner.

5. After up to a minute of exposure, retreat from the phobic scene to your peaceful scene. Spend about one minute in your peaceful scene or long enough to get fully relaxed. Then repeat your visualization of the same phobic scene as in step 4 for thirty seconds to one minute. Keep alternating between a given phobic scene and your peaceful scene (about one minute each) until the phobic scene loses its capacity

to elicit any (or more than minimal) anxiety. Then you are ready to proceed to the next step up in your hierarchy.

6.   If visualizing a particular scene causes strong anxiety, especially if you feel you're approaching panic (level 4 on the *Anxiety Scale*), do not spend more than ten seconds there. Retreat immediately to your peaceful scene and stay there until you're fully relaxed. Expose yourself gradually to the more difficult scenes, alternating short intervals of exposure with retreat to your peaceful scene. If a particular scene in your hierarchy continues to cause difficulty, you probably need to add another step—one that is intermediate in difficulty between the last step you completed successfully and the one that is troublesome.

7.   Continue progressing up your hierarchy step-by-step. Generally, it will take a minimum of two exposures to a scene to reduce your anxiety to it. Keep in mind that it's important not to go on to a more advanced step until you're fully comfortable with the preceding step.

Practice imagery desensitization for fifteen to twenty minutes each day. Begin each practice session not with a new step but with the last step you successfully negotiated. Then go on to a new step.

How to Get the Most Out of Imagery Desensitization

The process of desensitization will work best if you adhere to the following guidelines:

1.   Spend about fifteen to twenty minutes the first time you practice imagery desensitization. As you gain skill in relaxation and visualization, you can lengthen your sessions to thirty minutes. In this time period (on a good day), you can expect to master two or three scenes in your hierarchy.

2.   You need to be very relaxed for this sort of desensitization to be effective. If you feel that you aren't deeply relaxed, then you might spend more time—twenty to thirty minutes—relaxing at the outset, and spend more time relaxing in your peaceful scene after each exposure to a particular phobic scene. Make sure that you *fully* recover from any anxiety after each exposure.

3.   Take time to visualize each phobic scene in your hierarchy as much as possible. You may want to write a paragraph or two describing each scene to facilitate your visualization. You need to be able to visualize each phobic scene as well as your peaceful scene in detail, as if you were really there.

4.   Try to practice every day if possible. Desensitization through imagery will be most effective following your regular period of relaxation.

5.   Even if the first few scenes in your hierarchy don't elicit any anxiety at all, it's important to expose yourself to each of them at least once. (You can proceed from one to the next without retreating to your peaceful scene if your anxiety stays below level

2.) Imagery desensitization is at work even when you're not feeling any anxiety in response to a given scene, for you are still associating relaxation with your phobia.

6. Stop your session of imagery desensitization if you begin to feel overly tired or upset.

Summary of Things to Do

1. Decide on those phobias for which you're ready to undertake real-life desensitization.

2. Establish a hierarchy with at least eight steps for each phobia you wish to work on. If you haven't yet constructed any hierarchies for your phobias, use the examples in this chapter and in appendix 2 as models.

3. Review the section "Basic Procedure for Exposure" so that you're thoroughly familiar with the correct procedure for real-life desensitization.

4. Practice exposure 3 to 5 days per week. Monitor your progress by indicating the date you complete each step in your hierarchy on your hierarchy worksheet. Regular practice is the best way to ensure your success.

5. Rely on a support person (your spouse, your partner, a close friend, a recovered phobic, or a therapist) when you begin to work on your hierarchy and also the first time you confront each new step. Having a support person with you should help make exposure easier unless you have a strong preference for doing it on your own.

6. Review the section "Making the Most of Exposure" so that you fully understand all of the ingredients that contribute to success with real-life desensitization. Your willingness to deal with initial resistance, tolerate some discomfort, learn to retreat if necessary, practice regularly, and handle setbacks is particularly important.

7. Practice using coping statements when you're preparing to undertake an exposure session or during the exposure process itself.

8. Have your support person read the section "Guidelines for Your Support Person" before accompanying you on your practice sessions.

9. If you've utilized everything in this book up to and including this chapter, and you're still having a difficult time getting started with exposure, consult with your doctor about the possibility of using medication to help you move forward.

Further Reading

Barlow, David. *Anxiety and Its Disorders: The Nature and Treatment of Anxiety and Panic.* Second edition. New York: Guilford Press, 2004.

Beckfield, Denise F. *Master Your Panic and Take Back Your Life.* Second edition. San Luis Obispo, CA: Impact Publishers, 1998.

Bourne, Edmund J. *Overcoming Specific Phobia: Therapist Protocol* and *Client Manual.* Oakland, CA: New Harbinger Publications, l998.

Feninger, Mani. *Journey from Anxiety to Freedom.* Rocklin, CA: Prima Publishers, 1998.

Ross, Jerilyn. *Triumph Over Fear.* New York: Bantam Books, 1994.

Williams, Karen. *How to Help Your Loved One Recover from Agoraphobia.* Far Hills, NJ: New Horizon Press, 1993.

Zuercher-White, Elke. *An End to Panic.* Second edition. Oakland, CA: New Harbinger Publications, 1998.

8

Self-Talk

Imagine two individuals sitting in stop-and-go traffic at rush hour. One perceives himself as trapped, and says such things to himself as "I can't stand this," "I've got to get out of here," and "Why did I ever get myself into this commute?" What he feels is anxiety, anger, and frustration. The other perceives the situation as an opportunity to lie back, relax, and listen to music. He says, "I might as well just relax and adjust to the pace of the traffic" or "I can unwind by doing some deep breathing." What he feels is a sense of calm and acceptance. In both cases, the situation is exactly the same, but the feelings in response to that situation are vastly different because of each individual's internal monologue, or *self-talk*.

The truth is that it's *what we say to ourselves* in response to any particular situation that mainly determines our mood and feelings. Often we say it so quickly and automatically that we don't even notice, and so we get the impression that the external situation "makes" us feel the way we do. But it's really our interpretations and thoughts about what is happening that form the basis of our feelings. This sequence can be represented as a timeline:

External Events $\longrightarrow$ Interpretation of Events and Self-Talk $\longrightarrow$ Feelings and Reactions

In short, you are largely responsible for how you feel (barring physiological determinants, such as illness). This is a profound and very important truth—one that sometimes takes a long time to fully grasp. It's often much easier to blame the way you feel on something or someone outside yourself than to take responsibility for your reactions. Yet it is through your willingness to accept that responsibility that you begin to take charge and have mastery over your life. The realization that you are mostly responsible for how you feel is empowering once you fully accept it. It's one of the most important keys to living a happier, more effective, and anxiety-free life.

Anxiety and Self-Talk

People who suffer from phobias, panic attacks, and general anxiety are especially prone to engage in negative self-talk. Anxiety can be generated on the spur of the moment by repeatedly making statements to yourself that begin with the two words "what if." Any anxiety you experience in anticipation of confronting a difficult situation is manufactured out of your own "what-if statements" to yourself. When you decide to avoid a situation altogether, it is probably because of the scary questions you've asked yourself: "What if I panic?" "What if I can't handle it?" "What will other people think if they see me anxious?" Just noticing when you fall into "what-if thinking" is the first step toward gaining control over negative self-talk. The real change occurs when you begin to *counter* and *replace* negative "what-if statements" with positive, self-supportive statements that reinforce your ability to cope. For example, you might say, "So what," "These are just thoughts," "This is just scare-talk," "I can handle this," or "I can breathe, let go, and relax."

I want you to consider some basic facts about self-talk. Following these facts is a discussion of the different types of self-defeating inner monologues.

Some Basic Points About Self-Talk

- Self-talk is usually so automatic and subtle that you don't notice it or the effect it has on your moods and feelings. You react without noticing what you told yourself right before you reacted. Often it's only when you relax, take a step back, and really examine what you've been telling yourself that you can see the connection between self-talk and your feelings. What is important is that *you can learn to slow down and take note of your negative internal monologue.*

- Self-talk often *appears in telegraphic form.* One short word or image contains a whole series of thoughts, memories, or associations. For example, you feel your heart starting to beat faster and say to yourself, "Oh no!" Implicit within that momentary "Oh no!" is a whole series of associations concerning fears about panic, memories of previous panic attacks, and thoughts about how to escape the current situation. Identifying self-talk may require unraveling several distinct thoughts from a single word or image.

- Anxious self-talk is typically *irrational but almost always sounds like the truth.* What-if thinking may lead you to expect the worst possible outcome in a given situation, one that is highly unlikely to occur. Yet because the association takes place so quickly, it goes unchallenged and unquestioned. It's hard to evaluate the validity of a belief you're scarcely aware of—you just accept it as is.

- Negative self-talk *perpetuates avoidance.* You tell yourself that a situation such as the freeway is dangerous and so you avoid it. By continuing to avoid it, you reinforce the thought that it's dangerous. You may even project images of catastrophe around the prospect of confronting the situation. In short, anxious self-talk leads to avoidance, avoidance begets further anxious self-talk, and around and around the cycle goes.

Avoidance $\longleftrightarrow$ Self-Talk

- Self-talk can *initiate or aggravate a panic attack.* A panic attack often starts out with symptoms of increasing physiological arousal, such as a more rapid heartbeat, tightness in the chest, or sweaty palms. Biologically, this is the body's *natu*[*response to stress—the fight-or-flight response that all mammals, including human_, normally experience when subjected to a perceived threat. There is nothing inherently abnormal or dangerous about it. Yet these symptoms can remind you of previous panic attacks. Instead of simply allowing your body's physiological reaction to rise, peak, and subside in its own good time, you scare yourself into a considerably more intense panic attack with scary self-talk: "Oh no, it's happening again," "What if I lose control?" "I *have* to get out of here now," or "I'm going to fight this and make it go away." This scare-talk aggravates the initial physical symptoms, which in turn elicits further scare-talk. A severe panic attack might have been aborted or rendered much less intense had you made reassuring statements to yourself at the onset of your first symptoms: "I can accept what's happening even though it's uncomfortable," "I'll let my body do its thing," "This will pass," "I've gotten through this before and I will this time," or "This is just a burst of adrenaline that can metabolize and pass in a few minutes."

• Negative self-talk is a *series of bad habits*. You aren't born with a predisposition to fearful self-talk: you *learn* to think that way. Just as you can replace unhealthy *behavioral* habits, such as smoking or drinking excess coffee, with more positive, health-promoting behavior, so can you replace unhealthy thinking with more positive, supportive *mental* habits. Bear in mind that the acquisition of positive mental habits takes the same persistence and practice required for learning new behaviors.

Types of Negative Self-Talk

Not all negative self-talk is the same. Human beings are not only diverse but complex, with multifaceted personalities. These facets are sometimes referred to as "subpersonalities." Our different subpersonalities each play their own distinct role and possess their own voice in the complex workings of consciousness, memory, and dreams. Below I've outlined four of the more common subpersonality types that tend to be prominent in people who are prone to anxiety: the Worrier, the Critic, the Victim, and the Perfectionist.* Since the strength of these inner voices varies for different people, you might find it useful to rank them from strongest to weakest in yourself.

The Worrier (promotes anxiety)

Characteristics: This usually is the strongest subpersonality in people who are prone to anxiety. The Worrier creates anxiety by imagining the worst-case scenario. It scares you with fantasies of disaster or catastrophe when you imagine confronting something you fear. It also

---

* These subpersonalities are based on Reid Wilson's descriptions of the Worried, Critical, and Hopeless Observeres in his book *Don't Panic: Taking Control of Anxiety Attacks*.

aggravates panic by reacting to the first physical symptoms of a panic attack. The Worrier promotes your fears that what is happening is dangerous or embarrassing ("What if I have a heart attack?!" "What will they think if they see me?!").

In short, the Worrier's dominant tendencies include 1) anticipating the worst, 2) overestimating the odds of something bad or embarrassing happening, and 3) creating grandiose images of potential failure or catastrophe. The Worrier is always vigilant, watching with uneasy apprehension for any small symptoms or signs of trouble.

Favorite expression: By far the favorite expression of the Worrier is "what if …?".

Examples: Some typical dialogue from the Worrier might be: "Oh no, my heart's starting to beat faster! What if I panic and lose complete control of myself?" "What if I start stammering in the middle of my speech?" "What if they see me shaking?" "What if I'm alone and there's nobody to call?" "What if I just can't get over this phobia?" or "What if I'm restricted from going to work for the rest of my life?"

The Critic *(promotes low self-esteem)*

Characteristics: The Critic is that part of you that is constantly judging and evaluating your behavior (and in this sense may seem more "apart" from you than the other subpersonalities). It tends to point out your flaws and limitations whenever possible. It jumps on any mistake you make to remind you that you're a failure. The Critic generates anxiety by putting you down for not being able to handle your panic symptoms, for not being able to go places you used to go, for being unable to perform at your best, or for having to be dependent on someone else. It also likes to compare you with others and usually sees them coming out favorably. It tends to ignore your positive qualities and emphasizes your weaknesses and inadequacies. The Critic may be personified in your own dialogue as the voice of your mother or father, a dreaded teacher, or anyone who wounded you in the past with their criticism.

Favorite expressions: "What a disappointment you are!" "That was stupid!"

Examples: The following would be typical of the Critic's self-talk: "You stupid …" (The Critic relishes negative labels.) "Can't you ever get it right?" "Why are you always this way?" "Look at how capable _____ is," or "You could have done better." The Critic holds negative self-beliefs, such as "I'm inferior to others," "I'm not worth much," "There's something inherently wrong with me," or "I'm weak—I should be stronger."

The Victim *(promotes depression)*

Characteristics: The Victim is that part of you that feels helpless or hopeless. It generates anxiety by telling you that you're not making any progress, that your condition is incurable, or that the road is too long and steep for you to have a real chance at recovering. The Victim also plays a major role in creating depression. The Victim believes that there is something inherently wrong with you: you are in some way deprived, defective, or unworthy. The Victim always perceives insurmountable obstacles between you and your goals. Characteristically, it bemoans, complains, and regrets things as they are at present. It believes that nothing will ever change.

Favorite expressions: "I can't." "I'll never be able to."

Examples: The Victim will say such things as "I'll never be able to do that, so what's the point in even trying?" "I feel physically drained today—why bother doing anything?" "Maybe I could have done it if I'd had more initiative ten years ago—but it's too late now." The Victim holds such negative self-beliefs as "I'm hopeless," "I've had this problem too long—it will never get better," or "I've tried everything—nothing is ever going to work."

The Perfectionist (promotes chronic stress and burnout)

Characteristics: The Perfectionist is a close cousin of the Critic, but its concern is less to put you down than to push and goad you to do better. It generates anxiety by constantly telling you that your efforts aren't good enough, that you *should* be working harder, that you *should* always have everything under control, *should* always be competent, *should* always be pleasing, *should* always be _____ (fill in whatever you keep telling yourself that you "should" do or be). The Perfectionist is the hard-driving part of you that wants to be best and is intolerant of mistakes or setbacks. It has a tendency to try to convince you that your self-worth is dependent on *externals,* such as vocational achievement, money and status, acceptance by others, being loved, or your ability to be pleasing and nice to others, regardless of what they do. The Perfectionist isn't convinced by any notions of your inherent self-worth, but instead pushes you into stress, exhaustion, and burnout in pursuit of its goals. It likes to ignore warning signals from your body.

Favorite Expressions: "I should." "I have to." "I must."

Examples: The Perfectionist may provide such instructions as "I should always be on top of things," "I should always be considerate and unselfish," "I should always be pleasant and nice," or "I *have to* (get this job, make this amount of money, receive _____'s approval, etc.) or I'm not worth much." (See the discussion of "should statements" at the end of the next section.)

Exercise: What Are Your Subpersonalities Telling You?

Take some time to think about how each of the above subpersonalities plays a role in your thinking, feelings, and behavior. First, estimate how much each one affects you by rating its degree of influence from "not at all" to "very much" on a six-point scale (see the worksheets over the next few pages). Which subpersonality is strongest and which is weakest for you? Then think about what each subpersonality is saying to you to create or aggravate anxiety in each of four different situations.

1.   *Work* (on your job, at school, or in other performance situations)

2.   *Personal relationships* (with your spouse or partner, parents, children, and/or friends)

3.   *Anxiety symptoms* (on occasions when you experience panic, anxiety, or obsessive-compulsive symptoms)

4.   *Phobic situations* (either *in advance* of facing a phobia or while actually *confronting* the phobic situation)

Here are some examples for the Worrier:

The Worrier

Work:	"What if my boss finds out that I have agoraphobia? Will I get fired?"
Relationships:	"My husband is getting tired of having to take me places. What if he refuses? What if he leaves me?"
Anxiety symptoms:	"What if they see me panic? What if they think I'm weird?"
Phobic situation:	"What if I get into an accident the first time I try to drive on the freeway?"

You may find that the Worrier's self-talk in the latter two situations is by far the most common source of your anxiety. If you have panic attacks, the Worrier is prone to create anxiety about when and where your next one might occur. Should the bodily symptoms of panic actually start to come on, the Worrier will magnify them into something dangerous, which only creates more panic. Many of the coping strategies described in chapter 6 (in particular, the use of positive coping statements) are designed to help you deal with the Worrier during a panic attack.

If you have phobias, the Worrier is typically busy telling you about all kinds of things that might happen if you were to actually face your fear. As a result, you often experience "anticipatory anxiety" (anxiety in advance of facing a phobia) and try to avoid dealing with whatever your phobia may be. You'll find it helpful to do a separate analysis of what your Worrier is telling you (in other words, your "what-ifs") for *each* of your specific phobias. Ask yourself what you're afraid could happen if you faced each phobia.

Here are some examples of how other subpersonalities operate:

The Critic

Work:	"I'm incompetent because of my condition."
Relationships:	"I'm a burden to my husband."
Anxiety symptoms:	"I'm such a weakling—I go to pieces when I panic."
Phobic situation:	"Everybody else can drive—I feel like a loser."

The Victim

Work: "My situation at work is hopeless—sooner or later I'll be fired."

Relationships: "My parents really messed me up" or "I can't make it without my boyfriend."

Anxiety symptoms: "I'll *never* get over these panic attacks—there must be something very wrong with me."

Phobic situation: "It's useless going on any more job interviews. No one's going to hire me when they see that I'm so anxious."

The Perfectionist

Work: "I should be able to make sales like I used to, no matter how anxious I feel."

Relationships: "I shouldn't need to depend on my husband or anyone else to take me places."

Anxiety symptoms: "I *have to* be able to stop these thoughts from going through my mind."

Phobic situation: "I *have to* learn to drive like anyone else."

Use the worksheets that follow to write down the anxiety-provoking statements that your subpersonalities are using in each situation. You don't need to do this for all four subpersonalities or for all four types of situations in each case. Only include those subpersonalities and situations that you suspect are a problem for you. (You'll be filling in the right-hand columns of the worksheets later. Just complete the left-hand columns for now. Use additional sheets of paper if you need more room.)

Monitor what your subpersonalities are telling you for at least one week. Pay attention especially to occasions when you are feeling anxious (panicky), depressed, self-critical and ashamed, or otherwise upset. Look for the thoughts that were going through your mind that led you to feel the way you did. "I felt scared" is not a good example of self-talk because it doesn't indicate what you were thinking (telling yourself) that caused you to feel scared. On the other hand, the self-statement "What if I panic on the job today?" is an example of a thought that could have led you to feel scared. See step 4 in the section later in this chapter called "General Guidelines for Identifying and Countering Self-Talk" for further suggestions about separating thoughts from feelings.

Subpersonality: The Worrier

Affects me: not at all ———— 1 2 3 4 5 6 ———— very much

Negative Self-Talk	Positive Counterstatements
Situation	There are plenty of good jobs out there and I am a good worker.
Work/School What if I never find another good job.	
Relationships What if I'm always single?	I have a friendly demeanor that attracts people.
Anxiety Symptoms (give this special attention if you have panic attacks) What if I never stop worrying about the future	I need to be in the now.
Phobias (determine the Worrier's self-talk for each of your phobias— use a separate sheet if necessary) What if I mess up during interviews?	I need to stop projecting

Subpersonality: The Critic

Affects me: not at all ———————— very much
            1 2 3 4 5 6

Negative Self-Talk	Positive Counterstatements
Situation	
Work/School	I forgive myself for
I should have tried harder to do my job at Entravision.	reactions I've experienced.
Relationships	My family cares for
I'm making my family suffer.	my well being
My brother is doing better than me.	
Anxiety Symptoms	I'm working on making
I'm no longer the man I used to be, I fall to pieces easily.	myself **mentally** stronger.
Phobias	I'm working on
I had no trouble driving at night from San Jose and San Francisco.	conquering new fears

Subpersonality: The Victim

Affects me: not at all ——————— very much

1 2 3 4 ⑤ 6

Negative Self-Talk	Positive Counterstatements
Situation	
Work/School	
I can't perform as well as I used to before	I am working on myself to handle situations better.
Relationships	
I'm alone and have no girlfriend.	I have my family and loving friends.
Anxiety Symptoms	
I can't control my mind.	I'm practicing to control my emotions.
Phobias	
There are no jobs out there for me.	I will continue my career.

Subpersonality: The Perfectionist

Affects me: not at all ——————— very much
1 ②3 4 5 6

Negative Self-Talk	Positive Counterstatements
Situation	
Work/School	
I needed to have been working a good job right now.	I'm working on myself so I can do a good job in my next job.
Relationships	
I should have a girlfriend	I have friends that care deeply for me.
Anxiety Symptoms	
I should have conquered my anxiety	I'm working on controlling my anxiety
Phobias	
I should have stopped being affraid of not getting better ever	I'm learning to eliminate negative self talk.

Countering Negative Self-Talk

The most effective way to deal with the negative self-talk of your Worrier and other subpersonalities is to *counter* it with positive, supportive statements. Countering involves *writing down* and *rehearsing* positive statements that directly refute or invalidate your negative self-talk. If you're creating anxiety and other upsetting emotional states through negative mental programming, you can begin to change the way you feel by substituting positive programming. Doing this will take some *practice.* You've had years to practice your negative self-talk and naturally have developed some very strong habits. Your Worrier and other subpersonalities are likely to be very well entrenched. By starting to notice when you're engaging in negativity and then countering it with positive, supportive statements to yourself, you'll begin to turn your thinking around. With practice and consistent effort, you'll change both the way you think *and the way you feel* on an ongoing basis.

Sometimes countering comes naturally and easily. You are ready and willing to substitute positive, reasonable self-statements for ones that have been causing you anxiety and distress. You're more than ready to relinquish negative mental habits that aren't serving you. On the other hand, you may object to the idea of countering and say, "But what if what my Worrier (Critic, Victim, or Perfectionist) says is true? It's hard for me to believe otherwise." Or you may say, "How can I substitute positive self-statements for negative ones if I don't really believe them?"

Perhaps you're strongly attached to some of your negative self-talk. You've been telling yourself these things for years and it's difficult to give up both the habit and the belief. You're not someone who's easily persuaded. If that's the case, and you want to do something about your negative self-talk, it's important that you subject it to rational scrutiny. You can weaken the hold of your negative self-statements by exposing them to any of the following Socratic questions, or rational investigation.

1.   What is the evidence for this?

2.   Is this *always* true?

3.   Has this been true in the past?

4.   What are the odds of this really happening (or being true)?

5.   What is the very worst that could happen? What is so bad about that? What would you do if the worst happened?

6.   Are you looking at the whole picture?

7.   Are you being fully objective?

The validity of your negative self-statements has nothing to do with how attached you are to them or how ingrained they might be. Rather, it has to do with whether they stand up under careful, objective scrutiny. Consider the following examples:

Worrier: "What if I have a heart attack the next time I panic?"

Questioning:	"What is the evidence that panic attacks cause heart attacks?" (Answer: None—see chapter 6.)
Counterstatement:	"A panic attack, however uncomfortable, is not dangerous to my heart. I can let panic rise, fall, and pass, and my heart will be fine."
Critic:	"You're weak and neurotic because of your stupid phobias."
Questioning:	"What is the evidence for this?" (Answer: Phobias are caused by a conditioning process that occurs in a high-anxiety state—see chapter 2. "Weak" and "neurotic" are pejorative labels that explain nothing.)
Counterstatement:	"My phobias developed because of a conditioning process that caused me to be sensitized to certain situations. I'm learning to overcome my phobias through a process of gradual exposure."
Victim:	"I'll never get over this problem. I'll be limited in my mobility for the rest of my life."
Questioning:	"What is the evidence that agoraphobia is a lifelong condition? What other outcomes are possible?" (Answer: Ninety percent of agoraphobics recover with effective treatment.)
Counterstatement:	"My condition isn't hopeless. I can overcome it by establishing and committing myself to a program for recovery."
Perfectionist:	"I have to receive my parents' acceptance and approval or I'll be devastated."
Questioning:	"Am I being fully objective? Is it actually true that my parents' approval is absolutely necessary for my well-being? What is the worst that could happen?" (Answer: "I could still survive and have people who care for and support me even without my parents' approval.")
Counterstatement:	"I'm willing to go forward with my life and try to better myself regardless of what my parents think."

If you feel attached to your negative self-talk, use any of the above Socratic questions to evaluate the validity of what you're telling yourself. In most cases, you'll find that the negative statements of your Worrier, Critic, Victim, and Perfectionist have little basis in reality. At worst, they will be only partially or occasionally true. Once you've discredited a particular subpersonality's views, you will be ready to counter with positive, supportive statements.

Rules for Writing Positive Counterstatements

- *Avoid negatives* in writing your counterstatements. Instead of saying, "I'm not going to panic when I board the plane," try "I am confident and calm about boarding the plane." Telling yourself something will *not* happen is more likely to create anxiety than giving yourself a direct affirmation.

- Keep counterstatements in the *present tense* ("I can breathe and let these feelings pass" is preferable to "I will feel better in a few minutes"). Since much of your negative self-talk is in the here and now, it needs to be countered by statements that are also in the present tense. If you're not ready to *directly* affirm something, try beginning your positive statement with "I am willing to …" or "I am learning to …" or "I can …"

- Whenever possible, keep your statements in the *first person*. Begin them with "I" or refer to "I" somewhere in the statement. It's okay to write a sentence or two explaining the basis for your counterstatement (see the previous examples of counterstatements for the Worrier and Critic), but try to end with an "I-statement."

- It's important that you have some *belief* in your positive self-talk. Don't write something down just because it's positive if you don't actually believe it. If appropriate, use Socratic questions to challenge your negative self-talk first, and then follow this up with a positive counterstatement that holds some personal credibility for you.

To get you started, here are some more examples of positive counterstatements you can use with each of the above subpersonalities:

The Worrier

Instead of "what if …" you can say, "So what," "I can handle this," "I can be anxious and still do this," "This may be scary, but I can tolerate a little anxiety, knowing that it will pass," or "I'll get used to this with practice."

The Critic

Instead of putting yourself down, you can say, "I'm okay the way I am," "I'm lovable and capable," "I'm a unique and creative person," "I deserve the good things in life as much as anyone else," "I accept and believe in myself," or "I am worthy of the respect of others."

The Victim

Instead of feeling hopeless, you can say, "I don't have to be all better tomorrow," "I can continue to make progress one step at a time," "I acknowledge the progress I've made and will continue to improve," "It's never too late to change," or "I'm willing to see the glass as half full rather than half empty."

The Perfectionist

Instead of demanding perfection, you can say, "It's okay to make mistakes," "Life is too short to be taken too seriously," "Setbacks are part of the process and an important learning experience," "I don't have to always be …," or "My needs and feelings are as important as anyone else's."

Working with Counterstatements

Now you are ready to go back and counter all of the negative statements you recorded on the worksheets for your various subpersonalities. Write down counterstatements corresponding to each negative statement in the right-hand column. Use extra sheets of paper if you need to.

Once you've completed writing out positive self-talk for each subpersonality in each situation, there are several ways you can work with your positive counterstatements.

- Read through your list of positive counterstatements slowly and carefully for a few minutes each day for at least two weeks. See if you can feel some conviction about their truth as you read them. This will help you to integrate them more deeply into your consciousness.

- Make copies of your worksheets and post them in a conspicuous place. Take time once a day to carefully read through your positive counterstatements.

- Record your counterstatements, leaving about five seconds between each consecutive positive statement so that it has time to sink in. You can significantly enhance the effect of such a recording by giving yourself ten to fifteen minutes to become very relaxed before listening to your counterstatements. You will be more receptive to them in a relaxed state. You may want to record the instructions for progressive muscle relaxation or one of the relaxing visualizations described in chapter 4 on the first ten to fifteen minutes of the recording.

- If you're having a problem with a particular phobia, you might want to work with positive counterstatements that are *specific just to that phobia*. For example, if you're afraid of speaking before groups, make a list of all your fears about what could happen, and develop positive statements to counter each fear. Then read through your list of counterstatements carefully each day for two weeks or make a short recording as described in the preceding item.

Changing Self-Talk That Perpetuates Specific Fears and Phobias

Three factors tend to perpetuate fears and phobias: sensitization, avoidance, and negative, distorted self-talk. Chapter 7 focused on the first two conditions. A phobia develops when you become sensitized to a particular situation, object, or event—in other words, when anxiety becomes conditioned or associated with that situation, object, or event. If panic suddenly arises while you happen to be driving on the freeway or while you're home alone, you may start feeling anxious every time you're in either of these situations. Becoming *sensitized* means that the mere presence of—or even thinking about—a situation may be enough to trigger anxiety automatically.

After sensitization occurs, you may start to *avoid* the situation. Repeated avoidance is very rewarding, because it saves you from having to feel any anxiety. Avoidance is the most powerful way to hold on to a phobia, because it prevents you from ever learning that you can handle the situation.

The third factor that perpetuates fears and phobias is distorted self-talk. The more *worry* and *anticipatory anxiety* you experience about something you fear, the more likely you are to be involved in unconstructive self-talk connected with that fear. You may also have negative *images* about what could happen if you had to face what you fear or about your worst fears coming true. Both negative self-talk and negative images serve to perpetuate your fears, guaranteeing that you remain afraid. They also undermine your confidence that you can ever get over your fear. Without negative self-talk and negative images, you would be much more likely to overcome your avoidance and confront your fear.

Fears come in many forms, but the nature of fearful self-talk is always the same. Whether you are afraid of crossing bridges, speaking up in a social situation, the sensation of rapid heartbeat, the possibility of serious illness, or your children getting into trouble, the types of distorted thinking that perpetuate these fears are the same. *There are three basic distortions:*

1. Overestimating a Negative Outcome

Overestimating the odds of something bad happening is one type of distortion. Most of the time your worries consist of "what-if statements" that overestimate a particular negative outcome. For example, "What if I panic and lose complete control of myself?" "What if they see me panic and think I'm weird?" "What if I flunk the exam and have to drop out of school?"

2. Catastrophizing

The second distortion is thinking that if a negative outcome did occur, it would be catastrophic, overwhelming, and unmanageable. Catastrophic thoughts contain such statements as "I couldn't handle it," "I'd be overwhelmed," "I'd never live it down," or "They'll never forgive me."

3. Underestimating Your Ability to Cope

The third distortion is not recognizing or acknowledging your ability to cope if a negative outcome did, in fact, occur. This underestimation of your ability to cope is usually implicit in your catastrophic thoughts.

If you take any fear and examine the negative thinking that contributes to maintaining that fear, you'll probably find these three distortions. To the extent that you can overcome them with more reality-based thinking, the fear will tend to drop away. In essence, you can define fear as *the unreasonable overestimation of some threat, coupled with an underestimation of your ability to cope.*

Here are some examples of how the different types of distortions operate with various fears. In each example, the three types of distorted thoughts are identified. The distortions are then challenged in each case and modified with more appropriate, reality-based counterstatements.

Example 1: Fear of Having a Panic Attack While Driving on a Freeway

Overestimating Thoughts

"What if I can't handle the car? What if my attention wanders and I lose control of the car? What if I cause an accident and kill someone?"

Catastrophic Thoughts

"I couldn't handle it if I lost control of the car. It would be a totally unmanageable situation—the end of the world—if I caused an accident." (Note: An image of a horrendous accident can accompany and amplify the force of a catastrophic thought.)

Underestimating Your Ability to Cope

"I couldn't cope if I lost control of the car, especially if I got into an accident. I'll die of embarrassment if other drivers notice how frightened I am. What would I say to a policeman—that I'm phobic? I wouldn't be able to start driving again if I got stopped for a ticket. I couldn't live with myself if I caused physical injury to another person—and I know I couldn't face life in a wheelchair."

Refuting Distorted Thinking

It's possible to refute each of these types of distorted thinking with questions and counterstatements. Examples follow below:

Overestimating Thoughts

With overestimating thoughts, the appropriate question is, *"Viewing the situation objectively, what are the odds of the negative outcome actually happening?"*

In the case of the previous example, the question is, "If I did panic while driving, what are the true odds that I would lose control of the car?"

You could use this counterstatement: "It's unlikely that having a panic attack would cause me to lose complete control. The moment I felt my anxiety coming on, I could pull over to the shoulder on the side of the road and stop. If there weren't any shoulders, I could slow way down in the right lane, perhaps to forty-five miles per hour, put my flashers on, and keep a grip on myself until I reached the nearest exit. Once I got off the highway, my panic would begin to subside."

Catastrophic Thoughts

With catastrophizing, the relevant question to ask is, *"If the worst did happen, is it actually true that I couldn't handle it?"* The idea is to go ahead and imagine the worst that could happen and then ask yourself whether *in reality* you could handle the consequences or not.

In the above example, you would raise the question, "If the worst did happen—if I did get into an accident, one that even caused injury—would I be totally unable to handle it?"

You could then use a counterstatement, such as "As bad as having an accident would be, in most cases I would be able to handle it if I weren't injured. It's common for people to function in an emergency situation and then handle their anxiety later. So, in all likelihood, I would keep functioning in the event of an accident as long as I wasn't injured.

"Even if I were injured, and unable to handle the situation, the police and paramedics would soon arrive on the scene and take charge. There is simply no way in which the situation could become completely unmanageable."

Underestimating Your Ability to Cope

Countering the idea that you couldn't cope often takes place in the process of answering catastrophic thinking with a more objective appraisal. However, the process isn't complete until you actually *identify and list specific ways in which you could cope*. In the above example, some possible coping strategies could include the following:

- "If I did have a panic attack, I could cope by getting off the highway immediately or driving slowly to the nearest exit and getting off."

- "In the very unlikely case that I actually caused an accident, I would still cope. I would exchange names and addresses with other parties involved. If my car were undriveable, the police would likely drive me to a place where I could call to have the car towed. It would be a very unpleasant experience, to say the least, but, realistically, I would continue to function. I've functioned in emergencies in the past, and I could function in this case, if I weren't injured."

- "Even given the remote possibility that I were injured, I wouldn't 'go crazy' or 'totally lose it.' I would simply wait until the paramedics came and took charge of the situation."

Example 2: Fear of Panicking While Speaking Up in a Class or Meeting

Overestimating Thoughts

"What if I panicked while speaking? Wouldn't others think I was really weird or crazy?"

Questioning: "Realistically, how likely is it that I would panic while speaking? What are the odds, if I did panic, that people would be aware of what I was thinking or make any judgments about me at all?"

Counterstatements: "It is possible that I could start to panic while speaking. If I did, I could simply abbreviate what I wanted to say and sit back down. As people tend to be caught up in their own thoughts and fears, no one would likely notice my difficulty or judge that I'd cut my comments short.

"Even if people did see me panic—if they saw my face turn red or heard my voice trembling—the odds are very slim that they'd think I was weird or crazy. It's much more likely that they'd express concern."

Catastrophic Thoughts

"If I panicked while speaking and people thought I was weird, that would be terrible. *I'd never live it down.*"

Questioning: "Suppose the unlikely happened and people really thought I was strange or weird because I panicked. How terrible would that be?"

Counterstatements: "It's not going to be the end of the world if some people think I'm strange or that something's wrong with me. They have no way of knowing what it's like to have panic attacks, so they couldn't really understand. Even if people don't understand, or if they misperceive me, that doesn't decrease one bit my value or worth as a human being. If I believe in myself, then it really doesn't matter what others think. Certainly if others knew what it was like to have a panic attack, they would likely be sympathetic."

Underestimating Your Ability to Cope

"I couldn't cope if people thought I was strange."

Questioning: "Is it realistic to assume that I couldn't cope? Is it realistic to suppose I'd never live it down?"

Counterstatements: "Even if people thought I was strange or different because I panicked, I could explain to them that I sometimes have panic attacks in social situations. With all the publicity about anxiety disorders that's around these days, they would likely understand. Being totally honest is one way I could handle the situation. And no matter what happened, I would forget about it after a while. It's just not true that I would never live it down."

Example 3: Fear of Serious Illness

Overestimating Thoughts

"I have no energy and feel tired all the time. Maybe I have cancer and don't know it!"

Questioning: "What are the odds that symptoms of low energy and fatigue mean that I have cancer?"

Counterstatements: "Symptoms of fatigue and low energy can be indicative of all kinds of physical and psychological conditions, including a low-grade virus, anemia, adrenal exhaustion or hypothyroidism, depression, and food allergies, to name a few. There are many possible explanations of my condition, and I don't have any specific symptoms that would indicate cancer. So the odds of my fatigue and low energy indicating cancer are very low."

Catastrophic Thoughts

"If I were diagnosed with cancer, that would be the end. I couldn't take it. I'd be better off ending things quickly and killing myself."

Questioning: "If the unlikely happened and I really were diagnosed with cancer, how terrible could that be? Would I actually go to pieces and just want to die?"

Counterstatements: "As bad as a cancer diagnosis would be, it's unlikely that I would totally go to pieces. After an initial difficult adjustment to the fact—which might take days to weeks—I would most likely begin to think about what I needed to do to deal with the situation. It would certainly be difficult, yet it wouldn't be a situation that I was less equipped to handle than anyone else."

Underestimating Your Ability to Cope

"If I were given a diagnosis of cancer, I simply couldn't cope."

Questioning: "Realistically, is it actually true that I would have no way of coping with the situation?"

Counterstatements: "Of course I would cope. After an initial period of adjusting to the situation, my doctor and I would plan the most effective possible treatment strategies. I would join a local cancer support group and get lots of support from my friends and immediate family. I would try alternative methods, such as visualization and dietary changes, that could help. In short, I would try everything possible to attempt to heal the condition."

The above three examples illustrate how overestimating and catastrophic thoughts can be challenged and then countered by more realistic, less anxiety-provoking thinking. Now it's your turn. During the next two weeks, monitor the times when you feel anxious or panicky. Each time you do, use the following five steps to work with negative self-talk:

Step 1: If you're feeling anxious or upset, do something to relax, such as abdominal breathing, progressive muscle relaxation, or meditation. It's easier to notice your internal dialogue when you take time to slow down and relax.

Step 2: After you get somewhat relaxed, ask yourself, "What was I telling myself that made me anxious?" or "What was going through my mind?" Remember to separate thoughts from feelings. For example, "I felt terrified" describes a feeling, while "This panic will never end" is an overestimating thought that might have led you to feel terrified.

Step 3: Identify the three basic types of distortions among your anxious self-talk. Sort out *overestimating thoughts, catastrophic thoughts,* and *thoughts that underestimate your ability to cope.*

Step 4: When you've identified your anxious, distorted thoughts, challenge them with appropriate questions.

- *For overestimating thoughts:* "What are the realistic odds that this feared outcome would actually happen?"

- *For catastrophic thoughts:* "If the feared outcome actually did occur, how terrible would it be? Is it really true that I would go to pieces and lose my ability to cope?"

- *For thoughts underestimating your ability to cope:* "If the feared outcome did occur, what could I actually do to cope?"

Step 5: Write counterstatements to each of your anxious self-statements. These counterstatements should contain language and logic that reflect more balanced, realistic thinking.

Use *The Worry Worksheet* that follows to write down your anxious thoughts and corresponding counterstatements for any specific fear or phobia you choose to work with. In the section at the bottom, list ways in which you could cope if the negative (but unlikely) outcome you fear actually occurred.

It would be a good idea to make photocopies of the worksheet before you begin so that you can fill out a separate sheet for each specific fear or phobia you have.

The Worry Worksheet

Specific Fear or Phobia _____

Anxious Self-Talk	*Counterstatements*
Overestimating thoughts (or images) "What if ...?"	
Catastrophic thoughts (or images) "If the worst happened, then ..."	

Coping Strategies: List the ways in which you would cope if a negative (but unlikely) outcome did occur. Use the other side of the sheet if needed. Change "What if" to "What I would do if (one of the negative predictions) actually did come about."

Make copies of this worksheet before you start, and use a separate sheet for each of your phobias or fears.

Other Types of Distorted Thinking (Cognitive Distortions)

Overestimating and catastrophizing, along with underestimating your ability to cope, are the most common types of distortions in thinking that contribute to most phobias and fears. There are other types of distortions, however, that can skew the ways in which you perceive and evaluate both yourself and innumerable situations in everyday life. These distortions can contribute not only to anxiety but also to much of the depression, guilt, self-criticism, and/or cynicism you might feel. Learning to identify and counter these unhelpful modes of thinking with more realistic and constructive self-talk can go a long way toward helping you handle everyday stresses in a more balanced, objective fashion. This, in turn, will significantly reduce the amount of anxiety, depression, and other unpleasant emotional states you experience. Remember that your immediate experience of the outside world is largely shaped and colored by your own personal thoughts about it. Change your thoughts and you'll change the way your world appears.

Four additional cognitive distortions that are especially relevant to people dealing with anxiety disorders are described below. Use the examples given under each one to help you identify these distortions when they occur in your own self-talk. Then write out both your distorted thoughts and appropriate counterstatements, using the *Cognitive Distortion Worksheet* (below). You'll want to make copies of this worksheet, reserving several sheets for each of the four types of cognitive distortions.

Cognitive Distortion Worksheet

Type of Distorted Thinking: _____	Rational Counterstatements

Overgeneralizing

To overgeneralize is to assume (usually falsely) that because you've had one bad experience in a particular situation, your bad experience will always repeat itself in similar situations. This happens automatically in the process of developing a phobia—you have a panic attack in one store, and after a while you start to avoid all stores. (The generalizing of a phobia from one to all instances of a situation is also influenced by a conditioning phenomenon that behavioral psychologists call *stimulus generalization*.)

For example, you conclude that because you've had one bad experience with public speaking, you'll *never* be able to speak in public successfully. Or because you had one panic attack where you felt terrified and out of control, you assume that the next one and every one thereafter will be equally bad. Or because one person made an unflattering remark about your performance at work or school, you conclude that *everyone* must see it that way (which then leads you to believe that your work is "objectively" substandard).

The essence of overgeneralizing consists of jumping from one instance in the present to *all* instances in the future. You can tell that you're overgeneralizing when your self-talk includes words such as *never, always, all, every, none, no one, nobody, everyone,* and *everybody,* or absolute statements incorporating those words ("I'll never be able to drive again" or "No one would remain my friend if they really knew me").

Three types of Socratic questions are effective for rationally challenging and refuting overgeneralizations:

- What is the evidence for this?

- What are the odds of this really happening (or being true)?

- Has this been true in the past?

Most cases of overgeneralizing won't stand up in the face of these questions. The example below illustrates how to question and counter overgeneralizing thoughts.

Overgeneralizing:	"That panic attack I had on the freeway yesterday was so bad that I'll never be able to drive on freeways again."
Questioning:	"Is it really likely that because I had difficulty driving the freeway yesterday, I'll never be able to drive any freeway again? Has this been true in the past?"
Counterstatement:	"I may need to lay off driving freeways for a while. After some time has passed, I'll feel good enough to try it again. I believe I can succeed if I break the task down into small enough steps. After all, I was able to drive freeways in the past, so I know I can do so again."

Note that one of the keys to countering overgeneralizations is to look for balancing evidence—that is, balancing your negative outlook with other evidence that is more positive and compelling.

Exercise

Monitor your self-talk for one week and notice occasions when you use words such as *always, never, everyone, and no one*. Write down your overgeneralizations in the left-hand column of one of your copies of the *Cognitive Distortion Worksheet*, then write rational counterstatements in the right-hand column. Use balancing evidence and be as specific as possible in your counterstatements.

Filtering

Filtering involves selecting and focusing on one negative aspect of a situation so that you ignore any positive aspects. It is a favorite tactic of the Critic. Applied to yourself, you focus on a single fault and ignore any of your assets and strengths. Or at times you may filter out anything positive in your view of a personal relationship.

Filtering commonly occurs in the course of exposure to a phobic situation, when you focus on one setback and ignore all the progress you've made. Just because you were able to drive to work alone last week but can't do it this week, you begin to question the entire process of real-life desensitization. Or because you have one bad panic attack, you ignore the fact that you've had fewer panic attacks in the last two months than you did before. Another example would be if you received a job performance evaluation that was mostly positive, but you focused exclusively on the one or two criticisms it contained. It is as if you were wearing a special pair of eyeglasses that filtered out anything positive. It's like the old joke about the mother who gives her grown son two ties. When he shows up at her house wearing one of them, she asks him, "So what's wrong with the other tie?"

Be wary of filtering when the following words crop up in your self-talk: *worthless, pointless, hopeless, stupid, failure, dangerous, unfair*. In fact, any word you use that is globally negative in scope may indicate that you're filtering. If you describe someone or something in such terms, reexamine your thinking to see whether you're viewing things in a *balanced* way—one that takes both positive and negative aspects into full account.

Two Socratic questions are often helpful in challenging cognitive distortions due to filtering:

- Are you looking at the whole picture (or are you taking both sides of this into account)?

- Are there positive aspects of this situation (person, object) that you're ignoring?

Both questions remind you to look for other, more positive evidence and to consider both sides of an issue. The following example illustrates this:

Filtering: "I just flunked my midterm in calculus. I'm going down the tubes! I'll never make it through the semester!" (Note the use of catastrophizing as well as filtering.)

Questioning: "Am I looking at the whole picture?"

Counterstatement: "I'm doing satisfactory to good work in my other courses. In calculus, I'm doing well enough on the homework to offset bad grades on the exams, so I can at least pass. There's no basis for the idea that I can't make it through the semester."

The counterstatement in this example of filtering relied on balancing evidence, much like the counterstatement to overgeneralizing in the previous section. These two types of cognitive distortion are similar in that they both *ignore* refuting evidence.

Exercise

Monitor your self-talk for one week and notice any examples of filtering, especially when you find yourself viewing something exclusively in a negative light or using globally negative labels such as *failure, worthless,* or *hopeless.* Write your self-talk based on filtering in the left-hand column of one of your worksheets and then refute each negative statement with rational counterstatements that take the whole picture into account.

Emotional Reasoning

Emotional reasoning refers to the tendency to judge or evaluate something illogically, totally on the basis of your feelings. There may, of course, be some instances when relying on feelings alone can be useful and appropriate. For example, if you simply don't feel good about someone you're just meeting, interviewing, or dating, that may be sufficient reason for you to decide not to proceed with the relationship. In many other cases, though, going solely on feelings and suspending your reason can lead to erroneous conclusions.

One common example of this is to conclude that because you *feel* a certain way, then you necessarily *are* that way as well ("I feel useless, therefore I must *be* useless," "I feel incompetent, therefore I *am* incompetent," or "I feel ugly, therefore I *am* ugly"). To conclude from one negative feeling or a mood that you inherently and for all time possess that negative quality is like concluding from one rainy day that the sun never shines. "I feel, therefore I am" simply isn't accurate or true.

An indication of emotional reasoning is when you make decisions totally on impulse, without the mediation of reasoning. While spontaneity argues in favor of doing this on certain occasions, there are many situations where impulsive decisions can create problems. Be wary about making such snap judgments.

Questions you can use to challenge emotional reasoning include:

* Are you going solely by your feelings?

* Are you looking at this objectively?

* What is the evidence that your judgment (based on feelings) is completely accurate?

Note the use of such questions in the following examples:

Emotional Reasoning:	"It feels impossible to go in and participate in that meeting. I just can't do it."
Questioning:	"Am I going solely by my feelings? Am I looking at this objectively?"
Counterstatement:	"Just because it feels impossible doesn't mean facing this situation is impossible. If necessary, I can leave the meeting (saying I have to go to the bathroom) if I need to. Knowing that, I'll go in and give it a try."
Emotional Reasoning:	"I feel terrible today—there's got to be something seriously wrong with me."
Questioning:	"Am I being completely objective? What is the evidence for this?"
Counterstatement:	"Just because I feel bad doesn't mean that I'm inherently flawed. Even though I'm depressed, there's no evidence for the idea that I'm irrevocably defective. So what if I'm feeling bad? I know that there are things I can do (exercise, call a friend, work in the garden) to get myself out of this mood."

Exercise

During the next week, see if you can track down instances when you make judgments or draw conclusions solely on the basis of your feelings. Notice especially those occasions when you make snap judgments. Use the suggested questions above to dispute emotional reasoning, and write down your counterstatements in the right-hand column of one of your worksheets.

"Should Statements"

"Should statements" are the hallmark of the Perfectionist subpersonality described earlier. You are using them whenever you tell yourself "I should do this," "I must do that," or "I have to" in an attempt to motivate yourself to do something. In cases of ethical responsibility or common courtesy, shoulds *can* be appropriate. There's nothing wrong with such "should statements" as "I should let him know that I appreciate the favor he did," "I should be honest on my income tax," or "I should teach Johnny to look both ways when he crosses the street." The difficulty arises when you use "I should" or "I must" to pressure yourself to meet self-imposed expectations that are unreasonably high:

"I should always be pleasing and cheerful to others, despite my feelings."

"I should be totally competent."

"I should be a 'perfect' spouse, parent, lover, friend, worker, student ..."

"I should be totally self-reliant."

"I should never get tired or sick."

"I should never feel negative emotions like anger or jealousy."

"I should have achievements that bring me status and/or wealth."

"I should not be susceptible to panic attacks."

"I should never be afraid."

Imposing "should statements" on yourself such as the ones above is guaranteed to keep you anxious and tense. Such statements also lower your confidence and self-esteem. After the Perfectionist tells you what you should do, the Critic comes in to inform you about how far you fall short.

How can you tell when your "should statements" are appropriate and when they are reflections of a stress-inducing bad habit? In their book *Self-Esteem*, Matthew McKay and Patrick Fanning outline four criteria for determining when a "should" reflects "healthy" versus "unhealthy" standards:

1. Is the standard flexible—in other words, does it allow for exceptions, or is it rigid and global with no exceptions?

2. Is the standard based on your own experience or is it "inherited"—without your ever having questioned it—from your parents?

3. Is the standard realistic (does it take into account all the consequences its application may lead to), or is it based on an arbitrary sense of rightness, regardless of consequences?

4. Is the standard life-enhancing (does it acknowledge your needs and feelings)—or is it life-restricting (does it ignore your needs and feelings)?

When you find that you're telling yourself "I should" or "I must," you can evaluate the appropriateness of your self-talk according to these criteria. Failing even one of the criteria is enough to cast serious doubt on the reasonableness of a particular "should statement." Consider the following example:

Should Statement: "I should always be pleasing and positive toward others."

Questioning: "Is this something I've tested out for myself, or did I accept it unquestioningly from my parents? Does this acknowledge my needs and feelings or does it ignore them?"

Counterstatement: "My mother gave me the message that I should always be pleasing, no matter what the situation. In my own experience, I've learned that there are times when it's hypocritical to act this way. This 'should' also ignores my needs and feelings, as there are times when I don't really feel like being cheerful and pleasing. Conclusion: It's okay not to always be pleasing and cheerful."

Exercise

Notice during the course of a week how often you tell yourself "I should do this," "I must do that," or "I have to." Write these down in the left-hand column of one of your worksheets. Use the four criteria above to challenge "shoulds" involving excessively high and rigid standards you imposed on yourself. Use Socratic questions to refute "shoulds" involving unrealistic expectations about life. Write your counterstatements in the right-hand column of your worksheet.

General Guidelines for Identifying and Countering Self-Talk

Negative self-talk is nothing more than an accumulation of self-limiting mental habits. You can begin to break these habits by noticing occasions when you engage in unconstructive dialogues with yourself and then countering them, preferably in writing, with more positive, rational statements. It took repetition over many years to internalize your habits of negative self-talk; it will likewise take repetition and practice to learn more constructive and helpful ways of thinking.

Follow the steps below:

1. *Notice.* "Catch yourself in the act" of engaging in negative self-talk. Be aware of situations that are likely to be precipitated or aggravated by negative self-talk.

    - Any occasion when you're feeling anxious, including the onset of a panic attack (watch for the Worrier and the cognitive distortions of overestimating and catastrophizing)

    - When you anticipate having to face a difficult task or a phobic situation (again the Worrier, overestimating, and catastrophizing play a large role)

    - Occasions when you've made some kind of mistake and feel critical of yourself (watch for the Critic and overgeneralizing, filtering, and "should statements")

    - Occasions when you're feeling depressed or discouraged (watch for the Victim, overestimating, catastrophizing, filtering, and overgeneralizing)

    - Situations where you're angry at yourself or others (watch for the Critic, the Perfectionist, and any of the above-described cognitive distortions)

    - Situations where you feel guilty, ashamed, or embarrassed (watch especially for the Perfectionist and "should statements")

2. *Stop.* Ask yourself any or all of the following questions:

    "What am I telling myself that is making me feel this way?"

    "Do I really want to do this to myself?"

    "Do I really want to stay upset?"

If the answer to the last two questions is no, proceed to step 3.

Realize that sometimes your answers may actually be yes. You may actually wish to continue to be upset rather than change the underlying self-talk. Often this is because you're having strong feelings that you haven't allowed yourself to fully express. It's common to stay anxious, angry, or depressed for a period of time when there are strong feelings that you haven't fully acknowledged—let alone expressed.

If you're feeling too upset to easily undertake the task of identifying and countering self-talk, give yourself the opportunity to acknowledge and express your feelings. If there's no one available to share them with, try writing them down in a journal. When you've calmed down and are ready to relax, proceed with the steps below. (See chapter 12 for more guidelines and strategies.)

Another reason you may maintain your anxiety is because you perceive a strong need to "keep everything under control." Often you're overestimating some danger or preparing for an imagined catastrophe—and so staying tense and vigilant is the way in which you give yourself a sense of control. Your vigilance is validated by the feeling of control it gives you. Unfortunately, in the process you can make yourself more and more tense, until you reach a point where your mind seems to race out of control and you dwell on danger and catastrophe almost to the exclusion of anything else. This, in turn, leads to more anxiety and tension. The only way out of this vicious circle is to let go and relax. The next step, relaxation, is crucial for you to be able to slow down your mind and sort out patterns of negative self-talk.

3. **Relax.** *Disrupt* your train of negative thoughts by taking some deep abdominal breaths or using some methods of distraction. The point is to *let go, slow yourself down*, and *relax*. Negative self-talk is so rapid, automatic, and subtle that it can escape detection if you're feeling tense, speeded up, and unable to slow down. You'll find it difficult to recognize and undo such self-talk by merely thinking about it: it's necessary to physically relax first. In extreme cases, it may take fifteen to twenty minutes of deep relaxation, using breathing, progressive muscle relaxation, or meditation, to slow yourself down enough so that you can identify what you've been telling yourself. If you're not excessively wound up, you can probably do this step in a minute or two.

4. **Write down** the negative self-talk or inner dialogue that led you to feel anxious, upset, or depressed. It's often difficult to decipher what you're telling yourself by merely reflecting on it. The act of writing things down will help to clarify what specific statements you actually made to yourself. Use the *Daily Record of Dysfunctional Thoughts* in the exercise following this section to write down your self-talk.

This step may take some practice to learn. *It's important in identifying self-talk to be able to disentangle thoughts from feelings.* One way to do this is to write down just the feelings first and then uncover the thoughts that led to them. As a general rule, feeling statements contain words expressing emotions, such as "scared," "hurt," and "sad," while self-talk statements do not contain such words. For example, the statement "I feel stupid and irresponsible" is one in which thoughts and feelings are entangled. It can be broken down into a particular feeling ("I feel upset" or "I feel disappointed") and the thoughts (or self-talk) that logically produce such feelings ("I'm stupid" or "I'm irresponsible").

To give another example, the statement "I'm too scared to undertake this" mixes a feeling of fear with one or more thoughts. It can be broken down into the feeling ("I'm scared") which arises from the negative self-statement ("This is unmanageable" or "I can't undertake this"). You can ask yourself first, "What was I feeling?" and then ask, "What thoughts were going through my mind to cause me to feel the way I did?"

Always keep in mind that *self-talk consists of thoughts, not feelings.* Most of the time these thoughts are judgments or appraisals of a situation or yourself. The feelings are emotional reactions that *result* from these judgments and appraisals.

5. *Identify the type* of negative self-talk you engaged in. (Is it from the Worrier, the Critic, the Victim, or the Perfectionist?) Also, look for any *cognitive distortions* that were present (such as overestimating, catastrophizing, overgeneralizing, and filtering). After doing this for a while, you'll become aware of the particular types of negative inner dialogue and particular types of cognitive distortions you're especially prone to use. With practice, you'll identify them more quickly as they come up.

6. *Answer or dispute* your negative self-talk with positive, rational, self-supportive statements. Answer each negative statement you've written by *writing down* an opposing, positive statement. These counterstatements should be worded so that they avoid negatives and are in the present tense and first person. They should also be *believable* and *feel good* to you (in other words, you should feel comfortable with them).

In many cases, you'll find it helpful to question and refute your negative statements with the Socratic questions enumerated earlier in this chapter.

In other instances, you may imagine a positive counterstatement immediately, without going through a process of rational questioning. This is fine, so long as you have some degree of belief in your counterstatement.

Exercise: The Daily Record of Dysfunctional Thoughts

On the following page you'll find the *Daily Record of Dysfunctional Thoughts* designed by Aaron Beck, one of the pioneers in investigating self-talk. This form has been specifically designed to assist you in identifying and countering your negative thinking. The *Daily Record* is *particularly* appropriate to use at times when you're feeling anxious, depressed, self-critical, or otherwise upset. The columns should be filled in from left to right as follows:

1. *Situation:*   Describe in a few words the specific situation that led you to feel anxious or upset. If it was exclusively a matter of internal thoughts, anticipations, or memories that led you to feel upset, describe these instead.

Daily Record of Dysfunctional Thoughts

Date	Situation	Emotion(s)	Automatic Thought(s)	Rational Response	Outcome
	Describe: 1. Actual event leading to unpleasant emotion, or 2. Stream of thoughts, daydream, or recollection leading to unpleasant emotion	1. Specify sad, anxious/angry, etc. 2. Rate degree of emotion, 1 to 100.	1. Write automatic thought(s) that preceded emotion(s). 2. Rate belief in automatic thought(s), 0 to 100.	1. Write rational response to automatic thought(s). 2. Rate belief in rational response, 0 to 100.	1. Rerate belief in automatic thought(s), 0 to 100. 2. Specify and rate your subsequent emotions, 0 to 100.

Instructions: When you experience an unpleasant emotion, note the situation that seemed to stimulate the emotion. If the emotion occurred while you were thinking, daydreaming, etc., then note the automatic thought associated with the emotion. Record the degree to which you believe this thought: 0 = not at all; 100 = completely. In rating degree of emotion, 1 = a trace; 100 = the most intense possible.

2. *Emotion(s):* What emotions (for example, anxiety, depression, shame) did you experience while you were upset? On a scale of 0 to 100, how intense were your emotions?

3. *Automatic Thought(s):* Here is where you write down the negative self-talk that caused you to be anxious, depressed, or upset. Think back over what you were telling yourself when your strong emotions arose, and be careful to separate the actual thoughts that went through your mind from the resulting feelings. Ask yourself what thoughts led you to feel the way you did. If you're still feeling upset or tense as you're doing this exercise, give yourself time to relax before attempting to identify self-talk. After you've determined what you were saying to yourself, rate your degree of belief in it: How valid does it seem to you on a scale from 0 to 100?

4. *Rational Response:* In this column, write positive statements to counter your negative self-talk. Think about how you could take a more constructive, self-supportive outlook and write statements that reverse your negative thoughts. Use Socratic questions, if necessary, to challenge negative self-talk. Be sure that you actually have some belief in your positive counterstatements. Also specify your degree of belief in these statements on a scale from 0 to 100.

5. *Outcome:* First, rerate your degree of belief in your negative self-talk (as a result of having written positive counterstatements). Then rerate the initial feelings you experienced before doing the exercise. What is the intensity of your feelings now on a scale from 0 to 100?

Note: Before filling in the *Daily Record*, you will want to photocopy at least fifty copies for future use.

If you are serious about overcoming your habits of negative self-talk, I recommend that you use the *Daily Record of Dysfunctional Thoughts* on a *daily* basis for at least two weeks. After that, use it every time you find yourself anxious, depressed, self-critical, angry, or otherwise upset during the next two months. It will take some time and effort to write down your negative self-talk along with positive counterstatements—however, this will be time and effort well spent. The practice of writing down counterstatements repeatedly will help you to internalize a new habit of reversing your negative thinking whenever you notice it beginning to start. After a month or two of writing everything out, you'll find that you begin to counter negative self-talk automatically and effortlessly as it comes up. *Cultivating the habit of countering is one of the most significant steps you can take in dealing with all kinds of anxiety, as well as panic attacks.*

Disrupting Negative Self-Talk: Short Form

Using the *Daily Record of Dysfunctional Thoughts* will go a long way to help you overcome long-established mental habits that produce anxiety, depression, and low self-esteem. In many situations, however, you may have neither the time nor the opportunity to write down negative self-talk and positive counterstatements. Follow the three steps below whenever you wish to disrupt a negative train of thought "on the spot."

1. ***Notice*** that you are engaging in negative self-talk. The best time to catch yourself involved in negative inner dialogue is when you are feeling anxious, depressed, self-critical, or upset in general.

2. ***Stop.*** Ask yourself any or all of the following questions:

    "What am I telling myself that is making me feel this way?"

    "Do I really want to do this to myself?"

    "Do I really want to stay upset?"

3. ***Relax or distract yourself.*** In order to break a train of negative self-talk, you need to switch gears. This can be accomplished by slowing yourself down with deep, abdominal breathing *or* by finding some form of distraction to divert your mind from negative thoughts. Often doing something *physical* (such as exercise, dancing, or household chores) will have the greatest power to distract because it moves you out of your head and into your body. Other ready forms of distraction include engaging in conversation, reading, hobbies and games, relaxation recordings, and music.

    As an alternative to deep breathing or distraction, use a thought-stopping technique such as shouting "Stop!" or "Get out!" or stomping your foot or snapping a rubber band against your wrist to divert your mind.

    See appendix 4 for a more detailed list of methods for distracting yourself from anxious thinking and worrying.

The purpose of this section is to suggest convenient methods for disrupting negative self-talk "on the spot." It is *not* intended as a substitute for writing out counterstatements or using the *Daily Record of Dysfunctional Thoughts*. Only by using the latter and practicing over a period of weeks can you begin to effectively change your lifelong habits of negative thinking that arise from the subpersonalities and cognitive distortions described in this chapter.

Summary of Things to Do

1.   Reread the section "Some Basic Points About Self-Talk" to reinforce your understanding of the automatic nature of self-talk and its role in maintaining both phobias and panic attacks.

2.   Familiarize yourself with the four subpersonalities that contribute to much of your negative self-talk: the Worrier, the Critic, the Victim, and the Perfectionist. Determine their role in your daily life by completing the worksheets in the exercise "What Are Your Subpersonalities Telling You?" Then counter the negative self-talk of each subpersonality with positive statements. Read over your positive statements every day for a week or record them so that you can listen to them in the car or while going to sleep at night.

3.   Make a list of all your phobias and other specific fears, then rank them from the most to least bothersome. Complete *The Worry Worksheet* for each of your most difficult phobias or fears. For each one, write down overestimating and catastrophic thoughts that keep the fear going. Then refute these negative thoughts with more reasonable and positive counterstatements. Finally, write down ways in which you would cope if what you feared were actually to come about.

4.   Identify and challenge other types of cognitive distortions that may aggravate worry and anxiety. Use the *Cognitive Distortion Worksheet* to identify examples of overgeneralizing, filtering, emotional reasoning, and "should statements" that come up at times when you feel anxious, depressed, self-critical, or otherwise upset. Then use Socratic questions to challenge distorted self-statements and write down corresponding positive counterstatements.

5.   Become familiar with the six steps for identifying and countering negative self-talk: 1) *Notice*, 2) *Stop*, 3) *Relax* and slow down, 4) *Write down* negative self-statements, 5) *Identify* the relevant subpersonality or cognitive distortion, and 6) *Counter* each negative self-statement with a rational, positive alternative. After you've completed the exercises for the subpersonalities, *The Worry Worksheet*, and the other cognitive distortions (which should take a few weeks), spend at least two more weeks filling out the *Daily Record of Dysfunctional Thoughts* every day. Make about fifty copies of the *Daily Record* for this purpose and for future use. A thorough effort on your part here will pay off.

6.   Use the "short form" of disrupting negative self-talk when you want to quickly divert yourself from a train of negative thinking. Remember, this is not a substitute for doing the exercises in 2, 3, and 4 above.

Further Reading

Barlow, David, and Michelle Craske. *Mastery of Your Anxiety and Panic: Workbook.* Fourth edition. New York: Oxford University Press, 2007.

Beck, Aaron T. *Cognitive Therapy and the Emotional Disorders.* New York: Meridian, 1979.

Beck, Aaron T., and Gary Emery. *Anxiety Disorders and Phobias: A Cognitive Perspective.* New York: Basic Books, 1990. (This book is primarily intended for helping professionals.)

Burns, David. *Feeling Good.* New York: Avon, 1999. (The classic popular book on cognitive distortions.)

Helmstetter, Shad. *What to Say When You Talk to Yourself.* New York: Pocket Books, 1982. (This book is timely and easy to read.)

McKay, Matthew, Martha Davis, and Patrick Fanning. *Thoughts & Feelings: The Art of Cognitive Stress Intervention.* Third edition. Oakland, CA: New Harbinger Publications, 2007.

McKay, Matthew, and Patrick Fanning. *Self-Esteem.* Third edition. Oakland, CA: New Harbinger Publications, 2000.

Wilson, Reid. *Don't Panic: Taking Control of Anxiety Attacks.* Revised edition. New York: HarperCollins, 1996.

9

Mistaken Beliefs

By now you may have asked, "Where does negative self-talk come from?" In most cases, it's possible to trace negative thinking back to deeper-lying beliefs or assumptions about ourselves, others, and life in general. These basic assumptions have been variously called "scripts," "core beliefs," "life decisions," "fallacious beliefs," or "mistaken beliefs." While growing up, we learned them from our parents, teachers, and peers, as well as from the larger society around us. These beliefs are typically so basic to our thinking that we do not recognize them as *beliefs* at all—we just take them for granted and assume them to reflect reality. Examples of mistaken beliefs that you might hold are "I'm powerless," "Life is a struggle," or "I should always look good and act nice, no matter how I feel." There is nothing new about the idea of mistaken beliefs—they are a part of what people have in mind when they refer to your "attitude" or "outlook."

Mistaken beliefs are at the root of much of the anxiety you experience. As discussed in the preceding chapter, you talk yourself into much of your anxiety by anticipating the worst (what-if thinking), putting yourself down (self-critical thinking), and pushing yourself to meet unreasonable demands and expectations (perfectionist thinking). Underlying these destructive patterns of self-talk are some basic false assumptions about yourself and "the way life is."

You could save yourself quite a bit of worrying, for example, if you let go of the basic assumption, "I must worry about a problem before there's any chance it will go away." Similarly, you would feel more confident and secure if you discarded the mistaken belief "I'm nothing unless I succeed" or "I'm nothing unless others love and approve of me." Once again, life would be less stressful and tense if you would let go of the belief "I must do it perfectly or it's not worth bothering to try." You can go a long way toward creating a less anxious way of life by working on changing the basic assumptions that tend to perpetuate anxiety.

Mistaken beliefs often keep you from achieving your most important goals in life. You might ask yourself right now, "What is it that I really want out of life? What would I attempt to do if I knew I could not fail?" Take a few minutes to seriously reflect on this and write your answer in the space below. (Use a separate sheet of paper if you need more room.)

I want to live a life free from fear and anxiety. I want to have a good job again and grow on my profession. I want a loving partner.

Now, if you don't yet have what you want, ask yourself the simple question, "Why not?" List what reasons you can come up with in the space below or write them on another sheet of paper.

- I'm currently living with a lot of anxiety
- I'm affraid of going to job interviews
- I'm affraid of failing at a job
- I'm not confident enough to talk to girls

In the process of doing the above exercise, you may have discovered certain beliefs or assumptions that have been holding you back. Are these assumptions truly valid? Examples of assumptions that people hold themselves back with might include "I can't afford to have what I want," "I don't have the time to go back to school and study the subject that interests me," or "I don't have the talent to succeed." At a more unconscious level, you might even feel "I don't deserve to have what I truly want." None of these ideas necessarily reflects the true nature of reality—they all involve assumptions that might well turn out to be false if actually tested. Often you don't realize how such assumptions are affecting your behavior until someone else points them out to you.

Mistaken beliefs often set limits on your self-esteem and self-worth. Many such beliefs involve the idea that your self-worth depends on something outside yourself, such as social status, wealth, material possessions, the love of another person, or social approval in general. If you don't have these things, somehow you believe that you are not worth much. The belief that "Success is everything" or "My worth depends on what I accomplish" places the basis of your self-esteem outside of you. So does the belief "I'm nothing unless I'm loved (or approved of)."

The truth that takes some people a long time to realize is that self-worth is *inherent*. You have an essential value, worth, and dignity just by virtue of the fact that you're a human being. You have many qualities and talents, regardless of your outer accomplishments or the approval of others. Without thinking, we respect the inherent value of dogs and cats as animals. So, too, human beings have inherent value *just as they are,* apart from what they accomplish, what they possess, or whose approval they enjoy. As you grow in self-esteem, you can *learn* to respect and believe in yourself apart from what you have accomplished and without relying on others for your good feeling (or making others reliant on you).

Examples of Mistaken Beliefs

There are innumerable mistaken beliefs. You have your own collection as a result of what you learned from your parents, teachers, and peers during childhood and adolescence. Sometimes you take on a false belief directly from your parents, such as when you are told "Big boys don't cry" or "Nice girls don't get angry." At other times, you develop an attitude about yourself as a result of being frequently criticized (thus "I'm worthless"), ignored (thus "My needs don't matter"), or rejected (thus "I'm unlovable") over many years. The unfortunate thing is that you may live out these mistaken attitudes to the point where you act in ways—and get others to treat you in ways—that confirm them. Like computers, people can be "preprogrammed," and the mistaken beliefs of childhood can become self-fulfilling prophecies.

Below are some examples of fairly common mistaken beliefs that tend to influence many people. Following each are counterstatements that replace the negative belief with a positive one, much in the way negative self-talk was countered by positive self-statements in the preceding chapter. Positive statements that counter mistaken beliefs are known as *affirmations*.

- I'm powerless. I'm a victim of outside circumstances.

  I'm responsible and in control of my life. Circumstances are what they are, but I can determine my attitude toward them.

- Life is a struggle. Something must be wrong if life seems too easy, pleasurable, or fun.

  Life is full and pleasurable.
  It's okay for me to relax and have fun.
  Life is an adventure—and I'm learning to accept both the ups and the downs.

- If I take a risk, I'll fail. If I fail, others will reject me.

  It's okay for me to take risks.
  It's okay to fail—I can learn a lot from every mistake.
  It's okay for me to be a success.

- I'm unimportant. My feelings and needs are unimportant.

  I am a valuable and unique person.
  I deserve to have my feelings and needs taken care of as much as anyone else.

- I always should look good and act nice, no matter how I feel.

  It's okay simply to be myself.

- If I worry enough, this problem should get better or go away.

  Worrying has no effect on solving problems; taking action does.

- I can't cope with difficult or scary situations.

  I can learn to handle any scary situation if I approach it slowly, in small enough steps.

- The outside world is dangerous. There is safety only in what is known and familiar.

  I can learn to become more comfortable with the world outside. I look forward to new opportunities for learning and growth that the outside world can offer.

Just *recognizing* your own particular mistaken beliefs is the first and most important step toward letting go of them. The second step is to develop a positive affirmation to counter each mistaken belief and continue to impress it on your mind until you are "deprogrammed."

What follows is a questionnaire that will help you to identify some of your own unconstructive beliefs. Rate each statement on a 1 to 4 scale, according to how much you think it influences your feelings and behavior. Then go back and check off the beliefs you rated 3 or 4.

Mistaken Beliefs Questionnaire

How much does each of these unconstructive beliefs influence your feelings and behavior? Take your time to reflect about each belief.

1 = not at all   3 = strongly/frequently
2 = somewhat/sometimes   4 = very strongly

Place the appropriate number after each statement:

1.   I feel powerless or helpless. 4
2.   Often I feel like a victim of outside circumstances. 4
3.   I don't have the money to do what I really want. 2
4.   There is seldom enough time to do what I want. 2
5.   Life is very difficult—it's a struggle. 4
6.   If things are going well, watch out! 2
7.   I feel unworthy. I feel that I'm not good enough. 3
8.   Often I feel that I don't deserve to be successful or happy. 3
9.   Often I feel a sense of defeat and resignation, a sense of "Why bother?" 2
10. My condition seems hopeless. 4
11. There is something fundamentally wrong with me. 4
12. I feel ashamed of my condition. 4
13. If I take risks to get better, I'm afraid I'll fail. 4
14. If I take risks to get better, I'm afraid I'll succeed. 2
15. If I recover fully, I might have to deal with realities I'd rather not face. 3
16. I feel like I'm nothing (or can't make it) unless I'm loved. 2
17. I can't stand being separated from others. 2
18. If a person I love doesn't love me in return, I feel like it's my fault. 2
19. It's very hard to be alone. 2
20. What others think of me is very important. 2
21. I feel personally threatened when criticized. 2
22. It's important to please others. 3
23. People won't like me if they see who I really am. 3
24. I need to keep up a front or others will see my weaknesses. 2
25. I have to achieve or produce something significant in order to feel okay about myself. 4
26. My accomplishments at work/school are extremely important. 2
27. Success is everything. 4
28. I have to be the best at what I do. 3

29.   I have to be somebody—somebody outstanding. 3

30.   To fail is terrible. 2

31.   I can't rely on others for help. 2

32.   I can't receive from others. 2

33.   If I let someone get too close, I'm afraid of being controlled. 2

34.   I can't tolerate being out of control. 2

35.   I'm the only one who can solve my problems. 3

36.   I should always be very generous and unselfish. 2

37.   I should be the *perfect* … (Rate each below.)
   *   employee 3   *   lover 3
   *   professional 3   *   friend 3
   *   spouse   *   student
   *   parent   *   son/daughter 3

38.   I should be able to endure any hardship. 4

39.   I should be able to find a quick solution to every problem. 4

40.   I should never be tired or fatigued. 3

41.   I should always be efficient. 3

42.   I should always be competent. 3

43.   I should always be able to foresee everything. 4

44.   I should never be angry or irritable. Or: I don't like (or am afraid of) anger. 2

45.   I should always be pleasant or nice, no matter how I feel. 2

46.   I often feel … (Rate each below.)
   *   ugly 2   *   unintelligent 3
   *   inferior or defective 4   *   guilty or ashamed 4

47.   I'm just the way I am—I can't really change. 2

48.   The world outside is a dangerous place. 4

49.   Unless you worry about a problem, it just gets worse. 4

50.   It's risky to trust people. 2

51.   My problems will go away on their own with time. 2

52.   I feel anxious about making mistakes. 4

53.   I demand perfection of myself. 3

54.   If I didn't have my safe person (or safe place), I'm afraid I couldn't cope. 3

55.   If I stop worrying, I'm afraid something bad will happen. 2

56.   I'm afraid to face the world out there on my own. 4

57.   My self-worth isn't a given—it has to be earned. 2

You may have noticed that some of the beliefs on the questionnaire fall into specific groups, each of which reflects a very basic belief or attitude toward life.* Go back over your answers and see how you scored with respect to each of the groups of beliefs listed below.

Add up your scores for each of the following subgroups of beliefs. If your total score on the items in a particular subgroup exceeds the criterion value, then this is likely to be a problem area for you. It's important that you give this subgroup special attention when you begin to work with affirmations to start changing your mistaken beliefs.

If your total score for questions 1, 2, 7, 9, 10, 11 is over 15:	You likely believe that you are powerless, have little or no control over outside circumstances, or are unable to do much that could help your situation. In sum, "I'm powerless" or "I can't do much about my life."
If your total score for questions 16, 17, 18, 19, 54, 56 is over 15:	You likely believe that your self-worth is dependent on the love of someone else. You feel that you need another's (or others') love to feel okay about yourself and to cope. In sum, "My worth and security are dependent on being loved."
If your total score for questions 20, 21, 22, 23, 24, 45 is over 15:	You likely believe that your self-worth is dependent on others' approval. Being pleasing and getting acceptance from others is very important for your sense of security and your sense of who you are. In sum, "My worth and security depend on the approval of others."
If your total score for questions 25, 26, 27, 28, 29, 30, 41, 42 is over 20:	You likely believe that your self-worth is dependent on external achievements, such as school or career performance, status, or wealth. In sum, "My worth is dependent on my performance or achievements."
If your total score for questions 31, 32, 33, 34, 35, 50 is over 15:	You likely believe that you can't trust, rely on, or receive help from others. You may have a tendency to keep a distance from people and avoid intimacy for fear of losing control. In sum, "If I trust or get too close, I'll lose control."
If your total score for questions 37, 38, 39, 40, 52, 53 is over 25:	You likely believe that you have to be perfect in some or many areas of life. You make excessive demands on yourself. There is no room for mistakes. In sum, "I have to be perfect" or "It's not okay to make mistakes."

---

* The idea for defining subgroups of beliefs was adapted from David Burns, MD, *Feeling Good*. See his book for further details on how to counter and work with mistaken beliefs.

Countering Mistaken Beliefs

Now that you have an idea of those mistaken beliefs which have the greatest impact on you, how do you go about changing them? The first step is to ask yourself this question: *how strongly do you believe in them?* There are three possible ways to maintain a mistaken belief:

- You don't really believe it. You view the belief as a bad mental habit that you are truly ready to give up. You are convinced of the uselessness of the belief *and* you realize that it has no strong emotional hold on you.

  If that is the case, you are ready to develop a positive affirmation to counter the belief. You can proceed directly to the section "Guidelines for Constructing Affirmations" and follow the suggested steps for developing affirmations to counter a particular belief. You may also want to see the section "Examples of Affirmations" at the end of the chapter to get ideas for specific alternatives to any of the beliefs on the *Mistaken Beliefs Questionnaire.*

- You don't really subscribe to the belief on an intellectual level, but it still has an emotional grip on you and influences the way you act. You *don't want to believe* that "it's always important to be pleasing to others," for example, but you find that you continue to feel and act as if it were true. It's hard to "get the belief out of your system."

  If that is the case, it's important to subject the belief to questions 4 and 5 under "Five Questions for Challenging Mistaken Beliefs" listed below. Identify any belief you rated 3 or 4 that still affects you despite your intellectual doubts. Then use questions 4 and 5 to examine whether the belief is beneficial to your well-being and whether it developed out of your own choice or from your family history.

- You may really have faith in a particular belief. You're not convinced that it's inaccurate; you'll need some persuading before you'll consider giving it up. The idea of substituting a positive affirmation in place of an attitude you've long believed in seems superficial or naively optimistic.

  If that is the case, it's important to subject the belief to questions 1, 2, and 3 under "Five Questions for Challenging Mistaken Beliefs" listed below. These first three questions are taken from the Socratic questions described in chapter 8 and are especially useful for challenging a mistaken belief on a strictly logical level. If you discredit your belief on purely rational grounds, then proceed to questions 4 and 5. These questions will enable you to see how the belief affects your personal well-being and to determine whether it's your own belief or was acquired from your parents.

Five Questions for Challenging Mistaken Beliefs

1. What is the evidence for this belief? Looking objectively at all of your life experience, what is the evidence that this is true?

2. Does this belief *invariably* or *always* hold true for you?

3. Does this belief look at the whole picture? Does it take into account both positive and negative ramifications?

4. Does this belief promote your well-being and/or peace of mind?

5. Did you choose this belief on your own or did it develop out of your experience of growing up in your family?

A few words need to be said about this last question. Many of your mistaken beliefs were likely acquired from your family while you were growing up. There are at least two ways this could happen. First, one or both of your parents may have held the belief and you simply learned it from them. For example, beliefs such as "The world outside is a dangerous place" or "It's risky to trust people" might have been attitudes held by your parents that you adopted wholesale, because no alternative views were presented to you as a child.

The other way you might have acquired a mistaken belief is as a *reaction to what happened* and/or *the way you were treated* as a child. For example, if your father died and then your mother went to work when you were five years old, you may have felt abandoned and developed the belief that "Being alone means being abandoned and unloved." Or if your parents expected you to achieve and criticized your mistakes and performance at school, your reaction would likely involve developing such beliefs as "My accomplishments are extremely important" and "It's not okay to make mistakes."

It's often helpful in the process of evaluating mistaken beliefs to see how they arose from unfortunate or dysfunctional circumstances during childhood. While such beliefs may have helped you to survive as a child, *they have long lost their usefulness and only serve to create anxiety or stress for you now*. To investigate connections between your childhood and mistaken beliefs, refer to the section "Childhood Circumstances" in chapter 2, and complete the *Family Background Questionnaire* if you haven't done so already. You may also find it helpful to look at the section "Some Causes of Low Self-Esteem" in chapter 14 to get a clearer idea of the various types of dysfunctional childhood situations that can provide the basis for developing mistaken beliefs.

Examples

The following examples illustrate the application of the above questions in challenging mistaken beliefs.

Mistaken Belief: "I am powerless or helpless." (Note: In challenging beliefs from the *Mistaken Beliefs Questionnaire*, reword any belief beginning with the words "I feel ... " to "I am ... " This provides a more direct statement of the belief.)

Questioning: 1. "What is the evidence for this?"

2. "Is this *always* true for me?"

4. "Does this belief promote my well-being?"

Counterarguments:	1. "What is the evidence for this?"

"Though I often *feel* powerless or helpless, that doesn't necessarily mean that I *am* powerless or helpless." (Recognize that the mistaken belief is an example of an attitude typically held by the Victim subpersonality described in chapter 8. It is also an example of a cognitive distortion based on emotional reasoning.) "After all, I can work on mastering the strategies in this workbook and can consult a therapist specializing in anxiety disorders to help me overcome my condition. Also, I have the support of my family and friends who are backing me all the way. Thus, there is no strong evidence that I'm either powerless or helpless."

2. "Is this *always* true for me?"
"Some days I certainly *feel* powerless or helpless, but other days I feel more capable and optimistic. It's just not true that I *always* feel that way."

4. "Does this belief promote my well-being?"
"Believing that I'm powerless and helpless is destructive to developing confidence in myself and hope for recovery. Such a belief definitely does not promote my well-being or peace of mind."

Affirmations: *I believe in myself.*

I trust I have the capacity to overcome my problem with anxiety.

Mistaken Belief: "It's very important to please others."

Questioning: 2. "Is this *always* true for me?"

4. "Does this belief promote my well-being?"

5. "Did I choose this belief on my own or did it develop from my childhood?"

Counterarguments: 2. "Is this *always* true for me?"
"Certainly there are some situations where it's helpful to come across in a pleasing manner. If I'm interviewing for a job, going out on a first date, comforting my spouse, or hosting a party, I generally *want* to be pleasing. On the other hand, if I'm feeling exhausted or upset and need support from my partner or friends, it serves me better to ask them to be there for me rather than to have to deny my needs and keep up a pleasing front. In short, it's sometimes *more* important to attend to my own feelings."

Counterarguments:	4. "Does this belief promote my well-being?"

"In some situations, probably yes. I feel good about myself if I can be pleasant in situations where to come across as such might be appropriate. However, it doesn't serve me to try to be pleasing when I'm actually feeling upset or ill. I'll be more honest and in tune with myself to let people know what I'm feeling and ask for their support."

5. "Did I choose this belief on my own or did it develop from my childhood?"

"My mother was ill and frequently complained during much of my childhood. I felt I always had to be on guard to protect her from my own problems. It seemed that I had to be pleasing to maintain her approval. No wonder I grew up to be such a people pleaser! I guess that I didn't freely choose this belief, but rather it was imposed on me by the circumstances of my childhood."

Affirmations:	*It's okay to not always be pleasing.*
	I can enjoy being pleasing at those times when I genuinely feel like it.

Mistaken Belief: "My accomplishments at work/school are supremely important."

Questioning:
2. "Is this belief *always* true?"

3. "Does this belief look at the whole picture?"

4. "Does this belief promote my well-being?"

5. "Did I choose this belief on my own or did it develop from my childhood?"

Counterarguments:
2. "Is this belief *always* true?"

"No, in as much as other areas of my life (health, relationships, leisure time, creative pursuits) are also important. Accomplishing things at school or work is certainly important, but it's not *always important twenty-four hours a day, seven days a week.*"

3. "Does this belief look at the whole picture?"

"It's true that what I accomplish at school or work is important. I need to maintain a certain level of competence in school in order to earn the degree that will help me find a job." (Or "I need to maintain a certain level of performance at work to hold my job.") "But is it looking at the whole picture to regard my accomplishments as *supremely* important? If that were the case, they would be more important than my health, my peace of mind, my family, and everything else I value. Such an attitude would lead to an imbalanced and ultimately unhealthy lifestyle—a lifestyle where nothing else mattered except my success and accomplishments. Thus it's unreasonable to believe that my accomplishments are supremely important."

Counterarguments: 4. "Does this belief promote my well-being?"

"For reasons already mentioned, I recognize that an *exclusive* focus on accomplishments is unhealthy."

5. "Did I choose this belief on my own, or did it develop from my childhood?"

"My parents were both professionals who were successful in their careers and expected me to follow their example. I always had to do well in school to receive their approval and was criticized for any grade below a B. My attitude that achievement is so important came from living with them—I didn't freely choose it."

Affirmations: *My accomplishments are important and so are other things in my life.*

I am learning how to balance work and play in my life.

The above examples can serve as guidelines for challenging your own mistaken beliefs. If there is little evidence for a particular belief, if it is not always true, or if it doesn't promote your personal well-being, then it is most likely mistaken. If the belief was acquired out of dysfunctional family circumstances rather than freely chosen by you as an adult, it is equally likely to be mistaken. It is important to go through such a process of questioning if you feel at all attached to any particular belief.

Once you've completed the process of challenging all of those mistaken beliefs you rated 3 or 4, you're ready to develop positive affirmations to counter each one of them. The next section explains how to construct affirmations. Although it's preferable to develop your own affirmations, you can refer to the examples at the end of the chapter if you need help creating an affirmation for a particular mistaken belief.

After you've developed your affirmations, go back to the *Mistaken Beliefs Questionnaire* and write each affirmation in capital letters next to or under the particular mistaken belief it is intended to counter. (Refer to the examples of mistaken beliefs and affirmations earlier in this chapter.)

The process of countering mistaken beliefs with affirmations is very similar to that of countering negative self-talk with positive self-statements, which was described in chapter 8. The difference is that affirmations are very compact statements that you can easily rehearse (not unlike the coping statements for panic attacks listed in chapter 6). Writing affirmations repetitively on paper or listening to them repetitively on a recording can, with persistence, actually result in their supplanting unwanted mistaken beliefs in your mind. In the chapter on self-talk, the important process to master was "countering." By continually writing out counterstatements to negative self-talk, you eventually develop a *habit* of noticing and countering the anxiety-provoking things you tell yourself. In this chapter, the important process is working with affirmations. This will actually change the core beliefs that underlie your negative self-talk.

Guidelines for Constructing Affirmations

- An affirmation should be *short, simple,* and *direct.* "I believe in myself" is preferable to "There are a lot of good qualities I have that I believe in."

- Keep affirmations in the *present tense* ("I am prosperous") or *present progressive tense* ("I am becoming prosperous"). Telling yourself that some change you desire will happen in the future always keeps it one step removed.

- Try to *avoid negatives.* Instead of saying "I'm no longer afraid of public speaking," try "I'm free of fear about public speaking" or "I'm becoming fearless about public speaking." Similarly, instead of the negative statement "I'm not perfect," try "It's okay to be less than perfect" or "It's okay to make mistakes." Your unconscious mind is incapable of making the distinction between a positive and a negative statement. It can turn a negative statement, such as "I'm not afraid," into a positive statement that you don't want to affirm—that is, "I'm afraid."

- Start with a direct declaration of a positive change you want to make in your life ("I am making more time for myself every day"). If this feels a little too strong for you just yet, try changing it to "I am willing to make more time for myself." *Willingness* to change is the first step you need to take in order to actually make any substantial change in your life. A second alternative to a direct declaration is to affirm that you are *becoming* something or *learning* to do something. If you're not quite ready for a direct statement such as "I'm strong, confident, and secure," you can affirm "I am becoming strong, confident, and secure." Again, if you're not ready for "I face my fears willingly," try "I'm learning to face my fears."

- It's important that you have *some* belief in—or at least a willingness to believe in—your affirmations. It's by no means necessary, however, to believe in an affirmation 100 percent when you first start out. The whole point is to shift your beliefs and attitudes in favor of the affirmation.

I'm working on becoming mentally fit.

Ways to Work with Affirmations

Once you have made a list of affirmations, decide on a few that you would like to work with. In general, it's a good idea to work on only two or three at a time, unless you choose to make a recording containing all of them. Some of the more helpful ways you can utilize affirmations are listed below.

- Write an affirmation repetitively, about five or ten times every day, for a week or two. Each time you doubt your belief in the affirmation, write down your doubt on the reverse side of the paper. As you continue to write an affirmation over and over, giving yourself the opportunity to express any doubts, you'll find that your willingness to believe it increases. Here is an example:

I'm working on becoming healthier. I make progress every day

Affirmation	*Doubt*
"I'm learning to be fine by myself."	"Yes, for a few hours, but how will I ever manage for a whole day?"
"I'm learning to be fine by myself."	"What if I panic and no one is around?"
"I'm learning to be fine by myself."	"I'm not sure I'll be able to do this."
"I'm learning to be fine by myself."	

Later, go back and counter your doubts one by one with positive statements. In the example above, the three doubts might be countered by the following three affirmations:

"Gradually, I can learn to extend the time I'm okay being alone to an entire day."

"If I panic while I'm alone, I can do deep breathing, go with the feeling, and call _____."

"If I break this down into small enough steps, I know I can do it."

- Write your affirmation in giant letters with a magic marker on a blank sheet of paper (the words should be visible from at least twenty feet away). Then attach the sheet to your bathroom mirror, your refrigerator, or some other conspicuous place in your home. Constantly seeing the affirmation day in and day out, whether or not you actively attend to it, will help to reinforce it in your mind.

- Record a series of affirmations. If you develop twenty or so affirmations to counter statements on the *Mistaken Beliefs Questionnaire,* you may wish to put all of them on a recording. You can either use your own voice or have someone else do the recording. Make sure the affirmations are in the first person and that you allow five to ten seconds between them so that each one has time to sink in.

    Listening to the recording once a day for thirty days will lead to a major shift in your thinking and the way you feel about yourself. It's okay to play the recording at any time, even while cleaning the house or driving in your car. However, you can expedite the process by giving the recording your full attention in a very relaxed state when you've slowed yourself down enough to deeply feel each affirmation.

- Work with a partner. Have your partner say the affirmation to you in the *second* person while looking into your eyes. After she or he says it (for example, "You are learning to overcome your fears"), you respond, "Yes, I know." Your partner keeps repeating the affirmation to you until she or he is convinced that you really mean it when you say, "Yes, I know." After you've completed this, reverse roles. This time you repeat the affirmation in the *first* person while looking into your partner's eyes. After each time you say the affirmation (for example, "I'm learning to overcome my fears"), your partner responds with the statement "Yes, it's true!" Again, you need to continue this until your partner is convinced that you really mean what you're saying.

- Take a single affirmation with you into meditation. Repeating an affirmation slowly and with conviction while in a deep meditative state is a very powerful way of incorporating it into your consciousness. Meditation is a state in which you can experience yourself as a "whole being." Whatever you affirm or declare with your whole being will have the strongest tendency to come true.

Increasing the Power of an Affirmation

There are two fundamental ways of reinforcing an affirmation or any new habit of thinking—*repetition* and *feeling*.

Repetition   It took repetition to "program" mistaken beliefs in your mind originally. Being told numerous times by your parents to "shut up" or "behave yourself" reinforced the fallacious belief "I'm unworthy" or "I'm unimportant." By the same token, repeated exposure to a positive affirmation can help instill it in your mind until it replaces the original, false belief.

Feeling   Saying affirmations with deep conviction and feeling is the *most* powerful method, in my opinion, for strengthening them. Getting a new belief *into your heart*—as well as into your head—will give it the greatest power and efficacy. A good way to do this is to attain a deep state of relaxation first (through progressive muscle relaxation or meditation) and then to say the affirmation slowly, with feeling and a sense of conviction. It has been said before that what you believe in with your whole heart becomes a part of you.

Active Integration

You can also increase your conviction about an affirmation by keeping track of confirmations of it in real life. Select an affirmation you wish to work on and write it down on a note card. As you go through the day, write down on the other side of the card any event or situation, no matter how minor, that supports the affirmation. Keep this up for two or more weeks and see if you can compile a list of confirmations. For example, if you're working with the affirmation "I can recover by taking small risks at my own pace," then you might list all of your successes in reducing your anxiety and/or confronting phobic situations. Or if you're working with the statement "I'm learning that there is more to life than success in my career (or school)," you can list all the occasions when you derived enjoyment from other activities to demonstrate the truth of your new belief.

Reinforcing an affirmation by noting real-life events that confirm it will go a long way toward strengthening your conviction of its truth.

Examples of Affirmations

Below are examples of affirmations you can use to counter statements from the *Mistaken Beliefs Questionnaire*. Use any that feel right to you, or use them as guidelines for making up your own.

1. I'm responsible and in control of my life.

2. Circumstances are what they are, but I can choose my attitude toward them.

3. I am becoming prosperous. I am creating the financial resources I need.

4. I am setting priorities and making time for what is important.

5. Life has its challenges and its satisfactions—I enjoy the adventure of life. Every challenge that comes along is an opportunity to learn and grow.

6. I accept the natural ups and downs of life.

7. I love and accept myself the way I am.

8. I deserve the good things in life as much as anyone else.

9. I am open to discovering new meaning in my life.

10. It's never too late to change. I am improving one step at a time.

11. I am innately healthy, strong, and capable of fully recovering. I am getting better every day.

12. I am committed to overcoming my condition. I am working on recovering from my condition.

13. I can recover by taking small risks at my own pace.

14/ I am looking forward to the new freedom and opportunities I'll have when I've fully
15. recovered.

16. I am learning to love myself.

17. I am learning to be comfortable by myself.

18. If someone doesn't return my love, I let it go and move on.

19. I am learning to be at peace with myself when alone. I am learning how to enjoy myself when alone.

20. I respect and believe in myself apart from others' opinions.

21. I can accept and learn from constructive criticism.

22. I'm learning to be myself around others. It's important to take care of my own needs.

23/ It's okay to be myself around others. I'm willing to be myself around others.
24.

25. I appreciate my achievements, and I'm much more than all of them put together.

26. I am learning how to balance work and play in my life.

27. I am learning that there is more to life than success. The greatest success is living well.

28/ I'm a unique and capable person just as I am. I am satisfied doing the best I can.
29.

30. It's okay to make mistakes. I'm willing to accept my mistakes and learn from them.

31. I'm willing to allow others to help me. I acknowledge my need for other people.

32. I am open to receiving support from others.

33. I am willing to take the risk of getting close to someone.

34. I am learning to relax and let go. I'm learning to accept those things I can't control.

35. I am willing to let others assist me in solving my problems.

36. When I love and care for myself, I am best able to be generous to others.

37. I'm doing the best I can as a _____ (Optional: And I'm open to learning ways to improve.)

38. It's okay to be upset when things go wrong.

39. I'm okay if I don't always have a quick answer to every problem.

40. It's okay to make time to rest and relax.

41/ I do the best I can, and I'm satisfied with that.
42.

43. It's okay if I'm unable to always foresee everything.

44. It's okay to be angry sometimes. I am learning to accept and express my angry feelings appropriately.

45. I'm learning to be honest with others, even when I'm not feeling pleasant or nice.

46. I believe that I am an attractive, intelligent, and valuable person. I am learning to let go of guilt.

47. I believe that I can change. I am willing to change (or grow).

48. The world outside is a place to grow and have fun.

49. Worrying about a problem is the real problem. Doing something about it will make a difference for the better.

50. I am learning (or willing) to trust other people.

51. I'm making a commitment to myself to do what I can to overcome my problem with _____.

52. I'm learning that it's okay to make mistakes.

53.   Nobody's perfect—and I'm learning (or willing) to go easier on myself.

54.   I'm willing to become (or to learn to become) self-sufficient.

55.   I'm learning to let go of worrying. I can replace worrying with constructive action.

56.   I am learning, one step at a time, that I can deal with the outside world.

57.   I'm inherently worthy as a person. I accept myself just the way I am.

The purpose of this chapter has been to increase your awareness about mistaken beliefs and help you identify some of your own. Countering negative self-talk and mistaken beliefs with positive thinking and affirmations can go a long way toward helping you lead a calmer, more balanced, and anxiety-free life. While the earlier chapters on relaxation and exercise were designed to help you overcome the physiological bases of anxiety, the intent of the last two chapters has been to give you tools to deal with that part of anxiety that is in your mind—what you say to yourself and what you believe. Chapter 12 will examine the important relationship between anxiety and feelings.

Summary of Things to Do

1.   Complete the *Mistaken Beliefs Questionnaire*, checking off those beliefs you rated 3 or 4. Note any subgroupings of beliefs where your total score exceeds the criterion value for that group. The theme for that subgroup deserves your special attention.

2.   Reread the section "Countering Mistaken Beliefs" until you are thoroughly familiar with various ways to challenge them. Use the "Five Questions for Challenging Mistaken Beliefs" to call into question any belief that has an emotional hold on you or seems intellectually plausible.

3.   After challenging your mistaken beliefs, develop affirmations to counter each one of them. Use the "Guidelines for Constructing Affirmations" to assist you, and refer to the section "Examples of Affirmations" at the end of the chapter for a list of examples. On the questionnaire, write each of your affirmations in capital letters underneath the particular mistaken belief you're countering.

4.   Reread the section "Ways to Work with Affirmations" and decide which method of rehearsing affirmations you want to use—for example, writing them repetitively, listening to them on a recording, working with a partner, or taking your affirmations into meditation. Work with this method for two weeks to one month on a daily basis, and afterward whenever you feel the need.

Further Reading

Bloch, Douglas. *Words That Heal: Affirmations and Meditations for Daily Living*. Portland, OR: 1998. (The single best book on working with affirmations I've seen.)

Burns, David. *Feeling Good: The New Modern Therapy*. Revised edition. New York: Avon Books, 1999.

Handly, Robert, and Pauline Neff. *Anxiety and Panic Attacks: Their Cause and Cure*. New York: Random House, 1987. Rawson Associates, 1985. (Popular book for phobics on how to utilize affirmations and visualization.)

McKay, Matthew, and Patrick Fanning. *Prisoners of Belief*. Oakland, CA: New Harbinger Publications, 1991.

10

Personality Styles That Perpetuate Anxiety

People who are prone to anxiety disorders tend to share certain personality traits. Some of these traits are positive—such as creativity, intuitive ability, emotional sensitivity, empathy, and amiability. Such traits as these endear anxiety-prone people to their friends and relatives. Other common traits tend to aggravate anxiety and interfere with the self-confidence of people with anxiety disorders. This chapter focuses on four of these traits, all of which need to be addressed at some point in the process of recovery.

- Perfectionism

- Excessive need for approval

- Tendency to ignore physical and psychological signs of stress

- Excessive need for control

You may not possess all four of these traits. But if panic, phobias, or generalized anxiety have been part of your life for any length of time, you probably identify with at least two or three of them.

Origins of Anxiety-Provoking Traits

What's the origin of these traits that perpetuate anxiety? Such traits as creativity and emotional sensitivity may well be part of the hereditary component of anxiety disorders. On the other hand, perfectionism and excessive need for approval or control most likely have their origin in early childhood experiences. There are various ways in which you can acquire such traits. If your parents have these traits, you may learn them directly by following their example. If your mother and father are high achievers and demand perfection of themselves, you may have internalized their values and behave in a similar way. Alternatively, such traits may develop out of your *response* to the ways in which you were treated by one or both of your parents. If, for example, you were frequently criticized or reprimanded, you may have decided early on that nothing you could do was good enough. As a result, you strive to do everything perfectly. Or you might constantly seek reassurance and approval. In the process, you may have also learned to deny your feelings and ignore signs of stress.

If you would like to obtain more insight about how you developed any of the traits considered in this chapter, you can start by referring to the *Family Background Questionnaire* in chapter 2. Reflecting on your answers to the questions will help you better understand your past.

Below you'll find guidelines to help you identify, work with, and change each of the four traits that perpetuate anxiety: perfectionism, excessive need for approval, the tendency to ignore physical and psychological signs of stress, and the excessive need for control.*

Perfectionism

Perfectionism has two aspects. First, you have a tendency to have expectations about yourself, others, and life that are unrealistically high. When anything falls short, you become disappointed and/or critical. Second, you tend to be overconcerned with small flaws and mistakes in yourself or your accomplishments. In focusing on what's wrong, you tend to discount and ignore what's right.

Perfectionism is a common cause of low self-esteem. It is critical of every effort and convinces you that nothing is ever good enough. It can also cause you to drive yourself to the point of chronic stress, exhaustion, and burnout. Every time perfectionism counsels you that you "should," "have to," or "must," you tend to push yourself forward out of anxiety, rather than from natural desire and inclination. The more perfectionistic you are, the more often you're likely to feel anxious.

Overcoming perfectionism requires a fundamental shift in your attitude toward yourself and how you approach life in general. The following seven guidelines are intended as a starting point for making such a shift.

Let Go of the Idea That Your Worth Is Determined by Your Achievements and Accomplishments

Outer accomplishment may be how society measures a person's "worth" or social status. But are you going to allow society to have the last word on your value as a person? Work on reinforcing the idea that your worth is a given. People ascribe inherent worth to pets and plants just by virtue of their existence. You as a human being have the same inherent worth just because you're here. Be willing to recognize and affirm that you're lovable and acceptable as you are, apart from your outer accomplishments. When self-reflective people are near death, there are usually only two things that seem to have been important to them about their lives: learning how to love others and growing in wisdom. If you need to measure yourself against any standard, try these rather than society's definitions of value.

---

* Outlines of the sections on perfectionism and the excessive need for approval in this chapter were adapted with permission from chapters 6 and 8 of *Anxiety, Phobias, and Panic: Taking Charge and Conquering Fear* by Reneau Z. Peurifoy, MA, MFCC. See this useful book for more detailed discussions of these issues.

Recognize and Overcome Perfectionistic Thinking Styles

Perfectionism is expressed in the way you talk to yourself. "Should/must thinking," "all-or-nothing thinking," and "overgeneralization" characterize a perfectionist attitude. Below are examples of self-statements associated with each thinking style and corresponding, more realistic counterstatements.

Thinking Style	**Counterstatements**
Should/Must Thinking	
"I should be able to do this right."	"I'll do the best I can."
"I must not make mistakes."	"It's okay to make mistakes."
All-or-Nothing Thinking	
"This is all wrong."	"This is not *all* wrong. There are some parts of it that are okay and some that need attention."
"I just can't do it at all."	"If I break this down into small enough steps, I can do it."
Overgeneralization	
"I'll *always* foul things up."	"It's simply untrue that I *always* foul things up. In this particular case, I'll go back and make the necessary corrections."
"I'll *never* be able to do this."	"If I take small steps and keep making an effort, over time I'll accomplish what I set out to do."

Spend one week noticing all the instances when you get involved in should/must thinking, all-or-nothing thinking, or overgeneralization. Keep a notebook with you so that you can write down thoughts as they occur to you. Examine what you're telling yourself at times when you feel particularly anxious or stressed. Pay special attention to your use of the words "should," "must," "have to," "always," "never," "all," or "none." After you've spent a week writing down your perfectionist self-statements, compose counterstatements for each one. In subsequent weeks, read over your list of counterstatements frequently to encourage yourself to develop a less perfectionist approach to life. See chapter 8 for further information on how to develop and work with counterstatements.

Stop Magnifying the Importance of Small Errors

One of the most problematic aspects of perfectionism is its mandate to focus on small flaws or errors. Perfectionists are prone to come down very hard on themselves for a single, minute mistake that has few or no immediate consequences, let alone any long-term effects. When you really think about it, how important is a mistake you make today going to be one month from now? Or one year from now? In 99.9 percent of cases, the mistake will be forgotten within a short period of time. There is no real learning without mistakes or set-backs. No great success was ever attained without many failures and mistakes along the way.

Focus on Positives

In dwelling on small errors or mistakes, perfectionists tend to discount their positive accomplishments. They selectively ignore anything positive they've done. A way to counter this tendency is to take inventory near the end of each day of positive things you've accomplished. Think about what ways, small or large, you've been helpful or pleasant to people during the day. Think of any small steps you've taken toward achieving your goals. What other things got done? What insights did you have?

Pay attention to whether you disqualify something positive with a "but"—for example, "I had a good practice session, but I became anxious near the end." Learn to leave off the "but" in the assessments of your attitudes and behavior.

Work on Goals That Are Realistic

Are your goals realistically attainable, or have you set them too high? Would you expect of anyone else the goals you set for yourself? Sometimes it's difficult to recognize the overly lofty nature of certain goals. It can be helpful to do a "reality check" with a friend or counselor to determine whether any given goal is realistically attainable or even reasonable to strive for. Are you expecting too much of yourself and the world? You may need to adjust some of your goals a bit in line with the limiting factors of time, energy, and resources. If your determination of self-worth truly comes from within rather than from what you achieve, you will be able to do this. Acceptance of personal limitations is the ultimate act of self-love.

Cultivate More Pleasure and Recreation in Your Life

Perfectionism has a tendency to make people rigid and self-denying. Your own human needs get sacrificed in favor of the pursuit of external goals. Ultimately, this tendency can lead to a stifling of vitality and creativity. Pleasure—finding the enjoyment in life—reverses this trend.

The Sioux have a wise saying: "The first thing people say after their death is—'Why was I so serious?'" Are you taking yourself too seriously and not allowing yourself time for fun, recreation, play, and rest? How can you make more time for leisure and pleasure? You can change by taking time every day to do at least one thing you enjoy.

Develop a Process Orientation

If you engage in sports, do you play to win or just to enjoy the activity of playing? In your life in general, are you "playing to win"—channeling your energies into excelling at all costs—or are you enjoying the process of living day by day as you go along?

Most people find, especially as they get older, that to get the most enjoyment out of life, it works best to place value on the *process* of doing things—not just on the product or accomplishment. Popular expressions of this idea include "The journey is more important than the destination" and "Stop and smell the roses."

Excessive Need for Approval

All human beings need approval. Yet for many people struggling with anxiety and phobias, the need for approval can be excessive. Being overly concerned with approval often arises from an inner sense of being flawed or unworthy. This leads to the mistaken belief that you are unacceptable just the way you are ("If people really saw who I am, they wouldn't accept me"). Individuals with an excessive need for approval are always looking for validation from other people. In trying to be generally pleasing, they may conform so well to others' expectations that they often ignore their own needs and feelings. Frequently, they have a difficult time setting boundaries or saying no.

The long-term consequence of always accommodating and pleasing others at the expense of yourself is that you end up with a lot of withheld frustration and resentment over not having taken care of your own basic needs. Withheld frustration and resentment form the unconscious foundation for a lot of chronic anxiety and tension.

There are many ways to get over being excessively needy for approval. The following guidelines can help you start:

Develop a Realistic View of Other People's Approval

When people don't express approval toward you—or even act rude or critical—how do you receive it? Do you tend to take it personally, to see it as further evidence of your own ineptness or lack of worth? Below are some common attitudes characteristic of people who place excessive emphasis on always being liked. These might be called "people-pleasing" attitudes. Following each is an alternative view which represents, in most cases, a more realistic outlook.

Common Attitude: "If someone isn't friendly to me, it's because I did something wrong."

Alternative View: "People may be unable to express warmth or acceptance toward me for reasons having nothing to do with me. For example, their own problems, frustrations, or fatigue may get in the way of their being friendly and accepting."

Common Attitude: "Others' criticism only serves to underscore the fact that I really am unworthy."

Alternative View: "People who find fault with me may be projecting their own faults, which they can't admit to having, onto me. It's a human tendency to project unconscious flaws onto others."

Common Attitude: "I think I'm a nice person. Shouldn't everyone like me?"

Alternative View: "There will always be some people who just won't like me—no matter what I do. The process by which people are attracted to or repelled by others is often irrational."

Common Attitude: "Others' approval and acceptance of me is very important."

Alternative View: "It's not necessary to receive the approval of everyone I meet in order to live a happy and meaningful life—especially if I believe in and respect myself."

The next time you feel put off or rejected, take a moment to calm down and think about whether the person acting negatively is reacting to something you did or might simply be upset about something that has little or nothing to do with you. Ask yourself whether you might be taking the other person's inconsiderate remarks or behavior too personally.

Deal with Criticism in an Objective Fashion

An excessive need for approval is often accompanied by an inability to handle criticism. You can learn to change your attitude toward criticism, ignoring those critical remarks that are unfounded and accepting constructive criticism as a positive learning experience.

The following three guidelines may be helpful:

Evaluate the source of the criticism. If you find yourself criticized, it's important to ask *who* is making the criticism. Is this person qualified to criticize you? Does he or she know enough about you, your skills, or the subject involved to make a reasonable assessment? Does this person have a bias that would make it impossible for him or her to be objective? (The more emotionally charged the relationship, the more likely this is to be true.) Is this person speaking emotionally or rationally? You can often soothe the sting of criticism by exploring the answers to these questions.

Ask for details. This is especially important if you receive a blanket criticism, such as "That was a lousy job" or "I don't think you know what you're doing." Don't accept a global judgment. Ask the person offering the criticism to indicate specific behaviors or issues that seem to fall short. Ask that person's point of view about what actions you can take to improve your performance or correct the situation.

Decide whether the criticism has some validity. You've evaluated the source of criticism and also, in the case of a global criticism, asked for details. The next question to ask is whether the criticism has some merit. Usually when a criticism has some truth to it, it has a little more sting—you may feel somewhat pained or disturbed by it. If a criticism has no validity, you're likely to have little emotional reaction to it at all: you may dismiss it as irrelevant, absurd, or uninformed.

The best way to handle criticism that rings true is to view it as important feedback that can help you learn something about yourself. Also be sure to remind yourself that the criticism is—or should be—directed toward only one aspect of your behavior, not to you as a total person. Here are some good affirmations to help cultivate a positive response:

- This criticism is a good opportunity to learn something.

- This criticism concerns only a few of my actions, not my entire being.

- Although this criticism feels uncomfortable, it doesn't mean that I'm totally rejected or disapproved of.

Recognize and Let Go of Codependency

Check off any of the following statements that generally reflect your beliefs:

- ☐ If someone important to me expects me to do something, I should do it.
- ☐ I should not be irritable or unpleasant.
- ☐ I shouldn't do anything to make others angry at me.
- ☐ I should keep people I love happy.
- ☐ It's usually my fault if someone I care about is upset with me.
- ☐ My self-esteem comes from helping others solve their problems.
- ☐ I tend to overextend myself in taking care of others.
- ☐ If necessary, I'll put my own values or needs aside in order to preserve my relationship with my significant other.
- ☐ Giving is the most important way I have to feel good about myself.
- ☐ Fear of someone else's anger has a lot of influence on what I say or do.

If you checked three or more statements, codependency is likely to be one of the issues you need to deal with.

Codependency can be defined as the tendency to put others' needs before your own. You accommodate others to such a degree that you tend to discount or ignore your own feelings, desires, and basic needs. Your self-esteem depends largely on how well you please, take care of, and/or solve problems for someone else (or many others).

The consequence of maintaining a codependent approach to life is a lot of resentment, frustration, and unmet personal needs. When these feelings and needs remain unconscious, they often resurface as anxiety—especially *chronic, generalized anxiety.* The long-term effects of codependency are enduring stress, fatigue, burnout, and eventually serious physical illness.

Recovering from codependency in essence involves learning to love and take care of yourself. It means giving at least equal time to your own needs alongside the needs of others. It means setting limits on how much you will do or tolerate, and learning to say no when appropriate. The following list of affirmations will encourage you to develop a more self-nurturing attitude that can move you beyond codependency (see chapter 9 for suggestions on how to work with affirmations):

- I'm learning to take better care of myself.
- I recognize that my own needs are important.
- It's good for me to take time for myself.
- I'm finding a balance between my own needs and my concern for others.
- If I take good care of myself, I'll have more to offer others.

- It's okay to ask for what I want from others.

- I'm learning to accept myself just the way I am.

- It's okay to say no to others' demands when I need to.

- I don't have to be perfect to be accepted and loved.

- I can change myself, but I accept that I can't make another person change.

- I'm letting go of taking responsibility for other people's problems.

- I respect others enough to know that they can take responsibility for themselves.

- I'm letting go of guilt when I can't fulfill others' expectations.

- Compassion toward others is loving; feeling guilty about their feelings or reactions accomplishes nothing.

- I am learning to love myself more every day.

In order to work with your own codependency issues, you may want to read some of the classic books on the subject, such as *Codependent No More* by Melody Beattie, *Facing Codependence* by Pia Melody, and *Women Who Love Too Much* by Robin Norwood. Also consider attending a local meeting of Codependents Anonymous, which offers a 12-step approach to overcoming codependent attitudes.

The above three guidelines are only a start in the direction of learning to be less concerned with others' approval. The chapters on assertiveness and self-esteem in this book will also help you learn to rely on yourself rather than others for a sense of your inherent worth and acceptability.

Tendency to Ignore Physical and Psychological Signs of Stress

People with anxiety disorders are often out of touch with their bodies. If you are anxious or preoccupied with worrying, you may, as the expression goes, be "living in your head"—not feeling strongly connected with the rest of your body, below the neck. Try checking in with yourself as you are reading right now. Do you feel as if most of your energy—your "center of gravity"—is situated from your neck up? Or do you feel solidly connected with the rest of your body, in touch with your chest, stomach, arms, and legs?

To the extent that you are out of touch with your body, you may ignore—often unconsciously—an entire range of physical symptoms that arise when you're under stress. Examples of physical symptoms that may signify stress are fatigue, headaches, nervous stomach, tight muscles, cold hands, and diarrhea, to mention a few. Unfortunately, when you're unaware that you're under stress, you're likely to keep pushing yourself without taking time out or slowing down. You may keep going until you reach a state of exhaustion or illness.

Many individuals with anxiety disorders have a long history of pushing themselves very hard and continually overextending themselves—trying to fit too much into too little time. Driven by perfectionist standards, they keep striving to do more and be more for everyone.

Often they may go for months at a time—even years—without noticing, or simply ignoring, that they are under high levels of stress.

One possible outcome of chronic, cumulative stress is that the neuroendocrine regulatory systems in the brain begin to malfunction, and you develop panic attacks, generalized anxiety, depression, mood swings, or some combination of these three (see chapter 2). You might also develop ulcers, hypertension, headaches, or other psychosomatic illnesses under conditions of chronic stress. If it is your neurotransmitter systems that happen to be vulnerable, the effects of chronic stress are likely to show up in the form of an anxiety or mood disorder. Although these disorders cause significant distress in themselves, *they are, in fact, warning signs.* The body has built-in mechanisms for preventing its self-destruction. Developing panic disorder or depression may be viewed as a way in which your body forces you to slow down and alter your lifestyle before you push yourself into catastrophic illness or death.

One of the themes of this workbook is that your recovery from anxiety disorders depends in great measure on your ability to manage and cope with stress. And this, in turn, requires that you learn to *recognize* your own symptoms of stress and then *do* something about them—to relieve your symptoms through deep relaxation, exercise, downtime, supportive social interaction, recreation, and so on—so that stress does not become cumulative.

Stress can manifest itself not only in the form of physical symptoms but as emotional and psychological symptoms as well. The psychological symptoms are a *direct* indication that your nervous system (and possibly endocrine system) is being overtaxed. As previously mentioned, being out of touch with your body may cause you to miss physical symptoms of stress. It is more difficult to be unconscious about psychological symptoms, however, because they are so much a part of your immediate experience. The problem is that if you are too busy, rushed, driven, or preoccupied, you may choose to ignore both types of symptoms.

The *Stress Symptom Checklist* that follows is designed to help you increase your awareness of both physical and psychological symptoms of stress. You may want to make a number of copies of the checklist and complete it periodically to get a reading of your own stress level.

The *Life Events Survey* in chapter 2 measured your level of cumulative stress over a period of two years. The *Stress Symptom Checklist* will enable you to determine the stress load on your body and psyche over the past month. Take some time to complete the checklist now.

Handling stress involves two steps. The first is to *recognize and identify* your own symptoms of stress. The second is to *decide not to ignore* them. If you would truly like to find relief from anxiety disorders, you need to *do* something to reduce and better manage your stress. Some of the stress management strategies described in this workbook include deep relaxation, regular exercise, downtime and time management, cultivating constructive self-talk and attitudes, expressing feelings, learning assertiveness and self-nurturing skills, and good nutrition.

Many other strategies for coping with stress are available. You will find them described in books on stress management such as *Guide to Stress Reduction* by L. John Mason and *The Relaxation & Stress Reduction Workbook* by Martha Davis, Elizabeth Eshelman, and Matthew McKay. A list of twenty-four positive coping skills for dealing with stress is presented following the *Stress Symptom Checklist*.

Stress Symptom Checklist

Instructions: Check each item that describes a symptom you have experienced to any significant degree during the last month; then total the number of items checked.

Physical Symptoms

- ☐ Headaches (migraine or tension)
- ☐ Backaches
- ☐ Tight muscles
- ☐ Neck and shoulder pain
- ☐ Jaw tension
- ☐ Muscle cramps, spasms
- ☐ Nervous stomach
- ☐ Other pain
- ☐ Nausea
- ☐ Insomnia (sleeping poorly)
- ☐ Fatigue, lack of energy
- ☐ Cold hands and/or feet
- ☐ Tightness or pressure in the head
- ☐ High blood pressure
- ☐ Diarrhea
- ☐ Skin condition (e.g., rash)
- ☐ Allergies
- ☐ Teeth grinding
- ☐ Digestive upsets (cramps, bloating)
- ☐ Stomach pain or ulcer
- ☐ Constipation
- ☐ Hypoglycemia
- ☐ Appetite change
- ☐ Colds
- ☐ Profuse perspiration
- ☐ Heart beats rapidly or pounds, even at rest
- ☐ When nervous, use of alcohol, cigarettes, or so-called recreational drugs

Psychological Symptoms

- ☐ Anxiety
- ☐ Depression
- ☐ Confusion or "spaciness"
- ☐ Irrational fears
- ☐ Compulsive behavior
- ☐ Forgetfulness
- ☐ Feeling "overloaded" or "overwhelmed"
- ☐ Hyperactivity—feeling you can't slow down
- ☐ Mood swings
- ☐ Loneliness
- ☐ Problems with relationships
- ☐ Dissatisfied/unhappy with work
- ☐ Difficulty concentrating
- ☐ Frequent irritability
- ☐ Restlessness
- ☐ Frequent boredom
- ☐ Frequent worrying or obsessing
- ☐ Frequent guilt
- ☐ Temper flare-ups
- ☐ Crying spells
- ☐ Nightmares
- ☐ Apathy
- ☐ Sexual problems
- ☐ Weight change
- ☐ Overeating

Evaluate your stress level as follows:

Number of Items Checked	Stress Level
0–7	*Low*
8–14	*Moderate*
15–21	*High*
22+	*Very High*

24 Positive Coping Strategies for Stress

Physical and Lifestyle Strategies
(see chapters 4 and 5)

1. Abdominal breathing and relaxation

2. Low-stress diet

3. Regular exercise

4. Downtime
    (including "mental health days")

5. Mini-breaks (5–10-minute
    periods to relax during the day)

6. Time management
    (appropriate pacing)

7. Sleep hygiene (see chapter 16)

8. Choosing a nontoxic environment

9. Material security

Emotional Strategies
(see chapters 12, 13, and 14)

10. Social support and relatedness

11. Self-nurturing

12. Good communication

13. Assertiveness

14. Recreational activities ("playtime")

15. Emotional release

16. Sense of humor—ability to see things in
    perspective

Cognitive Strategies
(see chapters 8 and 9)

17. Constructive thinking—ability to
    counter negative thinking

18. Distraction—ability to distract
    yourself from negative preoccupations
    (see appendix 4)

19. Task-oriented (vs. reactive) approach
    to problems

20. Acceptance (ability to accept/cope
    with setbacks)

21. Tolerance for ambiguity—ability
    to see shades of gray

Philosophical/Spiritual Strategies
(see chapter 19)

22. Consistent goals or purposes to work
    toward

23. Positive philosophy of life

24. Religious/spiritual life and commitment

Excessive Need for Control

The excessive need for control makes you want to have everything in life be predictable. It's a kind of vigilance that requires all the bases to be covered—the opposite of letting go and trusting in the process of life.

Often an excessive need for control has its origins in a traumatic personal history. After living through experiences in which you felt frightened, vulnerable, or violated and powerless, it's easy to grow up feeling defensive and vigilant. You may go through life this way, ready to put up your defenses in response to any situation that seems to challenge your sense of security (whether it actually does or not). Survivors of severe trauma often develop highly controlled and/or controlling personalities; or else they may have been so distressed that they decided to give up, feeling depressed and discouraged about maintaining any control of their lives (the latter outcome has been referred to as "learned helplessness").

Overcoming the excessive need for control takes time and persistence. Four strategies that have been helpful to many people are described in the sections below.

Acceptance

Acceptance entails learning to live a little more comfortably with the unpredictability of life—with the unexpected changes that occur daily on a small scale and, less often, on a large scale. It's inevitable that you'll encounter changes in your environment, in the way others choose to behave, and in your own physical health that you are simply unable to predict or control. You may have resources to cope with these changes, but you are not always going to be prepared for them. There will be times when your personal life situation may seem relatively chaotic, disordered, or out of control. Developing acceptance means acquiring a willingness to take life as it comes. Rather than fearing and struggling with those occasions when circumstances don't obey your expectations, you can learn to go with the change. Popular expressions for this are "go with the flow" and "take things in stride." In a word, acceptance implies *nonresistance.*

There are numerous ways in which to cultivate greater acceptance. Certainly letting go of perfectionism, as described earlier in this chapter, will provide a good start. A willingness to let go of unrealistic expectations can save you a lot of disappointment. Relaxation is also an important key. The more relaxed you remain, the less likely you are to be fearful and defensive when circumstances suddenly change and don't go your way. When you're relaxed, you slow down, and it's easier to go with rather than balk against the unexpected.

Finally, a sense of humor toward life can be very helpful. Humor enables you to step back from those times when everything appears to be in disarray and to get some perspective. If you can remain relaxed and laugh a little at situations that appear out of control, your response begins to change from "Oh my God!" to "Oh well—that's the way it goes." Acceptance ensures that you will be able to cope better and sooner. You are likely to say, "Now what do I need to do?" a lot sooner after "Oh well …" than after "Oh my God!"

Affirmations that can help you develop acceptance include

- "I'm learning to take life as it comes."

- "It's okay to let go and trust that things will work out."

- "I can relax and tolerate a little disorder and ambiguity."

- "I'm learning not to take myself or life so seriously."

Cultivating Patience

People who have an overcontrolled approach to life's problems want to have them all figured out by tomorrow. Yet it's often true that difficult situations cannot be worked out immediately. All the pieces that contribute to a solution come together gradually over a period of time. Developing patience means allowing yourself to tolerate temporary muddles and ambiguity while you wait for all the necessary steps of the solution to unfold. As you develop patience, you learn to let go and wait for a resolution or an answer to emerge.

Trusting That Most Problems Eventually Work Out

Developing trust goes along with cultivating patience. You may not see the solution to a particular difficulty easily or quickly. But if you always need to see in advance how something is going to work out, you can end up making yourself very anxious. There is an old saying, "Life is a river—you can't always see what's coming around the bend." Developing trust means believing that just about everything *eventually does work out.* Either you find a solution, or, if the problem can't be changed externally, you learn to alter your attitude toward it so that coping becomes easier. When you look back over the problems you've encountered in your life, you'll find that in most, if not all cases, the problem eventually worked itself out.

Developing a Spiritual Approach to Life

Developing a spiritual approach to life can mean many things (for further discussion of this topic, see chapter 20). In essence, it means believing in a Higher Power, Force, or Intelligence that transcends the world as you ordinarily perceive and know it. Very often it also implies having a personal relationship—in your inner experience—with that Power, Force, or Intelligence.

Developing your spirituality offers at least two ways in which to reduce an excessive need for control. First, it gives you the option to "turn over" or let go of any problem that seems insoluble, overwhelming, or just plain worrisome to the care of your Higher Power. This possibility is expressed in the third step of all 12-step programs: "[We] made a decision to turn our will and our lives over to the care of a Higher Power as we understood that Power." This does *not* mean that you relinquish responsibility for handling the problems that come up in life. It does mean that there is a higher resource (higher in the sense of being beyond your own capabilities) that can be of support and assistance when you've reached the point where a problem appears insoluble, despite your best efforts. Faith in such a resource enables you to let go of the idea that you have to fully control everything. Some of my clients find that they can approach a phobic situation more easily by "turning over" their worry and anxiety to a Higher Power.

The second way in which developing your spirituality can reduce your need for control is in nurturing your belief that *there is a larger purpose in life beyond the overt appearance of what happens from day to day*. If you believe that there is no spiritual foundation to reality, then the unpredictable and unforeseen events of life can seem both random and capricious. You can feel distressed because there is no explanation for why this bad event happened or that apparent unfair situation occurred. Most forms of spirituality offer the alternative view that the universe is not random. Events that may appear meaningless and brutal from a human perspective have some meaning or purpose in a broader scheme of things.

A popular phrase that expresses this idea is "Everything happens for some purpose." Often hindsight provides us with clearer vision. When you reflect deeply on some of the unforeseen mishaps in your life, you may see in retrospect how they served you—either in an obvious way or simply in promoting your growth and development as a human being.

The four traits described in this chapter—perfectionism, excessive need for approval, tendency to ignore physical and psychological signs of stress, and excessive need for control—are shared by many people who deal with anxiety on a day-to-day basis. I hope by this point you've become more aware of which of these traits might be a problem for you. Actually changing traits such as perfectionism or the excessive need for control will take time and commitment on your part. Part of the process involves changing particular mistaken beliefs you may hold, as was described in chapter 9. Ultimately, though, you may need to reevaluate and shift certain basic values and priorities in your life.

Summary of Things to Do

1. What are you willing to do today—and each day—to relax your quest for perfection? Can you let go of some of the demands you put on yourself in order to make time for your anxiety recovery program—or simply for rest and relaxation? Each day, find something you would ordinarily do that doesn't *have to* get done (such as work or household chores) and defer it to another day.

2. If excessive need for approval is an important issue, be sure to spend extra time with the chapters on assertiveness and self-esteem in this book. It's important to work on developing 1) greater self-respect, 2) an ability to nurture yourself, 3) knowledge of your basic rights, and 4) a willingness to ask for what you want. If you suspect that codependency is an issue for you, consult the references on that subject below, or attend a Codependents Anonymous meeting in your area.

3. Complete the *Stress Symptom Checklist* to get an idea of your level of stress over the past month. If stress is a real problem, focus on the chapters on relaxation, exercise, and nutrition in this book to get started with a program of stress management. Working on mistaken beliefs (chapter 9) and perfectionism is also important. Consult the references on the subject of stress reduction below.

4. Learning to let go of the excessive need for control can be a challenge for people who are prone to anxiety. Cultivating a sense of humor and an ability to laugh at life's limitations is one way to get started. You tend to loosen up as you learn how to laugh and have more fun with your life. Another way to proceed, if you feel so inclined, is to develop your spirituality and trust in a Higher Power (see chapter 20).

Further Reading

Beattie, Melody. *Codependent No More.* San Francisco: Harper/Hazelden, 1987.

Davis, Martha, Elizabeth Robbins Eshelman, and Matthew McKay. *The Relaxation & Stress Reduction Workbook.* Sixth edition. Oakland, CA: New Harbinger Publications, 2008.

Mason, John. *Guide to Stress Reduction.* Berkeley, CA: Celestial Arts, 1985.

Mellody, Pia. *Facing Codependence.* San Francisco: Harper & Row, 1989.

Norwood, Robin. *Women Who Love Too Much.* New York: Pocket Books, 1985.

Peurifoy, Reneau. *Anxiety, Phobias, and Panic: Taking Charge and Conquering Fear.* Citrus Heights, CA: Lifeskills, 1988.

Ten Common Specific Phobias

A *specific phobia* involves a *fear of one particular type of object or situation*—for example, flying, a type of animal, or going to the dentist. You tend to avoid the situation altogether or else endure it with dread. The fear is of the situation itself, not of having a panic attack. If you avoid a situation primarily out of fear of having a panic attack, you are more likely to be dealing with agoraphobia (see chapter 1). Yet panic can occur if you unexpectedly find yourself confronted with a specific phobic situation you've routinely avoided.

Specific phobias affect many people. More than half of the population in the United States has some degree of performance anxiety, and fear of flying affects approximately 20 percent of the population. To be diagnosed with a specific phobia, however, not only do you have a strong fear and avoidance of a specific situation, but your phobia also interferes significantly with your occupational and/or social functioning. Using this stronger criterion, about 10 percent of the population have a diagnosable specific phobia that causes impairment at some time in their life.

There are many types of specific phobias, and phobia lists enumerate over a hundred types with exotic names. This chapter provides descriptions of ten common types of specific phobias, along with proposed causes and common approaches to their treatment. Resources such as books and audio programs relevant to a particular type of phobia are mentioned, when available. Although the list of common phobias described here is by no means complete, the cognitive behavioral principles and treatment strategies described can be applied to any type of phobia.

The phobias described include the following:

- Performance anxiety

- Fear of flying

- Claustrophobia

- Fear of disease (hypochondria)

- Dental phobia

- Blood/injection phobia

- Fear of vomiting (emetophobia)

- Fear of heights

- Animal and insect phobias
- Fear of death

Even if you are not dealing with any of the specific phobias described above, reading through the chapter will provide some insight into the variety of causes as well as the most common effective treatments for phobias of all kinds. For an in-depth description of the details and mechanics of facing phobias in general, see chapter 7.

Performance Anxiety

The fear of performing or speaking in front of an audience is the most common phobia, affecting up to 70 percent of the population worldwide. In the context of fear of public speaking, it's sometimes referred to as *glossophobia*. It's a complex fear and can involve any one or all of the following components:

- Fear of being judged as awkward or inadequate by others
- Fear of underperforming or making a mistake, as in a musical recital or sports performance
- Fear of having your anxiety be visible to others, as in sweating, stammering, or blushing
- Fear of failure and/or rejection, as in a job interview or oral examination
- Anxiety over uncertainty as to how you will do when you have to perform

Performance anxiety often has a strong anticipatory aspect, with considerable worry in advance of the performance or speaking presentation. The anxiety usually increases as the time of the performance approaches. For many, the anxiety goes away as soon as they actually start speaking, singing, or performing. Others, however, continue to have distracting symptoms during the performance such as pounding heart, hand tremors, sweating, nausea, or dry mouth. In the worst case, the anxiety becomes severe enough to interfere with the performance and/or disrupt speech.

Performance anxiety affects all kinds of people whether they are novices or professionals. Singer Barbra Streisand, for example, spent twenty-seven years avoiding any performance before a live audience.

Causes

The long-term cause of performance anxiety may be a single traumatic experience with speaking before a group or doing a musical recital as a child. Or you may simply be prone to social anxiety and shyness from early childhood. You consistently avoid speaking or performing in front of others, and, in the more extreme case, avoid being in groups in general.

Performance anxiety is a distinct problem from social phobia (see chapter 1), however, affecting large numbers of people who otherwise do not avoid or fear participating in groups.

The immediate cause of performance anxiety often lies in deep-seated core beliefs and images where you may think or picture yourself losing control or being incompetent in front of others. You may imagine that you will make dreadful mistakes, believe that your performance has to be perfect to be acceptable, or exaggerate the importance or status of the people you will speak to. These self-defeating thoughts can be very stubborn and persistent, leading to long-term avoidance of any situation where you might have the opportunity to perform or speak before others.

Treatment

Cognitive-behavioral treatment of performance anxiety consists of identifying self-defeating core beliefs (and images) and gradually internalizing more constructive beliefs that:

- You really do have the ability to perform well in front of others.

- It's possible to embrace or "flow with" anxiety when it comes up rather than resist it.

- It's human and okay to make mistakes.

- Others will approve of you if you are "just yourself."

- You will likely not appear anxious to others, even if you feel anxious inside.

- People are not scrutinizing you to see if you flub the speech or performance.

- By focusing on the message you want to convey, you can deflect attention away from anxiety.

- With practice and adequate rehearsal, you can assure a good performance.

The replacement of dysfunctional beliefs is then followed by a gradual hierarchy of exposures to progressively more challenging performance opportunities. For example, in the case of public speaking, you would start by speaking to one or two friends, then speak to a larger group of friends, and finally speak before a group of strangers. Also, the number and perhaps status of the people you speak to would be gradually increased.

An important facet of treatment includes learning to refocus away from excessive concern about yourself and your appearance and instead think about how what you do might benefit, help, or entertain the people in your audience. Refocusing on how you can help or benefit people can make a big difference. The more you can think about how you are contributing to your audience, the less you focus on your own internal thoughts and feelings.

Other practical tips often mentioned in programs on public speaking include:

- Spend plenty of time rehearsing your speech or performance in advance (ideally in front of a friend) to build confidence.

- Take a walk to release nervous energy an hour or two before your performance, and make sure you don't perform on an empty stomach. (Keep your blood sugar level up.)

- Have a glass of water available next to the podium so you have something to do should your mind get distracted by anxious thoughts or body symptoms.

- If you're afraid of your audience, imagine them as babies with bonnets or in their underwear to remind yourself they are just people.

- If it's part of your philosophy, say a prayer and turn your performance over to your deity.

Medication

Many performers use beta-blocker medications such as propranolol or metoprolol in advance of a performance to reduce body symptoms such as sweating, shaky hands, or pounding heart. These can be quite effective. Less common but sometimes useful are tranquilizers or sedatives the night before (to ensure sleep). While the latter can be helpful in reducing anxiety or aiding sleep, they have the downside of sometimes flattening access to your feelings and inner spontaneity. Too high a dose can also interfere with mental clarity.

Resources

The books and CDs of Janet Esposito are highly recommended for dealing with performance anxiety. Her first book, *In the Spotlight*, provides an excellent general introduction, while her recent book *Getting Over State Fright* provides specific affirmations and practices to help reframe your approach and attitude toward performing in front of others.

Fear of Flying

Fear of flying is the second most common phobia (after fear of public speaking) and affects about 20 percent of the population, who either avoid flying or do so with discomfort. It can cripple a person's life in major ways, such as avoiding desirable jobs that require flying or going on vacations to visit family and friends.

Frequently, the fear of flying overlaps with other phobias, particularly *claustrophobia*—the fear of being enclosed on a plane with no ability to exit for a set period of time. Fear of heights (*acrophobia*) may also play a role. For some, the main fear is of a plane crash, despite the realistic odds of a crash being less than one in ten million. Other fears can include a fear of encountering air turbulence, a fear of hijackers, or just a general fear of relinquishing control—putting one's life in the hands of the pilots.

Flying phobia can involve avoiding flights altogether or flying only with the aid of sedation from alcohol and/or prescription tranquilizers. Fearful fliers are often afraid they will have a full-blown panic attack while flying, and this may be based on a bad previous experience.

Causes

The most frequent cause of flying phobia is a traumatic experience with flying, either related to another phobia (such as heights or feeling enclosed) or as a result of encountering air turbulence, getting sick (vomiting) while in flight, and/or having a bad panic attack. Once you start to avoid flying, the longer you avoid it, the more formidable the idea of ever flying again seems to become.

Occasionally, witnessing scenes of an air crash on TV will be enough to initiate a phobia in certain individuals. Also, having a negative experience *after* the flight, such as flying to a meeting only to be told you are fired, could be traumatic enough to instigate a strong negative association with flying.

Treatment

Education and cognitive behavioral therapy are the mainstays of effective treatment for flying phobia. Education includes information on how planes fly and all of the multiple precautions that are taken to ensure safety. The fact that planes are designed to withstand several times the amount of air turbulence they would ever encounter is helpful in diminishing fears that come up around the prospect of a bumpy ride due to turbulence. Understanding that certain abrupt noises, such as putting the landing gear down, is just a routine part of the flight can help those who jump at any unexpected sound. Finally, just knowing that the statistical odds of any single commercial plane crashing are less than one in ten million (much more favorable odds than being killed or badly injured in an auto crash) helps many people.

Cognitive behavioral therapy consists of teaching people panic control strategies (see chapter 6) and then working to shift catastrophic cognitions based on the individual's specific fears. A hierarchy of progressive exposures to flying is set up, beginning with a trip to the airport and culminating with an actual flight, usually no more than one hour in duration. A typical hierarchy of exposures for fear of flying can be found in appendix 2. Sometimes therapists who specialize in flying phobia have an arrangement with an airline to allow their clients to enter and sit on a grounded plane a few days in advance of making an actual flight—an important intermediate exposure. On the day of the actual first flight, the therapist either accompanies or has a support person accompany the person.

Distraction is often helpful in facilitating a fearful flier's initial flight. The therapist or support person continuously talks to the phobic both before and during the flight to divert their attention away from fearful thoughts and body symptoms. The phobic may also take a "tool kit" on board the flight, with favorite forms of distraction such as magazines, a CD player with guided visualizations, or puzzle books.

Medication may be an additional treatment intervention in some cases. Tranquilizers such as Xanax or Ativan, or beta blockers such as propranolol or metoprolol, may be used to help both the subjective experience of anxiety as well as physical body symptoms prior to and during the flight. Many people uneasy with flying self-medicate with alcohol both before and during the flight. One problem is that alcohol has a stronger effect in a pressurized cabin (due to lower oxygen levels) so that one or two drinks may produce high levels of intoxication for some people.

Additional guidelines for fearful flyers:

- Educate yourself about how planes operate. For example, it's helpful to know that even if an engine fails, the plane can continue to fly. The SOAR program, mentioned below, provides detailed education about flying.

- If feeling confined is an issue, be sure to choose an aisle seat (also true if height above the ground is an issue).

- Give yourself plenty of time the day you make your initial flight—don't end up rushing.

- Have a support person go with you and talk to you (distraction) the first few times you fly.

- If possible, make your initial flight no more than one hour long each way.

- Have a "tool kit" of things that will distract you while on board the plane.

- Use prescription medication only if you feel you need to have an extra safety margin against anxiety. Avoid all caffeine the day you fly.

Resources

There are several special programs and websites that have a wealth of information (as well as paid programs) for flying phobia. Two of the better-known programs are the SOAR program (see fearofflying.com) and Reid Wilson's program Achieving Comfortable Flight (see anxieties.com).

Claustrophobia

Most people know that *claustrophobia* refers to a fear of being closed in and having no escape. It can take a variety of forms, including fear of small and/or crowded rooms, fear of being stuck in traffic, fear of tunnels, fear of subways, fear of being stuck waiting in line, or fear of sitting in a chair while receiving a procedure. It can overlap with other phobias. Many people who fear flying are really afraid of the forced confinement of being on board the plane for a set period of time. Or a fear of elevators may have a strong claustrophobic component. One of the best-known forms of claustrophobia occurs in the course of being confined in the small, tunnel-like chamber of an MRI scanner. This can be a serious problem if you need such a procedure.

For a certain proportion of claustrophobics, there is a second stage of the problem. The fear of confinement, if not relieved, leads to a fear of suffocation, of not getting enough air. Either the fear of confinement, or confinement combined with the fear of suffocation, can lead to panic attacks. Panic attacks include the usual array of symptoms such as sweating, shaking, and heart palpitations. With claustrophobia, you may also feel that the walls are closing in on you and you may experience a desperate urge to escape.

Claustrophobia can generalize to a whole range of situations. You may come to avoid crowds in general, or you may always sit near the door of any room containing other people in order to have easy access out. Traveling may be very difficult for some claustrophobics, since any form of traveling, whether by plane, train, or car, requires a sustained period of confinement.

Causes

There is no clear consensus on what causes claustrophobia. The most common explanation is a traumatic experience in childhood where you were frightened while being confined in some way. However, there are plenty of people with claustrophobia who cannot recall any such experience. Some degree of resistance to confinement is common for all animals and humans, but claustrophobia appears to be a very exaggerated form of this reaction.

Treatment

As with other phobias, cognitive behavioral therapy is used effectively to treat claustrophobia. In the cognitive component, the therapist would help you to identify and challenge catastrophic beliefs, such as the false idea that being confined to a crowded room or a crowded plane is potentially threatening or dangerous. You would work on strengthening the belief that there are many advantages to being able travel over avoiding travel simply because of your fear of confinement. After working on shifting your fearful beliefs, you would undergo a custom-made hierarchy of exposures progressing from simple to more difficult types of confinement situations that bother you. For example, in the case of tunnels, you would progress from short to longer ones, likely having a support person go with you at first. In the case of public transportation (buses or trains), you would progress from short trips with a support person eventually to longer trips alone.

Virtual reality has also been used effectively to treat claustrophobia. Researchers found that virtual reality—recreating a three-dimensional video experience on an MRI procedure—reduced anxiety when subjects subsequently went through the real procedure (Garcia-Palacios et al. 2007/2008).

Medications, including tranquilizers and beta blockers, are sometimes used to treat claustrophobia in instances where the situation you are afraid of occurs infrequently, such as making a flight.

Fear of Disease (Hypochondria)

Hypochondria is defined as excessive worry about having a serious disease, even after medical reassurance. Often a particular symptom, such as gastric discomfort, chronic headaches, or heart palpitations, is taken to be evidence of a life-threatening disease. Having a bad headache might be taken as evidence of a brain tumor, or a chronic cough as evidence for cancer. Forgetting where you put something might be taken as an indication of Alzheimer's disease.

Some people continuously seek out various doctors and have repeated exams to confirm whether they have the dreaded disease, while others avoid doctors altogether out of fear that their worst-case scenario will turn out to be true.

Hypochondria is often thought of as an OCD-spectrum disorder because it frequently involves intrusive fears followed by compulsive checking (such as feeling for lumps or continually retaking one's blood pressure). In other cases, it is more like a phobia, consisting of sensitization and avoidance around anything that reminds you of, for example, cancer. The more you tend to engage in self-monitoring, doctor-seeking, or reassurance-seeking behavior, the more the problem fits an OCD-spectrum disorder model. One difference between OCD and hypochondria is that OCD sufferers tend to fear getting a disease, while hypochondriacs fear they already have a disease.

About 3 to 5 percent of the population experience hypochondria at some point in their life. Men and women are about equally affected.

Causes

Many different kinds of factors can lead to hypochondria. It may develop through unconscious identification after the death or serious illness of a close family member. Suddenly you become afraid that you could develop the same or a similar disease. Even approaching the age at which a loved one's premature death occurred may be enough to trigger worry about oneself.

Predicted pandemics, such as a worldwide flu outbreak, lead some people to become obsessed with becoming ill. Even seeing a special on TV about a particular illness may be enough to trigger serious worry about that disease.

Family studies of hypochondria find little evidence of a genetic predisposition. However, having a first-degree relative with OCD increases the likelihood that you might develop obsessive preoccupation with a particular disease.

Treatment

Cognitive behavioral therapy is the first-line treatment for hypochondria. The cognitive component focuses on identifying and countering false beliefs that lead you to overestimate the threat posed by your symptoms. The risk of actually having a life-threatening disease is usually very low, much lower than your estimated risk. The behavioral part focuses on stopping the quest for continual reassurance from doctors and others. Also, you would work on stopping continuous monitoring of your body for evidence of the problem, which only reinforces your fear. Excessive research about the disease on the Internet would also be discontinued. Being frequently exposed to symptoms that evoke worry about disease—without engaging in body monitoring, reassurance seeking, or Internet research—is an approach very similar to exposure and response prevention utilized in the treatment of OCD.

Another approach used with hypochondria is imaginal exposure. Here you would write out your worst-case scenario of having the dread disease (such as cancer or AIDS) in vivid detail. Your script would be audio-recorded, and you would listen to the recording repeatedly until you desensitized to the fears and worries it evokes. While this can be an uncomfortable process at first, it ultimately reduces the frequency and intensity of intrusive worries about the disease.

Mindfulness-based therapy may be used to treat hypochondria just as it is in the case of OCD. The goal of mindfulness-based therapy (such as acceptance and commitment therapy) is to develop the ability to more willingly experience uncomfortable thoughts, feelings, and sensations without struggling with or trying to control them. This may naturally lead you to engage in less worry-based behavior such as doctor visits, body monitoring, or reassurance seeking. For more information about mindfulness-based therapy, see chapter 19.

Finally, as with OCD, SSRI (selective serotonin reuptake inhibitor) medications can be helpful in reducing anxiety (and depression) around excessive concern about having a disease.

Dental Phobia

Dental phobia can involve fear and avoidance of dentistry in general, or a more specific fear about having a particular dental procedure. In some cases, it appears that the problem is not a phobia at all but symptoms of post-traumatic stress disorder in response to a previous, traumatic dental experience.

More than half of adults in America experience some anxiety about going to the dentist, though a much smaller number are phobic to the point of avoiding dentists altogether unless they have an acute, painful dental emergency. Obviously, this can create very serious problems for dental health, resulting in much more serious and intrusive procedures down the road when you have not had regular cleanings and routine dental maintenance over the years.

Women and young children report a higher incidence of dental phobia than men. The more invasive the procedure (for example, oral surgery), the greater the likelihood of dental phobia or at least considerable anticipatory dental anxiety.

Causes

There are multiple ways you can develop a fear of going to the dentist. The most common is actually having had a painful or traumatic dental experience. A second factor is the personality of the dentist. Even in the absence of painful experiences, many people develop fears simply as the result of working with a dentist they found cold, impersonal, or uncaring.

Other causes can include hearing about someone else's bad experience or a generalization of fear from doctor phobia—that is, you can be afraid of receiving any procedure in an antiseptic clinic administered by a health professional.

Often a dental phobia can overlap with the fear of confinement (being in a chair you can't leave for a period of time) or a fear of loss of control (relinquishing complete control to the dentist, especially in the cases where you are sedated or put to sleep for the procedure). Sometimes there is a fear of surrendering to the effects of the anesthetic.

Treatment

As with other phobias, the first-line treatment for dental phobia is cognitive behavioral therapy. This would include three components.

1. Learn panic control techniques as described in chapter 6 of this book (for example, abdominal breathing and the use of specific coping statements).

2. Identify and challenge catastrophic fears about the phobic situation—the tendency both to overestimate the danger or threat of the situation and to underestimate your ability to cope, as described in chapter 8.

3. Gradual exposure to the phobic situation. A hierarchy of progressive exposures would be set up to the dentist's office, then the treatment room, and, finally, a specific procedure such as receiving an injection. In the latter case, you might first see the syringe, then handle it, then witness the dentist giving a "placebo" injection to himself, then finally receive the injection while in an induced state of relaxation. An example of a hierarchy of exposures relevant to dental phobia can be found in appendix 2.

There is one crucial variable beyond cognitive behavioral therapy that is critical for successful treatment: the personality and style of the dentist in caring for his or her patients.

Most dental phobics will attest to the fact that the most important factor in helping them to overcome their fear was the bedside or "chairside" manner of the dentist. Is she or he warm, caring, attentive, reassuring, and willing to explain things simply and clearly? Such personal qualities go a long way to mitigate anxiety. Other things that can be done to make the overall dental environment easier for phobics include dispensing with traditional antiseptic smells, having the staff wear nonclinical clothes, and playing relaxing music in the background.

Specialized clinics that claim to offer fear-free dentistry exist in many major metropolitan areas. It's helpful to ask friends if they have found a dentist with whom they feel an easy and comfortable rapport.

Medications are commonly used to manage anxiety about dental procedures. Nitrous oxide (or "laughing gas") may be used to help you relax, though some people are afraid of the mask that needs to be worn to administer the gas. Benzodiazepine tranquilizers such as Xanax or Valium may be administered orally or intravenously ahead of the procedure. While such medications help you to relax, you remain conscious and able to communicate with the dentist. In general, if you are prone to dental anxiety, ask your dentist about using a dental anesthetic that does not contain epinephrine.

General tips helpful for dental phobics:

*   When trying out a new dentist, meet in advance of any procedure to get a feel for him or her personally as well as to scope out how you feel about the office setting.

- Take a supportive friend along when you go to the dentist, but don't let your friend speak for you. Instead, be sure you communicate directly to the dentist.

- For any new procedure, have the dentist explain and demonstrate the procedure in some detail before actually performing it.

- Have a pre-agreed hand signal you can use to let the dentist know when you need to take a break or in case you need more local anesthetic.

- Expect that you can find a dentist who is caring, responsive to your needs, willing to explain everything, and who provides lots of positive reinforcement. If the dentist is not someone you can trust and feel comfortable with, look for someone else.

Resources

For further helpful information on dealing with dental phobias, go to dentalfearcentral. org. Also check out the many resources linked to this site.

Blood/Injection Phobia

Fears of blood, injuries associated with blood, and injections often go together. About 70 percent of people who are phobic of blood also have a phobia of injections. On the other hand, only about 30 percent of injection/needle phobics have fears of blood and injury. A phobia of injections can have very serious health consequences, if you refuse to receive blood tests or potentially life-saving medication that needs to be taken by injection or IV. About 25 percent of people with blood/injection phobias jeopardize their health by avoiding visits to doctors altogether (Thompson 1999).

Of all anxiety disorders, blood/injection phobia has the strongest degree of family association. Up to 60 percent of people with this type of phobia have a family member with the same problem, compared to about a 5 percent association rate among family members for claustrophobia or animal phobias. The overall incidence of blood-injection phobias in the general population is about 3 percent.

Another unusual characteristic of blood/injection phobias, distinguishing them from all other phobias, is that they often involve a fainting response. When confronted with the sight of blood (your own or another's) or the prospect of receiving an injection, there is a twofold response. The first phase is a normal anxiety response with increased heart rate, increased blood pressure, and other panic-like symptoms. This is followed by a sudden drop in blood pressure, slowing down of heart rate (called *bradycardia*), and reduced blood flow to the brain, which often results in fainting. (Referred to as a "vasovagal response," it appears that the vagus nerve stimulates the parasympathetic nervous system to overcompensate for the initial sympathetic nervous system arousal associated with anxiety.) About 75 percent of people with blood/injection phobias tend to faint, allowing them to escape from the feared stimulus.

Causes

Since phobias of blood, injury, and injections tend to run in families, the most likely cause is children learning and internalizing the fear from their parents and siblings.

Treatment

Cognitive behavioral therapy, emphasizing gradual exposure, works well for blood/injection phobias. However, because of the fainting response, an additional technique called *"applied tension"* is included. Upon the first sensation of possibly fainting, you are instructed to tense your feet, legs, and arms quickly all at once. This raises blood pressure and blocks the fainting response. Even more important, it gives you confidence that you have a coping strategy you can use to overcome fainting. With this confidence, it's much easier to negotiate exposure.

It takes some resourcefulness to come up with effective hierarchies for these types of phobias. A possible hierarchy for blood phobia would include:

1.   Read an article about bleeding.
2.   Look at photos of blood.
3.   Look at photos of injuries involving blood.
4.   Watch videos or movies involving blood and injuries.
5.   Hold a jar or test tube containing blood.
6.   Visit a blood bank.
7.   Witness a veterinary surgery (if this can be arranged).

For injection phobia, a possible hierarchy might include:

1.   Look at photos of people receiving a shot.
2.   Look at videos of people receiving a shot.
3.   Visit a doctor's office and watch someone get a shot.
4.   Visit a doctor's office and watch someone receive a blood draw.
5.   Handle syringes.
6.   Have a health professional touch a syringe needle to your skin without penetration.
7.   Receive a shot in the arm.
8.   Receive a blood draw.

As with other phobias, it is best to start the hierarchy at whatever step causes mild anxiety, and repeat any difficult steps several times until the anxiety subsides. A support person going with you to a medical setting can be quite helpful. Medication (a tranquilizer) can be used to help negotiate a particularly difficult step, but it's generally not recommended if you are prone to fainting. In order to gain confidence that you won't faint, applied tension should be used the moment you feel light-headed. As described above, this includes suddenly tensing your feet, legs, and arms together at once. In some cases where fainting is a difficult problem, the exposures may be done first lying down, then sitting up, and finally standing.

In medical and particularly dental settings, a variety of anesthetics may be used to reduce the fear of being injected. These usually include some kind of numbing gel applied to the gum followed by a very gradual injection of anesthetic. Often you aren't even aware of the needle at all. Most competent dentists are proficient in administering painless injections.

Fear of Vomiting (Emetophobia)

Fear of vomiting, sometimes called *emetophobia*, is surprisingly prevalent. It can take various forms, including the fear of vomiting itself, a fear of doing so in public, a fear of seeing vomit, or a fear of seeing someone else throw up.

Emetophobia can develop in childhood or adulthood and last for many years without treatment. Sometimes it accompanies other fears, such as the fear of eating, or other disorders, such as eating disorders (anorexia and/or bulimia) or obsessive-compulsive disorder.

Most people with emetophobia rarely actually vomit and may not have done so since childhood. Yet when the fear is severe, your life can be restricted in many ways. You may avoid long car trips or only go places where you know a restroom is easily available. Or you may be afraid to be around babies or sick people who you believe have an increased risk of throwing up. Frequently, you are hypervigilant around any gastrointestinal symptoms. In this phobia, nausea is the worst thing that can happen to you. You are afraid to vomit, which aggravates the nausea, which in turn increases the urge to vomit, and around the cycle goes until you may panic.

Causes

A general fear of losing control can often be found in the background of people who are fearful of vomiting. For some, the phobia begins with a particularly bad instance of vomiting in childhood, or seeing vomiting in a loved one who is very ill. The more traumatic the initial experience was, the more likely a phobia may develop. In other cases, no traumatic past incident can be found, and the fear seems to center more around losing control of oneself.

Treatment

If you are emetophobic, the first thing to find out is what it is you are truly afraid of. Is it vomiting itself, or is it a fear of rejection if others were to see you vomit? Or does it have to do more generally with losing control of your body? It's important to identify and work through the core fear or fears.

Next, it's important to make a list of all the situations you avoid because of your fear. For example, you might avoid long car trips, taking a boat cruise, eating certain foods that you think could make you sick, being around babies and young children, and going on amusement park rides. List all of the situations you avoid in order of difficulty and then gradually take the risk to face and enter each one of them. Working up such a hierarchy will help you to reclaim your life as well as reduce the fear of vomiting itself.

Finally, gradual exposure to the vomiting itself will help desensitize you to your fear. One way to do exposure is to write down a series of vomiting scenarios, starting off easy and progressing up to the worst-case vomiting scenario you can imagine (for example, you describe in graphic detail vomiting all over yourself and others while being in the presence of work associates who disapprove). Read through your written vomiting scenarios repeatedly, or, better yet, have someone read them to you over and over several times, until the scenes lose their ability to evoke much anxiety.

Another way to do exposure (not exclusive of the first) is to look at a series of vomiting scenes, progressing from color photos of vomiting to videos and movies that have graphic vomit scenes. Ultimately, you should progress to a live vomiting situation—for example, a nursery where babies are having lunch and spit up on themselves. If you are bold, you can progress to self-induced vomiting, though emetophobic experts are mixed on whether this is helpful.

By doing one or both types of exposure, you will begin to desensitize yourself to vomiting and shift your core belief around vomiting being something horrific to it merely being a normal bodily function.

Medications are generally not used for emetophobia (except sometimes in helping you to enter a previously avoided situation). Most emetophobics tend to avoid antianxiety medications for fear they will cause vomiting. Natural remedies for nausea, such as ginger tea or 7Up, may be helpful in reducing long-lasting symptoms of nausea that exacerbate anxiety.

Resources

Good information on emetophobia can be found at these websites: emetophobia-clinic. com and emetophobiaeraser.com.

Fear of Heights

The fear of heights, or *acrophobia*, is another very common phobia. Frequently, it combines with other phobias, such as the fear of flying, fear of riding elevators, or fear of driving over a high bridge. The most frequent form of the fear is being high up in a building.

Sometimes the fear of heights is confused with vertigo. *Vertigo* is a sensation of spinning usually caused by a medical condition, and it rarely occurs with acrophobia. A more common reaction to heights is dizziness and difficulty trusting your own sense of balance. Frequently, you may grab on to something to steady yourself, and if that doesn't help, you may panic.

People with acrophobia should avoid construction work at heights or climbing tall ladders. Unfortunately, this is one phobia where panic might, in some circumstances, lead to a dangerous fall.

Acrophobia can result in severe restrictions on your life if it causes you, for example, to avoid taking a job offer that would involve being high up in a building or visiting someone in the hospital on a high floor.

Causes

A certain amount of acrophobia is instinctive in all animals. It has an evolutionary advantage in preventing falls. However, a true phobia of heights is typically learned and is an exaggeration of the normal, adaptive fear response to heights. It may develop as the result of an actual fall or the memory of an incident where you were very afraid of falling as a child. People prone to having problems with balance may be more susceptible to developing a fear of heights, but the research on this is inconclusive.

Treatment

Cognitive behavioral therapy is effective in overcoming the fear of heights. The acrophobic is first taught panic-control strategies (see chapter 6) and then undergoes a gradual, progressive exposure to a hierarchy of situations that involve increasing heights. This can be done by going up successive floors in a building and looking out of a window or even walking onto balconies. As with other phobias, having a support person accompany you when you first attempt exposure can be very helpful. Here is an example of a hierarchy of exposures for the fear of heights:

1. Go to the second story of a building and look out a window for ten to sixty seconds. Have a support person go with you if you wish.

2. Look out of a second-story window for two to five minutes. Look straight out and then down. Have a support person go with you, if you wish.

3. Repeat steps 1 and 2 alone, or with phone access to a support person and then alone.

4. Go to the third floor of a building and look out of a window for ten to sixty seconds. Take someone with you, if you wish.

5. Repeat step 4 for two to five minutes. Look straight ahead and then down.

6. Repeat steps 4 and 5 with phone access to your support person, then alone.

7. Continue the process in steps 1 through 6 for progressively higher floors in a taller building. Beyond the fourth floor, take an elevator to higher floors.

8. Continue advancing to higher floors in small increments until you reach your desired goal (ideally, the highest floor of the tallest building in the area where you live).

9.   If possible, go out on a balcony or observation deck at your goal height (you may want to try balconies on lower floors first) with your support person, then alone.

10.   Repeat step 9 for longer durations and walking closer to the guardrail.

Virtual exposure has also been used effectively with the fear of heights. This involves recreating a hierarchy of height scenarios in virtual reality using special equipment. Clinics that can afford the equipment prefer this option because it allows therapists to treat more people in a more efficient and timely manner.

Animal and Insect Phobias

Phobias of specific types of animals or insects abound. The fear can be of snakes, bats, mice or rats, dogs, cats, certain birds, frogs, spiders, bees or cockroaches, to name some of the most common examples. People with this type of phobia avoid not only a particular animal/insect but areas where they believe they might be exposed to the feared creature. Evidence of the presence of the feared animal/insect, such as seeing a spiderweb, hearing a dog bark, or being near a zoo is enough to evoke strong fear. Sometimes merely seeing a picture of the animal will lead to a panic attack.

In childhood, many of these fears are so common that they are considered normal fears. Only when they significantly disrupt your life and/or cause you significant distress—as a child or an adult—do they qualify as a full-blown phobia. In general, animal and insect phobias tend to be more common in women than men, especially in regard to snakes, mice, spiders, and cockroaches.

Causes

It has been proposed that certain animal phobias, such as fear of snakes or large animals, are innate in all mammals because they confer an evolutionary advantage in promoting survival. In many cases, though, the cause of the phobia appears to be a previous traumatic experience, such as being bitten by a dog, scratched by a cat, or stung by a wasp. It's also possible for children to acquire fears of animals from their parents. Simply observing a parent express fear at the sight of a mouse or a spider may instill the same fear in the child. There have also been instances where simply watching a horror film that featured a particular animal was sufficient to cause a phobia.

Treatment

Overcoming animal and insect phobias is straightforward and involves gradual exposure to the feared creature. As with exposure to any other phobia, it's necessary to set up a hierarchy of incremental experiences of the animal, progressing from photos and videos to eventual live contact. A generic hierarchy applicable to any animal/insect phobia might run something like this:

1. Draw a picture of the animal.

2. Look at black and white photos.

3. View color photos.

4. Watch a video of the animal.

5. Handle a toy version of the animal.

6. Look at the animal from a distance (this could involve a trip to a pet store or zoo).

7. Move progressively closer to the live animal.

8. Watch someone touch or hold the animal.

9. Touch or hold the animal in a cage and, ultimately, directly.

Note: The last two steps may require a visit to a pet store, nature center, or zoo. In cases where it's not possible to touch the animal (bears, for example), sustained close observation at a zoo would be the highest step in the hierarchy.

As with all exposure hierarchies, working through the various steps requires commitment, perseverance, and a willingness to tolerate varying degrees of anxiety. If anxiety becomes extreme, it can be useful to have a support person accompany you through the most difficult steps. Sometimes medication, such as a beta blocker or a benzodiazepine, may be helpful to facilitate getting through a particularly challenging step, but the medication eventually needs to be relinquished. In beginning the hierarchy, it's best to start with whatever step evokes mild anxiety, skipping any early steps that do not elicit anxiety at all. Repeat a step more than once if you need to until anxiety diminishes to a low level.

In working through the hierarchy, it's also important to think about what it is about the animal or insect that you find particularly frightening. In the case of a dog, for example, is it the barking, the appearance, the size, the way they move, or mainly the idea of being attacked? Once you pinpoint what specific characteristics of the creature bother you the most, then it's important to focus on those characteristics as you progress through the exposure. Once you've desensitized to the most bothersome characteristics, you are more likely to remain free of the phobia indefinitely.

Fear of Death

The fear of death, sometimes referred to as *thanatophobia*, can involve any one or several of a variety of distinct fears. Here are some of the most common types of fear:

- Fear of nonexistence, a permanent end to life

- Fear of the unknown—not knowing what will happen after death

- Fear of negative afterlife based on religious beliefs, such as the idea of hell or purgatory

- Fear of sickness, pain, and suffering associated with death

- Fear of the death of a loved one to whom you are closely attached

- Fear of what will happen to loved ones in your family after your death

- Fear of dead things, such as a corpse or something associated with death, such as coffins, funeral homes, and cemeteries (this type of fear is referred to as *necrophobia*)

Sometimes the basic fear is simply one of losing control. Dying is out of your control, and you may attempt to hold death at bay through frequent visits to doctors and ritualistic health practices (an instance where the fear of death overlaps with hypochondria).

Causes

Causes of the fear of death vary depending on which of the above fears is dominant. Existentialist philosophy maintains that the fear of nonexistence is innate to the human condition and shared by all human beings at a deep level. Some have even gone so far as to claim that the fear of death (in the sense of permanent nonexistence) is the "core" or underlying fear behind all fears. There is certainly at least some truth to the existentialist point of view. All of us, at one point or another, have had anxiety about our eventual demise.

Other fears of death center around religious beliefs about punishment and hell in the afterlife. Counselors who deem these beliefs to be fictitious need to be sensitive in working with clients who take them quite seriously.

The fear of pain and suffering associated with death may arise from a traumatic experience of witnessing a loved one go through a protracted process of dying. Often the death of a loved one may lead to an increased fear of one's own death as well as fear of sights and objects associated with death.

Treatment

Treatment of thanatophobia, of course, depends on the specific nature of your particular fear. Working with the fear of nonexistence may require some deep philosophical reflection on the meaning of life and the recognition that probably the best way to deal with death is to live life as well as you can. It's also important to realize that none of us is unique in this regard; everyone has to deal with death.

Some people respond favorably to reading literature that provides evidence for the survival of consciousness following death. An extensive literature on near-death experiences, and numerous individual accounts of what people "saw" during such experiences, provides compelling evidence for many that death is not a permanent end to existence.

Among books that describe visions of the "other side" by people who have had near-death experiences, the following are a good place to start: *Life After Life* by Raymond Moody and *Evidence of the Afterlife* by Jeffrey Long and Paul J. Perry.

Fear of the death of a loved one can be difficult, but may be seen as a "spiritual call" to develop inner strength and the capacity to stand on your own even in the absence of someone dear. Some people are heartened by the belief that, after their death, they will be reunited with loved ones who "went before," a possibility that is clearly indicated by the literature on near-death experiences.

Finally, if your fear of death started with a traumatic experience of witnessing a friend or family member's death, it may be helpful to try hypnotherapy or eye-movement desensitization and reprocessing to work through and reconfigure traumatic memories.

Summary of Things to Do

1. Read about any specific phobia in this chapter that affects you. You may wish to work with a therapist or a supportive friend in actually undertaking a detailed exposure plan to overcome your fear. A Google search of any of the phobias described in this chapter will yield websites that offer further information, advice, and various treatment options.

2. Even if you don't struggle with any of the phobias described in this chapter, reading the treatment sections for all of the various phobia types may give you some new insights on how to work through whatever phobia(s) you do have. Also see chapter 7 for further information on the details of facing a phobia.

Further Reading

Bourne, Edmund J. *Overcoming Specific Phobia: Therapist and Client Protocols* (two-book set). Oakland, CA: New Harbinger Publications, 1998.

Brown, Duane. *Flying Without Fear*. Second edition. Oakland, CA: New Harbinger Publications, 2009.

Maisel, Eric. *Performance Anxiety*. New York: Back Stage Books, 2005.

12

Dealing with Feelings

As you progress in your recovery, you may notice unaccustomed emotions and feelings beginning to surface. This is particularly true if you're beginning to confront your phobias. It's entirely normal to experience feelings more intensely when you begin to face situations you've been avoiding for a long time. If this is happening to you, you're on the right track.

Many people who are phobic and prone to anxiety tend to have difficulty with feelings. You may have a problem just knowing *what* you're feeling. Or you may be able to identify your feelings but unable to express them. When feelings begin to come up in the course of facing phobias or dealing with panic, there is often a tendency to withhold them, which only aggravates your stress and anxiety. The purposes of this chapter are 1) to help you to increase your awareness of feelings and 2) to give you some tools and strategies for identifying and expressing them more readily.

Some Facts About Feelings

- Feelings, unlike thoughts, involve a *total body reaction*. They are mediated both by a part of your brain called the limbic system and by the involuntary, autonomic nervous system in your body. When you're emotionally excited, you "feel it all over" and experience bodily reactions such as increased heart rate, quickened respiration, perspiration, and even shaking or trembling (note the similarity to panic, which is another type of intense emotional state).

- Feelings do not come out of the blue but are *influenced by your thoughts and perceptions*. They arise from the way you perceive or interpret outer events and/or the way you react to your own inner thought processes or "self-talk" (see chapter 8), imagery, or memories. If you can't identify a stimulus for a particular emotional reaction (for example, a spontaneous panic attack), that stimulus may be unconscious. Feelings are also affected by stress. When you're under stress, your body is already in a state of physiological arousal similar to that which accompanies an emotion. Since you're already primed to have emotional reactions, it may not take much to set you off. The particular type of emotion you happen to experience will depend on your view of external events and what you tell yourself about them.

- Feelings can be divided into two groups—*simple* and *complex*. There is much controversy and disagreement about how to do this—and even whether it can be done—

but for our purposes here, a distinction will be made between *basic emotions* such as anger, grief, sadness, fear, love, excitement, or joy, and more *complex feelings* such as eagerness, relief, disappointment, or impatience. Complex feelings may involve a combination of more basic emotions and are also shaped by thoughts and imagery. Many of the feelings on *The Feeling List* presented later in this chapter are complex. Complex feelings can last a long time and are more tied to thought processes, while basic emotions tend to be short-lived, more reactive, and more tied to involuntary physical reactions mediated by the autonomic nervous system. Fear or panic is a basic emotion, while free-floating anxiety (anxiety without an object) is an example of a more complex feeling.

- Feelings are what give you *energy*. If you're in touch with your feelings and can express them, you'll feel more energetic. If you're out of touch with your feelings or unable to give them expression, you may feel lethargic, numb, tired, or depressed. As you'll see shortly, blocked or withheld feelings can lead to anxiety.

- Feelings often come in *mixtures* rather than in pure form. Sometimes you may experience a simple, basic emotion such as fear, sadness, or rage. More often, though, you'll find that you feel two or more emotions at the same time. For example, it's common to feel anger and fear at the same time when you're threatened. Or you may feel anger, guilt, and love all at the same time in response to arguing with your partner, parent, or close friend. The common expression *sorting out feelings* reflects the fact that you can feel several things at once.

- Feelings are often *contagious*. If you're close to someone who is crying, you may start to feel sad or even cry yourself. Or you may pick up on another's excitement or enthusiasm. Phobic and anxiety-prone individuals are often particularly susceptible to taking on the feelings of people around them. The more you learn to be in touch with and comfortable with your own feelings, the less prone you'll be to "catch" those of others.

- Feelings are *not* right or wrong. As reactions, feelings simply *exist*. Fear, joy, guilt, and anger are not in and of themselves valid or invalid—you just happen to have these feelings and usually will feel better if you can express them. The *perceptions* or *judgments* you made that *led* to your feelings, however, may be right or wrong, valid or invalid. Be careful not to make yourself or anyone else wrong for simply having a feeling, whatever that feeling may be.

- Feelings are often subject to *suppression*. Sometimes you may actively control or "hold in" your feelings. For example, you're still upset from an argument with your spouse and then you have to talk to a colleague at work. You deliberately and consciously hold back your feelings, because you know that it would be inappropriate for them to carry over into your work situation. On other occasions, you may start to experience feelings that are unpleasant and decide that you don't want to deal with them. Instead of deliberately suppressing them, you just get busy and put your mind on something else—in essence you ignore them. This avoidance or evasion of feelings is a subtler form of suppression (which some people speak of as "repression"). Over time, the practice of continually suppressing your feelings can lead to increased difficulty in expressing or even identifying them.* When the process of suppression begins in childhood, you tend to grow up being out of touch with your feelings and going through life experiencing a certain numbness or "emptiness."

Why Phobic and Anxiety-Prone People Have a Tendency to Suppress Their Feelings

People with anxiety disorders tend to withhold their feelings. There are several reasons for this.

First, many such people tend to have a very strong need for control and/or a fear of losing control. It's difficult to surrender to the partial loss of control involved in a full experience of your feelings. When feelings have been chronically denied for a long time, they can loom very large and overwhelming when they first begin to surface. You can even experience irrational fears of "going crazy" or "coming apart" when you give in to the full force of these long-withheld feelings. Note that these are the very same fears that occur during a panic attack. In fact, in some cases *panic itself may be a signal that suppressed feelings are trying to emerge*. Instead of dealing with feelings that seem overwhelming, you panic instead. It's important to learn that feelings only *seem* overwhelming or scary at the point when they first begin to surface. This scariness goes away as soon as you allow yourself to accept and *feel* them. It's simply not possible to "go crazy" by fully feeling your emotions. In fact, "craziness"—or severe emotional disturbance—is more likely to develop as an outcome of not experiencing your feelings.

A second reason why phobic people have difficulty expressing their feelings is because often they grew up in families with overly critical parents who set unrealistically high or perfectionist standards. In such a situation, a child doesn't feel free to express her or his natural impulses and feelings. Parental approval is so essential to every one of us that we will always suppress our natural reactions and feelings if they are in conflict with parental expectations. As adults, many of us continue to make that choice. Anger is typically the most common feeling to be withheld because it was frequently not tolerated in childhood or its expression was punished. To the child, anger becomes truly dangerous if its expression threatens the continued approval and affection of the parents, on whom that child is completely dependent for survival. More will be said about anger later in this chapter.

---

* In this workbook, the terms "repression" and "repressed feelings" are avoided because there is frequently confusion between the popular use of these terms (where what is meant is usually similar to the term "suppression"—the conscious withholding of feelings) and the more technical, psychoanalytic use of the word "repression" to refer to an unconscious defense mechanism.

Identifying, Expressing, and Communicating Feelings

Because phobic people, by their very nature, tend to be emotionally reactive and have very strong feelings, it is especially important for them to learn to express rather than withhold what they feel. Actually, a three-stage process is involved here.

Perhaps you have so withheld your emotions that much of the time you don't even know *what* you're feeling. An important first step is to learn how to *identify* your feelings. Once this awareness and your ability to identify feelings has developed, the second step is learning to *express* them. This usually involves being willing to share your feelings with another person. Alternatively, you may choose to "write out" your feelings in a journal, or physically discharge them (for example, by crying or venting anger into a pillow).

Once you've given some expression to your feelings, you're ready for the third and final step: *communicating* them to whomever you perceive to have contributed to "triggering" these particular emotions. For the purposes of this chapter, "communicating" a feeling means to let someone know that your feeling involves something he or she said or did. While *expressing* anger means simply finding a way to discharge it—for example, telling a neutral friend that you feel angry about something—*communicating* anger means to let someone know that you're angry about something he or she said or did.

The good news is that identifying, expressing, and communicating your feelings is something that can be learned—and something that can be improved upon with practice. It does take some time and perseverance, however, if you've been accustomed to withholding or ignoring feelings for much of your life.

To sum up, your ability to gain awareness of and express your feelings is an *essential* part of the process of recovering from anxiety disorders. It is just as important as relaxation, desensitization, and the cognitive skills discussed in previous chapters.

Identifying Your Feelings

How can you identify what you're feeling? It will help to follow these three steps:

1. Recognize the symptoms of suppressed feelings.

2. Tune in to your body.

3. Discriminate the exact feeling.

Recognize Symptoms of Suppressed Feelings

Held-in feelings frequently make themselves known through several types of bodily and psychological symptoms:

Free-floating anxiety. Anxiety arises from many sources. Sometimes it's simply fear in the face of uncertainty. Sometimes it's the result of anticipating a negative outcome ("what-if" thinking). If anxiety doesn't seem to relate to any specific situation—if it's only a vague, unde-fined uneasiness—this may be because it arises from strong but unexpressed feelings. Every feeling carries a charge of energy. When we hold that energy in and do not give it expression, it may create a state of tension or vague anxiety. The next time you hold in your anger toward someone, notice whether you feel anxious afterward. Holding in enthusiasm or excitement about something can also produce anxiety.

Depression. In his well-known book *The Road Less Traveled*, M. Scott Peck defines depres-sion as "stuck feelings." Often we feel depressed when we're holding in unexpressed grief or sadness over some loss. Letting out tears and crying often helps us to feel better—we effec-tively mourn the loss. Depression can also result from holding in anger. Gestalt psychologists were the first to point out that depression can mask anger turned in against the self. If you find yourself feeling depressed without any obvious recent loss, it may help to ask yourself what you're angry about. This is an especially good question if you find that you're attacking and criticizing yourself.

Psychosomatic symptoms. Common psychosomatic symptoms such as headaches, ulcers, high blood pressure, and asthma are often the end result of chronically withheld feelings. While psychosomatic symptoms can arise from any type of chronic stress, the holding in of feelings over many years is a form of stress that is especially likely to take its toll on your body. Learning to identify and express strong feelings can lead to a reduction or even a remis-sion of many types of psychosomatic symptoms.

Muscle tension. Stiff, tight muscles are an especially common symptom of chronically with-held feelings. We tend to tighten certain groups of muscles when we suppress and hold in what we feel. Different feelings are held in by tightening different muscle groups. Anger or frustration is often suppressed by tightening the back of your neck and shoulders. (These are the areas, incidentally, where tension is most commonly experienced in our society.) Grief and sadness can be held in by tightening muscles in the chest and around the eyes. Fear can be held in through tightening up in the stomach-diaphragm area. Withheld sexual feelings may be indicated by a tightening up of muscle groups in the pelvic region.

These correlations between areas of the body and suppression of specific feelings should not be viewed as absolute. Anger, for example, can be held in by tightening many different muscle groups from the eyes to the pelvis. The point is that tight muscles and physical tension in any region may be a sign of chronically bottled-up feelings. This relationship between suppressed feelings and muscular tension has been explored in great depth by the school of therapy known as *bioenergetics*. The books of Dr. Alexander Lowen provide a good introduc-tion to this approach.

Any of the above four symptoms may indicate that you've been withholding strong feel-ings. Once you've recognized this, the next step is to tune in to exactly what it is you're feeling.

Tune In to Your Body

Staying in your head, preoccupied with daily worries and concerns, tends to keep you out of touch with your feelings. To switch gears and gain access to your feelings, it's necessary to shift your focus from your head to your body. Again, feelings tend to be held in the body. Our use of language reflects this in expressions such as "heart-broken," "pain in the neck," and "gut-level feeling." By making time to tune in to your body, you can learn to get in touch with and identify your feelings. Many people have found the following steps to be useful. (They are based on a process called "experiential focusing" developed by Eugene Gendlin— see the reading list at the end of this chapter.)

1. Physically relax. It's difficult to know what you're feeling if your body is tense and your mind is racing. Spend five to ten minutes doing progressive muscle relaxation, meditation, or some other relaxation technique to slow yourself down.

2. Ask yourself, "What am I feeling right now?" or alternatively, "What is my main problem or concern right now?"

3. Tune in to that place in your body where you feel emotional sensations such as anger, fear, or sadness. Often this will be in the area of your heart or your gut (stomach/diaphragm), although it may be other areas higher or lower in the body. This is your "inner place of feelings."

4. Wait and listen to whatever you can sense or pick up on in your place of feelings. *Don't try to analyze or judge* what's there. Be an observer and allow yourself to sense any feelings or moods that are waiting to surface. Simply *wait* until something emerges.

5. If you draw a blank on steps 3 and 4 or are still stuck in your head (your thoughts are racing), go back to step 1 and start over again. Most likely you need more time to relax. A few minutes of slow, deep breathing will often help to increase your awareness of your feelings.

6. Once you've obtained a general sense of what you're feeling, it may help you to make it seem more concrete by answering the following questions:

    *   Where in my body is this feeling?

    *   What is the shape of this feeling?

    *   What is the size of this feeling?

    *   If this feeling had a color, what would it be?

If, after taking the time to relax and tune in to what you're feeling, you still have only a vague sense of what's there, it may be useful to look at a list of "feeling words" to help you to identify the exact feeling you're experiencing.

Identify the Exact Feeling: The Feeling List

The list of feeling words on the next page may help you to identify exactly what you're feeling. Use the list anytime you have a vague sense of some feeling but are unsure of exactly what it might be: read down the list until a particular feeling word stands out and then check to see if it matches your inner experience.

Expressing Feelings

Once you're able to identify what you're feeling, it's very important to express it. *Expressing* feelings, here, is defined as "letting them out" by 1) sharing them with someone else, 2) writing them out, or 3) physically discharging them (such as by hitting a plastic bat against your bed or crying into a pillow). Expressing your feelings does *not* mean "dumping" or directing them toward someone you perceive to be responsible for how you feel. The skill of letting someone know how you feel about them (or better, their behavior) is discussed later, in the section "Communicating Your Feelings to Someone."

Feelings can be compared to charges of energy that need physical release or discharge from the body. When unexpressed, they tend to be stored in your body in the form of tension, anxiety, or other symptoms previously described. Your physical health as well as your sense of well-being depends on your willingness to acknowledge and express feelings at or close to the time they occur. Here are some useful ways of expressing your feelings.

Talk It Out

Probably the best way to express feelings is to share them with a supportive friend, mate, or counselor. Sharing means not just talking *about* your feelings but actually letting them out. It's important that you have a high level of trust toward the person you share with in order to open up and fully disclose your true feelings. And it's important that they *listen carefully*—in other words, they do not offer advice, opinions, or suggestions while you're sharing. Your ability to share will in part be determined by your partner's willingness to do nothing more than "just listen." (This type of listening may still be "active," where the listener occasionally summarizes what you've said in order to confirm that it's been correctly understood.)

Write It Out

If your feelings are running high and there's no one immediately available to talk to, take a pen and paper and write out what you feel. You may wish to keep a "feeling journal" in which you enter your strong feelings from time to time (see exercise 2 at the end of this chapter). Weeks or months later it will be very instructive to go back and read through the journal to get an idea of broad patterns or themes running through your life. Whether you keep a journal or not, the act of writing out your feelings will often suffice as an outlet until you have the opportunity to talk them out.

The Feeling List

Positive Feelings

Affectionate	Great
Alive	Happy
Amused	Hopeful
Accepted	Hopeful
Beautiful	Joyful
Brave	Lovable
Calm	Loved
Capable	Loving
Caring	Loyal
Cheerful	Melancholy
Cherished	Passionate
Comfortable	Peaceful
Competent	Playful
Concerned	Pleased
Confident	Proud
Content	Quiet
Courageous	Relaxed
Curious	Relieved
Delighted	Respected
Desirable	Safe
Eager	Satisfied
Excited	Secure
Forgiving	Self-reliant
Friendly	Sexy
Fulfilled	Silly
Generous	Special
Glad	Strong
Good	Supportive
Grateful	Sympathetic
	Tender

Negative Feelings

Afraid	Hostile
Angry	Humiliated
Anxious	Hurt
Apprehensive	Ignored
Ashamed	Impatient
Awkward	Inadequate
Bitter	Incompetent
Bored	Indecisive
Confused	Inferior
Contempt	Inhibited
Defeated	Insecure
Dejected	Irritated
Dependent	Isolated
Depressed	Jealous
Despairing	Lonely
Desperate	Melancholy
Devastated	Miserable
Disappointed	Misunderstood
Discouraged	Muddled
Disgusted	Needy
Distrustful	Old
Embarrassed	Outraged
Exasperated	Overwhelmed
Fearful	Panicky
Foolish	Touchy
Frantic	Trapped
Frustrated	Troubled
Furious	Unappreciated
Guilty	Unattractive
Hateful	Uncertain
Helpless	Uncomfortable
Hopeless	Uneasy
Horrified	Unfulfilled

Discharging Sadness

You might want to ask yourself the following questions:

* Do you ever cry?

* Under what circumstances do you cry?

* Do you cry because someone hurt you? Because you feel lonely? Because you're scared?

* Do you cry for no apparent reason?

* Do you cry only when alone or do you permit someone else to see you crying?

Sometimes you may have a feeling of being on the verge of tears. You feel like you would like to cry but are having difficulty "getting it out." At this point, you may find that a particular artistic prodding will help. Evocative pieces of music that have personal significance can often help to elicit tears. Watching an emotional movie or reading poetry or literature or even certain television commercials may also bring an initially vague sense of sadness to the surface.

Discharging Anger

Often you may feel angry or frustrated but are reluctant to express it for fear of hurting others. It's quite possible, and often healthy, however, to discharge your anger in ways that are not destructive— ways that do not involve "dumping" your anger on someone else. *Going through the physical motions associated with aggression* will usually bring anger to the surface. The target of these motions, however, always needs to be an inanimate object. All of the following have been helpful to many people in ventilating angry feelings:

* Hitting a large pillow with both fists

* Screaming into a pillow

* Hitting a punching bag

* Throwing eggs against a wall or into a bathtub

* Yelling within the confines of a car

* Chopping wood

* Hitting a life-size inflatable doll

* Hitting an old tennis racket or a plastic bat against the bed

* Having a vigorous physical workout

I do not recommend that you engage in any of the above (with the exception of physical exercise) on a daily basis. There is evidence, reported by Carol Tavris in her book *Anger: The Misunderstood Emotion*, that excessive ventilation of anger only tends to produce more anger. The popular term "rageaholic" describes the type of person who has become addicted to anger through *excessive* expression. On the other hand, many phobic and anxiety-prone people have a tendency to withhold or deny angry feelings under any circumstances. Anger may be such a difficult emotion for you that some additional comments are warranted here.

Dealing with Anger

Of all the different emotions that can give rise to anxiety, anger is the most common and pervasive one. Anger comprises a continuum of emotions ranging from rage at one extreme to impatience and irritation at the other. Frustration is perhaps the most common form of anger that most of us experience.

A proneness to phobias and obsessive-compulsive behavior is often associated with withheld anger. *Your preoccupation with phobias, obsessions, and compulsions increases during those times when you're feeling most frustrated, thwarted, and otherwise angry with your situation in life.* Frequently, however, you are entirely (or almost entirely) unaware of these angry or frustrated feelings.

Why should people suffering from phobias and other anxiety disorders be predisposed to deny or withhold anger? There are several reasons:

- Individuals who are prone to phobias and anxiety tend to be "people pleasers." They want to think of themselves—and appear to others—as pleasant and nice. And that leaves very little room for experiencing, let alone expressing, anger.

- Such people, especially if they suffer from agoraphobia, are often unusually dependent on relationships with significant others. Outward expressions of anger are taboo because they might threaten to alienate the very person on whom the agoraphobic feels dependent for survival.

- People who are prone to anxiety have a high need for control. But anger, when full-blown, is probably the least rational and least controllable of our feelings. Giving in to anger, with the attendant loss of control, is very frightening if you are someone who always feels the need to "keep a grip" on yourself.

The consequences of withholding anger over time have been discussed in the previous section detailing the symptoms of suppressed feelings. Generalized anxiety can be a sign of suppressed anger. So can depression or psychosomatic symptoms such as ulcers, neck and upper back tension, or tension headaches. Some additional signs of withheld anger include

- An *increase* in phobic concerns or sensitization to new situations without any obvious reason

- An *increase* in obsessive thoughts and/or compulsive behaviors

- Self-defeating behaviors, such as excessive self-criticism, maximizing what's wrong with your life while discounting the good, complaining about problems without taking any action, passive-aggressive behavior such as procrastination or always being late, blaming others, and worrying about the future instead of enjoying the present

Some Guidelines for Learning to Deal with Anger

Once you've become aware of the signs and symptoms of suppressed anger, what can you do to better deal with these feelings? The following guidelines may be helpful:

1. *Be willing to let go of the standard of always having to be nice or pleasing in all situations.* Expand your self-concept so that you can allow yourself to express irritation or anger in situations when to do so might be appropriate. Examples would include occasions when someone keeps responding to you with snide remarks or subtle put-downs— or a situation where someone breaks an important agreement they made with you. Remember that expressing your anger does *not* mean dumping it on someone else, but rather sharing with someone (preferably *not* the person you feel angry at) that you're feeling angry. You need to do this with feeling, rather than merely talking in a detached manner about your anger. Expressing your anger might alternatively mean to write out or physically "exercise out" your angry feelings. When you're ready to tell people you're angry with them or their behavior, there are specific skills you can learn to communicate your feelings without hurting or belittling the other person. See the section below, "Communicating Your Feelings to Someone," and chapter 13 for guidelines about communicating anger or other feelings.

2. *Work on overcoming "what-ifs" about what might happen if you let your anger out.* Usually these what-ifs are exaggerated and unreasonable—for example, "What if I go berserk or crazy?" or "What if I do something terrible?" Remember that anger withheld for a long time may *seem* ominous at first. Its intensity may startle you during the first few moments you give it vent, but it is not going to cause you to "fall apart," "go crazy," or "do something destructive." The intensity of your angry feelings will diminish quickly as soon as you allow yourself to experience them. This is especially so if you express your anger in a benign way. If your anger is intense, try discharging it onto inanimate objects or on paper in the ways previously described, instead of "dumping" it onto someone you'd like to blame for your feelings.

3. *Work on overcoming fears about alienating people you care about when you allow your anger to show.* Being able to appropriately communicate angry feelings to significant others is, in fact, an indication that you do care about them. If you didn't care, you would be more likely to withdraw from them and withhold your true feelings. While over-expression of anger can be destructive to others or yourself, not ever communicating angry feelings to someone you love may convey either indifference or a kind of phony, "holier-than-thou" equanimity.

4. *Learn to communicate angry feelings assertively rather than aggressively.* It is quite possible to convey your anger or frustration toward other people in a way that respects their dignity—in a way that doesn't blame or put them down. One way is to begin what you say with *I* rather than *you*—in other words, "I feel angry when you break your agreements" instead of "You make me so mad when you break your agreements." "I-statements" maintain respect for the other person; "you-statements"

put people on the defensive and assign them the blame for your feelings.

Believe it or not, other people don't *make* you angry. You react angrily to your own interpretation of the significance of another person's behavior. Something they say or do goes against your standards of what is acceptable or just, and so you feel angry. You can learn to convey your angry feelings without hurting, judging, or blaming others by using the communication skills discussed in the next section.

5.　*Learn to discriminate different modes of expressing anger, depending on the intensity of your feelings.* If your anger is *very* intense, you're probably not ready to talk to someone yet. Instead, you need a direct and physical mode of expression such as pounding pillows, screaming into a pillow, or engaging in a vigorous physical workout. After your anger has lessened as a result of direct physical expression—or if it was moderate in the first place—talk it out with someone. If possible, it is best to share it with a neutral friend first before directly confronting the person with whom you're angry. If no such neutral person is available, use the communication guidelines that follow as well as those outlined in chapter 13. If, finally, your anger is only a mild irritation, you can use the tried-and-true method of deep breathing and counting to ten to dispel it—or communicate it directly if you wish.

A Caveat

This section on dealing with anger is intended for you if you have difficulty being aware of, or expressing, angry feelings. If you tend to withhold your anger, even when you are being taken advantage of or abused, then learning to be more in touch with your angry feelings can be empowering. If you have difficulty standing up for yourself in the face of manipulation or when your boundaries are violated, then appropriate, *assertive* communication of your anger is something that you will certainly want to learn.

On the other hand, if you feel angry often and find that your angry feelings interfere with your relationships, then obviously you don't need instructions on how to identify and express your anger! If you're tired of the emotional and physical toll that frequent anger can take, you're looking for a different solution. *When any emotion is excessive or destructive, the solution lies not in expressing it more but in changing the self-talk and mistaken beliefs that aggravate that emotion.* In brief, while this chapter will be useful if you have difficulty acknowledging or expressing feelings, a more cognitive approach is needed for any feeling that is excessive or destructive to you (for example, anxiety itself). Thus it may be useful, if anger comes too easily and interferes with your relationships, to review chapters 8 and 9.

Anger, like all other emotions, is determined by your perceptions and your internal monologue. Other people and situations don't, *in themselves*, "make" you angry: it is your interpretations of what others do and say and your internal commentary about them that stimulate anger. Often these interpretations and this self-talk contain an element of distortion. Any of the following cognitive distortions can trigger anger:

- *Global labeling*—When you describe someone to yourself as a "bum" or a "jerk," you write them off in a way that ignores the whole person.

- *Black-or-white thinking*—You see things in extreme terms, so that people or situations are either all good or all bad; there are no shades of gray. You thus often lose sight of the truth of a situation.

- *Magnification*—When you blow something out of proportion, you increase your sense of being wronged and victimized. This is a common way of fueling and maintaining anger.

- *Entitlement*—When you believe that you should always get what you want, everything should come easily, or life should always be fair, your thinking rests on the mistaken belief that you are *naturally entitled* to complete gratification of your needs all the time. This kind of misconception can lead to a lot of self-defeating anger and blame.

The above examples are just four among several types of distorted thinking that can lead to excessive and destructive anger. A more complete discussion of the mistaken beliefs that can trigger anger may be found in the book *When Anger Hurts* by Matthew McKay, Peter Rogers, and Judith McKay. If excess anger is interfering with your well-being and relationships, I highly recommend this book.

Communicating Your Feelings to Someone

Communicating your feelings, for the purposes of this chapter, means letting someone know that your feelings have something to do with what they said or did. This level of dealing with your feelings is usually riskier than simply expressing them to a third party or setting them down on paper. Yet when you let someone know how you feel toward him or her, you have the greatest likelihood of being able to work through or "complete" the feeling—in short, to be done with it. You can live in fear or anger toward someone for a long time without any change until you finally let the person know how you feel. Once you do, you no longer need to "hold" the feeling in secret or silence. Sometimes the person you have feelings toward is no longer available or alive, in which case you can still communicate your feelings by writing a letter (see exercise 3 at the end of this chapter).

There are two important rules for communicating your feelings:

1. Be sure that the person you disclose your feelings to is willing to hear you out and listen.

2. Avoid blaming or belittling the person you're addressing.

The first rule is important because your feelings are an intimate part of you that deserves respect. If someone isn't truly ready or willing to hear you, you're likely to go away feeling discounted and misunderstood. Your sadness, fear, or anger toward the person may even increase. When you're ready to tell someone how you feel, ask her or him to make time to listen to you. You might say, "I have something important to say and I'd appreciate it if you would listen." If the other person interrupts you, you might say, "Would you please wait until I'm finished?" When others truly listen to you, it means that they give you their undivided attention, don't interrupt, and don't offer any advice, opinions, or judgments. They just listen—silently and attentively. If they have any comments, these can wait until after you're finished with your communication. The only appropriate interruption by the other person would be an occasional summary of what you've said, just to confirm that they heard you accurately. This occasional summarizing by the listener is called *active listening* and is a skill that you can learn about in any basic book or course on communication. Good listening skills on the part of the person you're addressing will actually *enhance* your ability to disclose and communicate what you're feeling.

The second rule is important because the person you're speaking to can best listen if you respect him or her and refrain from blaming or making him or her responsible for your feelings. Three skills are needed to accomplish this: 1) using first-person statements, 2) referring how you feel to the other's behavior rather than to him or her personally, and 3) avoiding judging the other person.

1.   *Use first-person statements. When you communicate how you feel to someone, begin what you say with the expression "I feel ..." or "I'm feeling ..."* In this way, you take responsibility for your feelings rather than putting them off onto the other person. The moment you tell someone "You make me feel ..." or "You caused me to feel ..." you relinquish your responsibility and put the other person on the defensive. Even if part of you wants to cast blame, you'll get across more easily and get a better hearing if you begin with "I feel ..."

2.   *Refer to the other person's behavior rather than making a personal attack.* What do you have feelings about? Although initially it may seem that you're angry at or scared of the other person, this almost invariably turns out to be an overgeneralization. On further reflection, you'll find that you're angered or frightened by something specific that was *said* or *done*. Before communicating your feelings, it's important to determine what that something was. Then, when you actually speak, complete your first-person statement with a reference to that specific behavior or statement.

   "I'm feeling angry because you didn't call when you said you would."

   (*Not*: "I had a panic attack because you didn't call—not that you'd care" or "You didn't call, you jerk, and it made me feel awful.")

   "I felt threatened when I saw you dancing with your secretary at the party."

   (*Not*: "How could you dance with her when you knew how humiliated I'd feel?" or "You're so completely insensitive to my feelings.")

   "I feel scared when you talk about leaving."

   (*Not*: "I'm scared" or "How can you talk to me like that when you know how vulnerable I am?")

   Although right and wrong ways of stating your feelings can involve little more than a difference in wording, it is an important difference. Referring your feelings to people rather than their behavior results in putting either them or yourself in a one-down position. In the first example, dumping anger on the other person is likely to make him or her feel guilty or angry. Calling someone a jerk will certainly put him or her on the defensive. In the third example, telling someone you're afraid of her or him is likely to make *you* feel more defensive and to promote distance in the relationship. In brief, referring your feelings to a specific statement or behavior lets other people know that you're upset with *something they can change*—rather than with who they are personally.

3. *Avoid judgments.* This point speaks for itself and is an extension of the previous point. When telling people how you feel about what they said or did, avoid judging them. Your problem is with their behavior, not them. Refraining from judging others will greatly increase the likelihood of their hearing you out.

Looking for the Need Behind Your Feelings

Strong feelings are often a clue to unmet needs. Perhaps you're feeling anxious because you're afraid of what other people will think of you if you show signs of panic. The need for acceptance underlies your fear. You experience sadness or grief because you're alone after the departure of someone you felt close to. The need beneath your grief is for companionship and affection. Or you're feeling angry because your partner broke an important agreement you had. The need behind your anger is for respect and consideration. Or you may be feeling bored, empty, or depressed because your life seems too dull or routine. The need behind your boredom is for a greater sense of meaning and purpose in your life.

By looking for the need behind your feelings, you give your feelings a new and deeper perspective. You're not just feeling anger or sadness without reason: you know you have a particular need. Once you've gained more insight into your needs, you can begin to address how to go about meeting them. If you ignore or fail to address the needs behind a feeling, you'll find that the feeling will come up more and more, to the point that it feels as if it will never leave you. Once again, you can view your excessive feelings as a sign rather than a problem. When it gets to the point that you're asking yourself why you feel sad all the time—or angry all the time—that is a sure sign that you need to uncover some unmet need or needs. The subject of how to ask for what you need is dealt with in detail in the following chapter on assertiveness. More will be said about the nature of human needs and the importance of acknowledging and addressing them in the chapter on self-esteem. If anxiety plays too big a part in your life, take that as a sign that you're denying some of your basic needs.

Self-Evaluations

The following two self-evaluations are intended to help you gain more awareness about how you handle two important emotions—anger and sadness. Use them as a basis for identifying any attitudes or habits that stand in the way of your ability to express and communicate what you feel.

Self-Evaluation 1: Developing Awareness of Anger

1.   What messages did you receive as a child about expressing anger?

2.   What types of people, situations, and events tend to make you angry?

3.   Is it okay for you to feel anger?

4.   How do you feel about expressing angry feelings? To others? To inanimate objects?

5.   If you do express anger, how do you go about it? Are you aggressive? Assertive? Stubborn/resistant? Complaining? Rebellious?

6.   What are you willing to do to increase your ability to recognize angry feelings? Express anger? Communicate anger appropriately?

Self-Evaluation 2: Developing Awareness of Sad Feelings

1.   What messages did you receive as a child about crying?

2.   What types of situations might lead you to cry? Do you usually cry for a reason—or for no apparent reason?

3.   Do you always cry alone, or can you cry in the presence of another?

4.   How do you feel about crying? Relieved? Depressed? Ashamed? Other?

5.   What are you willing to do to improve your ability to recognize sad feelings? Express sad feelings? Communicate sad feelings appropriately?

Exercises

The following three exercises offer direct ways to express your feelings.

Exercise 1: Establish a Listening Partner

Make an arrangement with your spouse, your partner, or a close friend to set aside an hour or more each week for listening to each other. Then do a trade-off. First, your partner gives you his or her undivided attention for a half hour, while you express what you've been feeling during the week. Then you switch roles. As a speaker in this process, you need to focus on how you've actually been *feeling* about what's happening in your life, not just chat about or describe it. If you are the listener, you need to give the speaker your undivided attention without interruptions. For the duration of the period that you're listening, refrain altogether from offering your advice, opinions, or comments. You may ask the speaker for clarification if you're confused about what he or she is saying. It also helps occasionally to summarize what you hear the speaker say, beginning with, "Let's see if I'm following you. You said ..." Again, this is called *active listening*.

Exercise 2: The Feeling Journal

Set aside a notebook whose sole purpose is to provide a place where you can express your feelings. Make entries whenever you feel the need to release frustration, anger, anxiety, fear, sadness, or grief, as well as positive feelings such as joy, love, and excitement. Begin each entry with the words "I feel" or "I felt" and refer to *The Feeling List* to help identify the specific feelings you are experiencing.

Exercise 3: Write a Letter Communicating Your Feelings

Write a letter communicating your feelings to someone who is not available in person. Good candidates for this would be an ex-spouse or lover or a deceased parent. Make time to express *all* of your feelings toward this person, both positive and negative. Persist with the process until you feel that you've said everything you need to say. It's not uncommon for such a letter to run on for several pages.

When you've completed the letter, read it to a close friend or counselor, which will help make it more real. It's all right, on the other hand, if you prefer to keep the letter private.

Option: You may want to write a letter to someone who is available but to whom, for various reasons, you've avoided communicating your feelings. I suggest that you consult with a close friend or, even better, a counselor before deciding to send such a letter.

Summary of Things to Do

1. Reread the section "Symptoms of Suppressed Feelings" until you're familiar with both psychological and bodily signs of suppressed feelings: free-floating anxiety, depressed moods, psychosomatic symptoms such as headaches or ulcers, muscle tension, and so on.

2. If you have difficulty identifying your feelings, practice the focusing exercise in the section "Tune In to Your Body." Use *The Feeling List* to help you identify exactly what you're feeling.

3. Practice expressing your feelings on a daily basis. Establish a "listening partner" with whom you can talk out your feelings regularly (exercise 1) and/or keep a feeling journal (exercise 2). Notice changes in your level of bodily tension and mood after expressing what you feel.

4. If anger is an especially difficult feeling to deal with, reread "Some Guidelines for Learning to Deal with Anger." Practice getting comfortable expressing your anger to a neutral person or in a journal before attempting to communicate anger directly.

5. In communicating anger or any other feeling to people directly, remember to 1) make sure that they're willing to listen to you, 2) use first-person statements, 3) refer

your feeling to their behavior (or statements) rather than to them personally, and 4) avoid judging them.

6. Write a letter communicating your feelings to someone who was or is important in your life (exercise 3).

Further Reading

Gendlin, Eugene. *Focusing*. New York: Bantam Books, 2007.

McKay, Matthew, Martha Davis, and Patrick Fanning. *Messages: The Communication Skills Book*. Third edition. Oakland, CA: New Harbinger Publications, 2009.

McKay, Matthew, Peter Rogers, and Judith McKay. *When Anger Hurts*. Second edition. Oakland, CA: New Harbinger Publications, 2003.

Peck, M. Scott. *The Road Less Traveled*. Twenty-fifth anniversary edition. New York: Touchstone Books, 2003.

Rubin, Theodore I. *The Angry Book*. New York: Touchstone, 1997.

Tavris, Carol. *Anger: The Misunderstood Emotion*. Revised edition. New York: Touchstone, 1989.

13

Being Assertive

Assertiveness is an attitude and a way of acting in any situation where you need to

- Express your feelings

- Ask for what you want, or

- Say no to something you don't want

Becoming assertive involves self-awareness and knowing what you want. Behind this knowledge is the belief that you have the right to ask for what you want. When you are assertive, you are conscious of your basic rights as a human being. You give yourself and your particular needs the same respect and dignity you'd give anyone else's. Acting assertively is a way of developing self-respect and self-worth.

If you are phobic or anxiety-prone, you may act assertively in some situations but have difficulty making requests or saying no to family members or close friends. Having perhaps grown up in a family where you felt the need to be perfect and please your parents, you've remained a "people pleaser" as an adult. With your spouse or others, you often end up doing many things you don't really want to do. This creates resentment, which in turn produces tension and sometimes open conflict in your relationships. By learning to be assertive, you can begin to express your true feelings and needs more easily. You may be surprised when you begin to get more of what you want as a result of your assertiveness. You may also be surprised to learn that assertive behavior brings you increased respect from others.

Alternative Behavior Styles

Assertiveness is a way of acting that strikes a balance between two extremes: aggressiveness and submissiveness.

Nonassertive or *submissive* behavior involves yielding to someone else's preferences while discounting your own rights and needs. You don't express your feelings or let others know what you want. The result is that they remain ignorant of your feelings or wants (and thus can't be blamed for not responding to them). Submissive behavior also includes feeling guilty—or as if you are imposing—when you do attempt to ask for what you want. If you give others the message that you're *not sure* you have the right to express your needs, they will tend to discount them. Phobic and anxiety-prone people are often submissive because, as previously mentioned, they are overly invested in being "nice" or "pleasing" to everybody. Or they may be afraid that the open expression of their needs will alienate a spouse or partner on whom they feel dependent.

Aggressive behavior, on the other hand, may involve communicating in a demanding, abrasive, or even hostile way with others. Aggressive people typically are insensitive to others' rights and feelings and will attempt to obtain what they want through coercion or intimidation. Aggressiveness succeeds by sheer force, creating enemies and conflict along the way. It often puts others on the defensive, leading them to withdraw or fight back rather than cooperate. For example, an aggressive way of telling someone you want a particular assignment at work would be to say, "That assignment has my name written on it. If you so much as look at the boss when she brings it up during the staff meeting, you're going to regret it."

As an alternative to being openly aggressive, many people are *passive-aggressive*. If this is your style, instead of openly confronting an issue, you express angry, aggressive feelings in a covert fashion through passive resistance. You're angry at your boss, so you're perpetually late to work. You don't want to comply with your spouse's request, so you procrastinate or "forget" about the request altogether. Instead of asking for or doing something about what you really want, you perpetually complain or moan about what is lacking. Passive-aggressive people seldom get what they want because they never get it across. Their behavior tends to leave other people angry, confused, and resentful. A passive-aggressive way of asking for a particular assignment at work might be to point out how inappropriate someone *else* is for the job or to say to a coworker, "If I got more interesting assignments, I might be able to get somewhere in this organization."

A final nonassertive behavior style is being *manipulative*. Manipulative people attempt to get what they want by making others feel sorry for or guilty toward them. Instead of taking responsibility for meeting their own needs, they play the role of victim or martyr in an effort to get others to take care of them. When this doesn't work, they may become openly angry or feign indifference. Manipulation only works as long as those at whom it is targeted fail to recognize what is happening. The person being manipulated may feel confused or "crazy" up to this point; afterward they become angry and resentful toward the manipulator. A manipulative way of asking for a particular assignment at work would be to tell your boss, "Gee, if I get that assignment, I think my boyfriend will finally have some respect for me," or to tell a coworker, "Don't breathe a word about this—but if I don't get that assignment, I'm going to finally use those sleeping pills I've been saving up."

Assertive behavior, in contrast to the above-described styles, involves asking for what you want (or saying no) in a simple, direct fashion that does not negate, attack, or manipulate anyone else. You communicate your feelings and needs honestly and directly while maintaining respect and consideration for others. You stand up for yourself and your rights without apologizing or feeling guilty. In essence, assertiveness involves taking responsibility for getting your own needs met in a way that preserves the dignity of other people. Others feel comfortable when you're assertive because they know where you stand. They respect you for your honesty and forthrightness. Instead of demanding or commanding, an assertive statement makes a simple, direct request, such as "I would really like that assignment" or "I hope the boss decides to give that particular assignment to me."

Which of the above five descriptions (nonassertive/submissive, aggressive, passive-aggressive, or assertive) fits you most closely? Perhaps more than one behavior style applies depending on the situation. The following exercise will assist you in identifying your preferred behavior mode when you want something.

*What's Your Style?**

Think about each of the following situations, one at a time. How would you typically handle it? Would your approach be nonassertive (in other words, you wouldn't do anything about it), aggressive, passive-aggressive, or manipulative—or would you respond assertively? Note the style you'd use after each situation. If you have fewer than twenty-five out of thirty "assertive" responses, it would be useful for you to work on your assertiveness.

1. You're being kept on the phone by a salesperson who is trying to sell you something you don't want.

2. You would like to break off a relationship that is no longer working for you.

3. You're sitting in a movie and the people behind you are talking.

4. Your doctor keeps you waiting more than twenty minutes.

5. Your teenager has the stereo on too loud.

6. Your neighbor next door has the stereo on too loud.

7. You would like to return something to the store and get a refund.

8. You're standing in line, and someone moves in front of you.

9. Your friend has owed you money for a long time—money you could use.

10. You receive a bill that seems unusually high for the service you received.

11. Your home repair person is demanding payment but has done unsatisfactory work.

12. You receive food at a restaurant that is over- or undercooked.

13. You would like to ask a major favor of your partner or spouse.

14. You would like to ask a major favor of your friend.

15. Your friend asks you a favor that you don't feel like doing.

16. Your son/daughter/spouse/roommate is not doing their fair share of the work around the house.

17. You would like to ask a question but are concerned that someone else might think it's silly.

18. You're in a group and would like to speak up, but you don't know how your opinion will be received.

19. You would like to strike up a conversation at a gathering, but you don't know anyone.

20. You're sitting/standing next to someone who is smoking, and the smoke is beginning to bother you.

21. You find the behavior of your partner/spouse unacceptable.

22. You find your friend's behavior unacceptable.

23. Your friend drops by unexpectedly, just before you were about to leave to run some errands.

24. You're talking to someone about something important, but he or she doesn't seem to be listening.

25. Your friend stands you up for a lunch meeting.

26. You return an item you don't want to the department store and request a refund. The clerk diverts your request and offers to exchange the item for another.

27. You're speaking and someone interrupts you.

28. Your phone rings, but you don't feel like getting it.

29. Your partner or spouse "talks down" to you as if you were a child.

30. You receive an unjust criticism from someone.

---

* The idea for this questionnaire was adapted from Shirley J. Mangini, *Secrets of Self-Esteem.* Canoga Park, CA: N.O.V.A. Corp., 1986.

The Assertiveness Questionnaire

To further clarify those situations in which you could be more assertive, complete the following questionnaire, developed by Sharon and Gordon Bower in their book *Asserting Yourself*. Check those items that apply in column A, and then rate the comfort level of those situations for you in column B:

1 = comfortable
2 = mildly uncomfortable
3 = moderately uncomfortable
4 = very uncomfortable
5 = unbearably threatening

(Note that the varying degrees of discomfort can be expressed whether your feelings are angry, fearful, or passive.)

A) Check here if the item applies to you

B) Rate from 1 to 5 for comfort level

When do you behave nonassertively?

_____	_____	Asking for help
_____	_____	Stating a difference of opinion
_____	_____	Hearing or expressing negative feelings
_____	_____	Hearing or expressing positive feelings
_____	_____	Dealing with someone who refuses to cooperate
_____	_____	Speaking up about something that annoys you
_____	_____	Talking when all eyes are on you
_____	_____	Protesting a "rip-off"
_____	_____	Saying no
_____	_____	Responding to undeserved criticism
_____	_____	Making requests of authority figures
_____	_____	Negotiating for something you want
_____	_____	Having to take charge
_____	_____	Asking for cooperation
_____	_____	Proposing an idea
_____	_____	Asking questions

_____	_____	Dealing with attempts to make you feel guilty
_____	_____	Asking for service
_____	_____	Asking for a date or appointment
_____	_____	Asking for favors
_____	_____	Other _____

Who are the people with whom you are nonassertive?

_____	_____	Parents
_____	_____	Fellow workers, classmates
_____	_____	Strangers
_____	_____	Old friends
_____	_____	Spouse or significant other
_____	_____	Employer
_____	_____	Relatives
_____	_____	Children
_____	_____	Acquaintances
_____	_____	Salespeople, clerks, hired help
_____	_____	More than two or three people in a group
_____	_____	Other _____

What do you want that you have been unable to achieve with nonassertive styles?

_____	_____	Approval for things you've done well
_____	_____	To get help with certain tasks
_____	_____	More attention from, or time with, your partner
_____	_____	To be listened to and understood
_____	_____	To make boring or frustrating situations more satisfying
_____	_____	To not have to be nice all the time
_____	_____	Confidence in speaking up when something is important to you
_____	_____	Greater comfort with strangers, store clerks, mechanics, and so on
_____	_____	Confidence in asking for contact with people you find attractive
_____	_____	To get a new job, ask for interviews, raises, and so on
_____	_____	Comfort with people who supervise you or work under you

_____	_____	To not feel angry and bitter a lot of the time
_____	_____	To overcome a feeling of helplessness and the sense that nothing ever really changes
_____	_____	To initiate satisfying sexual experiences
_____	_____	To do something totally different and novel
_____	_____	To have time by yourself
_____	_____	To do things that are fun or relaxing for you
_____	_____	Other _____

Evaluating your responses. What do your answers tell you about areas in which you need to develop more assertiveness? How does nonassertive behavior contribute to the specific items you checked on the "What" list? In developing your own assertiveness program, you might initially want to focus on items you rated as falling in the 2 to 3 range. These situations are likely to be the easiest to change. Items you rated as very uncomfortable or threatening can be handled later.

Learning to Be Assertive

Learning to be assertive involves working on yourself in six distinct areas:

1. Developing nonverbal assertive behaviors

2. Recognizing and being willing to exercise your basic rights as a human being

3. Becoming aware of your own unique feelings, needs, and wants

4. Practicing assertive responses—first through writing and role-playing and then in real life

5. Assertiveness on the spot

6. Learning to say no

Each of these areas is considered in the remainder of this chapter.

Developing Nonverbal Assertive Behaviors

Some of the nonverbal aspects of assertiveness include

- *Looking directly at* another person when addressing them. Looking down or away conveys the message that you're not quite sure about asking for what you want. The opposite extreme, staring, is also unhelpful because it may put the other person on the defensive.

- Maintaining an *open* rather than closed *posture*. If you're sitting, don't cross your legs or arms. If standing, stand erect and on both feet. Face the person you're addressing directly rather than stand off to the side.

- While communicating assertively, do not back off or move away from the other person. The expression "standing your ground" applies quite literally here.

- *Stay calm.* Avoid getting overly emotional or excited. If you're feeling angry, discharge your angry feelings *somewhere else* before you attempt to be assertive. A calm but assertive request carries much more weight with most people than an angry outburst.

Try practicing the above nonverbal skills with a friend by using role-playing in situations that call for an assertive response. A list of such situations can be found at the end of the section "Assertiveness on the Spot."

Recognizing and Exercising Your Basic Rights

As adult human beings, we all have certain basic rights. Often, though, either we have forgotten them or else as children we were never taught to believe in them. Developing assertiveness involves recognizing that you, just as much as anyone else, have a right to all of the things listed under the *Personal Bill of Rights* that follows. Assertiveness also involves taking responsibility to *exercise* these rights in situations where they are threatened or infringed upon. Read through the *Personal Bill of Rights* and reflect on your willingness to believe in and exercise each one.

Personal Bill of Rights

1. I have the right to ask for what I want.

2. I have the right to say no to requests or demands I can't meet.

3. I have the right to express all of my feelings, positive or negative.

4. I have the right to change my mind.

5. I have the right to make mistakes and not have to be perfect.

6. I have the right to follow my own values and standards.

7. I have the right to say no to anything when I feel I am not ready, it is unsafe, or it violates my values.

8. I have the right to determine my own priorities.

9. I have the right *not* to be responsible for others' behavior, actions, feelings, or problems.

10. I have the right to expect honesty from others.

11. I have the right to be angry at someone I love.

12. I have the right to be uniquely myself.

13. I have the right to feel scared and say "I'm afraid."

14. I have the right to say "I don't know."

15. I have the right not to give excuses or reasons for my behavior.

16. I have the right to make decisions based on my feelings.

17. I have the right to my own needs for personal space and time.

18. I have the right to be playful and frivolous.

19. I have the right to be healthier than those around me.

20. I have the right to be in a nonabusive environment.

21. I have the right to make friends and be comfortable around people.

22. I have the right to change and grow.

23. I have the right to have my needs and wants respected by others.

24. I have the right to be treated with dignity and respect.

25. I have the right to be happy.

Photocopy the above list and post it in a conspicuous place. By taking time to carefully read through the list every day, you will eventually learn to accept that you are entitled to each one of the rights enumerated.

Becoming Aware of Your Own Unique Feelings, Needs, and Wants

Developing an awareness and ability to express your feelings was discussed in chapter 12. Being in touch with your feelings is an important prerequisite for becoming assertive. Learning to recognize and take care of your needs and wants will be considered in some detail in the following chapter, on self-esteem.

It's difficult to act assertively unless you're clear about 1) what it is you're feeling and 2) what it is you want or don't want.

Assertiveness involves saying how you feel inside *and* saying directly what changes you would like—such as "I'm feeling upset right now *and* I would like you to listen to me." If you're feeling confused or ambivalent about your wants or needs, take time to clarify them first by writing them out or talking them out with a supportive friend or counselor. You might also use role-playing with a friend to ask for what you want in advance. Be sure not to *assume* that other people already know what you want: you have to make your needs known. Other people aren't mind readers.

Practicing Assertive Responses

In learning to be more assertive it is often very helpful to play out your responses first on paper. Write out a problem situation that calls for an assertive response on your part. Then formulate in detail how you'll handle it. A trial run in writing can allow you to feel more prepared and confident when you actually confront the situation in real life.

Describing Your Problem Situation

In their book *Asserting Yourself,* Sharon and Gordon Bower suggest that you first select a problem situation from *The Assertiveness Questionnaire.* Write a description of that situation, including the person involved *(who),* the time and setting *(when), what* bothers you about the situation, *how* you would normally tend to deal with it, what *fears* you have about consequences that would follow if you were to be assertive, and finally, your behavior *goal.*

It's important to be specific in these descriptions. For instance, the following description of a problem situation is too vague:

> I have a lot of trouble persuading some of my friends to listen to *me* for a change. They never stop talking, and I never get a word in edgewise. It would be nice for me if I could participate more in the conversation. I feel that I'm just letting them run over me.

Notice that the description doesn't specify *who* the particular friend is, *when* this problem is most likely to occur, *how* the nonassertive person acts, what *fears* are involved in being assertive, and a specific *goal* for increased involvement in the conversation. A more well-defined problem situation might be as follows:

My friend Joan (*who*), when we meet for coffee after work (*when*), often goes on nonstop about her marriage problems (*what*). I just sit there and try to be interested (*how*). If I interrupt her, I'm afraid she'll think I just don't care (*fear*). I'd like to be able to change the subject and talk sometimes about my own life (*goal*).

Exercise: Specifying Your Problem Situations

On a sheet of paper, write up two or three of your own problem situations. Be sure to specify the "who," "when," "what," "how," "fear," and "goal," as described above. If possible, choose situations that are current for you. Begin with a situation that's not very uncomfortable or overwhelming.

Developing an Assertive Response

Now that you've defined your problem situations, the next step is to develop an assertive response for each one. For the purposes of learning assertiveness skills, such a response can be broken down into six steps (adapted from the Bowers' work):

1. Evaluate your rights within the situation at hand.

2. Designate a time for discussing what you want.

3. Address the main person involved and state the problem in terms of its consequences for you.

4. Express your feelings about the particular situation.

5. Make your request for changing the situation.

6. Tell this person the consequences of gaining (or not gaining) his or her cooperation.

Let's consider each of these points in greater detail:

1. **Evaluate your rights.** Refer back to the *Personal Bill of Rights*. What do you have a right to ask for in this situation?

2. **Designate a time.** Find a mutually convenient time to discuss the problem with the other person involved. This step, of course, would be omitted in situations when you need to be spontaneously assertive on the spot.

3. **State the problem situation in terms of its consequences for you.** Don't make the mistake of expecting other people to be mind readers. Most people are wrapped up in their own thoughts and problems and will have very little idea about what's going on with you unless you state your case explicitly. Clearly outline your point of view, even if what you're describing seems obvious to you. This will allow the other person to get a better idea of your position. Describe the problem as objectively as you can, without using language that blames or judges.

Examples

"I'm having a problem with your stereo. I need to study for an exam tomorrow and the stereo is so loud I can't concentrate."

"I don't have any way to get to the grocery store today. My support person is sick and I'm out of milk, vegetables, and meat."

"It seems to me that you do most of the talking when we're together. I'd like to have the chance to tell you some of my thoughts and feelings, too."

4. **Express your feelings.** By telling other people about your feelings, you let them know how greatly their behavior affects you and your reactions. Even if the person you're addressing completely disagrees with your position, he or she can at least appreciate your strong feelings on an issue.

    Each of us owns our personal feelings. Though it might at first seem hard to believe, nobody else *causes* you to have feelings of fear, anger, or sadness. Other people say and do all kinds of things, but it is your *perception*—your interpretation—of their behavior that is ultimately responsible for what you feel. You don't necessarily choose how you react to people—yet your reaction is based on your perception of the meaning of what they say or do.

    In expressing feelings, always be sure to own your reactions rather than blame them on someone else. You can still point out what the other person did to stimulate your feelings, but be willing to take ultimate responsibility for them.

    The best way to do this is to own your feelings by speaking about them in the first person (for example, "I felt sad when you forgot to call me at the time you said you would"). First-person statements acknowledge your responsibility for your feelings while second-person statements generally accuse or judge.

Examples

Instead of saying, "You make me angry when you don't hear what I say," you can say, "I feel angry when you don't listen to me."

Instead of saying, "You show that you have no respect for me or this household when you leave things lying around," you can say, "I feel demeaned and devalued when you leave things lying around."

Instead of saying, "You don't care about me or my getting better—you don't ever help," you can say, "I feel very sad and unloved when you don't seem to be helping me in my attempt to get better."

5. **Make your request.** This is the *key* step to being assertive. You simply ask for what you want (or don't want) in a direct, straightforward manner. Observe the following guidelines for making assertive requests:

    *   *Use assertive nonverbal behavior.* Stand squarely, establish eye contact, maintain an open posture, and work on staying calm and self-possessed.

- *Keep your request simple.* One or two easy-to-understand sentences will usually suffice: "I would like you to take the dog out for a walk tonight," or "I want us to go to a marriage counselor together."

- *Avoid asking for more than one thing at a time.*

- *Be specific.* Ask for exactly what you want—or the person you're addressing may misunderstand. Instead of saying, "I'd like you to help me with my practice sessions," specify what you want, such as "I'd like you to go with me when I practice driving on the freeway every Saturday morning." Or instead of "I would like you to come home by a reasonable hour," specify "I would like you to come home by twelve midnight."

- *Use "I-statements" of the form:*
    "I would like ..."
    "I want to ..."
    "I would appreciate it if ..."
    It's very important to avoid using "you-statements" at the point of actually making a request. Statements that are threatening ("You'll do this or else") or coercive ("You have to ...") will put the person you're addressing on the defensive and decrease the likelihood of your getting what you want.

- *Object to behaviors—not personalities.* When objecting to what someone is doing, object to the *specific behavior—not to the individual's personality.* Let the person know you're having a problem with something he or she is doing (or not doing), not with who he or she is as a person.

    It's preferable to say, "I have a problem when you don't call to let me know you're going to be late," rather than "I think you're inconsiderate for not calling me to let me know you'll be late."

    Referring to the problem *behavior* preserves respect for the other person. Judging others personally usually puts them on the defensive. When objecting to someone's behavior (for example, a lack of trustworthiness), always *follow up your complaint with a positive request,* such as "I would like you to keep your agreements with me."

- *Don't apologize* for your request. When you want to ask for something, do so directly. Say, "I would like you to ..." instead of "I know this might seem like an imposition, but I would like you to ..." When you want to decline a request, do so directly but politely. Don't apologize or make excuses. Simply say, "No, thank you," "No, I'm not interested," or "No, I'm not able to do that." If the other person's response is one of enticement, criticism, an appeal to guilt, or sarcasm, just repeat your statement firmly until you've made your point.

- *Make requests, not demands or commands.* Assertive behavior always respects the humanity and rights of the other person. Thus an assertive response is always a request rather than a demand. Demanding and commanding are aggressive modes of behavior based on the false assumption that you are always right or always entitled to get everything your way.

6. **State the consequences of gaining (or not gaining) the other person's cooperation.** With close friends or intimate partners, stating positive consequences of their compliance with your request can be an honest offer of give-and-take, rather than manipulation.

    Examples

    "If you take the dog out, I'll give you a back rub."

    "If you give me the time to finish this project, then we'll have more time to do something special together."

    In cases where you are dealing with someone with a history of being resistant and uncooperative, you may describe the *natural* consequences (usually negative) of a failure to cooperate. If at all possible, any negative consequences should naturally flow out of the objective reality of the situation rather than represent something that you arbitrarily impose. The latter will likely be perceived as a threat and may increase the other person's resistance.

    Examples

    "If we can't leave on time, then I'll have to leave without you."

    "If you keep talking to me like this, I'm going to leave. We'll talk again tomorrow."

Sample Scenarios

The six steps of an assertive response are illustrated below:

Jean would like a half hour of uninterrupted peace and quiet while she does her relaxation exercise. Her husband, Frank, has had the tendency to disrupt her quiet time with questions and other attention-getting maneuvers. Before confronting him, she wrote out an assertive response as follows:

1. *Evaluate your rights.*
    "I have a right to have some quiet time to myself."
    "I have a right to take care of my need for relaxation."
    "I have a right to have my husband respect my needs."

2. *Designate a time.*
    "When Frank gets home from work tonight, I'll ask him if we can sit down and discuss this issue. If it's not convenient for him tonight, we'll schedule a time within the next couple of days."

3. *State the problem situation in terms of its consequences.*
    "I've let you know several times that I need half an hour each day for relaxation and I've even shut the door, but you still come in and ask me questions. This disturbs my

concentration and interferes with an important part of my program for managing my anxiety."

4. *Express your feelings.*

"I feel frustrated when my attention is disrupted. I'm angry when you don't respect my right to have some time for relaxation."

5. *Make your request.*

"I would like to be uninterrupted during the time my door is closed, other than in cases of dire emergency. I'd like you to respect my right to have half an hour of quiet time each day. "

6. *State consequences of gaining cooperation.*

"If you respect my need to have some quiet time, I'll be much better able to spend some time with you afterward and to be a good companion."

Sharon would like her boyfriend, Jim, to assist her in regaining the ability to drive on the freeway. Specifically, she would like him to accompany her for a one-hour practice session every Saturday. She has been reluctant to ask him for several months because of heavy demands he has had from his job.

1. *Evaluate your rights.*

"I have a right to ask Jim to help me, even if he is very busy."

2. *Designate a time.*

"This Saturday morning I'll ask him whether he has time to discuss my need for getting his help. If that's not a good time, we'll arrange another time that's convenient for both of us."

3. *State the problem situation in terms of its consequences.*

"My progress in overcoming my fear of driving freeways has been slow. I've had difficulty finding someone who will go with me on Saturdays, which is the time I can most easily practice. In order to make progress at this stage, I need someone to accompany me, although later I'll be able to practice alone."

4. *Express your feelings.*

"I've been feeling very frustrated that I haven't had many opportunities to practice driving freeways. I feel very disappointed about my rate of progress."

5. *Make your request.*

"I'd like you to go with me to practice driving on freeways for one hour every Saturday. I would really appreciate it if you would help me out with this."

6. *State consequences of gaining cooperation.*

"If you help me with my practice sessions, I'm sure that I'll be able to get over my phobia of freeways sooner. It'll be great for us if I don't have to ask you anymore to take me to all those places that are only accessible by freeway."

Exercise: Developing an Assertive Response

Now it's your turn.

Select one of the problem situations you previously described and write up an assertive response following the six steps outlined above. You may want to make copies of this exercise before filling it in. (If you need more room, use a separate sheet of paper.)

1.   *Evaluate your rights.*

2.   *Designate a time.*

3.   *State the problem situation in terms of its consequences.*

4.   *Express your feelings.*

5.   *Make your request.*

6.   *State the consequences of gaining (or not gaining) the other person's cooperation.*

Once you've written out in detail your assertive response to a problem situation, you'll find that you feel more prepared and confident when you confront that situation in real life. This process of methodically writing out a preview of your assertive response is especially helpful during the time when you're learning to be assertive. Later on, when you have a fair degree of mastery, you may not need to write out your response in advance every time. It's never a bad idea, though, to prepare your response, especially when a lot is at stake. Attorneys do so as a way of life because they typically assert the rights of their clients in high-stakes situations.

Finally, an important *intermediate step* between writing out an assertive response and confronting a problem in real life is to *role-play* your response with a friend or counselor. This can be an invaluable tool for developing the nonverbal aspects of assertiveness described earlier in this chapter. It will further increase your confidence and sense of being well-prepared when you come to deal with the actual situation. Assertiveness training, whether done in the context of psychotherapy or in a classroom situation, relies primarily on role-playing as a teaching tool.

Assertiveness on the Spot

Many situations arise in the course of everyday life that challenge you to be assertive spontaneously. Someone smokes right next to you, making you uncomfortable. Someone blasts loud music while you're trying to go to sleep. Someone cuts in front of you in line. (Many of the situations listed in the *What's Your Style?* questionnaire at the beginning of this chapter fall into this category.) What do you do? Here are the steps you need to take to be assertive on the spot:

1. **Evaluate your rights.** Often you'll go through this step automatically, without the need to pause for reflection. The violation of your rights is obvious and perhaps flagrant. At other times, you may need to pause and think about which of your rights is at stake.

2. **Make your request.** This is the *key* step in on-the-spot assertiveness. In many cases your assertive response will consist *only* of this step. Someone interferes with your rights and you simply ask them, in a straightforward manner, for what you want or don't want. As discussed previously, your statement can begin with such words as

   "I would like ..."

   "I want ..."

   "I would appreciate ..."

   "Would you please ..."

   Your statement needs to be

   - Firm

   - Simple and to the point

   - Without apology

   - Nonjudgmental, nonblaming

   - Always a request, not a demand

   If the person doesn't immediately cooperate or pretends not to notice, simply *repeat* your statement. Repeating your request in a monotonous fashion will work better in getting what you want than becoming angry or aggressive if the person you're dealing with is a stranger. Avoid monotonous repetition if you're dealing with family or close friends (with the exception of small children).

3. **State the problem in terms of its consequences.** This step is optional but can be helpful in on-the-spot assertiveness. If you feel that the person you're addressing might be puzzled by your request, you might want to explain why his or her behavior has an adverse effect on you. The other person may gain empathy for your position in this way, leading to a greater chance of cooperation. Here are some examples:

   "Everyone here, including myself, has been waiting in line" (as a prelude to "Would you go to the back of the line, please?").

   "I am allergic to cigarette smoke" (as a prelude to "Would you please smoke somewhere else?").

4. **Express your feelings.** If you're dealing with a stranger with whom you don't wish to have any further relationship, it's usually okay to omit this step. The only occasion for using it with a stranger is if the person involved doesn't cooperate after you've made your assertive request (for example, "I've told you twice that I'm not interested in your product and you're still trying to sell it to me. I'm starting to feel

really irritated"). On the other hand, it's often a good idea to express your feelings when you need to be assertive on the spot with your spouse, child, or close friend ("I'm really disappointed that you didn't call when you said you would" or "I'm feeling too tired to clean up the kitchen right now").

5. **State the consequences of gaining (or not gaining) cooperation.** In situations with strangers, this step usually won't be necessary. On rare occasions, with someone resistant, you may choose to state negative consequences, although it will be difficult to keep this from coming across as a threat (for example, "If you continue smoking, I may have an asthma attack"). With family and friends, a statement of positive consequences may be used to strengthen your request ("If you get in bed by eight-thirty, I'll read you a story").*

The gist of being assertive on the spot is simply to *make your request* in as simple, specific, and straightforward a manner as possible. Whether you choose to mention your feelings or the consequences of the other person's behavior will largely depend on the situation. Mention consequences when you want the other person to better appreciate your position. Express your feelings when you want the other person to understand how strongly you feel about what they're doing (or not doing).

On-the-Spot Assertiveness Exercises

The exercises below are designed to give you practice in responding assertively on the spot. The situations presented are common ones which you may have encountered before in your life. The task is to fill in the blank with an assertive response. Alternatively, you may wish to role-play these situations with a friend. This will give you direct practice with both the verbal and the nonverbal aspects of assertive communication. As you practice, remember to stay calm.

1. You take your car to the garage for an oil change and receive a bill for that plus wheel alignment and new spark plugs. You say,

_____

_____

2. You arrange to take turns driving to work with a friend. Each day you drive, she has an errand to run on the way home. When she drives, there are no stops made. You say,

_____

_____

---

* Reproduced from the *TERRAP Program Manual* by permission of Dr. Arthur B. Hardy.

3. When you entertain your coworkers, the conversation always turns to shoptalk. You are planning a party and prefer to avoid the usual topics. You say,

_____

_____

4. You're in the bank. The teller asks, "Who's next?" It's your turn. A woman who came in after you says, "I am." You say,

_____

_____

5. You're in a taxi and you suspect that the driver is taking you by a roundabout route. You say,

_____

_____

6. You're in a restaurant, which, like most restaurants these days, is nonsmoking (even though nonsmoking signs are not visible). A person at the bar nearby lights up a cigarette. You say,

_____

_____

7. You've frequently had adverse reactions to medications in the past. Your doctor gives you a prescription without telling you what side effects to expect. You say,

_____

_____

8. You're buying some new clothes. The saleswoman is pressuring you into buying something that makes you look ten pounds heavier. You say,

_____

_____

9. You're playing miniature golf with your spouse. You're not doing very well but are having a good time. Your spouse is continually telling you how to do it "right." You say,

_____

_____

10. You've settled in for a quiet Sunday at home, the first in a long time. Your parents call and invite you over for the day. You don't want to go. You say,

_____

_____

11.   You receive a notice informing you that your child has been placed in the classroom of a teacher whom you know to be notoriously incompetent. You call the principal and you say,

_____

_____

12.   Someone rings your doorbell, wanting to convert you to their religion. You're not interested. You say,

_____

_____

13.   A friend asks you to babysit for her, but you have other plans for the day. You say,

_____

_____

14.   You're feeling lonely and "left out." Your spouse is in the living room, reading. You say,

_____

_____

15.   You've been rushing about all day. It's very hot and you don't have air conditioning. You prepare a salad for dinner because you don't want to turn the oven on. Your spouse comes home hungry and wants a hot meal. You say,

_____

_____

16.   Some friends dropped by without an invitation at five o'clock. It is now seven and you want to serve dinner to your family. You don't have enough to include the guests. You say,

_____

_____

Learning to Say No

An important aspect of being assertive is your ability to say no to requests that you don't want to meet. Saying no means that you *set limits* on other people's demands for your time and energy when such demands conflict with your own needs and desires. It also means that you can do this without feeling guilty.

In some cases, especially if you're dealing with someone with whom you don't want to promote a relationship, just saying "No, thank you" or "No, I'm not interested" in a firm, polite manner should suffice. If the other person persists, just repeat your statement calmly without apologizing. If you need to make your statement stronger and more emphatic, you may want to 1) look the person directly in the eyes, 2) raise the level of your voice slightly, and 3) assert your position: "I said no thank you."

In many other instances—with acquaintances, friends, and family—you may want to give the other person some explanation for turning down their request. Here it's often useful to follow a three-step procedure:

1. Acknowledge the other person's request by repeating it.

2. Explain your reason for declining.

3. Say no.

4. (Optional). If appropriate, suggest an alternative proposal where both your and the other person's needs will be met.

Use step 4 only if you can easily see a way for both you and the other person to meet each other halfway.

Examples

"I understand that you'd really like to get together tonight *(acknowledgment)*. It turns out I've had a really long day and feel exhausted *(explanation)*, so I need to pass on tonight *(saying no)*. Would there be another night later this week when we could get together?" *(alternative option)*

"I hear that you need some help with moving *(acknowledgment)*. I'd like to help out, but I promised my boyfriend we would go away for the weekend *(explanation)*, so I'm not going to be available *(saying no)*. I hope you can find someone else."

Note that in this example, the speaker not only acknowledges her friend's need, but indicates that she would have liked to help out if the circumstances had been different. Sometimes you may wish to let someone know that under different conditions you would have willingly responded to their request.

"I realize you would like to go out with me again *(acknowledgment)*. I think you're a fine person, but it seems to me that we don't have enough in common to pursue a relationship *(explanation)*, so I have to say no *(saying no)*."

"I know that you'd like me to take care of Johnny for the day *(acknowledgment)*, but I have some important errands I have to attend to *(explanation)*. So I can't babysit today *(saying no)*."

Are there any particular types of situations where you repeatedly have trouble saying no? Make a list of these situations in the space below:

Now take a sheet of paper and write a hypothetical assertive response for each of these situations where you say no, following the three-step procedure outlined above.

The following suggestions may also be helpful in learning to say no (adapted from Matthew McKay, Peter Rogers, and Judith McKay's *When Anger Hurts):*

1. *Take your time.* If you're the type of person who has difficulty saying no, give yourself some time to think and clarify what you want to say before responding to someone's request (for example, "I'll let you know by the end of the week" or "I'll call you back tomorrow morning after sleeping on it").

2. *Don't overapologize.* When you apologize to others for saying no, you give them the message that you're "not sure" that your own needs are just as important as theirs. This opens the door for them to put more pressure on you to comply with what they want. In some cases, they may even try to play upon your guilt to obtain other things or to get you to "make it up to them" for having said no in the first place.

3. *Be specific.* It's important to be very specific in stating what you will and won't do. For example: "I'm willing to help you move, but because of my back I can only carry lightweight items" or "I can take you to work, but only if you can meet me by eight-fifteen."

4. *Use assertive body language.* Be sure to face the person you're talking to squarely and maintain good eye contact. Work on speaking in a calm but firm tone of voice. Avoid becoming emotional.

5. *Watch out for guilt.* You may feel the impulse to do something *else* for someone after turning down their request. Take your time before offering to do so. Make sure that your offer comes out of genuine desire rather than guilt. You'll have fully mastered the skill of saying no to others when you reach the point that you can do so without feeling guilty.

Summary of Things to Do

Learning to be assertive will enable you to obtain more of what you want and will help minimize frustration and resentment in your relationships with partners, family, and friends. It will also help you to take more risks and to ask more of life, adding to your sense of autonomy and self-confidence.

Becoming assertive does, however, take *practice*. When you first attempt to act assertively with family and friends, be prepared to feel awkward. Also be prepared for them not to understand what you're doing and possibly even to take offense. If you explain as best you can and give them time to adjust to your new behavior, you may be pleasantly surprised when they come to respect you for your newfound directness and honesty.

To get the most out of this chapter, I suggest you do the following:

1. Determine your dominant behavior style (submissive, aggressive, passive-aggressive, manipulative, or assertive) by asking yourself how you'd respond to each of the thirty situations listed in the *What's Your Style?* questionnaire.

2. Clarify those situations and people with whom you'd like to be more assertive by completing *The Assertiveness Questionnaire.*

3. Make a copy of the *Personal Bill of Rights* and post it in a conspicuous place. Read it over a number of times until you feel thoroughly familiar with all of the rights listed.

4. Identify two or three problem situations in which you would like to be more assertive. Write them up under the exercise *Specifying Your Problem Situations*. Make your description of each situation specific, by indicating *who* it involves, *when* it occurs, *what* bothers you, *how* you'd normally deal with it, your *fears* about being assertive, and, finally, your particular *goal*.

5. Write out an assertive response to each of your problem situations. Your narrative for each assertive response should contain the six steps listed in the exercise *Developing an Assertive Response*.

6. Become thoroughly familiar with the guidelines for making an assertive request: using assertive nonverbal behaviors, keeping your request simple, being specific,

using first-person statements, objecting to behaviors (not personalities), not apologizing for being assertive, and making requests instead of demands.

7. Review the guidelines for being assertive on the spot and complete the *On-the-Spot Assertiveness Exercises.*

8. Role-play with a friend or counselor your assertive responses to your problem situations and/or the *On-the-Spot Assertiveness Exercises.*

9. Review the section "Learning to Say No" and, with a friend or counselor, role-play saying no to unreasonable requests.

10. Consult the books listed below under "Assertiveness Skills" for a more thorough coverage of the topic. If you feel the need to seek extra help beyond this workbook, you'll find that most adult education programs through local colleges or high schools offer workshops and classes in assertiveness training.

11. Consult the books listed below under "Communication Skills" or take a class in communication to back up your assertiveness training with other important interpersonal skills such as listening, self-disclosure, and negotiating.

Further Reading

Assertiveness Skills

Alberti, Robert E., and Michael Emmons. *Your Perfect Right*. Ninth edition. Atascadero, CA: Impact Press, 2008.

Bower, Sharon, and Gordon Bower. *Asserting Yourself*. Updated edition. Reading, MA: Perseus, 2004.

Davis, Martha, Elizabeth Robbins Eshelman, and Matthew McKay. *The Relaxation & Stress Reduction Workbook*. Sixth edition. Oakland, CA: New Harbinger Publications, 2008.

McKay, Matthew, Peter Rogers, and Judith McKay. *When Anger Hurts*. Second edition. Oakland, CA: New Harbinger Publications, 2003.

Smith, Manuel J. *When I Say No, I Feel Guilty*. New York: Bantam Books, 1985.

Communication Skills

Fisher, Roger, and William Ury. *Getting to Yes: Negotiating Agreement without Giving In*. Second edition. New York: Penguin, 1991.

McKay, Matthew, Martha Davis, and Patrick Fanning. *Messages: The Communication Skills Book*. Third edition. Oakland, CA: New Harbinger Publications, 2009.

14

Self-Esteem

Self-esteem is a way of thinking, feeling, and acting that implies that you accept, respect, trust, and believe in yourself. When you *accept* yourself, you can live comfortably with both your personal strengths and weaknesses without undue self-criticism. When you *respect* yourself, you acknowledge your own dignity and value as a unique human being. You treat yourself well in much the same way you would treat someone else you respect. *Self-trust* means that your behaviors and feelings are consistent enough to give you an inner sense of continuity and coherence despite changes and challenges in your external circumstances. To *believe* in yourself means that you feel you deserve to have the good things in life. It also means that you have confidence that you can fulfill your deepest personal needs, aspirations, and goals. To get a sense about your own level of self-esteem, think of someone (or imagine what it would be like to know someone) whom you *fully* accept, respect, trust, and believe in. Now ask yourself to what extent you hold these attitudes toward yourself. Where would you place yourself on the following scale:

Very Low Self-Esteem											Very High Self-Esteem
0	1	2	3	4	5	6	7	8	9	10	

A fundamental truth about self-esteem is that it needs to come from *within*. When self-esteem is low, the deficiency creates a feeling of emptiness that you may try to fill by latching on—often compulsively—to something external that provides a temporary sense of satisfaction and fulfillment. When the quest to fill your inner emptiness by appropriating something from outside becomes desperate, repetitive, or automatic, you have what is called an *addiction*. Broadly defined, addiction is an attachment to something or someone outside yourself that you feel you need to provide a sense of inner satisfaction or relief. Frequently, this attachment substitutes preoccupation with a substance or activity for healthy human relationships. It may also substitute a temporary feeling of control or power for a more lasting sense of inner confidence and strength.

A healthy alternative to addiction is to work on building your self-esteem. Growing in self-esteem means developing confidence and strength from within. While still enjoying life fully, you no longer need to appropriate or identify with something or someone outside yourself to feel okay. The basis for your self-worth is internal. As such, it is much more lasting and stable.

Ways to Build Self-Esteem

There are many pathways to self-esteem. It is not something that develops overnight or as a result of any single insight, decision, or modification in your behavior. Self-esteem is *built gradually* through a willingness to work on a number of areas in your life. This chapter considers—in three parts—a variety of ways to build self-esteem:

- Taking care of yourself

- Developing support and intimacy

- Other pathways to self-esteem

Most fundamental to your self-esteem are your willingness and ability to take care of yourself. This means first that you can *recognize* your basic needs as a human being and then *do* something about meeting them. Taking care of yourself also involves cultivating a relationship with that part of yourself known as the "inner child." Your inner child is a place deep inside that is the origin of your needs. It is the playful, spontaneous, and creative side of you—yet it also carries any emotional pain, fear, or sense of vulnerability you acquired from your childhood. By becoming a good parent to your own inner child now, you can overcome the limitations and deficiencies of your upbringing years ago. A popular saying these days aptly states, "It's never too late to have a happy childhood."

Part I of this chapter focuses on this theme of taking care of yourself. It begins by enumerating a variety of dysfunctional family situations that can cause low self-esteem. Following this is a discussion of basic human needs to help you identify those needs that are most important to address in your life right now. Finally, a variety of methods for cultivating a relationship with your inner child are offered. Learning to meet your needs—to care for and nurture yourself—is *the most fundamental and important thing you can do to build your self-esteem.*

Part II of this chapter is an extension of part I. Finding support and intimacy in your life is obviously a major part of taking care of yourself. Other people can't give you self-esteem, but their support, acceptance, validation, and love can go a long way toward reinforcing and strengthening your own self-affirmation. This part is divided into four sections. The first addresses the importance of developing a support system. The second presents ten conditions that I feel are critical to genuine intimacy. The third section offers a discussion of interpersonal boundaries. Having boundaries in your relationships is essential both to intimacy and to self-esteem. A final section underscores the relevance of assertiveness to self-esteem.

Part III presents four additional aspects of self-esteem:

- Personal wellness and body image

- Emotional self-expression

- Self-talk and affirmations for self-esteem

- Personal goals and a sense of accomplishment

Although these pathways to self-esteem are diverse among themselves, they can all be viewed as an extension of the basic idea of taking care of yourself.

Part I: Taking Care of Yourself

Taking care of yourself is the foundation on which all other pathways to self-esteem rest. Without a basic *willingness* and *ability* to care for, love, and nurture yourself, it is difficult to achieve a deep or lasting experience of self-worth.

Perhaps you had the good fortune to receive the love, acceptance, and nurturing from your parents that could provide you with a solid foundation for self-esteem as an adult. Presently, you are free of any deep-seated feelings of insecurity and your path to self-esteem is likely to be simple and short, involving certain changes in attitude, habits, and beliefs. For those who have carried a lifelong sense of insecurity, though, the way to self-worth involves developing the ability to give yourself what your parents could not. *It's possible to overcome deficits from your past only by becoming a good parent to yourself.*

Some Causes of Low Self-Esteem

What are some of the childhood circumstances that can lead you to grow up with feelings of insecurity or inadequacy?

1. **Overly Critical Parents**
   Parents who were constantly critical or set impossibly high standards of behavior may have left you feeling guilty; that somehow you could "never be good enough." As an adult, you will continue to strive for perfection to overcome a long-standing sense of inferiority. You may also have a strong tendency toward self-criticism.

2. **Significant Childhood Loss**
   If you were separated from a parent as a result of death or divorce, you may have been left feeling abandoned. You may have grown up with a sense of emptiness and insecurity that can be restimulated very intensely by losses of significant people in your adult life. As an adult, you may seek to overcome old feelings of abandonment by overdependency on a particular person or addiction to food, drugs, work, or whatever works to cover the pain.

3. **Parental Abuse**
   Physical and sexual abuse are extreme forms of deprivation. They may leave you with a complex mix of feelings, including inadequacy, insecurity, lack of trust, guilt, and/or rage. Adults who were physically abused as children may become perpetual victims or may themselves develop a hostile posture toward life, victimizing others. Adults—especially men—who were sexually abused as children sometimes express their rage by turning to rape and abuse as adults. Or they may turn that rage inward in deep feelings of self-loathing and inadequacy. Survivors of abusive childhoods often, and understandably, have difficulty with intimate relationships in their adult lives. While less flagrant, constant verbal abuse can have equally damaging effects.

4. **Parental Alcoholism or Drug Abuse**
   Much has been written in recent years on the effects of parental alcoholism on

children. Chronic drinking or substance abuse creates a chaotic, unreliable family atmosphere in which it is difficult for a child to develop a basic sense of trust or security. The attendant denial of the problem, often by both parents, teaches the child to deny his or her own feelings and pain connected to the family situation. Many such children grow up with poor self-esteem or a poor sense of personal identity. Fortunately, support groups are presently available to help adult children of alcoholics heal the adverse effects of their past. If one or both of your parents were alcoholic, you may wish to read the following books: *It Will Never Happen to Me* by Claudia Black, *Adult Children of Alcoholics* by Janet Woititz, and *Recovery: A Guide for Adult Children of Alcoholics* by Herbert Gravitz and Julie Bowden. You may also want to join a support group or therapy group for adult children of alcoholics in your area.

5. **Parental Neglect**

   Some parents, because they are preoccupied with themselves, their work, or other concerns, simply fail to give their children adequate attention and nurturing. Children left to their own devices often grow up feeling insecure, worthless, and lonely. As adults, they may have a tendency to discount or neglect their own needs.

6. **Parental Rejection**

   Even without physical, sexual, or verbal abuse, some parents impart a feeling to their children that they are unwanted. This profoundly damaging attitude teaches a child to grow up doubting his or her very right to exist. Such a person has a tendency toward self-rejection or self-sabotage. Adults with such pasts must learn to love and care for themselves if they are to overcome what their parents didn't give them.

7. **Parental Overprotectiveness**

   The child who is overprotected may never learn to risk independence and trust the world outside of the immediate family. As an adult, such a person may feel very insecure and afraid to venture far from a safe person or place. Through learning to acknowledge and care for their own needs, overprotected individuals can gain the confidence to make a life of their own and discover that the world is not such a dangerous place.

8. **Parental Overindulgence**

   The "spoiled" child of overindulgent parents is given insufficient exposure to deferred gratification or appropriate limits. As adults, such people tend to be bored, lack persistence, or have difficulty initiating and sustaining individual effort. They tend to expect the world to come to them rather than taking responsibility for creating their own lives. Until they are willing to take personal responsibility, such people feel cheated and very insecure because life does not continue to provide what they learned to expect during childhood.

Do any of the above categories seem to fit you? Does more than one? You may initially find it difficult to acknowledge problems in your past. Our memory of childhood is often hazy and indistinct—especially when we do not *want* to recall what actually happened. The point of remembering and acknowledging what happened to you as a child is not so that you can blame your parents. Most likely, your parents did the best they could with their available personal resources, which may have been severely limited as a result of deprivations they experienced with *their* parents. The purpose of remembering your past is to *release* it and *rebuild your present*. Old "tapes" or patterns based on fear, guilt, or anger will tend to interfere with your present life and relationships until you can identify and release them. Once you acknowledge and ultimately forgive your parents for what they were unable to give you, you can truly begin the journey of learning to care for yourself. In essence, this means becoming a good parent to yourself. The balance of this section will consider three important ways in which you can learn to take better care of yourself:

1.   Acknowledging and meeting your basic needs

2.   Discovering and cultivating a relationship with your inner child

3.   Making time for small acts of self-nurturing on a daily basis

Your Basic Needs

Basic human needs conjures an association with shelter, clothing, food, water, sleep, oxygen, and so on—in other words, what human beings require for their physical survival. It was not until the last few decades that higher-order *psychological needs* were identified. While not necessary for survival, meeting these needs is essential to your emotional well-being and a satisfying adjustment to life. The psychologist Abraham Maslow proposed five levels of human needs, with three levels beyond primary concerns for survival and security. He arranged these levels into a hierarchy, as follows:

Self-Actualization Needs (fulfillment of your potential in life, wholeness)

↑

Esteem Needs (self-respect, mastery, a sense of accomplishment)

↑

Belongingness and Love Needs (support and affection from others, intimacy, a sense of belonging)

Safety Needs (shelter, stable environment)

Physiological Needs (food, water, sleep, oxygen)

In Maslow's scheme, taking care of higher-level needs is dependent on having satisfied lower-level needs. It's difficult to satisfy belongingness and esteem needs if you're starving. On a subtler level, it's difficult to fulfill your full potential if you're feeling isolated and alienated for lack of having met needs for love and belongingness. Writing in the 1960s, Maslow estimated that the average American satisfied perhaps 90 percent of physiological needs, 70 percent of safety needs, 50 percent of love needs, 40 percent of esteem needs, and 10 percent of the need for self-actualization.

Although Maslow defined esteem narrowly in terms of a sense of accomplishment and mastery, I believe that self-esteem is dependent on *recognizing and taking care of all of your needs.*

How do you recognize what your needs are? How many of the following important human needs are you aware of?

1.   Physical safety and security

2.   Financial security

3.   Friendship

4.   The attention of others

5.   Being listened to

6.   Guidance

7.   Respect

8.   Validation

9.   Expressing and sharing your feelings

10. Sense of belonging

11. Nurturing

12. Physically touching and being touched

13. Intimacy

14. Sexual expression

15. Loyalty and trust

16. A sense of accomplishment

17. A sense of progress toward goals

18. Feeling competent or masterful in some area

19. Making a contribution

20. Fun and play

21. Sense of freedom, independence

22. Creativity

23. Spiritual awareness—connection with a Higher Power

24. Unconditional love

Now go back over the list carefully and ask yourself how many of these needs you are actually getting fulfilled at this time. In what areas do you come up short? What concrete steps can you take in the next few weeks and months to better satisfy those needs that are going unmet? Working up your exposure hierarchies to overcome your phobias will help you meet needs 17 and 18. Going dancing or to a movie tonight will help in a small way with your need for fun and play. The point is that learning to take care of yourself involves being able to 1) *recognize* and 2) *meet* your basic needs as a human being. The above list may give you ideas on areas of your life that need more attention. Use the following chart to plan what you will actually do in the next month about five (or more) of your needs that could be better met.

Need	What I'm willing to do in the next month to better meet this need

Cultivating a Relationship with Your Inner Child

The concept of the *inner child*—the childlike part of yourself—has been around for many decades. The psychologist Carl Jung referred to it as the "divine child," while the religious thinker Emmet Fox called it the "wonder child." But what is it? How would you recognize your own child within? Some characteristics of the inner child include

- That part of you which feels like a little girl or boy.

- That part of you which feels and expresses your deepest emotional needs for security, trust, nurturing, affection, touching, and so on.

- That part of you which is alive, energetic, creative, and playful (much as real children are when left free to play and be themselves).

- Finally, that part of you that still carries the pain and emotional trauma of your childhood. Strong feelings of insecurity, loneliness, fear, anger, shame, or guilt—even if triggered by present circumstances—belong to the inner child. Actually, there are very few new feelings. Especially when they are strong, most of our feelings reflect ways we reacted or failed to react a long time ago as a child.

How do you feel about the little child within you? If you are willing to allow the little girl or boy inside some freedom of expression, you'll find it easier to be more playful, fun loving, spontaneous, and creative. You'll find it natural to give and receive affection, to be vulnerable, and to trust. You'll be in touch with your feelings and free to grow. On the other hand, to the extent that you suppress and deny your inner child, you will likely find it difficult to be playful or have fun. You may tend to be conventional and conforming and act out painful patterns repeatedly. You may feel constricted and inhibited, unable to let go and expand. It will be hard to be vulnerable or trusting, hard to give and receive affection. Finally, you will likely be out of touch with your feelings, inclined to be overly logical or overly in need of keeping everything under tight control.

How can you bring out and cultivate a healthy relationship with your inner child? In my experience there are four steps to this process:

1. Overcoming attitudes of criticism, rejection, and/or denial of your child within

2. "Bringing out" your inner child

3. Reevaluating negative feeling states in terms of positive needs of your inner child

4. Nurturing your inner child on a daily basis

Overcoming Negative Attitudes Toward Your Inner Child

A basic truth is that you tend to treat your own inner child in much the same way that your parents treated you as a child. For better or worse, you internalize your parents' attitudes and behaviors. If they were overly critical toward you, you likely grew up overly self-critical, especially of your "childish" or less rational, impulsive side. If they neglected you, you likely grew up tending to ignore or neglect the needs of your own inner child. If they were too busy for you as a child, you're likely to be too busy for your inner child as an adult. If they abused you, you may have become self-destructive as an adult or else may be abusive of others. If your parents placed a taboo on acknowledging and expressing your feelings and impulses, you may have grown up denying your feelings. The list goes on. To cultivate a healing, caring relationship with your own inner child—to become a good parent to yourself—you need to overcome any internalized parental attitudes that cause you to criticize, abuse, neglect, or deny the needs and feelings of your child within.

Bringing Out Your Inner Child

While learning to overcome negative patterns internalized from your parents, you may wish to begin bringing out your inner child. It's useful to begin this even *before* you work through all of the limitations you've imposed on your child within. There are a number of good ways to go about doing this, including 1) visualizations, 2) writing a letter to your inner child, 3) using photos as a reminder, and 4) real-life activities that give your inner child expression. You may be surprised to find that caring for your own inner child is a lot less time and energy consuming than bringing up a real one!

Visualization

Below is a detailed visualization to help you foster a closer relationship with your own inner child. Record this visualization, pausing for a few moments between each sentence and for ten to twenty seconds when the instructions say "Pause." You can do this yourself, or find a friend whose voice you like to prerecord the script for you. Make sure that you give yourself ten to fifteen minutes to deeply relax before beginning the visualization, since your capacity to remember and see yourself as a child will be greatly enhanced by deep relaxation. (You can use progressive muscle relaxation, meditation, or any deep relaxation technique you wish. See chapter 4.)

Healing Your Inner Child*

Imagine sitting down in a rocking chair and getting very comfortable. Feel yourself rocking easily back and forth. As you continue rocking, you might find yourself starting to drift … drifting more and more. Rocking back and forth you might find yourself gently drifting back into time. Rocking gently and drifting … slowly drifting back into time. Year by year you might imagine yourself getting younger and younger. The years are going by … back through the 1990s … back through the 1980s … gently drifting back … feeling younger and younger. Back into time long ago. Drifting back to a time when you were perhaps very young. You're imagining now that you can see the little child you were a long time ago. Very soon you can imagine seeing yourself as a little child. Perhaps you can see her [him] there now. What does she look like? What is she wearing? About how old is she? Can you see where she is? Indoors or outdoors? Can you see what she's doing? Perhaps you can see her face, and, if you look carefully, you

---

* I am indebted to David Quigley for some of the ideas in this visualization.

can see the expression in her eyes. Can you tell how this little child is feeling right now? (Pause.) As you look at this little girl, can you recall anything that was missing in her life? Is there anything that kept her from being fully happy? (Pause.) If there was anyone or anything that got in the way of this little girl being completely happy and carefree, perhaps you can imagine seeing that person or situation. (Pause.) If no one is there yet, perhaps you can imagine your dad or your mom or whoever you would like standing in front of you right now. (Pause.) What does your little girl feel toward Dad, Mom, or whoever is standing in front of you right now? ... Is there anything that your child would like to say to that person right now? If so, it's okay to go ahead and say it right now ... you can go ahead and say it. (Pause.) If your little child is feeling scared or confused about saying anything, imagine that your present-day, adult self enters the scene right now and goes up and stands next to your little child. (Pause.) Now when you're ready, imagine your adult self, standing next to your little child, speaking up on your little child's behalf to whoever is there. Your adult self can say whatever she wants. Tell your parent—or whoever is there—whatever you need to say ... whatever it was that never got expressed. (Pause thirty seconds or longer.) If you wish, you might complete the sentence "How do you think it makes me feel that ..." (Pause twenty seconds or longer.) Or you might complete the sentence "I wish you had ..." (Pause twenty seconds or longer.) Tell your parent or whoever is there anything you wish they had done but didn't. When you speak up, speak loud and clear so you can be sure that whoever is there really hears you. (Pause twenty seconds or longer.) Does the person you're facing have any response? Listen to see if they have a response. (Pause twenty seconds or longer.) If so, you can respond to what they say. If not, you can just finish what you need to say. (Pause.) When you're finished speaking, you can ask whoever is there either to go away and leave you alone ... or to go away for a while until you're ready to talk again ... or else to stay ... and you're going to accept them as they are and give them a hug. (Pause.)

Now go back and see your present-day, adult self standing next to your little child. (Pause.) If you're willing, pick that little girl up in your arms this very second and love her. Wrap your arms around her and tell her that it's okay. Tell her that you know how she feels. Tell her that you understand. You're here and you're going to help her and you love her very much. (Pause.) If you could give a color to the love you feel, what color comes to mind? (Pause.) Surround your little child with a light of that color and let her feel the peace of being in your arms. (Pause.) Tell her that you think she's a great little girl ... that you love the way she talks, walks, laughs ... and does everything. Tell her that you care and that she's precious ... (Pause thirty seconds or longer.)

Optional: *Now sit your child on your lap and talk to her. She's got a good mind, and if someone would only explain things, she would understand. Tell her that because of the problems Mom and Dad had in their own childhood, they couldn't care for her and love her in the way she deserved to be loved. It wasn't that they didn't want to love her ... it was because of their own difficulties that they couldn't love her the way she wanted. This little child simply needs someone to explain to her ... nobody ever explained to her about the problems her parents had when they were growing up. (Pause.) Can your little child understand that because of their problems, Mom and Dad weren't able to love or take care of her in the way she truly deserved? Is your little child ready to forgive Mom and Dad for what happened? (Pause.) If she's not ready right now, perhaps she'll be ready later. If she is ready now, go ahead and picture Mom and Dad standing in front of you. (Pause.) Now tell them, in whatever way you wish, that you forgive them. You're willing to forgive them for their shortcomings because you know that their own problems interfered with their being the best parents they could. Go ahead and forgive them now ... (Pause thirty seconds or longer.)*

(Give yourself instructions to wake up. Move your arms and legs, then take a few deep breaths. Then, as you start to feel more alert, say to yourself a few times, "Wake up.")

Write a Letter to Your Inner Child

After having done the preceding visualization or as a result of looking at photos of yourself (see next section) as a child, you may wish to write a letter to your inner child. You can tell your child about 1) how you feel about her or him, 2) how you feel about what happened to her or him as a child, 3) how you would like to get to know her or him better, and 4) what you would like to learn from her or him. When you've completed this letter, open your mind and see if you can take the role of the little child. Then write a child's letter back to your adult self, saying how you feel about your adult self and what you would like from her or him. You might even try using a child's handwriting for this letter to help get more in touch with how your little child feels. You will be surprised at how well this works in opening up communication between your adult and inner child "selves." Here is an example of such a letter from an adult to her inner child:

Dear Little Child,

I have long wanted to reach back in time to tell you how much I love you and how much I want to protect you from all the pain and suffering you've been going through. You're much too small and vulnerable to be facing such pain by yourself. I want you to know that you'll have me beside you from now on, and whenever you're frightened you can run to me. I'll be there to hold you and comfort you and protect you.

I know that seeing your daddy lose his temper is very, very frightening. He makes as much noise as he can, and sometimes he hits your mommy or your brother. He doesn't hit you and in a way this just makes you feel guilty. It makes it seem as if you're on his side, and that every time he hits one of them, it's your fault too.

I wish you could tell me more about how you feel, about yourself, your daddy, your mommy, and your brother. I think that a lot of things have happened to you that you just can't remember—either because they didn't make sense at the time or they were just too horrible to remember. It's hard to remember things that don't have any pictures, words, or even concepts attached to them—it's like trying to remember dreams.

As you remember more, I'll be able to understand more about who I am and how I act and what I feel. I know that it's painful trying to remember, and I want you to know how grateful I am to you for trying. Remember that from now on we'll always be there for each other.

> *Love,*
(sign your name)

Photographs

Carry a photo of yourself as a child in your purse or wallet and take it out periodically as a reminder of your child within. Reflect on what was going on and how you felt in your life around the time the photo was taken. After a week or so with one photo, pick another from a different age and repeat the process.

Real-Life Activities

A number of real-life activities can foster increased awareness of and closeness to your inner child. Spending ten minutes daily doing any of the following may help:

- Hugging a teddy bear or another stuffed animal

- Going to a children's playground and using the swings or other playground equipment

- Playing with your own child as if you were a peer rather than an adult

- Having an ice cream cone

- Going to the zoo

- Climbing a tree

- Engaging in any other activity you enjoyed as a child

Try to get into the spirit of being a child as you do any of the above. Your feelings in doing so will tell you a lot about your attitude toward your own inner child.

Reevaluating Negative Feelings as Positive Needs of Your Inner Child

If you were to encounter a small child who appeared scared, confused, or abandoned, you would likely do everything in your power to nurture and comfort him or her. Yet how do you treat yourself when you feel insecure, scared, lonely, abandoned, or otherwise needy? Too often we simply deny these feelings; or else we become critical or rejecting toward ourselves for having them. One of the most profound transformations you can make along the road to greater self-esteem is to *re-perceive feelings of insecurity and inadequacy as pleas for attention from your inner child rather than as signs of weakness to be gotten rid of.* You will heal yourself faster by acknowledging and nurturing the needy child behind your negative feeling states instead of trying to push away your inner child's needs.

The next time you feel frightened, insecure, inadequate, vulnerable, or angry, frustrated, and fed up, try asking yourself, "What is the need behind this feeling? What is it that my inner child needs right now?" Then take the time to give your child within the attention, caring, or nurturing she or he needs, and you'll be surprised by how much better you feel.

Learning to re-perceive negative feelings as pleas for attention from your inner child will transform your life and contribute greatly to your self-esteem. This is what "becoming a good parent to yourself" is all about.

Examples of Disguised Pleas for Help from Your Inner Child

You've just come home from a hard day at work. You see yourself in the bathroom mirror and you can't stand the way you look. Your makeup looks too heavy and it's smeared besides. You look and feel like an old floozy. You begin to think, "What's the use." You could choose to sink into a depression, but instead you ask your inner child what she wants at that very moment. Instead of fixing your makeup, you decide to fill the bathtub with warm bubbly water. You feel a little silly doing it, but you put some bath toys in the tub with you—a little rubber ducky and a child's teapot. You had similar tub toys when you were a child. You soak in the warm water and play with the toys, pouring pretend cups of tea and making the duck talk, just as you did when you were little. You stay in the tub as long as you feel like it, letting your fingertips and toes get wrinkled like prunes. When you look in the mirror again, you look pink and warm. You feel more forgiving of the way you look—after all, you've had a hard day!

You've spent two hours preparing a special meal for your sister, who was coming over to spend the evening with you. But at the last minute, she calls and says she can't come because she's not feeling well. You suspect it's because she's been asked out on a date. Suddenly you feel a mixture of sadness and anger. You could indulge in these negative feelings, but instead you ask what your inner child needs. Instead of getting angry and throwing the food away, you decide to pretend that you're your own guest of honor, and you've just prepared this beautiful meal for yourself. You make yourself a paper tiara and sit at the head of the table between two candles. Several times during the meal, you raise your glass and make toasts to yourself. You eat slowly, enjoying every bite and noticing the texture, color, and taste—after all, you're in a good position to appreciate it. At the end of the meal, you thank yourself for providing such splendid company.

Nurturing Your Inner Child on a Daily Basis

How do you go about caring for and nurturing your child within? Earlier in this chapter, I talked about recognizing and meeting twenty-four basic human needs. Meeting these needs would certainly be a good start. If you were to meet all of those needs you would go a long way toward developing a healthy relationship with your inner child. The exercises described above for bringing out the inner child will also foster a closer and more supportive relationship with this important part of yourself. Beyond this, there are hundreds of small acts of self-nurturing that can serve to cultivate a more caring relationship with yourself and ultimately a much improved sense of self-worth. Just as you would offer small gestures of caring and nurturing to deepen your relationship with your spouse, your child, or a friend you love, you can do the same for yourself. The list below suggests fifty-one small ways in which you can nurture yourself on a daily basis.

Self-Nurturing Activities

The following list has been very helpful to many of my clients who suffer from anxiety disorders or depression. By performing at least one or two items from the list every day, or anything else you find pleasurable, you will grow in the important skill of becoming a good parent to yourself. You have nothing to lose but your sense of insecurity and inadequacy—and nothing to gain except increased self-esteem.

1. Take a warm bath.

2. Have breakfast in bed.

3. Take a sauna.

4. Get a massage.

5. Buy yourself a rose.

6. Take a bubble bath.

7. Go to a pet store and play with the animals.

8. Walk on a scenic path in a park.

9. Visit a zoo.

10. Have a manicure or pedicure.

11. Stop and smell some flowers.

12. Wake up early and watch the sunrise.

13. Watch the sunset.

14. Relax with a good book and/or soothing music.

15. Go rent a funny video.

16. Play your favorite music and dance to it by yourself.

17. Go to bed early.

18. Sleep outside under the stars.

19. Take a "mental health day" off from work.

20. Fix a special dinner just for yourself and eat by candlelight.

21. Go for a walk.

22. Call a good friend—or several good friends.

23. Go out to a fine restaurant just with yourself.

24. Go to the beach.

25. Take a scenic drive.

26. Meditate.

27. Buy new clothes.

28. Browse in a book or record store for as long as you want.

29. Buy yourself a cuddly stuffed animal and play with it.

30. Write yourself a love letter and mail it.

31. Ask a special person to nurture you (feed, cuddle, and/or read to you).

32. Buy yourself something special that you can afford.

33. Go see a good film or show.

34. Go to the park and feed the ducks, swing on the swings, and so on.

35. Visit a museum or another interesting place.

36. Give yourself more time than you need to accomplish whatever you're doing (let yourself dawdle).

37. Work on your favorite puzzle or puzzlebook.

38. Go into a hot tub or Jacuzzi.

39. Make a recording of affirmations.

40. Write out an ideal scenario concerning a goal, then visualize it.

41. Read an inspirational book.

42. Write a letter to an old friend.

43. Bake or cook something special.

44. Go window shopping.

45. Buy a meditation CD or download one.

46. Listen to a positive, motivational recording.

47. Write in a special diary about your accomplishments.

48. Apply fragrant lotion all over your body.

49. Masturbate.

50. Exercise.

51. Sit and hold your favorite stuffed animal.

Part II: Developing Support and Intimacy

While self-esteem is something we build within ourselves, much of our feeling of self-worth is determined by our significant personal relationships. Others cannot give you a feeling of adequacy and confidence, but their acceptance, respect, and validation of you can reaffirm and strengthen your own positive attitude and feelings about yourself. Self-love becomes narcissistic in isolation from others. Let's consider four pathways to self-esteem that involve relationships with others:

- Close friends and support

- Intimacy
- Boundaries
- Assertiveness

Close Friends and Support

When surveys of human values have been done, many people rank close friends near the top, along with career, a happy family life, and health. Each of us needs a support system of at least two or three close friends in addition to our immediate family. A close friend is someone you can deeply trust and confide in. It is someone who comfortably accepts you as you are in all your moods, behaviors, and roles. And it is someone who will stand by you no matter what is happening in your life. A close friend allows you the opportunity to share your feelings and perceptions about your life outside your immediate family. Such a person can help bring out aspects of your personality that might not be expressed with your spouse, children, or parents. At least two or three close friends of this sort, whom you can confide in on a regular basis, are an essential part of an adequate support system. Such friends can help provide continuity in your life through times of great transition, such as moving away from home, divorce, or death of a family member.

How many close friends of the type just described do you have? If you don't have at least two, what could you do to cultivate such friendships?

Intimacy

While some people seem content to go through life with a few close friends, most of us seek a special relationship with one particular person. It is in intimate relationships that we open ourselves most deeply and have the chance to discover the most about ourselves. Such relationships help overcome a certain loneliness that most of us would eventually feel—no matter how self-sufficient and strong we may be—without intimacy. The sense of belonging that we gain from intimate relationships contributes substantially to our feelings of self-worth. I want to reemphasize, however, that self-worth cannot be derived entirely from someone else. A healthy intimate relationship simply reinforces your own self-acceptance and belief in yourself.

Much has been written on the topic of intimacy and on what ingredients contribute to lasting intimate relationships. Some of the most important of these are listed below (not ranked in any order):

1. Common interests, especially leisure time and recreational interests. (A few differences in interests, though, can add some novelty and excitement.)

2. A sense of romance or "magic" between you and your partner. This is an intangible quality of attraction that goes well beyond the physical level. It's usually very strong and steady in the first three to six months of a relationship. The relationship then requires the ability to renew, refresh, or rediscover this magic as it matures.

3. You and your partner need to be well matched in your relative needs for togetherness versus independence. Conflict may arise if one of you has a much greater need for freedom and "space" than the other, or if one of you has a need for protection and coziness that the other doesn't want to provide. Some partners may hold a double standard—in other words, they're unwilling to allow you what they require for themselves (such as trust and freedom).

4. Mutual acceptance and support of each other's personal growth and change. It is well known that when only one person is growing in a relationship, or feels invalidated in their growth by the other, the relationship often ends.

5. Mutual acceptance of each other's faults and weaknesses. After the initial romantic months of a relationship are over, each partner must find enough good in the other to tolerate and accept the other's faults and weaknesses.

6. Regular expressions of affection and touching. An intimate relationship cannot be healthy without both partners being willing to overtly express affection. Nonsexual expressions such as hugging and cuddling are just as important as a sound sexual relationship.

7. Sharing of feelings. Genuine closeness between two people requires emotional vulnerability and a willingness to open up and share your deepest feelings.

8. Good communication. Entire books and courses are devoted to this subject. While there are many different aspects to good communication, the two most important criteria are that

   • The partners are genuinely willing to listen to each other, and

   • Both are able to express their feelings and ask for what they want directly (as opposed to complaining, threatening, demanding, and otherwise attempting to manipulate the other to meet their needs).

9. A strong sense of mutual trust. Each person needs to feel that he or she can rely on the other. Each also trusts the other with his or her deepest feelings. A sense of trust does not come automatically; it needs to be built over time and maintained.

10. Common values and a larger sense of purpose. An intimate relationship has the best opportunity to be lasting when two people have common values in important areas of life such as friendships, education, religion, finances, sex, health, and family life. The strongest relationships are usually bound by a common purpose that transcends the personal needs of each individual—for example, raising children, running a business, or commitment to a spiritual ideal.

How many of the above ten characteristics are present in your intimate relationship? Are there any, in particular, that you would like to work on?

Boundaries

Just as important as intimacy is the need for each of us to maintain appropriate boundaries within both intimate and other relationships. Boundaries simply mean that you know where you end and the other person begins. You don't define your identity in terms of the other person. And above all, you don't derive your sense of self-worth and self-authority by attempting to take care of, rescue, change, or control the other person. The terms "women who love too much" and "codependency" have been used to define those people who, because they lack a solid, internal basis of self-worth, attempt to validate themselves through taking care of, rescuing, or simply pleasing another person. The classic case of this is the person who attempts to organize his or her life around "rescuing" an alcoholic or otherwise addicted spouse or close relative. But loss of boundaries can occur in any relationship in which you attempt to gain self-worth and security by overextending yourself to take care of, control, rescue, or change someone else. Your own needs and feelings are set aside and discounted in the process. A good indication of loss of boundaries is when you spend more time talking or thinking about another's needs or problems than your own.

Two excellent books are recommended if you want to further explore boundary issues in your own relationships. In her best-selling book *Women Who Love Too Much*, Robin Norwood advocates the following steps in overcoming codependency in a close relationship:

1. Going for help—giving up the idea you can handle it alone

2. Making recovery from codependency your highest priority

3. Finding a support group of peers who understand the problem

4. Developing a personal spiritual life that allows you to let go of self-will and rely on a Higher Power

5. Learning to stop managing, controlling, or "running the life" of another or others you love

6. Learning to let go of playing the game of "rescuer" and/or "victim" with the other person

7. Facing and exploring your own personal problems and pain in depth

8. Cultivating yourself: developing a life of your own and pursuing your own interests

9. Becoming "selfish," not in the unhealthy sense of egoism but instead putting *your* well-being, desires, work, play, plans, and activities first instead of last

10. Sharing what you have learned with others

Another excellent book which carefully defines codependency and provides a series of steps for overcoming the problem is *Codependent No More* by Melody Beattie. Some of her recommendations include

1. Practicing "detachment"—letting go of obsessively worrying about someone else

2. Letting go of the need to control someone else—respecting that person enough to know that he or she can take responsibility for his or her own life

3. Taking care of yourself, which includes finishing up "unfinished business" from your own past and learning to nurture and cherish the needy, vulnerable child within

4. Improving communication—learning to state what you want and to say no

5. Dealing with anger—giving yourself permission to feel and express anger at loved ones when you need to

6. Discovering spirituality—finding and connecting with a Higher Power. Is codependency an issue for you? Have you considered joining a support group that focuses on codependency issues, such as Al-Anon or Codependents Anonymous?

Assertiveness

Cultivating assertiveness is critical to self-esteem. If you're unable to clearly get across to others what you want or do not want, you will end up feeling frustrated, helpless, and powerless. If you do nothing else, the practice of assertive behavior in and of itself can increase your feeling of *self-respect*. Honoring your own needs with other people in an assertive manner also increases *their* respect for you, and quickly overcomes any tendency on their part to take advantage of you.

The concept of assertiveness, along with exercises for developing an assertive style of communication, are presented in chapter 13 of this workbook.

Part III: Other Pathways to Self-Esteem

The first two parts of this chapter focused on taking care of your needs through honoring your inner child and developing support and intimacy in your relationships. In this final part, I want to emphasize four other pathways to self-esteem that involve different levels of your whole being.

- Body: physical well-being and body image

- Feelings: emotional self-expression

- Mind: positive self-talk and affirmations for self-esteem

- Whole self: personal goals and a sense of accomplishment

Although these areas have been considered elsewhere in this workbook, they are discussed briefly here for their relevance to self-esteem.

Physical Well-Being and Body Image

Physical health and a sense of personal wellness, vitality, and robustness compose one of the most important foundations of self-esteem. It's often difficult to feel good about yourself when you're feeling physically weak, tired, or ill. Current evidence points to the role of physiological imbalances—often caused by stress—in the genesis of panic attacks, agoraphobia, generalized anxiety, and obsessive-compulsive disorder. Upgrading your physical well-being will have a direct impact on your particular problem with anxiety, as well as contribute substantially to your self-esteem. The chapters on relaxation, exercise, and nutrition relate directly to physical well-being. Reading them and putting into practice the suggestions and guidelines offered will go a long way toward upgrading your personal wellness. The questionnaire below is intended to give you an overview of how you are doing in this area.

Personal Wellness Questionnaire

1. Are you exercising for at least one half hour three to five times per week?

2. Do you enjoy the exercise you do?

3. Do you give yourself the opportunity to deeply relax each day through progressive muscle relaxation, visualization, meditation, or some other relaxation method?

4. Do you give yourself at least one hour of downtime or leisure time each day?

5. Do you manage your time so that you are not perpetually rushed?

6. Do you handle stress, or do you feel that it has control of you?

7. Do you give yourself solitary time for personal reflection?

8. Do you get at least seven hours of sleep every night?

9. Are you satisfied with the quality and quantity of your sleep?

10. Are you eating three solid meals each day, including a good-sized breakfast?

11. Are you minimizing your consumption of stress-producing foods (those containing caffeine, sugar, salt, or processed "junk" foods)?

12. Do you take vitamin supplements on a regular basis to augment your diet—such as a multivitamin tablet and extra vitamin B-complex and vitamin C when you're under physical or emotional stress?

13. Do you like your living environment? Is the place where you live comfortable and relaxing?

14. Does smoking tobacco interfere with your physical well-being?

15. Does excessive use of alcohol or so-called recreational drugs compromise your well-being?

16. Are you comfortable with your present weight? If not, what can you do about it?

17. Do you value your personal appearance through good hygiene, grooming, and dressing in a way that feels comfortable and attractive?

18. Do you like your body and the way you appear?

Emotional Self-Expression

When you're out of touch with your feelings, it's hard to know who you are. You tend to feel internally detached from yourself and often fearful. By identifying and expressing the full range of your feelings, you can become better acquainted with your unique needs, desires, and yearnings. Literally you begin to *feel* yourself—your whole self—rather than walking around in a cloud of worried thoughts, fantasies, and anticipations. Learning to own and express your feelings takes time, courage, and a willingness to be vulnerable in the presence of others whom you trust. If you haven't already, read chapter 12 for suggestions on how to increase your awareness and ability to express your feelings. This is a very important pathway to self-esteem.

Self-Talk and Affirmations for Self-Esteem

What you tell yourself, and your beliefs about yourself, contribute in an obvious and literal way to your self-esteem. If you are feeling inadequate and powerless, it's very likely because you *believe* that you are. By the same token, you can raise your self-esteem *simply* by working on changing your self-talk and basic beliefs about yourself.

Exercises for identifying and altering your negative self-talk and mistaken beliefs have been presented in chapters 8 and 9. At this point, I'll simply highlight certain parts of those chapters that are relevant to self-esteem. First, I want you to consider two types of self-talk that are most damaging to your self-worth. Second, I will cover the use of affirmations to overcome negative beliefs and assumptions about yourself.

Of the four types of self-talk described in chapter 8—the Worrier, the Critic, the Victim, and the Perfectionist—the Critic and the Victim are the most potentially destructive to your self-esteem. Indeed, it has been my experience that people with low self-esteem invariably have a strong Critic, a strong Victim consciousness, or both. It's the Critic's specific function to talk you down into feeling inadequate, inferior, and incompetent. Then Victim self-talk may add insult to injury by telling you that you're hopeless and powerless.

First, go back to chapter 8 and review the section "Types of Negative Self-Talk" and the exercise "What Are Your Subpersonalities Telling You?" with particular attention to the Critic and Victim. Complete the worksheets for countering the destructive self-talk of each of these subpersonalities, if you haven't already. Then use the *Daily Record of Dysfunctional Thoughts* (make several copies) to track the occurrence of negative self-statements from your Critic and Victim as they occur spontaneously during a two-week time period.

When you catch yourself engaging in self-critical or self-victimizing inner dialogues, follow these three steps:

1. *Disrupt* the chain of negative thoughts with some method that diverts your attention away from your mind and helps you to be more in touch with your feelings and body. Any of the following may work:

    *   Physical activity—for example, household chores or exercise

    *   Taking a walk outside

    *   Abdominal breathing

    *   Five minutes of progressive muscle relaxation

    *   Shouting "Stop!" aloud or silently

    *   Snapping a rubber band against your wrist

    The point is to do *something* that slows you down and gives you a bit of distance from your negative thoughts. It's difficult to counter negative self-talk when you're tense and your mind is racing.

2. *Challenge* your negative self-talk with appropriate questioning, if necessary. Good questions to raise with your Critic or Victim might be "What's the evidence for this?" "Is this *always* true?" and "Am I looking at both [or all] sides of this issue?" Review the list of Socratic questions in chapter 8 for other examples of questions.

3. *Counter* your negative inner dialogue with positive, self-supportive statements. You may want to design your own positive statements specifically tailored to refute your Critic's or Victim's statements, one by one. Alternatively, you can draw positive counterstatements from the following list of affirmations.

Affirmations for Self-Esteem

What I Am

I am lovable and capable.

I fully accept and believe in myself just the way I am.

I am a unique and special person. There is no one else quite like me in the entire world.

I accept all the different parts of myself.

I'm already worthy as a person. I don't have to prove myself.

My feelings and needs are important.

It's okay to think about what I need.

It's good for me to take time for myself.

I have many good qualities.

I believe in my capabilities and value the unique talents I can offer the world.

I am a person of high integrity and sincere purpose.

I trust in my ability to succeed at my goals.

I am a valuable and important person, worthy of the respect of others.

Others perceive me as a good and likable person.

When other people really get to know me, they like me.

Other people like to be around me. They like to hear what I have to say and know what I think.

Others recognize that I have a lot to offer.

I deserve to be supported by those people who care for me.

I deserve the respect of others.

I trust and respect myself and am worthy of the respect of others.

I now receive assistance and cooperation from others.

I'm optimistic about life. I look forward to and enjoy new challenges.

I know what my values are and am confident of the decisions I make.

I easily accept compliments and praise from others.

I take pride in what I've accomplished and look forward to what I intend to achieve.

I believe in my ability to succeed.

I love myself just the way I am.

I don't have to be perfect to be loved.

The more I love myself, the more I am able to love others.

What I Am Learning

I am learning to love myself more every day.

I am learning to believe in my unique worth and capabilities.

I am learning to trust myself (and others).

I am learning to recognize and take care of my needs.

I am learning that my feelings and needs are just as important as anyone else's.

I am learning to ask others for what I need.

I am learning that it's okay to say no to others when I need to.

I am learning to take life one day at a time.

I am learning to approach my goals one day at a time.

I am learning to take better care of myself.

I am learning how to take more time for myself each day.

I am learning to let go of doubts and fear.

I am learning to let go of worry.

I am learning to let go of guilt (or shame).

I am learning that others respect and like me.

I am learning how to be more comfortable around others.

I am learning to feel more confident in _____
(name situation)

I am learning that I have a right to _____
(specify)

I am learning that it's okay to make mistakes.

I am learning that I don't have to be perfect to be loved.

I am learning to accept myself just the way I am.

There are several ways you might want to work with the above list. The chapter on mistaken beliefs contains a number of suggestions for working with affirmations. The following two methods have been especially popular with my clients:

- Select your favorite affirmations from the list and write them down individually on 3 by 5 index cards. Then read through the stack slowly and with feeling once or twice a day. Doing this while alternately looking at yourself in a mirror is an excellent idea. You may also want to reword each affirmation in the second person: "You are lovable and capable" (rather than "I am lovable and capable") when repeating the phrases to your mirror image.

- Alternatively, you can record the affirmations. Repeat each affirmation twice and leave about five to ten seconds between different statements. Listen to the recording once a day when you feel relaxed and receptive. You are most likely to internalize affirmations when you focus your attention on them fully while in a relaxed state. (Note that you may wish to construct your own list of self-esteem affirmations, drawing on those that are most meaningful to you from the above list; or make up new ones of your own.)

A Sense of Accomplishment

Accomplishment of personal goals always adds to your self-esteem. If you look back over your life to the times when you felt most confident, you'll find that they often followed the accomplishment of important personal goals. Although external achievements can never be the *sole* basis of a sense of self-worth, they certainly contribute to how you feel about yourself.

If you are dealing with phobias or panic attacks, a most significant accomplishment is the ability to enter into and handle situations that you previously avoided. An even more unassailable sense of achievement is reached when, in addition to confronting phobic situations, you become confident that you can handle any panic reaction that might arise. The mastery of phobias and panic reactions is a main theme of this book and is dealt with in detail in chapters 6 and 7. If you have fully recovered from agoraphobia, social phobias, or panic disorder through conscientiously facing the very things you feared most, you know how much self-confidence and inner strength there is to be gained. Facing your phobias (including the phobia of panic itself) through a process of gradual exposure will, *in and of itself*, add considerably to your self-esteem.

Beyond the important goal of overcoming phobias and panic, however, are all the other goals you might have in your life. Your sense of self-esteem depends on the feeling that you're making progress toward *all* of your goals. If you feel "stuck" and unable to move toward something important that you want, you may begin to doubt yourself and feel somewhat diminished.

Beyond the issue of recovery from phobias and panic, then, you might ask yourself two questions:

1. What are the most important things I want out of life—now and in the future?

2. What am I doing about these goals right now?

Let's consider each of these. To answer the first question, you need to define what your goals are. If this is presently unclear, thinking about what you want in each of the areas below might help you to be more specific:

Physical health	Friends	Psychological well-being
Career	Finances and money	Education
Intimate relationships	Personal growth	Family
Recreation and leisure	Living environment	Spiritual life

Give yourself some time—up to several days if necessary—to clarify what your most important goals are in these areas over the following time intervals: the next month, the next six months, the next year, and the next three years. You may find the *Personal Values Inventory* in chapter 20 to be helpful in making an exploration of your lifelong goals. The focus of the present section is on your more immediate goals.

Write down your most important goals for each time period, using the chart below. You may wish to talk with a close friend or perhaps a counselor to assist you with the process of clarifying your specific personal goals.

The second question involves honestly evaluating what steps you're currently taking—or not taking—toward attaining your immediate and longer-range goals. Are you genuinely working toward what you want? Or are you making excuses and setting up obstacles to the attainment of what you want? The popular phrase "taking responsibility for your life" simply means that you take full responsibility for working toward your own goals. Avoiding self-responsibility is to not do anything about what you want and/or to expect someone else to do it for you. Avoiding self-responsibility will guarantee that you'll have feelings of power-lessness, inadequacy, and even hopelessness. A sense of personal self-worth is dependent on taking responsibility for yourself.

Your Most Important Personal Goals

For the next month:

For the next six months:

For the next year:

For the next three years:

What are some of the obstacles you might be putting in the way of going after what you want? *Fear* is the greatest impediment to doing something about your goals, just as it is in the case of overcoming phobias. If you don't see yourself moving toward what you want, ask whether you're letting any of the following fears get in your way:

- Fear of losing present security

- Fear of failure

- Fear of personal rejection or the disapproval of others

- Fear of succeeding (*then* what would you have to deal with!)

- Fear of your goal involving too much work

- Fear of your goal involving too much time

- Fear of your goal involving too much energy

- Fear that your goal is too unrealistic—for example, that others will discourage you

- Fear of change itself

The solution to any of these fears about taking action on your life goals is exactly the same as the solution to dealing with a phobia: *face the fear and go forward in small steps*. There is no way to eliminate some risk and discomfort, but breaking a goal down into sufficiently small steps (much like an exposure hierarchy) will enable you to go forward.

While fear is the biggest obstacle to moving forward on goals, guilt can also be an impediment. You may wish to consider whether any of the following beliefs are keeping you from seeking what you want:

"I'm not good enough to have _____."

"I don't deserve to have _____."

"No one in my family has ever done something like that before."

"Others won't approve if I go after _____."

"No one will accept this idea if I try to put it into practice."

The latter two beliefs really could have been listed under fears, but they also involve guilt. To overcome the feeling of not deserving to achieve your goal, I suggest that you work intensively with the simple affirmation "I deserve _____." or "I deserve to have _____." Don't be sparing in the use of repetition with this particular affirmation. Continue to work with it until you develop an emotional conviction that it is true. Developing the belief that you deserve what you truly want will add significantly to your self-esteem.

After you've worked through your specific obstacles to taking action on your goals, it's time to develop a plan of action. Just as you would with a desensitization hierarchy, break down your goal into a series of small steps. Remember that this is a long-range plan. As an option, you may wish to specify a time frame for accomplishing each step. Be sure that you reward yourself after the accomplishment of each step, just as you would with a phobia hierarchy. You might ask family or friends for their support in your undertaking, much as you would rely on a support person in tackling a phobia.

For example, you might be feeling increasingly dissatisfied with your present line of work and would like to be doing something else. Yet you're not quite sure about what you want to do, let alone how to go about training for it. The broad goal of "getting into another line of work" might seem a bit overwhelming, taken as a whole. But if you break it down into its component parts, it becomes more manageable:

1. Find a career counselor you respect (or take a course in exploring career options at a local college).

2. Explore different options by

    *   Working with the counselor or taking an appropriate course

    *   Reading about different vocations in such books as *What Color Is Your Parachute?* and the *Occupational Outlook Handbook*

    *   Talking to people who hold positions in vocations you feel drawn to

3. Narrow down vocational options to one particular type of work (obtain whatever help you need to do this)—focus is extremely important in achieving goals.

4. Obtain education or training for the line of work you've chosen.

    *   Find out where training is available in your area (your local library is a good resource for doing your research).

    *   Apply to appropriate schools or training programs.

    *   Apply for an educational grant or loan if your education or training will require a full-time commitment.

5. Complete your education or training (if possible while maintaining your current job).

6. Search for an entry-level position in your new career.

    *   Obtain resources that tell you where jobs are available (professional or trade newsletters, journals, alumni organizations, newspapers, and job hotlines and websites are all good resources).

    *   Prepare a professional-looking resume.

    *   Apply for jobs.

    *   Go for interviews.

7. Begin your new career.

Provided it's physically possible, you can make any major goal manageable by breaking it down into sufficiently small steps. Use the worksheet below to list specific steps you might take to progress toward an important personal goal. Make photocopies of the sheet if there is more than one goal you want to pursue. You may find that you can clarify specific steps more easily by talking about them with a friend or counselor.

The advantage of developing a plan of action is that you then have a map to follow in going after what you want; you can refer to it as you monitor your progress or if you get stuck at any time along the way. If you have trouble with any particular step, you may need to investigate once again any sense of guilt or fears that are getting in your way.

Taking personal responsibility for achieving the things you want most out of life—and making tangible progress toward obtaining them—will add greatly to your sense of self-esteem. An excellent book for getting started that I've often recommended to my clients is Susan Jeffers' *Feel the Fear and Do It Anyway*.

Plan of Action: Steps Toward Your Goal

1. Your goal (be as specific as possible):

_____

_____

2. What small step can you take right now to make some progress toward achieving this goal?

_____

_____

3. What other steps will you need to take to achieve this goal? (Estimate the time required to complete each step.)

_____

_____

_____

_____

Remembering Previous Accomplishments

In identifying goals for the future, it's important not to lose sight of what you've already accomplished in your life. It's common to forget about past attainments at those times when you're feeling dissatisfied with yourself. You can raise your self-esteem in a few minutes by thinking about your life and giving yourself credit for those goals you've already achieved.

The following exercise is designed to help you do this. Think about your entire life as you review each area and make a list of your accomplishments. Keep in mind that while it's gratifying to have external, "socially recognized" achievements, the most important attainments are more intangible and internal. What you've given to others (for example, love, assistance, or guidance) and the life lessons you've gained on the road to maturity and wisdom are ultimately your most important accomplishments.

List of Personal Accomplishments

For each of the following areas, list any accomplishments you've had up to the present. Use a separate sheet of paper if you need to.

School

Work and career

Home and family (for example, raising a child or taking care of a sick in-law)

Athletics

Arts and hobbies

Leadership

Prizes or awards

Personal growth and self-improvement

Charitable activities

Intangibles given to others

Important life lessons learned

Other

Summary of Things to Do

So many different strategies for raising your self-esteem have been presented in this chapter that it would be impractical to summarize each one of them here. The following worksheet is intended to help you organize what you've learned from this chapter and decide which particular strategies for building self-esteem you want to try out in the immediate future.

Strategies for Building Self-Esteem

Go back through the chapter and decide which of the following strategies you want to implement in raising your self-esteem over the next month. I recommend that you stick with no more than three or four strategies and devote at least one week to each. In the spaces provided below, or on a separate sheet of paper, write out specifically what actions you'll take with respect to each intervention. When you're finished, design your own four-week self-esteem program by writing down which strategy you'll work with over each of the next four weeks.

1. Identify no more than three or four needs from the list of needs mentioned earlier in this chapter that you'd like to give special attention to. Then take action to do something about meeting those needs you've singled out. What specifically will you do?

2. Work on bringing out your inner child.

   • Record and listen to the inner child visualization.

   • Write a letter to your inner child.

   • Carry around a photo of yourself as a child.

   • Engage in playful activities that give expression to your inner child. What activities will you practice?

3. Work on redescribing negative feeling states as pleas for attention from your inner child. Describe examples of when you do this over a period of at least one week.

4. Do one or more things from the list of self-nurturing activities. What will you do for each day of a given week?

5. Work on building your support system. How will you specifically do this?

6. Work on cultivating or enhancing an intimate relationship (for example, spending quality time with your partner, taking a course in communication skills, attending a marriage enrichment weekend). How will you do this?

7. Work on improving your understanding and ability to maintain appropriate boundaries (for example, read the suggested books by Robin Norwood and Melody Beattie, attend Al-Anon or Codependents Anonymous meetings, attend a workshop on codependency). How will you specifically do this?

8. Learn and practice assertiveness skills (see chapter 13). What specifically will you do?

9. Work on upgrading your personal wellness and body image (for example, implement relaxation, exercise, and nutritional improvements in your life—see chapters 4, 5, and 15). What are you willing to do in the next month?

10. Work on identifying and expressing your feelings (see chapter 12). What specifically will you do?

11. Counter negative self-talk of your Critic or Victim subpersonalities (use the *Daily Record of Dysfunctional Thoughts* in chapter 8).

12. Work with self-esteem affirmations by

    • Writing one or two of them out several times each day

    • Reading them daily from a list

    • Putting them on a recording that you listen to daily.

    Which one will you do?

13. Define your important personal goals over the next month, six months, year, and three years using the goals worksheet in this chapter. Then take action on one or more goals. What specifically will you do?

14. List personal accomplishments you've achieved to date, using the worksheet in this chapter.

Four-Week Self-Esteem Program

Which of the above interventions will you implement over the next four weeks?

Week 1:

Week 2:

Week 3:

Week 4:

Further Reading

Beattie, Melody. *Codependent No More*. San Francisco: Harper/Hazelden, 1987.

Black, Claudia. *It Will Never Happen to Me*. New York: Ballantine, 1981.

Bradshaw, John. *Homecoming: Reclaiming and Championing Your Inner Child*. New York: Bantam Books, 1990.

Brandon, Nathaniel. *The Psychology of Self-Esteem*. New York: Nash, 1969.

Gravitz, Herbert L., and Julie D. Bowden. *Recovery: A Guide for Adult Children of Alcoholics*. New York: Simon & Schuster (Fireside), 1985.

Jeffers, Susan. *Feel the Fear and Do It Anyway*. San Diego: Harcourt Brace Jovanovich, 1987.

Mangini, Shirley. *Secrets of Self-Esteem*. Canoga Park, CA: N.O.V.A. Corp., 1985.

Maslow, Abraham. *Toward a Psychology of Being*. Second edition. New York: Van Nostrand Reinhold, 1968.

McKay, Matthew, and Patrick Fanning. *Self-Esteem*. Third edition. Oakland, CA: New Harbinger Publications, 2000.

Missildine, Hugh. *Your Inner Child of the Past*. New York: Simon & Schuster, 1963.

Norwood, Robin. *Women Who Love Too Much*. New York: Pocket Books, 1985.

Whitfield, Charles. *Healing the Child Within*. Pompano Beach, FL: Health Communications, 1987.

Woititz, Janet. *Adult Children of Alcoholics*. Hollywood, FL: Health Communications, 1983.

15

Nutrition

Relatively little has been written on the subject of nutrition and anxiety disorders. Yet if it is assumed that there is at least some biological basis for panic attacks and anxiety, the subject of nutrition becomes important. What you eat has a very direct and significant impact on your physiology and biochemistry.

In the last twenty years, the relationship between diet, stress, and mood has been well documented. It's known that certain foods and substances tend to create additional stress and anxiety, while others promote a calmer and steadier mood. Certain natural substances have a directly calming effect and others are known to have an antidepressant effect. You may not yet recognize connections between how you feel and what you eat. You simply may not notice that the amount of coffee or cola beverages you drink aggravates your anxiety level. Or you may be unaware of any connection between your consumption of sugar and your anxiety, depression, or PMS symptoms. This chapter may clarify some of these connections and help you to make positive changes in the way you feel.

The discussion of nutrition in this chapter covers three main topics:

- Foods, substances, and conditions that aggravate anxiety

- Dietary guidelines for reducing anxiety

- Supplements for reducing anxiety

The information in these sections is based on my personal experience and reading in the field of nutrition. It is intended to be suggestive only—not prescriptive. If you wish to make an in-depth assessment and reevaluation of your diet, I recommend that you consult a nutritionist, or a physician who is knowledgeable about nutrition.

Substances That Aggravate Anxiety

Stimulants: Caffeine

Of all the dietary factors that can aggravate anxiety and trigger panic attacks, caffeine is the most notorious. Several of my clients can trace their first panic attack to an excessive intake of caffeine. Many people find that they feel calmer and sleep better after they've reduced their caffeine consumption. Caffeine has a directly stimulating effect on several different systems in your body. It increases the level of the neurotransmitter norepinephrine in your brain, causing you to feel alert and awake. It also produces the very same physiological arousal response that is triggered when you are subjected to stress—increased sympathetic nervous system activity and a release of adrenaline.

In short, too much caffeine can keep you in a chronically tense, aroused condition, leaving you more vulnerable to generalized anxiety, as well as panic attacks. Caffeine further contributes to stress by causing a depletion of vitamin B_1 (thiamine), which is one of the so-called antistress vitamins.

Caffeine is contained not only in coffee but in many types of tea, cola beverages, chocolate candy, cocoa, and over-the-counter drugs. Use the chart on the next page to determine your total daily caffeine consumption in milligrams (mg).

If you are prone either to generalized anxiety or to panic attacks, I suggest that you reduce your total caffeine consumption to *less than 100 mg per day*. For example, one cup of percolated coffee or one diet cola beverage a day would be a maximum. For coffee lovers, this may seem like a major sacrifice, but you may be surprised to find how much better you feel if you can wean yourself down to a single cup in the morning. The sacrifice may well be worth it if you have fewer panic attacks. If you are very sensitive to caffeine, eliminating it altogether would be advisable.

Please note that there are tremendous individual differences in sensitivity to caffeine. As with any addictive drug, chronic caffeine consumption leads to increased tolerance and a potential for withdrawal symptoms. If you have been drinking five cups of coffee a day and abruptly cut down to one a day, you may have withdrawal reactions including fatigue, depression, and headaches. It's better to taper off gradually over a period of a few months—for example, from five cups to four cups per day for a month, then two or three cups per day for the next month, and so on. Some people like to substitute decaffeinated coffee, which has about 3 mg of caffeine per cup, while others drink herbal teas. At the opposite extreme of the sensitivity continuum are people who are made jittery by a single cola or cup of tea. Some of my clients have found that even small amounts of caffeine predispose them to panic or a sleepless night. So it's important that you experiment to find out what your own optimal daily caffeine intake might be. For most people prone to anxiety or panic, this turns out to be less than 100 mg per day.

Nicotine

Nicotine is as strong a stimulant as caffeine. It causes increased physiological arousal, vasoconstriction, and makes your heart work harder. Smokers often object to this notion and claim that having a cigarette tends to calm their nerves. Research has proven, however, that smokers tend to be more anxious than nonsmokers, even when there are no differences in their intake of other stimulants, such as coffee and over-the-counter drugs. They also tend to sleep less well than nonsmokers. I have found that smokers, after quitting, not only feel healthier and more vital but are less prone to anxiety states and panic. In short, if you presently smoke, here is one more reason for stopping.

Caffeine Chart

Coffee   _____cups   @ _____mg = _____mg

Tea   _____cups   @ _____mg = _____mg

Cola drinks   _____cups   @ _____mg = _____mg

Over-the-counter drugs   _____tablets @ _____mg = _____mg

Other sources (chocolate 25 mg per bar, cocoa 13 mg per cup)   _____ mg

                                                    Daily Total   _____ mg

Caffeine content of coffee, tea, and cocoa (milligrams per cup)

Coffee, instant	66 mg
Coffee, percolated	110 mg
Coffee, drip	146 mg
Teabag—five-minute brew	46 mg
Teabag—one-minute brew	28 mg
Loose tea—five-minute brew	40 mg
Cocoa	13 mg
Decaffeinated Coffee	4 mg

Caffeine content of cola beverages (milligrams per twelve-ounce can)

Coca-Cola	65 mg
Dr. Pepper	61 mg
Mountain Dew	55 mg
Diet Dr. Pepper	54 mg
Diet Coke	49 mg
Pepsi-Cola	43 mg

Caffeine content of over-the-counter drugs (per tablet)

Anacin	32 mg
Caffedrine	200 mg
Empirin	32 mg
Excedrin	65 mg
No-Doz	100 mg
Pre-mens Forte	100 mg
Vanquish	33 mg
Vivarin	200 mg

Stimulant Drugs

Over-the-counter drugs containing caffeine have already been mentioned. In addition to these medicines, you should be aware of prescription drugs that contain amphetamines, including Benzedrine, Dexedrine, Methedrine, and Ritalin. While these drugs used to be widely prescribed as appetite suppressants as well as antidepressants, they are rarely used today. Being strong stimulants, they are risky to use if you have a history of anxiety or panic attacks.

The same is especially true for cocaine, whose nonmedicinal use remains widespread. Cocaine use has been the initial cause of recurring panic attacks in countless people, including several whom I've treated personally. If you are at all concerned about panic, this is definitely a drug to avoid.

Substances That Stress the Body

Salt

Excessive salt (sodium chloride) stresses the body in two ways: 1) it can deplete your body of potassium, a mineral that's important to the proper functioning of the nervous system, and 2) it raises blood pressure, putting extra strain on your heart and arteries and hastening arteriosclerosis. You can reduce the amount of salt you consume by avoiding the use of table salt, using a natural salt substitute (such as tamari) both in cooking and on the table, and limiting, as much as possible, salty meats, salty snack foods, and other processed foods containing salt. As a rule of thumb, it's good to limit your salt intake to one gram or teaspoon per day. If you must buy processed foods, choose those that are labeled low sodium or salt-free.

Preservatives

There are presently about five thousand chemical additives used in commercial food processing. Common artificial preservatives include nitrites, nitrates, potassium bisulfite, monosodium glutamate (MSG), BHT, BHA, and artificial colorings and flavorings. Our bodies are simply not equipped to handle these artificial substances, and, in most cases, very little is known about their long-term biological effects. To date, some that have been thoroughly tested have been found to be carcinogenic and thus have been removed from the market. Others currently in use, especially monosodium glutamate, nitrites, and nitrates, produce allergic reactions in many people. It is known that traditional societies that eat strictly whole foods without additives have a lower incidence of cancer. You should try to eat whole, unprocessed foods as much as possible—the foods your body was designed to handle. Try to purchase vegetables and fruits that haven't been treated with pesticides (organically grown) if these are available in your area.

Hormones in Meat

Red meat, pork, and most commercially available forms of chicken are derived from animals that have been fed hormones to promote fast weight gain and growth. There is evidence that such hormones stress these animals (steers and hogs sometimes die of heart attacks on the loading platform). While there is at present no conclusive evidence, many people believe that these hormones might also have harmful effects for the human consumers of meat and meat products. One particular hormone, diethylstilbestrol (DES), has come to the public's attention because it has been implicated in the development of breast cancer and fibroid tumors.

Try to reduce your consumption of red meat, pork, and commercially available poultry, replacing it with organically raised beef, poultry, and fish such as cod, halibut, salmon, snapper, sole, trout, or turbot.

Stressful Eating Habits

Stress and anxiety can be aggravated not only by what you eat but by the way you eat. In our modern, fast-paced society, many of us simply do not give ourselves enough time for eating. Any of the following habits can aggravate your daily level of stress:

- Eating too fast or on the run

- Not chewing food at least fifteen to twenty times per mouthful (food must be partially predigested in your mouth to be adequately digested later)

- Eating too much, to the point of feeling stuffed or bloated

- Drinking too much fluid with a meal, which can dilute stomach acid and digestive enzymes; one cup of fluid with a meal is sufficient

All of the above put a strain on your stomach and intestines in their attempt to properly digest and assimilate food. This adds to your stress level in two ways:

- Directly, through indigestion, bloating, and cramping

- Indirectly, through *malabsorption* of essential nutrients

If food is not properly digested in your mouth and stomach, much of it will pass undigested through your intestines and will subsequently putrefy and ferment—causing bloating, cramps, and gas. The result is that you will get only a limited portion of the nutrition potentially available in your food, leading to a subtle form of undernourishment that you're not likely to be aware of.

So, in addition to reconsidering what you eat, you can decrease stress and a probable malabsorption problem by giving yourself adequate time to eat, chewing your food thoroughly, and not overtaxing your body by eating excessive amounts.

Sugar, Hypoglycemia, and Anxiety

Among nutritionally conscious people these days, sugar has become somewhat of a dirty word. The fact is, however, that your body and brain need glucose—or naturally occurring sugar—in order to operate. Glucose is the fuel your body burns; it provides the energy that sustains life. Much of this glucose is derived from carbohydrate foods in your diet such as bread, cereal, potatoes, vegetables, fruits, and pasta. The starches in these foods are broken down *gradually* into glucose.

Simple sugars, on the other hand, such as refined white sugar, brown sugar, and honey, break down very quickly into glucose. These simple sugars can cause problems because they tend to overload your system with too much sugar too quickly. Our bodies are simply not equipped to process large amounts of sugar rapidly, and, in fact, it was not until the twentieth century that most of us (other than the very wealthy) consumed large amounts of refined sugar. Today, the standard American diet includes white sugar in most beverages (coffee, tea, cola), sugar in cereal, sugar in salad dressings, and sugar in processed meat, along with one or two desserts per day and perhaps a donut or a cookie on coffee breaks. In fact, the average American consumes about *120 pounds* of sugar per year! The result of continually bombarding the body with this much sugar is the creation of a chronic disregulation in sugar metabolism. For some people, this disregulation can lead to excessively high levels of blood sugar, or diabetes (the prevalence of which has increased dramatically in this century). For an even larger number of individuals, the problem is just the opposite—periodic drops in blood sugar level *below* normal, a condition that is popularly termed *hypoglycemia*.

The symptoms of hypoglycemia tend to appear when your blood sugar drops below 50 to 60 milligrams per deciliter—or when it drops very rapidly from a higher to a lower level. Typically, this occurs about two to three hours after eating a meal. It can also occur *simply in response to stress,* since your body burns up sugar very rapidly under stress. The most common subjective symptoms of hypoglycemia are

- Light-headedness

- Anxiety

- Trembling

- Feelings of unsteadiness or weakness

- Irritability

- Palpitations

Do the symptoms look familiar? All of them are symptoms that can accompany a panic attack! In fact, for *some* people panic reactions may actually be caused by hypoglycemia. Generally, such people recover from panic simply by having something to eat. Their blood sugar rises and they feel better. (In fact, an informal, nonclinical way to diagnose hypoglycemia is to determine whether you have any of the above symptoms three or four hours after a meal and whether they then go away as soon as you have something to eat.)

The majority of people with panic disorder or agoraphobia find that their panic reactions do *not* necessarily correlate with bouts of low blood sugar. Yet hypoglycemia can aggravate both generalized anxiety and panic attacks that have been caused for other reasons.

What causes blood sugar to fall below normal is an excessive release of insulin by the pancreas. Insulin is a hormone that causes sugar in the bloodstream to be taken up by the cells. (Insulin is used in the treatment of diabetes to lower excessive blood sugar levels.) In hypoglycemia, the pancreas tends to overshoot in its production of insulin. This can happen if you ingest too much sugar, with the result that you feel a temporary sugar high followed a half hour later by a crash. This can also happen in response to sudden or chronic stress. Stress can cause a rapid depletion of blood sugar. You then experience confusion, anxiety, spaciness, and tremulousness because 1) your brain is not getting enough sugar *and* 2) a secondary stress response occurs. When blood sugar falls too low, your adrenal glands kick in and release adrenaline and cortisol, which causes you to feel more anxious and aroused and also has the specific purpose of causing your liver to release stored sugar in order to bring your blood sugar level back to normal. So the subjective symptoms of hypoglycemia arise from *both* a deficit of blood sugar *and* a secondary stress response mediated by the adrenal glands.

Hypoglycemia can be formally diagnosed through a clinical test called the six-hour glucose tolerance test. After a twelve-hour fast you drink a highly concentrated sugar solution. Your blood sugar is then measured at half-hour intervals over a six-hour period. You will likely get a positive result on this test if you have a moderate to severe problem with hypoglycemia. Unfortunately, many *milder* cases of hypoglycemia are missed by the test. It's quite possible to have subjective symptoms of low blood sugar and to test negative on a glucose tolerance test. Any of the following subjective symptoms are suggestive of hypoglycemia:

- You feel anxious, light-headed, weak, or irritable several hours after a meal (or in the middle of the night); these symptoms disappear within a few minutes of eating.

- You get a high feeling from consuming sugar and this changes to a depressed, irritable, or spacey feeling twenty to thirty minutes later.

- You experience anxiety, restlessness, or even palpitations and panic in the early morning hours, between four and seven. (Your blood sugar is lowest in the early morning because you have fasted all night.)

How do you deal with hypoglycemia? Fortunately, it's quite possible to overcome problems with low blood sugar by 1) making several significant dietary changes and 2) taking certain supplements. If you suspect that you have hypoglycemia or have had it formally diagnosed, you may want to implement the following guidelines. Doing so may result in a calmer disposition—less generalized anxiety, less emotional volatility, and less vulnerability to panic. You may also notice that you are less prone to depression and mood swings.

Dietary Modifications for Hypoglycemia

- Eliminate as much as possible all types of simple sugar from your diet. This includes foods that obviously contain white sugar, such as candy, ice cream, desserts, Coke, or Pepsi. It also includes subtler forms of sugar, such as honey, corn syrup, corn sweeteners, molasses, and high fructose. Be sure to read labels on any and all processed foods to detect these various forms of sugar.

- Substitute fruits (other than dried fruits, which are too concentrated in sugar) for sweets. Avoid fruit juices or dilute them 1:1 with water.

- Reduce or eliminate simple starches such as pasta, refined cereals, potato chips, and white bread. Substitute instead complex carbohydrates such as whole-grain breads and cereals, vegetables, and brown rice or other whole grains.

- Have a complex carbohydrate or protein snack (nuts or whole-grain toast and cheese, for example) halfway between meals—around ten-thirty to eleven in the morning and especially around four to five in the afternoon. If you awaken early in the morning at four or five, you may also find that a small snack will help you to get back to sleep for a couple of hours. As an alternative to snacks between meals, you can try having four or five small meals per day no more than two to three hours apart. The point of either of these alternatives is to maintain a steadier blood sugar level.

Supplements

1. Vitamin B-complex: 50 to 100 mg of all eleven B vitamins once per day with meals.

2. Vitamin C: 1000 mg once or twice per day with meals.

3. Chromium (often called *glucose tolerance factor*): 200 mcg per day. This is available at your local health food store.

4. Glutamine: 500 mg once or twice per day.

5. A combination of glycogenic amino acids (including L-glycine, L-glutamic acid, L-tyrosine, L-leucine, L-alanine, L-methionine, L-lysine). These combinations are available at many health food stores under the name of *hypoglycemia balancer* or *glycemic factors*. Take it as recommended either on the bottle or by a qualified nutritionist.

Vitamin B-complex and vitamin C help to increase your resiliency to stress, which can aggravate blood sugar swings. The B vitamins also help regulate the metabolic processes that convert carbohydrates to sugar in your body.

The mineral chromium and the glycogenic amino acids have a direct, stabilizing effect on your blood sugar level. Glutamine, an amino acid, is quite helpful in reducing cravings for sweets. (If you have an alcohol problem, it helps reduce cravings for alcohol as well.)

If you're interested in exploring the subject of hypoglycemia in greater depth, you might want to read the book *Sugar Blues* by William Dufty.

Food Allergies and Anxiety

An allergic reaction occurs when the body attempts to resist the intrusion of a foreign substance. For some people, certain foods affect the body like a foreign substance, causing not only classic allergic symptoms, such as runny nose, mucus, and sneezing, but a host of psychological or psychosomatic symptoms, including any of the following:

- Anxiety or panic

- Depression or mood swings

- Dizziness

- Irritability

- Insomnia

- Headaches

- Confusion and disorientation

- Fatigue

Such reactions occur in many individuals only when they eat an excessive amount of a particular food, eat a combination of offending foods, or have excessively low resistance due to a cold or infection. Other people are so highly sensitive that only a small amount of the wrong food can cause debilitating symptoms. Often the subtler, psychological symptoms have a delayed onset, making it difficult to connect them with the offending foods.

In our culture, the two most common foods causing allergic reactions are milk or dairy products and wheat. It is casein in milk and gluten in wheat that tend to cause problems. Other foods that can be a source of allergic response include alcohol, chocolate, citrus fruits, corn, eggs, garlic, peanuts, yeast, shellfish, soy products, and tomatoes. One of the most telling signs of food allergy is addiction. You tend to crave and are addicted to the very foods you are allergic to! While chocolate is the most flagrant example of this, you might also take pause if you find yourself tending to crave bread (wheat), dairy products, or another specific type of food. Many people go for years without recognizing that the very foods they crave the most have a subtle but toxic effect on their mood and well-being.

How can you find out whether food allergies are aggravating your problems with anxiety? As in the case of hypoglycemia, there are both formal tests you can obtain from a nutritionally oriented doctor as well as informal tests you can conduct on your own.

Among formal clinical tests for food allergies, the RAST test (radioallergosorbent test) is probably the most reliable. This is a blood test that measures the presence of antibodies to a wide range of foods. Elevated levels of antibodies to specific foods suggest that you are allergic to those foods. Although expensive, the RAST test provides a detailed profile of all of the foods to which you're allergic and can be a very helpful diagnostic tool.

A less formal and expensive way to assess food allergies is to conduct your own elimination tests. If you want to determine whether you are allergic to wheat, simply eliminate all products containing wheat from your diet for two weeks and notice whether you feel better. Then, at the end of the two weeks, suddenly eat a large amount of wheat and carefully monitor any symptoms that appear in the next few hours. After trying out wheat, you might want to try out milk and milk products. It's important to experiment with only one potentially allergic type of food at a time so that you don't confound your results.

It's also a good idea to keep a diary of symptoms comparing how you feel before, during, and following the elimination of a particular food type. Many people feel worse immediately after they eliminate a food for a few days, as though their body is going through withdrawal symptoms. This is a telltale sign of food allergy. In severe cases, such withdrawal symptoms may persist for several weeks, and the period for eliminating the food may need to be lengthened. If this happens, I suggest that you consult a nutritionist to assist you in conducting elimination tests.

An alternative way to test for food allergies is to take your pulse after eating a meal. If it is elevated more than ten beats per minute above your normal rate, it's likely that you ate something you're allergic to.

The good news is that you do not have to permanently abstain from a food to which you are allergic. After a period of several months away from a food, it is possible to eat it again occasionally without adverse effects. For example, instead of having bread at almost every meal, you'll find that you feel better having it only two or three times per week.

For some people, food allergies can definitely be a contributing factor to excessive anxiety and mood swings. If you suspect this to be a problem, try experimenting with the elimination method and/or consult a qualified nutritionist.

Note: Although the emphasis of this section has been on food allergies, some people have allergic symptoms to other environmental substances, both organic and inorganic, which can precipitate a host of psychological symptoms *including anxiety* and *panic.* Offending substances can include food preservatives, natural gas, synthetic fabrics, household cleaners and detergents, hydrocarbons in smog, gasoline fumes, insect sprays, molds, newspaper print, kerosene, turpentine, tar or asphalt, asbestos, cosmetics, shampoos, perfumes, colognes, and hair sprays, to name a few. If you suspect that you might be chemically sensitive to any of these substances, you might want to consult an allergy specialist.

Move Your Diet in the Direction of Vegetarianism

It has been frequently observed that vegetarians tend to be somewhat calmer and more easygoing than their meat-eating counterparts. It might be argued that low-stress, laid-back types are more attracted to vegetarianism in the first place. However, impressions from clients and personal experience suggest otherwise. A dietary change toward vegetarianism can definitely promote a calmer, less anxiety-prone disposition.

If you're used to eating meat, dairy, cheese, and egg products, it is not necessary—or even advisable—to give up *all* sources of animal protein from your diet. Giving up red meat alone, for example, or restricting your consumption of cow's milk (and using soy or rice milk instead)—can have a noticeable and beneficial effect.

How can vegetarianism lead to a calmer disposition? Earlier in this chapter, it was mentioned that steroid hormone residues in red meat can exert an effect not unlike the body's own steroid hormones, activating natural defenses against stress and suppressing immunity. Another reason, however, is that meat, poultry, dairy and cheese products, and eggs—along with sugar and refined flour products—are all *acid-forming* foods. These foods are not necessarily acid in composition, but they leave an acid residue in the body after they are metabolized, making the body itself more acid. This can create two kinds of problems:

When the body is more acid, the transit time of food through the digestive tract can increase to the point where vitamins and minerals are not adequately assimilated. This selective underabsorption of vitamins—especially B vitamins, vitamin C, and minerals—can subtly add to the body's stress load and eventually lead to low-grade malnutrition. Taking supplements will not necessarily correct this condition unless you are able to adequately digest and absorb them.

Acid-forming foods, especially meats, can create metabolic breakdown products that are congestive to the body. This is especially true if you are already under stress and unable to properly digest protein foods. The result is that you tend to end up feeling more sluggish or tired and may have excess mucus or sinus problems. Although it's true that this congestion is not exactly the same thing as anxiety, it can certainly add stress to the body, which in turn aggravates tension and anxiety. The freer your body is from congestion due to acid-forming foods, the lighter and more clear-headed you'll be likely to feel. Be aware, also, that many medications have an acid reaction in the body and may lead to the same types of problems as acid-forming foods.

To maintain a proper acid–alkaline balance in the body, it helps to decrease consumption of acid-forming foods—most animal-based foods, sugar, and refined flour products—and increase the amount of alkaline-forming foods in your diet. Prominent among alkaline foods are all vegetables; most fruits, except plums and prunes; whole grains such as brown rice, millet, and buckwheat; and bean sprouts. Ideally, about 50 to 60 percent of the calories you consume should come from these foods, although in the winter it is okay to eat a slightly higher percentage of animal proteins. Try including more of the alkaline foods in your diet and see if it makes a difference in the way you feel.

Increase Protein Relative to Carbohydrates

Until recently, many nutritionists advocated eating a high amount of complex carbohydrates (whole grains, pastas, bread)—as much as 70 percent of total calories. The prevailing idea was that too much fat promoted cardiovascular disease and too much protein led to excessive acidity and toxicity in the body. The ideal diet was thought to consist of 15 to 20 percent fat, 15 to 20 percent protein, and the rest carbohydrates.

In the past few years, however, evidence has mounted against the idea of eating high quantities of carbohydrates, especially by themselves. Carbohydrates are used by the body to produce *glucose,* the form of sugar the body and brain use for fuel. In order to transport glucose to the cells, your pancreas secretes insulin. Eating high levels of carbohydrates means your body produces higher levels of insulin, and too much insulin has an adverse effect on some of the body's most basic hormonal and neuroendocrine systems, especially prostaglandins and serotonin.

In brief, eating high amounts of cereals, breads, pastas, or even starches such as white rice, corn, and potatoes can raise your insulin levels to the point that other basic systems are thrown out of balance. The answer is not to eliminate complex carbohydrates but to reduce them *proportionately* to the amounts of protein and fat you consume, *without increasing the total number of calories in your diet.* By doing this, you won't end up eating a diet that is too high in fat or protein. Instead, you'll continue to eat fats and protein in moderation *while decreasing the amount of carbohydrate you have at each meal relative to the amount of fat and protein.* The optimal ratio may be 40 percent carbohydrates, 30 percent protein, and 30 percent fat.

Dr. Barry Sears, in his book *The Zone,* presents considerable research supporting the value of reducing the proportion of carbohydrates relative to protein and fat. Many people report that they feel better and have more energy when they increase the ratio of protein to carbohydrates in their diets. Several clients of mine have noticed that increasing protein relative to carbohydrates at each meal had a favorable effect on both anxiety and depression. This isn't surprising because anxiety and mood disorders often involve deficiencies in neurotransmitters, especially serotonin. The body has no way to make neurotransmitters (and serotonin in particular) without a steady supply of amino acids, which are derived from protein. Whether or not you agree with Dr. Sears' approach or choose to adopt a 40:30:30 diet, I highly recommend you have some protein (preferably in the form of fish, organic poultry, eggs, protein powder, tofu, tempeh, or beans and grains) at every meal. On the other hand, aim not to exceed 30 percent of your calories as protein—especially in the form of meat, chicken, or fish—as this may tend to make your body overly acidic.

What to Do When You Eat Out

The pressures and constraints of modern life require that many of us eat lunch or dinner out. Unfortunately, most restaurant food, even at its best, provides too many calories, too much saturated fat, too much salt, and often food that has been cooked in stale or rancid oils. Much restaurant food is less fresh than what you can obtain on your own. For the most part, eating in restaurants is not optimal for taking care of your health.

If you need to eat in restaurants often, observe the following guidelines:

- Avoid all fast food or "junk food" concessions.

- Whenever possible, eat out at natural food or health food restaurants that use whole, preferably organic foods.

- If natural food restaurants are unavailable, go to high-quality seafood restaurants and order fresh fish, preferably broiled without butter or oil. Accompany the fish with fresh vegetables, potatoes or rice, and a green salad. On the salad, avoid creamy or dairy-based dressings.

- As a third choice, try a high-quality Chinese or Japanese restaurant and have a meal consisting of rice, vegetables, and fresh fish or tofu (bean curd). In Chinese restaurants, be sure to ask the waitress to leave off MSG (monosodium glutamate), a flavor enhancer to which many people are allergic.

- As a general rule, when eating out, have no more than one roll with one pat of butter, and minimize ordering cream-based soups, such as clam chowder. Get your salad dressings on the side, using oil and vinegar or a low-fat Italian dressing. Stick with simple entrees such as chicken or whitefish without elaborate sauces or toppings. If possible, try to avoid high-fat desserts. Don't hesitate to ask your server for assistance in having food prepared according to your needs. Learn to enjoy the subtle tastes of simple foods. You'll find this becomes easier and desirable after a while when you omit rich, high-fat, and sugary foods.

As you think back over all of the guidelines for improving your nutrition, keep in mind that it's unnecessary to try to adopt them all at once. Begin by decreasing your caffeine and sugar consumption, which will have the most direct impact on reducing your vulnerability to stress and anxiety. Beyond these suggestions, go at your own pace in upgrading your diet. You're more likely to *maintain* a dietary change that you've decided you truly *want* to make—instead of pressuring yourself.

Summary: Low Stress/Anxiety Dietary Guidelines

As with the rest of the information in this chapter, the following guidelines are intended to be suggestive rather than prescriptive. These guidelines are not intended to take the place of a detailed dietary assessment, recommendations, and the creation of a meal plan by a competent nutritionist, dietician, or nutritionally oriented physician. Although all of the guidelines below are important, they are listed in order of their direct relevance to anxiety reduction.

1. Eliminate as far as possible the stimulants and stress-inducing substances described in the first section of this chapter—caffeine, nicotine, other stimulants, salt (down to one gram or teaspoon per day), and preservatives. (Elimination of caffeine and nicotine is the most critical for reducing anxiety.)

2. Eliminate or reduce to a minimum your consumption of refined sugar, brown sugar, honey, sucrose, dextrose, and other sweeteners such as corn syrup, corn sweeteners, and high fructose. Replace desserts, sugary beverages, and sweet snacks with fresh fruit and sugar-free beverages. Moderate alcohol consumption, since your body converts alcohol to sugar. Also eliminate artificial sweeteners such as aspartame (Nutrasweet) and saccharin. Aspartame, in particular, can aggravate panic attacks and may, over time, cause damage to the nervous system. For a natural sweetener with no proven adverse effects, try stevia.

3. Reduce or eliminate refined and processed foods from your diet as much as possible. Replace with whole and fresh foods (preferably organic). Even many apparent "health food" items, such as protein powder, are highly processed.

4. Eliminate or reduce to a minimum any food that you establish as an allergen. Notice particularly how you feel if you eliminate wheat and/or dairy products from your diet. Be mindful of any food that causes you to feel tired or produce mucus after eating it.

5. Reduce consumption of red meat as well as poultry containing steroid hormones and other chemicals. Replace these with organic poultry and/or seafood (fish such as halibut, salmon, snapper, sole, trout, and turbot are recommended). Avoid large sea fish such as swordfish, marlin, and tuna, which contain excessive levels of mercury.

6. Increase your intake of dietary fiber by eating whole grains, brans, and raw vegetables. (Note, though, that too much fiber can cause gas and bloating and interfere with the body's ability to absorb protein.)

7. Drink the equivalent of at least six eight-ounce glasses of bottled spring water or purified water per day. Reverse osmosis and activated carbon are good methods of filtration. When possible, avoid drinking water sold in plastic bottles. If you do, drink all of the water after opening the bottle—don't leave water in a plastic bottle for days (even in the refrigerator) to have later.

8. Increase your intake of raw, fresh vegetables. A mixed-vegetable salad every day is an excellent idea. Include one fresh (not frozen or canned) cooked vegetable in your diet each day.

9. Whenever possible, buy produce that is organic.

10. Reduce all fat in your diet (oils, nuts, salad dressings, and so on) to no more than 20 to 30 percent of your total calories. Animal fat and cholesterol-containing foods such as red meat, organ meats, gravy, cheeses, butter, eggs, whole milk, and shellfish should make up no more than 10 percent of your total calories. Avoid foods containing trans-fatty acids altogether (contained in deep fried foods, chips, mayonnaise, margarine, and all processed foods that contain partially hydrogenated oils.)

11. To avoid excessive weight gain, consume only as much energy (calories) as you expend. Decrease caloric intake and increase aerobic exercise if you're already overweight.

12. Select foods from the four major food groups: 1) fruits and vegetables (four to five servings daily), 2) whole grains, including whole-grain rice, cereals, and whole-grain breads (two to three servings daily), 3) animal proteins, emphasizing organic poultry, seafood, and eggs, or legume equivalents if you are vegetarian (two to three servings daily), and 4) dairy products, emphasizing low-fat or nonfat dairy products (one or two servings daily). If you are sensitive to cow's milk, try substituting soy, rice, or almond milk instead. Your diet should emphasize the first two categories and moderate amounts of the latter two. In general, it's a good idea to move your diet in the direction of vegetarianism and away from excess consumption of animal-based foods. At the same time, you should increase the ratio of protein to carbohydrates in your diet. Protein should make up approximately 20 to 30 percent of what you eat, fat 20 to 30 percent (or less if your cholesterol is above 220), and complex carbohydrates about 40 to 60 percent.

Use the *Food Diary* on the next page to monitor what you eat for at least three days. In what ways might you improve your dietary habits? What would you actually be willing to change in the next month?

Food Diary

Instructions: Use the following chart to evaluate your eating habits for three days. The areas in which your average daily consumption varies the most from the ideal are the areas in which you can make the greatest improvement in what you eat. Make copies of this form so that you can track your diet for one or two weeks.

For three days, keep track of how many servings you have of each of these food categories. For each category, divide the total servings by 3 to get your daily average for the period. Compare your eating pattern to the ideal.

Week of: _____ (dates)	Day one servings	Day two servings	Day three servings	Average servings per day	Ideal servings per day
Caffeine serving = 1 cup coffee or black tea, or caffeinated cola beverage					
Sweets serving = 1 candy bar, 1 piece of pie, 1 cup ice cream					
Alcohol serving = 1 beer, 1 glass of wine, or cocktail					
Vegetables and fruits serving = 1 cup string beans, 1 apple, 1 orange, medium potato					
Whole-grain breads and cereal serving = 1 slice of bread, ¾ cup cereal					
Milk, cheese, yogurt serving = 1 cup milk, 1 medium slice cheese					
Meat, poultry, fish, eggs, beans, and nuts serving = 3 oz. lean meat or fish, two eggs, 1¼ cup cooked beans, ¾ cup nuts					

Supplements for Anxiety

B Vitamins* and Vitamin C

It is widely known that during times of stress your body tends to rapidly deplete stores of B vitamins and vitamin C. I recommend to all of my clients that they take a high-potency B-complex vitamin and a high dose of vitamin C every day. Many of them find that doing so makes a noticeable difference in their energy level and resiliency to stress. The B vitamins are necessary to help maintain the proper functioning of the nervous system. Deficiencies, especially of vitamin B_1, B_2, B_6, and B_{12}, can lead to anxiety, irritability, restlessness, fatigue, and even emotional instability. It's best to take all eleven of the B vitamins together in a B-complex supplement, since they tend to work together synergistically. Vitamin C is well known for enhancing the immune system and promoting healing from infection, disease, and injury. Less well known is the fact that vitamin C helps to support the adrenal glands, whose proper functioning is necessary to your ability to cope with stress. Vitamin B_5 (pantothenic acid) also supports the adrenal glands, and many people find that it is helpful in dealing with excess stress. (A high dose—such as 1000 mg—of B_5 actually has a calming effect for many individuals.)

Based on personal experience and work with clients, I would suggest that you try a B-complex and vitamin C in the following doses on a regular basis:

- B-complex: 50 to 100 mg of all eleven B vitamins once a day (twice a day under high stress)

- Vitamin C: 1000 mg in a time-release form, twice a day (double this dose under high stress). Vitamin C in combination with bioflavonoids is preferred.

When under unusual stress, it is also a good idea to take extra B_5 (pantothenic acid). Up to 1000 mg in a time-release form may be needed to help mitigate the effects of pronounced anxiety and stress.

Please note that it is not possible to overdose on B vitamins, since they are water soluble. The one exception to this is vitamin B_6. It is important not to exceed 100 mg per day if you're taking B_6 on a long-term basis. (Higher doses of B_6 may be taken on a short-term basis to relieve premenstrual symptoms, however.) High daily doses of vitamin C are generally harmless and a good hedge against infections and colds. However, repeated daily doses in *excess of 8000 mg per day* have been associated with stomach complaints and even kidney stones in some people.

It's important that you take B vitamins, vitamin C, and other vitamins *with meals*. Stomach acids and enzymes produced while digesting food are necessary to help break down and assimilate vitamins. Do not take vitamins on an empty stomach (with the exception of amino acids, as discussed in the section on amino acids). Capsule forms of vitamins are probably easier on the stomach than tablets.

---

* B vitamins include: thiamine (B_1), riboflavin (B_2), niacin or niacinamide (B_3), pantothenic acid (B_5), pyridoxine (B_6), biotin, folic acid, choline, inositol, cyanocobalamin (B_{12}), and PABA (para-aminobenzoic acid).

Calcium

It is widely known that calcium can act as a tranquilizer, having a calming effect on the nervous system. Calcium, along with neurotransmitter substances, is involved in the process of transmitting nerve signals across the synapse between nerve cells. Depletion of calcium can result in nerve cell overactivity, which may be one of the underlying physiological bases of anxiety. It's important that you get at least 1000 mg of calcium per day, either in calcium-rich foods, such as dairy products, eggs, and leafy vegetables, or by taking calcium supplements (chelates are preferred to calcium carbonate). If you take a calcium supplement, be sure to take it in combination with magnesium, as these two minerals balance each other and work in tandem. For some people, magnesium can have a relaxing effect equal to that of calcium. In your supplement, the ratio of calcium to magnesium should be either two to one or one to one. You may also want to try taking liquid calcium-magnesium, available in most health food stores, as a natural tranquilizer.

Note: You may want to have your nutritionist or doctor perform a hair analysis test if you are concerned about having a deficiency of calcium or other minerals. Utilizing a hair sample, the test detects deficiencies of a large number of different minerals. The presence of certain mineral deficiencies can be used to detect other conditions. For example, too little chromium suggests a problem in carbohydrate metabolism and possible hypoglycemia. Too little cobalt suggests a possible vitamin B_{12} deficiency. The test can also detect excesses of toxic metals such as aluminum, lead, or mercury in your body. High levels of mercury, in particular, have been associated with anxiety.

Relaxing Herbs

Herbs have been used for hundreds of years to promote calmness and relaxation. While usually not as potent as prescription tranquilizers, such as Xanax or Klonopin (with the exception of kava), they have few side effects and are nonaddictive. Many people benefit from using herbs for mild to moderate states of anxiety. The following herbs have been most helpful to my clients.

Kava: Relaxing Herb from the Pacific Islands

Kava (or kava kava) is a natural tranquilizer that has become quite popular in the United States in recent years. Several clients of mine have testified that it's as potent a relaxer as Xanax. A member of the pepper tree family, kava is native to the South Pacific. Polynesians have used it for centuries both in ceremonial rituals and as a social relaxer. Small doses produce a sense of well-being, while large doses can produce lethargy, incur drowsiness, and reduce muscle tension.

In European countries, such as Germany and Switzerland, kava has been approved for treatment of insomnia and anxiety. It appears from the limited research available that kava may tone down the activity of the limbic system, particularly the amygdala, which is a brain center associated with anxiety (see chapter 2). Detailed neurophysiological effects of kava are not known at this time.

Kava's principal advantage over such tranquilizers as Xanax or Klonopin is that it's not addictive. It's also less likely to impair memory or aggravate depression as tranquilizers sometimes can. Research indicates that it is an effective treatment for mild to moderate anxiety (not panic attacks), insomnia, headaches and muscle tension, and gastrointestinal spasms and can even help relieve urinary tract infections.

When buying kava, it's preferable to obtain a standardized extract with a specified percentage of kavalactones, the active ingredient. The percentage of kavalactones can vary from 30 to 70 percent. If you multiply the total number of milligrams of kava in each capsule or tablet by the percentage of kavalactones, you get the actual strength of the dose. For example, a 200 mg capsule with 70 percent kavalactones would actually be a 140 mg dose.

Most kava supplements at your health food store contain on the order of 50 to 70 mg kavalactones per capsule. Research in Europe has found that taking three or four doses of this strength daily may be as effective as a tranquilizer.

At present, there is little hard data on the long-term effects of taking kava on a daily basis. In the Polynesian islands, where residents use kava in high doses daily for long periods of time, skin discoloration can occur. Sometimes this progresses to scaling dermatitis, which is relieved when kava is discontinued. If you notice any ill effects, please stop using kava immediately, and do not resume without consulting a naturopath or an informed physician. I would recommend that you not use kava on a *daily* basis for more than six months. On an intermittent basis, however, you can use it indefinitely.

In general, it's not a good idea to use kava in combination with tranquilizers. While not dangerous, such a combination can produce grogginess and even disorientation. Especially if you're taking a moderate to high dose of Xanax or Klonopin (more than 1.5 mg a day), refrain from using kava.

Kava should also not be taken if you have Parkinson's disease, are pregnant, or are breastfeeding. It should be used with caution before driving or operating machinery.

Several years ago there were widespread concerns that kava might cause liver problems. In Europe, some manufacturers used the stems and leaves of the kava plant, which contain a liver toxin, and a few people subsequently developed liver disease. American-based companies then used and now continue to use only the root of the plant (as the Polynesians have done for centuries), which is safe. Kava has never been banned in the United States. However, the FDA still warns that people with a history of liver problems should not use kava without first consulting with their physician.

Valerian

Valerian is an herbal tranquilizer and sedative that is widely used in Europe. In recent years, it has gained popularity in the United States. Clinical studies, mostly in Europe, have found it to be as effective as tranquilizers in alleviating mild to moderate anxiety and insomnia, as Jonathan Davidson and Kathryn Connor discuss in *Herbs for the Mind*. Yet it has fewer side effects and is nonaddictive.

Valerian is also not as likely as prescription tranquilizers to impair memory and concentration or cause lethargy and drowsiness. It will generally not cause a hangover the next day if used for sleep, though a few people have reported being affected that way. In general, valerian can work well for mild to moderate anxiety but may be less effective for more severe cases.

Derived from the plant *Valeriana officinalis,* valerian has numerous chemical constituents, including essential oil, iridoids, and alkaloids. No one of these constituents is responsible for its sedative properties; the overall impression is that all of the components work synergistically. It's therefore unlikely that a single component will be isolated and manufactured synthetically.

Valerian has a good reputation for promoting sleep. Numerous studies have shown that it can reduce the time it takes to get to sleep, as well as improve the quality of sleep. If you try valerian for sleep and it doesn't seem to work, don't give up. Some studies indicate that it may take from two to three weeks of regular use for the herb to achieve its full benefit, whether you're taking it for insomnia or anxiety.

Valerian can be obtained at any health food store in three forms: capsules, liquid extract, or tea. In treating anxiety or insomnia, try each of these forms to see which you like best, following the instructions given on the bottle or package. Capsules are the most convenient, but some people swear by the efficacy of the tinctures and teas. Frequently, you'll find valerian combined with other relaxing herbs such as passionflower, skullcap, hops, or chamomile. You may find these combinations to be more palatable or effective.

The effective dose for valerian ranges from 200 to 400 mg for anxiety relief during the day and 400 to 800 mg for help with sleeping at night. For sleep, it's best to take it about an hour before retiring. For mild to moderate anxiety during the day, you might take two or three doses in the 200 to 400 mg range.

Be sure to buy a valerian product with sufficient potency. Generally, a statement on the bottle indicating that the product has been standardized to at least 0.5 percent of *valerenic acid* is an indication that it has reasonable potency. Also note the expiration date, as older products tend to lose potency. If the product contains other herbs or ingredients besides valerian, it should offer a complete listing of these along with the amount in each recommended dose. Avoid products that don't provide a full listing of ingredients.

As a general rule, you should avoid using valerian daily for over six months. Long-term use at high doses has been associated with side effects such as headache, excitability, restlessness, agitation, and palpitations. You can use it three to four times per week, however, indefinitely. Also, valerian should not be taken together with benzodiazepine tranquilizers such as Xanax, Ativan (lorazepam), and Klonopin or sedatives such as Restoril (temazepam), Ambien (zolpidem), and Sonata (zaleplon). It can be combined with other herbs, such as kava, Saint-John's-wort, and especially hops or passionflower.

Long experience in Europe indicates valerian is an especially safe herb. Still, there are occasional reports of paradoxical reactions of increased anxiety, restlessness, or heart palpitations, possibly due to allergy. Stop using valerian or any other herb if it causes such reactions.

Saint-John's-Wort

Saint-John's-wort, or *hypericum,* has a long history of use. It was recommended by Hippocrates for anxiety more than two thousand years ago. Currently, it is being used widely in Europe and the United States to treat symptoms of mild to moderate depression, as well as anxiety. In Germany, it has outstripped even Prozac and accounts for over 50 percent of the antidepressant market. This fact alone testifies to its effectiveness.

Hypericum has a direct effect on relieving depression and appears to reduce anxiety as a secondary effect. European studies have found it to have antianxiety properties comparable to tranquilizers, although this finding has not yet been confirmed in the United States. There is evidence that hypericum enhances levels of all three neurotransmitters implicated in anxiety disorders: serotonin, norepinephrine, and dopamine. On this basis, it might be seen as preferable to SSRI antidepressants, which raise only serotonin levels.

Saint-John's-wort is available in health food stores and many drugstores. Be sure to obtain brands that are standardized to contain 0.3 percent hypericin, the active ingredient. The standard dose is three 300 mg capsules per day.

When starting out, you may want to try two capsules per day to get used to the herb, then raise the dose to three capsules, or 900 mg per day. If you find hypericum upsets your stomach, take each dose with a meal.

It's important to keep in mind that hypericum takes four to six weeks to reach therapeutic effectiveness. If you're not seeing any benefit in the first two to three weeks, don't get discouraged and stop; you need to stick with it for at least one month.

Hypericum has had a very good safety record over the hundreds of years it has been used. For some people, though, it can cause photosensitivity, an increased sensitivity to sunlight. If you are using hypericum and are in direct sunlight frequently, you may want to limit your exposure or use a sunscreen with 30 SPF or higher. Other side effects occasionally reported are stomach upset, dizziness, dry mouth, and mild allergic reactions. These reports are rare and, in general, side effects are less likely to occur with Saint-John's-wort than with SSRI and especially tricyclic antidepressants.

If you're already taking an SSRI or tricyclic antidepressant and want to switch to Saint-John's-wort, it's best to wean yourself off the prescription drug before starting to take the herb. In general, do not take an SSRI and Saint-John's-wort together without your doctor's approval.

It's okay to take Saint-John's-wort in conjunction with relaxing herbs such as kava or valerian. There is no strong evidence against combining Saint-John's-wort with tranquilizers, such as Xanax and Klonopin, though some doctors are wary of doing so. However, if you are taking an MAO-inhibitor antidepressant, such as Nardil or Parnate, do *not* take hypericum.

In conclusion, Saint-John's-wort is likely to be helpful if you're dealing with mild to moderate depression. It may also alleviate mild to moderate levels of anxiety after four to six weeks' use, although it is probably not effective in relieving panic attacks, obsessive-compulsive disorder, or symptoms of post-traumatic stress disorder. If you are suffering from more severe anxiety symptoms and have not obtained sufficient help from cognitive behavioral therapy and other natural strategies, consult a qualified psychiatrist and consider a trial of an SSRI medication (see chapter 17).

For further information on Saint-John's-wort, see the book *Hypericum and Depression* by Harold Bloomfield, Mikael Nordfors, and Peter McWilliams.

Other Helpful Herbs

Passionflower

Passionflower is a good natural tranquilizer considered by many to be as effective as valerian. In higher doses, it is often used to treat insomnia, as it both relieves nervous tension and relaxes muscles. It's available either in capsules or in liquid extract at your health food store. Sometimes you'll find products that combine it with valerian or other relaxing herbs. Use as directed on the bottle or package.

Gotu Kola

Gotu kola has been popular for thousands of years in India. It has a mildly relaxing effect and helps revitalize a weakened nervous system. It has also been found to help improve circulation and memory function, and it has been found to promote healing following child-birth. You can find it in most health food stores in capsules or extracts. I personally use gotu kola and find it to be beneficial.

Ginkgo Biloba

Derived from the ginkgo tree, ginkgo biloba can indirectly help reduce anxiety by improving concentration and mental clarity. It does this by increasing the flow of blood, oxygen, and nutrients to the brain. Studies have found that it can improve mental function in elderly people and also help tinnitus or "ringing in the ears." Available in 60 mg tablets, I recommend taking one to three 60 mg doses per day. If you're taking aspirin regularly, limit your use of ginkgo, since the combination can inhibit blood clotting.

In using any of the herbs described above, be sure not to exceed the recommended dose. For further information on herbs, consult the books by Harold Bloomfield, Michael Tierra, or Earl Mindell listed at the end of this chapter or see a doctor (usually a holistic physician or naturopath) who is well versed in the use of herbs.

SAM-e: Fast-Acting Natural Antidepressant

Unlike the herbs just described, S-adenosyl-methionine (abbreviated SAM-e, pronounced "Sammy") is a substance that occurs naturally in the body. Widely popular in Europe for over two decades, it first became available in the United States in 1999. Extensive research done in Europe has found it to be as effective in treating depression as prescription SSRI antidepressants. In Italy, in fact, it's more frequently prescribed for depression than Prozac.

SAM-e appears to work by increasing serotonin and dopamine activity in the brain. While healthy people manufacture enough of their own SAM-e, research has found that clinically depressed people are often deficient.

A major advantage of SAM-e is that it has almost no side effects. Since it occurs naturally in the body, adverse reactions are rare. Some people occasionally report nausea or queasiness when starting it, but this tends to go away after a few days. SAM-e also works very quickly. Unlike prescription antidepressants and Saint-John's-wort, the benefits are usually felt within a few days of starting to take it.

In addition to helping with depression, SAM-e has been found useful in the treatment of osteoarthritis and fibromyalgia. It appears to restore and maintain healthy joint function by contributing to regeneration of cartilage. SAM-e also has potent antioxidant properties. It's used by the body to help synthesize glutathione, an important antioxidant involved in protecting cells from free-radical damage. Finally, SAM-e is beneficial to the liver and can assist in detoxifying the body from alcohol, drugs, and environmental toxins.

At present, information on the use of SAM-e to treat anxiety is limited. Most available research has evaluated its effectiveness as an antidepressant. If it functions at all like the SSRIs, I would expect it to have antianxiety as well as antidepressant effects.

SAM-e is available in most health food stores and drugstores in 200 mg tablets. The recommended dose for depression is 400 to 1200 mg a day. Because it can cause nausea and gastrointestinal (GI) disturbances for some people, start with 200 mg per day at first (for this reason, enteric coated tablets are preferable). After two days, raise the dose to 200 mg twice per day. If you do not experience benefits after a week at this dose, you can raise the dose again to 800 to 1200 mg per day. If you're taking it primarily for arthritis or fibromyalgia, 800 mg per day is probably sufficient.

People with bipolar disorder (manic depressives) should take SAM-e only under the supervision of a knowledgeable physician, as it can aggravate manic states.

For detailed information on SAM-e, see the book *Stop Depression Now* by Dr. Richard Brown.

Amino Acids

In the past few years, amino acids, which are the natural constituents of protein, have come into use in the treatment of both anxiety disorders and depression. Many people prefer them to prescription drugs because they have fewer side effects and are nonaddictive. You may wish to talk to a holistic doctor, a naturopath, or the staff at your local health food store to expand on the information presented below.

Tryptophan

The amino acid tryptophan is a natural precursor to the neurotransmitter serotonin. Serotonin is involved in regulating many body functions, including mood, sleep, appetite, and pain threshold. It produces a feeling of calmness and well-being, and deficiencies have been linked to anxiety.

A number of studies have found tryptophan to be as effective as prescription antidepressants and sedatives in relieving insomnia, generalized anxiety, and depression.

Tryptophan is available in two forms: 5-hydroxytryptophan (5-HT) and L-tryptophan. You can find 5-HT in most health food stores. The recommended dose is 50 to 100 mg two to three times per day (or in a single combined dose at bedtime for insomnia), with or without food. L-tryptophan was widely used in the 1980s and then taken off the market in 1989 by the FDA: an impurity in the manufacturing process at a single company caused a rare blood disease that resulted in severe illness for several thousand people. In the mid-nineties, L-tryptophan was reintroduced in the United States under strict manufacturing standards and only by prescription. In the past two years, it has become available again to the public and can be obtained at some health food stores and over the Internet. Many people (including the author) find L-tryptophan to be more sedating than 5-HT and so prefer it for insomnia. The recommended dose is 1000 to 2000 mg at bedtime, taken with a carbohydrate snack or fruit juice. If you take either 5-HT or L-tryptophan, effectiveness can be improved by taking it along with vitamin B_3 (niacinamide) (100 to 500 mg) and vitamin B_6 (100 mg). If you are taking an SSRI, tricyclic, or MAO-inhibitor antidepressant, do not take either form of tryptophan except under the supervision of a physician.

Gamma-Aminobutyric Acid

As an alternative to tryptophan, you may want to consider trying gamma-aminobutyric acid (GABA, for short), an amino acid that is available at most health food stores. GABA has a mildly tranquilizing effect, and many people have used it as an alternative to prescription tranquilizers such as Xanax and Ativan. Although it is not as potent as prescription drugs, GABA does have the advantage of having few side effects and being nonaddictive.

The usual dose of GABA recommended for its calming effect is 200 to 500 mg. It is fine to take it in this dose once or twice per day (do not exceed 1000 mg in a twenty-four-hour period).

It's a good idea to take GABA either on an empty stomach or with a carbohydrate snack (such as a piece of toast, crackers, cereal, or rice cakes). Carbohydrate foods actually enhance the calming or sedative effect. Avoid taking GABA with protein. There is nothing harmful in doing so, but the protein (which is made up of many different amino acids) will tend to compete with absorption of GABA.

Phenylalanine and Tyrosine as Natural Antidepressants

Since depression frequently accompanies anxiety, it's important to consider two amino acids that have been used effectively to treat depression. Both DL-phenylalanine and tyrosine increase the amount of a neurotransmitter substance in the brain known as *norepinephrine*, a substance whose deficiency has been implicated as a contributing cause of depression.

Many mild to moderately depressed people benefit from taking one or the other of these amino acids. These supplements may allow you to feel better without resorting to prescription antidepressant drugs which, while effective, have numerous side effects.

DL-phenylalanine (DLPA) and tyrosine are available in 500 mg capsules or tablets in most health food stores. If you are interested in experimenting with either of them, please observe the following guidelines:

- Do not take either of them if you are pregnant, have PKU (a disease requiring a phenylalanine-free diet), or are taking an MAO-inhibitor medication (such as Nardil or Parnate). If you have high blood pressure, take them only under a doctor's supervision.

- Take them with a carbohydrate snack or at least one half hour before or after any meal containing protein. As with GABA, protein interferes with the absorption of DLPA and tyrosine.

- Start with a dose of 500 mg per day and increase it to 1500 mg per day over three or four days. If you experience no benefit, increase the dose to 2000 to 3000 mg per day after four days. Stay with one amino acid for at least two weeks (unless you experience an adverse reaction). If you experience no noticeable effect after two weeks, try the other one.

- It's likely that you'll experience some benefit from either tyrosine or DL-phenylalanine after a few weeks if taken at the right dosage. Do not exceed 3000 mg per day of either amino acid except under the supervision of a doctor who is familiar with the use of amino acid therapy for the treatment of depression. If you are severely depressed and/or have suicidal thoughts, do not rely on amino acids alone to deal with your problem. Please consult a professional.

An in-depth discussion of the use of amino acids in the treatment of depression can be found in the books by Joan Mathews Larson and Julia Ross at the end of this chapter.

Omega-3 Fatty Acids

Omega-3 fatty acids, especially DHA and EPA, are important for brain and neurological health. Without sufficient levels of omega-3 fatty acids, nerve cell membranes are less fluid and may cause nerve cells to react slowly and misfire. Recent studies have found omega-3 supplementation to be helpful in diminishing symptoms of depression. The best source of omega-3 fatty acids is wild fish (especially salmon and sardines), meat, and fowl. Taking fish oil in liquid (two tablespoons per day) or capsules (two or three per day, or a combined dose of 1000 to 2000 mg per day) may help alleviate depression and mood instability. Oils should be stored in the freezer or refrigerator to protect them from damaging oxidations. Taking 400 IU daily of vitamin E (mixed tocopherol form) can also provide protection from oxidation.

Hormone Supplements

A variety of hormones are available to supplement presumed deficiencies. You've probably seen many of them at your local drugstore or health food store. Some may promote relaxation and aid sleep. Two of the most common are discussed below.

Melatonin

Melatonin is a hormone secreted at night by the pineal gland to signal the brain that it is time to go to sleep. Supplemental melatonin can help regulate sleep cycles. It is taken in doses from 0.5 to 3 mg. While some people find it useful, others say that they get no benefit from it and that it leaves them feeling groggy in the morning. If you experience no benefit from 2 to 3 mg, try lowering your dose to 0.5 mg.

Summary of Things to Do

1. Evaluate the amount of caffeine in your diet, using the *Caffeine Chart* in this chapter, and attempt to gradually reduce your intake to less than 100 mg per day. If you are especially sensitive, you may want to eliminate caffeine altogether, substituting decaf coffee (or decaf teas) for regular coffee and decaf soft drinks for caffeinated ones.

2. Stop smoking. In addition to significantly reducing your risk for cardiovascular disease and cancer, you will lower your susceptibility to panic attacks and anxiety.

3. Reduce your consumption of substances that stress your body. Decrease your intake of salt to one gram per day. Replace processed foods containing preservatives with (preferably organic) vegetables and fruits and whole grains. If possible, substitute organic beef, poultry, and fish for commercially available meats. Avoid processed meats.

4. Allow eating to be a relaxing activity. Avoid eating on the run or eating excessively. Chew your food thoroughly and limit your fluid intake during a meal to eight ounces.

5. Evaluate whether you experience the subjective symptoms of hypoglycemia—such as light-headedness, anxiety, depression, weakness, or shakiness—three or four hours after a meal (or in the early morning hours) and whether they are quickly relieved by eating. You may want to follow this up with a formal six-hour glucose tolerance test. If you suspect that hypoglycemia is contributing to your problem with anxiety, strive to eliminate from your diet all forms of white sugar as well as brown sugar, honey, corn syrup, corn sweeteners, molasses, and high fructose. (Be careful also about aspartame, or Nutrasweet. A recent study found a link between this substance and panic disorder for certain people.) Most fresh, whole fruits (not dried) are fine if you're hypoglycemic, although fruit juices should be diluted with water. Observe the "Dietary Modifications for Hypoglycemia" recommended in this chapter and consider taking the suggested supplements. You may want to consult a qualified nutritionist to assist you in setting up an appropriate dietary and supplement regime.

6. Evaluate your susceptibility to food allergies. Take note of any types of food that you crave (paying attention particularly to wheat and dairy products) and try eliminating that food from your diet for two weeks. Then reintroduce the food and notice if you have any symptoms.

7. Work toward complying with the "Low Stress/Anxiety Dietary Guidelines" described in this chapter. Use the *Food Diary* to monitor your intake of caffeine, fats, sweets, and alcohol, and try for a balanced number of servings of each major food group for several weeks. *Avoid pushing yourself to radically change your diet all at once,* or you may end up rebelling against the idea of making any changes. Introduce one small change each week—or perhaps even each month—so that you gradually modify your dietary habits.

8. Consider taking the supplements recommended for anxiety and stress, especially the B vitamins, vitamin C, and calcium-magnesium. You may want to consult with a nutritionist or physician who is supportive of the idea of high-potency vitamins (not everyone is) to assist you in this.

9. You may want to try the herbs kava or valerian as a mild tranquilizer to relieve anxiety. Or you may want to try SAM-e or Saint-John's-wort as a treatment for mild to moderate depression. Fish oil capsules (high in omega-3 fatty acids) can also be helpful for depression. All of these substances can be found at your local drugstore or health food store. Avoid exceeding recommended levels unless you consult with a knowledgeable professional.

10. You may want to explore whether amino acids can be helpful—specifically, GABA or L-tryptophan for anxiety and tyrosine or DL-phenylalanine for depression. Consult the books by Joan Mathews Larson and Julia Ross listed below for in-depth information on the use of amino acids to treat anxiety and depression.

11. Of the many things your brain needs in order to function properly, the following three criteria are of particular importance to people who have panic attacks, phobias, and/or anxiety:

    • **An adequate level of serotonin**
      Adequate levels can be accomplished, if necessary, via the selective serotonin reuptake inhibitor medications, such as Prozac, Zoloft, or Paxil (see chapter 17). Natural alternatives for increasing serotonin include the use of the herb Saint-John's-wort, the enzyme S-adenosyl-methionine (SAM-e), or the amino acid L-tryptophan. You can also increase your serotonin levels by eating tryptophan-rich foods such as turkey, tuna, eggs, or milk, getting plenty of exercise, getting at least one hour per day of exposure to sunshine, and last, but not least, having that magic ingredient in your life known as love and affection.

    • **An adequate, stable level of blood sugar**
      Review the sections on hypoglycemia and dietary guidelines for hypoglycemia. Eliminate sweets other than fruits from your diet. Always have a nonsugar

snack with you (in your car, at work, and so on) such as unsalted nuts or crackers and cheese should you start to experience hypoglycemic symptoms. Be sure to take supplemental B-complex and chromium.

- **Sufficient light**
  Review the section in chapter 16 on seasonal affective disorder to determine whether light deficiency is an issue for you. If so, read the book by Norman Rosenthal cited below. In the meantime, increase your exposure to sunlight or bright light during fall and winter, if possible.

Further Reading

Balch, Phyllis. *Prescription for Nutritional Healing*. Fourth edition. Garden City Park, NY: Avery Trade, 2006. (A comprehensive reference book.)

Bloomfield, Harold. *Healing Anxiety Naturally*. New York: HarperPerennial, 1999.

Bourne, Edmund J., Arlen Brownstein, and Lorna Garano. *Natural Relief for Anxiety*. Oakland, CA: New Harbinger Publications, 2004.

Brown, Richard. *Stop Depression Now*. New York: Berkeley Trade, 2000.

Crook, William. *The Yeast Connection*. Third edition. Jackson, TN: Professional Books, 1989.

Dufty, William. *Sugar Blues*. New York: Warner Books, 1986. (Classic popular book on hypoglycemia.)

Haas, Elson M. *Staying Healthy with Nutrition*. Twenty-first century edition. Berkeley, CA: Celestial Arts, 2006.

Mathews Larson, Joan. *Depression-Free, Naturally*. New York: Ballantine, 2001.

Mindell, Earl. *Herb Bible*. New York: Fireside, 2002.

———. *Earl Mindell's New Vitamin Bible*. New York: Warner Books, 2004.

Robbins, John. *The Food Revolution*. York Beach, ME: Conari Press, 2001.

Rosenthal, Norman. *Winter Blues: Everything You Need to Know to Beat Seasonal Affective Disorder*. New York: Guilford Press, 2006.

Ross, Julia. *The Mood Cure*. New York: Penguin Books, 2003.

Sears, Barry. *The Zone*. New York: Regan Books, 1995.

Tierra, Michael. *The Way of Herbs*. New York: Pocket Books, 1998.

Weil, Andrew. *Natural Health, Natural Medicine*. Revised edition. Boston: Houghton Mifflin, 2004.

16

Health Conditions That May
Contribute to Anxiety

It's likely that rather than having one identifiable cause, your anxiety springs from a variety of lifestyle, physical, and psychological factors. This chapter examines a number of common physical conditions that can aggravate anxiety or tax your system and make you more vulnerable to its effects. These conditions include adrenal exhaustion, thyroid imbalance, candidiasis, body toxicity, premenstrual syndrome, menopause, seasonal affective disorder, and insomnia. Hypoglycemia and food allergies, discussed in chapter 15, can have similar effects. In order to adequately address your problem with panic, phobias, generalized anxiety, or depression, it's important to deal with these conditions as well, since any one or more of them can aggravate your anxiety problems. While this list is by no means exhaustive of all of the conditions that can complicate anxiety, it includes some of the more common ones I've seen in my practice. Some of these conditions are obvious, while others are not. You know it if you can't sleep or if you suffer from PMS, but you (and your therapist) may not be aware of conditions such as adrenal exhaustion, candidiasis, body toxicity, thyroid imbalances, or seasonal affective disorder. Anyone who suffers from anxiety should be aware of the symptoms, causes, and treatments of all of the disorders discussed in this chapter.

Adrenal Exhaustion

Prolonged and unremitting stress taxes your adrenal glands. In *The Stress of Life*, stress expert Hans Selye describes how protracted stress on the adrenal glands results in a state of chronic underfunctioning or exhaustion. Insufficient adrenal resources, in turn, tend to affect how you handle stressful situations, making it more likely that you will become anxious in the face of stress. Inadequate sleep; prolonged exposure to heat or cold; exposure to toxins, pollutants, or substances you're allergic to; and taking cortisone over a period of time can also contribute to adrenal exhaustion. Sudden trauma or severe physical illness can initiate or worsen adrenal exhaustion. Notice that many of these factors, particularly sudden trauma, such as losses or life transitions, also play a role in the onset of anxiety disorders. Anxiety disorders and adrenal exhaustion frequently occur together.

Adrenal exhaustion develops in stages. When you're combating stress, the adrenal glands tend to hyperfunction, producing large amounts of adrenaline and noradrenaline, as well as steroid hormones such as *cortisol*. As stress becomes prolonged, the glands begin to be overtaxed and go into a state of temporary underfunctioning. If you are relatively healthy, the glands will try to compensate and can actually rebuild themselves to the point of *hypertrophy* (growing larger). However, if high levels of stress continue, the glands will eventually exhaust themselves again and then remain in a chronic state of underfunctioning. At this stage, they can oscillate between overproducing adrenaline, which can cause panic or mood swings, and underproducing adrenaline. The ultimate outcome of prolonged adrenal exhaustion can be chronic fatigue syndrome, fibromyalgia, chronic bronchitis or sinusitis, and autoimmune disorders, ranging from lupus to rheumatoid arthritis.

Symptoms of adrenal exhaustion include

- Low stress tolerance (little things that didn't use to bother you get to you)

- Lethargy and fatigue (often manifested in difficulty getting up in the morning)

- Light-headedness when standing up quickly (called *postural hypotension*)

- Light sensitivity (difficulty adjusting to bright light outdoors)

- Difficulties with concentration and memory

- Insomnia

- Hypoglycemia

- Allergies (to foods, environmental substances, pollens, molds, and so on)

- Increased symptoms of premenstrual syndrome

- More frequent colds and respiratory conditions

Hypoglycemia and adrenal exhaustion. Hypoglycemia and adrenal exhaustion often go hand in hand. The adrenals function along with the pancreas in helping to maintain stable blood sugar levels. When the adrenals underfunction, blood sugar levels tend to become erratic. As adrenal fatigue worsens, the immune system is compromised, leading to increased susceptibility to allergies, asthma, respiratory infections, and colds.

Addictions and adrenal exhaustion. Addiction to caffeine, tobacco, alcohol, or recreational drugs is frequently associated with adrenal exhaustion, as is the physiological craving for sugar. Continued use of any of these substances tends to worsen the condition. If you have any of these addictions, your risk of adrenal insufficiency is higher than average.

Your day-to-day life and adrenal exhaustion. A day-to-day life that is chronically stressful and demanding due to perfectionism and self-imposed pressure to achieve also often leads to adrenal exhaustion.

Recovery from Adrenal Exhaustion

To recover from adrenal exhaustion, you have to address it on a few different fronts. Certain lifestyle changes, supplementation, and dietary modifications can be helpful. These are outlined below:

Simplify your life. Ask yourself which of your habits, practices, and obligations clutter your life rather than enrich it.

Regularly practice your preferred form of relaxation. Whether this is progressive muscle relaxation, guided visualization, yoga, or meditation, try to commit to practicing it daily.

Give yourself downtime daily. Remember that downtime is not a luxury, it is necessary for maintaining a vibrant, fulfilling life (see chapter 4). Break up your day with two or three twenty- to thirty-minute periods of relaxation.

Strive to get eight hours of sleep at night. Sufficient sleep is not a luxury, either. Turn in by ten or eleven at night if possible. Whenever you can sleep late in the morning, let yourself do so.

Exercise regularly. Get twenty to thirty minutes of moderate exercise every day, preferably outdoors (see chapter 5).

Eliminate caffeine, nicotine, alcohol, and recreational drugs. Substitute herb teas for caffeinated beverages. Licorice tea is especially good if you're hypoglycemic.

For three months, eliminate all forms of sugar except xylitol or stevia. This includes white and brown sugar, honey, chocolate, molasses, corn syrup, maple syrup, and dried fruit. Substitute fresh fruits in moderation. Xylitol is a sugar that is made from the fiber of the birch tree. It produces only a small increase in blood sugar and no rise in insulin levels. Stevia is derived from a South American herb and is many times sweeter than sugar. It has no calories and is much safer that artificial sweeteners like aspartame and saccharin. Both xylitol and stevia are available at most health food stores. After three months, you can reintroduce natural sugars such as honey in very small amounts.

Eat a healthy, balanced diet. As much as possible, eliminate processed foods and foods to which you're allergic. Emphasize whole grains, fresh vegetables, and fresh fruits in your diet. Eat protein in the form of beans and grains; eggs; organic poultry; free-range, hormone- and antibiotic-free meat; or fish. Do not overeat carbohydrates. Reduce your consumption of simple starches: pasta, bread, chips, potatoes, cereal, crackers, rolls, and so on. Combine a fat, protein, and complex carbohydrate source at every meal. Avoid eating just fruit first thing in the morning and avoid fruit juices (see chapter 15).

If you have hypoglycemia, eat the appropriate diet. Be sure to eat a protein-carbohydrate snack two to three hours after each main meal (see chapter 15).

Supplements for Adrenal Exhaustion

Certain supplements can help relieve adrenal exhaustion. Talk to your health professional about taking the supplements and quantities listed below:

- Vitamin C with bioflavonoids: 500 to 1000 mg three times per day with meals
- Zinc: 30 mg daily

- Vitamin B$_6$ in the form of P5P (pyridoxal-5-phosphate): 50 mg twice daily

- Calcium with magnesium (preferably in chelated forms such as citrate or aspartate): 1000 mg calcium and 500 to 1000 mg magnesium at bedtime

- Pantothenic acid: 100 to 500 mg daily

With the assistance of a holistic physician, naturopath, or other professional health practitioner, you may want to try an adrenal cortical glandular supplement. Recommended companies for this include Bezwecken, Allergy Research, and Enzymatic Therapy. Adrenal cortical glandulars are preferable to whole adrenal glandulars, which can be overstimulating for some people.

Some people find licorice, in the form of whole licorice root capsules, to be helpful in treating adrenal exhaustion. Do not take licorice, though, if you have high blood pressure or high estrogen levels.

Thyroid Imbalances

Your thyroid gland sits above your breastbone and directs metabolic reactions throughout your body. It secretes two hormones, thyroxine and triiodothyronine, which play a role in regulating your body temperature and metabolic rate, among many other things.

The thyroid gland can be out of balance in two ways: either it can become sluggish and not secrete enough hormones, a condition called *hypothyroidism,* or it can become overly active, which, as you might have guessed, is referred to as *hyperthyroidism* (or *thyrotoxecosis*). According to Dr. Ridha Arem, author of *The Thyroid Solution,* approximately 10 to 20 percent of the adult population suffers from some kind of thyroid imbalance.

Low thyroid function is associated with depression, low energy, weight gain, fatigue, and lethargy. You may be inclined to feel cold, especially in your hands and feet, and tend to gain weight easily. Other symptoms can include menstrual problems in women, water retention, and poor concentration and memory. *An overly active thyroid, on the other hand, is associated with anxiety, hyperactivity, restlessness, difficulty sleeping, weight loss, increased heart rate, and a tendency toward profuse sweating and elevated body temperatures.*

Hyperthyroidism is a condition that is occasionally mistaken for generalized anxiety. If you're not only anxious but feel "hyper," have recently lost weight despite good or increased appetite, or you tend to sweat a lot, it would be a good idea to have your thyroid function evaluated.

If you suspect you might have a thyroid problem, it's best to consult with a physician. Your doctor should do a *complete* thyroid blood panel, preferably one that measures the following four factors:

- *TSH (thyroid stimulating hormone).* A hormone released by your pituitary gland that tells your thyroid gland to make more or less of its hormones. A TSH value of three or higher is considered to be indicative of hypothyroidism. A value below one suggests a hyperthyroid condition.

- *T4 (free thyroxine).* This is a less active form of thyroid hormone which you have on hand to convert to the more active thyroid hormone, T3.

- *T3 (free triiodothyronine).* This is the active form of thyroid hormone. Low levels of T3 are commonly associated with depression and other symptoms of hypothyroidism. Many doctors may suspect you have a problem even if your T3 level is at the low end of the normal range.

- *Antithyroglobulin* and *antithyroperoxidase.* These are two factors that measure the number of antibodies you may be making that can attack your thyroid gland and suppress its function. High levels of these antibodies are indicative of a condition called Hashimoto's thyroiditis, which can lead to either hypo- or hyperthyroid conditions, and needs to be treated medically.

Treating Thyroid Imbalance

If your thyroid panel indicates abnormal thyroid function, your doctor may choose from among several alternative treatments. If blood test results indicate a *hypothyroid* condition, you will usually be put on a ninety-day trial of thyroid medication. This might be a natural form of thyroid hormone derived from pigs' thyroid glands, such as Armour Thyroid, or a synthetic form such as Levoxyl or Synthroid. Some people do better on the natural form of the hormone, while others do better with the synthetic forms. Beginning thyroid hormone replacement, whether natural or synthetic, is usually accompanied by a period of a month or two adjusting the dose upward or downward to determine the precise dose that you need. If you find you're too jittery on the medicine, your doctor will lower the dose to the minimum level you need to relieve symptoms of sluggishness, depression, and weight gain. Or you may try two or three different types of thyroid hormone. Generally, you need to stay on thyroid hormone for a year. At that point, you can try going off and see how you do. About two-thirds of people with hypothyroidism need to keep taking the hormone long term.

Some doctors will try dessicated natural thyroid before trying a synthetic drug. These natural extracts are available in some health food stores as well as over the Internet and appear to work for some people with milder forms of hypothyroidism. If you are hypothyroid, it's also a good idea to take zinc (15 to 30 mg per day), vitamin E (400 IU per day), and vitamin A (10,000 IU per day), all of which are needed in the manufacture of thyroid hormone. Finally, exercise is very important if you are hypothyroid. It stimulates thyroid gland secretion and enhances cellular sensitivity to thyroid hormone.

If test results indicate you are *hyperthyroid*, your doctor will want to perform further tests to rule out problems such as Graves' disease (another type of autoimmune problem). Mild cases of hyperthyroidism may resolve on their own over time. Sometimes beta blockers such as Inderal (propranolol) are given to reduce symptoms of anxiety, rapid heart rate, and sweating. In more severe cases, treatment can involve antithyroid medications, radioactive iodine (which destroys the thyroid and thus stops the excessive production of hormones), or surgery to remove part or all of the thyroid. If your thyroid gland has to be removed, you would need to take synthetic or natural thyroid hormone indefinitely to avoid developing hypothyroidism.

Candidiasis

Candidiasis, or "yeast syndrome," is the result of an overgrowth of a particular yeast, *Candida albicans*, in the intestinal tract, genitourinary tract, or both. Normally, candida lives in a healthy balance with bacteria in the gut, but certain conditions can lead it to multiply, first proliferating throughout the intestinal tract and then moving beyond the gut to invade tissues and organ systems throughout the body. Candidiasis is common, especially among women.

In the early stages of candidiasis, localized infections—particularly skin rashes and "yeast infections" (vaginitis)—are common. Other symptoms include

- Chronic fungal infections such as athlete's foot, ringworm, or jock itch

- Fatigue or feeling drained

- Depression or mood swings

- Gastrointestinal problems such as bloating, cramps, chronic diarrhea, or constipation

- Chronic anxiety and tension

- Food allergies

- Poor memory

- Headaches

- Rectal itching

- Extreme sensitivity to chemicals, perfumes, or tobacco smoke

- Severe premenstrual syndrome symptoms

- Muscle or joint pain

- Cravings for sweets, bread, or alcohol

A characteristic feature of candidiasis is that the symptoms worsen after you eat sugar or drink alcohol. All forms of sugar (except for xylitol) and alcohol feed the yeast and cause it to spread. Symptoms also tend to worsen in damp, moldy climates or environments. If you have five or more of the above symptoms, you may be dealing with candidiasis. If you have two or three of these symptoms, you may want to consult with a health professional to rule out the possibility of this problem.

What Causes Candidiasis?

Factors that increase your risk of developing candidiasis include frequent past use of broad-spectrum antibiotics such as ampicillin, amoxicillin, Ceclor (cefaclon), Bactrim (sulfamethoxazole), or Septra (sulfamethoxazole and trimethoprim); the use of birth control pills for more than a year; frequent or prolonged use of steroid hormones such as cortisone, prednisone, or other corticosteroids; living in a damp, moldy environment; heavy consumption of sweets or alcohol; and having certain diseases such as diabetes, cancer, or AIDS.

Diagnosing Candidiasis

There are three ways to diagnose candidiasis. One is to use a diagnostic questionnaire such as the one developed by William Crook in his classic book *The Yeast Connection.* Alternatively, your doctor can measure antibodies to candida (IgG, IgM, and IgA) with a blood test. Elevated IgG antibody levels indicate that the candida organism has proliferated to excessively high levels in the gut. Elevated IgM antibodies indicate that the candida has ventured beyond the intestine and become systemic. High levels of IgA antibodies are indicative of mucosal involvement, such as in vaginal yeast infections. Candidiasis can also be diagnosed through a stool analysis, which may show high levels of the yeast. However, the stool test may be negative, even when other indications are present.

Recovery from Candidiasis

Recovery from chronic candidiasis can be achieved with a three-pronged program. First, for three months, eliminate from your diet foods that the candida organism feeds on. This includes all kinds of sugar except xylitol or stevia: sucrose, fructose, dextrose, maltose, galactose, dried fruits, and fruit juices. (Xylitol and stevia do not feed candida.) Alcohol, yeast, fermented foods, cheese, vinegar, and refined flour products (including bread) should also be avoided, as they feed candida too. After three months you can reintroduce these foods in small quantities. See the section on the candida diet below.

Second, it is often necessary to take an antifungal medication, such as nystatin or Nizoral (ketoconazole), which would be prescribed by your doctor for a period of several months. Note that there is some controversy among health practitioners about the use of these drugs. Medical doctors are often more inclined to use these drugs in high doses, whereas some naturopaths and alternative health practitioners use nystatin modestly or not at all. One problem is that nystatin kills candida only in the gut and does not directly affect systemic proliferation. Another is that after you use nystatin six months or longer, the yeast may mutate to other forms that are resistant to the drug. An alternative to nystatin used by some health practitioners is *caprylic acid.* Since it is absorbed through the intestine, it can have a greater effect on systemic candidiasis. In addition, many practitioners use goldenseal and grapefruit seed extract. These plants contain *berberine,* which battles candida. Some people also like to add pau d'arco tea to their treatment program because of its antibacterial and fungicidal properties. Taking a multivitamin and multimineral capsule, vitamin C, vitamin E, and zinc can also be helpful, as can increasing your intake of essential fatty acids. Discuss these options with your doctor, and remember that they should be used in conjunction with the candida diet.

Finally, candida tends to crowd out healthy intestinal bacteria, so you need to restore normal bacterial ecology in the intestine by implanting useful bacteria such as *Lactobacillus acidophilus* and *Lactobacillus bifidus.* Probiotic supplements are usually part of the treatment. Talk to your doctor about these. After one to three months on this regimen, you should be retested to see if your candida levels have returned to normal.

The Candida Diet

What follows is a series of dietary principles that help in the recovery from candidiasis. You may need to modify them to fit your particular needs or lifestyle, but in general they provide a good rule of thumb.

Foods that should be *avoided* include

- Milk and other dairy products

- Sweets and all forms of sugar, except xylitol or stevia

- Alcohol

- Fruit and fruit juices (with the possible exception of grapefruit)

- Honey, molasses, artificial sweeteners

- Chocolate

- Foods containing yeast, including all forms of bread made with yeast

- Aged cheese

- Peanut butter

- Smoked or processed nuts

- Vinegar

- Mushrooms

- Carrot juice

- Peanuts

- Starchy foods, such as pastas, chips, or potatoes, in large quantities

- Leftovers (except if they've been frozen)

The following are foods that you should *include* in your diet:

- Chicken or fish

- Raw or cooked vegetables

- Grains in moderation (whole-grain rice is preferable to wheat)

- Eggs

- Beans

- Lemon- or oil-based salad dressings (without vinegar)

- Raw nuts

- Yeast-free breads (available in most health food stores)

- Unaged cheeses (such as Monterey Jack)

- Garlic

- Enteric-coated volatile oil preparations (for example, oregano oil)

Some people call the candida diet the "can't eat it" diet because it seems so restrictive. If you're used to eating large quantities of sweets, you may find yourself calling it this in the week or so after you begin. After a few weeks, however, you'll find that a diet free of sugar can still be enjoyable, and your cravings will begin to dissipate.

If you are like many people who successfully recover from candidiasis, you are likely to find that you have increased energy, less depression, fewer gastrointestinal problems, and more overall vitality. These benefits will also make the dietary trade-offs easier to bear.

Body Toxicity

Excessive body toxicity may not directly increase anxiety, but it adds to the physical stress level of your body and thus makes the impact of anxiety symptoms greater. Body toxicity often aggravates allergies and chemical sensitivities, which in turn can aggravate anxiety. Factors that can cause toxins to build up in your body include consumption of chemicals, additives, and pesticides in food; exposure to environmental pollutants in the air and water; exposure to substances used indoors, such as household cleaners, deodorants, hairsprays, cosmetics, and even carpeting (which may outgas toxic chemicals); use of either prescription or recreational drugs; and buildup of your own metabolic waste products, which are produced in abundance when you're under stress.

Those who have reached a high level of cumulative toxicity may experience any of the following symptoms frequently:

- Fatigue and low energy

- Joint or muscle pain

- Headaches

- "Brain fog" or mental confusion

- Irritability and moodiness

- Insomnia

- Sensitivity to chemicals in the environment

- Depression

- Heavily coated tongue or abnormal body odor

- Excess mucus (coughing and wheezing)

- Allergies

- Sinus or respiratory problems

The liver and colon are believed to be the organs most affected by toxic buildup. Next to the brain and heart, the liver is probably the most important organ in your body. It is the metabolic "factory" in which hundreds of functions necessary for life take place. Some of the more important ones include

- Filtration of the blood

- Secretion of bile, which is necessary to digest fats

- Extraction and storage of vitamins (such as vitamins A, D, and E) from nutrients in your bloodstream

- Synthesis of fatty acids from amino acids and sugar

- Oxidation of fat to produce energy

- Storage of sugar in the form of *glycogen,* which can be used when the body is depleted of blood sugar or glucose

- Detoxification of the by-products of digestion (such as ammonia from protein digestion)

- Detoxification of metabolic waste products as well as all chemicals and foreign substances to which you are exposed

Exposure to toxins, some drugs, poor diet, and overeating can cause accumulations of fatty deposits on the liver and interfere with its functioning. Regular consumption of large quantities of alcohol can damage the liver and eventually lead to cirrhosis. Chronic overeating forces the liver to work harder and may weaken it over time, especially if you are eating foods laden with preservatives and additives. Eating a lot of fried or processed foods containing trans fats can also be hard on the liver.

Detoxifying Your Lifestyle

Some of the most important measures you can take to decrease the level of toxicity in your body are everyday diet and lifestyle changes.

Avoid foods containing preservatives and additives. Try to eat unprocessed, whole foods as much as possible. Be sure to include plenty of fresh fruits and vegetables, preferably five servings a day.

Reduce or eliminate caffeine, nicotine, sugar, and alcohol. Aside from other health problems these substances can contribute to, they leave toxic waste products in your body.

Minimize your use of drugs. Take only necessary medications prescribed by your physician and avoid recreational drug use.

Reduce animal proteins (especially red meat) and increase vegetable sources of protein (tofu, tempeh, and beans). When metabolized, animal proteins can produce toxic by-products, especially if not properly digested.

Drink purified or filtered water. Eight eight-ounce glasses a day will assist your kidneys in their natural process of elimination. Your kidneys are critically involved in ridding your body of various toxic waste products.

Include ample fiber in your diet. Make sure your diet contains high-fiber foods such as whole-grain cereals, all kinds of bran, most fresh fruit, fresh raw vegetables, nuts and seeds, and legumes such as beans, lentils, or peas. You may also want to take a fiber supplement recommended by your health practitioner.

Move away from acid-forming, congestive foods toward more alkaline-forming, detoxifying foods. This means reducing your consumption of red meat, sweets, fried foods, fatty foods, milk, cheese, eggs, refined flour, and salty foods, as well as any foods you know you're allergic to, such as wheat or dairy.

Increase your consumption of fresh vegetables, fruits, whole grains, beans, nuts, and seeds, and increase the proportion of raw to cooked foods that you eat. It's good to have some raw, fresh vegetables or fruit at each meal. Be aware that the degree to which you move from acid- to alkaline-forming foods should be tailored to your individual constitution and needs. If you've been highly toxic in your eating habits, make the change gradually. You can have one day a week in which you lighten your diet.

Get regular, vigorous exercise. This helps to clear your body of toxins through sweating, and it aids the digestive, renal, and lymphatic systems.

Discuss the use of antioxidant supplements with your doctor. These supplements include vitamin C, vitamin E, beta-carotene, selenium, zinc, lipoic acid, coenzyme Q_{10}, and the amino acids cysteine and methionine.

Investigate various herbs that can help detoxify your body. Consult a naturally oriented physician or a qualified nutritionist or herbologist before using any herbs or supplements. Some herbs believed to aid detoxification are milk thistle, dandelion root, burdock, cayenne, ginger, licorice, echinacea, and goldenseal. A high-potency multivitamin and mineral supplement can help combat heavy metal poisoning and help the liver detoxify.

Support colon detoxification. Consider a natural laxative, which may contain bentonite, senna, or cascara sagrada. Psyllium seed husks, available in most health food stores, also cleanse mucus along the small intestine and pull toxins from both the small and large intestines. Discuss these options with your doctor or health practitioner. Remember that even natural laxatives can be habit-forming, so use them sparingly. Some people report benefits from receiving *colonics* from a certified colon therapist. In a colonic, your colon is irrigated and cleansed with water using a special machine.

Support liver detoxification. Eat foods that protect the liver and improve its function. These include vegetables in the *brassica* family, such as cabbage, broccoli, and brussels sprouts, and high-sulfur foods like garlic, onions, eggs, and legumes. Herbs such as dandelion root, burdock, and milk thistle are often used to help detoxify the liver.

Premenstrual Syndrome

Premenstrual syndrome (PMS) involves a constellation of disruptive physical and psychological symptoms that many women experience in the days or week prior to menstruation. Common physical symptoms include water retention, breast soreness, bloating, acne, headaches, increased hunger, and a craving for sweets. Psychological symptoms can include depression, irritability, anxiety and tension, mood swings, distractibility and forgetfulness, fatigue, and even a feeling of "going crazy." Up to half of all women experience a premenstrual increase in depression, anxiety, or irritability in addition to some of the above physical symptoms. Panic reactions can also be a symptom of PMS. The question to ask is whether your panic attacks typically occur—or increase in frequency and intensity—during the days before menstruation. If so, treating your PMS may help to reduce or eliminate panic attacks.

Most medical theories relate PMS to an imbalance in the amount of estrogen and progesterone in a woman's body, particularly during the second half of the menstrual cycle. During this fourteen-day period, women with PMS tend to experience elevated estrogen levels, while progesterone is reduced. Insufficient levels of progesterone relative to the amount of estrogen tend to promote water retention, reduced levels of serotonin in the brain, lower endorphin levels, impaired vitamin B_6 activity, and alterations in other hormone levels.

Other theories about PMS suggest that menstruation allows the body to throw off excess toxins accumulated through improper diet, as well as from exposure to environmental contaminants and pollutants. Thus the symptoms experienced just prior to menstruation reflect the body's reaction to excess toxicity. The implication is that eating a healthy diet and reducing exposure to other toxins should help lessen PMS symptoms.

Both theories are probably valid. PMS symptoms can definitely be helped by eliminating foods that tend to aggravate them. Symptoms can also be alleviated in many cases with the aid of supplemental vitamins, minerals, and herbs, particularly those that raise the body's level of progesterone. Recommendations for treating PMS follow. Before undertaking any of them, consult a physician, nutritionist, or qualified practitioner of Chinese medicine who is well versed in treating this problem.

Dietary Help for PMS

Avoid or minimize the following foods:

- Foods high in sugar as well as large amounts of simple carbohydrates (bread, chips, or pasta). It's especially important to avoid the impulse to binge on sweets and carbohydrate foods, including chocolate, for one week before the expected onset of symptoms.

- Salty foods and table salt. This will help reduce bloating and water retention.

- High-fat foods. Reducing calories consumed as fat will help to reduce estrogen levels.

- Caffeinated drinks, including coffee, tea, and colas. Caffeine is linked to breast tenderness as well as psychological symptoms such as anxiety, depression, and irritability.

- Alcohol.

Eat plenty of fresh fruits and vegetables, whole-grain breads and cereals, and legumes, nuts, free-range poultry, and fish. Consume soy foods, such as tofu or soy milk, in moderation.

Vitamin and Mineral Supplements for PMS

What follows is a list of vitamin and mineral supplements that can help relieve PMS symptoms.

Vitamin B$_6$. The recommended dose is 200 mg daily during the week before menstruation, but you should avoid taking this much vitamin B$_6$ for more than one week out of every month.

Beta-carotene (provitamin A). During the entire month, take 25,000 IU per day.

A high-potency B-complex in conjunction with calcium and magnesium (1000 mg calcium to 500 mg magnesium). Supplementing with calcium and magnesium may help reduce menstrual cramps.

Zinc. During the entire month, take 15 to 20 mg per day.

Essential fatty acids. A good source of essential fatty acids can be found in fish oils, which contain both EPA and DHA omega-3 fatty acids. You can take 500 to 2000 mg per day of combined EPA/DHA in the form of fish oil capsules. An alternative is flaxseed oil, which provides a plant-based form of omega-3 fatty acids. However, the conversion to EPA and DHA is nowhere near as efficient as occurs with fish oils. Borage oil, black currant seed oil, or evening primrose oil are sources of GLA, a special form of omega-6 fatty acid that is essential for humans. You can take 300 to 900 mg of any one of these daily.

Herbs for PMS

The following herbs can help reduce the physical and psychological symptoms of PMS:

- Dong quai *(Angelica sinensis)*. This herb can boost energy and stabilize your mood during PMS. It will also help relieve menstrual cramps. It can be taken in capsule form (follow dosage recommendations given on the label), in a tincture, in a liquid extract, or as a tea.

- Licorice root, taken three times per day in a powdered root form, as a tea, or as a liquid extract. It will help stabilize hormone levels and can also relieve cramps.

- Rosemary, cramp bark, and kava have been known to reduce cramps.

- Kombucha tea. This provides energy and stimulates the immune system. It has been reported to be helpful for some women.

Regular Exercise

A program of regular physical exercise will liven up your metabolism, help your mood, and reduce stress levels. If you can't do vigorous exercise, try walking at least one mile each day. See chapter 5.

Prescription Treatments for PMS

Below is a list of treatments prescribed by doctors to relieve PMS.

Oral contraceptives. These help to maintain proper estrogen-to-progesterone balance. Be aware that the effectiveness of oral contraceptives in preventing pregnancy can be reduced by some antibiotics and perhaps by Saint-John's-wort. Oral contraceptives have a number of short- and long-term side effects that you may wish to avoid.

Diuretics. These reduce water retention and breast swelling.

Natural progesterone. Natural progesterone creams are used effectively by many women to increase levels of progesterone prior to menstruation. These creams are available over the counter, but it's best if you consult with a health professional experienced in the use of these creams before you try one on your own. It's also important to monitor your progesterone levels after using progesterone cream for a month to be sure your progesterone levels aren't elevated and to determine the proper dose and frequency of use of the cream. For further information on PMS and on the use of natural progesterone to treat it, go to womenshealth. com.

For further information on PMS, see the books *Taking Back the Month* and *PMS: Solving the Puzzle* in the reading list at the end of the chapter.

Menopause

Menopause is medically defined as the cessation of menstrual periods for at least six months. On the average, it begins when a woman reaches the age of fifty to fifty-one, though it can start as early as forty or as late as fifty-five. Common symptoms that accompany menopause include

- Hot flashes
- Headaches
- Vaginal dryness
- Bladder or urinary tract infections
- Cold hands and feet
- Forgetfulness and the inability to concentrate
- Reduced libido

- Anxiety and/or depression

The main underlying cause of menopause is reduced production of the two main female hormones, estrogen and progesterone. Interestingly, the undesirable symptoms of menopause appear only in countries where aging of women is devalued, particularly in the United States and Western Europe. In many traditional cultures, where youthfulness and sex appeal are not worshipped and women receive increasing respect with aging, menopausal symptoms are mostly nonexistent. This is a clear example of the effect of culture on symptomatology, even though the underlying physiological basis of menopause is universal. In the United States, 60 to 85 percent of menopausal women experience hot flashes. Among Mayan Indian women, no one does.

Back in the 1950s and 1960s, the American medical establishment decided menopause is a "disease" based on estrogen deficiency. In his 1965 book, *Feminine Forever*, Robert A. Wilson declared that menopause renders women sexless "caricatures of their former selves—the equivalent of a eunuch." This view has remained the dominant outlook among Western doctors to this day. The medical establishment's answer to the problem of menopause is hormone replacement therapy.

Estrogen replacement therapy, as a treatment for menopause, began back in the 1950s with the administration of synthetic estrogen to women. After about twenty years, doctors finally realized that estrogen replacement is associated with up to thirteen times increased risk of developing endometrial cancer. Thus, in the 1970s, it became fashionable to add synthetic progesterone (progestin) to the estrogen, and so the treatment came to be called "hormone" replacement therapy. HRT is an effective treatment. It reduces hot flashes and other symptoms of menopause and has the added advantage of reducing women's risk of developing osteoporosis (loss of bone density that comes with age). After another twenty years, however, it became apparent that HRT significantly increases the risk of breast cancer, especially in women who are at risk for developing it. Worse yet, a more recent study (Women's Health Initiative 2002) found that the risk of heart disease and stroke increased with HRT, enough so that investigators halted the study and told all subjects to stop taking Premarin and Provera (brand names of synthetic estrogen and progesterone) immediately. Additional side effects of synthetic estrogen and progesterone can include nausea, breast tenderness, depression, liver disorder, fluid retention, and blood sugar disturbances. Because of all of these problems, many doctors currently do not recommend HRT except for women with severe risk of osteoporosis.

As with PMS, menopause symptoms can be helped effectively through a combination of diet, exercise, supplements (including *natural* hormone replacement), and herbs.

You may find all of the following to be helpful:

Natural Hormones

You can obtain natural progesterone in the form of creams, drops, or pills from health professionals who are conscious about natural alternatives or from some health food stores. As with PMS, natural progesterone appears to help many women with menopause. Natural forms of estrogen, including estriol and TriEst, are available by prescription and may be associated with a slightly increased risk of breast cancer, though not to the same extent as with synthetic estrogen. When using natural hormone replacement, it's a good idea to have your doctor measure your estrogen and progesterone levels every three to six months to assure that your levels do not get too high. Many women use natural hormones in a "two weeks on, two weeks off" cycle to assure hormone levels remain in normal range.

Herbs

Many women find *black cohosh* to be an effective herb in reducing symptoms of menopause. Used by American Indians for centuries, black cohosh is effective in reducing hot flashes and other menopausal symptoms such as depression, headaches, and vaginal dryness. If you use black cohosh, it's recommended you purchase a product standardized to contain at least 1 mg of *triterpenes*, the active ingredient. *Dong quai* (angelica) also can be very helpful in relieving hot flashes and other symptoms of menopause. Licorice and chasteberry are additionally helpful in stabilizing hormone levels, although it's not clear that any herb can actually raise deficient levels of estrogen and progesterone up to normal.

Supplements

You may find the following supplements to be helpful in alleviating menopause symptoms:

- Vitamin E—400 to 800 IU per day

- Hesperidin (a bioflavonoid)—900 mg per day combined with 2000 mg vitamin C per day

- Gamma-oryzanol (ferulic acid)—300 mg per day

Diet

Along with the healthy diet recommended in chapter 15, it's good to eat foods that are high in phytoestrogens, which bind to estrogen receptors just like estrogen does in your body. Such foods include soy products, flaxseed oil, apples, whole grains, celery, parsley, and alfalfa. In general, vegetables and plant-based foods tend to be high in phytoestrogens relative to animal-based foods, which may explain why cultures whose diets are predominantly plant based (including soy) tend to have low incidence of menopausal symptoms.

Exercise

Regular physical exercise, so helpful in reducing symptoms of anxiety and depression, is also helpful in reducing the severity and frequency of hot flashes.

See the books by Christiane Northrup and John Lee in the references at the end of the chapter for further information on menopause.

Seasonal Affective Disorder

When the seasons change from spring and summer to fall and winter, do you develop the following symptoms? Check off the symptoms that are familiar.

- ☐ Lower energy than usual

- ☐ Awakening feeling tired, although you sleep more

- ☐ Mood changes such as feeling more anxious, irritable, sad, or depressed

- ☐ Diminished productivity or creativity

- ☐ Feeling that you have little control over your appetite or weight

- ☐ More memory and concentration problems

- ☐ Lowered interest in socializing

- ☐ Lessened ability to cope with stress

- ☐ Less enthusiasm about the future or reduced enjoyment in your life

If you checked off two or more of these, you may be one of the many people affected by *seasonal affective disorder* (SAD) or a milder form of this disorder known as *subsyndromal SAD*. Seasonal affective disorder is a cyclical depression that occurs during the winter months, typically between November and March. It's brought on by insufficient exposure to light. As the days get shorter and the angle of the sun changes during the fall, the symptoms of SAD begin to appear. An estimated 20 percent of the American adult population, or 36 million people, are affected by SAD and subsyndromal SAD. The farther from the equator you happen to live, the more susceptible you are.

Anxiety and SAD

Many individuals dealing with anxiety disorders experience an aggravation of their condition during the late fall and winter. Panic attacks may occur more often, and generalized anxiety may increase along with depression. It's not surprising that this is so, because the same systems of the brain that contribute to the neurobiological basis of depression, the *noradrenergic system* and the *serotonin system*, are also implicated in anxiety disorders, particularly panic disorder, generalized anxiety disorder, and obsessive-compulsive disorder. Biochemical imbalances in these systems tipped one way may cause depression; tipped the other way, they may aggravate anxiety disorders. And for many individuals, unfortunately, problems with anxiety and depression coexist, both becoming aggravated during the winter months.

Whether they manifest as depression or anxiety, the symptoms of SAD are caused by decreased availability of light. SAD can be aggravated not only by reduced light outside during the winter months but by spending too much time in indoor environments that have low levels of light, whether at home or work. SAD symptoms have been reported even in the summer among people who work in environments without windows. They can also occur in sensitive individuals at any time of year after a succession of cloudy days.

It used to be thought that SAD was caused by insufficient suppression of a hormone in the brain called *melatonin.* Melatonin is secreted by the pineal gland in the brain at night after several hours of darkness. It is one of the mechanisms by which your brain lets you know it is time to go to sleep. With light in the morning, melatonin secretion is suppressed, and you know that it's time to wake up. Although popular for many years, the hypothesis that SAD is caused by insufficient melatonin suppression has not been borne out by systematic research. Results of studies have been mixed, and researchers have looked in other directions to find clues to the cause of SAD. The hypothesis that is currently receiving the most attention is that light insufficiency can cause a reduction in levels of serotonin in the brain. Norman Rosenthal, one of the leading researchers in this field, writes in *Winter Blues* that when susceptible individuals are exposed to too little environmental light—such as during winter—they produce too little serotonin. Rosenthal and others believe that these low levels of serotonin are responsible for the symptoms of SAD.

Serotonin deficiencies are frequently associated with symptoms of depression, anxiety, or both; that is why drugs that block the reuptake of serotonin in the brain—drugs such as Prozac (fluoxetine), Zoloft (sertraline), or Paxil (paroxetine)—often alleviate depression and many of the anxiety disorders. But why should reduced light affect serotonin? And why only in certain individuals? The answer to the first question is still being researched. In answer to the second question, there is some evidence that people who are susceptible to SAD may have difficulty receiving or processing light at a neurological level.

During the winter, people with SAD tend to crave sweets and carbohydrates. Eating large amounts of carbohydrates usually increases the amount of *tryptophan* (an essential amino acid derived naturally from protein foods) that gets into the brain. Once in the brain, tryptophan becomes serotonin, the neurotransmitter that is so critical to psychological well-being. Eating sweets and carbohydrates gives tryptophan a competitive edge over the body's other amino acids in getting into the brain. So, if you tend to be drawn to sweets and starches in the wintertime, it may be your body's attempt to raise your levels of serotonin.

Light Therapy for SAD

The treatment that most effectively reduces the symptoms of SAD is *light therapy.* In principle, it would be possible to reduce SAD in the winter by spending prolonged periods of time outdoors every day. Unless you're a ski instructor or a snowplow operator, however, this is pretty impractical. Light therapy involves the use of one or more specific devices indoors to increase your exposure to bright light. Sometimes light-sensitive individuals can experience an improvement simply by increasing normal room light or installing brighter lightbulbs. However, most SAD sufferers seem to require exposure to higher light levels—at least four times brighter than normal household and office light.

Light boxes are commonly used to alleviate symptoms of SAD. A light box is a set of fluorescent bulbs in a box, with a diffusing plastic screen. Most of these devices deliver between 2,500 and 10,000 lux of light energy—considerably above the usual range of indoor lighting (approximately 200 to 1,000 lux). A typical light therapy session involves sitting within two or three feet of a light box for a period of half an hour to two hours in the morning. It's neither necessary nor advisable to look directly at the light; rather, you can use the time to read, write, eat, sew, or do whatever you need to do. The amount of daily light exposure needed to achieve a reduction in symptoms varies from one person to another. Experiment with varying the duration of exposure according to your own needs.

Other devices used in light therapy are *dawn simulators* and *light visors*. The dawn simulator creates an artificial dawn in your bedroom by having a light come on very dimly at, say, six in the morning and gradually brightening until seven o'clock. The light visor is a lightweight source of light that you can wear on your head. It allows you to have more mobility than with the light box.

Light therapy is very effective when administered properly, as Norman Rosenthal documents. In experimental trials, it has been shown to help 75 to 80 percent of SAD sufferers within a week if used regularly. Before undertaking light therapy on your own, you should consult with a physician or another health professional who is knowledgeable about this therapy and its application. Although light therapy devices are available without a prescription, you can save yourself time—as well as such possible side effects as headache, eyestrain, irritability, or insomnia—by getting assistance in using them properly.

Coping with SAD

The National Organization for Seasonal Affective Disorder (NOSAD) offers the following suggestions:

- Discuss your symptoms with your physician. You may be referred to a psychiatrist who may diagnose seasonal affective disorder or subsyndromal SAD and prescribe special light treatments to help relieve your symptoms. Certain SSRI antidepressants also can be helpful in treating some people with seasonal depression.

- If you have a medical diagnosis of SAD or subsyndromal SAD and your doctor prescribes light treatment, do not skip or shorten treatment because you're feeling better; you may relapse. Work with your doctor in adjusting the length of time, time of day, distance, and intensity of light for your own individualized treatment.

- Get as much light as possible and avoid dark environments during daylight hours in winter.

- Reduce mild winter depressive symptoms by exercising daily, preferably outdoors, to take advantage of natural light.

- If you are unable to exercise outdoors in the winter due to extreme cold, exercise inside. If possible, try sitting in sunlight from a south-facing window for short but frequent periods during the day.

- Rearrange work spaces at home, and work near a window, or set up bright lights in your work area.

- Stay on a regular sleep–wake schedule. People with SAD report being more alert and less fatigued when they get up and go to sleep at preset hours than when they vary their schedules.

- Be aware of cold outside temperatures and dress to conserve energy and warmth. Many people affected by seasonal changes report sensitivity to extreme temperatures.

- Arrange family outings and social occasions for daytime and early evening in winter. Avoid staying up late, which disrupts your sleep schedule and biological clock.

- Conserve energy by managing time wisely and avoiding or minimizing unnecessary stress.

- Try putting lights on a timer in your bedroom or use a dawn simulator set to switch on a half hour or more before you get up. Some people with SAD report that this light technique has an antidepressant effect and helps them awaken more easily.

- When possible, postpone making major life changes until spring or summer.

- Share experiences regarding SAD as a way to get information, understanding, validation, and support.

- If you are able, arrange a vacation during the winter to a warm, sunny climate.

During the winter months you may find it helpful to boost your serotonin levels either naturally or with prescription medication. For the natural approach, try taking 5-hydroxy-tryptophan (5-HT). You can start with 50 mg per day and go as high as 300 mg per day (see chapter 15 for more information on tryptophan). If you feel you're not getting help from 5-HT, consult with your doctor about trying a selective serotonin reuptake inhibitor (SSRI) medication such as Zoloft, Celexa, Luvox, or Paxil (see chapter 17 for more information on SSRIs).

Insomnia

Insomnia affects about 30 percent of adults and is the most common condition that can aggravate anxiety disorders. Anxiety problems of all kinds are generally worse after a poor night's sleep.

Most of us need seven to eight hours of sleep per night, at least six of which are uninterrupted. It is during the early hours of the night that we get the deep sleep needed to replenish our body systems for another day, while during the latter part of the night we get proportionately more REM (rapid eye movement) or dream sleep, which is necessary for the brain to integrate and work through "unfinished business" from the previous day. Sleep actually goes through a series of stages: four stages of progressively deeper sleep, followed by one stage of REM sleep. This five-stage cycle repeats itself three or four times during the night.

If you can't sleep, the problem may be either with *getting* to sleep, in which case it takes you more than twenty minutes to fall asleep, or in *staying* asleep, where you may fall asleep easily but awaken hours before dawn and not be able to get back to sleep. Typically anxiety is more associated with the first type of problem, while depression is associated with "early morning awakening." However, it's not uncommon to have both types of problems if you're anxious or depressed.

Ten Common Problems

Why is it that you are unable to sleep? Insomnia is complex and can have a very large variety of causes. In most cases there are, in fact, several causes operating at once. What follows are ten of the more common origins of sleeplessness.

1. *Too much caffeine during the day.* Excessive consumption of coffee, tea, cola beverages, and other foods or medicines containing caffeine is a very common culprit behind insomnia. Everyone, of course, is different. You may be so highly sensitive to caffeine that even one cup of coffee in the morning can keep you awake the following night. At the opposite extreme, you may be able to have coffee at bedtime. As a general rule, it's best to avoid caffeine after noon if you're having problems with sleep, and you may even want to consider cutting down your consumption in the morning. (See the *Caffeine Chart* in chapter 15 to determine how much caffeine you consume in a day.)

2. *Insufficient exercise.* When clients ask me what they can do to improve their sleep, the first thing I suggest is that they do an aerobic workout during the day. Vigorous exercise helps to release muscle tension and burn off excess stress hormones (such as adrenaline and thyroxine), both of which can interfere with sleep. It can also release pent-up frustration that can keep your mind racing at night. If you're not working out during the day, you may be surprised to find how much such a workout can help your sleep and help you with your anxiety, as well (see chapter 5). The one precaution is to avoid vigorous exercise within three hours of bedtime, as it can be overstimulating and interfere with getting to sleep.

3. *Excess stimulation in the evening.* Anything that overstimulates you after eight in the evening can keep you from getting to sleep (or staying asleep) later that night. This could include a dramatic or violent TV show, surfing the Web, doing difficult tasks (including difficult reading), a stimulating phone conversation, or a domestic quarrel. You can also keep yourself awake by exposing yourself to bright light (such as a computer screen) late at night. It's best to turn yourself down during the last two or three hours of the day with soothing TV programs, reading, or conversation. Better yet, try a warm bath or shower before bedtime to unwind.

4. *Excess worry about sleep.* Sleep is an automatic process that requires letting go. The more you try to pursue it, the more it tends to get away from you. In general, worrying about sleep will prevent you from falling asleep, whether at bedtime or at four in the morning. Telling yourself to stop worrying probably won't be very helpful, so the best solution is some kind of diversion tactic. The various relaxation

techniques described in chapter 4 can all be helpful toward that end. Progressive muscle relaxation is helpful if your muscles feel tight, while mantra meditation or a guided visualization can be useful for a racing, anxious mind. For some people, just listening to soothing music or the drone of the TV can put them to sleep, while for others a boring novel does the trick. If you find yourself worrying, experiment with different diversionary tactics to redirect your mind away from it.

A famous, time-honored sleep principle is that if you're lying awake in bed for very long (more than thirty minutes to an hour), don't stay there. Get up and do a listening relaxation, meditation, or light reading in an easy chair or on the couch until you feel genuinely drowsy. Then get back in bed. That way your bed will become associated only with sleep—instead of with wakefulness.

5. *Serotonin and/or melatonin deficiency.* Over time, stress can deplete your brain's stores of the neurotransmitter serotonin and the hormone melatonin. Both are needed for sleep. Serotonin is needed to activate the parts of the brain that are responsible for sleep onset, and it's also needed to make melatonin. Melatonin is made from serotonin by your pineal gland, usually late in the day with the onset of darkness. It's the chemical your brain uses to signal to itself that it's time to sleep. In short, without melatonin, it's hard to get to sleep, and without serotonin, it's hard to make melatonin.

It's easy to increase your supplies of serotonin or melatonin with natural supplements available at your health food store or drugstore. Tryptophan, in the form of 5-hydroxytryptophan (50 to 150 mg) or L-tryptophan (500 to 1500 mg), is an amino acid that naturally converts to serotonin in your brain. Try 5-HT first at the suggested dose at bedtime, and if you aren't satisfied with the results, try L-tryptophan, which is available at some health food stores and over the Internet. The effect of tryptophan can be enhanced by taking it with a carbohydrate snack (such as orange juice or crackers) along with 100 mg vitamin B_6 and 100 mg vitamin B_3. The hormone melatonin is available in health food stores in tablets ranging from 0.5 to 3 mg. Experiment with the dose to determine what is best for you, since people vary a lot in what constitutes an optimal dose. If doses of 2 to 3 mg give you side effects, then lower the dose down to 0.5 or 1 mg. Keep in mind that it's okay to take both tryptophan and melatonin at bedtime to enhance your sleep.

If you find that natural supplements are ineffective in helping you to sleep, you may want to consult your doctor about prescription medications that boost serotonin. Any of the selective serotonin reuptake inhibitors (SSRIs such as Celexa or Zoloft)—medications commonly used to treat anxiety disorders—can also be helpful for insomnia. (See chapter 17 for a more detailed description of SSRIs.) Particularly if you're dealing with protracted depression along with insomnia, you may benefit from trying an SSRI. Generally when you take SSRIs, you need to take them on a daily basis for a period of six months to one year (or longer). If you are looking for a medication that can help you sleep without having the addictive problems associated with prescription sedatives (such as Restoril or Ambien), you may want to try trazodone, 25 to 100 mg, at bedtime.

6. *Excess levels of stress hormones.* Your adrenal glands manufacture two types of stress hormones. Adrenaline and noradrenaline give you a sudden burst of energy necessary to respond to an emergency with a quick reaction of fight or flight. As explained in chapter 2, these hormones are implicated in panic attacks. The other type of stress hormones includes the steroid hormones, of which cortisol is perhaps the most important. You need cortisol to help you wake up and address the various challenges life brings you throughout the day. The problem is that under high stress, your cortisol can stay too high day and night, with the consequence that you're too activated round the clock to sleep easily. If your cortisol is too high at bedtime, you may have difficulty falling asleep; if it's too high early in the morning, you may wake up prematurely.

    With the assistance of your doctor, you can have your cortisol levels measured at various intervals throughout the day to assess whether elevated cortisol is interfering with your sleep. If so, you can try a cortisol-regulating supplement called "phosphorylated serine" (not the same as phosphatidyl serine), which can be obtained under the brand name Seriphos. In consultation with your doctor, take Seriphos at dinnertime for about one month to gradually turn down your cortisol levels. Beyond this, it's important to utilize all the stress reduction measures described earlier in this chapter in the section on adrenal exhaustion.

    A common reason for high levels of cortisol during the night is nocturnal hypoglycemia. When there is a drop in blood glucose levels during the night, you release hormones that regulate glucose levels, such as adrenaline, glucagon, cortisol, and growth hormone. If too much of these hormones is released, they may wake you up. By following the recommendations listed in chapter 15 for hypoglycemia, you may help your sleep. If you wake up in the early morning hours feeling hungry, or feeling that your blood sugar level is down, try having a protein-carbohydrate snack, such as bread and nut butter or cheese and crackers.

7. *Irregular bedtimes.* A very common problem for people who suffer insomnia is going to bed and getting up at irregular times. The body sleeps better when it has a routine, going to bed and getting up at approximately the same time every day. If you sleep in too late, you may find it hard to get to sleep the following night. That's why many people have difficulty sleeping Sunday night before Monday, having stayed up late on the two weekend nights. The extreme case of sleep disruption is working different shifts back to back. Unless you must, it's best to avoid jobs that require you to continually change your shift. Over time, you will lose a lot of sleep and compromise your health.

    The body has a sleep-wakefulness cycle, called the *circadian* cycle, which it goes through every day—ideally about sixteen to seventeen hours out of bed and seven to eight in bed. This cycle will function much more smoothly, ensuring better sleep, if you retire and get up at the same times every day.

8. *Inadequate sleep environment.* There may be problems with your sleep environment that subtly undermine your sleep without your realizing it. A common problem

is a mattress that is either too soft or too firm. If at all possible, invest in a quality mattress that feels truly comfortable to you. The same applies for pillows (you want something more comfortable than what you'd find in the average motel). Room temperature is also an important variable; many people have problems sleeping if the temperature of their room is over 80 degrees. If you don't have air conditioning, use a fan to cool your room. The optimal temperature for sleep is about 70 degrees. Noise and light can also be problems. If you can't escape noise, get a fan or "white noise" machine to help mask it. In the case of excess light, dark curtains or eye shades will often help.

9.   *Noisy partners.* One critical part of your sleep environment is your bed partner, if you have one. Loud snoring is a very common disrupter of sleep that affects millions of people who simply lie there and put up with it. There are many solutions to snoring, including sprays and nose guards that you can get at your local drugstore. On the Internet, you'll find hundreds of devices that can help snoring. Or you may want to go to an otolaryngologist who specializes in the treatment of snoring. For more severe cases, laser surgery or surgical techniques using high-frequency radio waves have been used effectively. Snoring is not something you have to live with. For more information, see the books *No More Snoring* and *Snoring from A to ZZzz* listed at the end of the chapter.

10. *Sleeping pills.* Sleeping pills include benzodiazepine tranquilizers and sedatives, such as Xanax, Ativan, Klonopin, Valium, Librium, Restoril and Dalmane, as well as nonbenzodiazepine sedatives, such as Ambien, Lunesta, and Sonata. Millions of people use sleeping pills, and they can be a lifesaver on certain occasions, such as night flights, or when negotiating highly stressful times. The problem comes when they are used on a long-term regular basis. They all have three major problems. One is that they eventually lose their effectiveness when used nightly. If you take them every night, you'll find that sooner or later they don't work very well. Also, even though they put you to sleep, they interfere with the quality of your sleep by reducing the amount of time you spend in deeper stages of sleep (or increasing your time in shallower sleep stages). Finally, they are all highly addictive unless used on only an occasional basis. Whether Xanax, Klonopin, Ambien, or Lunesta, if you take a prescription sedative for more than a few weeks, you're likely to become hooked on it. You may find you are unable to sleep without it. Eventually you may need to go through a difficult process of weaning yourself off the medication.

So these are some of the more common problems that can interfere with sleep. Others, beyond the scope of this section, include specific sleep disorders such as sleep apnea and restless leg syndrome, or specific health conditions, such as asthma and allergies, acid reflux, or chronic pain. For an in-depth discussion of sleep, sleep problems, and measures for improving sleep, see the books *No More Sleepless Nights* by Peter Hauri, or *The Promise of Sleep* by William Dement.

General Guidelines for a Good Night's Sleep

Sleep is as integral to physical and mental well-being as proper nutrition and regular exercise. The guidelines below are designed to help you maintain a healthy sleep routine.

Do:

* Exercise during the day. Twenty minutes or more of aerobic exercise midday or in the late afternoon before dinner is optimal. At minimum, forty-five minutes to an hour of brisk walking daily will suffice. Many people find a short walk (twenty to thirty minutes) before bedtime to be helpful.

* Go to bed and get up at regular times. Even if you're tired in the morning, make an effort to stick to your scheduled wake-up time, and don't vary your nightly bedtime. The next day, you can resume whatever you're working on or doing. Your body prefers a regular cycle of sleep and wakefulness.

* Turn yourself down during the last hour or two of the day. Avoid vigorous physical or mental activity, emotional upsets, and so on.

* Try a hot shower or bath before bedtime.

* Develop a sleep ritual before bedtime. This is some activity you do nightly before turning in.

* Reduce noise. Use earplugs or a noise-masking machine, like a fan, if necessary.

* Block out excess light.

* Keep your room temperature between 65 and 70 degrees. Too warm or cold a room tends to interfere with sleep. Use fans for a hot room if air conditioning is unavailable. Your room should be ventilated, not stuffy.

* Purchase a quality mattress. Try varying the firmness of your mattress. Invest in a new one or insert a board underneath one that sags or is too soft. For a mattress that is too hard, place an egg-crate foam pad between the mattress surface and the mattress cover.

* Pillows should not be too high or too puffy. Feather pillows, which compress, are best.

* Have separate beds if your partner snores, kicks, or tosses and turns. Discuss this with him or her and decide on a mutually acceptable distance.

* Have physically and emotionally satisfying sex. This often aids sleep.

* See a psychotherapist if necessary. Anxiety and depressive disorders commonly produce insomnia. Talking to a competent psychotherapist can help. Getting more emotional support and expressing your feelings to someone you trust often helps sleep.

Don't:

- Try to force yourself to sleep. If you're unable to fall asleep after twenty to thirty minutes in bed, leave your bed, engage in some relaxing activity (such as watching TV, sitting in a chair and listening to a relaxation recording, meditating, or having a cup of herbal tea), and return to bed only when you're sleepy. The same applies for waking up in the middle of the night and having difficulty going back to sleep.

- Have a heavy meal before bedtime or go to bed hungry. A small, healthy snack just before bedtime can be helpful.

- Indulge in heavy alcohol consumption before bedtime. For some people, a small glass of wine before bed may help, but your alcohol consumption should not exceed this.

- Consume too much caffeine. Try to limit caffeine intake to the mornings. If you're sensitive to caffeine, avoid it altogether and try decaf coffee or herb teas.

- Smoke cigarettes. Nicotine is a mild stimulant, and apart from its more publicized health risks, it can interfere with sleep. If you are a smoker, talk to your doctor about the best ways to curtail this habit.

- Engage in nonsleep activities in bed. Unless they are part of your sleep ritual, avoid activities such as working or reading in bed. This will help to strengthen the association between bed and sleep.

- Nap during the day. Short catnaps (fifteen to twenty minutes) are okay, but long naps of an hour or more may interfere with sleep the following night.

- Let yourself be afraid of insomnia. Work on *accepting* those nights when you don't sleep so well. You can still function the next day, even if you had only a couple of hours of sleep. The less you fight, resist, or fear sleeplessness, the more it will tend to go away.

In General:

- With your doctor's or health practitioner's approval, try natural supplements that can foster sleep. Herbs such as kava and valerian, in higher doses, can induce sleep. (See chapter 15 for more detailed information on these herbs.) Do not exceed recommended doses and be sure to discuss all herbs with your doctor before taking them.

- Some people find 0.5 to 3 mg of the hormone melatonin at bedtime to be helpful. Experiment with the dose to determine the amount that works best for you.

- The amino acid tryptophan is very helpful for many people in getting to sleep. You can obtain it at most health food stores either in the form of 5-hydroxytryptophan or in L-tryptophan. If you try 5-HT, take 50 to 150 mg at bedtime; for L-tryptophan, try 500 to 1500 mg before going to bed. The effects of either form of tryptophan can be enhanced by taking it with a carbohydrate snack and 100 mg of vitamins B_6 and B_3. You can take tryptophan every night if you need to. Finally, the amino acid GABA,

500 to 1000 mg before bedtime, may induce sleep for some people. Vary the dose, as some people find higher doses to cause agitation.

- For relaxing tense muscles or a racing mind, use deep relaxation techniques. Specifically, progressive muscle relaxation or recorded guided visualization exercises can be helpful (see chapter 4). Use a device that can play the recording in a continuous loop.

- If pain is causing sleeplessness, try an analgesic. In the case of pain, this is more appropriate than a sleeping pill.

- Avoid sleeping pills such as Restoril or Ambien except for occasional emergencies. Prescription sedatives such as these can interfere with your sleep cycle and ultimately aggravate insomnia. If you must take a prescription medication for sleep, try trazodone at 25 to 100 mg.

- If you're dependent on a sleeping pill and feel that it's interfering with your sleep, consult a competent physician or psychiatrist experienced with helping people discontinue these medications.

Summary of Things to Do

1. If you suspect you are suffering from adrenal exhaustion, you need to eliminate caffeine and sugar from your diet as much as possible, as well as deal with any food allergies (see chapter 15). Strive to have a high-protein, low-carbohydrate diet and eliminate all processed or junk foods. It's important to simplify your life as much as possible in order to reduce stress, and make sure you get adequate sleep and exercise every day. Take the supplements recommended in the section on adrenal exhaustion and talk to your health professional about taking an adrenal cortical glandular supplement.

2. If you believe you have symptoms of either hypothyroidism or hyperthyroidism, have your doctor do a complete thyroid blood panel. Use the medications your doctor recommends and be sure to get adequate exercise.

3. Symptoms such as fatigue, fungal or yeast infections, abdominal bloating and cramps, and feeling ill after you consume sugar or are in a damp environment all suggest a problem with candidiasis. You may want to have your doctor confirm the diagnosis by doing a blood test for candida antibodies. If you have candida, follow the dietary recommendations listed in the section on candidiasis. You may also need to take nystatin for a while, as well as natural anticandida supplements, such as caprylic acid, grapefruit seed extract, and oregano oil capsules.

4. Symptoms such as fatigue, headaches, "brain fog" or confusion, muscle aches and pains, chemical sensitivity, irritability, rashes, and allergies all suggest your body may be overly toxic. Follow all of the dietary and lifestyle recommendations listed

in the section "Detoxifying Your Lifestyle." It's particularly important to eliminate caffeine, nicotine, alcohol and recreational drugs, refined sugar, and junk foods from your diet as much as possible. With your doctor's assistance, use only those prescription medications that you really need. Regular exercise accompanied by sweating is also very important. In consultation with your doctor or health care professional, you may want to try a week on raw foods or a four-day juice fast, take antioxidant supplements, work with detoxifying herbs such as milk thistle, dandelion, and burdock, and support colon detoxification by using psyllium seed products or receiving a series of colonics.

5.   To relieve symptoms of PMS, reduce or eliminate sweets and refined carbohydrates from your diet as much as possible. You'll find reducing caffeine, alcohol, and salt also to be helpful. Increase vegetables, fresh fruits, and soy foods in your diet. Also increase your daily exercise. Take the supplements recommended in the section on PMS, including B-complex, B_6, vitamin A, calcium-magnesium, fish oil capsules, and GLA. Many women find the herb dong quai to be helpful. In consultation with your doctor or health care professional, use natural progesterone creams. For further information, visit womenshealth.com or call Madison Pharmacy Associates at 1-800-558-7046.

6.   If you're dealing with menopause, discuss natural progesterone and possibly natural estrogen replacement with a doctor or health professional who is knowledgeable about these alternatives to synthetic hormone replacement. Black cohosh is an herb that can be very helpful for menopause; you can use it alone or in combination with other herbs, such as dong quai and licorice. Eat a diet that is high in phytoestrogens and get regular exercise.

7.   For seasonal affective disorder (SAD), follow all of the suggestions listed in this chapter. Be sure to get exposure to the outdoors or to an indoor light box for at least one hour each day during the winter months. If the recommendations listed here are not enough, consider boosting your serotonin levels in the winter. This can be done either naturally, by taking tryptophan or Saint-John's-wort, or by consulting with your doctor about taking an SSRI medication such as Zoloft, Lexapro, Celexa, or Luvox (see chapter 17 for further information on SSRIs).

8.   The causes and cures for insomnia are complex. Review the section on insomnia carefully to determine the possible cause of your problem with sleep. Then try out all of the different suggestions listed in the general guidelines section. If you feel you aren't getting sufficient help, take a look at the books by Peter Hauri and William Dement in the references and/or consult a sleep specialist.

Further Reading

Arem, Ridha. *The Thyroid Solution*. New York: Ballantine Books, 2007.

Bourne, Edmund J., Arlen Brownstein, and Lorna Garano. *Natural Relief for Anxiety*. Oakland, CA: New Harbinger Publications, 2004.

Crook, William. *The Yeast Connection*. Third edition. Jackson, TN: Professional Books, 1989.

Dement, William C. *The Promise of Sleep*. New York: Delacorte Press, 2000.

Hahn, Linaya, and Allan Warshowsky. *PMS: Solving the Puzzle: Sixteen Causes of PMS and What to Do About It*. Chicago: Chicago Spectrum Press, 1995.

Hauri, Peter, and Shirley Linde. *No More Sleepless Nights*. Revised edition. New York: John Wiley and Sons, 1996.

Hoffstein, Victor, and Shirley Linde. *No More Snoring*. New York: John Wiley and Sons, 1998.

Lee, John R. *What Your Doctor May Not Tell You about Menopause*. Revised edition. New York: Warner, 2004.

Lipman, Derek S. *Snoring from A to ZZzz*. Portland, OR: Spencer Press, 2002.

Murray, Michael, and Joseph Pizzorno. *Encyclopedia of Natural Medicine*. Revised second edition. Roseville, CA: Prima Publishing, 1998. (An outstanding reference for most of the conditions described in this chapter and many others.)

Northrup, Christiane. *The Wisdom of Menopause*. New York: Bantam Books, 2003.

Rosenthal, Norman. *Winter Blues: Everything You Need to Know to Beat Seasonal Affective Disorder*. Revised edition. New York: Guilford Press, 2006.

Taylor, Diana, and Stacey Colino. *Taking Back the Month: A Personalized Solution for Managing PMS and Enhancing Your Health*. New York: Perigee, 2002.

Wilson, James L. *Adrenal Fatigue*. Petaluma, CA: Smart Publications, 2001.

Women's Health Initiative. "Risks and Benefits of Estrogen Plus Progestin in Healthy Postmenopausal Women." *Journal of the American Medical Association* 288 (2002): 321–333.

17

Medication for Anxiety

The use of medication is a critical issue among those who struggle with anxiety on a daily basis, as well as for professionals treating anxiety disorders. For many people, medication is a positive turning point along the path to recovery. For others, medication can confuse and complicate the recovery process, when freedom from anxiety is purchased at the cost of long-term addiction to tranquilizers. For still other people—those who are either phobic of or philosophically opposed to all types of drugs—medication may seem not to be an option, even when it's needed. One thing is clear: the pros and cons of relying on medication are unique and variable in each individual case.

As you will have gathered, this workbook offers a range of nonmedical strategies to help you overcome anxiety, panic, and phobias. My personal view is that natural methods should always be thoroughly explored before you develop a reliance on prescription drugs. Medications can induce unnatural changes in your body's physiology, with attendant short- and long-term side effects.

Quite a few people find that they can avoid drugs—or eliminate those they have been taking—by implementing a comprehensive personal health program that includes

- Positive changes in nutrition and the use of appropriate supplements

- A program of daily, vigorous exercise

- A daily practice of deep relaxation or meditation

- Changes in self-talk and basic beliefs encouraging a less driven, more relaxed approach to life

- Human support from family and/or friends

- Simplifying your life and environment to reduce stress

Such approaches may be all you need if your anxiety symptoms are relatively mild. By "mild," I mean that your problem does not significantly interfere with your ability to work or interfere with important personal relationships. Also, the problem does not cause you serious and/or constant distress.

If, on the other hand, you have a more severe problem with anxiety, *appropriate* use of medication may be an important part of your treatment. This is particularly true if you're dealing with panic disorder, agoraphobia, or obsessive-compulsive disorder. It's also true for social phobia and generalized anxiety disorder when these problems interfere with the quality of your life in a major way. Approximately 50 to 60 percent of my clients take medication. For them, my impression is that a *combination* of natural methods and medication provides the most helpful, effective, and compassionate approach to recovery.

Be aware that it's often unnecessary to take medications indefinitely. However, the use of the right medication for the right period of time can help you to turn a corner toward improving your condition. In this chapter, I first want to present some information about the various types of medication used to treat anxiety problems. Beyond this, you'll find a number of guidelines to help you decide whether medication is something you should consider.

When to Consider Medication

In my experience, there are certain types of individuals, in certain types of situations, for whom medications are appropriate. What follows is a list of situations in which I would refer a client to a physician or psychiatrist for medication, along with the types of medication that might appropriately be used.

1. You have panic attacks that are so frequent (for example, one or more per day) and severe that they impede your ability to work and earn a living, your primary personal relationships, and/or your sense of basic security and control over your life. It is particularly important to consider medication if you have *severe* symptoms of panic or anxiety that have not improved over a period of two or three weeks. "Severe" means that you have difficulty functioning and/or are suffering considerable distress. Enduring severe levels of anxiety for long periods of time can, unfortunately, predispose your nervous system to *stay* anxious much longer than it would if the anxiety were reduced by medication early on.

    Two types of medication are most frequently used to treat panic attacks. The first type is antidepressants. Even though they're labeled "antidepressants," such medications also have a potent effect in reducing anxiety. The most commonly used antidepressants are *SSRIs* (selective serotonin reuptake inhibitors), such as Paxil (paroxetine), Zoloft (sertraline), Luvox (fluvoxamine), Celexa (citalopram), and Lexapro (escitalopram). Another class of antidepressant medications sometimes used is the *tricyclics*, such as Tofranil (imipramine) or Pamelor (nortriptyline); these days, however, they are a second choice after SSRIs have been tried.

    The other type of medication used to treat panic (and other anxiety disorders) is the *benzodiazepine tranquilizers*. Among these, Xanax (alprazolam), Klonopin (clonazepam), or Ativan (lorazepam) are typically used. (Descriptions of the major types of drugs used to treat anxiety disorders follow this section.) Usually, tranquilizers are prescribed for a period of six months to two years at a high enough dose to significantly reduce the frequency and severity of panic, as well as anxiety about panic.

2. You are agoraphobic and have a difficult time undertaking real-life exposure to phobic situations (See chapter 7). That is, you've tried for some time without medication and not gotten very far. *Low* doses of a benzodiazepine tranquilizer, such

as Klonopin (in the range of 0.25 to 0.5 mg per day), may enable you to negotiate graded exposure to your phobias. The benefits of exposure are likely to be retained even after the medication is discontinued, if the dose has been sufficiently low. This is less likely, however, for higher doses of tranquilizers (that is, more than 2 mg per day). You need to feel at least mild anxiety while undertaking exposure for the technique to be effective. After exposure hierarchies have been completed with tranquilizers, it's important to rework them without medication, to ensure a full and permanent recovery from your phobias.

The SSRI antidepressants (see below) can also be highly effective in helping people undertake exposure. In fact, many psychiatrists consider SSRI medications to be an essential part of the treatment of agoraphobia.

3. You're dealing with acute anxiety in response to a crisis situation. You may benefit from relying on a benzodiazepine tranquilizer on a *short-term* basis to get you through a particularly stressful time (such as interviewing for a new job, dealing with a significant health crisis, the death of a close relative, or other such major life events). Alternatively, a sedative (Restoril or Ambien, for example) might be prescribed to help you sleep during such a time.

4. If you have chronic or severe depression accompanying panic disorder, agoraphobia, or any other anxiety disorder, you will usually benefit from a prescription antidepressant medication. Milder cases of depression (that is, you do not lose your appetite, your ability to sleep, or your interest in simple pleasures, and/or do not have suicidal thoughts) may respond to the herb Saint-John's-wort, the supplement S-adenosyl-methionine (SAM-e), or amino acids such as tryptophan, tyrosine, or DL-phenylalanine (see the section "The Use of Natural Supplements" at the end of this chapter). Moderate to severe cases of depression are best treated with SSRI, tricyclic, or another type of antidepressant medications. Such medications will help relieve depression, panic, and anxiety at the same time.

5. If you suffer from performance anxiety in public speaking or other performance situations—especially if the anxiety involves heart palpitations—you may be helped by short-term doses of beta-blocking drugs, such as Inderal (propranolol). A benzodiazepine tranquilizer, such as Xanax or Klonopin, may also be used on occasion (not regularly) to help you negotiate high-performance situations.

6. Difficult cases of social phobia or social anxiety (for example, you avoid a wide range of social situations or you are unable to attend important meetings at work) may be helped by SSRI antidepressant medications or another class of antidepressant drugs called MAO-inhibitors. These medications should be taken in conjunction with individual or, preferably, group cognitive behavioral therapy (see chapter 1, the section on social phobia).

7. Those with obsessive-compulsive disorder often benefit from the use of antidepressant medication, usually in combination with cognitive therapy, exposure, and response prevention. Medications such as Anafranil (clomipramine), Prozac (fluox-

etine), Paxil (paroxetine), or Luvox (fluvoxamine) are frequently used in the treatment of this disorder. From 60 to 70 percent of persons with obsessive-compulsive disorder experience an improvement in their symptoms while taking one of these drugs. All of these medications appear to be helpful in treating obsessive-compulsive disorder itself, whether or not it is accompanied by depression. Anafranil, however, does have some undesirable side effects.

For further information on various factors that can affect your decision to rely on medication, see the section "The Choice to Use Medication: What to Consider" later in this chapter.

Types of Medication Used to Treat Anxiety Disorders

What follows is a description of the major classes of prescription medications used in the treatment of anxiety disorders. Potential advantages and drawbacks of each type of medication are considered.

SSRI Antidepressant Medications

The SSRI (selective serotonin reuptake inhibitor) antidepressant medications include Prozac (fluoxetine), Zoloft (sertraline), Paxil (paroxetine), Luvox (fluvoxamine), Celexa (citalopram), and Lexapro (escitalopram). In the past fifteen years, they have become the first-line medications used by most psychiatrists to treat anxiety disorders. The SSRIs all increase levels of the neurotransmitter serotonin in the brain by preventing the reabsorption of serotonin at synapses (spaces between nerve cells). With increased serotonin, the number of serotonin receptors on nerve cells in the brain can decrease (not as many are needed). The reduction in serotonin receptors takes place over the first month or two of taking an SSRI and is technically called *downregulation*.

Downregulation allows the millions of nerve cells in the serotonin receptor system (particularly those in parts of the brain responsible for anxiety) to become less sensitive to changes in the neurochemical environment of the brain created by stress. That means less dramatic shifts in mood and less vulnerability to anxiety.

The SSRIs tend to be as effective—sometimes more effective—than the older cyclic antidepressants that have been used to treat panic (for example, imipramine, desipramine, nortriptyline). They also have the distinct advantage of causing fewer side effects for most people than the older antidepressants. SSRIs are used most often to treat panic, panic with agoraphobia, or obsessive-compulsive disorder. They have also found use with social phobia, particularly generalized social phobia, in which a person is phobic of most types of social situations and encounters. Sometimes they are used to treat post-traumatic stress disorder or generalized anxiety disorder, especially when these difficulties are accompanied by depression. People differ quite a lot in their response to the SSRIs. If you try one and experience no benefit, be willing to try another. To gain full benefit from an SSRI, you may need to take it for *one to two years*. Relapse with SSRI medications appears to be low when the medication is taken for at least eighteen months; however, reliable data on the exact percentage of relapse is not available at the time of this writing. Typical effective daily doses for SSRIs are Prozac, 20 to 40 mg; Paxil, 20 to 40 mg; Zoloft, 50 to 100 mg; Luvox, 50 to 100 mg; Celexa, 20 to 40 mg; and Lexapro, 10 to 20 mg. Effective doses of these medications for OCD tend to be somewhat higher. However, some OCD clients find that they obtain good results from lower doses.

Advantages

The SSRIs can be helpful for any of the anxiety disorders or depression. They have been particularly helpful for people with panic disorder, agoraphobia, or obsessive-compulsive disorder. SSRIs are easily tolerated and safe for medically ill or elderly persons. They are not addictive. They do not cause problems when taken long term. In most cases, they do not lead to weight gain.

Drawbacks

Although SSRIs have fewer side effects than the older cyclic antidepressants, they can cause side effects in some people, including jitteriness, agitation, restlessness, dizziness, drowsiness, headaches, nausea, gastrointestinal distress, and sexual dysfunction. These side effects tend to go away after two weeks, so it's important to try to ride them out during the early phase of treatment. *All of these side effects can be minimized by starting off with a very low dose of the medication and increasing it, over time, to therapeutic levels.* For example, doses might start at 5 mg per day for Prozac or Paxil and 10 mg for Zoloft or Luvox. To achieve such doses, you need to start with a quarter of a tablet per day in most cases, then gradually increase up to a tablet per day over a period of several weeks. Be willing to take plenty of time in increasing the dose gradually. (You may notice side effects increase for a day or two after each dose increase.)

The one side effect that can be problematic over time is reduced sexual motivation and/ or sexual dysfunction (for example, absent or delayed orgasm). This can be upsetting to many people and, in some cases, leads them to discontinue the medication. For a certain percentage of people who take SSRIs, normal sexual functioning will resume after two or three months on the medication, so it's a good idea to stay with an SSRI even if at first you experience diminished sex drive. If the problem doesn't get better, it can be mitigated in one of four ways, under the supervision of your doctor: 1) reducing the dose of the SSRI by half on days you choose to be sexually active, 2) augmenting the use of the SSRI with 5 to 10 mg per day of BuSpar, 3) supplementing the SSRI with the medications amantidine or cyproheptidine, or 4) trying the supplement DHEA, available at most health food stores, at 25 to 50 mg per day. Many people find that one or two of these interventions can help them restore more normal sexual activity while continuing to take an SSRI.

A third disadvantage is that SSRIs, while often effective, take four to five weeks to produce any significant therapeutic benefit. Sometimes the full therapeutic potential is not achieved until the medication has been taken for twelve weeks or longer. (There is some evidence that even further benefits occur over the course of one year.) If you're suffering from severe and disabling panic, your doctor may recommend you take a tranquilizer (most likely a high-potency benzodiazepine—see below) while waiting for the SSRI to take effect.

In the past few years, many people have found the medication Paxil to be especially difficult to discontinue. Approximately 5 to 10 percent of persons withdrawing from Paxil may experience severe symptoms such as panic attacks, mood swings, profuse sweating, depersonalization, and "electric shock"-like sensations. Before deciding to use Paxil, be sure to discuss this potential problem with your physician.

A final drawback of SSRIs is their expense. Without insurance, you can pay upward of $200 per month for some SSRIs. The optimal duration for taking an SSRI medication is one to two years. You increase your risk of a return of symptoms if you take the medication for a shorter time period.

Note: People with bipolar disorder (manic depression) should take SSRIs only under the supervision of a knowledgeable physician, as SSRIs can aggravate manic states.

High-Potency Benzodiazepines

The high-potency benzodiazepine tranquilizers (BZs) Xanax (alprazolam), Ativan (lorazepam), and Klonopin (clonazepam) are commonly used to treat anxiety disorders. Older benzodiazepine drugs, such as Valium, Librium, or Tranxene, are occasionally tried when someone is sensitive to the side effects of the newer BZs. The benzodiazepines are often used in conjunction with SSRI antidepressants (or older tricyclic antidepressants) to treat severe cases of panic disorder. Frequently, it's possible to gradually withdraw from use of the BZ after the antidepressant medication has achieved its full antianxiety benefit (that is, from four to six weeks after starting the drug).

Benzodiazepine drugs generally depress the activity of the entire central nervous system and thus directly and efficiently decrease anxiety. They do so by binding with receptors in the brain that function to tone down or suppress activity in those parts of the brain responsible for anxiety—the amygdala, locus coeruleus, and limbic system, in general. In higher doses, BZ tranquilizers act like sedatives and may promote sleep. Lower doses tend to simply reduce anxiety without sedation. The main difference between various benzodiazepines is each medication's "half-life," or the length of time their chemical metabolites stay in your body (for example, Xanax has a half-life of eight hours, Klonopin eighteen to twenty-four hours, and Valium forty-eight to seventy-two hours).

At present, the most common tranquilizer used to treat anxiety disorders is Xanax (alprazolam). Alprazolam differs from other BZs in that it has an antidepressant effect, as well as the ability to relieve anxiety. It also tends to have a less sedating effect than other tranquilizers. Because Xanax has a short half-life, two or three doses per day are usually prescribed. If you take only one dose per day, you may experience "rebound anxiety"—the tendency to experience heightened levels of anxiety as the medication wears off. BZs with longer half-lives, such as Klonopin, tend to cause less rebound anxiety and can often be taken in a single dose per day. Research indicates that high doses of Xanax, 2 to 9 mg per day, are necessary to fully suppress panic attacks. In clinical practice, however, it's common to administer low doses: in the range of 0.25 to 1 mg two or three times per day. (Daily doses of Xanax tend to be higher than for Klonopin.) Such doses can significantly reduce the symptoms of panic attacks with less sedating side effects.

Advantages

BZs work very quickly, reducing symptoms of anxiety within fifteen to twenty minutes. Unlike antidepressants, which need to be taken regularly, BZs can be taken on an as-needed basis. That is, you can take a small dose of Xanax, Ativan, or Klonopin only when you have to confront a challenging situation, such as a graded exposure task, going to a job interview, or taking a flight.

The BZs tend to have less bothersome side effects for many people than the antidepressant medications (especially the tricyclic antidepressants). Sometimes they are the only medication that can provide relief when a person is unable to take any of the antidepressant medications. Generic forms of BZs are available, reducing their cost.

Drawbacks

BZs, unlike antidepressant medications, tend to be addictive. The higher the dose (that is, more than 1 mg per day for high-potency BZs) and the longer you take them (that is, more than one month), the more likely you are to become physically dependent. Physical dependency means that if you stop taking the medication abruptly, severe anxiety symptoms are likely to occur. Many people who have taken Xanax (or other BZs) in high doses for a month or low doses for several months report that it's very difficult getting off the medication. (There is some evidence that withdrawal from Klonopin, because of its longer half-life, may be slightly easier and less protracted than withdrawal from Xanax.) *Abrupt* withdrawal from these medications is *dangerous* and may produce panic attacks, severe anxiety, confusion, muscle tension, irritability, insomnia, and even seizures. A more gradual tapering of the dose, stretched out over many weeks or even months, is what makes withdrawal possible. The ease with which people can withdraw from Xanax varies, but as a general rule, it's best to taper off *very* gradually over a period of one to four months under medical supervision. During this withdrawal period, you may suffer a recurrence of panic attacks or other anxiety symptoms for which the drug was originally prescribed.

If a BZ medication is tapered off too quickly, you can experience *rebound anxiety*. Rebound is the occurrence of anxiety symptoms *greater* than those you experienced prior to taking the drug in the first place. Rebound may lead to *relapse*, a return of your anxiety disorder at equal or greater severity than what you experienced before taking the medication. To minimize the risk of rebound, it is critical to withdraw from your dose of a BZ very gradually, preferably over several months. (For example, if you have been taking 1.5 mg of Xanax per day for six months, reduce your dose by 0.25 mg every two to three weeks.)

Another drawback of BZs is that they are effective only as long as you take them. When you stop taking them, your anxiety disorder has virtually a 100 percent chance of returning, unless you have learned coping skills (that is, abdominal breathing, relaxation, exercise, stress management, working with self-talk, assertiveness, and so on) and made lifestyle changes that will result in long-term anxiety relief. Taking a BZ only, without doing anything else, amounts to merely suppressing your symptoms without getting at the cause of your difficulty.

A final problem with benzodiazepines is that they tend to have a blunting effect, not only on anxiety but on feelings in general. Many people report that their emotional responses are muted while they are taking these drugs (for example, they may have trouble crying or getting angry, even at times when these reactions are appropriate). To the extent that anxiety is related to suppressed and unresolved feelings, taking these drugs will tend only to alleviate symptoms rather than relieve the cause of the problem. (Some people have a paradoxical reaction to benzodiazepines, during which they actually become *more* emotional or impulsive, although this tends to happen infrequently). Emotional blunting is somewhat less likely with antidepressant medications, although it may occur.

Long-term use of BZs (more than two years) is sometimes necessary in those cases of severe panic and anxiety that do not respond to any other type of medication. While enabling many people to function, long-term BZ use has several problems. Many long-term BZ users report that they feel depressed and/or less vital and energetic than they would like. It is as though the medication tends to sap them of a certain degree of energy. Often, if they are able to switch to an antidepressant medication to help manage their anxiety, they regain a sense of vitality and enthusiasm for life. In my experience, the BZs are most appropriate for treating short-term, acute anxiety and stress rather than longer-lasting conditions, such as agoraphobia, post-traumatic stress disorder, or obsessive-compulsive disorder. Wherever possible, chronic, long-term anxiety disorders are most appropriately treated with SSRI antidepressants. There are, however, certain individuals who seem to need to take a low dose of a BZ over the long term in order to function. They accept the addiction and other side effects in exchange for protection from the anxiety that they have been unable to manage using solely natural techniques or other types of medication. If you are over fifty years old and have been taking a BZ medication for more than two years, you should periodically receive medical checkups, including an evaluation of your liver function.

Serotonin-Norepinephrine Reuptake Inhibitor (SNRI) Antidepressants

SNRI antidepressants work by blocking the reuptake of two major neurotransmitters, serotonin and norepinephrine. At present, the three most commonly used SNRIs are Cymbalta (duloxetine), Effexor (venlafaxine), and Pristiq (desvenlafaxine). Desvenlafaxine is the mirror-image isomer of venlafaxine, and is claimed by some to have fewer side effects than venlafaxine, though there is no systematic research on this. The SNRIs are potent medications and may be tried when response to SSRIs is insufficient. They are most commonly used to treat depression and/or generalized anxiety disorder but may be used to treat other anxiety disorders such as panic disorder or OCD.

The main advantage of SNRIs over the SSRIs is that they can stabilize both the norepinephrine and serotonin receptor systems, instead of just the serotonin system alone. So for certain people, they are more powerful anxiolytics than the SSRIs. They have the same disadvantages as the SSRIs, with side effects including dizziness, nausea, weakness, dry mouth, insomnia, and sexual dysfunction. Like the SSRIs, the dose needs to be tapered gradually when SNRIs are discontinued. Abrupt discontinuation is associated with withdrawal symptoms.

Tricyclic Antidepressants

Tricyclic antidepressants include Tofranil (imipramine), Pamelor (nortriptyline), Norpramin (desipramine), Anafranil (clomipramine), Elavil (amitriptyline), and Sinequan (doxepin), among others. These medications (especially imipramine) are frequently used to treat panic attacks, whether such attacks occur by themselves or in conjunction with agoraphobia. Tricyclic antidepressants seem to reduce both the frequency and intensity of panic reactions for many people. They are also effective in reducing the depression that often accompanies panic disorder and agoraphobia. While it used to be believed that Tofranil was the most effective antidepressant for treating panic, more recent evidence indicates that any of the tricyclic antidepressant medications can be helpful, depending on the individual. Anafranil tends to be specifically helpful in treating OCD.

The tricyclic antidepressants are used less these days than SSRI antidepressants because they tend to have more troublesome side effects. For example, in studies of imipramine, usually about one-third of the subjects drop out because they cannot tolerate side effects (only about 10 percent do in studies using SSRIs). On the other hand, tricyclic antidepressants are sometimes a better choice than SSRIs for certain people because most of them (other than Anafranil) modify a different receptor system in the brain (the noradrenergic system instead of the serotonin system). As with SSRIs, tricyclic antidepressants are best tolerated by starting with a very low dose (for example, 5 mg per day of imipramine) and gradually working up to a therapeutic dose level (approximately 100 to 200 mg per day).

Advantages

Tricyclic antidepressants, like the SSRIs, do not lead to physical dependence. They have a beneficial effect on depression as well as on panic and anxiety. They block panic attacks, even if you are not depressed. Because generic forms are available, they are inexpensive.

Drawbacks

Tricyclic antidepressants (unlike SSRIs) tend to produce anticholinergic side effects, including dry mouth, blurred vision, dizziness or disorientation, and postural hypotension (causing dizziness). Weight gain and sexual dysfunction can also occur. With imipramine, in particular, anxiety may *increase* during the first few days of administration. With clomipramine (effective for OCD), side effects can be particularly bothersome.

Although these side effects tend to diminish after one or two weeks, they persist for 25 to 30 percent of people who take tricyclic antidepressants after the initial adjustment period.

Like the SSRIs, tricyclic antidepressants take about three to four weeks to offer therapeutic benefits. While able to block panic attacks, these medications may not be as effective as SSRIs and benzodiazepine tranquilizers in reducing anticipatory anxiety about the possibility of having a panic attack or having to face a phobic situation.

Finally, about 30 to 50 percent of people will relapse (experience a return of panic or anxiety symptoms) after discontinuing tricyclic antidepressant medications. This is, however, a much lower relapse rate than occurs when benzodiazepines are discontinued.

MAO-Inhibitor Antidepressants

If you have given SSRIs and cyclic antidepressants a fair trial and still have obtained no benefit, your doctor may try the oldest class of antidepressant medications—the MAO-inhibitors (MAOIs). Nardil (phenelzine) is the MAOI most commonly used to treat panic, although Parnate (tranylcypromine) is sometimes used. While MAOIs are potent medications, they are frequently last in line to be tried because they can cause serious or even fatal rises in blood pressure when combined with 1) foods that contain the amino acid tyramine, such as wine, aged cheeses, and certain meats, and 2) certain medications, including some over-the-counter analgesics. If you are taking an MAOI, you should be under close supervision by your doctor.

Advantages

MAOIs have a potent panic-blocking effect and are sometimes effective when other types of antidepressants have failed. There is also some research indicating that they are helpful in treating social phobia, especially generalized social phobia (a tendency to be phobic toward a wide range of interpersonal situations or encounters). They may also help severe depression that has been unresponsive to other classes of antidepressants.

Drawbacks

Side effects include weight gain, hypotension (low blood pressure), sexual dysfunction, headache, fatigue, and insomnia. These side effects may be most pronounced during the third and fourth weeks of treatment and then are likely to diminish.

Dietary restrictions are critical. When taking an MAOI, you need to avoid foods containing tyramine, including most cheeses, homemade yogurt, most alcoholic beverages, aged meats and fish, liver, ripe bananas, and certain vegetables. Over-the-counter cold medicines, diet pills, and certain antihistamines need to be avoided. Prescription amphetamines and SSRI or cyclic antidepressants should be avoided as well.

Other Antidepressants

Other antidepressant medications occasionally used with anxiety disorders include Remeron (mirtazapine), Wellbutrin (bupropion), Serzone (nefazodone), and Desyrel (trazodone). Remeron is classified as a noradrenergic/specific serotonergic antidepressant (NaSSA), and, like Effexor, it has a dual action, increasing the levels of both norepinephrine and serotonin at the synapse. Remeron is very sedating at lower doses and may be used to promote sleep. At higher doses, it is an effective antidepressant, and may be used when Effexor is not well tolerated. Psychiatrists sometimes use it in combination with an SSRI, like Paxil or Celexa, to enhance the antianxiety and/or antidepressant effects of the SSRI, a strategy called *augmentation*.

Wellbutrin is often helpful for depression but can be difficult for people with anxiety disorders to tolerate, since its side effects can include anxiety and insomnia. On the positive side, Wellbutrin is the only newer antidepressant that does not have sexual side effects.

Serzone was widely used in the 1990s as both an antidepressant and an antianxiety medication but has recently fallen out of favor because of reports of liver damage or failure associated with its usage. Trazodone is an older antidepressant medication that has been around since the early 1980s. While not frequently prescribed for anxiety, it can be a highly effective sedative for many people. It has the advantage of not being addictive, like Restoril, Ambien, or Lunesta, and may be more potent for some people than natural sedatives like melatonin and tryptophan. Its side effects are similar to those listed for the tricylic antidepressants.

Beta Blockers

Although there are several different beta-adrenergic blocking drugs (popularly called *beta blockers*), the two most commonly used with anxiety disorders are Inderal (propranolol) and Tenormin (atenolol). These medications can be helpful for anxiety conditions with marked body symptoms, especially heart palpitations (rapid or irregular heartbeat) and sweating. Beta blockers are quite effective in blocking these peripheral manifestations of anxiety, but are less effective in reducing the internal experience of anxiety mediated by the central nervous system. Inderal or Tenormin may be used in conjunction with a benzodiazepine tranquilizer, such as Xanax, in treating panic disorder when heart palpitations are prominent. By themselves, beta blockers are often given in a single dose (for example, 20 to 40 mg Inderal) to relieve body symptoms of anxiety (rapid heartbeat, shaking, or blushing) prior to a high-performance situation, such as public speaking, a job interview, final examinations, or a musical recital. Beta blockers are also often used to treat mitral valve prolapse, a benign heart arrhythmia that sometimes accompanies panic disorder.

Although these medications are relatively safe, they can produce side effects, such as the excessive lowering of blood pressure (causing dizziness or light-headedness), fatigue, and drowsiness. In some people, they can also cause depression. Unlike tranquilizers, these medications do not tend to be physically addictive. Still, if you've been taking them for a while, it's preferable to taper your dose gradually to avoid rebound elevations of blood pressure. Beta blockers are not recommended for people with asthma or other respiratory illnesses that cause wheezing or for diabetics.

BuSpar

BuSpar (buspirone) has been available for about twenty years. To date, it has been found useful in diminishing generalized anxiety but is not effective in reducing the frequency or intensity of panic attacks. Some research indicates that BuSpar can be helpful in treating social phobia or in augmenting the effects of SSRI medications used to treat OCD. Some practitioners prefer it over Xanax (and other benzodiazepines) for treating generalized anxiety because it is less prone to cause drowsiness and is nonaddictive. There is little risk of your becoming physically dependent on BuSpar or requiring a protracted period of time to withdraw from it.

Research in recent years, however, has not found BuSpar to be any more effective than SSRIs in treating generalized anxiety.

An ordinary starting dose for BuSpar is 5 mg two or three times per day. It takes from two to three weeks before the full antianxiety effect of this medication is achieved. Some people with generalized anxiety respond well to BuSpar, while others report side effects (lethargy, nausea, dizziness, or paradoxical anxiety).

Other Medications Used to Treat Anxiety

When antidepressant medications and/or BZ tranquilizers are ineffective or not fully effective in treating panic disorder, psychiatrists may try other medications such as Depakote (valproic acid), Neurontin (gabapentin), Gabitril (tiagabine), or Lyrica (pregabalin). Although such medications are often used to treat seizure disorders or bipolar disorder, they also have an antianxiety effect. It's thought that they work by increasing levels or activity of the neurotransmitter GABA in the brain. (Tiagabine is actually a selective GABA reuptake inhibitor.) Certain clients, most often those with generalized anxiety disorder, seem to benefit from one or another of these medications, taken either alone or with an SSRI antidepressant. Effective dose ranges for Depakote are 700 to 1500 mg per day, Neurontin 300 to 1800 mg per day, Gabitril 4 to 10 mg per day, and Lyrica 150 to 300 mg per day.

The advantage of these medications is that they work rapidly, are nonaddictive, and are not associated with sexual side effects. Numerous people receive genuine help from these drugs. On the downside, some people report that Neurontin or Gabitril makes them feel tired, lethargic, or otherwise "out of it." If you have not had a good response to antidepressants and want to avoid the addictive problems associated with benzodiazepines, these medications are worth trying.

The Choice to Use Medication: What to Consider

The decision to include medication in your effort to recover from anxiety involves many considerations. First and foremost, it's always a decision to be made in consultation with your physician. Your doctor, preferably a psychiatrist, should be knowledgeable and experienced in treating anxiety disorders and should work with you in a collaborative (not authoritarian) way. Second, your decision depends on a number of personal factors, including 1) the severity of your problem with anxiety, 2) your personal outlook and values regarding medication, and 3) your patience, which may be tested in those situations where several medications need to be tried before the right one for you can be found.

Be wary of pat answers and simple generalizations when you consider undertaking a course of medication. The following twelve vignettes illustrate the complex range of situations that might lead a person to decide for or against taking medication.

1. A busy physician has numerous duties at work, at home, and in his community. He takes time to meditate, jog, express feelings, and work with self-talk, but still has

debilitating panic attacks. He finds that an SSRI antidepressant helps him to sleep better and carry out his round of daily responsibilities with less anxiety.

2.   A mother who has been housebound with agoraphobia for a long time has a difficult time beginning exposure therapy. She finds that taking an SSRI medication helps her to get started. After one year of exposure, she is confident enough to continue without medication.

3.   A secretary who has been taking medication for mixed anxiety and depression for a year discovers she is pregnant. She stops her medication and puts up with intensified symptoms for nine months in order to have a healthy baby.

4.   A husband going through a divorce has a heart attack followed by mixed anxiety and depression. Although he has been opposed to taking medication up to this time, he decides to rely on a benzodiazepine medication to help him negotiate this severe crisis.

5.   A woman who has just been promoted to a more demanding job learns her mother has died. She elects to take medication for a period of several months to handle her stressful life circumstances.

6.   A chiropractor who teaches classes in nutrition and is heavily involved in alternative health practices has obsessive-compulsive disorder. He finds that he needs to take an SSRI antidepressant in order to handle his work.

7.   A student who decides to enroll in a certificate program to be an acupuncturist has a strong desire, despite her panic attacks, to embrace only natural methods (such as herbs, nutrition, tai chi, and meditation) to handle her anxiety. She decides not to use medication.

8.   A man who has been taking various SSRI antidepressants for panic disorder over five years wants to evaluate how he might do without medication. He discontinues it over a period of two months and does well.

9.   A long-term user of benzodiazepines feels they are causing her to be depressed and decides she would rather have some anxiety and emotional intensity in her life than feel numbed or de-energized by a tranquilizer.

10.   A minister with panic disorder is unable to tolerate any antidepressant medication. He finds he is best able to function taking a low dose of a tranquilizer every day over the long term.

11.   A woman who belongs to a religious group that espouses that prayer and right living are the answer to life's difficulties has a strong philosophical belief that medications are unnecessary for her recovery. She elects not to use medication for her panic attacks.

12.   A recovering alcoholic with two years' sobriety begins taking Xanax to manage his anxiety. Within two months, he starts escalating the dose. Both his doctor and his

12-step program friends advise him to discontinue the medication. In the interest of maintaining a commitment to a substance-free lifestyle, he does so.

Whether you're considering starting medication or thinking about stopping medication you've been taking for a while, the two most important factors to look at in making a decision for yourself are your own *personal values* and the *severity of your condition.* Each of these is considered below.

Personal Values

What are your personal values about medication? Are you open to including medication as a part of your recovery program, or do you feel strongly about adhering to natural methods alone? While your symptoms may warrant trying medication and while your doctor might encourage you to do so, the decision is ultimately your own. If you happen to be committed to the ideal of natural healing without the aid of medication, that is a perfectly legitimate option. Many people can recover from anxiety disorders by natural methods alone if they have sufficient motivation, persistence, and diligence in practicing natural methods, such as those outlined in this book. At the opposite extreme, there are people who lack sufficient interest or motivation to put in the time and effort involved in practicing relaxation, exercise, desensitization, and cognitive skills on a daily basis. They seek immediate relief of symptoms through taking a drug. In many cases, this is also a viable choice. It is not for anyone to judge a person's decision to seek relief from anxiety disorders through medication. Medications certainly do provide a great deal of relief for many people.

In making a choice about whether to rely on medication, it's important to have all the information that you need to make the most informed and enlightened decision possible. Such a decision should not be based solely on impulse—for example, a desire to take a high dose of medication to eliminate all symptoms of anxiety as soon as possible. Nor should it be based upon fear or avoidance of medication because you have a phobia of it. The purpose of this chapter is to give you as much information as possible so that you can make the optimal decision for yourself.

Severity of Your Condition

Apart from your personal values, the next thing to look at in considering medication is the severity of your symptoms. As a general rule, the more severe your problem, the more likely you will benefit from a trial of medication. Severity can be defined in two ways: your ability to function and your level of distress. Use the following questions to evaluate the severity of your own condition.

First, does your problem with anxiety significantly interfere with your ability to function in your everyday life? Are you having a hard time working, or are you unable to work at all? Is your ability to raise your children or be responsive to your spouse impaired by your anxiety? Do you have a hard time organizing your thoughts to complete basic tasks, such as cooking or paying bills?

Second, does your problem with anxiety cause you considerable distress to the point that you have two or more hours every day during which you feel *very uncomfortable*? Is it hard for you just to make it through each day? Do you wake up each morning in a state of dread? If your answer to *any* of these questions is yes, you may want to consider medication.

Another factor in considering medication is depression. Significant depression accompanies anxiety disorders in about 50 percent of cases. It is especially common with panic disorder, agoraphobia, obsessive-compulsive disorder, and post-traumatic stress disorder. There is also a syndrome—mixed anxiety and depression—that has received attention in recent years. Criteria for depression include lack of energy, continuous low mood or apathy, loss of appetite, disturbed sleep, frequent self-criticism, difficulty concentrating, and possibly suicidal thoughts. If you are depressed, antidepressant medication can be especially helpful because it tends to restore the motivation and energy you need to practice the skills promoted in this book, such as abdominal breathing, relaxation, exercise, cognitive restructuring, and graded exposure. If you have had suicidal thoughts, your doctor will most certainly recommend medication.

In addition to severity of symptoms, *chronicity*—how long you've had your problem— is another important factor to consider. If your anxiety is of recent origin and a response to stressful circumstances, it may pass when you learn stress-management techniques and work through whatever problem instigated the stress. On the other hand, if you've been suffering for more than a year—and especially if you've tried cognitive behavioral therapy and have not yet received the benefit you wanted—a trial of medication may be helpful. *To conclude, the more severe and/or the more chronic (long-standing) your condition, the more likely you may respond favorably to medication.*

How Long to Continue Medication

For anyone who is considering trying or is presently taking a prescription medication, how long to take it is a very important issue. Unfortunately, there is no simple answer. The length of time you need to take medication depends on at least three different factors:

- *What type of medication* (for example, tranquilizer or antidepressant)
- *What type of anxiety disorder* (for example, panic, social phobia, or obsessive-compulsive disorder)
- *Your motivation and commitment to utilize natural approaches* (a committed program of nonmedication approaches may help you to stop relying on medication or else reduce your dose)

What Type of Medication

Some types of medication, such as tranquilizers or beta blockers, can be used on an as-needed basis only. That is, you only use the medication when dealing with an acute, anxiety-provoking situation, such as confronting a phobia. Tranquilizers can also be used over a period of a few weeks to help you get through a particularly difficult situation, such as the death of a loved one or taking the bar exam. For a period of one to two years, tranquilizers may be useful if you are unable to take any type of antidepressant medication for anxiety. Long-term use of tranquilizers (more than two years), while having certain problems, may even be justified in some cases (see the previous section on benzodiazepine tranquilizers).

Antidepressant medications are usually taken on a daily basis for a minimum of six months. In my experience, they are *most effective in treating anxiety disorders when taken for a period of eighteen months to two years*. Risk of relapse once you discontinue the antidepressants is lower if you've taken them for this length of time. For some people, long-term use (more than two years) of antidepressant medication, at a maintenance dose level, offers an optimal quality of life.

What Type of Anxiety

If you have a fairly mild case of agoraphobia, you may need to take medication (a tranquilizer or an antidepressant) only up to and during the early stages of graded exposure to your phobic situation. Then, during later stages, you may wean yourself off the medication and work through your exposure hierarchies on your own. Being able to do so without the use of medication will enhance your sense of mastery over your phobias. On the other hand, if you are having frequent panic attacks and/or are practically housebound, you may benefit from taking medication for a longer time. For SSRI antidepressant medications, the eighteen-month to two-year period mentioned above is optimal. Long-term maintenance on a low dose of antidepressant medication may be necessary in some cases.

For social phobia, you may take an antidepressant (SSRI antidepressant or MAO-inhibitor) or a benzodiazepine, especially if you suffer from generalized social phobia (anxiety in a wide variety of social situations). One to two years on the medication will likely optimize your treatment. Long-term maintenance at a low dose, as with agoraphobia, may be necessary in some cases.

With obsessive-compulsive disorder, long-term use of an SSRI medication at a higher dose is often the best strategy. After two years, you can try lowering the dose to see what is the minimum you need to correct the neurobiological problem associated with OCD. On the other hand, some people with OCD are able to manage their problem with cognitive behavioral strategies alone—sometimes from the outset and sometimes after a year or two on medication. (See the book *Brain Lock* by Jeffrey Schwartz, cited at the end of this chapter.)

Generalized anxiety disorder will require medication only in moderate to severe cases or in situations where you are unmotivated or unwilling to make the behavioral and lifestyle modifications that can help.

Finally, post-traumatic stress disorder may frequently be helped by antidepressant medication in conjunction with cognitive behavioral therapy; severe cases may need a long-term maintenance dose.

Your Motivation and Commitment to Natural Approaches

In many cases, it's possible to eliminate or at least reduce your need for medication over the long term, if you maintain a committed program of natural approaches. *The brain has an inherent ability to heal from the stress-induced imbalances that may have led to your original need for medication.* While it may take your brain somewhat longer to recover than would be the case for a broken bone or a torn ligament, the brain can regain, with proper cognitive, behavioral, and lifestyle modifications, much or all of its natural integrity over time. Your very belief that you can recover from anxiety and eventually wean yourself off medication will help make it more likely that you do. The popular idea of "mind over matter" is not an idle notion. Any of the approaches suggested in this book will help you to heal yourself naturally. The more of these approaches you are able to implement on a regular basis, the sooner and more powerfully you will be able to foster a state of natural health in body and mind.

Discontinuing Medication

If you've decided that you want to stop relying on prescription medications, observe the following guidelines:

1. *Be sure you've gained some level of mastery of the basic strategies for overcoming anxiety and panic presented in this book.* In particular, it would be a good idea to have established a daily practice of deep relaxation and exercise, along with skills in using abdominal breathing and countering fearful self-talk to overcome anxiety symptoms. If you plan to withdraw from Xanax or a BZ tranquilizer, these skills will serve you well in dealing with possible recurrences of anxiety during the withdrawal period, as well as over the long run. Be assured that any resurgence of high anxiety during withdrawal from a tranquilizer is temporary and should not persist if you proceed through your withdrawal in a sufficiently gradual manner.

2. *Consult with your doctor to set up a program for gradually tapering off the dosage of your medication.* This is especially important if you've been taking a BZ tranquilizer (the tapering-off period is dose-dependent but may need to be as long as six months). A tapering-off period (usually a month or two) also needs to be observed if you're curtailing your use of an antidepressant medication like Paxil or a beta blocker such as Inderal.

    For many people, benzodiazepine tapering can be difficult. The nervous system adapts to these drugs, and it may take you quite some time to readapt to living without them. Often psychiatrists prescribe an SSRI antidepressant, or other nonaddictive antianxiety medication such as Neurontin, during and after the BZ tapering-off process in order to ease withdrawal symptoms. For people unable to tolerate these prescription medications, sometimes high doses of the amino acids tryptophan, GABA, taurine, and glycine—administered either intravenously or orally—can be helpful both during and for some time after the tapering-off period.

    There are two approaches to withdrawing from the benzodiazepines. One is to reduce the dose very slowly over a period of several months, preferably with the aid of a nonaddictive antianxiety medication, as described. Alternatively, drug rehabilitation programs do a more rapid taper over a period of two to three weeks and use an alternative (long half-life) benzodiazepine, such as Valium, or else phenobarbital in lieu of the high-potency benzodiazepine (such as Xanax or Klonopin) that is being withdrawn. After withdrawal from the secondary drug, an antidepressant or other nonaddictive antianxiety medication may be used to assist adjustment for several months after the taper is finished. For more detailed information on benzodiazepine tapering, see the book by C. Heather Ashton listed at the end of this chapter.

3.   *Be prepared to increase your reliance on strategies described in this workbook during your tapering-off period.* Especially important are abdominal breathing, relaxation, exercise, coping strategies for anxiety, and countering negative self-talk. Your withdrawal from medication is an opportunity to practice and improve your skills at using these strategies. You'll gain increased self-confidence by learning to use self-activated strategies to master anxiety and panic without having to rely on medication.

4.   *Don't be disappointed if you need to rely on medication during future periods of acute anxiety or stress.* Stopping regular use of a medication doesn't necessarily mean that you might not benefit from the *short-term* use of that medication in the future. For example, using a tranquilizer or sleep medication for two weeks during a time of acute stress due to a traumatic experience is appropriate and unlikely to lead to dependence. If you're subject to seasonal affective disorder, you may stand to benefit from taking an antidepressant medication during the winter months. Don't consider it a sign of weakness or a lack of self-control if you occasionally need to rely on prescription medications for a limited period of time. Given the stress and pressures of modern life, there are quite a few people who occasionally use prescription medications to help them cope.

Working with Your Doctor

The purpose of this chapter has been to provide a balanced view of the role of medications in treating anxiety. There are certainly a variety of situations where the benefits of prescription drugs outweigh their associated risks and drawbacks. It's important, however, that before taking *any* medication you become fully aware of all of its potential side effects and limitations. It is your doctor's responsibility to 1) obtain a complete history of your symptoms, 2) inform you of the possible side effects and limitations of any particular drug, and 3) obtain your *informed consent* to try out a medication. It's your responsibility not to withhold information your doctor requests in taking your medical history, as well as to let him or her know, should he or she fail to ask, whether 1) you have allergic reactions to any drugs, 2) you are pregnant, 3) you are taking any other prescription or over-the-counter medications, or 4) you are taking any natural supplements.

Once this exchange of information has taken place between you and your physician, both of you will be in a position to make a *fully informed and mutual decision* about whether taking a particular prescription medication is in your best interest. If your doctor is unwilling to take a collaborative, rather than authoritarian, stance or to allow for your informed consent, I strongly recommend that you find another doctor who will. Medications may enable you to turn the corner in recovering from your particular problem, but it is essential that they be used with the utmost care and responsibility.

Note: The Internet offers websites that distribute various antianxiety medications, especially tranquilizers, without a prescription. I urge you not to do business with these sites, as they may take your money without sending you anything, send you the wrong medication, or send you an inferior or toxic version of the medication you ordered. It is worth your time and money to consult with an experienced physician or psychiatrist when you are in need of medication, and to utilize reputable pharmacies that require a prescription.

In Conclusion

Appropriate use of medication does not conflict with holistic values or a natural lifestyle. There is a time and place for the use of medication in treating anxiety disorders, and not to use them at those times is equivalent to not taking good care of yourself. The real question to ask, in my opinion, is this: *what is the most compassionate thing you can do for yourself?* In some cases, the answer may be to wean yourself off medication—especially if you have become overly dependent on or addicted to a drug for several years without having evaluated how you might fare without it. In some cases, the answer may be to use medication for a period of several months (up to a year) to get through a difficult time or to jump-start your motivation to utilize cognitive behavioral and other natural approaches. In other cases, long-term use of medication (particularly the SSRIs), *in conjunction with the full spectrum of cognitive, natural, and lifestyle changes suggested in this book*, may be the most compassionate response you can have to yourself.

There are few set answers when it comes to the subject of medication. Getting all the information you can, working with a competent physician whom you can trust, and then listening to your own intuition is the best you can do.

The Use of Natural Supplements

Since this chapter is about prescription medications, I have not included information here on natural substances that can be useful in the treatment of anxiety problems. There are two classes of such substances. *Natural tranquilizers* include herbs such as kava, valerian, passion-flower, and chamomile, as well as the amino acid GABA. *Natural antidepressants*, which can have an anxiety-reducing effect as well, include the herb Saint-John's-wort, S-adenosyl-methionine (abbreviated as SAM-e), and the amino acids tryptophan, tyrosine, and DL-phenylalanine (abbreviated as DLPA). You may find any of these supplements at your local health food store or drugstore. Any one or a combination of them may be quite helpful as an alternative to prescription drugs in treating your problem with anxiety or depression. The key consideration in deciding to try natural supplements is whether you consider your anxiety problem to be in the *mild to moderate* range of severity. *If anxiety is more of a nuisance—a discomfort or inconvenience in your life—*and not a debilitating or highly distressing condition, I suggest you consider natural supplements first before consulting with a psychiatrist about prescription drugs. If you are already taking an SSRI antidepressant or BZ tranquilizer, do not try natural supplements without first consulting with a doctor well versed in combining prescription medications with supplements.

Full descriptions of all of the natural supplements used to treat anxiety and depression may be found in the section "Supplements for Anxiety" in chapter 15.

Summary of Things to Do

1. Review this chapter to provide yourself with an overview of the various types of medications used to treat anxiety disorders. Be familiar with the benefits and limitations of those medications that may have relevance for your particular issue.

2. If you are not currently taking medication but wonder if you could benefit from doing so, contact a psychiatrist who is knowledgeable about anxiety disorders to discuss your options. A *National Professional Membership Directory*, published by the Anxiety Disorders Association of America, lists psychiatrists who specialize in anxiety disorders, as well as other professionals who would know of such psychiatrists (see appendix 1).

3. If you are currently taking a medication and would like to stop, consult your prescribing physician to discuss the appropriateness of doing so. If you and your physician jointly decide that you are ready to discontinue the medication, follow the guidelines in the section "Discontinuing Medication." Remember, it's preferable to stop medication only after you've gained some mastery of the skills discussed in chapters 4 through 15 of this book. If you wish to withdraw from a benzodiazepine medication that you have been taking for more than three months, prepare to take some time tapering off the dose gradually, possibly over a period of several months. Consult the book by C. Heather Ashton listed below.

4. If you feel your problem with anxiety is relatively mild (if it's more of an inconvenience or nuisance than a debilitating or highly distressing condition), consider trying natural supplements, as described in chapter 15, before resorting to drugs. You may also want to take a look at the books *Healing Anxiety Naturally* by Harold Bloomfield or *Natural Alternatives to Prozac* by Michael Murray.

Further Reading

Ashton, C. Heather. *Benzodiazepines: How They Work and How to Withdraw*. Boston: Benzodiazepine Awareness Network, 2002. (Call 1-603-679-9595 or download from benzo.org.uk.)

Bloomfield, Harold. *Healing Anxiety Naturally*. New York: HarperPerennial, 1999.

Murray, Michael T. *Natural Alternatives to Prozac*. New York: Quill/William Morrow, 1999.

Norden, Michael. *Beyond Prozac*. Revised and updated edition. New York: HarperPerennial, 1996.

Preston, John, John H. O'Neal, and Mary C. Talaga. *Handbook of Clinical Psychopharmacology for Therapists*. Sixth edition. Oakland, CA: New Harbinger Publications, 2010.

Schwartz, Jeffrey. *Brain Lock: Free Yourself from Obsessive-Compulsive Behavior*. New York: ReganBooks/HarperPerennial, 1997.

18

Meditation

Meditation has been practiced for over three thousand years for the purpose of training and calming the mind. As you may know, it originated as a spiritual practice within Hinduism and Buddhism, though it was later practiced in various forms in many other religions. Eastern philosophy has taught that the origin of human suffering is in our automatic, conditioned thoughts (the term "automatic thoughts" in cognitive therapy is similar to this notion). Nothing in life is inherently bad except that we think about it or react to it as such. The purpose of meditation practice is to learn to step back and simply witness your automatic thoughts and reactive patterns without judgment. If you are caught up in your mind's automatic patterns, regular meditation practice can help you to become gradually freer of them. Acceptance and commitment therapy, described in chapter 19, borrows the principle of self-observation from meditation; it refers to the process of observing and disentangling from one's thoughts as "defusion." However, the process itself—learning to become a nonjudgmental witness of your ongoing experience—has been utilized in many cultures throughout the world for millennia. The goal of such practice in its many forms has always been to achieve a state of freedom or "liberation" from the suffering we create in our minds.

How does meditation help to achieve this freedom? In a word, you can say that it is by the enlargement or "expansion" of awareness. Awareness can be defined as a pure, unconditioned state of consciousness that you can experience deep within yourself. It exists "beneath" or prior to the conditioned patterns of thinking and emotional reactivity you've learned over a lifetime. This unconditioned awareness is always available to you, but most of the time it's clouded over by the incessant stream of mental chatter and emotional reactions that make up your ordinary, moment-to-moment experience. Only when you become very quiet and still, willing to "just be," observing your inner experience in the present moment and without judgment, and without striving to do anything, can this uncluttered awareness that underlies your thoughts and feelings begin to reemerge.

When you experience this unconditioned state of awareness, you simply feel a deep sense of peace. Out of this place of inner peace can arise other unconditioned states such as unconditional love, wisdom, deep insight, and joy. In itself, this state of inner peace is nothing you need to develop. You were born with it. It's always there, deep inside of you. You can discover it if you simply become still and quiet long enough to allow it to emerge. The practice of meditation is one of the most direct, straightforward ways to do this.

Meditation practice allows you to expand your awareness to the point where it's larger—or more "spacious"—than your fearful thoughts or emotional reactions. As soon as your awareness is larger than your fear, you are no longer claimed by the fear but can stand outside of it (in your mind) and merely witness it. It's as though you're identified with a part of your inner being that's larger than the part that's constricted by fearful thoughts. As you continue to practice meditation and enlarge your awareness, it becomes easier on an ongoing basis to observe the stream of thoughts and feelings that make up your experience. You are less prone to get "stuck" or lost in them.

You might be concerned that increasing your ability to observe your inner thoughts and feelings sounds like becoming internally divided rather than more connected with yourself. In fact, the opposite is true. It's your reactive thoughts and conditioned emotional patterns that tend to pull you away from your own center—to lead you away from your deeper inner self and into what has been popularly termed "mind trips" or "personal dramas." To practice meditation is to cultivate greater self-integration and wholeness. As you deepen and enlarge your awareness, you begin to be in touch with more of yourself. Your reactive thoughts and feelings still occur, but you're not so strongly swept up by them. You're more free to truly enjoy your life because you don't get quite as stuck—or stuck as long—in any particular state of anxiety, worry, anger, guilt, shame, grief, and so on. Rather, you're able to simply acknowledge your reaction, allow it to move through your experience, and let it go. Your inner consciousness becomes spacious enough so that you can observe a worried thought, then take action if it's reasonable to act or choose to let the thought go if it's unreasonable. You begin to have more choice over what you think and experience. You are not quite so scattered by your mind's endless cascade of reactive thoughts and feelings. While these thoughts and feelings still occur, your relationship to them is different. Your inner awareness becomes spacious enough so that you can more easily step back and accept your thoughts and feelings rather than be carried away by them.

Benefits of Meditation

Meditation was first popularized in the United States in the mid-1960s in the form of Transcendental Meditation or TM. In Transcendental Meditation, an instructor selects a Sanskrit mantra (a word or sound) for you, such as "Om Shanti" or "So-Hum." You are then instructed to repeat the sound mentally while sitting upright in a quiet place. You must concentrate completely—but unforcefully—on the mantra while letting any distractions just pass through your mind.

In the 1970s, Herbert Benson did research on Transcendental Meditation, which he published in his well-known book *The Relaxation Response*. Benson developed his own version of meditation, which involved mentally repeating the word "one" on each exhalation of the breath. He documented a number of physiological effects of meditation, including

- A decrease in heart rate

- A decrease in blood pressure

- A decrease in oxygen consumption

- A decrease in metabolic rate

- A decrease in the concentration of lactic acid in the blood (associated with anxiety reduction)

- An increase in forearm blood flow and hand temperature

- An increase in electrical resistance of the skin (associated with deep relaxation)

- An increase in alpha brain wave activity (also associated with relaxation)

Benson established that the positive benefits of meditation are not exclusive to TM, and that an individually selected mantra is unnecessary. His own "respiratory-one" method achieved the same physiological effects as Transcendental Meditation. He referred to the deep state of physiological relaxation induced by meditation as the "relaxation response."

Since the time of Benson's work, considerable research on the long-term benefits of meditation has established that it can alter personality traits, behaviors, and attitudes. If you suffer from an anxiety disorder, meditation can break up obsessional mental patterns and help you restructure your thoughts more productively. (Regular meditation has an even greater impact on repetitive mental patterns than the practice of progressive muscle relaxation, which is directed more to relieving muscle tension.)

Meditation has repeatedly been found to reduce chronic anxiety and worry. Often the dosage of tranquilizers or other medications can be reduced if you are meditating daily. Other long-range benefits include

- Sharpened alertness

- Increased energy level and productivity

- Decreased self-criticism

- Increased objectivity (the capacity to view situations nonjudgmentally)

- Decreased dependence on alcohol, recreational drugs, and prescription drugs

- Increased accessibility of emotions

- Heightened self-esteem and sense of identity

In the 1980s and 1990s, Jon Kabat-Zinn did extensive research on meditation as a method of stress management. Utilizing an approach to meditation he referred to as "mindfulness," Kabat-Zinn developed a comprehensive program for stress management known as "mindfulness-based stress reduction" (MBSR), which has been taught at universities and clinics throughout the United States. (The term "mindfulness" refers to the basic stance of all forms of meditation: silently witnessing the ongoing stream of your inner experience with complete acceptance and without judgment. Some people prefer this term because it is a purely psychological concept without the "Eastern" overtones of the word "meditation.") Two of Kabat-Zinn's books, *Full Catastrophe Living* and *Wherever You Go, There You Are*, have been widely influential in bringing meditation or mindfulness practice into mainstream society.

More recently meditation practice has been shown to prevent relapse among people who have had three or more episodes of major depression (Segal, Williams, and Teasdale 2002). It is one of the few interventions, apart from medication, that have been empirically demonstrated to help prevent recurrence of depression. At present, meditation and mindfulness practice are being used by many physicians and psychotherapists as an adjunct to treatment of a wide variety of physical and psychological problems. In short, meditation/mindfulness practice is a powerful psychological technique for calming the mind. Although it has origins in spiritual traditions, you do not have to adopt any particular spiritual perspective in order to practice and benefit from meditation.

Types of Meditation

There are two broad types of meditation: concentrative and nonconcentrative. Sometimes these are referred to as structured and unstructured meditation. The concentrative approach emphasizes concentrating your attention during meditation by maintaining a specific focus on a particular object. Every time your mind starts to wander during a meditation session, you bring your attention back to a particular object of focus. For example, you might focus on a particular word which you repeat over and over, such as "one," "now," or "relax." Another popular and widely practiced form of concentrative meditation involves focusing on the sensation of the breath. As you meditate, you simply keep bringing your attention back to the cycle of your breath, experiencing the rising and falling of your breath, preferably from your abdomen.

The nonconcentrative, unstructured approach to meditation does not narrow attention to a particular object. Instead the total content of experience—whatever comes up in awareness—becomes the object of focus. You simply witness whatever thoughts, feelings, desires, or physical sensations arise in your experience without resisting them or judging them in any way. You carefully pay attention in a way so that you are aware of the present moment, and all that is contained in your present experience, without any judgment.

The term "mindfulness" is sometimes used to refer to the nonconcentrative type of meditation, since mindfulness means to pay attention on purpose to whatever arises in the present moment, without judgment (Kabat-Zinn 2005). For the purpose of this chapter, mindfulness is understood more as an attitude, stance, or approach you can take in any form of meditation, whether concentrative or nonconcentrative. For example, you can maintain a mindful stance toward the thoughts, feelings, and sensations that arise in your experience while focusing on your breath or on a specific word. Mindfulness is a nonjudgmental, accepting stance you can assume in any type of meditation, and in fact at any time in your ongoing experience outside of meditation. Meditation is a deliberate process that you set aside a specific time for. Mindfulness is a stance, approach, or attitude you can take in meditation practice as well as toward all of your waking experience.

Learning to Meditate

Learning to meditate is a process that involves at least three distinct stages:

- Right attitude

- Right technique

- Cultivating mindfulness

Right attitude is a mind-set or mental stance that you bring to meditation. Such an attitude takes time and commitment to develop. Fortunately, the practice of meditation itself helps you to learn right attitude. Right technique involves learning specific methods of sitting and focusing your awareness that facilitate meditation. Cultivating mindfulness is the process of making a fundamental shift in your relationship with your own inner experience. It is to develop a nonjudgmental "inner observer" within yourself that enables you to simply witness rather than react to the ups and downs of everyday existence.

Right Attitude

The attitude that you bring to the practice of meditation is critical. In fact, cultivating right attitude is a part of the practice. Your success and ability to persevere with meditation practice will in large part be determined by the way you approach it. The following eight aspects of right attitude are based on the writings of a prominent educator in the field of meditation, Jon Kabat-Zinn. His books *Full Catastrophe Living* and *Wherever You Go, There You Are* are highly recommended if you're serious about undertaking a regular meditation practice.

Beginner's Mind

To observe your immediate, ongoing experience without any judgments, preconceptions, or projections is often referred to as "beginner's mind." In essence, with beginner's mind you perceive something with the freshness you would bring to it if you were seeing it for the very first time. It's seeing—and accepting—things as they actually are in the present moment, without the veil of your own assumptions or judgments about them. For example, next time you're in the presence of someone familiar, consider seeing them as much as possible as they actually are, apart from your feelings, thoughts, projections, or judgments. How would you see them if you were meeting them for the first time?

Nonstriving

Almost everything you do during your day is likely to be goal-directed. Meditation is one thing that is not. Although meditation takes effort to practice, it has no aim other than to "just be." When you sit down to meditate, it's best to clear your mind of any goals. You are not trying to relax, blank your mind, relieve stress, or reach enlightenment. You don't need to evaluate the quality of your meditation according to whether you reach such goals. The only intention you bring to meditation is simply to be—to observe your "here and now" experience just as it is, perhaps using the repetition of a mantra or observing your breath to assist your focus. If you are tense, anxious, or in pain, you don't strive to get rid of these sensations; instead you simply observe them and be with them as best you can. You let them remain simply as they are. In so doing, you cease resisting or struggling with them.

Acceptance

Acceptance is the opposite of striving. As you learn to simply be with whatever you experience in the moment, you cultivate acceptance. Acceptance does not mean that you have to like whatever comes up (such as tension or pain, for example); it simply means you're willing to be with it without trying to push it away. You may be familiar with the saying, "What you resist persists." As long as you resist or struggle with something, whether in meditation or life in general, you actually energize and magnify it. Acceptance allows the discomfort or problem to just be. While it may not go away, it becomes easier to deal with because you cease to struggle with and/or avoid it.

In meditation practice, acceptance develops as you learn to embrace each moment as it comes, without moving away from it. As you learn to do this, you discover that whatever was there for a given moment will soon change—more quickly, in fact, than if you tried to resist it.

In life, acceptance does not mean that you resign yourself to the way things are and cease trying to change and grow. On the contrary, acceptance can clear a space in your life for you to reflect clearly and act appropriately. Energy is freed up to act when you are no longer reacting to or struggling with the difficulty. Sometimes, of course, it's necessary to go through a range of emotional reactions around a problem first before you can get to acceptance.

Nonjudgment

An important prerequisite for acceptance is nonjudgment. When you pay attention to your ongoing experience through the day, you'll notice that you frequently judge things—both outer circumstances as well as inner circumstances (your own moods and feelings). These judgments are based on your personal values and standards of what is "good" and "bad." If you doubt this, try taking just five minutes to notice how many things you judge during that short time interval. To practice meditation, it's important to learn not so much to stop judging but to gain some distance from the process. You can simply observe your inner judgments without reacting to them, least of all judging them! Instead you cultivate a suspension of any judgment, watching whatever comes up, including your own judging thoughts. You allow such thoughts to come and go, while continuing to observe your breathing or whatever other object you have selected as a focus for meditation.

Patience

Patience is a close cousin to acceptance and nonstriving. It means allowing things to unfold in their own natural time. It is letting your meditation practice be whatever it is without rushing it.

Patience is needed to make time to meditate for a half hour to an hour every day. Patience is also required to persist with your meditation practice through the days or weeks when nothing particularly interesting happens. To be patient is to stop hurrying. This often means going against the grain of a fast-paced society where rushing from one destination to another is the norm.

The patience you can bring to your meditation practice will help assure its success and permanence. Sitting in meditation regularly will help you develop patience, as it will help you cultivate all of the characteristics described in this section. The attitudes that help you develop your meditation practice are the very same attitudes that are deepened by the practice itself.

Letting Go

Our minds are often like the monkey. We grab on to a particular thought or emotional state—sometimes one that is actually painful—and then we don't let go. Cultivating the ability to let go is crucial to meditation practice, not to mention a less anxious life. When you hold on to any experience, whether pleasant or painful, you impede your ability to simply be present in the here and now without judgment or striving. Learning to let go of things is assisted by learning to accept them. Letting go is a natural consequence of a willingness to accept things as they are. If you find that, prior to meditation, you have a hard time letting go of some concern, you can actually use your meditation as a means to witness the thoughts and feelings you're creating around the concern—including the process of "holding on" itself. The more minutely you observe the specific thoughts and feelings you have created around a problem, the more quickly you'll be able to expand your awareness around that problem and let it go. When the concern is intensely charged emotionally, it's probably best to release your feelings by talking or writing in a journal about them before you sit down to meditate. Cultivating all of the attitudes described in this section will help with letting go.

Commitment and Self-Discipline

A strong commitment to work on yourself, along with the discipline to persevere and follow through with the process, is essential to establishing a meditation practice. While meditation is very simple in nature, it's not always easy in practice. Learning to value and make time for "just being" on a regular basis requires a commitment in the midst of a society that is strongly oriented toward doing. Few of us have grown up with values that cherished nonstriving, and so learning to stop goal-directed activity, even for just thirty minutes per day, requires commitment and discipline. The commitment is similar to that which is required in athletic training. An athlete in training doesn't practice only when he or she just feels like it, when there is time enough to fit it in or other people to keep her company. The training requires the athlete to practice every day, regardless of how she feels or whether there is any immediate sense of accomplishment.

To establish a meditation practice, it's best to sit whether you feel like it or not—whether it's convenient or not—six or seven days per week, for at least two months. (If you find you're unable to sit that often at first, don't chastise yourself—just do your best.) You will likely find it easier if you set aside a particular time of day to do your practice, such as first thing in the morning or before dinner in the evening. At the end of two months, if you've practiced regularly, the process will likely have become enough of a habit (and sufficiently self-reinforcing) to continue. The experience of meditation varies from session to session: sometimes it feels good, sometimes it seems ordinary, and other times you will find it difficult to meditate at all.

Although the point is not to strive for anything, a long-term commitment to regular meditation practice will transform your life fundamentally. Without changing anything that might happen in your life, meditation will change your relationship to everything you experience, on a deep level.

Right Technique: Guidelines for Practicing Meditation

There is a technique to proper meditation. Probably the most important aspect is to sit in the right fashion, which means sitting upright with your back straight either on the floor in a cross-legged position or in a chair with your feet flat on the floor. There seems to be a certain energetic alignment within the body that occurs from sitting up straight. It's not as likely to happen when you're lying down, although lying down is fine for other forms of relaxation (and for the body scan exercise described later in the chapter). It's also helpful to relax tight muscles before you meditate. One way to do this is through practicing yoga. In historic times, the main purpose of yoga postures was to relax and energetically balance the body prior to meditating. The guidelines that follow are intended to help make your meditation practice easier and more effective.

- Find a quiet environment. Do what you can do to reduce external noises and distractions. If this is not completely possible, play a recording of soft, instrumental sounds or sounds from nature. The sound of ocean waves also makes a good background.

- Reduce muscle tension. If you're feeling tense, take some time (no more than ten minutes) to relax your muscles. Yoga postures, if you're familiar with them, are an excellent way to unwind. Progressive muscle relaxation of the upper portion of the body—your head, neck, and shoulders—is often helpful (see chapter 4). If you feel too much energy or your mind is racing, doing some physical exercise first can make it easier to meditate afterward.

- Sit properly. Eastern style: Sit cross-legged on the floor with a cushion or pillow supporting your buttocks. Rest your hands on your thighs. Lean slightly forward so that some of your weight is supported by your thighs as well as your buttocks. Western style (preferred by most Americans): Sit in a comfortable, straight-backed chair, with your feet on the floor and legs uncrossed, hands on your thighs (palms down or up, whichever you prefer).

   In either position, keep your back and neck straight without straining to do so. Do not assume a tight, inflexible posture. If you need to scratch or move, do so. In general, do not lie down or support your head; this will tend to promote sleep.

- Set aside twenty to thirty minutes for meditation (beginners might wish to start out with ten minutes). You may wish to set a timer (within reach) or run a background recording that is twenty to thirty minutes long so that you'll know when you're done. If having a clock or watch available to look at makes you more comfortable, that's okay. After you have practiced twenty to thirty minutes per day for several weeks, you may wish to try longer periods of meditation up to an hour.

- Make it a regular practice to meditate every day. Even if you meditate for only five minutes, it's important to do it every day. It's ideal if you can find a set time to practice meditating. Twice a day is optimal; once per day is a minimum.

- Don't meditate on a full stomach. Meditation is easier if you don't practice on a full stomach or when you're tired. If you are unable to meditate prior to a meal, wait at least a half hour after eating to do so.

- Select a focus for your attention. The most common devices are your own breathing cycle or a mantra. The structured meditation exercises below use both of these techniques. Other common objects of meditation include pictures, repetitive music or chants, or a sacred object.

- During meditation, it can be helpful to close your eyes in order to reduce outside distractions. Some people, however, find they prefer to keep their eyes slightly open— just enough to see external objects indistinctly. This can reduce the tendency to be distracted by inner thoughts, feelings, and daydreams. Try this if you are having difficulty with distractibility.

- During meditation, you will find you are often distracted by extraneous thoughts, feelings, and bodily sensations. When this happens, don't judge yourself. Just gently bring your attention back to whatever you have selected as your focus. If an unpleasant thought or feeling tries to capture your attention, try reminding yourself "This is just a thought" or "This is just a feeling." Just be present with the thought or feeling without going into it. Eventually, it will shift and pass. Good questions to ask to yourself occasionally are "Can I just be the space for whatever comes up?" and "Can I just be fully present with this?"

- Distraction, boredom, restlessness, sleepiness, and impatience are common reactions during meditation. When these states come up, just notice them, allow them to be as they are, and then return to being fully present in the moment.

- When you've finished with your practice for the day, open your eyes gently (if they've been closed) and stretch your body. Notice how you are feeling, but whether the feeling is positive or negative, don't judge it. If you feel good after your practice, refrain from setting any expectation that your next practice should be the same way. Let each practice session be a unique experience unto itself.

Ultimately, meditation practice has no goal other than just to be—to be fully aware in the present moment. However, an important benefit of regular meditation is the cultivation of mindfulness: the capacity to stand back and observe the ongoing stream of your experience without getting caught up in it.

You are unlikely to be aware of just how distractible your mind is until you first sit down to meditate. Using structured meditation techniques will build your capacity to concentrate in the beginning. Later you may want to drop these forms and focus more directly on simply observing the ongoing stream of your experience.

Cultivating Mindfulness: Meditation Exercises

Mindfulness is paying attention without judgment to whatever comes up in the present moment of your experience. It is witnessing your immediate experience just as it is, without trying to change, react to, or interfere with it. A good way to appreciate mindfulness is to realize that it encompasses all of the attitudes described in the section on right attitude: nonstriving, acceptance, nonjudgment, beginner's mind, patience, letting go, commitment, and self-discipline. Mindfulness is not something that you have to strive hard to attain. If you strive for it, it will tend to elude your grasp. By relaxing, letting go and simply observing the ongoing stream of your experience without judgment, you will begin to experience what mindfulness actually is. Words cannot teach the meaning of mindfulness nearly so well as direct experience.

Ultimately, mindfulness can change the way you deal with fear and pain in a profound way. As your practice strengthens, you can learn to relax and stay present even when fear and pain move through the present moment.

The following meditation exercises were inspired by Jon Kabat-Zinn, Jack Kornfield, and other teachers of meditation. They derive from basic practices that have been used by students of meditation for many centuries. The exercises described here emphasize maintaining a focus on your breathing cycle—continually bringing your attention back to your breath each time you become distracted. It is probably best to do the exercises in sequence. Once you've gained some experience with meditation, you can incorporate aspects of both of the exercises into your daily practice.

Basic Meditation Exercise

The basic instruction for this exercise is simple—to gently pay attention to your breath cycle. You simply observe your breath as it flows in and out. You give your full attention to the feeling of your breath as it comes in and your full attention to the feeling of your breath as it goes out. See if you can feel your breath from your abdomen or your chest. You don't try to deepen your breath or do anything with it (unless you are using a breath-counting technique initially to help you focus). The idea is simply to observe the process of your breathing without force or effort, experiencing all the sensations, gross and subtle, associated with it.

Staying with your own breathing cycle is simple, although it's not always easy. After two or three minutes, you're likely to find that your mind gets bored and wants to go on to do something else. Or your body will have had enough and want to shift your position or get up and do something. It's just at this point that the "work" of meditation begins. Instead of giving in to the impulse to do something else, you simply observe the impulse itself and then gently bring your attention back to your breathing, observing your breath from moment to moment.

The tendency to become distracted and stop observing your breath is inevitable. In five minutes, it may happen ten or perhaps fifty times. It's very important not to judge yourself when you get distracted. Simply notice that you did and then gently bring your attention back to your breathing. If you don't like the fact that you're so distractible, simply notice your not liking it and then bring your focus back to your breath. If you're really enjoying how you feel, simply observe that and return to your inhalation and exhalation. Be aware that there is no such thing as a "good" meditation session or a "bad" one. Often you will notice that you feel "good" or "bad" about how a particular session went. Yet keep in mind that the whole point of meditation is to simply witness your experience in the present moment without striving to achieve anything or evaluating how well the experience went.

Here are the steps of the exercise:

1. Sit in a comfortable, upright position with your feet flat on the floor. Focus on your breathing as you breathe slowly from your abdomen. (If you can't feel your breath from your abdomen, try feeling it from your chest.) As you focus on your abdomen, let it relax and become soft. Let the sensations of inhaling and exhaling be the object of your focus. (This process is quite similar to the *Abdominal Breathing Exercise* in chapter 4.) Allow yourself twenty to thirty minutes for this exercise in a place where you are free of distractions and interruptions.

2. Keep in mind the basic attitudes that form the foundation of meditation: acceptance, nonstriving, nonjudgment, patience, trust, letting go, and so on. Let go of any expectations about how your practice will go. If you're feeling anxious, let go of any goal of trying to make your anxiety go away.

3. You may want to close your eyes, or you may prefer to leave them slightly open. If you find that closing your eyes causes you to feel sleepy, it may help to keep them open and focused on a particular spot in the room.

4. Focus on the place in your body where you can feel your breath come and go. This might be your abdomen or your chest. Just be with the place in your body where you are most comfortable paying attention to your breath. If you're not sure about this, your abdomen is a good place to start.

5. Just allow your breath to come and go without trying to control it. When your mind starts to wander away from the focus on your breath (which it will), let it do so without judging it. Then gently bring your attention back to your breath. Do this as many times as you need to during the course of your meditation. Recognizing when your mind wanders and then bringing your attention back to your breath is what normally goes on in meditation practice. You can expect it to happen many times.

6. If a fearful thought comes up and tries to capture your attention, it may help to remind yourself "this is just a thought" or "I am not my thoughts." Just breathe with the fearful thought or feeling without going into it. Eventually, it will shift and pass. With practice, it will get easier to let go of distracting thoughts, even fearful ones.

7.   Distraction, boredom, restlessness, sleepiness, and impatience are common reactions during meditation. When they come up, just notice them, try to let them be, and return your attention to your breath.

8.   Begin practicing this exercise for ten minutes and gradually work up to thirty minutes. It may take you a few weeks to become comfortable with a thirty-minute session, but that is a good time period to maintain for your practice over the long term. You may find it useful to set a timer or play a thirty-minute recording of meditative music so that you'll know when you're done. Some people prefer forty-five minutes or even an hour for their daily meditation practice. Experiment with what time period feels best for you; at least thirty minutes at least once every day is highly recommended.

9.   When you've finished with your practice for the day, open your eyes gently (if they've been closed) and stretch your body. Notice how you are feeling, but don't judge that feeling, whether it's positive or negative. If you feel good after your practice, refrain from setting any expectation that your next practice "should" be the same way. Expect that you will enjoy some practice sessions more than others. Let each practice session be a unique experience unto itself.

The Body Scan: Sensing Your Body During Meditation

The body scan is another very useful exercise in developing mindful awareness.

By bringing your attention slowly and deliberately to each part of your body, you are able to deeply reconnect with your body and foster increased mind–body integration. Many of us have an ambivalent relationship with our bodies, viewing them as an object and judging them as too big, the wrong size, or out of shape. We also tend to store negative feelings in our bodies, in the form of muscle tension, poor posture, or feelings of heaviness. The body scan exercise promotes making friends with your body, allowing feelings suppressed or held in your body to come to the surface where they can be released.

The body scan is best done by lying down or sitting back in an easy chair or recliner with your head supported. Start first by focusing on breathing from your abdomen for a minute or so, making sure you are in a comfortable position. Then begin the exercise by focusing on the toes of your left foot. Notice whatever sensations you're aware of in your left toes. Then, take a breath in and imagine breathing those sensations out through your left toes. Simply visualize your left toes and imagine breathing down through your left leg and foot and out through your left toes. While this may seem odd at first, it becomes easier with practice. Once you've experienced several exhalations through your left toes, continue the body-scan process with your left foot. Again, notice the sensations or tension you experience in your left foot for a few moments, then breathe those sensations or tension out through your left foot several times. Once you've completed the process with your left foot, continue on with each part of your body. A suggested order for proceeding through your body is provided below. Keep in mind that with each part, you want to focus on whatever sensations, tensions, or feelings you notice, and then breathe those sensations out of your body.

1. Left toes	12. Left hand
2. Left foot	13. Left forearm
3. Left calf	14. Left upper arm
4. Left thigh	15. Left shoulder
	16. Right hand
5. Right toes	17. Right forearm
6. Right foot	18 Right upper arm
7. Right calf	19. Right shoulder
8. Right thigh	20. Neck
9. Pelvic area	21. Mouth and jaw
10. Lower abdomen	22. Eyes and forehead
11. Chest	23. Top of head

When you get to the top of your head, imagine breathing in and out through the top of your head. Some people find it helpful to use a recording of instructions for the body scan. Jon Kabat-Zinn offers an excellent series of recordings on mindfulness meditation, which includes the body scan. (See "Further Reading and Resources" at the end of this chapter.)

As you do these exercises, experience whatever you're experiencing in the present moment. The more you can let go and fully accept anxiety or worry being there, the more space you are going to be able to create around it.

Maintaining a Meditation Practice

The motivation, commitment, and self-discipline necessary to establish a meditation practice was mentioned already in the section on right attitude. Learning to meditate can be compared with learning a sport like baseball, racquetball, or golf. A significant amount of time in training is necessary before you become proficient. This involves a commitment to keep sitting on those days when you don't feel like it or find it inconvenient to do. Setting aside a regular time to practice for thirty minutes to one hour each day makes this easier. The best times are generally first thing in the morning upon awakening or in the evening before you go to bed, provided you are not too tired. Other good times would be before lunch or dinner, or on a break at work. By setting aside a regular time, you build in a place for meditation in your life.

Besides your own personal commitment and self-discipline, there are several things that can greatly support your practice. Probably most supportive is to find a local class or group that meditates regularly. You may find such a class at a local hospital or college (adult education program) in your area. Or there may be a free-standing meditation group within driving distance. Programs in Transcendental Meditation, or TM (a specific form of mantra meditation that has been around for many years), are offered in many areas. Having the support of a group with whom you meditate regularly will help motivate you at those times when it seems hard to keep up with your daily practice.

In some areas, you may be fortunate to be close to a teacher thoroughly grounded and skilled in the practice of meditation. If you are interested in finding a group or teacher in your area, you can contact the Insight Meditation Society or Spirit Rock Meditation Center, listed in the resources at the end of this chapter.

The Insight Meditation Society offers meditation retreats in various places throughout the United States. A meditation retreat generally involves being in meditation for eight to twelve hours per day (with hourly breaks), alternating between sitting and walking forms of meditation. Retreats can go from one to ten consecutive days, although a few go even longer. Doing a retreat is a powerful way to deepen your ongoing meditation practice. It is generally not recommended for beginners.

Finally, there are a number of excellent books and tapes that can support your practice. Jeffrey Brantley's book *Calming Your Anxious Mind* (see "Further Reading and Resources" at the end of this chapter) explores specifically how meditation practice can be helpful in dealing with anxiety, fear, and worry.

Common Concerns That May Come Up

As you undertake to meditate regularly, you may have many questions and concerns. The following is based on a list compiled by Jeffrey Brantley in *Calming Your Anxious Mind*.

- *I don't have time to meditate.*
  Usually when you say you don't have time for something, it means that it doesn't have enough priority for you to give it time. It's likely that meditation and mindfulness, practiced regularly, will gradually transform your life and your ability to handle your anxiety. The question you have to answer is how much of a priority are you willing to give to meditation. How committed are you to giving it a regular place in your life?

- *Meditation is too boring.*
  Sometimes meditation can be boring. This is to be expected. The question in this case is whether you have unreasonable expectations about what meditation ought to be. If you are being mindful, the solution to boredom is to carefully witness your state of boredom when it comes up. By carefully investigating it, you may learn some things about the boredom. For example, boredom usually contains specific negative self-talk and judgments. By carefully investigating your thoughts and reactions around your state of boredom to see what's there—instead of just reacting—you may find yourself less bored.

- *When I sit still and meditate, it makes me more anxious.*
  Does meditation really make you more anxious? Or is it possible that by stopping and sitting still, you begin to become more aware of anxiety that was already present? When you're not distracted, any anxiety that was covered up by distraction is likely to come forward. Now you have the opportunity to work with your anxiety instead

of running from it or trying to avoid it. By accepting your anxiety—and making it the object of your attention and awareness—you have the opportunity to change the way you relate to it. You have the opportunity to just be with it until it shifts. You can allow your mind to become spacious enough to contain it, rather than to react to it.

One of the most important ways in which meditation practice can help you to better deal with anxiety is by training you simply to accept anxiety states instead of trying to run from them. The more you learn to accept and work with your anxiety as it arises, the less it becomes an "enemy" that you're trying to combat. Ultimately, the less you struggle against anxiety, the easier it will be to deal with. So if you feel more anxious during meditation, just breathe with it and allow it to be. You will learn a whole new way to deal with anxiety and worry by doing so.

- *I'm too anxious and agitated to meditate.*
  What if mindfulness practice does not seem to help you quiet down? What if you continue to feel highly agitated and distracted after ten or more minutes of meditation? If this happens, your body may indeed be too charged up to sit still. The best thing to do is to get physical. Try doing some form of aerobic exercise (see chapter 5) or take twenty minutes to do a sequence of yoga postures. After you've discharged the energy from your body, try sitting in meditation again.

- *I just don't have the discipline to meditate regularly.*
  While the goal is to meditate seven days per week, you may find yourself unable to do this at first. Don't try to be perfect, just do the best you can. As you continue to practice, you'll begin to experience some of the benefits of meditation and perhaps find yourself motivated to keep it up every day. It's true that meditation practice takes discipline, just like learning to play the piano or mastering a sport. You need to make a commitment to yourself to practice regularly in order to keep meditating over the long term. However, don't chastise yourself if you can't do it every day at first. Do the best you can. Read books, listen to recordings, or, best of all, find a local group that sits regularly. All of these things will help you sustain your motivation to practice regularly.

Meditation and Compassion

An important aspect of developing a capacity to observe your mind is to bring compassion into your observation. It may not be enough to learn merely to observe your reactive thoughts and feelings. Without cultivating compassion toward your reactivity, you may remain at war with it. To bring compassion and heart into your self-observation is to begin to make peace with yourself.

Many people, especially if they are perfectionistic, treat themselves as though they were a harsh drill sergeant disciplining a new recruit. If this seems hard to imagine, watch yourself to see how much time you spend criticizing yourself, putting yourself down, or pushing and driving yourself to do what you don't really want to do. When you're not pushing or criticizing yourself, you may fall into a more passive stance of fear—or of being a victim. Out of fear, your mind constantly scares you with "What if this ..." or "What if that ..." When you fall into a victim stance, you may depress yourself with "It's no use ..." "It's hopeless ..." "It's a lost cause ..." As soon as you start to feel less depressed, your perfectionism may keep you on a treadmill with "I should ..." "I must ..." "I have to ..." Notice how much you criticize, scare, depress, or push yourself, and you'll learn quite a bit about your own mind. Unfortunately, all of the cognitive therapy in the world is not going to help if you are still basically at war with yourself.

Cultivating compassion in self-observation is fundamental to changing your relationship with yourself. Compassion allows you to move away from judgment, criticism, and even contempt and toward tolerance, acceptance, and love. Compassion depends on accepting yourself—and the rest of the world—as it is, an attitude that can be cultivated through meditation practice. Living with your limitations and embracing your humanness is something you can learn. For a more in-depth statement about the role of compassion in meditation, see Jack Kornfield's book *A Path with Heart*.

Meditation and Medication

Few, if any, books on meditation address the question of how prescription medications affect the experience of meditation. Some formal meditation training programs, such as Transcendental Meditation, request that beginners get off all nonessential prescription drugs before learning to meditate. My own observation, based on personal experience as well as the experience of clients, is that different medications affect people in different ways.

Two generalizations, however, might be made:

1. Benzodiazepine medications such as Xanax, Ativan, or Klonopin seem to increase distractibility, making it more difficult to focus during meditation. It has been found that the benzodiazepines tend to increase beta wave activity in the brain (rapid, nonsynchronous brain waves associated with thinking) and reduce the ability to enter into alpha brain-wave states (synchronous brain waves associated with relaxed states as well as meditation). While it's certainly not impossible to meditate while taking a benzodiazepine medication, you may find it somewhat more difficult.

2. SSRI antidepressant medications (such as Prozac, Zoloft, Paxil, or Celexa) do not seem to impede meditation for most people. There are a few people who report that meditation is more difficult while taking an SSRI medication. On the other hand, I've also heard reports that some people find it easier to meditate after taking SSRIs because they feel calmer and less subject to intrusive thoughts and feelings. In general, it seems that SSRI medications do not pose a significant impediment to cultivating a meditation practice.

Information is hard to find on the effects of tricyclic antidepressants (such as imipramine or nortriptyline) or other antianxiety medications such as Neurontin, Gabitril, or Buspar on meditation. It's possible to evaluate the effects of such medications if you reduce your dose for a few days while meditating and then resume taking your normal dose. Please consult with your prescribing physician before you try this.

Conclusion

The purpose of this chapter has been to present meditation practice as one additional strategy you can use to help better deal with anxiety, fear, and worry. Though meditation is a powerful coping strategy, it in no way supersedes any of the other methods for dealing with anxiety and fear presented in this book. Abdominal breathing, exercise, working with fearful self-talk, facing fears through exposure, utilizing good nutrition, dealing with conditions that can aggravate anxiety, working on assertiveness and self-esteem, and, finally, relying on medication, if needed, can all be very helpful to your recovery from your anxiety difficulties, just as meditation can be. Ultimately, you will discover for yourself what role meditation plays in your journey to overcome anxiety by making time to practice it every day. You may find it to be a quite powerful tool, if you stick with it over the long run.

Keep in mind that "success" in meditation is just doing it. The more often you do it, the more quickly you will train your mind to be less reactive, more stable, and better able to observe. You will be training it to be able to take each moment as it comes, without valuing any one above any other. Working regularly with the resistance of your mind builds inner strength. Regular meditation practice will foster the development of the very attitudes that help facilitate the practice in the beginning: acceptance, patience, nonjudgment, letting go, and trust.

Summary of Things to Do

1. To begin a meditation practice, follow the guidelines in the section "Right Technique" for the first week or two. You may want to begin with ten-minute meditation periods and gradually increase the duration up to thirty minutes. Make a commitment to yourself to practice every day. It's best to find a specific time of day and a specific place for your practice where you're free of distractions. Review the section on "Right Attitude" to help cultivate the proper approach to take toward your practice.

2. After a week or two—or when you feel you have gained some familiarity and comfort with meditation—try the meditation exercises in the section "Cultivating Mindfulness." Alternatively, you may want to order professionally made recordings for meditation (see below). After you've spent time practicing one of the exercises several times, you will begin to work out your own preferred style of practice.

3. To support your practice, find a class or group that meditates regularly. If this is unavailable, you may want to work with recordings relevant to meditation and read some of the books on meditation listed below, perhaps starting with those by Brantley, Kabat-Zinn, Kornfield, and Goldstein.

Further Reading and Resources

Books

Brantley, Jeffrey. *Calming Your Anxious Mind*. Second edition. Oakland, CA: New Harbinger Publications, 2007. (Directly examines how meditation practice can help deal with anxiety and worry.)

Goldstein, Joseph. *Insight Meditation*. Boston: Shambhala, 1993.

Harp, David, and Nina Smiley. *The Three-Minute Meditator*. Fifth edition. Oakland, CA: New Harbinger Publications, 2007.

Kabat-Zinn, Jon. *Full Catastrophe Living*. New York: Delta, 2005.

Kabat-Zinn, Jon. *Wherever You Go, There You Are*. Tenth anniversary edition. New York: Hyperion, 2005. (Kabat-Zinn's books provide a good introduction to meditation and mindfulness practice.)

Kornfield, Jack. *A Path with Heart*. New York: Bantam, 1993.

Levine, Stephen. *A Gradual Awakening*. New York: Anchor Books, 1989.

Salzberg, Sharon. *A Heart as Wide as the World*. Boston: Shambhala, 1997.

Thich Nhat Hanh. *The Miracle of Mindfulness*. Boston: Beacon Press, 1999.

Thich Nhat Hanh. *Being Peace*. Berkeley, CA: Parallax Press, 2005.

Meditation CDs and Programs

A good collection of meditation CDs is available through Sounds True in Boulder, Colorado. You can call them at 1-800-333-9185 or go to shop.soundstrue.com (click on "Meditation & Guided Practices" or "Music" for background music for meditation). Meditation programs and CDs by Jon Kabat-Zinn can be ordered by going to mindfulnesstapes.com.

Meditation Retreats

Two major centers for meditation retreats are the Insight Meditation Society in Barre, Massachusetts (dharma.org) and Spirit Rock Meditation Center in Woodacre, California (spirit rock.org). Contact either of these centers to find out about meditation retreats in other parts of the country.

19

Taking a Step Back from Anxiety

Suppose that instead of struggling so hard with your anxiety difficulties, you take a step back and *entirely change the way you relate to them*. You already know that you can't overcome anxiety by avoiding or resisting it—that only makes it bigger. Suppose you decide that you are also going to stop struggling as much with your anxiety. This does not mean giving up or resigning yourself to it—it just means letting go of the struggle.

Imagine that you could actually *accept* your condition and embrace the discomfort it causes as something that's potentially vital in your life. You may ask: *Accept* my condition? What could that possibly mean?

Again, it does not mean resigning yourself and giving up. Instead, it means stepping back and learning how to better *observe* your anxious thoughts, images, and feelings instead of becoming embroiled and entangled in them. This is a relatively new approach to anxiety: stepping back and learning how to "be with" your difficult thoughts, feelings, and sensations rather than struggling against them. You *can* learn to be with your anxiety with more compassion and gentleness toward yourself.

Another word used to describe the approach of witnessing anxious thoughts and feelings is *mindfulness*—a concept described at length in the previous chapter on meditation. Mindfulness can be defined as paying attention, without any judgment, to the ongoing content of your experience in the present moment. In this definition, "paying attention" and "in the present moment" go together. The tendency is for distractions—either the thoughts/feelings/sensations within us or stimuli in the outer environment—to quickly pull us out of the present moment and away from simple observation of what is going on. Our mind is also constantly judging our experience of ourselves, others, or situations as "good" or "bad" and "right" or 'wrong." In mindfulness, we relax and simply observe what is going on with no judgment. Mindfulness is at the heart of a new approach to anxiety called "acceptance and commitment therapy," described in this chapter.

Understanding Acceptance and Commitment Therapy

Acceptance and commitment therapy (spoken of as a single word, "ACT") is an empirically based form of therapy that uses mindfulness strategies along with commitment and behavior change strategies to work with anxiety disorders, depression, and a variety of other psychological problems. ACT differs from traditional cognitive behavioral therapy (CBT). Instead of teaching you to modify your thoughts and beliefs, ACT emphasizes a mindfulness approach:

just noticing and fully accepting your difficult thoughts and feelings, which helps you gain a certain distance from them in order to be less entangled with them. *Acceptance* of uncomfortable thoughts, images, feelings, and sensations is critical to ACT. It is the opposite of *experiential avoidance*—the tendency to ignore or avoid our uncomfortable thoughts and feelings, which contributes to many forms of psychological difficulty. Beyond learning to observe your immediate stream of experience and cease avoiding unpleasant or painful thoughts and feelings, ACT stresses self-knowledge: knowing your true values and taking action on those values. In brief, the basic idea of ACT is that personal suffering is caused by experiential avoidance, as well as entanglement or *fusion* with dysfunctional thoughts (see below), and a resulting psychological rigidity. This rigidity and avoidance can lead to further confusion about your true values as well as an inability to take needed action to express those values.

In the past decade, acceptance and commitment therapy has been utilized by many therapists and also garnered considerable research support. The term "ACT" is not only an abbreviation for acceptance and commitment therapy, it is an acronym that emphasizes three core principles of ACT: accept, choose, and take action. Let's take a closer look at each of these principles.

Accept. Accept your anxiety condition, whether that be panic, phobias, worry, or obsessions and compulsions. Be with it (without resignation), even if uncomfortable, instead of struggling to get rid of it. Dropping the struggle frees up energy, which can then be redirected toward constructive goals—for example, getting on with other things in your life that you would like to do.

Choose. Choose the most important directions for your life. Get in touch with what you truly value and want your life to stand for. ACT isn't only about mindfulness and stepping back from painful thoughts and feelings. It's also about knowing your true values and being willing to take the necessary risks you need to take in order to live by them.

Take action. Take committed action to change what you truly want to change in your life. An important premise of ACT, which you have probably heard before, is the maxim "If you continue to do what you've done before, you're going to keep getting what you've always got." Again, ACT is not only about choosing to embrace your true values, it's also about taking actions—including risks—to change your life so that you can live by these values.

If you are fearful, taking action begins with facing your fears so that your life is not limited by them. Yet ACT goes beyond this. It's a practice of accepting—"taking along"—the inevitable discomfort life brings and even using it in the service of your goals and dreams.

Does all of this sound intimidating? Do you balk at taking risks and potentially experiencing more discomfort and pain? Perhaps you wonder how you could ever fully embrace your anxieties and fears rather than avoid them. If so, consider the alternative of keeping your life exactly where it is right now. Allow your fearful thoughts about truly changing your life to "just be." Simply take a deep abdominal breath and allow your fearful thoughts to arise—sort of let them "hang out" in your ongoing stream of experience—without pushing them away. By doing this, you've taken the first step in making a fundamental change in your relationship with your anxiety that ACT encourages. Rather than pushing away painful experience, you accept it and stay with it.

Mindful acceptance is fundamental to meditation practices (both Eastern and Western) that have been used for thousands of years to gain freedom from mental and emotional suffering. To this, ACT adds a wide array of its own techniques to enhance skill with mindful acceptance. Then it goes further to help you clarify your personal values and to encourage you to take committed actions so you can fulfill those values.

The ACT Approach to Fearful Self-Talk

Acceptance and commitment therapy works on your fearful self-talk in a different way than standard cognitive behavioral therapy. (Recall the four subpersonalities described in chapter 8 on self-talk: Worrier, Critic, Victim, and Perfectionist.) Instead of challenging and changing your self-talk, you *simply step back from it and observe it.* You are not trying to change your self-talk; instead, you *reduce its impact* on you by stepping back from it and just "witnessing" it. Of course, this might not be so easy in the midst of a full-blown panic attack. But what about worry? Instead of always getting caught up or entangled in your worries, suppose you could learn to take a step back from them, let go of your struggle with them, and just let them pass through your mind. This is what ACT aims for, and it teaches a variety of specific techniques to help you disentangle from worried thoughts. Some of these techniques borrow directly from mindfulness meditation techniques; others are quite unique.

Note: The idea of simply observing your anxious thoughts or feelings might put you off if you associate it with detachment, depersonalization, or derealization. These are states that can accompany high anxiety where you feel cut off from everything and may have a sense of unreality. The witnessing or observing of your anxious states encouraged by ACT, however, is very different from depersonalization states and *can only occur in a relative state of relaxation.*

In ACT (and in cognitive behavioral therapy), you start with *identifying dysfunctional thoughts* that cause you problems. For example, common anxious thoughts might include "what if'" fears such as "What if I go crazy from this panic attack?" or "What will they think if I sweat and blush while giving my presentation?" The very act of identifying them immediately gives you some distance from them—something that ACT emphasizes as important. In fact, even being aware of the four inner voices described in chapter 8—Worrier, Critic, Victim, and Perfectionist—and the kinds of self-talk they engage in is a step in the direction of greater self-awareness. On the other hand, when you get some distance from your thoughts, you are more free to choose helpful, constructive thoughts, if you wish.

Fusion and Defusion

Fusion is a state of two things being merged or joined together. Much of the time, our thoughts are fused with our ongoing awareness. We don't see or recognize our thoughts; instead we just act and react *from* them. When we are "fused" with our thoughts, we tend to *believe them as if they were absolute truth*, even if they refer to some future danger that hasn't even happened (and isn't likely to). For example, if your heart races when you're anxious, you may be fused with the idea that you are going to have a heart attack. You may absolutely believe this, even if the true probability of it happening is remote.

Another type of fusion includes *adherence to rigid rules* about what you should or shouldn't feel or do. This type of fusion is typical of the Perfectionist subpersonality described in chapter 8. It reveals itself in self-talk that includes the words "should," "must," and "have to." Common examples include "I shouldn't be feeling this way" and "I have to do this right, or it's not worth trying at all."

Yet another type of fusion is to be closely *identified with the negative judgments of your "inner critic."* In this case, you really believe negative self-judgments such as "I'm worthless," "I'm weak," "I'm a failure," or "I can't cope." Fusion with such self-critical statements can lead to severe depression and feelings of hopelessness.

The problem with fusion is that *what you take to be absolutely true and real are simply strings of words and images in your head.* These strings of words and images that your mind creates may have nothing to do with reality, and yet you whole-heartedly believe them as if they were utterly true. Being enmeshed or "entangled" with such thoughts can lead to a lot of suffering. The way out is to stop believing everything you think.

Defusion helps you to "stop believing everything you think." It is a process of disentangling—ceasing to fuse—with unhelpful thoughts. When you defuse a thought, you recognize it for what it is—nothing more than a bunch of words and pictures "inside your head." You step back from your thoughts enough to see them for what they are.

Defusion begins by simply asking yourself to notice what you're thinking. You might say to yourself:

- "So what is my mind telling me right now?"

- "What thoughts are going through my mind right now?"

- "Just notice what my mind is saying."

- "What judgments am I making right now?"

Once you've identified your thoughts—perhaps even written them down—the next important question to ask is whether they are *helpful* or not—whether they *work* for you or not. In contrast with cognitive behavioral therapy, ACT is less concerned with the truth or falsity of a given thought than whether it is *workable—whether it is helpful and leads to a richer, fuller or more meaningful life* (as opposed to leading to more stress and suffering). If you are fused with the thought "I'm fat," ACT is not concerned with whether this thought is true or not (unlike your counselor at the local Jenny Craig program); rather, it's concerned with whether the thought is helpful. Does it lead you to feel better and do things to improve your life? Or does fusion with that thought lead to depression and inactivity, such as more time in front of the TV eating ice cream?

So ACT is concerned with loosening up around—disidentifying with—unworkable thoughts, whether they are true or not. The whole point is *to hold painful/critical/fearful thoughts less tightly* so that they are less likely to run your life.

Common Defusion Techniques

Acceptance and commitment therapy offers a wide array of specific techniques to facilitate defusion. Some of these draw heavily from mindfulness meditation techniques while others do not. Here are some common defusion techniques you can use:

Noticing. Just notice what your mind is telling you right now.

Writing thoughts down. When you feel upset, notice your thoughts and write them down on a index card or piece of paper.

Bracketing a thought. Take a thought that you notice and preface it with the phrase "I'm having the thought that …" For example, you could take the self-destructive thought "I'm a loser" and defuse it or gain some distance from it by saying to yourself, "I'm having the thought: 'I'm a loser.'"

Leaves on a stream. Imagine that you're sitting on the bank of gentle stream. Leaves drop into the stream and float by you. Now, for the next few minutes, take every thought that pops into your head, place it on a leaf, and let it flow by. Whether you like the thought or not, place it on a leaf and let it float by. If a leaf gets stuck, let it hang around. Don't force it to float away. If you start to feel bored or impatient, just acknowledge that thought: "Here's a feeling of boredom" or "Here's a feeling of impatience." Then place that thought on a leaf, and let the leaf float by.

Watching your thinking (adapted from Russ Harris, *ACT Made Simple*). Relax, center yourself in your body, and engage in abdominal breathing for one minute. Now shift your attention to your thoughts. Where are they? Where do they seem located in space? Are they inside your head? Are they floating around in "mental space" in your mind? Are they someplace else? Notice the form your thoughts take. Are they more like words, pictures, or sounds? Notice whether your thoughts are moving or still. If they are moving, at what speed and in what direction are they moving? Notice what is above and below your thoughts. Are there any gaps between them? From time to time, you may find you get caught up in your thoughts. This is perfectly natural and normal. When it happens, just gently acknowledge it, and go back to watching your thoughts.

Computer screen. Imagine your thought on a computer screen. Change the font, color, and format. Animate the words.

Sing the thought. For example, take the thought "I'm a loser" and sing it to the tune of "Happy Birthday." (This is one of the zanier defusion techniques, which may or may not appeal to you, but it works for many people.)

Workability. Ask yourself these questions: "If I go along with a particular thought, buy into it, and let it control me, where does that leave me? What do I get for buying into it? Does buying into that thought lead me to a better and more meaningful life?"

Defusion techniques like these can be used at any time, but they work really well in the context of meditation practices (see chapter 18). For thousands of years, one of the principal aims of meditation practice has been to develop mindfulness—the capacity to witness and disentangle from conditioned thoughts. This is, of course, the whole point of defusion as well.

Acceptance

What really matters to you? Are your fears and anxiety causing you to avoid pursuing goals or taking actions in your life that are truly important to you? How much of your life have you given up to your anxiety? Think about two or three things in your life that really matter but that you are missing out on because you've given up on them due to your anxiety.

Acceptance involves a fundamental shift in attitude. Instead of restricting your life by giving in to your fears, you decide to take the scary step of facing your anxiety. Why? Because having a full life—living in accord with your true values—becomes more important to you than staying safe and comfortable in your anxiety. Embracing acceptance means you deliberately chose to overcome your avoidances, step by step.

While defusion helps you to disentangle yourself from painful thoughts, acceptance helps you to develop the skill to "be with" your feelings—especially fearful feelings—"just as they are," whether pleasant or painful. In the process of acceptance, you open up and make room for your anxious feelings, stop resisting or pushing against them, and "soften up" around them. Even in the case of panicky feelings, acceptance means letting the feeling be, "hanging out with it" (even if it doesn't go away quickly), and refraining from avoiding it or pushing it away. In short, you *accept* it instead of struggling with or against it. This does not mean you just give up and resign yourself to it. Acceptance is the first thing to do when you move *with* anxiety rather than avoiding and running from it. (After acceptance, you may also choose to engage other coping techniques, as described in chapter 6.) For example, if you wish to stop avoiding flying, going to the grocery store, or giving talks because of a fear that you might panic, your first step toward facing these situations is accept—rather than resist—the anxious feelings that are likely to come up in these situations.

The more you try to avoid fear and anxiety, the bigger they usually become. The longer you run from something you're anxious about, the larger and more foreboding it becomes. ACT reverses this process by empowering you to stop running from fear. When you face and deal with your fear, your fear tends—eventually—to get smaller and less ominous. Though initially you may find it difficult to face your fear, in the long run your fear will diminish. In this case, acceptance with regard to anxiety and fear is very closely related to exposure. As such, it needs to be done gently and gradually—in an incremental progression—rather than all at once.

An important principle of ACT is that making changes in your life usually brings up anxiety. The more you are inclined to avoid anxiety in general, the more you will tend to avoid taking risks to make changes in your life, even if they could be very positive. Acceptance means being willing to embrace the necessary anxiety that often accompanies change. This may not be easy—and it can be painful—but the alternative of staying the same and not risking change is, in many cases, even worse. For example, think of someone afraid to take elevators above the fifth floor. Imagine all the situations they could not deal with if they held on to their phobia, especially if they lived in a large city. Visiting friends in apartment buildings, going on some job interviews, even obtaining medical care from some doctors, would all be unavailable to them. Such was the situation for the late Jerilyn Ross before she decided to face her fear of elevators. After overcoming her phobia, she went on to be president of the Anxiety Disorders Association of America for almost thirty years.

Common Acceptance Techniques

You can develop your capacity for acceptance in a variety of ways. Here are some commonly used acceptance techniques:

Notice the form of the feeling. Observe your feeling and notice where it's in your body. In your chest or in your gut? In your head or in your throat? What is its shape and size? Is it heavy or light? Is it at the surface of your body or deep inside? Notice different sensations within the feeling. If it just stays there without changing, allow it to be. Make room for it without pushing it away. For example, if you feel a sensation of nausea or queasiness in your stomach, just allow it to be there for five minutes without doing anything to try to diminish or change it. Just "be with" the sensation and observe whether it changes on its own.

Healing Hand. Lay your hand on the part of your body where you feel the feeling most intensely. Send some warmth and nurturance into the area—not to get rid of the feeling but to make room for it.

Softening. See if you can soften up around the feeling, loosen up, and hold it gently.

Allowing. Just allow yourself to be with the feeling—to "hang out" with it for a while. Even if you don't like it or want it, just leave it alone and allow it to be.

The choice to feel. If you could choose to turn off all of your painful feelings, you would also gradually lose your capacity to love and care. However, you can choose to be fully open to loving and caring, and when there is a gap between what you want and what you've got, painful feelings may arise.

Note: All of these acceptance techniques can be used to make space for an unpleasant physical sensation in your body, just as readily as they can be used to accept unpleasant feelings. As with defusion techniques, it is easier to implement acceptance techniques when you are relaxed, instead of caught up in a state of stress. So, if you are feeling highly stressed and have difficulty implementing these techniques, try doing some relaxation techniques first, such as abdominal breathing or progressive muscle relaxation, or, alternatively, release stress through aerobic exercise or yoga. Even better, carve out some time to do some meditation practice. This will enhance utilizing both defusion and acceptance techniques of all kinds.

We all feel anxiety at times. ACT offers us an approach and a set of techniques that allow us to take a step back from our anxiety and move with it rather than struggling so much against it. ACT emphasizes that an important part of overcoming anxiety is learning to stop running from it.

Commitment

The "commitment" part of acceptance and commitment therapy means taking constructive action, based on your values. After you've clarified your most important values in life, you decide whether you are ready and willing to overcome any obstacles to realizing them, including your fears and avoidances. If so, you take committed action—"doing what it takes"—to live by your values even if this brings up pain and discomfort. Acceptance, as we discussed above, is a big part of this. Instead of "declaring war" on your anxiety, you accept uncomfortable anxious feelings when they come up. Doing so is what allows you to "take action" to realize your cherished values, to live your life fully. This is ultimately what acceptance and commitment therapy is all about. Without acceptance of anxious feelings and sensations, you will continue give into experiential avoidance. Acceptance is what empowers commitment.

Acceptance and commitment means you may have to face some discomfort. How do you do this? Any and all of the cognitive and behavioral interventions described elsewhere in this book can be used to assist you in doing what it takes to stop avoiding life and live fully by your values. If you feel you are not really clear about what your true values are, then see the following chapter, "Personal Meaning," and spend some time with the *Personal Values Inventory*. Once you've clarified your values, write down specific goals that you are willing to set to realize those values in your life. Then break each goal down into specific actions to take. For each action, identify any fears or avoidances to taking that action and use ACT and/ or CBT processes (on your own or with the assistance of a therapist) to overcome your fears.

So, the commitment sequence goes something like this:

1. Define values

2. Set goals

3. Specify actions to achieve goals

4. Identify fears or avoidances that block goal attainment

5. Work through fears using ACT/CBT

6. Take committed action

To sum up, commitment means taking action to live in accord with your true values. It does not mean striving toward total perfection or pressuring yourself to reach every goal you can imagine. It is simply making a commitment to valued living, returning again and again to your most important values—giving them priority over other things that might distract you from them, including your anxiety and fears.

If you are interested in learning more about ACT, see the books listed under "Further Reading" below. If you would like to get in touch with a therapist who specializes in ACT, a directory is available online at contextualpsychology.org.

Summary of Things to Do

1. Think about how the three core principles—accept, choose, take action—of ACT apply to your life. How much are you able to accept or just "be with" your anxiety (and other life challenges) as opposed to struggling with them? Do you choose—do you give priority to—your most important values in life and feel committed to doing whatever it takes to realize them? What actions have you taken to reach the goals and live out the values that are most important to you?

2. Practice defusion. After relaxing for a few moments (using abdominal breathing, muscle relaxation, visualization, yoga, or calming music—see chapter 4), take a step back from your anxious thoughts using one or more of the defusion techniques listed in the section "Common Defusion Techniques."

3. Practice acceptance. Again, after relaxing for a few moments, practice one of the acceptance techniques listed in the section "Common Acceptance Techniques." Use this technique with whatever feelings and/or physical body sensations are coming up for you at the moment.

4. Make a commitment to take action in accord with your personal values. If you are unclear about your values, see chapter 20 and spend some time with the *Personal Values Inventory*. Then, on your own or with the assistance of a therapist, define goals that would fulfill your most important values. For each goal, specify actions that need to be taken to realize the goal as well as any obstacles that get in the way of taking those actions. Again, on your own or with the help of a therapist, *choose one action* that would be the most important for you to undertake now. Make a commitment to work through the obstacles and complete that action.

Further Reading

The following two books provide an excellent introduction to ACT:

Forsyth, John P., and Georg H. Eifert. *The Mindfulness & Acceptance Workbook for Anxiety*. Oakland, CA: New Harbinger Publications, 2007.

Harris, Russ. *ACT Made Simple*. Oakland, CA: New Harbinger Publications, 2009.

The Forsyth and Eifert book is a very practical application of ACT principles and techniques to anxiety disorders, while the Harris book, although intended for therapists, is written in a very clear, accessible, and well-organized fashion, making ACT easy to grasp.

20

Personal Meaning

The chapters of this book up to this point have considered the physical, emotional, behavioral, and mental aspects of anxiety disorders. Guidelines have been offered for dealing with these various levels of the problem. On a bodily level, anxiety, panic, and phobias can be helped through abdominal breathing, relaxation, exercise, and/or medication. Emotionally, learning to identify and express feelings can relieve the tension that lies behind anxiety. Behaviorally, exposure can overcome phobic avoidance. On a mental level, replacing fearful self-talk and beliefs with realistic thoughts and assumptions can help reduce anxiety in all of its diverse forms.

For many people, the wide range of approaches presented up to this point will be enough to ensure recovery. Making a commitment to follow through with the program outlined in this book, whether on your own or with a therapist, will help you to take back your life from anxiety. You may require a bit more, however. All the techniques described so far can help a great deal, yet for certain people they aren't quite enough. An underlying level of anxiety remains—an anxiety that comes from not having answered basic questions about the meaning and purpose of your life.

Existential psychologists such as Rollo May have used the term "existential anxiety" to refer to the type of anxiety that arises from having been unable to reach your full potential in life. This is a vague sense of tension, boredom, perhaps even "quiet desperation" that arises from feeling held back, for one reason or another, from being all that you can be. You live with a feeling of incompleteness—a sense that something vital is missing—although you may not consciously recognize what it is. If someone were to ask you, "Where is your life going?" or "What do you think your life is about?" you would tend to have trouble answering. Or you might think of things that, on further reflection, don't seem "quite enough" to make your life as meaningful as you would like it to be.

For some people, a lack of purpose or meaning in life can provide fertile ground for the development of panic attacks and phobias. Although panic may be caused by a number of factors, it sometimes reflects a sudden revelation (and desperation) that your life has no obvious direction. Similarly, the fear of being trapped or confined, or "unable to escape," that underlies so many phobias *may* reflect a deeper fear of being trapped by your current circumstances in life, whether involving a dead-end career, a relationship, or any other situation that feels confining yet would require substantial risks to move out of. Phobic avoidance, in turn, *may* reflect a deeper avoidance of the very risks that are necessary to realize your full potential and life purpose. It has been my experience with a number of clients that their anxiety disorders (it doesn't seem to matter which particular type) did not fully resolve until they found something that could give their life a greater sense of meaning *and* they took the necessary risks to embrace it. In one case, this involved a career change, and in still another it meant cultivating a creative talent with music.

The purpose of this chapter is to give you the opportunity to reflect on the question of your life's meaning, as well as to explore whether spirituality might provide at least one direction in which to find answers. Spirituality is a universal concept. It refers not to any particular religion but to a basic sense of there being a larger purpose to life, as well as a larger power—a "Higher Power," if you will—that transcends the human order of things. Not only may spirituality provide life with greater meaning, but it can help overcome anxiety directly because it leads to qualities such as inner peace, serenity, faith, and unconditional love.

If you feel that meaning and spirituality are important, you may want to take a look at my book *Beyond Anxiety & Phobia: A New Spectrum of Holistic Approaches to Long-Term Recovery*, which explores these topics in considerably more depth. In fact, this book presents a wide range of approaches intended to go beyond what is presented in *The Anxiety & Phobia Workbook*. It was written as a supplement or companion to the workbook. See the "Further Reading" section of this chapter.

Finding Your Unique Purpose

Each of us has one or more special purposes to fulfill that can give our life a sense of completeness. Those people who fully realize their special purpose often say, by the time they reach their senior years, that they feel satisfied with their life—that they did as much as they could to accomplish what they set out to do. Common examples of life purposes might include raising a family, succeeding in a fulfilling career, making a contribution to your community, developing and expressing an artistic talent, completing an educational goal and using what you've learned to serve others, overcoming an addiction or the problems of a dysfunctional childhood, and conveying what you've learned to others. Life purposes appear to have a twofold function: 1) allowing you to feel more complete and whole, and 2) allowing you in some way to serve or contribute to the betterment of others. Realizing what truly gives your life meaning and purpose is likely to carry you beyond your own personal needs and to have a beneficial impact on someone else—whether that someone is a child, the people you work for, your community, or anyone to whom you convey what you've learned from your experience. In discovering your true purpose and potential, you move beyond immediate concerns for personal security and satisfaction toward making a meaningful contribution.

If you currently feel out of touch with your life purpose, how do you go about discovering what it is? The questionnaire that follows is designed to stimulate your thinking in ways that can help you to formulate your own unique goals. Your answers to the questions may give you some insights into what it is that is most important for you to do with your life. Give yourself at least one full day to reflect on these questions and write out your answers. You may even want to ponder these questions for a week or a month. After you've arrived at the answers for yourself, practice visualizing what your life would look like if you were truly fulfilling your special purpose. Then you might share your answers to these questions with a close personal friend or counselor and get that person's input and feedback. If realizing your purpose involves making a career change, it might be helpful to work with a career counselor. If it involves going back to school, you'll want to talk to an academic guidance counselor at the school you're considering.

Personal Values Inventory

1.   Does the work you're presently doing express what you truly want to be doing? If not, how can you begin to take steps toward discovering and doing work that would be more personally fulfilling?

2.   Are you satisfied with the education you've obtained? Would you like to go back to school and increase your education and training? If so, how can you begin to move in that direction?

3.   Do you have creative outlets? Are there any areas of your life where you feel you can be creative? If not, what creative activities could you develop?

4.   Have you developed your spiritual life? Is doing so something you would like to explore further?

5.   What would you like to do with your life if you could do what you truly wanted? (Assume, for the purpose of this question, that money and the responsibilities of your current job and family are not a limitation.)

6.   What would you like to accomplish with your life? What would you like to have accomplished by the time you reach seventy in order to feel that your life has been productive and meaningful?

7.   What are your most important values? What values give your life the greatest meaning? Some examples of values include

Happy family life	Material success
Intimacy	Career achievement
Friendship	Creative expression
Good health	Personal growth
Peace of mind	Spiritual awareness
Serving others	Dedication to a social cause

8.   Is there anything that you deeply value and yet feel you haven't fully experienced or realized in your life? What changes do you need to make—or what risks do you need to take—to more fully realize your most important values?

9. Do you have any special talents or skills that you haven't fully developed or expressed? What changes do you need to make—or what risks do you need to take—in order to develop and express your special talents and skills?

10. In the light of the above questions, your most important life purposes would include (list):

11. What obstacles exist to pursuing and realizing your life purposes?

12. What are you willing to *commit* to doing in the next month, year, and three years to eliminate the obstacles in question 11 and move toward realizing your special purposes?

    One month:

    One year:

    Three years:

Life Purpose Visualization

Write a scenario on a separate sheet of paper of what your life would look like if you were to fully realize your unique life purposes. You can design separate visualizations for each purpose or incorporate the realization of all of your life purposes into a single description. Be sure to make your scenario sufficiently detailed to include where you're living and working, whom you are with, what activities make up your day, and what a typical day would look like. Once you've completed a detailed description, record it, preferably in your own voice. You may want to record it after a few minutes of preliminary instructions to relax. Visualizing the fulfillment of your life purpose on a regular, consistent basis will go a long way toward accelerating the process of actually realizing your goal.

Spirituality

This section on spirituality is included because many clients of mine have achieved break-throughs in their condition as the result of developing their spiritual life. If this section speaks to you, then it may serve to motivate you to cultivate your spirituality. If you already have a deep spiritual commitment, what follows may simply reinforce what you know rather than teach you anything new. Conversely, if this section seems repellent or inapplicable, you need not feel compelled to read it or incorporate it into your recovery program. You can entirely overcome your particular problem with anxiety by relying on the strategies and guidelines presented in previous chapters of this workbook.

Spirituality involves the recognition and acceptance of a Higher Power beyond your own intelligence and will, with whom you can have a relationship. This Higher Power can provide you with an experience of inspiration, joy, security, peace of mind, and guidance that goes beyond what is possible in the absence of the conviction that such a power exists.

For our purposes here, spirituality can be seen as being distinct from religion. Different world religions have proposed various doctrines and belief systems about the nature of a Higher Power and humanity's relationship with it. Spirituality, on the other hand, refers to the *common experience* behind these various points of view—an experience involving an awareness of and relationship with something that transcends your personal self as well as the human order of things. This "something" has been given various names ("God" being the most popular in Western society) and defined in ways that are too numerous to count. For the purposes of this chapter, it can be referred to as a (or "your") *Higher Power.* You can choose to define what that means for yourself in whatever way feels most appropriate. Your own sense of a Higher Power can be as abstract as "cosmic consciousness" or as down-to-earth as the beauty of the ocean or mountains. It can be quite personal, as in the case of Jesus or Krishna. Even if you regard yourself as an agnostic or atheist, you may get a sense of inspiration from taking a walk in the forest or contemplating a beautiful sunset. Or a small child's smile may give you a special sense of joy. Whatever inspires you and takes you beyond yourself into a larger perspective points in the direction of what is referred to here as your Higher Power.

The purpose of this section is to emphasize that there is much healing and benefit to be obtained by cultivating your spiritual life (if that is something you feel drawn to or that feels right for you). Of all the methods and guidelines suggested in this workbook, a personal spiritual commitment is likely to reach the deepest in helping you to overcome the basic sense of fear or insecurity that underlies the various types of anxiety disorders. Whereas other methods described in previous chapters work at different levels—body, feelings, mind, or behavior—spiritual awareness and growth can effect a transformation in your whole being. It can help you to develop a basic trust and faith that is unshakable. Of course, the other methods described in previous chapters are still important and necessary. Please keep in mind that the ideas and exercises presented in this chapter are not a substitute for working with all of the other strategies and skills in this book.

A number of my clients have experienced major turnarounds in their condition as a result of cultivating their spirituality. Developing a relationship with their Higher Power did not necessarily cure a specific phobia or obsession, but it provided the moral support, courage, hope, and faith for them to follow through with their personal recovery program. It provided them with a sense that they are not alone in the universe and that there is a source of guidance and support that is available at times of confusion and discouragement.

What are some of the specific benefits to be gained by developing your spirituality? Before enumerating several of these, it is important to understand that no one pursues spiritual growth in order to "get" such benefits. You will develop yourself spiritually only because you feel a deep, inner prompting to do so. The benefits are simply a consequence that follows from choosing to cultivate a relationship with your Higher Power. If you have already developed your spiritual life, you will understand the benefits listed below.

Security and Safety

A sense of inner security and safety is especially important if you frequently deal with anxiety, worries, panic attacks, or phobias. Through developing a connection with your Higher Power, you gain security through the conviction that you are not all alone in the universe, even at those times when you feel temporarily separated from other people. You feel increasingly safe as you come to believe that there is a source you can always turn to in times of difficulty. There is much security to be gained through the understanding that there is no problem or difficulty, however great, that cannot be resolved through the help of your Higher Power.

Peace of Mind

Peace of mind is the result of feeling a deep, abiding sense of security and safety. The more reliance and trust you develop in your Higher Power, the easier it becomes to deal without fear or worry with the inevitable challenges life brings. It is not that you give up your self or your will to such a power; rather you simply learn that you can "let go" and turn to your Higher Power when you feel stuck with a problem in living and don't know how to proceed. Learning how to let go when solutions to problems aren't immediately apparent can go a long way toward reducing worry and anxiety in your life. Peace of mind is what develops in the absence of such anxiety.

Self-Confidence

As you develop a relationship with your Higher Power, you come to remember that you did not create yourself. You are reminded that you are a part of the universe of creation, as much so as the birds, stars, and trees. If this is a benign and supportive universe we live in—and developing a relationship with your Higher Power will help you to believe that it is—then in essence you're good, lovable, and worthy of respect just by virtue of the fact that you're here. However you behave—whatever choices you make—you are still inherently good and worthwhile. Your own judgments of yourself, however negative, do not ultimately count if you are a creation of the universe like everything else. As one person humorously put it, "God doesn't make junk." (It is, of course, a mistake to assume that this type of reasoning can be used to justify ignorant or unethical behavior. It's important to keep in mind the distinction between how a person behaves and what a person is in essence.)

The Capacity to Give and Receive Unconditional Love

The most fundamental characteristic of your Higher Power is that it offers you an experience of unconditional love. This is a kind of love that differs from romantic love or even ordinary friendship. It entails an absolute caring for the welfare of another, without any conditions. That is, no matter how another person appears or acts, you have compassion and care for him or her without judgment. As you develop a deeper connection with your Higher Power, you come to experience greater degrees of unconditional love in your life. You feel your heart opening more easily to people and their concerns. You feel freer of judgment toward them or of making comparisons among them. Unconditional love shows up in your increased capacity both to give love to others and to experience more of it coming into your life. You begin to experience less fear and more joy in your life and help to inspire others to experience their own capacity for unconditional love. This kind of love also manifests itself through the experience of having everything you need in your life to get on with what you want to do. This is spoken of in the Bible by the saying "Seek ye first the Kingdom, and all will be added unto you."

Guidance

Developing a relationship with your Higher Power will provide you with guidance for making decisions and solving problems. Your Higher Power has a universal wisdom that goes beyond what you can accomplish through your own intellect. In traditional religions, this has been referred to as the "all-knowingness of God" or "divine intelligence." Through connecting with your Higher Power, you can draw upon this greater wisdom to help you resolve all kinds of difficulties. You have probably already experienced this aspect of your Higher Power at moments when you've felt a deep conviction about something or have had an intuitive flash that turns out to be quite accurate. By learning to ask your Higher Power for guidance, you'll be surprised to find that every sincere request sooner or later is answered. And the quality of that answer generally exceeds what you could have figured out through your own conscious intellect or will.

These are some—by no means all—of the characteristics that define a close relationship with your Higher Power. All of them can contribute in a significant way to your personal recovery process. Keep in mind that there are many different paths you can take in coming into a greater awareness of your Higher Power. The particular path you choose, whether traditional or nontraditional, is up to you. The extent and sincerity of your commitment to your chosen path will determine the degree of personal healing you experience.

Changes in Beliefs Associated with Spirituality

Developing spiritually not only leads to new experiences and changes in the way you feel, it also can lead to a shift in your basic beliefs and assumptions about life and the world. As you develop spiritually, many of your beliefs about the meaning of life in general, and what your life is about specifically, can shift dramatically. And as these basic beliefs change, your view of your condition—your personal struggle with anxiety—also begins to change.

These shifts in beliefs can lead to having more compassion and tolerance toward yourself, as well as to finding a deeper meaning in the challenges you face, instead of viewing them as arbitrary and meaningless. You may feel less like a victim who has a particular problem with anxiety. Instead, you may come to regard your condition as an *opportunity* to grow and expand who you are.

What follows is a list of ten assumptions that are frequently associated with spirituality. They are not taken from any one source, tradition, or creed, but are based on my personal experience. Although they represent my own personal point of view, these ideas have been useful points of departure for discussion with a number of my clients. As you read through the ideas, give consideration to those that fit or make sense to you and feel free to discard those that do not. Each of us has a basic philosophy about life that we have to formulate on our own.

Some of these ideas may stimulate questions that you may want to discuss with a significant other, a trusted friend, or even a minister, priest, or rabbi. All of the ideas can lead to a more optimistic and tolerant view of life. As you adopt any of these ideas that fit for you, you may find your attitude about your condition—as well as life in general—becoming a little more positive and a little less burdensome.

1. Life is a school. The primary meaning and purpose of life is that it is a "classroom" for growth in consciousness.

Most people tend to define their life's meaning in terms of those people, activities, self-images, or objects to which they attach the greatest value. Whatever you value most in life—whether family, another individual, work, a particular role or self-image, your health, or material possessions—these things are probably what define your life's meaning. If you lost what you valued the most, your life might seem to lose its meaning. Think for a moment about what you value most highly in your life and what gives you the greatest satisfaction and comfort. Then imagine what your life would be like if these things were all suddenly taken away.

The truth, of course, is that everything you value most *will* eventually pass away. Nothing that you cherish lasts forever. Yet if everything you value must someday cease to be, what is the *ultimate* meaning of life? And as long as you assume that there is nothing more to existence than your present life—what there is right now—then there doesn't seem to be *any* ultimate meaning. You end up saying (along with Jean-Paul Sartre and other existentialists) that the only meaning life has is what you make of it in the present moment. Apart from this, life appears to have no meaning in and of itself. Since everything, including life itself, eventually passes away, how can there be any ultimate point to any of it?

Most forms of spirituality, traditional and modern, move beyond this existential predicament. Most of them make some kind of assumption that human life is *not* all there is. Something of us persists beyond human life, and so life comes to be seen as a temporary sojourn—not the final destination. Life comes to be understood as a preparation or training ground for something else that cannot be fully understood or revealed while you are alive.

It is this particular interpretation of life's "ultimate" meaning that I have found to be most valid and helpful. If the final meaning of life is that it is a classroom or school for growth in consciousness—for the development of wisdom and the capacity to love—then the fact that everything passes away takes on an entirely new meaning. The tasks and challenges that come up in life, and your response to them, do not have eternal repercussions. Nor do they have no meaning at all. They are more like lessons in a school, lessons to which you apply yourself and which you try to master as best you can. Each lesson is repeated until it is mastered. As you master old lessons, new ones are put before you. This "earth school" is thus a place where you learn and grow; it is not your final dwelling place. Eventually it is time to leave this classroom and move on.

2. Adversity and difficult situations are lessons designed for your growth—they are not random, capricious acts of fate. In the larger scheme of things, everything happens for a purpose.

If you accept the idea that life is a classroom, then the adversity and difficulties that come into your life may be viewed as part of the curriculum—as lessons for growth. This is a very different point of view from one that sees life's misfortunes as random quirks of fate. The latter perspective leads to a sense of victimization. You can end up feeling powerless in a capricious world which appears to be completely inequitable in its treatment of people, some of whom have such good luck, while others have misfortune heaped upon them.

The view proposed here is that the difficulties of life are lessons to promote growth in wisdom, compassion, love, and other positive qualities (some religious traditions refer to "tests" or "lessons"). The greater the difficulty, the greater the potential for learning and growth. If you accept this idea, then the next question you may ask is, who establishes the curriculum or "assigns" your life lessons? Many of us may ask this question in one form or another when a given life challenge seems particularly difficult. We tend to protest and even rail against some of the misfortunes and limitations we're faced with. The question arises: "How could a loving God permit this?"

There is no easy answer to this question. None of us can fully understand how our life lessons are administered and assigned, though different spiritual traditions have different views on this matter (Eastern traditions speak of "karma," while Judeo-Christian traditions speak of "tests" and "temptations"). Each of us has to struggle with the challenges life brings without fully understanding why. What does seem apparent is that growth could not occur if the lessons were *always* easy. If the purpose of life is for us to grow in wisdom, consciousness, and compassion, then at least some of the lessons need to be difficult. This may not be an altogether consoling view, but it at least makes some sense out of the difficult situations that occur in life.

Given this view, you can stop asking, "Why did this happen to me?" and instead ask the more constructive questions: "What is this meant to teach me? What can be learned from this?" You might take whatever worry or concern is bothering you the most in your life at this time and try asking the latter two questions instead of the first.

3. Your personal limitations and flaws are the grist you have to work with for your inner growth. Sometimes you can heal and overcome them with modest effort. In other cases, they may stay with you for a long time in order to push you to evolve and develop to your fullest potential. You are not wrong or in any way to blame because of your limitations.

Think for a moment about some of your own personal limitations—the ones you find most difficult to live with. If you are dealing with an anxiety disorder, think about your condition. You may ask why anyone should have to deal with a difficult condition such as panic disorder, agoraphobia, social phobia, or an obsessive-compulsive disorder for even a few months, let alone a longer time. Hopefully you have utilized all of the best treatments—including medication, if necessary—and have experienced a significant and genuine recovery. In many cases, a full recovery from an anxiety disorder is certainly possible. Suppose, however, that you have received all the best treatments, worked very hard for one or two years, and have experienced *some* improvement—yet you are still dealing with your condition to a degree. Is that a reason for you to think of yourself as a failure? A reason to think that you are somehow less skillful or persistent than those people who overcame their condition quickly?

If you've worked hard on overcoming your condition but are still troubled by it, perhaps there is some significant growth experience to find in the process of having to work with your difficulty for a long time. It all depends upon the lesson you happen to be learning. Having a difficult condition that is easily dispensed with in a short time would certainly help develop your confidence in your own self-mastery—an important lesson in itself. Yet it wouldn't necessarily develop qualities of compassion or patience. It often seems that only through having to struggle with our own infirmities for a time can we learn fully how to feel compassion or have patience with others' difficulties.

As a second example, suppose that your lesson is to learn how to let go of the excessive need for control—even more, to learn how to let go and allow your Higher Power or God to have an impact on your life. One way (not the only way) this might be learned is to have to deal with a difficult situation in which all your efforts to control it just don't work. The ability to let go of control is often fostered by those very difficulties in life that are most challenging. Some conditions and situations are so challenging that they *compel* us to let go. There is no other alternative. To struggle or fight against the condition only creates more distress and suffering. It is often at the exact moment when you fully let go of your worry or stop struggling that you may experience some kind of response or relief from your Higher Power. To let go and trust in your Higher Power should not be thought of as relinquishing responsibility for your life. Rather, it involves doing all you can to help yourself first, and then turning things over to another source of assistance.

In sum, it is a mistake to fault yourself for having any intractable condition, no matter how disabling or how long you've had it. It is there to foster and deepen certain qualities of your inner self. *How you respond to it and what you learn from it is what's important—not the condition itself.*

4. Your life has a creative purpose and mission. There is something creative that is yours to develop and offer.

Your life is not a random sequence of accidental events but follows a plan. This plan is *created* from a level that none of us can fully understand. Part of this plan consists of the lessons for growth in consciousness that were described in the preceding three sections.

Another very important aspect of the plan is your creative endowments, talents, or "gifts." Each of us has at least one personal form of creativity that can give our life meaning and purpose. The development and full expression of your creative talents and gifts is your "life purpose" or "life mission" spoken of earlier in this chapter.

Your life purpose is something that you feel you *need* to do in order to feel whole, complete, and fulfilled in your life. It's uniquely your own—something that can't be duplicated. Only you can do it. It comes from within, and it has nothing to do with what your parents, partner, or friends might want you to do. Generally, it moves you beyond yourself and has an impact on something or someone else.

Your purpose or mission can be a vocation or avocation—its scope can extend to the entire world or to just one other person. Examples include raising a family, mastering a musical instrument, volunteering your services to help youth or the elderly, writing poems, speaking eloquently before groups, or tending the garden in your backyard.

Until you develop and express your creative gifts, your life will seem incomplete. You will feel more anxiety because you are not making time to do what you truly want to do, what you were, in fact, born to do. The first part of this chapter was designed to help you get in touch with your creative purpose and mission. If you are not quite sure yet what it is, you may want to discuss your answers to the *Personal Values Inventory* at the beginning of this chapter with a trusted friend or counselor. You may also find the book *Fulfill Your Soul's Purpose* by Naomi Stephan to be useful.

5. A Higher Source of support and guidance is always available.

This idea is the basis of this entire section on spirituality. Much fear and anxiety is based on the perception that you are separate and alone—or else it is based on the anticipation of rejection or loss that might eventually result in your being separate and alone. The truth is that you are not alone. Even at those times when you might find it difficult to turn to other human beings for support, there remains another source of support that can always be called on. Your Higher Power is not merely an abstract entity that created and sustains the universe.

It is a force, power, or presence with which you can enter into a personal relationship. This relationship is as personal as any you could have with another human being.

In this personal relationship, you can experience both *support* and *guidance*. Support often appears in the form of inspiration or enthusiasm that can help lift and sustain you at times of low motivation and discouragement. Guidance can come in the form of clear insights and intuitions that provide discrimination and direction about what you need to do. Frequently, this type of inspired insight or realization is wiser than anything you might have figured out with your rational mind.

You may experience a dilemma about this. If you think of inspiration and intuition originating in your own subconscious mind, how do they come then from a Higher Power—from something seemingly separate from you? Certainly from the perspective of the conscious mind, everything does seem separate—you perceive yourself as separate from others, from the world, and most likely from a Higher Power. There is another level, though, that the conscious mind can't comprehend, where all things are joined. Eastern philosophy refers to this as "the One in which all things reside." The modern physicist David Bohm speaks of the "implicate order" in which everything is connected. In the Bible (New Testament), this idea is expressed in the statement "The Kingdom of Heaven is within you."

To receive support and guidance from your Higher Power, you simply need to ask. Nothing more is necessary. While this might seem easy enough, it may not be in practice if you believe that you're supposed to figure out and handle everything entirely on your own. Or it may not be easy if you feel that it's irrational, weak, or in some other way beneath your dignity to rely on an invisible power for support. To trust and rely on your Higher Power takes a certain willingness to let go of control as well as a certain humility (it's often humbling to come to the realization that you can't handle something completely on your own). The ability to let go and trust is something that can be learned. Often the life lessons that are the hardest—the ones that push you to your absolute limit—tend to be the ones that have the most to teach about letting go.

As you increasingly learn to allow your Higher Power (Spirit) to assist in your life, you can grow in trusting that it is sometimes appropriate to relinquish control.

6. Contact with your Higher Power is directly available within your personal experience.

You can discover a personal relationship with your Higher Power within your own immediate experience. It is as personal a relationship as any you might have with another human being. It is a two-way relationship. You can receive support, guidance, inspiration, peace of mind, inner strength, hope, and many other gifts from your Higher Power; you can also communicate your needs to Spirit through prayer and directly communicate feelings of gratitude and reverence. Such a relationship can deepen and grow to the extent that you choose to give it attention and time.

There are numerous ways in which your Higher Power can manifest in your personal experience. Some fairly common examples follow:

- Feeling supported by a loving presence.

- An inner knowing or intuitive recognition. Some deep insight comes to you and you have a clear, unequivocal sense that it is true.

- After a period of stress or struggle, you suddenly feel an influx of calmness or peace. Because it comes to you without any effort on your part, there is a sense that it comes from a place beyond your personal ego.

- Feelings of awe and wonder when beholding the beauty of nature.

- Visionary experiences—actually having a visual impression within or outside of your mind of a spiritual being or presence.

- Synchronicities—something in the outside world coincidentally matches what is going on in your mind. It feels like more than just a coincidence. For example, you're obsessively worrying about something while driving and a car pulls in front of you with a personalized license plate that says, "Let Go."

- Miracles—for example, spontaneous healings that defy medical explanation.

As you read this, think about some of the ways in which you have experienced the presence of a Higher Power within your own experience. There are many forms other than those listed above.

7. Questions sincerely asked of your Higher Power are answered.

This idea is really an extension of the previous point about your Higher Power being a source of support and guidance. The reason for making this point separately is to underscore the fact that your Higher Power's support and guidance is not only bestowed on you—you can deliberately ask for it. The famous quote of Jesus "Ask and you shall receive" is true regardless of the particular spiritual tradition or orientation you follow.

It is the assumption of all religious approaches that incorporate prayer that prayer will be answered. Perhaps you have had experiences of your prayers being answered. It often seems that the degree of earnestness of your request has something to do with how readily the prayer receives a response. A common example is when you feel overwhelmed with some situation and you almost literally cry out for help to your Higher Power. In many, if not most, cases, something about the situation improves or shifts, often within a short time.

There is actually scientific research that confirms the efficacy of prayer. Several well-controlled empirical studies of prayer are reported in the book *Recovering the Soul: A Scientific and Spiritual Search* by Larry Dossey, MD.

In sum, there is both anecdotal and research support for the idea that prayer is effective. This doesn't mean that whatever you pray for will come true. There are some qualifications that, in this author's experience, need to be kept in mind: 1) the request or plea needs to be made with genuine earnestness and sincerity, 2) the "answer" or response to prayer may not come immediately—it may take days, weeks, or months, and 3) the answer may not come all at once—instead, only a step in the direction of the answer may come (for example, if you're praying for healing from chronic pain, the answer may come in the form of a strong intuition to visit a particular doctor or healing practitioner). Prayer can be answered in many ways, and sometimes the answer may not be what you expected. It is not possible to know in advance how a particular prayer will be answered (that is when faith comes in). What can be trusted is that there will be an answer, and that answer will serve your highest good.

8. What you truly ask for or intend from the deepest level of yourself—from your heart—will tend to come to you.

One of the most powerful things that can foster positive change and healing is a sincerely held intention. With clients and in my own experience, I have observed how the power of intention can promote miraculous consequences. What you believe in and commit to with your whole heart tends to come true. When the intention is for your own highest good—and when it doesn't conflict with anyone else's highest good—it is most likely to become manifest.

A deeply held intention shifts and focuses your own consciousness. It also appears to have ramifications on events in the world apart from you. Events in the outer world will tend to align with your most deeply held intention. Goethe summed this up in his famous remark:

Concerning all acts of initiative or creation,
there is one elementary truth;

The ignorance of which kills countless ideas and splendid plans:
the moment one definitely commits oneself,
then Providence moves too.

All sorts of things occur to help one
that would never otherwise have occurred.

A whole stream of events issue from the decision,
raising in one's favor
all manner of unforeseen incidents and assistance,
which no person could have dreamt
would have come their way.

9. Love is stronger than fear. Pure, unconditional love emanates from your Higher Power (God) and is at the very center of your being and all beings. All fears can be understood as different forms of separation: separation from others, ourselves, and God—separation from the love that unites all things.

Love is stronger than fear because it goes deeper. On a conscious level, love is the experience of feeling your heart go out toward unity with someone or something other than yourself. On a deeper level, love is the "ground state" or essential foundation of the entire universe. This is a view that is common both to Eastern and Western religions. Love is not something we either possess or do not possess, because it literally *defines* what we are at our core and in essence. Fear may go deep but never as deep as love, because fear arises only when we feel separate from the ground state that unifies us with everything else.

The popular phrase "We are all one" expresses the truth about love and is, on a level beyond what our conscious mind can fully comprehend, literally true.

Most of the anxiety you experience may be related to specific fears of abandonment, rejection and humiliation, loss of control, confinement, injury, or death. Fear can take on any of these forms, based on your conditioning and past experience. Yet none of these fears could ever arise if you did not experience separation. The existence of fear always points to a degree of separation—separation of your conscious mind from your innermost being, separation from others, and/or separation from God. If it is true that in essence all of us are united as one, then every fear we feel—no matter how much we believe it—is, in fact, just an illusion. If we could perceive things the way they truly are, there would be no reason to have any more fear.

Love and fear constitute perhaps the most profound duality in human existence. Yet the former can always overcome the latter.

10. Death is not an end but a transition. Our essential nature or soul survives physical death. (To fear death as "the end" is simply an illusion.)

This basic idea is shared by all of the world's religions. They all assume that an individual's soul continues to exist after physical death, although they differ somewhat in their conceptions about the nature of the afterlife.

Actual evidence for this view has emerged in the past twenty-five years from the widespread research on "near-death experiences." As you most likely already know, near-death experiences are based on reports of what people experienced between the time when their vital signs indicated imminent or actual death and when they were subsequently revived. These reports all share several things, such as passing through a tunnel, meeting a being of light that radiates love and understanding, witnessing a scene-by-scene review of your entire life, and sometimes meeting relatives who have already died. A smaller number of these reports describe otherworldly scenes and locales associated with the events that are experienced. Though the thousands of such reports that have been collected worldwide don't "prove" that consciousness survives death, they certainly make a strong case in that direction. Further evidence that near-death survivors get a peek into an afterlife comes from the fact that many of them lose their fear of death and become more deeply spiritual following their experience. If what they went through was simply a dream, why would it have such a deep and lasting impact?

Does fear of death come up for you or underlie other fears you might have about sickness or injury? If so, you might want to look at the literature on near-death experiences and come to your own conclusions about life after death. The classic book in the field is *Life After Life* by Raymond Moody, but there are large number of other good books on the topic.

Exercise 1: Spirituality and Your View of Your Condition

Go back over the ten assumptions above. Decide which ones fit for you, which ones you would want to question or discuss, and which, if any, don't fit or make sense to you.

If some of these ideas strike you as true, how would believing them change your view of your anxiety condition? Your view of life in general? On a separate sheet of paper, write down your answers to these two questions.

Exercise 2: Connecting with Your Higher Power

The following exercise is intended to help you get in touch with your Higher Power and obtain assistance to deal with any issue causing you worry or anxiety. Use the exercise only if it feels appropriate to you. (You may have your own methods of prayer and meditation that you prefer.) Give yourself time to get relaxed and centered first before working with the affirmations and visualization.

1. Get comfortable in a seated position (or lie down if you prefer). Spend at least five minutes using any technique you wish to get relaxed. You can do abdominal breathing, do progressive muscle relaxation, visualize going to your peaceful place, or meditate. (See chapter 4 for instructions for specific relaxation techniques.)

2. If you're not already aware of it, bring to mind the situation, the person, or whatever it is that you are worried or anxious about. Focus on this for several moments until you have it clearly in mind. If feelings of anxiety come up, allow yourself to feel them.

3. Affirm over and over, with as much conviction as you can,

   "I turn this over to my Higher Power (or God)."

   "I release this problem to my Higher Power (or God)."

   Simply repeat these statements slowly, calmly, and with feeling as many times as you wish until you begin to feel better. While doing this, it is good to bring to mind the following ideas about your Higher Power:

   • It is "all knowing"—in other words, it has wisdom and intelligence that go beyond your conscious capacity to perceive solutions to problems.

   • In its greater wisdom, your Higher Power has a solution to whatever you're worried about.

   • Even though you can't see the solution to your worry right now, you can affirm faith that there is no problem that can't be resolved through the help of your Higher Power.

4. If you are visually inclined, imagine that you're going to meet your Higher Power. You might see yourself in a garden or a beautiful setting of your choice, and then imagine that you see a figure—your Higher Power—approaching you. It may be indistinct at first and grow gradually clearer. You may notice that this figure exudes love and wisdom. It might be a wise old man or woman, a being of light, Jesus, the supreme being in your particular religion, or any other presence that adequately represents your Higher Power.

5. While in the presence of your Higher Power—whether you visualize it or not—simply find a way to ask for help. For example, you might say, "I ask for your help and guidance with _____." Keep repeating your request until you feel better.

You may want to listen to see if your Higher Power has an immediate answer or an insight to offer you about your request. It is quite all right, though, simply to make your request and ask for help without getting an answer. The purpose of this process is to develop trust and belief in your Higher Power (what has traditionally been called "faith in God").

The key to this part of the process is an attitude of genuine humility. By asking for help from your Higher Power, you relinquish some of your conscious control of the situation and exercise a willingness to trust.

6. *Optional*: If it feels appropriate, visualize a beam of white light going to that place in your body that feels anxious or worried. Often this will be the solar plexus region (in the middle of your trunk right below the center of your rib cage) or the "pit" of your stomach. Let that area be filled with the light until the anxiety dissolves or fades away. Keep directing white light to that region until it completely settles down and is free of anxiety.

Give this entire process time. It may be necessary to persist with it for as long as a half hour to forty-five minutes in order to feel a genuine connection with your Higher Power and a deeply felt trust that the problem you're worried about can truly be resolved. If, after completing this process, your worry comes back the next day, simply repeat the exercise every day until you've mastered your worry.

Options for Developing Your Spiritual Life

You can deepen your commitment to spirituality through any of the following means:

1. Regular participation in church or your preferred spiritually based organization.

2. Regular reading of inspirational literature of your preference. It's good to do this at least once per day—upon awakening, during your lunch break, or before retiring.

3. Regular practice of meditation (see chapter 18).

4. Regular practice of prayer or spiritual affirmations (see the books by Louise Hay and Shakti Gawain below for how to work with spiritual affirmations).

5. Involvement in a 12-step program that is relevant to your needs. The 12-step programs offer many people a well-conceived and effective approach for healing addictions. Although they began with Alcoholics Anonymous fifty years ago, they now include a wide range of programs, such as Emotions Anonymous, Codependents Anonymous, Overeaters Anonymous, Sex and Love Addictions Anonymous, and Workaholics Anonymous. Consult your local chapter of the National Council on Alcoholism for a list of 12-step groups in your area.

A Final Caveat

Reading the previous sections may have made spirituality sound as if it were a cure-all. You might even be left with the idea that developing a relationship with your Higher Power is *all* that is necessary for you to overcome your problem with panic, phobias, or anxiety. This is very unlikely to be true. You're still going to need to draw on all of the strategies presented in this workbook to deal with your particular problem with anxiety. Relaxation, exercise, coping strategies for panic, imagery and real-life desensitization, changing self-talk and mistaken beliefs, expressing feelings, developing assertiveness, and working on self-esteem will all be necessary.

What developing your spirituality can do is give you the inspiration and hope to persist in following through with your recovery program. It can also provide you with a powerful means for breaking through to your next step forward at those times when you're feeling stuck, discouraged, or confused.

Summary of Things to Do

1. Do you feel aware of your own unique life purpose or purposes? Use the *Personal Values Inventory* to assist you in clarifying what you would most like to do with your life.

2. Reflect on the ten ideas presented in the section "Changes in Beliefs Associated with Spirituality" and complete exercise 1.

3. Practice the meditation "Connecting with Your Higher Power" in exercise 2 when you feel up against a personal issue that you've been unable to resolve through your own conscious efforts.

4. Among the list of options for developing your spiritual life, decide which one(s) you'd be willing to commit more time to during the next month.

Further Reading

If you are on a traditional religious path, you probably are already familiar with a number of written sources of inspiration and guidance. The Bible has a tremendous amount of insight and wisdom to offer if you are of Christian or Jewish faith. Islamic, Buddhist, Hindu, and other traditional cultures all possess a rich literature of spiritual wisdom. The books listed below are not aligned with any particular religion, but, like this chapter, speak to a universal spirituality.

Bourne, Edmund J. *Beyond Anxiety & Phobia*. Oakland, CA: New Harbinger Publications, 2001.

Dass, Ram, and Paul Gorman. *How Can I Help?* New York: Alfred A. Knopf, 1985.

Dossey, Larry. *Recovering the Soul: A Scientific and Spiritual Search.* New York: Bantam Books, 1989.

Gawain, Shakti. *Creative Visualization.* Novato, CA: New World Library, 2002.

Gawain, Shakti, with Laurel King. *Living in the Light.* Revised edition. Novato, CA: New World Library, 1998.

Hay, Louise. *You Can Heal Your Life.* Carlsbad, CA: Hay House, 1999. (Includes many helpful tools and affirmations for developing self-worth.)

Jampolsky, Gerald. *Good-bye to Guilt.* New York: Bantam Books, 1985.

———. *Love Is Letting Go of Fear.* 25th anniversary edition. Berkeley, CA: Celestial Arts, 2004.

Moody, Raymond. *Life After Life.* 25th anniversary edition. San Francisco: HarperSanFrancisco, 2001.

Rodegast, Pat, and Judith Stanton. *Emmanuel's Book.* New York: Bantam Books, 1987.

Roman, Sanaya. *Spiritual Growth.* Tiburon, CA: H J Kramer, 1989.

Stephan, Naomi. *Fulfill Your Soul's Purpose.* Nevada City, CA: Blue Dolphin, 1999.

Tolle, Eckhart. *The Power of Now.* Novato, CA: New World Library, 1999. (An excellent resource for going beyond the conditioned mind and developing awareness.)

Williamson, Marianne. *Illuminata.* New York: Riverhead Books, 1994. (An outstanding collection of thoughts and prayers for modern times.)

Zukav, Gary. *The Seat of the Soul.* New York: Fireside Books, 1990.

Appendix 1

Resources

The Anxiety Disorders Association of America

The Anxiety Disorders Association of America (ADAA) is a nonprofit, charitable organization founded in 1980 by leaders in the field of treatment for phobias, agoraphobia, and panic/anxiety disorders. Its purpose is to promote public awareness about anxiety disorders, stimulate research and development of effective treatments, and offer assistance to sufferers and their families in gaining access to available specialists and treatment programs.

The association publishes a quarterly newsletter and a *National Professional Membership Directory* which lists professionals and programs throughout the United States and Canada specializing in the treatment of anxiety disorders. It also publishes several relevant books and pamphlets.

For further information about the Anxiety Disorders Association of America, its services, publications, and conferences, as well as how to join, please contact

The Anxiety Disorders Association of America
8730 Georgia Ave.
Silver Spring, MD 20910
1-240-485-1001

For a comprehensive listing of professionals specializing in the treatment of anxiety disorders, organized by zip code, go to ADAA's website: adaa.org. You can also find support groups for anxiety disorders, listed by state, at the ADAA's website.

For comprehensive information about obsessive-compulsive disorder and a list of therapists who specialize in treating OCD, see the website of the International Obsessive Compulsive Foundation at ocfoundation.org.

Appendix 2

Additional Hierarchies*

Use the following hierarchies as guidelines for attaining your own goals. You may want to add steps or develop your own hierarchies. Space is left between the steps of each hierarchy for adding in additional steps.

Remember to repeat each step in the hierarchy until you become comfortable with it. *Do not advance to the next step until you are comfortable with all of the preceding steps.*

Being in a Supermarket

1. With your partner, sit in the parking lot and look at the store.

2. With your partner, walk to the door and remain there for one to five minutes.

3. Without your partner, walk in and out of the door. (In steps 3–8, have your partner wait outside the store.)

4. Walk to the checkout area alone.

5. Walk to the first aisle alone.

6. Walk one-quarter of the way to the back of the store alone.

7. Walk halfway to the back of the store alone.

8. Walk all the way to the back of the store alone.

9. With your partner, remain in the back of the store for one to five minutes.

10. Remain in the store, browsing in different areas, alone, for five to ten minutes.

---

* These additional hierarchies are adapted from the *TERRAP Program Manual,* Menlo Park, CA: TSC Publications, 1986, with the permission of Dr. Arthur B. Hardy.

Shopping in a Supermarket

Work through the steps first with your partner accompanying you or waiting outside the store. Then repeat on your own.

1. Spend five minutes in the store alone, browsing.

2. Purchase one item through the express line (with no more than one person ahead of you).

3. Purchase two to five items through the express line (with no more than one person ahead of you).

4. Purchase six to ten items through the express line (with one to three people ahead of you).

5. Purchase two or three items through the regular checkout line (with one or two people ahead of you).

6. Purchase five to ten items through the regular checkout line (with two to four people ahead of you).

7. Purchase ten or more items through the regular checkout line.

8. Select ten or more items and change checkout lines while waiting to purchase them.

9. Purchase ten or more items through the regular checkout line and ask the clerk to take back one item you've decided you don't want.

10. At a different supermarket, purchase ten or more items through the regular checkout line (with two to four people ahead and behind).

Riding As a Passenger in a Car

1. Sit in a car for one to five minutes with your partner in the driver's seat.

2. Ride, with your partner driving, for one block.

3. Ride with your partner in a residential area for ten to fifteen minutes.

4. Ride with your partner on a minor arterial for five to ten minutes.

5. Ride with your partner on a major arterial for ten to fifteen minutes.

6. Ride with your partner on the freeway for ten to fifteen minutes.

7. Ride with your partner on the freeway in heavy traffic.

8. Ride with your partner on a curving, mountainous road.

9. Do all of the above with a less familiar person driving.

10. Extend the distance that you ride away from home.

Driving with a Partner As Passenger

1. Sit in a car for one to five minutes, with your partner in the passenger seat.

2. Drive one block, making smooth stops and starts.

3. Drive in a residential area, making right turns.

4. Drive in a residential area, making left turns.

5. Drive in the right lane of a minor arterial.

6. Drive on a minor arterial, making left turns at a stop sign or traffic light.

7. Drive on a major arterial in the right lane.

8. Drive on a major arterial, changing lanes and making left and U-turns.

9. Drive on the freeway in the right lane for one to two exits.

10. Drive on the freeway, changing lanes and passing cars for two to five exits.

Driving Alone

When you practice driving alone, first have your partner follow you in another car as you go through the steps. When you feel comfortable, have your partner wait for you at your pre-established destination and then follow you back home. When you're comfortable with this, then practice by yourself.

1. Sit in the car for one to five minutes alone.

2. Drive one block, making smooth stops and starts.

3. Drive in a residential area, making right turns.

4. Drive in a residential area, making left turns.

5. Drive in the right lane of a minor arterial.

6. Drive on a minor arterial, making left turns at a stop sign or traffic light.

7. Drive on a major arterial in the right lane.

8. Drive on a major arterial, changing lanes and making left and U-turns.

9. Drive on the freeway in the right lane for one or two exits.

10. Drive on the freeway, changing lanes and passing cars for two to five exits.

People

1. Go to a street or mall where there are stores and look around.

2. In the same area, look at the people walking around.

3. In the same area, pick out one person and look at what that person is doing.

4. In the same area, pick out one person and look at what that person is wearing.

5. In the same area, pick out one person and make eye contact.

6. In the same area, pick out one person and smile, making eye contact.

7. In the same area, go into a store and make eye contact with the clerk and smile.

8. In the same area, go into a store and talk to a clerk, making eye contact and smiling.

9. In the same area, pick out a person, go over, smile, make eye contact, and ask the person a question, such as what time it is.

10. In a different area, pick out a person, go over, smile, make eye contact, and ask the person a question.

Crowds

1. With your partner, approach a small store with a few people inside.

2. With your partner nearby, remain in the small store for two to five minutes.

3. Approach and enter a small store alone for five to ten minutes.

4. With your partner, approach a busier store (such as a department store) and remain for one to five minutes.

5. Approach a crowded store alone (or with your partner waiting in the car), and remain nearby for five to ten minutes.

6. With your partner, approach a large shopping center and go inside and out for five to fifteen minutes.

7. Approach and enter a store in a large shopping center and browse for five to fifteen minutes. Do this with your partner, then alone.

8. Approach and enter a large department store in a shopping mall and browse for five to fifteen minutes. Do this with your partner, then alone.

9. Attend a small sporting event, party, or concert with your partner.

10. Attend a larger sporting event, party, or concert with your partner and then try steps 9 and 10 alone.

Groups

1. With your partner, join a small group of acquaintances and remain five to ten minutes, participating only minimally (for example, commenting on the weather).

2. Without your partner, join a small group of acquaintances and remain ten to thirty minutes, participating only minimally.

3. With your partner, enter into conversation with one or two friends for five minutes.

4. With your partner, talk with two to four people for five to ten minutes.

5. Talk with one to three friends in a group alone.

6. With your partner, talk with a less familiar person or a total stranger for one to five minutes.

7. Talk with some less familiar people alone for five to ten minutes (such as people you see every day around your place of work, but aren't acquainted with personally).

8. Enter a larger group of people with your partner and talk with them for five to fifteen minutes.

9. Enter a larger group of people without your partner and talk with them for ten to thirty minutes. (You'll probably have to search around for an opportunity like this. A church social, a group meeting such as Al-Anon, and a community college seminar would all be possibilities.)

10. Enter a larger group of people without your partner and give a short presentation on some topic on which you have some expertise.

Restaurants

1. With your partner, drive around the outside of a restaurant.

2. With your partner, sit in the restaurant parking lot for one to five minutes.

3. With your partner, enter the restaurant, stand inside for thirty to sixty seconds, then leave.

4. Enter the restaurant alone, stand inside for one to two minutes, then leave.

5. Enter the restaurant alone, select a table near the door, and order a beverage.

6. Enter the restaurant alone, select a table near the door, and order one item of food.

7. After ordering food, wait for it to arrive and eat it.

8. Enter the restaurant alone, select a table away from the door, and order a beverage.

9.   Enter the restaurant alone, select a table away from the door, and order a small meal; wait for it and eat it.

10.   Enter a larger restaurant, select a table away from the door, order a small meal, wait for it, and eat it.

Elevators

1.   Approach an elevator with your partner; look at it, and then retreat.

2.   Walk with your partner into an elevator with the door remaining open (have your partner make sure the door remains open).

3.   Walk with your partner into an elevator and allow the door to close.

4.   With your partner, ride up one floor and then return to the ground floor.

5.   With your partner, ride up two or more floors and then return to the ground floor

6.   Ride up two or more floors with your partner and exit the elevator at the second or higher floor. Then return, using the elevator, to the ground floor.

7.   Ride up two or more floors alone with your partner waiting at the floor where you exit the elevator.

8.   Ride up two or more floors alone with your partner waiting on the ground floor.

9.   Ride the elevator two or more floors while your partner is somewhere else in the building. (Repeat steps 4–9 going to progressively higher floors.)

10.   Ride the elevator alone for two or more floors without your partner being available.

11.   Ride a less familiar elevator alone, without your partner being available.

Bridges

1.   With your partner driving, approach a short bridge, stop, walk around, and look at the bridge.

2.   With you driving, approach a short bridge, stop, and look at the bridge.

3.   With your partner driving, drive across the same short bridge and return.

4.   With you driving, drive across the same short bridge and return.

5.   With your partner following in another car, drive across the same bridge and return.

6.   With your partner waiting at one end of the same bridge, drive across the bridge. Have your partner move to the other end of the bridge, and then return.

7.   Without your partner around, drive across the same bridge and return.

8.   Repeat the above procedure with a longer and/or higher bridge.

Buses and Trains

This hierarchy is described for buses but can be used in the same manner for trains.

1.   With your partner, ride on a bus for one stop, sitting on the aisle near the door.

2.   With your partner, ride the bus for two to five stops, sitting on the aisle near the door.

3.   With your partner, ride the bus for five or more stops, sitting in the back of the bus.

4.   With your partner following in a car, ride the bus one stop, sitting on the aisle near the door.

5.   With your partner following in a car, ride the bus for two to five stops, sitting on the aisle near the door.

6.   With your partner following in a car, ride the bus five or more stops, sitting in the back of the bus.

7.   Alone, without your partner following, ride the bus one stop, sitting on the aisle near the door.

8.   Alone, without your partner following, ride the bus two to five stops, sitting on the aisle near the door.

9.   Alone, without your partner following, ride the bus two to five stops, sitting in the back of the bus.

10.   Alone, without your partner following, ride the bus more than five stops, sitting in the back of the bus.

Dentists and Doctors

This hierarchy is designed for people with a fear of dentists but can be used in the same manner for doctor phobias.

1.   With your partner, walk in and out of a dentist's office.

2.   With your partner, sit in the waiting room for two to five minutes.

3.   With your partner, sit in the waiting room for ten to fifteen minutes.

4.   Make an appointment with the dentist just to talk to him or her for five to ten minutes. Tell the dentist about your problem and explain that you are trying to desensitize yourself. Ask for his or her cooperation.

5. With your partner, sit in the dentist's chair five to ten minutes without the dentist being in attendance, then leave.

6. With your partner, sit in the dentist's chair ten to twenty minutes without the dentist being in attendance, then leave.

7. Make an appointment with your dentist to just look in your mouth, and not to do any work, with your partner staying with you.

8. Make an appointment with your dentist to clean your teeth only, with your partner staying with you.

9. Make an appointment for the dentist to do more work while your partner is with you.

10. Repeat steps 7 through 9 without your partner.

Airports and Flying

1. Approach the airport with your partner and drive around it.

2. Park in the airport garage or lot; remain, observing people, for five minutes.

3. Park in the airport lot, enter the terminal with your partner, and remain one to five minutes.

4. Enter the terminal alone and remain five minutes, browsing and observing.

5. Arrange to visit a grounded plane; enter with your partner. (If you can't arrange this with a commercial airline, try a small, private airport that offers flying lessons.)

6. Enter a grounded plane alone and remain inside for five minutes.

7. Enter a grounded plane with your partner and get buckled into a seat. Remain five minutes.

8. Enter a grounded plane alone, browse, and then stay buckled into a seat for ten to fifteen minutes.

9. Schedule a short flight (ten to thirty minutes) and go with your partner.

10. Schedule a longer flight and go with your partner.

11. Repeat steps 9 and 10 alone.

Note: Many areas have fear of flying programs that will take you through a hierarchy similar to the one above. Also, imagery desensitization can be helpful for fear of flying.

Appendix 3

Resources for Relaxation

There are a wide variety of resources for training yourself to achieve a deep state of relaxation, available either in CD format or as MP3 downloads.

A good resource for guided visualizations that can induce deep relaxation is the website of Dr. Emmett Miller: drmiller.com.

A large variety of CDs and downloads that facilitate deep relaxation can be found at Sounds True (go to shop.soundstrue.com). Or you can go to amazon.com and do a search under the keyword "Relaxation CDs."

For peaceful, calming music, try the music of Steve Halpern, Enya, Michael Jones, David Lanz, or George Winston.

Finally, if you have access to iTunes radio, check out one of the author's favorite online radio stations for relaxation: calmradio.com (you will find it under one of the seventy-five classical music streams).

In general, compilations of music by *Windham Hill* and *Narada* are usually conducive to relaxation.

For classical enthusiasts, see *The Most Relaxing Classical Album in the World ... Ever!* (Virgin Records).

Appendix 4

How to Stop Obsessive Worry

Obsessive worry is like a *negative spiral*. The longer you spend time with it, the deeper into it you can get. It may also be viewed as a form of trance. The more you induce it by repetition, the more entranced you get, and the more difficult it may be to "break the spell."

It takes a deliberate act of will to stop it. You need to make a deliberate effort to move away from circular mental activity and *get out of your head* by "shifting gears" to another modality of experience, such as bodily activity, expressing emotions, interpersonal communication, sensory distraction, or a specific ritual. (In some cases, an alternative obsession will do.)

The downward pull of an obsessive spiral can be very compelling. Following the path of least resistance is likely to keep you going round and round. Although deliberately choosing to break out of the obsessive thinking may be difficult at first (especially if you're highly anxious), with practice it will get easier.

Below are some examples of alternative activities and experiences that can help you shift out of your mind and away from obsessive thinking.

1. *Do physical exercise.* This can be your favorite outdoor or indoor exercise, dancing, or just household chores.

2. *Do progressive muscle relaxation alone or in combination with abdominal breathing.* See chapter 4 for more detail. Keep this up for five to ten minutes until you feel fully relaxed and freer from obsessive thoughts.

3. *Use evocative music to release repressed feelings.* Such feelings—usually sadness or anger—may underlie and "drive" worry or obsessive thinking.

4. *Talk to someone.* Converse about something other than the worry, unless you want to express your feelings about it, as in point 3.

5. *Use visual distractions.* This can be TV, movies, video games, your computer, uplifting reading, or even a rock garden.

6. *Use sensory-motor distraction.* Try arts and crafts, repairing something, or gardening.

7. *Find an alternative, positive obsession.* For example, work out a crossword or jigsaw puzzle.

8. *Practice healthy rituals.* Combine abdominal breathing with a positive affirmation that has personal significance. Keep this up for five to ten minutes, or until you're

fully relaxed. (This is actually a positive trance induction to overcome the negative trance enforced by the obsessive worry.)

Examples of Affirmations:	*For the Spiritually Inclined:*
"Let it go."	"Let go and let God."
"These are just thoughts— they're fading away."	"I abide in Spirit (God)."
"I'm whole, relaxed, and free of worry."	"I release this negativity to God."

Appendix 5

Affirmations for Overcoming Anxiety

The following affirmations and script are intended to help you change your attitude and respond constructively to the kinds of negative self-talk that can feed anxiety. Reading through them once or twice probably won't make much difference. Rehearsing some or all of them daily for a few weeks or months will begin to help you change your basic outlook about fear in a constructive direction. One way to do this is to read through one of the three sections below slowly once or twice each day, giving yourself time to reflect on each affirmation. Even better, record one or all three sections, leaving a few seconds of silence between each affirmation. Then listen to the recording once daily, when relaxed, to reinforce a more positive and confident attitude about mastering your anxiety.

Negative Thoughts and Positive Affirmations to Combat Them

(Use only the affirmations if you make a recording.)

This is unbearable.	I can learn how to cope better with this.
What if this goes on without letting up?	I'll deal with this one day at a time. I don't have to project into the future.
I feel damaged, inadequate relative to others.	Some of us have steeper paths to walk than others. That doesn't make me less valuable as a human being—even if I accomplish less in the outer world.
Why do I have to deal with this? Other people seem freer to enjoy their lives.	Life is a school. For whatever reasons, at least for now, I've been given a steeper path—a tougher curriculum. That doesn't make me wrong. In fact, adversity develops qualities of strength and compassion.
Having this condition seems unfair.	Life can appear unfair from a human perspective. If we could see the bigger picture, we'd see that everything is proceeding according to plan.
I don't know how to cope with this.	I can *learn* to cope better—with this and any difficulty life brings.

I feel so inadequate relative to others.	Let people do what they do in the outer world. I'm following a path of inner growth and transformation, which is at least equally valuable. Finding peace in myself can be a gift to others.
Each day seems like a major challenge.	I'm learning to take things more slowly. I make time to take care of myself. I make time to do small things to nurture myself.
I don't understand why I'm this way—why this happened to me.	The causes are many, including heredity, early environment, and cumulative stress. Understanding causes satisfies the intellect, but it's not what heals.
I feel like I'm going crazy.	When anxiety is high, I *feel* like I'm losing control. But that feeling has nothing to do with going crazy. Anxiety disorders are a long way from the category of disorders labeled "crazy."
I have to really fight this.	Struggling with a problem won't help as much as making more time in my life to better care for myself.
I shouldn't have let this happen to me.	The long-term causes of this problem lie in heredity and childhood environment, so I didn't cause this condition. I *can* now take responsibility for getting better.

Antianxiety Affirmations

- I am learning to let go of worry.

- Each day I'm growing in my capacity to master worry and anxiety.

- I am learning not to feed my worries—to choose peace over fear.

- I am learning to consciously choose what I think, and I choose thoughts that are supportive and beneficial for me.

- When anxious thoughts come up, I can slow down, breathe, and let them go.

- When anxious thoughts come up, I can make time to relax and release them.

- Deep relaxation gives me the freedom of choice to move out of fear.

- Anxiety is made of illusory thoughts—thoughts I can let go of.

- When I see most situations as they truly are, there is nothing to be afraid of.

- Fearful thoughts are usually exaggerated, and I'm growing in my ability to turn them off at will.

- More and more, it's becoming easier to relax and talk myself out of anxiety.

- I keep my mind too busy thinking positive and constructive thoughts to have much time for worry.

- I'm learning to control my mind and choose the thoughts that I think.

- I am gaining more confidence in myself, knowing I can handle any situation that comes along.

- Fear is dissolving and vanishing from my life. I am calm, confident, and secure.

- As I take life more slowly and easily, I have more ease and peace in my life.

- As I grow in my ability to relax and feel secure, I realize that there is truly nothing to fear.

- More and more, I'm growing in confidence, knowing that I can handle any situation that comes up.

Script for Overcoming Fear

Focusing on a fear always makes it worse. When I can relax enough, I become able to change my focus. I can put my mind on loving, supportive, constructive ideas. I can't make fearful thoughts go away. Struggling with them makes them loom larger. Instead, I can redirect my mind to more peaceful, calming thoughts and circumstances. Every time I do this, I am choosing peace instead of fear. The more I choose peace, the more it becomes a part of my life. With practice, I get better at redirecting my mind. I learn how to spend less time focusing on fear. I grow stronger in my ability to choose wholesome, helpful thoughts over fearful ones. I make time to relax ... to reconnect with that place deep within myself that is always at peace.

When I make the time to do this, I can choose to move away from fearful thoughts. I can allow my mind to expand into a wider place that is much larger than my fearful thoughts. Fear requires a narrow, small focus of my mind. When I relax or meditate, my mind becomes deep enough—and large enough—to transcend fear. I'm learning to see that my fearful thoughts grossly overestimate risk or threat. The true risk I face in most situations is actually very small. True, it's impossible to eliminate risk from life altogether. Being in a physical body in the physical world necessitates some risk. Only in heaven is there an eternal risk-free state. I'm learning to recognize my tendency to exaggerate risks—to blow them out of proportion. Every fear involves both overestimating the risk of danger—and underestimating my ability to cope. If I take the time to examine my fearful thoughts, I'll discover that in most cases they are unrealistic. When I choose to see most situations as they truly are, I see that they are not dangerous. If I practice replacing my fearful thoughts with real thoughts, eventually my fearful thoughts will diminish. Every time I feel afraid, I recognize the unreality of my fearful thoughts and let go of them more easily.

The important thing is not to feed fear ... not to dwell on it or give it energy. Instead I can practice redirecting my attention to something—anything—that makes me feel better. I can focus on talking to a friend, reading something uplifting, working with my hands, listening to a recording, or any number of activities which help me take my mind off fear. With practice, I become more and more adept at moving away from fearful thoughts—of not indulging in them. I begin to become master rather than victim of my mind. I learn that I have more and more choice about fear. I can step into it or out of it. And, as time passes, I learn to step out of it.

Reference List

Cameron, Alasdair. (2004). *Crash Course Psychiatry*. Philadelphia: Elsevier.

Garcia-Palacios, A., H. Hoffman, T. Richards, E. Seibel, and S. Sharar. (June 1, 2007/May 5, 2008). Use of virtual reality distraction to reduce claustrophobia symptoms during a mock magnetic resonance imaging brain scan: A case report. *CyberPsychology and Behavior* 10(3): 485–88.

Isensee, B., H. U. Wittchen, M. Stein, M. Hofler, and R. Leib. (2003). Smoking increases the risk of panic: Findings from a prospective community study. *Archives of General Psychiatry* 60(7):692–700.

Kabat-Zinn, J. (2005). *Wherever You Go, There You Are*. Tenth anniversary edition. New York: Hyperion, 2005.

Kendler, K., L. Karkowski, and C. Prescott. (1999). Fears and phobias: Reliability and heritability. *Psychological Medicine* 29(3):539–53.

Mental Health America. (2007). Factsheet: Panic disorder. July 7. Available at reprint archives at nmha.org.

Seidler, G. H., and F. E. Wagner. (2006). Comparing the efficacy of EMDR and trauma-focused cognitive behavioral therapy in the treatment of PTSD: A meta-analytic study. *Psychological Medicine* 36(11):1515–22.

Segal, Z. V., J. M. G. Williams, and J. D. Teasdale. (2002). *Mindfulness-Based Cognitive Therapy for Depression: A New Approach to Preventing Relapse*. New York: Guilford Press.

Thompson, Alandra. (1999). Cognitive behavioral treatment of blood-injury-injection phobia: A case study. *Behavior Change* 36(3): 182–90.

True, W. R., J. Rice, and S. A. Eisen. (1993). A twin study of genetic and environmental contributions to liability for post-traumatic stress symptoms. *Archives of General Psychiatry* 50(4):257–64.

U.S. Department of Health and Human Services, Office of the Surgeon General. (1999). Adults and Mental Health (chapter 4). In *Mental Health: A report of the Surgeon General*. Washington, DC: U.S. Department of Health and Human Services.

Weekes. Claire. (1991). Hope for Your Nerves. New York: Signet.

Women's Health Initiative. (2002). Risks and benefits of estrogen plus progestin in healthy postmenopausal women. *Journal of the American Medical Association* 288: 321–33.

About the Author

Edmund J. Bourne, Ph.D., has specialized in the treatment of anxiety, phobias, and other stress-related disorders for over two decades. His self-help books have helped over a million people and have been translated into numerous languages. He currently resides in California and southern Florida.

Phone counseling for problems with panic attacks, phobias, and other anxiety difficulties is available with Dr. Bourne. For information, please call 1-800-334-1847. For resources in your local area, please see Appendix 1. Further information about Dr. Bourne's work may be found at helpforanxiety.com.

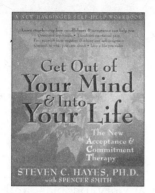